# PREJUDICE, POLEMIC
# OR PROGRESS?

# Cultural Diversity and the Schools

*Editors*: *James Lynch, Celia Modgil and Sohan Modgil*

# CULTURAL DIVERSITY AND THE SCHOOLS

VOLUME TWO

PREJUDICE, POLEMIC OR PROGRESS?

EDITED BY

James Lynch, Celia Modgil and Sohan Modgil

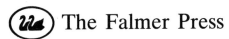 The Falmer Press

(A member of the Taylor & Francis Group)
London • Washington, D.C.

UK        The Falmer Press, 4 John St, London WC1N 2ET

USA       The Falmer Press, Taylor & Francis Inc., 1900 Frost Road, Suite 101,
          Bristol, PA 19007

First published 1992

**British Library Cataloguing-in-Publication Data**
Cultural diversity and the schools: Vol 2.
Prejudice, polemic or progress?.
  I. Lynch, James   II. Modgil, Celia
  III. Modgil, Sohan
  370.19

  ISBN 1–85000–991–0

**Library of Congress Cataloging-in-Publication data are available on request**

Jacket design by Caroline Archer

Typeset in 10/12 pt Times by
Graphicraft Typesetters Ltd, Hong Kong

*Printed in Great Britain by
Taylor & Francis (Printers) Ltd, Basingstoke*

# Contributors

Marcia Albert is Lecturer in the Psychology Department, Chapman University, Orange, California.

Elliot Aronson is Professor at the University of California, Santa Cruz.

Mike Bottery is Lecturer in Moral Education at the University of Hull.

Carlos E. Cortés is Professor of History at the University of California, Riverside.

Pierre R. Dasen is Professor of Anthropology of Education at the University of Geneva.

Brenda Derby is Research Specialist in Employee and Organizational Research at Hughes Aircraft Company.

H.J. Eysenck is Professor Emeritus of Psychology at the University of London.

Harold D. Fishbein is Professor in the Department of Psychology at the University of Cincinnati.

Geneva Gay is Professor of Education at the University of Washington, Seattle.

Hugh Jordan Harrington works for the Hughes Aircraft Company.

David W. Johnson is Professor of Educational Psychology at the University of Minnesota.

Roger T. Johnson is Professor of Curriculum and Instruction at the University of Minnesota.

Yaacov J. Katz is Director, Division of Educational Counselling at the School of Education, Bar Ilan University, Israel.

James Lynch works for the World Bank in Washington, specializing in education projects in least developed countries in Asia. His work on this volume is carried out in his personal capacity.

Norman Miller is Silberburg Professor of Psychology at the University of Southern California.

David Milner is Professor and Head of the Department of Psychology, Polytechnic of Central London.

Celia Modgil is Senior Lecturer in Education and Head of Department of Undergraduate Teacher Education at Goldsmith's College, University of London.

Sohan Modgil is Reader in Educational Research and Development at Brighton Polytechnic.

Fritz K. Oser is Professor of Education at the University of Fribourg, Switzerland.

Raphael Schneller is Senior Lecturer in the School of Education, Bar Ilan University, Israel.

Basil R. Singh is Senior Lecturer in the School of Education at Sunderland Polytechnic.

Robert E. Slavin is Director of the Elementary School Program, Centre for Research on Effective Schooling for Disadvantaged Students, Johns Hopkins University.

Cookie White Stephan is Professor in the Department of Sociology and Anthropology at New Mexico State University.

Ruth Thibodeau is a PhD candidate in social psychology at the University of California, Santa Cruz.

Herbert J. Walberg is Research Professor of Education at the University of Illinois at Chicago.

John Wilson is Fellow of Mansfield College, Oxford and Lecturer in Educational Studies at the University of Oxford.

# Contents

# Editors' Introduction

JAMES LYNCH, CELIA MODGIL AND SOHAN MODGIL

## THE AIM OF THE SERIES

One of the major problems facing societies in almost all parts of the world is the inadequate accommodation of social equity with cultural diversity. The crisis emanating from neglect of this issue can be seen in societies as different and wide apart as the Soviet Union, India, Pakistan, the United States and the United Kingdom. The lack of discourse between the two systems, cultural and social, means that there are fewer shared ideologies on the basis of which accommodations can be negotiated, for ideologies themselves are not static; the very process of discourse for accommodation can generate a greater overlap between the two systems. Its absence inevitably reduces that overlap.

Regardless of their political orientation, societies have by and large failed to generate the political means to engage creatively with this issue, and the consequence has been political disarray, social stagnation and civil unrest, sometimes even civil war and genocide. Neglect of interdependence between the two systems also leads to the education system becoming increasingly ectopic to the changing cultural biography of society and dysfunctional to its real needs. Some countries have tried to enter the problem through the language issue, including national language, mother tongue and bilingual approaches. Some have tried curricular apartheid. Some have attempted a 'trinkets and tokens' approach to curricular adornment. More realistically, others have sought to gain purchase on it through the human rights dimension, including women's rights and those of children. Some have begun to use the regional or international covenants, to which they are signatories, as the spur to cultural accommodation and social change. Some have secured the rights to be different of significant old-established minorities in their constitutions and legislation. Some have tried through curricular initiatives, backed up with cash, to sustain and legitimate cultural pluralism. Some have established separate school systems. A few have tried to match their political and educational systems to the profile of their emerging cultural pluralism. Fewer still have sought to set their own national aspirations for equity in diversity into the wider context of a global perspective and interdependence.

It is the inadequacy of those responses which is, in essence, the issue addressed by this series of books. It seeks to contribute, through joint publication and the stimulation of greater discourse, to identify the pathways to a less selfish and parochial response to the continuing dilemma of equity and diversity, not solely within the nation state, but also internationally. The books in the series aim to engage with a broad audience, aiming at new 'laicized' paradigms of under- standing, capable of being shared with a wider international public. They advocate new approaches and novel policies and seek to identify new strategies in pursuit of political change to share power more widely and to encourage participation and change outdated structures. The series takes as a central tenet the need to recognize as indivisible, and to implement, international agreements and cove- nants on human rights, to render critical focus on loopholes to national and international compliance with the provisions of those instruments, and to facilitate educational progress for respect for human rights and the concomitant change in values and attitudes, as the core of a new internationalized curriculum,[1] designed to respond to an era when political competition is gradually being replaced by cooperation, and where education has a central role to play in preparing people to support that new ideological climate.


## BROADENING THE DEBATE

The focus on issues of cultural diversity has increased in intensity over the recent past, as nations in Eastern Europe, formerly locked in political bondage, and with manifestations of their inherent cultural diversity deep-frozen for almost half a century, have thrown off the yoke of political uniformity and enforced, cultural monism, and sought to rediscover a pluralist political and economic order, un- known to a whole generation. The corollary of the movement to political plural- ism has been a re-emergence of their cultural diversity, and of social and cultural, territorial and environmental conflicts long suppressed. Even, or perhaps especial- ly, the giant Soviet Union has found itself no longer able to deny the heritage of its history, namely its dynamic of cultural diversity. It has appeared, at times, like a giant bound by cultural conflict, rooted in historical precursors, predating the Soviet state by many hundreds of years.

At the same time the societies of Western Europe and North America have continued to encounter their own problems with cultural diversity, as they have struggled to accommodate, both culturally and socially, to the arrival of large numbers of new immigrants in the post-war period. That influx and consequent demographic change have thrust a new concept of cultural pluralism to the fore and forced them to re-examine their fundamental cultural values and assump- tions, not least those cultural presuppositions that are embedded in the hegemony of their élites over the institutions of cultural transmission. But their failure to initiate their own 'perestroika' has led to increasing legitimation problems. In the United States one in five of the population of this rich nation lives below the poverty level; of Latinos, it is almost one in three, and of Blacks, approximately 45 per cent. Almost 90 per cent of Black children at some time in their childhood will be cared for by a single parent. A massive study, released in the summer of 1989, criticizes the slowing in movement to greater equity for Blacks in American society which has taken place in the 1980s.[2] It charts the progress which can be made by a mixture of legislative and structural approaches. In 1940, 77 per cent of Blacks lived in the South, socially segregated and legally discriminated against.

Three-quarters of the few Blacks who attended college went into the professions of cleric or teaching. In 1940 there were 300 Black engineers, by 1980 there were 36,019. Black families with incomes above $35,000 per annum constituted 13.1 per cent in 1967 and 22.3 per cent in 1987 of all Black families. Of course, poverty has not been erased, and economically induced housing segregation remains in many areas. The civil rights era certainly did not remove all barriers to equality. Gains have been made, however, by a combination of legislation, political pressure, educational initiative, economic investment and financial incentive, and the vast majority of Whites support racial equality in the attitude polls.

Perhaps of all Western countries Canada has established a backcloth of instrumental regulation, which is aimed at achieving greater normative regulation of human behaviour and addressing the dilemmas of equity and diversity. A Charter of Rights and Freedoms was attached to the Constitution, when it was patriated to Canada, which affords all citizens defence and redress against the infringement of their rights by other citizens or the state. Accompanying this has been the development of a national strategy on multiculturalism, embracing race relations and comprising legislation recognizing the multiculturalism of Canada as one of its basic norm-generating characteristics. In turn, this has been linked with the further development of human rights legislation and structures, including educational initiatives.[3] Such composite approaches, representing a broad social coalition, addressing many structures in society simultaneously and building on a broad ideological consensus, are rare.

In the developing world, too, the unifying euphoria of the early post-independence era has given way to a realization of the dynamic pluralism which comprises their cultural and historical biography. Even apparently homogeneous religious societies are by no means free from the conflicts of political, ethnic, linguistic and other forms of cultural diversity. Whatever their pretensions to cultural unity in understandable pursuit of political cohesion, most are far from being culturally monist. Those culturally diverse societies in the developing world seeking to pursue monist policies, whether in the form of single-party government or denial of cultural, ethnic and linguistic diversity in their education systems, have often paid a very high price for their attempted denial of pluralism in civil war and internal strife. At the end of the 1980s developing countries were expending five times the amount on armaments that they were receiving in aid. Almost a billion people were living in poverty in the developing world, and primary enrolment rates were falling or static in many countries, especially those which had been afflicted by war or internal strife.[4] Educational expenditure continued to favour the tertiary level of education, against the evidence that investment in that level of education yields the lowest rate of social return, in comparison with primary education, where the rates of return are highest. Moreover, human capital investment in health, education and nutrition achieves an effect of synergy leading both to higher income and to overall economic development.

Those societies, however, also face other problems of equity, focusing on their child and women populations. While in the 1960s and 1970s primary school enrolments in those countries increased substantially, that progress began to reverse in the 1980s, as population growth outstripped the financial capacity to respond, and massive resources were allocated to debt servicing and military spending. Several dozen of the world's poorest countries cut health spending by 50 per cent and educational spending by 25 per cent in the final years of the decade.[5] As the decade closed, almost 40,000 children a day were dying because of lack of food, shelter or adequate health facilities, millions of children lived on the streets, forced into work, military service, religious conversion, bondage or abuse, discriminated against on racial or religious grounds.[6] At the end of the same decade the educational enrolment of women and girls still lagged substantially behind that of the men and boys. Women still comprised the overwhelming majority of the unenrolled in developing countries, and their economic contribution to those societies was underrecognized and inaccurately recorded.[7]

Looked at globally, few countries have taken minorities into partnership in the design of their broader social and narrower educational strategies. Fewer still have tried a coordinated, global set of initiatives to achieve systematic and deliberate change towards agreed goals, based on a national convenant of acceptable norms and values, drawn against their international obligations. Yet such codifications are available in the many international agreements and conventions to which most Western countries are signatories. This stricture applies, of course, less to the 'newer' migrant countries and more to the older Eurocentric countries, still imprisoned by their perceptions of immigrants rather than fellow citizens and by the impedimenta of their nineteenth century values and a consequent outdated calibration of human beings and their worth.

If, however, we broaden the concept of equity to the global level, the discussion has hardly commenced on the interrelated responsibilities of North and South, East and West for greater economic and educational equity. Rather, the most powerful nations are still locked into introverted consideration of their own human rights, including educational equity, rather than a broader world-wide entitlement which can address the ingrained social, economic and educational prejudice and discrimination against women and children in their own and many developing countries. Thus, even in those Western societies where discussion of cultural pluralism is less recent and has resulted in structural policies in response to new perceptions, the debate has not progressed significantly beyond the frontiers of the nation state. In those societies, for example, discourse has not spread beyond dialogue among the academic cognoscenti about whether the issue of equity and cultural diversity can really be one-dimensional, and, if not, how it can best be understood and what are the structural implications of such cultural diversity. When the level of debate is raised to the infringement of the human rights of those in developing countries by the continued failure of the rich nations to embrace policies of sustainable development, by realizing the relationship between their profligate consumerism and the destitution of the poor world-wide, schools are silent and educators lose their eloquence.[8]

## THE DIVERSITY OF DIVERSITY[9]

Because especially sharp and unproductive controversy has surrounded the issue of whether cultural diversity can be realistically understood in the context of single factor explanations, it would be important for a series of books, such as this, to avoid the impression of a false convergence as much as the claim of some academics in the field to have found the holy grail of final resolution. Such utopian and millennial pretensions do not assist discussion of what is likely to be the major political and cultural topic of the last decade of the twentieth century: equity and diversity on a global stage. Contrary imaginations may exist about which factors should carry the heaviest weighting, or through which factors new policies and insights may best be accessed, or even which disciplinary traditions might serve best in studying and gaining purchase on cultural diversity, but not about the multidimensionality of cultural diversity itself.

If we consider the overlapping dimensions of cultural diversity which have seized headlines even in the recent past — racial, religious, linguistic, regional, ethnic, gender, age, social class and more recently caste — we cannot avoid the conclusion that, not only are most nation states culturally diverse, but that the world's population as a whole manifests a rich diversity across a large number of overlapping cultural factors and dimensions, representing a pluralism of pluralisms which are not usually embraced within the academic and political discourse about diversity in Western critical pedagogy.[10] Thus social policy options are needlessly constrained, political responses to the new-found pluralism of others needlessly impeded, and social policies and educational practice unnecessarily limited by a false perception, one could say an inadequate apprehension, of what cultural pluralism actually means in the daily construction and negotiation of reality in the lives of ordinary citizens, not least in the developing world, and thus how culturally diverse the world really is.

But the issue of equity and diversity must not be restricted myopically and parochially to a uniquely European phenomenon of contemporary arrival.[11] The social and political manifestations of cultural diversity and its interrelationship with equity are now becoming increasingly apparent in countries of East and West, North and South, in widely differing social systems and economic contexts, of diverse political persuasions and religious ideologies. Moreover, richer nations are gradually beginning to realize that on space-bus earth human welfare may be less divisible than they have assumed. Sometimes diversity and the right to greater equity are expressed in peaceful and creative tension, with cultural and social pluralism providing the momentum for social change, the liberation of the human spirit and greater human justice; sometimes the result is cultural bigotry, repressive hegemony, violent conflict, and even civil war, where diversity is used to legitimate economic and political conflict.

Accompanying the 'renaissance' of cultural diversity is a burgeoning of differing intellectual perspectives, which seek to complement and extend the already extensive literature of the past half-century. Sadly, almost exclusively, they address the issues from the point of the industrialized countries and ignore the broader international context and implications. Yet, can one really demand greater equity for oneself or one's own, and not for one's neighbour? It is the premise of this series of books that discourse about equity and diversity has to be brought to the bar of a global stage. True, the prevailing and countervailing dimensions of cultural diversity and the way in which it is apprehended vary considerably; its cultural composition diverges greatly in different countries and regions; and it is almost invariably complex and multifaceted. Yet deep-frozen cultural and intellectual paradigms have been slower to adapt to the need to apprehend diversity and equity as global issues than the pace of events necessitates. The upshot of that social, cultural and intellectual 'ice-age' in some Western countries has been a resort by academics to static, single factor models and explanations, the reinforce-ment of false stereotypes, overcategorization and enhancement of social category salience, and the only gentle reworking of essentially androcentric theories:[12] all rather ill-suited to reflect the dynamism of cultural diversity, let alone to combat the prejudice and bigotry which inevitably arise as a cultural by-product of that diversity.

In the case of educators such analyses have led to simplistic, and in some cases harmful and counterproductive, pedagogical panaceas, where both left and right have allocated a predominantly technicist role to the 'in-country' teacher, and where a Western hegemonic approach to social value positions has resulted in their being seen as absolutes rather than the field of competition of varying ideological perceptions and aspirations. Politically, the upshot has been a back-lash by socially conservative and culturally exclusive dominant groups. This has caused even less consideration of the global interactions and implications of in-flationary demands for equity in the 'North' for the achievement of equity in the 'South'.

For the above reasons it is important to regard with some scepticism percep-tions of the field of cultural diversity which seek to explain and propose policies for appropriate responses to that diversity on the basis of single factor analyses and one-dimensional perspectives within a single nation state.[13] Is it, for example, really conceivable that the overlays of factors — gender, religious, racial, ethnic, linguistic, social class, regional, caste and other circumambient cultural influences — can be coalesced into a meaningful and realistic single factor explanatory schema? Or do such analyses lead to a skewed and simplistic chimera that provides neither increased understanding nor improved policies?

This enigma applies in particular, to approaches in a very small number of countries which have labelled themselves antiracist, and taken on the exclusive mantel of legitimate commitment to combatting racial prejudice, bigotry and inequality in the face of a reality which includes many different groups and approaches, whose efforts and aspirations have often been spurned by antiracists. True, a more cooperative, less illiberal and coercive, ridiculous and authoritarian antiracist education is beginning to emerge than the variety which has done so much damage to race relations and the cause of an effective response to cultural diversity in the United Kingdom. More recent publications have sought, for example, to set antiracist education within the context of a broader civic, moral and political education, which 'seeks to extend participation in the democratic process by equipping young people with the range of skills and dispositions needed to become, decent, fairminded, responsible and informed citizens.'[14] That movement has not yet, however, begun to set such issues within a context of global rights and responsibilities.

The movement evinces major but usually unacknowledged similarities with Dewey and scholars such as Kohlberg, as well as the feminist and other critiques of that work by such writers as Gilligan,[15] and the work of such research practi-tioners as Sharan. There are strains of the work of the Centre for Social Integration at Bar Ilan, led by such scholars as Amir,[16] or of other schools of collaborative group work in the United States, such as that led by the Johnson brothers.[17] But there is still a rather worrying exclusion of the global dimension and a con-centration on cognitive, as opposed to affective, means of engaging with issues of race, when the literature of the last fifty years eloquently and extensively indicates the cognitive, affective and conative dimensions of prejudice and the efficacy of tackling it at those levels.[18] The movement's fetish-like zeal for a kind of Shavian 'brute sanity', or worse, even downright antidemocratic coercion in some cases, rather than for empowering people as a means to change their own prejudiced attitudes, flies in the face of what we know about systematic change and how to achieve it. Now, of course, there are differences between different forms of prejudice; but there are also commonalities and similarities, both nationally and globally.

The parlous state of human rights in the majority of the countries of the world, not to mention women's and children's rights,[19] owes much to that same spring of human cruelty and irrationality which nurtures racism. But it also owes much to that form of human endeavour which seeks to advance through coercion and intimidation rather than persuasion and normative re-education. Citizenship education, values education and law-related education, or even curriculum developments in the field of global education and world studies, made common cause against such human aberrations long before anyone dreamed up the term 'antiracist education'. Yet they are treated as 'Stalinist' non-movements by anti-racists. The global war on women and children remains unaddressed in the work of antiracists, because every human issue has to be forced through the gossamer of a biologically dubious racial interpretation of the human enterprise, a strategy which, far from decreasing racial prejudice, increases the dubious biological theory that there are different human 'races', strengthens the social category salience of that definition and thus increases prejudice.

This series of books is committed to the premise that racism and all other forms of negative prejudice are detrimental to a harmonious and healthy pluralist world society, and that it is the duty of all good democratic citizens to combat them, but that there are many valid routes by which such prejudice can be challenged, and that there are other kinds of prejudice and abuse which must also be combatted. It is also committed to the need for a fundamental review of the way in which the attenuation and eradication of all prejudice and discrimination have thus far been approached in educational systems and schools around the world. It is a deep sense of disappointment with the debate on diversity and equity thus far, seen internationally, which has been the motivation for almost 100 scholars, from many different societies, agreeing to contribute to the series and to seek to identify new ways of responding to cultural diversity and of combatting racism, sexism and 'childism' on a broader than national basis.

A rather superficial perspective on cultural diversity is also sometimes offered by organized religion, which sometimes runs for cover at the first signs of conflict even in the face of downright undemocratic demands which infringe the human and civic rights of citizens. A random and balkanized series of religious perspectives on society and its cultural diversity does not and cannot provide that core of common values, which can hold together a newly emerging highly diverse world society.[20] There has to be something more fundamental than a Babel of self-righteous organizations each despising the other and claiming to possess the truth. This is not to deny the importance of the spiritual dimension of life to millions of citizens, but to highlight the need for answers as to where human society as a whole stands, when that spiritual perspective denies the human rights of women or enslaves children in cultural bondage to their parents. In the Indian subcontinent the tradition of bride-burning is as potent as that of non-violence, but both cannot be acceptable to a more democratic global society which agrees to respect the human rights of all and recognizes the supra-statal rights of its citizens beyond national legitimation and legislation.

Some books, written from a religious perspective, convey a compelling and depressing impression that the soft religious tradition will only serve to increase false social and cultural category salience, and will, therefore, only augment the very typecasting and prejudice which it seeks to combat. It certainly cannot make significant contributions to that dialogue to which the world must commit itself if it is to survive as a multifaith democracy, multicultural, multiracial, multilingual and politically pluralist, yet not balkanized, where at the same time basic freedoms, such as the right to disagree fundamentally without being subject to threat and intimidation, can be safeguarded and extended: a society, in other words, which can serve to liberate the human spirit rather than find new means to enslave it.

## SOCIAL AND CULTURAL DIVERSITY?

The term 'cultural diversity' is used to describe the presence within one geographical area of a number of different cultural dimensions: linguistic, credal, racial, etc. Sometimes the term 'cultural pluralism' is used to describe what is called 'cultural diversity'. As Bullivant points out, there is a huge literature on cultural pluralism, drawn from many different disciplines and intellectual traditions.[21] Many models of cultural pluralism have been devised, all of them resting on implicit or explicit ideological assumptions, often expressive of contemporary fashions of their time in the social sciences. All seek, however, to develop a definition of pluralism according to major referents or descriptors. These referents, or an amalgam of such cultural referents, such as race and religion, class and gender, language and race, are then used by groups as what Bullivant calls 'boundary markers' for inclusion in, or exclusion from, the group and to advance the claims to rewards and resources of that group, as also its claims to justice and to representation for its value positions. But individuals each have a unique cultural biography, which comprises several different cultural referents, predisposes them to pre-judge members of other groups according to that cultural biography, and leads them to believe that their values are correct, when in reality they are contested positions within socio-cultural political arenas.[22] Not only cultural, but also social and economic demands may be levied by individuals and groups on the basis of their value positions.

Cultural pluralism is often confused with 'structural pluralism', which refers to what is made of cultural pluralism, so to speak, in structural or social terms — how we as social beings organize the cultural raw materials and fashion them into the shapes that we call institutions, organizations and societies. This is not a fact or a given in the way that cultural pluralism is. In other words, we are speaking of the social stratification of a society, which is partly planned, partly historically determined and partly culturally located. It is the way that we organize our culture, including values and meanings, to build our social and physical environment. The shape of our schools, for example, reflects — rather expresses — the educational epistemology of its time. Stratification may be on the basis of such referents as caste or socio-economic status, or, as in the United Kingdom, on the basis of birth into self-perpetuating monarchic, aristocratic or other élite groups. It does not necessarily imply that there is a different set of vertical structures in society for each group, for example, armies, financial structures, currencies, legal systems, to match the horizontal structure, although social and economic stratification are normally closely related and the allocation of life chances, jobs and economic and other rewards usually takes place on the basis of that stratification. Not many members of the aristocracy are to be found in the ranks of private soldiers in the army, and not many working-class people become generals. Social stratification is, however, a universal phenomenon, and it should not be assumed that it is found solely in Western societies.

In practice, individuals occupy several different kinds of groupings in society with overlapping membership, using them as means of advancing their claims to the satisfaction of their economic, political, cultural and other needs and demands. Such strivings, however, take place in the context of, one might almost say under the watch of, fairly constant élites, supporting and dominating the existing social order and exercising hegemonic social, and to a less extent cultural, control, sorting out and influencing life chances and the distribution of rewards and resources, as well as excluding or including different values and expressions of social reality, allocating high status to certain aspects of culture and not to others. In some culturally diverse societies, political stability may rely on a delicate but implicit social contract, under which certain groups are granted economic power, provided that they do not compete for political power, or under which they may mimic, but not threaten, the existing political structure.

Of course, each structure has its own distinctive culture, including the shared norms, values, ideologies, assumptions, symbols, meanings, language and other cultural capital which hold it together and enable it to function as a coherent unit without disintegrating. Groups then compete with each other, using ideologies as the means whereby they exercise leverage on each other and on the composite of all groups and individuals that we call society. Ideologies take the place of coercion as the means, in democratic societies, of persuading people to undertake particular courses of action or accept particular policies or fates. Groups or individuals have to be appealed to on the basis of overlap with their idealogy, or they will not accept the arguments and will remain unmotivated. So the 'trick' for the would-be social reformer is to marshall arguments and evidence that play maximally on the espoused values and ideologies of the groups or societies to be changed.

Thus 'democratic pluralism' is an essentially political concept, relating in particular to Western democratic societies, and expressive of the existence within one nation state of several political parties and many political ideologies. The term, however, is not an absolute, but only one varying point on a continuum. One might argue that democratic centralism, as practised until recently by all socialist countries, is at the opposite end of that same continuum. Often democratic pluralism is accompanied by economic pluralism, along a continuum from market to centralized economies, but the correspondence between cultural and economic location is by no means simple and direct. Thus members of minorities may define their social location along both cultural and economic dimensions. They may wish to retain as much of their own values and ideologies as are compatible with a democratic pluralism, but may wish to integrate politically and economically to maximize their access to rewards and resources. Groups and individuals use the gap between the espoused and declared values in a democratic society to gain purchase on change to influence it in the direction which they wish.

When we speak of structural pluralism, we are describing the extent to which the pluralism of different value positions can be accommodated within the social, economic and political make-up of any society. Too much accommodation and society disintegrates; too little, and it cannot legitimate itself and violent eruption or even revolution occurs. That is, at the same time, the fulcrum for creative social change and the dilemma for social policy-makers. How much, of what kind, to what extent can the cultural interests of minorities be expressed in structural terms? Should each have its own police force, or army, or schools, or legal system? This dilemma is subject to continual re-resolution, with different parties making different cultural, social and political accommodations, majorities as well as minorities, in different constellations of groupings. In some cases the aim may be social, political and economic inclusion, as in the claim for equal pay for equal work; in some cases it may be greater independence, as in the demand for separate schools. We are not faced with an either/or situation, but one of continual rebalancing and social accommodation, between the poles of unity and diversity, homogeneity and heterogeneity, cohesion and fragmentation. The distinction made by Gordon is useful when he writes of liberal and corporate forms of cultural pluralism.[23] By the first, he means a society where diversity is tolerated, but not officially recognized. By the second, he means a society where there is explicit recognition of cultural groups as a basis for the allocation of social and political power and economic resources. We might call the one 'passive cultural pluralism' and the other 'active cultural pluralism', where there is a continuum between the one and the other. The decision which has to be made is which cultural characteristics should be included as criteria for power and resources and which should not. Clearly, an infinite number of groups may exist in a situation of passive cultural pluralism, without any detriment to society, but there is a limit to the number which can be recognized for purposes of political and economic power without total balkanization and disintegration. Each group cannot really have its own legislation, or courts or police force, or army with no central control and coordination. That would be unworkable.

Once again we are faced with the need for an accommodation between total cultural pluralism across all social structures, at one extreme, and, at the other, exclusion of all cultural characteristics from all social structures, such as was tried until the recent past in the Soviet Union and to a greater extent in North Korea. Let us call these two poles total cultural and social heterogeneity and total cultural and social homogeneity. There are a number of forms of democratic structural pluralism, expressing the resolution of social tensions and dilemmas towards unity and towards diversity. The big question we must face today is which form of democratic social pluralism we would prefer to advocate. Which strategies for social inclusion and social differentiation can enable us to achieve that goal, bearing in mind the need to utilize appropriate ideologies to mobilize and convince the bulk of the population, that is, to legitimate those policies? Revolution is anathema within a society where democratic values are espoused or convincingly legitimated with the majority of the population.

Thus the question arises: how far can any society accommodate the needs of minority communities in what amount of structural pluralism, expressive of the needs of minorities, which can be legitimated by reference to democratic ideologies with a majority of the population, including the powerful hegemonic groups in society? In effect, the options for action available to both minorities and societies are very limited. Each has the choice of engaging in discourse by reference to shared ideologies, making technical accommodations to buy time or seeking to adopt coercive measures. A combination is also possible, but to the extent that either party adopts policies inclusive of the last option, it risks endangering its objectives, because its actions conflict with a major legitimating ideology of democratic society, that is, conflict resolution by discourse and not violence or coercion.

## THE CONTENTS OF THIS VOLUME

In this volume, the second volume of this series, the above considerations are woven into two major foci within the field of education and schooling: prejudice and its genesis, and the reduction and, if possible, eradication of prejudice and discrimination. Authors have been invited to review, critically discuss and seek to extend the theoretical and ideological approaches to these two themes, while accepting that containment of prejudice and its active mode discrimination may be as far as educational policy and practice can reach at the moment. Where it exists, they have been asked to examine critically the assumptions underlying policy and practice in their chosen field, within the context of these two foci. Their brief includes an admonition to pay particular attention to the identification of theories and policies which can express generic insights and approaches across a number of different areas of prejudice and discrimination, and which can be protective or expressive of human rights, while at the same time engendering a recognition of the need for social responsibility, national cohesion and international responsibility. Thus, authors are attentive to the synergy which these prejudices exert in support of each other.

Their focus includes the many dilemmas inherent in the concept of education for citizenship within democratic, culturally diverse societies, as well as the setting of those considerations in a wider international context and responsibility, so as to stimulate debate around the three levels of collective identity associated with membership of an ethnic group, and national and world citizenship across the issues of equity and diversity, seen as influenced by cultural, social and economic dimensions. Within those complex parameters, the contributions address some of the major policy issues in education and cultural diversity, grounded in up-to-date research and speculative writing in the field. The emphasis is on innovative approaches which have a wider applicability or transferability. Contributors have been invited to identify promising or novel approaches and to indicate the possibility for middle range theories which may assist educators, other practitioners and policy-makers in their professional enterprise of overcoming socially dysfunctional prejudices which sustain local, national and global inequity, exploitation and pollution.

The aim of their testimony is to place the life experience of prejudice and discrimination among teachers and children within a more globally responsible and world-sensitive context, drawing out the connections between personal, local, national and international analyses and initiatives, and seeking a continual rebalancing and social accommodation between the poles of unity and diversity, homogeneity and heterogeneity, cohesion and fragmentation. The overarching message of the volume is that the struggle to eradicate prejudice and discrimination is part of the overall struggle for human rights, democracy and environmentally sustainable development, and that it is a global one. It is not possible to support the aspiration to one without the other. All are indivisible for all human beings, and in these respects our future is a common one, or we do not have one.[24]

In Part One, directed to a consideration of the roots of prejudice, Eysenck considers certain fundamental problems relating to the causes of prejudice. He dismisses the almost universal assumption that prejudice is due to environmental factors and maintains that genetic factors are at least as important as environmental ones. Eysenck examines some theories concerning the hypothesized environmental causes of prejudice, in particular the famous frustration/aggression hypothesis, and seeks to show to what extent that hypothesis is applicable, and to what extent it can be used to reduce prejudice. Fishbein presents and elaborates an evolutionary model for understanding the development of prejudice and discrimination in children; and elucidates the facts about the development of prejudice and discrimination by children towards peers who are of the opposite sex, of another race, hearing impaired or mentally retarded.

Milner reflects that revealing the roots of racism is, in the first instance, a theoretical and educational exercise, as well as the first, necessary, phase in the process of their 'excavation'. It would, however, be naively utopian to believe that mere exposure to the light will eradicate them. The fact that racism fulfils an important function for dominant groups cannot be ignored, for it provides some of the essential raw material with which the structure of a competitive society is built. Milner concludes that racism is not simply a matter of cognitive errors which need to be corrected. While education must address such symptoms, only the political will for racial justice and social equality can begin to eradicate its roots.

Albert and Derby focus on the development of racial awareness, racial preferences and, subsequently, racial attitudes, including prejudice, that develop during a child's first twelve years. Historical studies on racial attitudes among children focused on Black and White children are considered as well as more recent research which has broadened its focus to include other groups under the rubric of ethnic attitudes. This new emphasis parallels awareness and concern in schools and workplaces with relations among different ethnic groups that has arisen in response to the tremendous increase in ethnic diversity in major American cities. Albert and Derby suggest that the lessons learned in studies of Black and White children provide a foundation for understanding ethnic diversity, but they also demonstrate the need for theories to take into account historical and cultural factors in understanding how children develop attitudes about their own and other groups.

Gay discusses some of the manifestations, causes and effects of female and male inequities, and how they can be remediated. She documents how gender discrimination is expressed in literacy rates, students' interactions with teachers, textbooks, and teaching and school leadership assignments. The causes of gender discrimination discussed include gender role socialization, teacher expectations, inappropriate role models, gender-typing of school subjects, and teaching styles. The author proposes that the remediation of these inequities requires system-wide and multidimensional strategies which give priority to making the processes of education more comparable in accessibility and quality for female and male students. Schneller's chapter offers evidence for the pancultural extent of cross-cultural misinterpretation of non-verbal language signs, and evaluates its impact on interethnic relations.

In the consideration of prejudice reduction with respect to intergroup relations in Part Two, Cookie White Stephan argues that intergroup anxiety is responsible for many of the unique effects of intergroup contact, including the superficial and formal nature of such interactions, the difficulty of changing intergroup attitudes and cognitions in intergroup interactions, and the intense emotional and evaluative reactions people experience in such interactions. She presents a model in which the causes of intergroup anxiety are traced to prior intergroup relations, prior intergroup cognitions and situational factors. The model also suggests that high levels of intergroup anxiety amplify normative intergroup behaviour patterns, cause cognitive and motivational information processing biases, lead to augmented emotional reactions and polarize evaluations of outgroup members. In revisiting the contact hypothesis (that previously segregated groups would benefit from mutual contact, Allport, 1954[25]), Harrington and Miller state that the expanded contact hypothesis is important in at least two respects. First, it focuses on conditions that promote harmony and, therefore, has implications for intervention strategies. Second, it articulates an array of variables that influence the intergroup setting. Harrington and Miller use these contingencies as a framework for organizing their discussion of intergroup work and for focusing on issues of controversy, particularly as they relate to educational settings.

Johnson and Johnson present their theoretical model of the processes of acceptance and rejection. The reason that cooperative experiences promote more positive crossethnic relationships than do competitive or individualistic experiences may be that cooperation promotes a process of acceptance rather than a process of rejection. Social judgment theory states that individuals become involved in a process of acceptance or rejection that determines whether they like or dislike each other. The processes of acceptance or rejection are a gestalt within which any part of the process tends to elicit all other parts of the process. When individuals cooperate with each other, the positive interdependence and promotive interaction result in frequent and accurate communication, accurate perspective-taking, inducibility, multidimensional views of each other, feelings of psychological acceptance and self-esteem, psychological success, and expectations of rewarding and productive future interaction. When individuals compete or work individualistically, the negative and no interdependence and oppositional or no interaction tendencies result in an absence of or inaccurate communication, egocentrism, resistance to influence, monopolistic and static views of each other, feelings of psychological rejection and low self-esteem, psychological failure, and expectations for oppositional interaction in the future.

Dasen argues that crosscultural psychology should become a part of teacher training towards an education for cultural diversity. Crosscultural psychology is defined as the scientific study of the ways in which social and cultural forces shape human behaviour. Two complementary theoretical frameworks are presented. The eco-cultural framework links individual behaviour to culture and the ecological and socio-historical contexts through the processes of acculturation and cultural transmission. The latter occurs through enculturation and socialization. The model of the developmental niche expands on these concepts in the area of developmental psychology. An understanding of these concepts and frameworks will help teachers to attain the necessary decentration from their own ethnocentrism, and will foster attitudes of respect for cultural diversity and solidarity. It is argued that, given these general principles, teachers should themselves be able to derive the educational implications appropriate to their particular multicultural context.

One of the main assumptions of Singh's paper is that denials of positive self-esteem or moral worth to others diminish one's own worth as a rational, moral, self-forming being. In Part Three, concerned with educational approaches to prejudice reduction, Singh analyzes teaching methods that enhance human dignity, self-respect and academic achievement. It is for the good of everyone that teachers and others should declare discriminatory acts against others invalid. The school community must express its denial of validity to the injurious discriminatory acts, uphold the rights of the injured and thereby the rights of all others as well. For the ultimate moral ground for the existence of any community of individuals is constituted by a collection of specific individuals valuing each other as ends and as members having rights in civic society. In such a society, individuals' values consist of their common will and mutual valuing.

In 'The Jigsaw Classroom: A Cooperative Strategy for Reducing Prejudice', Aronson and Thibodeau focus on the Jigsaw method, a cooperative teaching technique for reducing intergroup prejudice in the classroom. They also identify a selection of similar cooperative teaching strategies that have proved successful in fostering more harmonious relationships between minority and majority school children. Aronson and Thibodeau offer practical guidance for teachers wishing to implement the Jigsaw technique. Psycho-educational principles, educational interventions on the classroom level and teacher training for the promotion of integration and prejudice reduction are reviewed by Katz in the light of the initial disappointing results of the integrational process. Katz describes an apparently successful integration programme in an Israeli elementary school in which educational interventions, based on relevant key psycho-educational principles, were conducted.

In Part Four, which focuses on values in relation to prejudice reduction, Bottery argues that the promotion of an attitude of racial, cultural and ethnic tolerance will only be possible when a number of issues are addressed and changed at the same time. First, unfair structural and institutional practices which prolong discriminatory attitudes must be acknowledged and dealt with. Second, people's needs for cultural continuity and security must be understood and accepted. Third, an initial spirit of open enquiry into the unfamiliar must be generally adopted. Finally, a logically rigorous and critical values-based educational policy must be pursued which, while respecting the feelings and sensitivities of different groups, nevertheless explicitly confronts and questions practices within all cultures. Thus within values education there is a genuine need for an awareness by both pupils and teachers of the different value stances which people may adopt.

Wilson distinguishes between educational and political (social) values. After considering basic questions about the criteria to be used for differentiating pupils, Wilson argues that the aims of multicultural education involve questioning the very idea that one's identity should be conceived racially or culturally, and questioning the merits of one culture against another. The importance of 'local attachments' does not justify taking these criteria for granted. Schools must be made sufficiently potent — like families — to resist the importation of unacceptable social criteria and practices. They need to be based on the concept of education, and should encourage children to attach themselves to what is of central and permanent importance to human beings.

Oser formulates a number of theses that could provide a basis for an educational programme aiming at a reduction of prejudice in social reasoning. It seems to Oser: (1) that any education for reducing prejudice should be related to a developmental theory; (2) the fostering of unprejudiced action in educational settings can be based on direct stimulation of action tendencies as well as on developmental growth; (3) education for tolerance and understanding can only succeed in educational settings that are informed by high moral standards warranting an unprejudiced social climate; and (4) social psychological research gives strong suggestions as to what factors can help to reduce prejudice in society.

In Part Five Slavin reviews research on instructional methods designed to operationalize the principal elements of Allport's (*op. cit.*) contact theory of intergroup relations. Field experimental research on these methods in desegregated elementary and secondary schools has found relatively consistent positive effects on intergroup relations, as well as on the achievement of minority and majority students.

Walberg summarizes thirty-five years of results of major empirical studies and scholarly commissions on the controversial question of the possible dependence of Black students' learning on the student racial composition of schools. The inconsistency and inconclusiveness of research are traced from the early research to recent work that appears to present a reasonable resolution of the question. Cortés draws attention to the numerous complexities which arise concerning the media's role in contributing to ethnic pride and intergroup prejudice. He deals with five of these questions. How do the media fit within the larger process of educating the public about race, ethnicity, culture and foreignness? What dilemmas must be faced in attempting to assess media impact in these areas? What is the nature of that media influence? What forms of evidence provide insight into that influence? What effective actions can be adopted to address that influence?

The first volume in this series sought to give a panoramic overview of the differing perceptions and social constructions of cultural diversity, generated by the varying cultural, social and disciplinary positions of the authors. It sought to identify the divergence of policies and practices, but also the convergences in the form of the commitment to equal justice, to human dignity and rights and to the interdependence of humankind. In this volume, the second in the series, the relay of those earlier arguments about how to apprehend and respond to cultural diversity is retrieved and refocused through an intellectual and social lens, which sharpens the view that there can be no real human rights, justice and progress where human bigotry and its corollaries, discrimination, exploitation and enslavement, hold sway, either within societies or between them.

Neglect by school and society of the currently burgeoning diversity of human culture and the role of that diversity in prejudice 'production' is tantamount to supporting, or at the least conniving at, human injustice for others. It is a certain pathway to conflict, disaster and further human misery, through the legitimation of existing inequity, injustice and denial of human dignity and rights, above all to those who 'are different' in skin colour, ethnicity, religion, language, perhaps not least those who are less in economic power and military might. It is a path which leads to continuing human, economic and environmental degradation and economic decline, ultimately for all humankind, because education is silent on the pollution, deprivation and human misery visited on the poor by the rich.

The contributions to this volume, complete in themselves, also prepare the ground for the thrust of the final volume of this series, in the sense that they advocate the need to harness cultural diversity to a universal international, intergroup and personal commitment to human rights and social responsibilities, rather than to continued squandering of human potential for reasons of prejudice based on gender, race, class, caste, ethnicity, religion or other cultural factors. Their contributions embody the message that the campaign to eradicate human prejudice and discrimination is part of the unending struggle for human rights, democracy and environmentally sustainable development, and that it is a global and indivisible struggle for all human beings in pursuit of a common birthright.

## NOTES

1  This issue of a new internationalized curriculum with its ethical foundations bedded in human rights is dealt with in J. Lynch (1992) *Education for Gobal Citizenship in a Multicultural Society*, Lewes, Falmer Press.
2  National Research Council (1989) *A Common Destiny: Blacks and American Society*, Washington, D.C., National Academy Press.
3  Some of the human rights legislation in Canada pre-dates the Universal Declaration of Human Rights. A number of the main initiatives are summarized in J. Lynch (1986) *Multicultural Education: Principles and Practice*, London, Routledge; New York, Methuen.
4  The World Bank (1990) *World Development Report 1990*, Oxford, Oxford University Press.
5  N. Sadik (1989) 'Women: The Focus of the Nineties', *Populi*, 16, 2, pp. 5–19.
6  A useful primer on the rights of children, for use in schools and with an illustrated commentary on the International Convention on the Rights of the Child, is K. Castelle (1989) *In the Child's Best Interest*, New York, Foster Parents Plan International, Inc. and Defence for Children International.
7  A recent article argues the coincidence of equity and economic gain from greater investment in the education of women and girls. See B. Herz (1989) 'Bringing Women into the Economic Mainstream: Guidelines for Policymakers and Development Institutions', *Finance and Development*, December, pp. 22–25.
8  See the advocacy of the World Commission on Environment and Development (1986) *Our Common Future*, Oxford, Oxford University Press.
9  Some sequences of this section of the 'Editors' Introduction' were published previously in an earlier form. See J. Lynch (1990) 'Cultural Pluralism, Structural Pluralism and the United Kingdom', in Commission for Racial Equality, *Britain: A Plural Society* (A Report of a Seminar), London, CRE.
10  A recent critique of the highly abstract and utopian lines along which critical pedagogy has developed, its distance from the daily reality of education and its contribution to repressive pedagogical strategies and relationships of dominance in classrooms is contained in E. Ellsworth (1989) 'Why Doesn't This Feel Empowering? Working through the Repressive Myths of Critical Pedagogy', *Harvard Educational Review*, 59, 3, pp. 297–324.
11  A more extensive discussion of Lynch's views on the need to set educational policies to respond to

cultural diversity within a more international context is to be found in J. Lynch (1989) *Multicultural Education in a Global Society*, Basingstoke, Falmer Press. In particular, it seems that those advocating policies responsive to cultural diversity must come to creative terms with the implications of their own economic and cultural hegemony *vis-à-vis* developing countries.

12  A recent exposition of the encounter of feminist theory with liberalism and Marxism is A. Nye (1988) *Feminist Theory and the Philosophies of Man*, New York, Croom Helm.

13  One recent empirical study of the reasons why American Blacks tend to have high self-esteem but low personal efficacy emphasizes the importance of developing such research in a multidimensional framework. See M. Hughes and D.H. Demo (1989) 'Self-Perceptions of Black Americans: Self Esteem and Personal Efficacy', *American Journal of Sociology*, 95, 1, pp. 132–159.

14  The former illiberal rhetoric, urge to coercion and revolutionary purity and millenialism is beginning to be cast aside in favour of cooperation with other movements, sharing similar and in many cases wider aspirations to social change. See, for example, B. Carrington and G. Short (1989) *Race and the Primary School*, Windsor, NFER-Nelson.

15  See, for example, C. Gilligan (1982) *In a Different Voice*: *Psychological Theory and Women's Development*, Cambridge, Mass., Harvard University Press.

16  Y. Amir and S. Sharan (with the collaboration of Rachel Ben-Ari) (1984) *School Desegregation*, Hillsdale, N.J., Lawrence Erlbaum Associates.

17  D.W. Johnson, G. Mariyama, D. Johnson, D. Nelson and L. Skon (1981) 'The Effects of Cooperative, Competitive and Individual Goal Structures on Achievement: A Meta-Analysis', *Psychological Bulletin*, 89, pp. 47–62.

18  For a résumé of research and writing up to the mid-1970s, see P.A. Katz (Ed.) (1976) *Towards the Elimination of Racism*, New York, Pergamon Press.

19  See, for example, United Nations Children's Fund (1991) *The State of the World's Children*, Oxford, Oxford University Press, the statement made on 12 December 1989 by the General Secretary of UNICEF, and the United Nations Convention on the Rights of the Child, adopted in November 1989.

20  See E. Hulmes (1989) *Education and Cultural Diversity*, London, Longman.

21  B.M. Bullivant (1984) *Pluralism, Cultural Maintenance and Evolution*, Clevedon, Avon, Multilingual Matters Ltd.

22  It has been argued elsewhere that it should be the role of the school par excellence in a pluralist society to combat those predispositions and prejudices which are incompatible with creative membership of a democratic, pluralist society. See J. Lynch (1987) *Prejudice Reduction and the Schools*, London, Cassell.

23  M. Gordon (1964) *Assimilation in American Life*: *The Role of Race, Religion and National Origins*, New York, Oxford University Press.

24  See the commentary on our common future, The Global Tomorrow Coalition (1989) *Sustainable Development*, Washington, D.C.

25  G.W. Allport (1954) *The Nature of Prejudice*, Reading, Mass., Addison-Wesley.

# Part One: The Roots of Prejudice

# 1. Roots of Prejudice: Genetic or Environmental?

H.J. EYSENCK

## INTRODUCTION

In this chapter I propose to consider certain fundamental problems relating to the causes of prejudice. In particular, I shall examine the almost universal assumption that prejudice is based on an individual's historical experiences, i.e., is due to environmental factors. As we shall see, this is not so; genetic factors are at least as important as environmental ones. I shall also look at some theories concerning the hypothesized environmental causes of prejudice, in particular the famous frustration/aggression hypothesis, and seek to show to what extent that hypothesis is applicable, and to what extent it can be used to reduce prejudice.

Prejudice has been defined as 'an antipathy based on faulty and inflexible generalization. It may be felt or expressed. It may be directed toward a group as a whole, or toward an individual because he is a member of that group' (Allport, 1954, p. 9). Similarly, Ashmore defined it as 'a negative attitude toward a socially defined group and toward any person perceived to be a member of that group' (Ashmore, 1970, p. 253). Thus prejudice is an attitude which may or may not lead to discrimination, depending on many external circumstances. A fuller discussion of prejudice, discrimination and racism is given in a recent book by Dovidio and Gaertner (1986).

Prejudice is often linked with stereotyping, as in a definition given by Jones (1986), who uses the term 'prejudice' in the sense of 'a faulty generalization from a group characterization (stereotype) to an individual member of the group irrespective of either (a) the accuracy of the group stereotype in the first place, and (b) the applicability of the group characterization to the individual in question.' Stereotyping may be regarded as one of the *cognitive* components of prejudice; there are also *affective* components, such as dislike, and *conative* components, such as avoiding behaviour (Harding *et al.*, 1969). The recent book on *Stereotyping and Prejudice* by Bar-Tal, Graumann and Kruglandski (1989) spells out in detail the assumed connections between these variables.

Two assumptions are often made in the definition of 'prejudice' and 'stereotypes', namely that prejudices are always negative, i.e., disfavour a particular group, and that 'stereotypes' are always incorrect. Both these assumptions are false. Hitler had an obvious prejudice against the Jews, but he had an equal and contrary prejudice in favour of the hypothetical 'Aryan' race which was positive and extremely favourable. Prejudice *against* a given group normally implies a prejudice *favourable* to another group, and both should be considered. This is equally true of actions taken against or for a given group. Thus those in the apartheid tradition discriminate against Blacks, which is evidence of prejudice against them; in a similar way laws favouring Blacks, such as 'affirmative action', might be regarded as prejudice in favour of Blacks. Both types of law have been defended by its supporters on what are supposed to be rational grounds, but insofar as the laws favour one group against another they must be considered prejudicial.

As regards stereotypes, Eysenck and Crown (1948) have drawn attention to the dubious methodology on which many of the studies that have been carried out in this area depend. However that may be, stereotypes should not be considered 'true' or 'false' unless there is compelling evidence one way or the other; the fact that an attitude is stereotyped in a given group does not say anything about its truth or falsity. We have a stereotype of Japanese as hard workers, and it seems that this stereotype is perfectly valid. To act on this assumption would, therefore, not be evidence of prejudice, although an assumption that *every* Japanese is more hardworking than *any* American or European would of course be absurd. In Malaysia the stereotype of the bright Chinese and the dull Malays is widespread, but it does seem to have strong evidence in its favour, from IQ studies, from scholastic achievement, etc. Thus the whole field is very much more complex than is often assumed, and these assumptions themselves may be evidence of stereotype thinking and of prejudice.

American psychologists (e.g., Allport, 1954) identified a variety of approaches to the understanding of racial prejudice. These embraced (1) the historical approach, (2) the socio-cultural approach, (3) the situational approach, (4) personality structure and dynamics, (5) the phenomenological approach, (6) the stimulus-object approach. Theories based on these different approaches have burgeoned in recent years, and a detailed listing of some of them will be found in Dovidio and Gaertner's book on *Prejudice, Discrimination, and Racism* (1986). Here let us merely note that all these approaches without exception emphasize *environmental* determinants, whether related to the family or to the wider environment, and here, as in other books on prejudice, there is no mention of the possibility that genetic factors might exert an influence on the person's standing as far as prejudice is concerned.

## GENETIC FACTORS IN THE GENESIS OF PREJUDICE

In an early study of monozygotic and dizygotic twins, Eaves and Eysenck (1974) found evidence for a strong genetic component of the two major factors in the attitude field, namely, radicalism-conservatism and tough-vs.-tendermindedness, and more recently much more extensive studies of the field, with particular reference to prejudice, have been published in a book entitled *Genes, Culture and Personality* by Eaves, Eysenck and Martin (1989). Let us consider some major findings from the studies there summarized, which have bearing on the problem in question.

The instruments used for thses studies were the Eysenck Public Opinion Inventory, taken from *The Psychology of Politics* (Eysenck, 1954), and the Wilson-Patterson Conservatism Scale, taken from *The Psychology of Conservatism* by Wilson (1973). The former contained a series of attitude questions, the latter a series of fifty words presumably having positive or negative meaning for the respondent, such as 'chastity', 'royalty', 'socialism', etc. Subjects are requested to say 'yes' or 'no' in response to each item, according to whether they favour or believe in that item. Both the Eysenck and Wilson-Patterson scales contain items relevant to the question of prejudice. Details concerning the questionnaires, the factors they give rise to, their application in many different countries, etc., may be found in *The Psychological Basis of Ideology* by Eysenck and Wilson (1978).

The questionnaires were administered to large groups of monozygotic and dizygotic twins in England (the Eysenck Social Attitudes Scale only) and in Australia (both questionnaires). An analysis of the Australian data in particular has been published by Martin *et al.* (1986). Details concerning populations, selection, etc., as well as details of the genetical analyses made, can be obtained from these sources; this is not the place for a detailed discussion of these matters.

Essentially, the analysis consisted of constructing models embodying varying combinations of possible genetic and environmental factors, and then testing these models against the observed variables. Personality studies in general have shown that models containing only two major components are sufficient to account for the observed phenotypic values with sufficient accuracy (Eaves, Eysenck and Martin, 1989). These variables are first of all additive genetic variance ($V_A$), and secondly within-family environmental variance ($E_W$). There was little evidence for between-family environmental variance ($E_B$). Analysis of the various items reflecting prejudice in our study seemed to conform to a similar model.

The difference between within-family environmental variance and between-family environmental variance is implicit in the description of $E_W$ and $E_B$. Between-family environmental variance refers to those variables which, in the environment of the child, differentiate one family from another, i.e., the personalities and abilities of the parents, their socio-economic status, their living conditions, the amount of encouragement or otherwise they give to the scholastic endeavours of their children, the number of books and newspapers in the house, the interaction between parents and children, the schooling these children achieve, etc. Within-family environmental variance refers to those more or less accidental factors in the life of the child which differentiate him from other children in the same family, such as, for instance, having a particularly good or bad teacher, suffering or not suffering some illnesses, marrying a suitable or unsuitable partner, being in a satisfactory or unsatisfactory type of employment, etc.

In the nature of things, $E_B$ factors are much easier to study than $E_W$ factors, because the former can be defined systematically, whereas the latter are much more specific, random and unclassifiable. It is perhaps for this reason that $E_B$ factors have been researched much more readily than $E_W$ factors, and in relation to intelligence, for instance, it seems to be true that $E_B$ factors are more important than $E_W$ factors (Eysenck, 1979). However, for personality and social

**Table 1.** *Six Items from the Eysenck Social Attitudes Scale Relating to Prejudice, together with a Proportion of the Total Variance Explained by Genetic Factors ($V_a$), Between-Family Environmental Factors ($E_B$) and Within-Family Environmental Factors ($E_W$)*

| Item number | | $V_A$ | $E_B$ | $E_W$ |
|---|---|---|---|---|
| 2 | Coloured people are innately inferior to white people. | .50 | — | .50 |
| 15 | It would be a mistake to have coloured people as foremen over whites. | .41 | — | .59 |
| 19 | There may be a few exceptions, but in general Jews are pretty much alike. | .39 | — | .61 |
| 44 | All forms of discrimination against the coloured races, the Jews, etc., should be made illegal, and subject to heavy penalties. | .33 | — | .67 |
| 46 | Jews are as valuable citizens as any other group. | .44 | .01 | .55 |
| 54 | It would be best to keep coloured people in their own districts and schools, in order to prevent too much contact with whites. | .21 | .25 | .54 |

**Table 2.** *Three Items from the Wilson-Patterson Conservatism Scale Dealing with Prejudice, together with the Proportion of the Total Variance Explained by $V_A$, $E_B$ and $E_W$*

| Item number | | $V_A$ | $E_B$ | $E_W$ |
|---|---|---|---|---|
| 17 | White superiority | .50 | — | .50 |
| 33 | Apartheid | .49 | — | .51 |
| 40 | Mixed marriage | .33 | .12 | .55 |

attitudes, conditions seem to be different, and however difficult the field of $E_W$ factors may be, we have no choice but to attempt to postulate and test the importance of such factors.

Table 1 shows the six items of the Eysenck Social Attitudes Scale which are related to racial prejudice, and the results of the genetic analysis carried out on these items. It will be clear that genetic factors $V_A$ are somewhat less potent than within-family environmental factors $E_W$, but that between-family environmental factors $E_B$ are almost non-existent. These data establish the importance of genetic factors, although they underestimate the importance of the $V_A$ as compared to $E_B$ and $E_W$; as I shall show later, certain corrections need to be made.

Table 2 gives three main items from the Wilson-Patterson Conservatism Scale which are relevant, and again shows that $V_A$ is just slightly less important than $E_W$, with $E_B$ practically non-existent. The factor analysis of the Wilson-Patterson Conservatism Scale isolated a prejudice factor (Wilson, 1973; Eaves, Eysenck and Martin, 1989), and this factor showed a genetic contribution of 59 per cent, a within-family environmental component of 41 per cent and no evidence of a between-family environmental component.

The Eysenck Social Attitudes Scale, when factor analyzed, gives rise to a conservatism factor which is related to prejudice, and three studies have been done to demonstrate the environmental and genetic factors entering into its determination. On average, the $V_A$ amounts to 41 per cent, $E_W$ to 31 per cent and $E_B$ to 28 per cent. However, as previously pointed out, all these values require some correction because two additional factors have to be included in the

**Table 3.**  *Sources of Variance for Age-corrected Conservatism Scores (percentages)*

|  |  | Females | Males |
|---|---|---|---|
| $E_1$ < error | | 36 < 18 / 18 | 41 < 9 / 32 |
| $V_A$ | assortative mating \| total genetic | 35 ] 49 | 27 ] 38 |
| $E_2$ < assortative mating / family environment | | 29 < 14] / 15 | 32 < 11] / 21 |

calculation. One of these is measurement error (unreliability of the measure-ment), which is compounded with $E_W$, and assortative mating, which is com-pounded with $E_B$.

Table 3 shows a typical analysis carried out on the Eysenck Social Attitudes Scale. The results are given separately for females and males, and it will be seen that when correction is made for errors of measurement and for assortative mating, $V_A$ increases from 35 per cent to 49 per cent for females, and from 27 per cent to 38 per cent for males. This is not the place to describe how models are tested, or to discuss in detail the statistical methods employed; all these details will be found in Eaves, Eysenck and Martin (1989). The important point is that when these corrections are made for the values in Tables 1 and 2, it becomes clear that $V_A$ is at least as important in determining prejudice as is $E_W$, while $E_B$ is eliminated completely. Even without these corrections it is quite clear that genetic factors play a very important part in predisposing individuals to express opinions prejudical to the various racial groups in question, i.e., Jews and Blacks, and that between-family environmental variance plays little if any part in determining these prejudices.

The genetic determination, in part, of prejudice and ethnocentrism suggests that perhaps socio-biological evidence might be relevant, and that such prejudice might be the inevitable effect of group formation (Eibl-Eibesfeldt, 1986), i.e., the universal tendency for human beings to organize themselves into tribal national units, which are normally in competition with each other, thus creating a certain amount of enmity between them. When differences between groups become emphasized through racial characteristics, enmity and prejudice would seen to be magnified by easily recognizable features of the groups in question, such as skin colour. Prejudice would thus seem to have a biological, evolutionary root, which at the other extreme would give rise to friendship and altruism. A detailed discussion of the theory has been given by Rushton (1985, 1986, 1989; Rushton *et al.*, 1986) who provides a good deal of evidence in its favour, as well as supporting the hypothesis that genetic factors are involved in friendships and altruistic be-haviour towards people in groups similar in gene structure. Genetic findings related to attitudes thus fit well into a broader socio-biological and evolutionary picture.

These findings, replicated several times, throw a good deal of light on the roots of prejudice, and lead us to re-evaluate previous conceptions. It is curious that students of prejudice have themselves shown evidence of a very marked prejudice, namely, an avowal of 100 per cent environmentalism, and a refusal even to consider the possibility of genetic determination of prejudice. A reading of the now very large literature on the topic reveals hardly any mention of the very possibility that genetic causes might have been important in causing racial and other types of prejudice; the environmentalist position has been taken without any evidence in its favour, and in the absence of any effort to determine whether such a view was in fact justified. We may with justification call that position 'stereotyped'.

Equally, most writers have assumed, again in the absence of any evidence, that between-family environmental variance was a crucially important cause of individual differences in prejudice. This is particularly true of the 'dynamic' theories which rely heavily on parent-child relations, particularly during early life, and thus would seem to imply very strongly $E_B$ type factors as contributing to the total variance. Our studies have shown that this belief is mistaken, and would thus seem to rule out of court a number of widely popular theories, such as those associated with the concept of the 'authoritarian personality' (Adorno *et al.*, 1950).

One reason for these failures to take into account important research possibilities and methodologies is that psychologists often misperceive the way in which behaviour geneticists work, and the kind of problem they attempt to solve. It is often assumed that behaviour geneticists are concerned only to discover the degree of heritability of a given ability, trait or attitude pattern, a task which may easily appear unimportant to social psychologists, and which indeed would be of limited use. However, this is not how behaviour geneticists look upon their work. Faced with the phenotypic expression of certain abilities, personality traits or attitudes, they seek to partition the total variance into a number of portions, such as additive genetic variance, dominance, epistasis, or assortative mating on the genetic side, within-family environmental effects and between-family environmental effects on the environmental side, and various interaction factors between the two sides. Thus it may be argued (Eaves, Eysenck and Martin, 1989) that *no* model other than the type of model tested by behaviour geneticists is adequate for the causal analysis of any behaviour pattern whatsoever. It will be equally clear that behavioural geneticists do not concentrate on genetic factors but are equally concerned with environmental ones. Indeed, they are concerned with phenotypic behaviour and forces, and they are paying attention to both sides of the coin, as it is impossible to carry out any meaningful analysis paying attention only to one side. The implication is that no analysis re.,.ng only on environmental features can tell us very much about the roots of prejudice, or indeed about causal factors in the field of personality and ability; such partial analyses rely entirely on unrealistic assumptions and on improbable interpretations of partial data. This is a vital contribution that behavioural genetics has made to the study of individual differences in psychology, and to the causal analysis of social data.

The fact that prejudice and ethnocentrism are genetically determined to a large extent, and are linked with evolutionary events, does not, of course, serve to justify them in a moral or ethical sense. The main purpose of advanced civilizations is to curb natural, biologically determined tendencies in order to make civilized and communal living possible. The greater strength of males makes it possible for them to impose their will on females in most mammalian groups, but this biologically determined relationship is rightly curbed by law in civilized societies. Behaviours which may have been useful and successful in an evolutionary manner a million years ago are not necessarily so now. There is no way in which prejudices can be excused or justified because they have a biological underpinning.

In the following sections we will be concerned with the methodological consequences as far as research in this field is concerned, i.e., the indication that if we wish to look for environmental influences on prejudice, then we must look for $E_W$ rather than for $E_B$ factors, thus clearly delineating the field of research, and suggesting research possibilities which have hitherto often been neglected in favour of the less promising $E_B$ type of environmental variable.

One further comment may be appropriate here. It is often suggested that if genetic factors play an important part in the causation of individual differences in ability, personality or social attitudes, then this makes it impossible for environmental effects to change the observed patterns. This cleary is not so. Genetic factors determine social attitudes to the extent of between 50 and 60 per cent, when corrected for the various intruding factors mentioned above; this leaves a good deal of the total phenotypic variance to be accounted for in environmental terms which are subject to change. Even a very strong determination of a given phenotypic behaviour in genetic terms does not rule out considerable change if novel environmental factors are brought to bear. Heritability is a population statistic which describes the proportion of variance attributable to various genetic and environmental factors in a given population, at a given time; it has no absolute value, and may change from time to time in a given population, and at a given time from population to population. Bringing to bear new methods of social intervention would change the situation, and might lead to a lowering of genetic contribution and an increase in environmental contribution. Thus in a country showing great inequality of provision for primary, secondary and tertiary education, genetic factors would be much less effective in producing differences in IQ than in a country having a very egalitarian system of school and university education (Heath *et al.*, 1985). We are always dealing with a complex, interacting system in which there are no absolutes, in which any change in one variable produces changes in other variables. Hence the possibilities of personal intervention are not limited by the fact that genetic factors play a part in the creation of the phenotype. But such successful intervention only becomes possible when we gain a better understanding of the relative contributions of the various genetic and environmental factors, and of their interaction.

## PERSONALITY, STRESS AND PREJUDICE

There is a good deal of evidence that the different types of racial, national and religious prejudice are related together (Bierly, 1985; Ray and Lovejoy, 1986), and can be found in the tough-minded sector of the social attitude space (Eysenck, 1944, 1950, 1951, 1954). There is also evidence that such attitudes are related to personality (Eysenck, 1961; Eysenck and Coulter, 1972; Eaves and Eysenck, 1974). In this last study, prejudice was found to be part of 'tough-mindedness', and to be related to aggressive behaviour and attitudes. Eysenck and Wilson (1978) have reviewed some of the more recent literature, as have Wilson (1973), Oskamp (1977) and Pettigrew *et al.* (1980).

Among the personality variables studied were self-esteem (Bagley, Verma and Mallick, 1981); locus of control (Duckitt, 1984); repression-sensitization (Chesan, Stricker and Fry, 1970); punitiveness (Snortum and Ashear, 1982); adjustment (Sharan and Karan, 1974; Duckitt, 1985); as well as a variety of other personality characteristics (Chabassol, 1970; Heaven, 1976; Hesselbart and Schuman, 1976; Maykovich, 1975; Sinha and Hassan, 1975; Sarma, 1973; Serum and Myers, 1970; and many others). Krech, Crutchfield and Ballachey (1972) summarize a number of studies by stating: 'Racial prejudice is often found among the mentally ill' (p. 182).

Another source of prejudice and ethnocentrism which has been suggested in the literature is weak socio-economic position, uncertainty about future employment and earnings, and other similar aspects of social alienation and insecurity (Oskamp, 1977; Pettigrew *et al.*, 1980). Connected with these hypotheses is Campbell's view that aggression induced by frustration may be a powerful influence in racial prejudice towards the Jews (Campbell, 1947), or indeed generally.

Of the various causes suggested in the literature, the one that appears to agree best with the $E_W$ factor seems to be that suggested by Campbell (1947), which in turn is based on the well-known frustration-aggression hypothesis originally suggested by Dollard *et al.* (1939), who proposed the hypothesis that *frustration always leads to aggression, and aggression is always the result of frustration*. This very general theory has had to be modified in recent years, as research demonstrates that frustration does not always lead to aggression, but may cause alternative reactions like depression, feelings of helplessness and hopelessness (Seligman, 1975). Similarly, aggression is not always the result of frustration, but may have other causes. Berkowitz (1962, 1969, 1979) has suggested that frustration leads to anger, not aggression, but that anger may easily instigate aggression if suitable aggressive cues exist, including, for instance, pain or frustrative non-reward, or the presence of guns, swords or other arms.

In the latest examination and reformulation of the frustration-aggression hypothesis test reported by Berkowitz (1989), he concludes that there is a good deal of evidence consistent with the classic frustration-aggression hypothesis: '. . . when one, first, confines their thesis to (a) that part of the formulation dealing with frustrating reactions, or (b) those acts that are primarily hostile (emotional or expressive) aggression rather than instrumental aggression and, second, recognizes that the frustration involves the non-attainment of an unexpected gratification rather than a mere deprivation' (p. 71). Berkowitz also maintains that 'contrary to the widespread contention that only arbitrary, illegitimate, or personally directed interferences give rise to aggression, aggression is at times displayed when the thwarting is socially justified or is not directed against the subject personally' (p. 71). Berkowitz does suggest a major modification to the Dollard *et al.* formulation: 'Frustrations are perversive events and generate aggressive inclinations only to the extent that they produce negative affect' (p. 71). This modification agrees well with the results of the experiment described above, as 'negative affect' is characteristic of the reactions of Types 1, 2 and 3 to frustrating events.

One recent large-scale experiment (Grossarth-Maticek, Eysenck and Vetter, 1989) has attempted to test this hypothesis and demonstrated that frustration leads to racial prejudice, which is regarded as a form of implicit aggression which may easily turn into explicit aggression. The experiment is based on a series of findings demonstrating that certain personality types characterized by stress and frustration, resulting in feelings of hopelessness, helplessness and depression, are more likely than others to die of cancer and coronary heart disease (Eysenck, 1985, 1987a, 1987b, 1988; Grossarth-Maticek, Bastiaans and Kanazir, 1985; Grossarth-Maticek, Eysenck, Vetter and Frentzel Beyme, 1988; Grossarth-Maticek, Eysenck and Vetter, 1988; Grossarth-Maticek, Eysenck, Vetter and Schmidt, 1988; Grossarth-Maticek, Frentzel-Beyme and Becker, 1989). Three large-scale prospective studies were carried out, in each of which data concerning personality, stress, smoking and drinking habits, cholesterol level and other medical factors were assessed at the beginning of the studies, using only healthy probands, and death and cause of death were investigated ten years later to see the extent to which these variables predicted death and cause of death. Probands were at the beginning divided into four types, the cancer-prone type (Type 1), the coronary heart disease-prone (Type 2), a mixed or psychopathic type which proved to be relatively healthy (Type 3), and an autonomous or healthy type (Type 4). Types 1, 2 and 3 shared the experience of strong interpersonal stress, with Types 1 and 2 showing also suppression of emotion and inability to react appropriately to stress, but rather giving up and demonstrating feelings of hopelessness, helplessness and depression. The emotions suppressed were anxiety in the case of Type 1, and anger in the case of Type 2. Type 3 showed alternation between the behaviours characteristic of Type 1 and Type 2, and this alternation might have influenced its lower rate of illness.

Grossarth-Maticek, Eysenck and Vetter (1989) considered that degrees of frustration which could be implemented in a laboratory setting would be quite inadequate to produce the strong effects of prejudice, ethnocentrism, etc., which are the subjects of study, and felt that life events inducing intolerable stress and frustration would be much more likely to lead to measurable consequences in the field of social attitudes. For that reason they used probands taking part in the health studies already mentioned as subjects for the experiment, without mentioning the purpose of the additional investigations to the subject who throughout considered it merely a study of relationship between personality, stress and health. In this section we will be concerned primarily with the predicted relationship between personality and stress, on the one hand, and prejudice, on the other. In the next section we will deal with the possibility of prophylactic treatment of cancer-prone and coronary heart disease-prone probands, on the one hand, and the effectiveness of their treatment for health, and also for prejudice, on the other.

**Personality**

(a) Subjects of the experiment were 6796 males, aged from 45 to 55, interviewed and tested in the years from 1972 to 1983. Every year between 400 and 800 persons were interviewed, constituting a representative sample of the German

**Table 4.** *Eight Questions Constituting the Political Prejudice Inventory to Assess Social and Political Prejudice*

1   In the leading industrial countries of the West, is Parliamentary Democracy the major cause of the cultural deterioration and the accumulation of more and more unsolvable problems which are leading to the destruction of civilization altogether?

2   Would you agree that International Jewry carried the main responsibility for the growing number of crises and misunderstandings in the industrialized countries of the West, so that one might perhaps have to say that Hitler was not all that wrong in his judgment of the Jews?

3   Do the Arabs constitute the greatest threat to peace in Western Industrial society, because with their aggressive religion and their malicious mentality they intend to destroy Western culture?

4   Do the Slavs constitute the greatest threat to peace in the Western World because with their panslavistic attitudes they want to subjugate Germanic and Romanic countries and force upon the Western World an inferior culture?

5   Would you say that the Christian religion is a major cause of the difficulties and troubles to be found in the Western Industrial countries?

6   Do you believe that different races are so different in their abilities and qualities that it would be perfectly justified and desirable to speak of superior and inferior races?

7   Is the behaviour of the United States in the whole world one of the major causes of misunderstandings, crises and unsolvable problems?

8   Is the Communist ideology and practice such a cause of misunderstandings and crises in the whole world that we would be justified in trying to destroy communist governments and communist movements by force?

The questionnaire used is published elsewhere (Grossarth-Maticek, Eysenck and Vetter, 1989). Only some of the results are discussed here.

town of Heidelberg between the ages of 45 and 55. An additional 3625 persons refused to take part in the study. Interviewers were specially trained students who had taken part in similar studies concerned with stress and physical health (Grossarth-Maticek, Eysenck and Vetter, 1988; Eysenck, 1987a, 1987b).

(b) Attitudes towards possible sources of prejudice were obtained by means of an eight-point questionnaire, to be answered 'Yes', or 'No', which is reproduced as Table 4. The questions were intentionally put in a rather extreme manner, to obtain extreme judgments of prejudice. An additional twelve neutral questions relating to political and social problems were intermixed with the eight questions in Table 4, to make the intention of the questionnaire less obvious; these are irrelevant buffer items and have not been analyzed.

(c) One question was put to ascertain the socio-economic status and attitudes towards security-insecurity of the persons interviewed. The question was as follows: 'Looking at the last three years of life, do you find an increasing deterioration of your material situation and your social position, so that in comparison with earlier years you are becoming poorer and less integrated?'

(d) Subjects of the experiment were also given a detailed questionnaire to determine to what extent they belonged to one of four major types of personality previously studied in relation to physical health, particularly cancer and coronary heart disease.

Table 5 shows the number of persons of Types 1, 2, 3 and 4 who answered positively any of the eight items relating to prejudice, and who felt socio-

**Table 5.**  *Numbers of Subjects Agreeing with Each of the Eight Prejudice Statements, Subdivided According to Personality Type, and Numbers Showing Socio-Economic Insecurity*

| Political prejudice | Type 1 | Type 2 | Type 3 | Type 4 |
|---|---|---|---|---|
| Attitude | | | | |
| 1  Anti-democratic | 52 | 121 | 195 | 15 |
| 2  Anti-Semitic | 81 | 165 | 103 | 10 |
| 3  Anti-Arab | 75 | 76 | 54 | 6 |
| 4  Anti-Slav | 51 | 148 | 37 | 2 |
| 5  Anti-Christian | 77 | 48 | 67 | 1 |
| 6  Anti-racist | 88 | 157 | 105 | 2 |
| 7  Anti-American | 40 | 194 | 213 | 3 |
| 8  Anti-Communist | 105 | 207 | 121 | 5 |
| Total | 1590 | 1720 | 1970 | 1516 |
| Socio-economic uncertainty | 268 | 351 | 312 | 201 |
| Average age | 52.1 | 50.5 | 48.1 | 49.4 |

**Table 6.**  *Relationship between Typology and Prejudice*

| | Type 1 | Type 2 | Type 3 | Type 4 | Total |
|---|---|---|---|---|---|
| Any prejudice | 218 | 401 | 384 | 21 | |
| Total | | 1066 | | 21 | 1087 |
| No prejudice | 1309 | 1319 | 1548 | 1495 | |
| Total | | 4212 | | 1495 | 5707 |
| $X^2$: $P < 0.001$ | | | | Total: | 6794 |

economically uncertain. The average ages for the persons belonging to each of the four types showed no significant differences (mean age = 51 years).

Socio-economic uncertainty is significantly more frequently found among Types 1, 2 and 3 than in Type 4. Political prejudice is almost absent among persons of Type 4, most frequent among persons of Types 2 and 3, and intermediate among persons of Type 1.

These relations become more apparent when treated as percentages. Of Type 1, 36 per cent answered at least one question in the prejudiced direction. Of Type 2, 65 per cent did so; of Type 3, 45 per cent and of Type 4 less than a third of 1 per cent. Thus Type 2 is the most prejudiced, followed by Type 3, then Type 1, with Type 4 being almost free of prejudice.

There is some patterning to the relationships between prejudice and personality. There appears to be a suggestion that Type 1 is particularly characterized by anti-Arab and anti-Christian attitudes, and relatively little by anti-American attitudes. Type 3, on the other hand, shows little anti-Arab or anti-Slav prejudice. While these results, like all the others mentioned, are fully significant statistically, they were not predicted, and would required replication before being taken too seriously.

Table 6 shows the relationship between type and prejudice, this time using persons and not judgments indicative of prejudice as the variables plotted. In

**Table 7.**  *Intercorrelations (phi) between Eight Prejudiced Attitudes*

| Prejudice | 1 | 2 | 3 | 4 | 5 | 6 | 7 | 8 |
|---|---|---|---|---|---|---|---|---|
| 1 | — | 0.65 | 0.31 | 0.44 | 0.41 | 0.55 | 0.79 | 0.40 |
| 2 | 0.65 | — | 0.14 | 0.66 | 0.43 | 0.81 | 0.71 | 0.73 |
| 3 | 0.31 | 0.14 | — | 0.45 | 0.41 | 0.67 | 0.19 | 0.28 |
| 4 | 0.44 | 0.66 | 0.45 | — | 0.30 | 0.48 | 0.39 | 0.61 |
| 5 | 0.41 | 0.43 | 0.41 | 0.30 | — | 0.51 | 0.37 | 0.22 |
| 6 | 0.55 | 0.81 | 0.67 | 0.48 | 0.51 | — | 0.53 | 0.43 |
| 7 | 0.79 | 0.71 | 0.19 | 0.39 | 0.37 | 0.53 | — | 0.34 |
| 8 | 0.40 | 0.73 | 0.28 | 0.61 | 0.22 | 0.43 | 0.34 | — |

**Table 8.**  *Socio-Economic Insecurity and Prejudice*

|  | Type 1 | Type 2 | Type 3 | Type 4 |
|---|---|---|---|---|
| Socio-economic security | 1322 | 1369 | 1658 | 1315 |
| Total | | ----------v---------- 4349 | | 1315 |
| Socio-economic insecurity | 268 | 351 | 312 | 201 |
| | | ----------v---------- 931 | | 201 |
| $X^2$:P < 0.01 | | | Total | 6796 |

other words, any person showing even one prejudice is counted as prejudiced, demonstrating that approximately one person in five is prejudiced according to this differentiation. Chi square shows the significance of these results.

Table 7 shows the intercorrelations (phi coefficients) between the eight types of prejudice. It will be seen that the table constitutes a positive manifold; there are no negative correlations. Some are quite low, such as that between anti-Semitic and anti-Arab attitudes (0.14); one might have thought that this correlation would turn out to be negative, but this was not so. Others are very high, such as that between anti-democratic and anti-American attitudes (0.79), or that between anti-democratic and anti-Semitic attitudes (0.65). The pattern of correlations is not very different from what one might have expected, although the absence of any negative correlations may be surprising. The table demonstrates very clearly the prominence of a generalized prejudicial type of reaction, characteristic of certain types of individual.

## Socio-Economic Uncertainty and Prejudice

Table 8 shows the relationship between socio-economic insecurity and our personality typology. There is a significant relationship between insecurity and Types 1, 2 and 3, and security and Type 4. Chi square is fully significant for this differentiation.

**Table 9.**  *Prejudice, Typology and Socio-Economic Insecurity*

| | Prejudice | | | | | | | |
|---|---|---|---|---|---|---|---|---|
| | Any | | | | No | | | |
| Types | 1 | 2 | 3 | 4 | 1 | 2 | 3 | 4 |
| Socio-economic security | 91 | 100 | 134 | 4 | 1231 | 1269 | 1524 | 1311 |
| | ------v------ | | | | --------v-------- | | | |
| Total | 329 | | | | 5335 | | | |
| Socio-economic insecurity | 190 | 301 | 250 | 5 | 78 | 50 | 62 | 196 |
| | ------v------ | | | | --------v-------- | | | |
| Total | 746 | | | | 386 | | | |

$X^2: P < 0.01$

Table 9 shows the relationship between prejudice and socio-economic insecurity; there is a very significant relationship in the sense that socio-economic insecurity is related to high prejudice. Personality and socio-economic insecurity contribute jointly and severally to political prejudice.

The data in Table 10 were submitted to a log-linear analysis (Everitt, 1977), specifically testing the interaction between personality type and socio-economic security. The underlying distribution of the data was assumed to be multinominal, with significance testing implemented via the $Chi^2$ distribution. Brown's (1976) screening procedure (outlined in Lavic, 1986) was used to assess the relative contribution of the interaction parameter over and above an additive main effect model. Model fitting was accomplished using the SYSTAT statistical package (Wilkinson, 1987). For the additive main effect model of PERSONALITY TYPE = SOCIOECONOMIC SECURITY, the Likelihood ratio $Chi^2$ was 6119.69, with 11df and P,0.00001. For the model PERSONALITY TYPE × SOCIOECONOMIC SECURITY, the Likelihood value was 6088.81, with 8 df and P,0.00001. Use of Brown's screening method for assessing the significance of the interaction yielded a $Chi^2$ test statistic of 30.88, with 3 df with $P < 0.0001$.

This method of analysis is probably more appropriate to the type of data considered, and gives clear answers to our questions. The main outcome of the analysis, other than supporting the simple $Chi^2$ type of analysis reported in Tables 9 and 10, is the strong finding that the interaction between personality type and socio-economic security contributes a considerable portion of the variance, over and above the separate contributions of personality type and socio-economic security. Thus the influence of economic insecurity in causing prejudice would seem to be particularly strong in personality Types 1, 2 and 3, as opposed to personality Type 4.

The data suggest very strongly that prejudice and ethnocentrism are not entirely specific as far as given populations are concerned, but extend to all populations, at least to some extent, thus giving evidence of a general factor of prejudice-ethnocentrism. It is equally clear that this general factor is related to stress-induced frustration, and the particular type of personality structure which makes it difficult for a person to react positively and constructively to stress. It would seem that the frustration-aggression hypothesis finds some support in these data, although the aggression involved is more implied than explicit.


## INTERVENTION TO PREVENT PREJUDICE


There have been many suggestions as to how prejudicial attitudes might be altered, and how prejudice might be reduced (e.g., Katz and Zalk, 1978; Griffit and Garcia, 1979; Langer, Baschner and Chamowitz, 1985). Interracial contact has been a favourite in this connection (e.g., Foley, 1977; Moore, Hauck and Donne, 1984). Unfortunately, as Ford (1986) has shown, favourable intergroup contact does not always reduce prejudice, and on the whole the evidence is inconclusive; intergroup contact may have favourable or unfavourable effects, depending on circumstances which are not clearly understood.

There is a good deal of evidence to suggest that a certain type of cognitive behaviour therapy can alter in the direction of Type 4, the behaviour of persons typically answering questionnaires in the direction of Types 1, 2 and 3, and it has been demonstrated quite clearly that doing so acts as a very significant prophylactic device against cancer and heart disease (Eysenck, 1987a, 1987b, 1988, 1991 Grossarth-Maticek, Eysenck and Vetter, 1988; Grossarth-Maticek and Eysenck, 1989).

It was hypothesized that if frustration was a characteristic of Types 1, 2 and 3, and if frustration was causally implicated in producing prejudice, then treatment by behaviour therapy designed to lower frustration would also incidentally lower prejudice. Evidence for the prophylactic efficacy of behaviour therapy in preventing cancer and coronary heart disease from developing in probands of Types 1 and 2 (Eysenck, 1987a, 1987b, 1991; Grossarth-Maticek, Eysenck and Vetter, 1988) suggests that the treatment may be successful in partly removing frustration through improving coping behaviour.

People showing at least one political prejudice in the questionnaire were divided on a random basis into a control group and a therapy group, each consisting of 265 persons. Pairs were formed on an age basis, and one member was randomly assigned to the treatment group, the other to the control group. Pairs were also equated for type of prejudice; in other words, both were anti-Semitic, or whatever. Training was given to groups of twenty to thirty persons at a time, and lasted altogether between twenty and twenty-five hours. Roughly speaking, the training consisted of five hours of therapy, regarding the differences between autonomous and dependent behaviour, self-regulation, etc. Ten hours were spent on the identification of object dependence in individuals, and the discovery of alternative behaviour patterns which should be aimed at to avoid such object dependence. The last ten hours were spent formulating precise aims for each person, suggesting coping mechanisms, and dealing with general and specific methods of attaining the person's aims. A more detailed description of the methods and aims of the cognitive behaviour therapy employed is given in the references above. After this training was completed, the prejudice questionnaire was repeatedly applied to these groups after six months, one year and two years

**Table 10.** *Decline of Prejudice over Two Years in Control and Therapy groups*

| | Group without any prejudice | |
| --- | --- | --- |
| | Therapy | Control |
| Prior to treatment | 0 | 0 |
| Six months later | 124 | 1 |
| One year later | 153 | 2 |
| Two years later | 179 | 0 |

from the completion of the training. It should be noted that in both the therapy group and the control group there are fifty-five persons of Type 1, 100 persons of Type 2, and 110 persons of Type 3.

It is important to note that the therapy training was offered in the course of an investigation into the posibility of using such training as a prophylactic measure against cancer and coronary heart disease (Eysenck, 1987a, 1987b); it was not given as a 'cure' for racist prejudice, and indeed during the training political and social attitudes were never mentioned. Thus therapy was offered as an aid to physical health, and it was accepted or rejected *exclusively* on this basis. Of the 440 pairs originally approached, 175 refused to take part in the training; a pair was excluded from the experiment if one of the two refused participation.

Table 10 shows the main results. It will be seen that at the beginning of the therapy none of the 265 persons in either group was without at least one political prejudice, but two years after the training 179 people in the trained group did not have any political prejudice, while in the control group all 265 persons still showed at least one political prejudice. In other words, there was no change in the control group, but a very marked one in the therapy group. See also Figure 1.

Table 11 gives the number of persons showing anti-Semitism. Before the training there was no significant difference between the two groups, but while the control group does not show any change over the next two years, the therapy group shows a very significant reduction of about 70 per cent in anti-Semitic prejudice. See also Figure 2.

These data demonstrate fairly conclusively that it is possible to alter prejudice and ethnocentrism to a very marked extent by suitable environmental interventions in people displaying extreme forms of prejudice. This demonstration indicates that while genetic factors are important, they do not preclude changes from being produced by suitable methodology, taking into account important and well-validated theories and principles. Replication of this study would be important in validating these conclusions.

## DISCUSSION

I propose in this discussion to concentrate on methodological points which arise from the findings discussed above. Some of the points have already been made in passing, but may usefully be discussed in some detail. Our first point is that no proper study of topics in social psychology, such as prejudice, ethnocentrism or

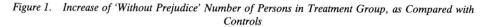

*Figure 1.   Increase of 'Without Prejudice' Number of Persons in Treatment Group, as Compared with Controls*

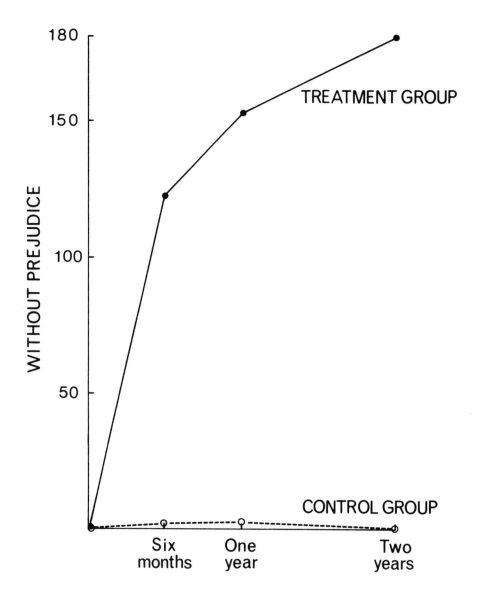

attitudes in general, is possible which does not use the methodology of behaviour-al genetics. Theories stressing environmental factors are incapable of proof unless genetic factors can be ruled out, and a suitable model constructed which can be shown to fit the data better than models involving genetic factors. Knowing the relative contributions of the various genetic and environmental factors studied is a *sine qua non* for designing specific experiments and developing specific theories concerning causal effects.

Given that in the field of prejudice we deal with two major causal factors, namely additive genetic variance ($V_A$) and within-family environmental variance

**Table 11.** *Decline in Anti-Semitic Prejudice over Two years in Therapy Groups*

| | Anti-Semitic | |
| --- | --- | --- |
| | Therapy group | Control group |
| Prior to treatment | 169 | 163 |
| Six months later | 101 | 165 |
| One year later | 67 | 168 |
| Two years later | 51 | 164 |

*Figure 2. Decline of Anti-Semitism in Treatment Group, as Compared with Controls*

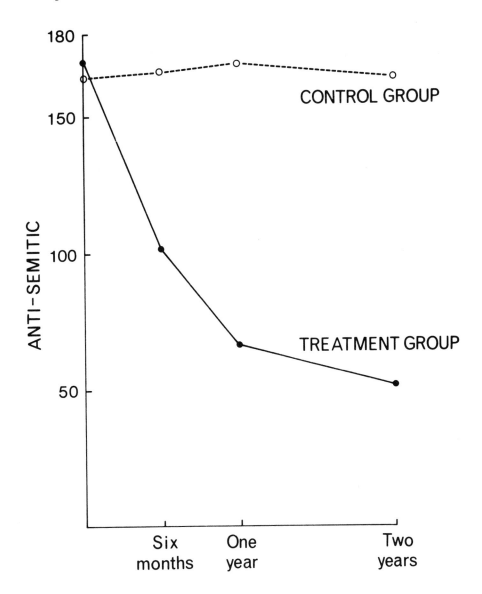

($E_W$), and may rule out between-family environmental variance ($E_B$), we can design hypotheses concerning likely influences, and then test these in real-life populations, rather than laboratory situations, by suitable prospective studies using such variables as stress and personality reaction to stress. It has been demonstrated that under these conditions prejudices of a racial or national kind form a cluster which is closely related to experiences of stress, poor reactions to stress, where stress may be of an interpersonal kind, such as is shown by individuals of Types 1, 2 and 3, or may be of a socio-economic sort, i.e., lack of financial security. In addition to the separate contributions of personality type and socio-economic security, there is a considerable interaction effect between interpersonal stress and socio-economic insecurity.

Frustration thus produced is a psychological factor that can be diminished or even abolished using certain types of behaviour therapy, and the use of these methods enables us to reduce the frustration-induced aggression, expressing itself in the form of prejudice, to a considerable extent. This type of intervention study directly attacks the problem of *causation*, and transforms the study from the well-known restrictions of being purely *correlational*. Even intervention studies cannot *prove* a given causal hypothesis, but they can render it more and more likely that true causal factors have been isolated. It is recommended that intervention studies must accompany any correlational studies claiming to isolate the causes of prejudice.

It may be concluded that our search for the roots of prejudice, by using the *genetic* method, has given us new insight into this complex field, and that the method of *intervention* has shown results to have a truly causal significance. Replication of this work is of course required to put our findings on a more secure basis.

## REFERENCES

Adorno, T.W., Frenkel-Brunswick, E., Levinson, D.J. and Sandford, R.N. (1950) *The Authoritarian Personality*, New York, Harper and Drew.
Allport, G. (1954) *The Nature of Prejudice*, Reading, Mass., Addison-Wesley.
Ashmore, R.D. (1970) 'Prejudice: Causes and Cures', in B.E. Collins (Ed.), *Social Psychology: Social Influence, Attitude Change, Group Processes, and Prejudice*, Reading, Mass., Addison-Wesley, pp. 245–339.
Bagley, L., Verma, C.K. and Mallick, R. (1989) 'Personality, Self-Esteem, and Prejudice', *Journal of Personality Assessment*, 45, pp. 320–321.
Bar-Tal, D., Graumann, C.T. and Kruglandski, A.W. (1989) *Stereotyping and Prejudice*, New York, Springer.
Berkowitz, L. (1962) *Aggression: A Social Psychological Analysis*, New York: McGraw-Hill.
Berkowitz, L. (1969) 'The Frustration-Aggression Hypothesis Revisited', in L. Berkowitz (Ed.), *Roots of Aggression*, New York, Atherton Press.
Berkowitz, L. (1979) *A Survey of Social Psychology*, 2nd ed. New York, Holt, Rinehart and Winston.
Berkowitz, L. (1989) 'Frustration-Aggression Hypothesis: Examination and Re-formulation', *Psychology Bulletin*, 106, pp. 59–73.
Bierly, M.M. (1985) 'Prejudice toward Contemporary Anti-Groups as a Generalized Attitude', *Journal of Applied Social Psychology*, 15, pp. 189–199.
Brown, M.B. (1976) 'Screening Effects in Multi-Dimensional Contingency Tables', *Applied Statistics*, 25, pp. 37–46.

Campbell, A.A. (1947) 'Factors Associated with Attitudes towards Jews', in T.M. Newcomb and E.L. Hartley (Eds), *Readings in Social Psychology*, New York, Holt.

Chabassol, D. (1970) 'Prejudice and Personality in Adolescents', *Alberta Journal of Educational Research*, 16, pp. 3–12.

Chesan, B.D., Stricker, G. and Fry, L.L. (1970) 'The Regression-Sensitization Scale and Measures of Prejudice', *Journal of Social Psychology*, 80, pp. 197–200.

Dollard, J., Doob, L., Miller, N., Mowrer, O. and Sears, R. (1939) *Frustration and Aggression*, New Haven, Conn., Yale University Press.

Dovidio, J.F. and Gaertner, S.L. (1986) *Prejudice, Discrimination, and Racism*, London, Academic Press.

Duckitt, J.H. (1984) 'Locus of Control and Racial Prejudice', *Psychological Reports*, 59, p. 462.

Duckitt, J.H. (1985) 'Prejudice and Neurotic Symptomatology among White South Africans', *Journal of Psychology*, 119, pp. 15–20.

Eaves, L.J. and Eysenck, H.J. (1974) 'Genetics and the Development of Social Attitudes', *Nature*, 249, pp. 288–289.

Eaves, L.J., Eysenck, H.J. and Martin, N.G. (1989) *Genes, Culture and Personality*, London, Academic Press.

Eibl-Eibsfeldt, I. (1986) *Die Biologie des Meuschlichen Verhaltens*, Munich, Piper.

Everitt, B.S. (1977) *The Analysis of Contingency Tables*, London, Chapman-Hall.

Eysenck, H.J. (1944) 'General Social Attitudes', *Journal of Social Attitudes*, 19, pp. 207–227.

Eysenck, H.J. (1950) 'Social Attitude and Social Class', *British Journal of Sociology*, 1, pp. 56–66.

Eysenck, H.J. (1951) 'Primary Social Attitudes as Related to Social Class and Political Party', *British Journal of Sociology*, 2, pp. 198–209.

Eysenck, H.J. (1954) *The Psychology of Politics*, London, Routledge and Kegan Paul.

Eysenck, H.J. (1961) 'Personality and Social Attitudes', *Journal of Social Psychology*, 53, pp. 243–248.

Eysenck, H.J. (1979) *The Structure and Measurement of Intelligence*, New York, Springer.

Eysenck, H.J. (1985) 'Personality, Cancer and Cardiovascular Disease: A Causal Analysis', *Personality and Individual Differences*, 5, pp. 535–556.

Eysenck, H.J. (1987a) 'Anxiety, "Learned Helplessness" and Cancer — a Causal Theory', *Journal of Anxiety Disorders*, 1, pp. 87–104.

Eysenck, H.J. (1987b) 'Personality as a Predictor of Cancer and Cardiovascular Disease and the Application of Behaviour Therapy in Prophylaxis', *European Journal of Psychiatry*, 1, pp. 29–41.

Eysenck, H.J. (1988) 'The Respective Importance of Personality, Cigarette Smoking and Interaction Effects for the Genesis of Cancer and Coronary Heart Disease', *Personality and Individual Differences*, 9, pp. 453–464.

Eysenck, H.J. (1991) *Smoking, Personality and Stress: Psychosocial Factors in the Prevention of Cancer and Coronary Heart Disease*, New York, Springer Verlag.

Eysenck, H.J. and Coulter, T. (1972) 'The Personality and Attitudes of Working-Class British Communists and Fascists', *Journal of Social Psychology*, 87, pp. 59–73.

Eysenck, H.J. and Crown, S. (1948) 'National Stereotypes: An Experimental and Methodological Study', *International Journal of Opinion and Attitude Research*, 7, pp. 26–39.

Eysenck, H.J. and Wilson, G.D. (Eds) (1978) *The Psychological Basis of Ideology*, Lancaster, MTB Press.

Foley, L. (1977) 'Personality Characteristics and Inter-Racial Contact as Determinants of Black Prejudice towards Whites', *Human Relations*, 30, pp. 709–720.

Ford, W.S. (1986) 'Favorable Inter-Group Contact May Not Reduce Prejudice — Inconclusive Journal Evidence, 1960–1984', *Sociology and Social Research*, 70, pp. 256–258.

Griffit, W. and Garcia, L. (1979) 'Reversing Authoritarian Punitiveness: The Impact of Verbal Conditioning', *Social Psychology Quarterly*, 42, pp. 55–61.

Grossarth-Maticek, R., Bastiaans, J. and Kanazir, D.T. (1985) 'Psychosocial Factors as Strong Predictors of Mortality from Cancer, Ischaemic Heart Disease and Stroke: The Yugoslav Prospective Study', *Journal of Psychosomatic Research*, 29, pp. 167–176.

Grossarth-Maticek, R., Eysenck, H.J. and Vetter, H. (1988) 'Personality Type, Smoking Habit and Their Interaction on Predictors of Cancer and Coronary Heart Disease', *Personality and Individual Differences*, 9, pp. 479–495.

Grossarth-Maticek, R., Eysenck, H.J. and Vetter, H. (1989) 'The Causes and Cures of Prejudice: An

Empirical Study of the Frustration-Aggression Hypothesis', *Personality and Individual Differences*, 10, pp. 547–558.

Grossarth-Maticek, R., Eysenck, H.J., Vetter, H. and Frentzel-Beyme, R. (1988) 'The Heidelberg Prospective Intervention Study', in W.J. Eylenbosch, N. van Larabeke and A.M. Depoorter (Eds), *Primary Prevention of Cancer*, New York, Raven Press, pp. 199–211.

Grossarth-Maticek, R., Eysenck, H.J., Vetter, H. and Schmidt, P. (1988) 'Psychosocial Types and Chronic Diseases: Results of the Heidelberg Prospective Psychosomatic Intervention Study', in S. Maes, C.D. Spielberger, P.B. Defares and I.G. Sarasan (Eds), *Topics in Health Psychology*, New York, John Wiley and Sons, pp. 57–75.

Grossarth-Maticek, R., Frentzel-Beyme, R. and Becker, N. (1989) 'Cancer Risks Associated with Life Events and Conflict Solutions', *Cancer Detection and Prevention*, 7, pp. 201–209.

Hamilton, D.L. and Trolier, T.K. (1986) 'Stereotypes and Stereotyping: An Overview of the Cognitive Approach', in J.F. Dovidio and S.I. Gaertner (Eds), *Prejudice, Discrimination, and Racism*, London, Academic Press, pp. 127–163.

Heath, A., Berg, K., Eaves, L., Solaas, M., Corby, L., Sundet, J., Magus, D. and Nance, W. (1985) 'Education Policy and the Heritability of Educational Attainment', *Nature*, 319, pp. 734–736.

Heaven, P.C. (1976) 'Personality, Prejudice and Cultural Factors', *Psychological Reports*, 39, p. 724.

Hesselbart, S. and Schuman, H. (1976) 'Racial Attitudes, Educational Level, and a Personality Measure', *Public Opinion Quarterly*, 40, pp. 108–114.

Jones, J.M. (1986) 'Racism: A Cultural Analysis of the Problem', in J.F. Dovidio and S.L. Gaertner (Eds), *Prejudice, Discrimination, and Racism*, London, Academic Press, pp. 279–314.

Katz, P. and Zalk, S.R. (1978) 'Modification of Children's Racial Attitudes', *Developmental Psychology*, 14, pp. 447–461.

Krampen, G. (1986) 'Politische Psychologie: Geschichte, Defizite, Perspektiven', *Psychologische Rundschau*, 37, pp. 138–150.

Krech, D., Crutchfield, R.S. and Ballachey, E.L. (1962) 'Racial Prejudice Is Often Found among the Mentally-Ill', *in Individual in Society*, New York, McGraw-Hill, p. 182.

Langer, E.J., Bashner, R.S. and Chanowitz, B. (1985) 'Decreasing Prejudice by Increasing Discrimination', *Journal of Personality and Social Psychology*, 49, pp. 113–120.

Lavic, A.D. (1986) *New Developments in Statistics for Psychology and the Social Sciences*, London, Methuen.

Martin, N.G., Eaves, L.J., Jardine, R., Heath, A.C., Feingold, L.F. and Eysenck, H.J. (1986) 'Transmission of Social Attitudes', *Proceedings of the National Academy of Sciences of the USA*, 83, pp. 4364–4368.

Maykovich, M.K. (1975) 'Correlated Racial Prejudice', *Journal of Personality and Social Psychology*, 32, pp. 1014–1020.

Moore, J., Hauck, W.E. and Donne, T.C. (1984) 'Racial Prejudice, Inter-Racial Contact, and Personality Variables', *Journal of Experimental Education*, 53, pp. 168–173.

Oskamp, S. (1977) *Attitudes and Opinions*, Englewood Cliffs, N.J., Prentice-Hall.

Pettigrew, T.F., Fredrickson, G.M., Knobel, D.T., Glazer, N. and Veda, R. (Eds) (1980) *Prejudice*, Cambridge, Mass., Harvard University Press.

Ray, J.J. and Lovejoy, F.H. (1986) 'The Generality of Racial Prejudice', *Journal of Social Psychology*, 126, pp. 563–564.

Rushton, J.P. (1985) 'Differential K Theory: The Sociobiology of Individual Group Differences', *Personality and Individual Differences*, 6, pp. 441–452.

Rushton, J.P. (1986) 'Gene Culture Co-evolution and Genetic Similarity Theory: Implications for Ideology, Ethnic Nepotism, and Geopolitics', *Politics and the Life Sciences*, 4, pp. 144–148.

Rushton, J.P. (1989) 'Genetic Similarity in Male Friendships', *Ethnology and Sociobiology*, 10, pp. 361–373.

Rushton, J.P., Fulker, D.W., Neale, M.C., Nias, D. and Eysenck, H.J. (1986) 'Altruism and Aggression: The Heritability of Individual Differences', *Journal of Personality and Social Psychology*, 50, pp. 1192–1198.

Sarma, S.C. (1973) 'Prejudice and Personality', in T.E. Shanmugan (Ed.), *Researches in Personality and Social Problems in Madras*, London, University of London.

Seligman, M.E.O. (1975) *Helplessness: On Depression, Development and Death*, San Francisco, Calif., Freeman.

Serum, C.S. and Myers, D.G. (1970) 'Note on Prejudice and Personality', *Psychological Reports*, 26, pp. 65–66.

Sharan, M.B. and Karan, L.W. (1974) 'Relationship between Prejudice and Adjustment', *Psychologia*, 17, pp. 99–102.

Sinha, R.D. and Hassan, M.K. (1975) 'Some Personality Correlates of Social Prejudice', *Journal of Social and Economic Studies*, 3, pp. 225–231.

Snortum, J.R. and Ashear, V.H. (1972) 'Prejudice, Punitiveness, and Personality', *Journal of Personality Assessment*, 36, pp. 291–296.

Wilkinson, L. (1987) *SYSTAT: The System for Statistics*. Evanston, Ill: SYSTAT.

Wilson, G.D. (Ed.) (1973) *The Psychology of Conservatism*, London, Academic Press.

# 2. The Development of Peer Prejudice and Discrimination in Children

HAROLD D. FISHBEIN

An inevitable by-product of living in a culturally diverse society is the differential socialization of its children. Socialization processes lead to the development of particular attitudes and behavioural preferences. These in turn may lead to the development of prejudice and discrimination towards peers with different socialization experiences. In order to be effective in either preventing the development of peer prejudice and discrimination or in modifying them once they occur, it is essential to understand how they develop.

The two major goals of this chapter are: to present and elaborate an evolutionary model for understanding the development of prejudice and discrimination in children; and to elucidate the facts about the development of prejudice and discrimination by children towards peers who are of the opposite sex, of another race, hearing impaired or mentally retarded. These four groups have been chosen for the following reasons. First, their diversity will allow useful insights to be gained into the development of prejudice and discrimination. Second, there is a substantial and methodologically adequate literature for each. Third, these groups have never before been considered together. Fourth, the common focus is on peers, which produces a focused discussion, and it is hoped, clear conclusions.

Allport (1954) defined *prejudice* as: '. . . an antipathy based upon a faulty and inflexible generalization. It may be felt or expressed. It may be directed toward a group as a whole, or toward an individual because he is a member of that group' (p. 9). *Discrimination*, for Allport, is the negative action that a person carries out, based on prejudices. Discrimination often takes the form of excluding others from some activity or group. Aboud (1988), a student of children's racial prejudice, defined it as '. . . an organized predisposition to respond in an unfavorable manner toward people from an ethnic group because of their ethnic affiliation' (p. 4). There is substantial agreement between the two definitions; however, there are differences in emphasis. For Allport, the negative evaluation must be 'faulty and inflexible', whereas for Aboud, it must be 'organized'. There are other definitions of prejudice, but the common core can be summarized as: an unjustified negative evaluation of others because of their membership in a particular outgroup. Discrimination involves the negative actions which follow from the underlying prejudice.

Prejudice and discrimination are not all-or-none phenomena. Rather, they are graded. The extent to which children will be prejudiced at any one time depends on their specific experiences with outgroup members, their personalities, and the prejudicial attitudes expressed to them by family and friends, as well as by other cultural means, e.g., television, books and schools. Prejudice, of necessity, will change over time, because children have new experiences and their cognitive, social and emotional understandings and capacities change with maturation and experience. In this chapter we address the issue whether there is anything systematic about observed age-related changes in prejudice and discrimination.

The measurement of prejudice and discrimination, as defined above, has rarely been successfully accomplished with children and adolescents. The stumbling block has been assessing the 'unjustified' aspect of the negative attitudes, beliefs or actions. There appear to be no relevant studies which have directly attempted this assessment. The research efforts seem to assume, as an example, that negative attitudes directed towards Blacks or Whites are unjustified. From an adult viewpoint they may be, but from a child's viewpoint the negative evaluation may be justified. In a simple case, a child is told by its parents that drinking milk is good, crossing streets without looking both ways is bad, policemen can be trusted, strangers in cars are dangerous, and that Whites will try to hurt you. Is it justified to have positive attitudes towards police, negative attitudes towards strangers in cars, and yet unjustified to have negative attitudes towards White children?

In another simple example, if a child has had a number of unpleasant encounters with hearing impaired children, are negative evaluations of hearing impaired peers justified or unjustified? Categorization is inevitable, normal and necessary for adaptive functioning (Allport, 1954). It would be concluded that in the second example the child's negative evaluations toward the hearing impaired were justified in that they were based on a consistent generalization. Is the child prejudiced? Allport would argue that if the attitudes were inflexible and did not change with new and different information, then the child would be considered prejudiced (because the attitudes would now be unjustified).

Following the lead of other researchers, this chapter will consider children's negative attitudes and beliefs as indicators of prejudice, and their negative actions as indicators of discrimination. However, the reader must bear in mind that a crucial element — 'unjustified' — is uncertain.

Before discussion of the evolutionary model of prejudice and discrimination, one additional point should be made. There are multiple causes of prejudice and discrimination, and many theories to account for the facts of their development. Allport, Aboud and other scholars describe and discuss these causes and theories. There is considerable controversy concerning some of the theories, as might be expected. For example, Williams and Morland (1976) argue that there is a biological basis for negative evaluations of dark colours, which may develop into racial prejudice. Milner (1983) equally convincingly argues that a case can be made for a biologically determined positive bias towards darkness. Owing to space limitations, there will be no discussion here of alternative theories. The evolutionary theory is one, and not the only, valid theory of the development of prejudice and discrimination. It is a theory which has been given little systematic treatment in this arena, but which, owing to its importance, deserves emphasis.

## AN EVOLUTIONARY MODEL FOR THE DEVELOPMENT OF PREJUDICE AND DISCRIMINATION

### The Primate Evolutionary Heritage

The primates evolved about 60 million years ago from mammalian ancestors probably resembling contemporary tree shrews (Andrews, 1985). Four major events occurred within that time span: (1) the New World and Old World primates were separated (about 50 million years ago); (2) the Old World monkey-ape split occurred (about 40 million years ago); (3) the common Old World ancestors of gorillas, chimpanzees and humans emerged (about 12–16 million years ago); and (4) the evolutionary lines leading to distinct gorilla, chimpanzee and human species appeared (about 6–10 million years ago).

Apart from obvious anatomical and physiological similarities, the key common denominator of nearly all the Old World primates, including humans, is that they are members of long-duration subsistence groups, comprising the young and old of both sexes. The major types of social structures of these groups are as follows (Fishbein, 1976, 1984).

1  For the chimpanzee, a mother and one or two young offspring comprise a family. The social group as a whole consists of many of these families, along with free-ranging juveniles and young and older adults, most in hearing distance of one another.
2  For the gorillas and most monkeys who live on the ground of forests and savannas, the social group consists of many adult males and females and their offspring, all in close visual proximity to one another.
3  For monkeys living on the ground in very dry areas, the basic social group is a 'harem' consisting of one adult male, several adult females and their offspring. The Hamadryas and gelada baboon harems gather in the evening and sleep in large groups.
4  For human hunter-gatherers — the mode of living which comprises at least 99 per cent of human existence — the family consists of a monogamous couple and their children, with several families forming a social group.

The subsistence group provides food or opportunities for food, protection, reproduction and socialization for its members. Charlesworth (1988) refers to these opportunities as 'resources'. There are several important characteristics of these groups.

1  Mothers and their pre-adolescent offspring form the core of the group (infants are nearly always born singly). Relative to other mammals, mother-offspring involvement is very long, nearly always extending beyond the period of infancy. This produces not only strong mother-child bonding, but often strong bonding between siblings as well.
2  Members of these groups are all well-known to one another and, relative

to outsiders, have strong bonds with each other. These bonds are often based on caring interactions. Group cohesion is also maintained through dominance relations, which checks aggression between group members. Group cohesiveness is essential for subsistence groups to carry out their necessary functions.

3   Socialization occurs primarily through play, observation, imitation and interactions with group members. The major task of pre-adults is to learn to fit into and contribute to the stability of the social group. To accomplish this task they have to develop: (a) knowledge of who are group members; (b) a set of social skills important to the group; (c) an enduring set of social relationships with many, if not most, members; (d) knowledge of the rules of social interaction and of the roles appropriate to self and others.

Threats to group cohesion put in jeopardy the viability of the group and are met by fear and hostility from group members (Van der Dennen, 1986). Two primary within-group threats are challenges to the established dominance hierarchy and to rules of interaction. Regarding the latter, for example, behaviour accepted in young primates is often punished when practised by adolescents. A major outgroup threat is the potential intrusion of same-species adult male or female strangers and non-group members into the group. This intrusion would not only disrupt established dominance and affiliative relations, but it has been observed for many primate species that strange males or non-group male adults may either kill infants or capture female group members (for the mountain gorilla, Fossey, 1979; for the chimpanzee, Goodall *et al.*, 1979; for Hamadryas baboons, Kummer, Gotz and Angst, 1974; and for human hunter-gatherers, Chagnon, 1983).

Given the importance of protecting group members and maintaining group cohesion, it is assumed that a set of genetically determined negative reactions to the presence of strangers evolved in the primates (Hamilton, 1975). These always include wariness and agitation, but often fear and hostility as well. These reactions serve to place a psychological and physical distance between the group and outsiders and to enhance within-group bonding (Lorenz, 1966). Group members do not have to experience negative consequences produced by strangers or non-group members to have negative reactions to them. Rather, these reactions are automatically triggered prior to interactions but can be modified by subsequent encounters that individual members of the group have with the outsiders.

To summarize, social cohesion is an essential evolutionary feature of human and non-human primate subsistence groups. It is maintained by the development of strong bonds between members, by the existence of a dominance hierarchy, by members learning and practising the rules and social roles of the group, and by reacting negatively to strangers and outsiders.

As previously noted, approximately 99 per cent of human existence has involved living in small subsistence groups in which members are all well-known to and bonded with one another. For individuals growing up in this setting, the people they usually interact with are members of a single social group. Because of this stability, children readily develop a group identity. Visits with other subsistence groups may temporarily extend the size of the primary group. With the exception of these visits, virtually every person encountered who is not a member of the subsistence group is an outsider, and will be responded to negatively.

The contemporary urban industrial situation contrasts dramatically with the narrow and well-defined setting in which children of hunter-gatherer groups are socialized. Here children move in and out of many settings involving a large and varied number of people, e.g., in stores, markets, playgrounds, streets, homes, schools, public transportation. Because of this variability, it is probably difficult for young children to determine which groups they are members of.

When children are placed in relatively stable settings such as daycare centres, camps and schools, involving few adults and many peers, group formation and membership become central issues. In the process of forming a group, children learn the appropriate interaction rules and roles of that group and determine its membership. They may decide to include some peers and exclude others in the new group. Even very young children show definite interaction preferences. They form friendships. These play preferences and friendships, along with parental attitudes and societal values, are probably the basis for group formation and membership. As these group processes unfold, evolutionarily determined negative reactions to peers who are not group members will emerge. What evolved as behaviourally protective mechanisms for supporting cohesion of the single sub-sistence group will manifest themselves in all settings in which group membership is an issue.

What is the psychological evidence to support these conclusions? The experiments by the Sherifs and by Tajfel are examined towards this end. Their research was not carried out within an evolutionary framework, but as will shortly be seen, their conclusions are highly supportive of this framework.

## The Sherifs' and Tajfel Experiments

The Sherifs' experiments (Sherif and Sherif, 1953; Sherif *et al.*, 1961) are among the most imaginative and important in the field of group development and intergroup relations. From the point of view of the subjects, they were not participants in experiments, but rather, in real-life experiences shared with other pre-adolescent or adolescent boys. In the first experiment (Sherif and Sherif, 1953) a number of middle-class boys were invited to attend an overnight camp. In the first phase, which lasted less than a week, the children participated in the usual camp activities, ate together, and were given great freedom in choosing their friends. The counsellors/experimenters paid special attention to friendship patterns and social networks.

In the second phase, which also lasted less than a week, close male friends were placed in two separate groups. The groups were kept isolated from each other as much as possible, eating, sleeping and carrying out activities in separate locations. One group named itself the Bulldogs, the other the Blue Devils. Each of the groups developed a set of norms which distinguished it from the other group. For example, the Bulldogs refused to use the colour blue, which they associated with the Blue Devils. Most of the boys talked in an 'us versus them' fashion and depreciated the other group. Boys who attempted to socialize with members of the other groups were called 'traitors' by their own group. Within each group, status hierarchies emerged. This system served to enhance group identification and cohesiveness, and to produce at least mild antagonism towards the other group.

In the third phase the two groups were brought into competition with each other to win points for the group as a whole and prizes for its individual members. The boys competed in sports, tournaments and camp chores. During this phase intergroup antagonism escalated to such a degree that the Sherifs made strong attempts to create intergroup harmony. They accomplished this by assigning the groups cooperative tasks necessary for the betterment of the camp as a whole.

In the second experiment (Sherif *et al.*, 1961) two groups of boys were brought into the camp separately, unaware of each other's presence during the first phase. As in the earlier experiment, a status hierarchy emerged, which included the development of group norms, cooperation, group identity and group loyalty. In the second phase the groups were brought together for a number of athletic competitions. As in the first study, strong negative attitudes and behaviours developed toward the other group. Even neutral contacts turned into conflict, such as a garbage-throwing war following a meal together. At the same time intragroup feelings were strengthened, often leading to overestimates of the group's competitive abilities. As in the first experiment, the third phase involved having the two groups work together cooperatively, which had the effect of improving intergroup relations.

In summary, by substituting the phrase 'outgroup member' for the word 'stranger' the results of these experiments are completley consistent with the findings of the studies on the functioning of primate subsistence groups. In the process of group formation, pre-adolescent and adolescent boys develop strong bonds between group members. A status hierarchy emerges, they develop and adhere to group norms, and then react negatively to outgroup members, some of whom were previously friends. Competition between groups serves to exaggerate these effects. The Sherifs' research indicates that for pre-adolescents and adolescents antagonism towards non-group members is an integral part of group formation and social cohesion. The groups studied carried out a large number of activities together, and ultimately were placed in competition with other groups.

Tajfel's (1981) research indicates that for adolescents, discrimination against outsiders is produced even when identification with a group is based on trivial characteristics, and the members of the 'group' had never met, nor would ever do so. In one of the experiments the adolescents were individually shown slides of paintings by Klee and Kandinsky and asked for their preferences. They were then told that they were being placed in the group who preferred the same painter as they. In another experiment the adolescents were shown pictures of dots and asked to state their number. They were then told that they were being placed in a group which had either underestimated or overestimated the number shown in the same manner as they. The adolescents were then individually tested on a number of tasks in which they had to determine the monetary rewards for other members of their group as well as for those in the second group. In all the experiments a consistent preference was shown to reward more highly ingroup as opposed to outgroup members. Moreover, in order to discriminate against the other group, the adolescents frequently made chocies that were less than optimal for their own group. Thus, even when adolescents are assigned membership in artificaly constructed groups, they discriminate against non-group members in favour of their own group.

The Sherifs' and Tajfel findings have important implications for the study of the development of prejudice and discrimination. Being a member of a group, however natural or imagined that may be, leads to negative reactions towards non-group members. These reactions are not restricted to responses elicited in experiments with adolescent and pre-adolescent humans. Rather, they are characteristic, instead, of human and non-human primate groups with an evolutionary history, and hence genetic heritage, dating back 60 million years. In other words, prejudice and discrimination against outsiders is a natural, indeed inevitable, consequence of being a member of a group. It is likely that this characteristic reaction to outsiders evolved in the service of maintaining group cohesion.

As was shown elsewhere (Fishbein, 1976, 1984), virtually all complex evolved behavioural characteristics have a developmental trajectory within each individual. Piaget's period of sensory-motor development takes about one and a half years to complete. The development of cognitive empathy, from simple to flexible, continues over the course of at least seven years. Language development extends over an even longer period. Regarding prejudice and discrimination against outsiders, a central question is: what is the developmental path of these reactions? The analysis of the evolutionary and human experimental data indicates that a highly significant aspect of this development is being a group member. That is, when children join a group, thus creating for themselves a group identity, they will manifest negative reactions to non-group members. Prior to this period of group identification, prejudice and discrimination against other groups should be minimal. Once prejudice and discrimination emerge, their subsequent development will be related to changes in group cohesion, the particular experiences individuals have had with members of outgroups, and the values expressed toward particular outgroups by family, friends and important members of the culture.

## Fear of Strangers

An argument can be made that the prejudice and discrimination shown by children towards various target groups are merely a continuation of the fear of strangers which first appears in infants. Lewis (1987) has briefly summarized his own and the work of others on the fear of strangers by infants between 8 and 15 months of age. Infants do not respond uniformly to all strangers, although younger babies usually react negatively to them. Children respond differently from each other due to variations in their temperaments, and to their prior experiences with strangers. They are also affected by the sex, age and physical characteristics of a stranger. Infants are influenced as well by their mother's interactions with strangers. Positive mother-stranger interactions typically lead to positive infant-stranger interactions.

In an independent series of studies Lamb (1976a, 1976b, 1977a, 1977b) compared 7- to 24-month-old infants' reactions to strangers, mothers and fathers in the laboratory and in the home. Lamb distinguishes between affiliation and attachment towards others. Affiliation social behaviours, such as smiling, looking, talking and pointing, occur at a distance from the child. Attachment behaviours, such as touching, approaching within arm's reach, reaching up and holding on, occur at a close range. In the laboratory setting, for both attachment and affiliation, infants of all ages prefer their parents to a stranger. In the home all the children prefer to affiliate more with their fathers and strangers than their mothers. However, for attachment, all the children prefer both parents to the stranger. These results strongly support the view that strangers evoke both interest and wariness in infants and young children. In the laboratory, which is a moderately stressful setting, wariness predominates. But at home, a safe and low stress environment, interest in strangers is the stronger response.

By 3 years of age, even in a laboratory setting, children show little wariness of strangers. Plunkett, Klein and Meisels (1988) brought children and their mothers into the laboratory for a short time. Mother was asked to sit and read, take no play initiatives toward her child, and to remain neutral when a strange woman entered the room. Children were encouraged to play with any of a variety of toys available to them. The stranger entered, eventually approached the child, offered to play with some toys with the child, and left after eight and a half minutes. In general, children reacted with a moderately pleasant mood throughout this period, had some positive interactions with the stranger and showed little stress. There was a slight decrease in toy play, perhaps indicating wariness, as the stranger moved close to the child. From these and the above results it is safe to conclude that prejudice and discrimination towards non-group members by children 3 years or older are quite different from their developmentally earlier reactions to strangers.

### Development of a Group Identity

According to the evolutionary model, development of a group identity should precede the development of prejudice and discrimination, but at what age do children begin to identify with a group? This question presents issues different from those concerned with the age at which children identify certain self-characteristics such as gender. A child may view herself as being a girl, see herself as being similar to other girls and yet not identify herself as a member of the girls' group. To be a member of a group, at a minimum entails the social cohesion of group members — bonding and a dominance hierarchy.

There appear to be only two experiments in the English language which directly evaluate the age-related development of group identity for young children. Abramenkova (1983) compares 5–6-year-olds with 6–7-year-olds, and Strayer and Trudel (1984) compare children between the ages of 1 and 6. There are several other studies, however, dealing with the development of children's knowledge of group functioning which bear indirectly on group identity. The assumption is made that if children have knowledge of group processes, then it is likely that they have experienced group identification.

Strayer and Trudel's research has its origin in the study of primate groups in naturalistic settings. Their subjects were ten daycare groups whose average ages ranged from approximately 1½ to 5½ years. There were two groups at each age level. The researchers focused on dominance and affiliative behaviour within the group, because these are central features of primate group social cohesion.

Affiliation includes close-in interactions such as touching, holding and kissing, as well as more distant interactions; dominance includes attacks, threats, competition, submission and retreat. The central idea of the research, from the present view, is that if children interact with each other in stable and systematic ways — ways that support social cohesion — then they are operating as members of a social group. This implies that they experience a group identity. If these dominance and affiliative interactions are unstable or unsystematic, they probably have not attained a group identity.

Strayer and Trudel measured several types of behavioural interactions that relate to this issue: frequency of conflict; stability of dominance relations; number of dyadic encounters in which dominance is depicted; the relation between dominance status and the amount of affiliation directed towards the child; and the relation between dominance status and number of unreciprocated affiliation behaviours received. The results are straightforward: children under age 3 do not operate as if they are members of groups, for both dominance and affiliation. Groups comprising 3-, 4- or 5-year-olds behave similarly regarding dominance relations, but there are more conflicts and more struggles over dominance within groups of 3-year-olds than within the older groups. This means that the dominance hierarchy for 3-year-olds is not functioning as effectively as it is for 4- and 5-year-olds. For affiliation, there is a trend from the 3-year-olds to the 5-year-olds for affiliation to be more frequently directed toward the high status members. In stable human and non-human primate groups, high status members receive more attention and/or affiliation than low status members. These patterns of results indicate that group identity starts to emerge at age 3 and is well developed by age 5. In general, the group interactions of the 4- and 5-year-olds were more similar to each other than to the younger children.

Abramenkova's (1983) study, carried out in the Soviet Union, assessed whether 5–7-year-old children would work as hard on a task when only the group leader would be punished for poor performance as compared to when each individual would be punished. The assumption made is that if individuals identify themselves as members of a group, they will act in a 'humane' way toward other members of the group — i.e., they will work as hard to protect their group leader as to protect themselves. Moreover, this humane attitude should more likely occur when the members have to interact cooperatively with each other, as opposed to when they work alone, parallel to each other.

The children were placed in groups of four, based on age and gender, and tested on either a brief interactive task or a brief parallel task. For each task, two conditions were compared: only the experimenter-appointed leader could be punished versus all members could be punished. The measure of a humane attitude compared speed and accuracy of performance when only the leader could be punished relative to when the entire group could be punished. The results indicate that: a humane attitude was much more likely to occur on the interactive than parallel task; groups of 6–7-year-olds showed more of this attitude, and more stably, than groups of 5–6-year-olds; but the humane attitude was present in even the younger groups. These findings indicate that by 5 years of age children readily develop and identify with a group which is externally formed and lasts for only a brief time. It would not be surprising to find evidence of a humane attitude in younger children, especially for long-standing groups in non-laboratory settings.

The remaining studies only indirectly bear on the development of a group identity. Sluckin and Smith (1977) were interested in the way 3- and 4-year-olds in two preschool play groups formed a dominance hierarchy. Pairwise dominance was measured by observing the ability of one child to win in aggressive encounters with another. Children's perception of dominance was measured by asking each child to evaluate the 'toughness' of each member in his or her playgroup by ranking photographs of all the playmates.

In both groups a clear dominance hierarchy was found, in the sense that all dominance relations were transitive. That is, if *A* was dominant over *B*, and *B* over *C*, *A* was found to be dominant over *C*. The toughness rankings were carried out twice in the same day, as a check on reliability. Only eight of the twenty children were reliable, i.e., consistently rank-ordered their peers in the two evaluations. Seven of these eight children were over 4 years old. Only one of the ten 3-year-olds was consistent in his rankings. Especially important was the validity of the rankings, i.e., the statistical relationship between toughness rankings (the two reliability rankings were averaged) and the observed dominance hierarchy. If children can accurately perceive this important dimension of group functioning, it may be inferred that they both perceive their playmates as a group and identify with that group. The data analyses showed that the children who were reliable in their rankings (predominantly 4-year-olds) also had valid rankings, and that the children unreliable in their rankings (predominantly 3-year-olds) did not have valid rankings. These findings, consistent with the Strayer and Trudel findings, indicate that group identity emerges at approximately 4 years of age.

The study by Watson and Fischer (1980) deals with the development of an understanding of social roles in children between 1½ and 7½ years of age. In their research, a sequence of eight levels was presented which describes children's social understanding in preschool play settings. Of particular importance is the distinction made between *behavioural role* and *social role* understanding. The former concept means that a child can perform several actions in play that fit a particular social role, e.g., doctor, nurse. The latter concept means that a child understands the complementary nature of social roles, e.g., that doctors and nurses interact with each other in particular ways. A child who demonstrates knowledge of a behavioural role may not understand that the role coordinates with other roles. It can be argued that for groups to function properly, social roles and not merely behavioural roles must be understood. If a child understandings social roles, it may be inferred that he has knowledge of group functioning. It is further assumed that he has probably experienced membership in a group.

The basic technique used by Watson and Fischer to study these issues was a modelling and imitation procedure. The experimenter would act out a brief story using dolls and then ask the child to act out her own similar story using the same dolls. The portrayed story reflected each of the eight levels in social understanding. If a child could successfully imitate the experimenter's story at a particular level, then it was assumed that the child had social understanding at that level. The results were consistent and straightforward: the maximum level attained by 3 and 3½-year-olds was that of behavioural roles, and for 4- and 4½-year-olds, social roles. Thus, consistent with Sluckin and Smith (1977) and Strayer and Trudel (1984), 4 years of age appears to be the age at which a group identity first emerges.

The last research to be discussed was carried out by Piaget in the areas of symbolic play (1962) and games with rules (1932). Piaget divides the development of symbolic play into two periods: from 1½ to 4 years, and from 4 to 7 years. The first period involves the simple and often haphazard, but novel use of language and non-verbal symbols with objects. For example, a child places a doll in a pan, covers it with a postcard and says, 'Baby, blanket, cold.' The pan is symbolic of a bed, and the postcard of a blanket. In the second period, relative to the first, the symbolic combinations are more orderly; the characters and objects used are more realistic, and collective symbolism appears. That is, children can now play together using the same symbols, all taking on roles that complement each other, such as that of mother and father. In this latter period there is evidence consistent with the findings of Watson and Fischer that the use of complementary roles emerges at about age 4.

In the practice of rules of games, Piaget again distinguishes between behaviour characteristic of 1½–4-year-olds and that of 4–7-year-olds. For the purposes of this discussion, the importance of games with rules is that they provide symbolic guides for group interaction. To play a game with other children implies that each player sees the rules binding in relation to their collective behaviour. Because the rules are somewhat abstract, young children could be expected to have difficulty with them — and they do. But Piaget points out substantial differences between the pre- and post-4-year-olds in their use of rules. Younger children evidence no understanding of a game governed by rules. Older children play together, claim they are playing by the rules, and even state some of the rules, but do not play as if the rules were binding, or even shared. It is not until children are about 7 years old that rules regulate their play interactions.

In all the above research the age of 4 continues to appear as the age at which understanding of group functioning clearly occurs. These findings support the conclusions based on the Strayer and Trudel experiment that a sense of group identity emerges at that age. Since understanding of group processes grows appreciably over the next three years, it might be expected that the nature of group identity also changes considerably between the ages of 4 and 7. Two predictions are thus made based on the above conclusions: the appearance of prejudice and/or discrimination against specific target groups will first reliably appear in 4-year-olds; and the nature of this prejudice/discrimination will change in systematic ways between the ages of 4 and 7.

## DEVELOPMENT OF PREJUDICE AND DISCRIMINATION

Prejudice and discrimination emerge from normal social developmental processes. During a child's first two years of life he attains several major social accomplishments: attachment to primary caretakers and to other family members; the development of positive social bonds to peers and adults with whom he is in frequent contact; social speech and understanding; the emergence of a personal identity; the beginnings of an understanding of rules of social interaction; and the start of age and sex-appropriate role behaviour.

During a child's third and fourth years she is developing a deeper and clearer understanding of social roles, and of the way that status (or dominance) varies with those roles. Thus children see themselves as boys or girls, as young children as opposed to older siblings or adults. They view themselves as having a certain status relative to peers, and a different status relative to older siblings and adults. Friendship with peers solidifies, as does the attraction to peer-play. The self-concept starts to become more closely identified with the social roles and status that the child experiences.

Of major importance is the emergence at about age 4 of the group self (group identity) for children who participate in play groups. The child now starts to think of herself as a member of a peer group. She strives to develop those attributes which will lead to maximum acceptance by and enhanced status within the group. Group identification exaggerates the importance of both appropriate role be-haviours and of the physical characteristics associated with that group. The sense of group membership is primarily based on friendship and perceived similarity of physical and behavioural attributes. Thus people who look and/or act differently are not considered to be members of the peer group. The implicit and explicit values of parents, teachers and older siblings are also incorporated into and help to define the child's group identity.

Prior to the emergence of the group self, awareness of differentness in others may have little emotional or motivational impact. But after group identification occurs, it brings increased consciousness of role, status and group membership. This new awareness produces positive attraction towards group members and prejudice and discrimination towards non-members. The child's self-esteem becomes related to the group norms. By following the internalized norms, self-esteem is enhanced; ignoring these standards lowers self-esteem. Peers and adults also reinforce the group norms, which further strengthens their internalization.

## Opposite-Sex Prejudice and Discrimination

This section deals with children between the ages of 2 and 7. The section focusing on race includes a discussion of opposite-sex effects for children of 7 and older. The research to be discussed in the present section was *not* carried out with the intention of studying prejudice or discrimination. Rather, researchers were in-terested in either the development of knowledge of sex role stereotypes or of sex segregation in play groups. Methodologically, however, this research is similar to the various approaches used in the study of prejudice and discrimination.

Sex role stereotypes are generalizations people make about gender-related behaviour irrespective of their accuracy. Sex role stereotypes are clearly related to sex roles — i.e., cultural prescriptions for appropriate gender-related behaviour. Parents, peers, teachers, neighbours and television all influence knowledge of sex roles and sex role stereotypes. These sources do not always convey the same message; therefore, children will vary in their gender-related knowledge.

Opposite-sex prejudice is examined in this paper by looking at the negative and positive sex role stereotypes that boys and girls hold for themselves and for the opposite sex. For example, if boys hold stronger negative female sex role stereotypes than girls do, and weaker positive female sex role stereotypes than girls do, it may be inferred that boys have prejudiced attitudes towards girls. The following two studies deal with this issue. In the first, Kuhn, Nash and Brucken (1978) compared knowledge of sex role stereotypes for 2½- and 3½-year-old boys and girls involved in a nursery school. The children were shown two paper dolls — one clearly resembling a girl, the other a boy — and asked to identify them. All did so correctly. The children were then read a list of seventy-two statements which dealt with *traits*, e.g., 'I'm strong'; *activities*, e.g., 'I like to play ball'; or *future roles*, e.g., 'when I grow up, I'll fly an airplane'. These were all items which adults and older children had clearly identified as being sex role stereotyped. For each statement, the children were asked to point to the doll that best fit in.

The results showed that children agreed with adult stereotypes about two-thirds of the time, which is statistically well above the range of chance. There were no age or sex differences in amount of stereotyping. Significantly, boys and girls sometimes disagreed about the statements that they stereotyped. Boys, but not girls, believed that girls cried, were slow, complained about hurt feelings and not having a turn at play. Girls, but not boys, believed that girls looked nice, gave kisses, never fought, and said, 'I can do it best.' Thus boys held more negative attitudes and fewer positive attitudes towards girls than girls held about themselves.

How do beliefs about boys fit into this picture? Girls, but not boys, believed that boys enjoy fighting, are mean, weak, and say, 'I did wrong.' Boys, but not girls, believe that boys enjoy hard work, are loud, naughty, and make people cry. Except for the last three items, which may be too ambiguous to categorize accurately, girls held more negative attitudes and fewer positive attitudes towards boys than boys held for themselves. It can be inferred from these findings that 2½- and 3½-year-olds do hold oppositive-sex prejudices.

The study by Albert and Porter (1988) deals with sex role stereotypes among 4-, 5- and 6-year-olds enrolled in preschool programmes. The children were shown both a male and a female doll and told two stories, one concerning the child's home, and the other the school environment. Intermittently throughout the stories the child was asked to point to the doll that engaged in the activity or event just described. In all, thirty-two activities were noted, all judged by adults to be either positive or negative as well as clearly sex role stereotyped. For example, the item 'which one throws toys around when told not to?' is a negative male sex role stereotype; 'which one goes over to take care of the little child?' is a positive female sex role stereotype.

Overall, children were found to be more accurate, i.e. to agree with adult ratings, in the sex role stereotyping of their own than of the opposite sex. Older children were also more accurate in their sex role stereotypes than were younger children. Girls were more likely than boys to associate all the negative male sex role stereotypes with the male doll. Moreover, the strength of these judgments was greater for older than for younger girls. For all of the positive male sex role stereotypes, boys scored higher than, or the same as, girls. As was the case with the negative stereotypes, older girls were less positive than younger ones.

A similar pattern was found for female sex role stereotypes, with boys and girls holding reversed positions. That is, boys generally view girls more negatively and less positively than girls see themselves. The opposite-sex disparity, however, was not as great as that seen for male sex role stereotypes. Taken together, the results of this research strongly indicate that 4-, 5- and 6-year-olds manifest opposite-sex prejudice, and that this increases with increasing age. This prejudice is clearly seen in 4-year-olds and, as shown by the Kuhn *et al.* study, is also present in 2½-year-olds.

The study of opposite-sex discrimination uses essentially the same methods as those employed for researching race or handicap discrimination. The basic hypothesis is that if children are given opportunitites to associate freely with others, their choices reflect positive and negative affiliations. Thus if boys choose to play with boys, and not to play with girls, it has been assumed by researchers that they are discriminating against girls. The phenomenon of sex segregation in play groups has been widely observed. It appears in early childhood, increases with age and reaches its maximum during pre-adolescence (Hartup, 1983; Maccoby and Jacklin, 1987). Several recent studies provide detailed analyses of this phenomenon.

LaFreniere, Strayer and Gauthier (1984) studied fifteen long-standing play groups of children 1½, 2¼, 3, 4 and 5½ years old. They observed how frequently children directed positive social initiatives to same- and opposite-sex peers. For the 1½-year-olds, no sex preferences were shown; 2¼-year-old girls, but not boys, showed same-sex preferences; by age 3 both boys and girls were directing twice as many initiatives to same-sex as to opposite-sex peers. This ratio remained stable for the girls; for the 5½-year-old boys, however, it changed to three to one. Thus 3-year-olds of both sexes are reliably showing opposite-sex discrimination.

Maccoby and Jacklin (1987) studied the social play of groups of 4½-year-old nursery school children and 6½-year-old kindergarten children. For each child engaging in either parallel or interactive play it was noted whether the child's partner was the same or opposite sex or whether the child was part of a mixed sex group. Both age groups participated in mixed sex groups approximately one-third of the time. The 4½-year-olds were about two and a half times more likely to be playing with a same-sex than with an opposite-sex partner, but the 6½-year-olds were eleven times more likely to be doing so. The results for the 4½-year-olds are consistent with those reported by LaFreniere *et al.*, and those for the 6½-year-olds are consistent with other published data. Thus a dramatic increase in opposite-sex discrimination occurs between the ages of 4½ and 6½.

The results of the research on both opposite-sex prejudice and opposite-sex discrimination are very consistent. By age 2½ children show same-sex to opposite-sex attitudinal and behavioural preferences. These remain relatively stable until about age 4½, after which they grow stronger. By age 6½ the phenomenon of opposite-sex discrimination is striking. The dramatic increase in children's sex discrimination after age 4½ is consistent with the argument that group identity emerges between the ages of 3 and 4 and increases between 4 and 5. How does one explain, however, the presence of opposite-sex prejudice and discrimination in 2½-year-olds?

Between the ages of 2 and 4 children appear to be learning what is appropriate and what is inappropriate sex role behaviour. In addition, through interactions with same- and opposite-sex play partners, they are learning to prefer playing with members of the same sex rather than with those of the opposite sex. As this learning occurs, children are being rewarded for same-sex play and punished for opposite-sex play. This induces them to value positively same-sex role stereotypes and same-sex play, and to value negatively opposite-sex role stereotypes and play. Thus the age 2–4 phenomena are based on the acquisition of sex role behaviour, and not to the emergence of a group identity. What is the evidence to support this argument? There are two types of support.

First, Lamb, Easterbrooks and Holden (1980) for 2½–5-year-olds in free play settings, and Langlois and Downs (1980) for 3–5-year-olds in a laboratory setting, studied sex role socialization. Lamb *et al.* observed how same- and opposite-sex peers responded to male-typed and female-typed activities. Consistently, both boys and girls socially rewarded boys for male-typed (appropriate) activities, and socially punished them for carrying out female-typed (inappropriate) activities. A similar pattern was found for girls engaging, respectively, in appropriate and inappropriate sex-typed activities. Langlois and Downs observed how mothers, fathers and peers reacted to children's sex-appropriate and sex-inappropriate toy play. In general, a similar pattern was found for the three socializing agents: sex-appropriate play was socially rewarded, and sex-inappropriate play was socially punished.

Second, Maccoby (1988, 1990) has summarized her own research and that of other scholars concerning play styles and interaction styles of 2½–4½-year-old children. Boys in this age range are more likely than girls to enjoy rough and tumble play and to orient more toward competitive and dominance-related activities. Girls seem to find these activities less pleasurable and often even distasteful. Boys tend to be more excitable, and girls calmer and quieter in their experiencing of these activities. In addition, by age 3½ (younger children have not been studied) girls find that they are not able to influence readily the play activities of boys, but can do so with girls. Boys can influence both sexes. But there is a difference between the approaches of the two sexes: girls make polite suggestions, while boys make direct physical and vocal demands. Thus boys learn to enjoy being with boys, and girls with girls, in approximately a 2 to 1 ratio. This ratio remains stable for about two and a half to three years, and then dramatically increases when boys develop a male group identity and girls a female group identity.

## Racial Prejudice and Discrimination

The literature concerning racial prejudice and discrimination is enormous. To make the topic manageable, this section limits its consideration to Black and White racial groups. Moreover, in dealing with racial prejudice, priority will be placed on the research of four scholars: Williams and Morland (1976), Milner (1983) and Aboud (1988). Most of the research carried out since the 1960s has been strongly influenced by the materials and methods developed by Williams and Morland, which they fully describe in their book.

In the study of racial prejudice, researchers use variants of two basic tests: the Color Meaning Test (CMT) and the Preschool Racial Attitude Measure (PRAM) (Williams and Morland, 1976). In the CMT, children are shown different coloured photographs of two animals which are identical except for colouring: one is black and the other white. After the experimenter reads a short story about each of these animals, the child is asked to identify the animal described. For example, 'Here are two cats. One of them is a bad cat and scratches on the furniture. Which is the bad cat?' Half the stories depict positive qualities, and half negative qualities. If a child consistently chooses one colour for the positive qualities, e.g., black, and the other colour for the negative qualities, e.g., white, the child is assumed to have, in this example, a pro-black colour bias.

In the PRAM, children are shown photographs of two nearly identical drawings of humans — male and/or female, young and/or old — except that one has a pinkish-tan skin colour and the other medium-brown. The children are read brief stories about one of the people and asked to make a choice. For example, 'Here are two little girls. One of them is an ugly little girl. People do not like to look at her. Which is the ugly little girl?' As with the CMT, half the qualities are positive, and half negative. It is assumed by researchers that consistent pro-White or pro-Black choices reflect racial bias.

Photographs and/or dolls have also been used to evaluate children's verbal awareness of different racial groups, of their own racial identity, of racial play-mate acceptance and playmate preference, and racial self-preference (e.g., 'of all the children in this picture, which one would you most rather be?'). Of these measures, racial bias on the PRAM and playmate acceptance seem most clearly related to racial prejudice. Responses to most other measures — e.g., playmate preference, preferring one race over another — do not signify prejudice *against* the non-preferred race. In addition, methodologically, if children show consistent colour biases on the CMT and these scores are correlated with the two racial bias scores, it is not obvious whether the latter measures indicate colour bias or racial bias.

Another issue concerns the relationship between racial labelling and the non-verbal measure of racial bias (e.g., pointing to photographs). The present view concurs with writers such as Aboud (1988) and Williams and Morland (1976) who consider verbal racial awareness to be a prerequisite to racial pre-judice. Children may have an apparent racial bias — e.g., preferring the pinkish-tan pictures —but unless they can link that skin colour preference to a particular labelled race, the apparent racial bias may be only a colour bias. For example, if a child shows a consistent preference for pinkish-tan pictures over the medium-brown ones, but is unable to point correctly to the pictures which look like 'Blacks' or 'Whites', then it is difficult to argue that the colour preferences are based on race.

The pattern of results is complex, but fairly consistent. First, regarding ac-ceptance of different racial playmates — e.g., 'Here is a picture of some children, would you like to play with them?' — about 80 per cent of 3–6-year-old Black and White children from North America answer positively to pictures of both races. As children move into the primary grades, a decline is seen in cross-racial acceptance, but most children through pre-adolescence are accepting of both races. When children are shown pictures of White and Black children and asked to choose one over the other, preschool children of both races generally choose the White child. For grade school children, with increasing age Blacks come to prefer Blacks and Whites retain their White preferences.

Second, the majority of 4–6-year-old Black and White children from North America show positive-white/negative-black attitudes on the PRAM and similar measures. There are few studies dealing with 3-year-olds, and the data are somewhat conflicting for them. From age 7 to 12 children show a decline in this pro-White bias, and many Black children start to show a pro-Black bias.

Third, on the CMT type of tests (drawings of black and white animals) North American children as young as 3 years old show a positive-white/negative-black bias. It is rare for even Black children to show the opposite bias. There is some increase in the pro-white bias to age 6, but it is apparently not substantial. Little research has been carried out with older children using the CMT. A recent study by Bagley and Young (1988) strongly indicates that the positive-white bias is culturally linked. They found that 4–7-year-old Black children of Ghanaian parents, living in England, Canada or Ghana, generally had a black-positive/white-negative bias on both the CMT and the PRAM.

Fourth, Bagley and Young and other researchers have found the correlation between CMT and PRAM scores to average only about .30. This indicates some independence between the two measures. The above set of results indicates that in North America and England 4-year-old White and Black children show an apparent pro-White racial bias. There is some doubt as to whether 3-year-olds have this bias. Despite the apparent racial bias, 3–6-year-olds say they are willing to play with children of both races.

Racial awareness literature is now considered in order to determine whether the apparent racial bias is based on prejudice. First, when Black and White North American and English children are shown pictures of dolls depicting Black and White races, 3-year-olds are usually unable racially to classify them accurately. The ability to do so increases dramatically in 4-year-old children, and by age 6 nearly all can classify accurately. Second, when White children are shown pictures of dolls depicting both races, and asked to point to the doll they are most similar to, 3-year-olds can do this at a level above the range of chance. By age 6 nearly all children are always accurate. However, when Black children are asked to perform this task, the results of most studies have shown that 3–5-year-olds are unable to do this consistently. Children between 6 and 10 are generally consistent in their responses, but rarely do they exceed 90 per cent in accuracy. The latter results suggest that the non-verbal test of racial self-identification is influenced by a pro-White racial bias that is not related to racial prejudice. The Black children may be, to some extent, interpreting the question, 'Whom do you look like?' as 'Whom would you prefer to look like?' This interpretation is supported by Williams and Morland's (1976) research. When preschool children are shown pictures of Black and White children and asked, 'Point to the child you'd rather be', both Black and White children point to the White child more frequently than to the Black one.

When all the results are considered together, the following picture emerges. Both Black and White children in North America and England have developed by age 3 a strong positive-white/negative-black colour bias. By age 4 both racial groups have developed corresponding racial biases. These biases increase over the next two years, stabilize and then decline for both racial groups. The racial bias for the White children from age 4 and older is now based on group identification with the White race and can thus be characterized as racial prejudice. Accurate racial identification for Black children emerges at about age 6 and continues to develop thereafter. This last conclusion is consistent with research dealing with other North American ethnic groups — e.g., Asians and native Americans — who often identify with Whites until age 6.

Basically, there are two kinds of research dealing with racial discrimination, one based on sociometric ratings, the other on observations of behavioural interactions. The sociometric procedures are of two types (Singleton and Asher, 1977). In the first or 'best friends' type, children and adolescents are given the names of all their classmates and asked to identify their best friends or those they most prefer playing with. In the second — roster and rating — children and adolescents are given the names of all their classmates and asked to rate on a five-

or seven-point scale how much they like to play with or to work with each of them. These two procedures lead to very different conclusions about racial discrimination, but *not* about opposite-sex discrimination. In the behavioural research, of which there are relatively few studies, the children and adolescents are observed in the classroom, school playground and cafeteria. The researcher notes with whom they are interacting.

Studies in the United States yield the folliwing information. First, for observational data, for preschool children during free play no systematic relationship has been found between play partner preferences and race (Stevenson and Stevenson, 1960, for 2½-year-olds; Goodman, 1952, for 4-year-olds; and Porter, 1971, for 5-year-olds). However, the sample sizes in these studies were small, and gender preferences were not controlled. Thus the existence of same-race preferences within each gender is still an open question. For grade school children and adolescents observed during recess, in the cafeteria and after school, Blacks and Whites moderately to strongly prefer interacting with same-race rather than other-race peers (e.g., Finklestein and Haskins, 1983; Schofield, 1979; Silverman and Shaw, 1973). Finklestein and Haskins observed kindergarten children during recess in the fall and spring and found this voluntary segregation to increase over the academic year. The 'best friends' sociometric data support these observations. However, roster and rating methods indicate that both Blacks and Whites show a willingness to interact socially with other-race peers (e.g., Jarrett and Quay, 1984; Singleton and Asher, 1979; Carter *et al.*, 1975). This pattern of results indicates that generally the behavioural racial discrimination observed is based on same-race affiliation preferences as opposed to different-race hostility.

Second, on the basis of classroom observational data, there are only slight tendencies for children and adolescents to prefer interacting with same-race rather than different-race peers (e.g., Singleton and Asher, 1977; Schofield and Francis, 1982). In the Schofield and Francis study it was found that same-race interactions tend to be more social than task oriented, whereas the reverse applies for different-race interaction. These observations are consistent with roster and rating methods which ask students about their willingness to work with same-race and different-race classmates. Thus, in a structured task oriented environment where students have some choice about with whom they will interact, the task requirements override racial considerations.

Third, the results of most studies using behavioural or sociometric measurements show that same-sex preferences are always considerably stronger than same-race preferences. For example, Singleton and Asher (1977) in their study of third grade children in a school that had been integrated since kindergarten found that 40 per cent of the variation in sociometric (roster and rating) preferences were accounted for by sex and less than 1 per cent by race. Differences exist between males and females in degree of same-race preferences. Damico and Sparks (1986) and Schofield (1982) show that Black females in classroom settings are the most racially isolated group. Other studies show no differences between Black and White female isolation, but note that females are more racially isolated than males (e.g., Schofield and Francis, 1982). It can at least be concluded that males are more likely to cross racial lines than females. One possible explanation for this sex difference is that females tend to associate with a few close friends, whereas males tend to interact in larger groups. In casting a wider social net, males are more likely to take in different-racial friends than are females.

Fourth, there is some evidence that Black and White children have different behaviour styles and preferred modes of social interaction. These differences may in part underlie same-race preferences (Finkelstein and Haskins, 1983; Patchen, 1982; Schofield, 1982). In their observational studies of kindergarten children, Finkelstein and Haskins found that White children from middle-income families were more verbal than Black children from low-income families in their interactions, whereas Blacks used more commands and were physically more aggressive. Both Patchen, for senior high school students, and Schofield, for junior high school students, found that Black students were much more likely than Whites to engage in roughhousing and mild physical aggression. The White students were more fearful of physical aggression than Blacks and readily interpreted playful acts by Blacks as threats. These perceptions often led to avoidance by, or withdrawal of, Whites from Blacks. These observations are significant because they parallel those made in relation to opposite-sex prejudice and discrimination. Children and adolescents prefer to interact and identify with those whose behaviour is similar to their own. These behavioural differences may be related to social class as well as racial differences.

Fifth, gender and race discrimination run different time courses from the primary grades through high school. We rely on Shrum, Check and Hunter's (1988) study of over 2000 students in Grades 3 to 12 as a summary. In their research a 'best friend' sociometric measure was used. Shrum *et al.* found that same-sex preferences were rated highest in Grades 3–6, began to decline in junior high school and continued to decline throughout high school. Same-race preferences were rated lowest in Grades 3 and 4, and showed a marked increase through Grade 7 where they stabilized at very high levels. The greatest differences in these trends for males versus females and Blacks versus Whites occurred in relation to Grades 6, 7 and 8 — when children begin puberty. The post-pubertal decline in same-sex best friends is readily understood as being a function of growing attraction to the opposite sex. The increase and stabilization of same-race best friends is probably much more complexly determined, having sexual, economic and group identity components.

Sixth, and finally, the extent of racial discrimination in school settings is affected by peers, family, classroom structure and school personnel. Patchen's (1982) study of the Indianapolis Public High Schools presents a summary of these influences. This study included over 5000 students, 1800 teachers, and administrators from all twelve public schools. For both White and Black students, results indicate that those with prior positive interracial experiences in either their neighbourhood or previous school were likely to have friendly interracial contacts in high school. Those with prior negative experiences tended either to avoid their different race peers or to have unfriendly contacts in high school. Similarly, students whose friends and family had positive attitudes towards different-race members tended to have positive contacts with them. Those whose parents and friends had negative attitudes tended either to avoid different-race peers or to have unfriendly contacts with them. Classroom structure was measured by the ratio of Black to White students and had somewhat different effects for Blacks and Whites. Overall, classrooms with a Black majority led to higher positive interracial contacts and lower negative interracial contacts than other structures. Finally, where Black students perceived that the teachers and administrators accepted them as being equal to White students, and where the White students perceived that they were physically safe and would receive a good quality education, interracial contacts tended to be positive.

Although generally the developmental results for racial prejudice and racial discrimination are consistent, some discrepancies do exist. First, there is no evidence of racial discrimination among preschoolers, but there is of racial prejudice. Moreover, prejudice appears to decline during junior high school, whereas discrimination increases and then stabilizes. These differences may be a function of the use of different tests for measuring prejudice and discrimination. Second, there is no clear evidence in the prejudice literature that males and females respond differentially, as was seen in the discrimination research. There is no obvious explanation for this finding. Third, Schofield (1982) has pointed out that interracial behaviour and attitudes may change in opposite ways. Thus students may develop different-race friendships, and yet maintain racial prejudice.

An overview of these research areas indicates that there is a strong undercurrent of racial tolerance just below the surface of racial antagonism. Whites and Blacks, in structured and safe settings, show a willingness to work with and socialize with members of the other race. In these settings behavioural similarities replace behavioural differences, and individuals come to be responded to individually rather than as members of an outside group.

### Discrimination towards the Hearing Impaired

This section reviews practically all the recent research which involves hearing impaired and normal hearing children in integrated settings. These studies have utilized either behavioural observations or sociometric techniques for comparing these two groups. None of the studies evaluated prejudice of normal hearing children towards the hearing impaired. There is some literature bearing on this issue, but the attitude measures are embedded in scales dealing with prejudice towards the 'physically handicapped'. In that research little information is given about the experiences the children have had with the hearing impaired, and as a consequence, is of limited value for the present purposes.

Three of the papers using observational methods deal with preschool children aged 3½–5 years (Brackett and Henniges, 1976; Vandall and George, 1981; Vandall *et al.*, 1982). One of the papers deals with first and second graders (McCauley, Bruininks and Kennedy, 1976), and one with first through sixth graders (Antia, 1982). Age effects are not reported in any of these studies, primarily because of the small number of hearing impaired children involved. In the Brackett and Henniges paper all the impaired children used hearing aids and had mild to profound hearing losses. Both the impaired and normal children spent part of each day in a structured language learning class and part in a free play setting. Each child's behaviour was observed in both settings. For purposes of analysis, the impaired children were divided into two groups based on their language abilities. The major finding relative to discrimination was that the normal hearing children interacted more with impaired children having good language abilities than with those having poor language abilities. The latter children interacted mainly with their teachers and with other hearing impaired children.

Cause and effect relationships are difficult to determine in this research. Do normal children reject the hearing impaired with poor language abilities, or do the latter only seek out teachers and other impaired children to interact with? Brackett and Henniges (1976) do not provide enough clues to answer this. The Vandall and George (1981) and Vandall *et al.* (1982) studies do help with this question. These studies took place in the same setting — an integrated preschool focused on the hearing impaired. Equal numbers of impaired and normal children were involved and spent part of each day together. The children were systematically observed in pairs in a separate playroom. In the first experiment the focus was on children's interaction initiatives — their frequency, type and success. The major findings were: pairs of normal children had the highest levels of interaction, and mixed pairs — i.e., normal with impaired — the lowest levels. Hearing impaired children initiated more interactions with normal children than normals towards impaired; however, the impaired children were more likely to be ignored or rejected by the normal children than were the normals by the impaired. Both groups of children used the same kinds of initiatives, and the impaired children were more persistent in their attempts to interact. Finally, mixed pairs were more likely to use inappropriate initiatives — e.g., signalling to a peer when his back was turned — than were pairs of normals or pairs of hearing impaired. These results indicate that normal hearing children would rather interact with other normal children than with impaired children, despite the persistence of the latter in initiating interactions.

The Vandall *et al.* (1982) experiment dealt with attempts to modify the 'frequent and persistent refusal of normal children to interact with profoundly deaf peers' (p. 1354). The researchers spent fifteen to thirty minutes a day for fifteen consecutive days with half of the normal children training them to be more knowledgeable about and to develop more appropriate communication skills for interacting with hearing impaired children. The other half of the normal children received no special training. The results were striking. In virtually every measure concerning interaction success between impaired and normal children, the trained normals performed more *poorly* than the untrained normals. It appears that sensitizing normally hearing children to the needs of impaired peers makes them less willing to interact with them.

McCauley *et al.* (1976) observed first and second graders in the classroom, with one hearing impaired child per class. The impaired children had moderate to profound hearing losses, all wore hearing aids and all were receiving speech therapy. McCauley *et al.* do not report the relative frequency with which normal children interacted with the impaired child. Rather, they report on the type of interactions both groups had — i.e., positive versus negative, verbal versus non-verbal — and with whom they interacted — i.e., peers versus teachers. The normal and impaired children were similar in all ways but one: the normal children interacted more with their peers than with the teacher, whereas the reverse was the case for the hearing impaired children. The authors suggest that the impaired children seek out teachers because interactions with them are more rewarding than those with normal hearing children.

Antia (1982) observed hearing impaired and normal children in integrated classes and the same hearing impaired children in special segregated classrooms. Antia took essentially the same kinds of measures as McCauley *et al.* and additionally noted the frequency with which each child was physically isolated in the classroom. The major findings were: normal and impaired children were rarely isolated within the classroom, and thus had ample opportunity for peer interactions. As in McCauley *et al.* the impaired children were more likely to interact with teachers than were the normal children, and less likely to interact with peers. The normal children also interacted more frequently with other normal hearing children than with their impaired peers. The normal children used verbal communications more frequently than the impaired children, and used gestures less frequently. In the special classes the impaired children increased their verbal communications, but not the frequency of peer interactions. Rather, they increased their interactions with teachers.

The above studies point to the following conclusions. Normal hearing children prefer interacting with other normal hearing peers rather than with the hearing impaired. The latter children prefer interacting with teachers and with other hearing impaired peers rather than with normal hearing peers. The motivation behind these choices seems to be based on ease of communication and the rewards of the interaction. In a sense, both groups of children follow the path of least effort.

Four studies used sociometric methods. Three occured in school settings (Kennedy and Bruininks, 1974; Kennedy *et al.*, 1976; Elser, 1959) and one, Hus (1979), in a summer day camp. The Kennedy *et al.* research is a longitudinal follow-up study of the same children assessed by Kennedy and Bruininks. Thus there are only three independent groups of children. Additionally, Hus' study assessed only five hearing impaired and four normal hearing children. Across all studies the age range of the children was 7 to 12 years, but no age effects are reported. In all cases the hearing impaired child was the only impaired person in his class or play group. Most, but not all, of the hearing impaired children wore hearing aids, and had moderate to profound hearing losses.

The following are the major results of this research. Elser (1959), measuring both friendship choices and reputation, found that the hearing impaired were not as well accepted or highly regarded as their normally hearing peers. They generally were perceived as being in the bottom third of their classes on these measures. Kennedy and Bruininks (1974) and Kennedy *et al.* (1976), however, found that the hearing impaired children in their studies, using both 'best friends' and roster and rating methods, were at least as socially accepted as their normal hearing classmates. Indeed, the hearing impaired children scored higher than the normal children with the best friends methodology. Kennedy *et al.* also made behavioural observations and found results similar to the behavioural observations reported above — i.e., normal children interact more with peers than do hearing impaired children, with the reverse holding for interactions with teachers. Thus the sociometric ratings do not give the same picture of peer preference as the observational measures. Finally, Hus (1979) found that the four normal hearing daycampers preferred playing with other normal children more than with their impaired peers. The camp lasted four weeks, and the children were placed in groups of one hearing impaired child and six to nine normal children.

The sociometric data do not give a consistent picture of the social acceptance of hearing impaired children by their normal hearing peers. They can be well liked or poorly liked, and this difference may lie mainly in personality characteristics and not in hearing status. The hearing impaired children in the Kennedy studies all had extensive experience in preschool with normal hearing peers, and extensive language training as well; and their parents, with the advice of counsellors, enrolled them in integrated schools. It is likely that they had developed social skills highly compatible for interactions with normally hearing children. The clear message that emerges is that hearing impairment per se is not an impediment to membership in normally hearing children's social groups.


## Prejudice and Discrimination towards the Mentally Retarded

Unlike research concerned with the hearing impaired, there is a substantial literature dealing with attitudes and behaviours of normal children in relation to their mentally retarded peers. However, this literature is not nearly as complete as that concerned with either race or gender. Unlike the gender studies, researchers here consciously address issues of prejudice and discrimination. Nine recent experiments have been identified involving large numbers of subjects, which focus on prejudice against the mentally retarded. For some areas of interest their results provide a very consistent picture; for others there is some inconsistency.

The studies by Graffi and Minnes (1988), Condon *et al.* (1986), Voeltz (1980, 1982) and Gottlieb and Switsky (1982) in part deal with the effects of normal children's age. Unfortunately, the youngest age group studied was kindergarten children, and that group was only included by Graffi and Minnes. The other studies include children between the second and sixth grade (approximately ages 8–12). Across these studies several different kinds of attitude measures were used. These include an adjective checklist, an acceptance scale of the mentally retarded, and various forms of a friendship scale which assesses the types of activities that normal children would be willing to carry out with mentally retarded peers. With one exception, in all these experiments older normals showed increasing positive attitudes and decreasing negative attitudes towards the mentally retarded. In the Graffi and Minnes study, third graders had more positive attitudes than kindergarten children towards peers who were described as mentally retarded, consistent with the above. However, the kindergartners had more positive attitudes towards peers who were shown in photographs to have Down's syndrome. These results are particularly puzzling because, unlike all the other research findings, the kindergarten children had more positive attitudes towards children with Down's syndrome than towards normally appearing children.

In addition to the above studies, the experiments by Bak and Siperstein (1987a), Siperstein and Chatillon (1982) and Siperstein, Budoff and Bak (1980) evaluated gender effects. In these studies, where audiotapes or videotapes were used, normal boys were presented with mentally retarded boys, and normal girls with mentally retarded girls. Again, with one exception (Graffi and Minnis, where no gender effects were found), all the research points to the same conclusion: girls have either more positive attitudes or less negative attitudes towards their retarded peers than do boys. This gender effect is quite different than any gender results observed either for racial or opposite-sex prejudice. One plausible explanation for the mental retardation effects is that in all cultures, including the United States and Canada where these studies were carried out, girls are socialized to be more nurturant and responsible towards dependent individuals than are boys (Fishbein, 1984). Mentally retarded peers probably fall in this category, and hence would elicit more positive feelings by girls than by boys.

The studies by Condon *et al.* (1986), Siperstein and Chatillon, and Voeltz compared children who had either no school contact with mentally retarded peers, low contact (classes for the retarded were located in the school, but there was no mainstreaming) or substantial contact (mainstreaming and/or special programmes involving normal and retarded peers). The results consistently show that the greater the current contact that normals have with retarded peers, the more positive and/or less negative are their attitudes towards the retarded. Graffi and Minnes, Condon *et al.* and Bourgondien (1987) examined the effects of normal children's self-reports of prior non-school contact with mentally retarded individuals on their attitudes towards retarded peers. The results across these studies are inconsistent: Bourgondien found positive effects, whereas the other two studies found no effects.

Finally, the highly imaginative studies by Bourgondien (1987); Bak and Siperstein (1987a, 1987b) and Siperstein *et al.* (1980) investigated the effects of the social skills manifested by mentally retarded peers on the attitudes of normals towards them. Bourgondien showed videotapes to normal girls of two normal-appearing girls interacting. In one tape one of the girls acted inappropriately — e.g., she spoke too loud, stared more, moved too close to the other girl; in the other tape both girls acted appropriately. Half the subjects were told that the inappropriately acting girl was in a special class for the retarded, and the other half were only told that she was in the same grade as they. In the Bak and Siperstein study, normal children were shown videotapes of normal peers, normal appearing but mildly retarded peers, and peers with Down's syndrome. They were first shown reading, and then discussing personal interests. The normals read with ease, the mildly retarded made some errors, and those with Down's syndrome showed some difficulty reading a much lower level text. In Siperstein *et al.* normal children listened to an audiotape of two children participating in a spelling bee. One child (control) was always a competent speller, whereas the other child (target child) was either competent with difficult words, or incompetent with easy words. The subjects were shown photographs of the spellers. The control speller was always normal appearing, whereas the target child was either normal appearing or had Down's syndrome. In addition, the target child was either labelled as 'mentally retarded' or as a 'retard'.

In all these experiments, irrespective of the label given the depicted children by the researchers, normal children showed more positive attitudes towards the competent and/or socially appropriate peer than towards the incompetent and/or inappropriate peer. In the Bourgondien study, labelling the target child as being retarded or normal had no effect on a measure of willingness by normals to interact with her. In Bak and Siperstein's study, normal children showed similar attitudes towards the mildly retarded and Down's syndrome child, both less positive than towards the normal child. In the Siperstein *et al.* study, labelling a normal appearing child a 'retard' had negative effects on children's attitudes, but labelling a Down's syndrome child a 'retard' had no differential effects as compared to labelling him 'mentally retarded'. These studies clearly indicate that normal children's negative attitudes towards their mentally retarded peers are primarily based on the intellectually incompetent or socially inappropriate behaviours of the retarded. Appearance differences from the normal seem secondary to behaviour differences in eliciting negative attitudes.

A number of recent studies have dealt with discrimination towards mentally retarded peers, using either observational or sociometric techniques. In most cases the retarded children and adolescents were members of the same classroom, but in one experiment (Rynders *et al.*, 1980) adolescents from different schools were brought together for weekly bowling lessons. Only one of the experiments (Acton and Zarbatany, 1988) had a sufficiently wide range of normal and retarded children to assess age effects on discrimination. Using rating and roster socio-metric methods with Grades 2 through 6 children, no age effects were found. The retarded children in this study were only mildly retarded, but on the basis of other research it is likely that retardation level was not a factor in the results. In essentially all the reported research, normal children in the primary and second-ary grades are much more likely to choose normal peers for friends than even mainstreamed mildly retarded ones.

These findings are discrepant with the age-related results concerned with prejudice. One plausible explanation of this discrepancy is that as children get older they acquire a societal value of compassion for the handicapped. This increase in compassion is readily translated into more positive attitudes towards the mentally retarded. However, being compassionate does not translate into being friends. In a sense, with increasing age, retarded peers 'look better' to normals, but only at a distance.

Only two of these studies (Acton and Zarbatany, 1988; Siperstein, Bak and O'Keefe, 1988) mention gender effects on discrimination. In both cases no differ-ences in sociometric ratings were found by middle school age normals towards their mildly retarded mainstreamed peers. Given that other studies included large numbers of males and females and did not report any gender analyses, it is likely that gender effects are at most minimal. This is a surprising conclusion in view of the prejudice results above; girls uniformly held more favourable attitudes to-wards retarded peers than did boys. The relatively positive attitudes girls hold are not translated into friendships. The explanation of the discrepancy is essentially the same as that for age effects. Girls develop more nurturing feelings and hence more positive attitudes towards retarded peers than boys, but these attitudes operate at a social distance.

In the prejudice literature it was found that the more contact normal children had with mentally retarded peers, the more positive were their attitudes towards the mentally retarded. Three of the recent studies bear on this issue (Beckman and Kohl, 1987, for preschool children; Acton and Zarbatany, 1988, for children in Grades 2 through 6; and Stager and Young, 1981, for senior high school students). Beckman and Kohl observed mildly to moderately retarded and normal children during free play throughout the school year. The number of positive interations between the normal and mentally retarded children increased over time, consistent with the prejudice findings. Acton and Zarbatany brought pairs of either normal children or normal and mildly retarded children into a laboratory setting in which they were asked to cooperate on a bean bag tossing game. Sociometric (rating and roster) measures were taken before and after the labora-tory experiences. Normal children rated their partners more highly after the game, but did not change their ratings towards children they had not played with. These findings are consistent with the prejudice results.

In the third study, Stager and Young, using a best friends sociometric method at the beginning and end of an academic semester, found no changes over time by normal adolescents towards their mildly retarded peers. As was discussed before, the best friends technique usually overestimates the amount of discrimination of one group towards another relative to the rating and roster technique. Hence the different pattern of results found in this study may be explained by methodological differences. On the other hand, it is possible that normal senior high school students do not change their friendship choices towards the mentally retarded based only on classroom experiences.

The Rynders *et al.* (1980) experiment bears on this issue. They compared behaviour interactions and sociometric ratings (rating and roster) for three mixed groups of 13–15-year-old normal and Down's syndrome adolescents. One of the groups learned to bowl in a cooperative method which encouraged mutual support; one of the groups learned in a competitive manner; and the last in an individualistic manner. Normal adolescents in the cooperative group gave substantially higher sociometric ratings and behaved more positively towards their mentally retarded peers than normals in the other two groups. Thus the nature of the contact between normals and mentally retarded peers is a strong determinant in changing the behaviour of normal children.

In the prejudice literature it was found that competence of the mentally retarded and positive attitudes were highly related. What effect does competence of the retarded have on normal children's friendship choices and behaviour? The research consistently shows that in preschool, normal 3–6-year-old children prefer to play with other normal children rather than even mildly retarded peers (e.g., Cavallaro and Porter, 1980; Garalnick, 1980; Garalnick and Groom, 1987). These preferences continue through senior high school. The research with preschoolers supports the view, consistent with the prejudice results, that mentally retarded children with higher social, intellectual or play skills are preferred more by normal children than those with lower abilities. Garalnick (1980) showed that normal preschoolers played more with mildly retarded peers than with either moderately or severely retarded peers. Normals had almost no interactions with the latter children. Strain (1985) measured various social and non-social behaviours of two groups of moderately retarded preschoolers. One group received relatively high sociometric ratings from their normal peers, and the other group relatively low ratings. Children in the higher group were often observed to organize play, to share, to show affection, to help and to act less negatively than children in the lower group.

Research with children in Grades 2 through 6 gives an apparently inconsistent picture of the effects of competence on peer preferences. Bak and Siperstein (1987b) and Acton and Zarbatany (1988) asked normals and mildly retarded children to participate in a bean bag tossing game. Scores could be rigged so that the mentally retarded children appeared to perform excellently or only average. Bak and Siperstein found that normals more often chose the excellent mentally retarded players than the average ones for future partners. Acton and Zarbatany found no effects on normal children's ratings of their mentally retarded peers on a global measure of play as a function of bean bag tossing performance. Thus 7–12-year-old normal children link mentally retarded competence to the specific behaviours in which that competence is shown, and do not generalize beyond that situation. With the preschool research, playmate preferences were linked with competence of play behaviours. Unfortunately, in the research dealing with older children, measures of social competence of mentally retarded peers as related to friendship choices of normal peers are not reported. It is highly likely that these measures would correspond consistently with the prejudice literature.

Finally, there is research showing that discrimination against mentally retarded peers by normals undergoes a marked shift between ages 3 and 4. Garalnick and Groom (1987) formed eight playgroups of previously unacquainted male children, each comprised of three normal 3-year-olds, three normal 4½-year-olds and two mildly retarded 4½-year-olds matched in mental age with the 3-year-olds. The groups met for two hours a day, five days a week, for four weeks, during which time they were systematically observed. At the end of the fourth week each child was asked to carry out a modified roster and rating sociometric test concerning playmate preferences for members of his playgroup. For the observational data, the 4½-year-old normals showed a much stronger preference to play with other 4½-year-old normals than with either the 3-year-old normals or the mentally retarded children. The 3-year-old normals showed mild and equivalent preferences to play with the 3-year-old and 4½-year-old normals, as compared to playing with their mentally retarded peers. The latter showed mild preferences to play with the 4½-year-old normals and their mentally retarded peers relative to the 3-year-olds.

The sociometric ratings give a somewhat different picture. Here the mentally retarded children received lower ratings than both normal groups, whose scores were very similar to each other. The difference between the observational and sociometric data can largely be attributed to the sociometric ratings of the 4½-year-old normals. Instead of rating the 3-year-olds and the mentally retarded children similarly, they rated both normal groups similarly. On balance, the results of this experiment show that 4½-year-old normals are much more likely to discriminate behaviourally against mentally retarded peers than are 3-year-old normals.

A comparison of the prejudice and discrimination literature leads to the following conclusions. First, attitudes and friendship choices by normals towards their mentally retarded peers are primarily determined by the perceived competence of the mentally retarded by normals. Second, attitudes and friendship choices by normals towards their mentally retarded peers are influenced by positive contacts between the two groups. However, in nearly all studies normals prefer normal to mentally retarded peers. Third, age and gender effects of normals toward mentally retarded peers differ for prejudice and discrimination. Socialization processes lead to positive attitude changes towards the mentally retarded, but these occur at some social distance. The close involvement which occurs with friends is unaffected by these attitude shifts.

## SUMMARY AND CONCLUSIONS

The development of prejudice and discrimination is determined in many complex ways, and thus theories pointing to one major causal factor are necessarily incomplete. It is useful, however, to focus on one factor in order to achieve a clear understanding. It has been argued in this chapter that the underlying evolutionary basis for the development of prejudice and discrimination was the social cohesion of subsistence groups. The appearance of non-group members is a major threat to this cohesion and is responded to by group members with wariness or hostility. Children display two types of responses to strangers and non-group members: an early fear of strangers which essentially disappears by age 3, and a later rejection of peers which starts to emerge at age 3 and is based on the development of a group identity. A child's group identity appears to be well developed by age 4, but continues to grow thereafter.

The development of peer prejudice and discrimination towards the opposite sex, other races, the mentally retarded, and the development of discrimination against the hearing impaired were examined. The most extensive literature is available for opposite sex and race, and the least extensive for the hearing impaired. From the opposite-sex research it was found that by 2½ years of age boys and girls show same-sex over opposite-sex attitudinal and behavioural preferences. These patterns remain relatively stable for the next two to three years and then undergo a marked increase. Same-sex preferences reach their peak between 9 and 12 years of age and decline thereafter. It was concluded that the marked changes occurring after age 4 were related to the development of a same-sex group identity. The declines shown after age 12 are largely attributable to the onset of puberty and its psychological concomitants.

The Black-White racial prejudice and discrimination research leads to much more complicated conclusions. In the United States the data indicate White prejudice against Blacks by age 4 (i.e., based on group identity), which increases until about age 12 and declines thereafter. Black children do not start to show prejudice against Whites until about age 6, after which it follows the same pattern as that of White to Black prejudice. There is no evidence of Black-White discrimination among preschool children. Interracial discrimination has been found for 6-year-olds. It increases to about age 13 and remains stable throughout high school. Racial discrimination is much lower for school-related tasks than it is for social activities. Additionally, racial discrimination in school settings is much weaker than opposite-sex discrimination.

Discrimination by normal hearing against hearing impaired children has reliably been observed in 3½-year-old preschoolers. No age effects are reported in any of the studies. The observational and sociometric measures give a somewhat different picture. Behaviourally, normals prefer interacting with other normally hearing children, and hearing impaired children prefer interacting with teachers and other impaired children. Sociometrically, normal children may rate their impaired peers below average, average or above average, depending upon the study examined. Thus hearing impairment, as such, is not an impediment for membership in normally hearing children's social groups.

Regarding prejudice of normal children towards mentally retarded peers, the youngest group studied were kindergartners. Discrimination data (behavioural and sociometric) are available for preschoolers. The prejudice research indicates that between the ages of 6 and 12 normal children are prejudiced towards their mentally retarded peers; but within this age range older children show increasing positive attitudes towards the retarded. The discrimination research indicates that 3-year-old normals prefer interacting with normals to mentally retarded peers, but this preference markedly increases in 4½-year-olds. Only one study evaluated age effects in older normal children (between the ages of 8 and 12), and no age-related differences were found; however, all groups of normals preferred interacting with other normal children.

The above research indicates that the developmental courses of peer prejudice and discrimination, respectively, differ as a function of the outgroup focused on. The two crucial factors determining these developmental changes are the cultural values children are exposed to and the specific kinds of behavioural experiences that children have with outgroup members. Regarding the latter, it appears that children develop prejudice and discrimination against groups of individuals who have different behavioural styles of interacting from the ones they possess. Children prefer to be with others who are behaviourally similar to themselves. Thus hearing impaired children who develop good language skills and 'normal' social skills will be highly valued by their normal hearing peers. Contact alone between ingroup and outgroup members is usually not sufficient to change prejudice and discrimination. Regarding cultural values, it appears that these influences have a greater impact on the development of prejudice than of discrimination. Thus children's attitudes towards the mentally retarded become more positive with increasing age, but children's discriminatory behaviour remains unchanged. Black-White interracial prejudice remains high in junior and senior high school, yet discrimination is often quite low.

From an evolutionary view, the most pressing theoretical research to be done concerns the emergence of a group identity, and its links to the development of prejudice and discrimination. Additionally, there is a pressing need to include in this research area development of criteria for and assessments of the 'justifiability' of the observed prejudice and discrimination. From a practical point of view, scholars need to think through the social implications of the evolutionary framework. To argue that the development of prejudice and discrimination is inevitable does not mean that they are not modifiable. Schools provide the common setting for children in a culturally diverse society. As such, they have a potentially important role in modifying peer prejudice and discrimination. The present findings need to be examined from this perspective. Teaching methods and whole-school strategies should be developed with the goal of ameliorating the individual and social problems produced by peer prejudice and discrimination.

## REFERENCES

Aboud, F. (1988) *Children and Prejudice*, Oxford, Basil Blackwell.

Abramenkova, V.V. (1983) 'Joint Activity in the Development of a Humane Attitude toward Preschool Peers', *Soviet Psychology*, 22, pp. 38–55.

Acton, H.M. and Zarbatany, L. (1988) 'Interaction and Performance within Cooperative Groups: Effects on Nonhandicapped Students' Attitudes toward Their Mildly Mentally Retarded Peers', *American Journal of Mental Retardation*, 93, pp. 16–23.

Albert, A.A. and Porter, J.R. (1988) 'Children's Gender-role Stereotypes: A Sociological Investigation of Psychological Models', *Sociological Forum*, 3, pp. 184–210.

Allport, G.W. (1954) *The Nature of Prejudice*, Cambridge, Mass., Addison-Wesley.

Andrews, P. (1985) 'Improved Timing of Homonoid Evolution with a DNA Clock', *Nature*, 314, pp. 498–499.

Antia, S.D. (1982) 'Social Interations of Partially Mainstreamed Hearing-Impaired Children', *American Annals of the Deaf*, 127, pp. 18–25.

Bagley, C. and Young, L. (1988) 'Evaluation of Color and Ethnicity in Young Children in Jamaica, Ghana, England, and Canada', *International Journal of Intercultural Relations*, 12, pp. 45–60.

Bak, J.J. and Siperstein, G.N. (1987a) 'Similarity as a Factor Effecting Change in Children's Attitudes toward Mentally Retarded Peers', *American Journal of Mental Deficiency*, 91, pp. 524–531.

Bak, J.J. and Siperstein, G.N. (1987b) 'Effects of Mentally Retarded Children's Behavioral Competence on Nonretarded Peers' Behaviors and Attitudes: Toward Establishing Ecological Validity in Attitude Research', *American Journal of Mental Deficiency*, 92, pp. 31–39.

Beckman, P.J. and Kohl, F.L. (1987) 'Interactions of Preschollers with and without Handicaps in Integrated and Segregated Settings: A Longitudinal Study', *Mental Retardation*, 25, pp. 5–11.

Bourgondien, M.E. Van (1987) 'Children's Responses to Retarded Peers as a Function of Social Behaviors, Labeling, and Age', *Exceptional Children*, 53, pp. 432–439.

Brackett, D. and Henniges, M. (1976) 'Communicative Interaction of Preschool Hearing Impaired Children in an Integrated Setting', *The Volta Review*, 78, pp. 276–285.

Carter, D.E., DeTine, S.L., Spero, J. and Benson, F.W. (1975) 'Peer Acceptance and School-related Variables in an Integrated Junior High School', *Journal of Educational Psychology*, 67, pp. 267–273.

Cavallaro, S.A. and Porter, R.H. (1980) 'Peer Preferences of At-Risk and Normally Developing Children in a Preschool Mainstream Classroom', *American Journal of Mental Deficiency*, 84, pp. 357–366.

Chagnon, N. (1983) *Yanomamo: The Fierce People*, 3rd ed., New York, Holt, Rinehart and Winston.

Charlesworth, W.R. (1988) 'Resources and Resources Acquisition during Ontogeny', in K.B. Mac-Donald (ed.), *Sociobiological Perspectives on Human Development*, New York, Springer-Verlag.

Condon, M.E., York, R., Heal, L.W. and Fortschneider, J. (1986) 'Acceptance of Severely Handicapped Students by Nonhandicapped Peers', *Journal of the Association for Persons with Severe Handicaps*, 11, pp. 216–219.

Damico, S.B. and Sparks, C. (1986) 'Cross-Group Contact Opportunities: Impact on Interpersonal Relationships in Desegregated Middle Schools', *Sociology of Education*, 59, pp. 113–123.

Elser, R. (1959) 'The Social Position of Hearing Handicapped Children in the Regular Grades', *Exceptional Children*, 25, pp. 305–309.

Finkelstein, N.W. and Haskins, R. (1983) 'Kindergarten Children Prefer Same-Color Peers', *Child Development*, 54, pp. 502–508.

Fishbein, H.D. (1976) *Evolution, Development and Children's Learning*, Pacific Palisades, Calif., Goodyear Publishing.

Fishbein, H.D. (1984) *The Psychology of Infancy and Childhood*, Hillsdale, N.J., Lawrence Erlbaum Associates.

Fossey, D. (1979) 'Development of the Mountain Gorilla (Gorilla, Gorilla Beringu)', in D.A. Hamburg and E.R. McCown (Eds), *The Great Apes*, Menlo Park, Calif., Benjamin/Cummings Publishing Company.

Garalnick, M.J. (1980) 'Social Interations among Preschool Children', *Exceptional Children*, 46, pp. 248–253.

Garalnick, M.J. and Groom, J.M. (1987) 'The Peer Relations of Mildly Delayed and Nonhandicapped Preschool Children in Mainstreamed Playgroups', *Child Development*, 58, pp. 1556–1572.

Goodall, J., Bandora, A., Bergmann, E., Busse, C., Metama, H., Mpongo, E., Pierce, A. and Riss, D. (1979) 'Intercommunity Interactions of the Chimpanzee Population of the Gombe National Park', in D.A. Hamburg and E.R. McCown (Eds), *The Great Apes*, Menlo Park, Calif., Benjamin/Cummings Publishing Company.

Goodman, M.E. (1952) *Racial Awareness in Young Children*, Cambridge, Mass., Addison-Wesley,

Gottlieb, J. and Switsky, H.N. (1982) 'Development of School-Age Children's Stereotypic Attitudes toward Mentally Retarded Children', *American Journal of Mental Deficiency*, 86, pp. 546–600.

Graffi, S. and Minnes, P.M. (1988) 'Attitudes of Primary School Children toward the Physical Appearance and Labels Associated with Down Syndrome', *American Journal of Mental Retardation*, 93, pp. 28–35.

Hamilton, W.D. (1975) 'Innate Social Aptitudes of Man: An Approach from Evolutionary Genetics', in R. Fox (Ed.), *Biosocial Anthropology*, London, Malaby Press.

Hartup, W.W. (1983) 'Peer Relations', in P.H. Mussen (Series Ed.) and E.M. Hetherington (Vol. Ed.), *Handbook of Child Psychology: Vol. 4. Socialization, Personality and Social Development*, 4th ed., New York, Wiley.

Hus, Y. (1979) 'The Socialization Process of Hearing-Impaired Children in a Summer Day Camp', *The Volta Review*, 81, pp. 146–156.

Jarrett, O.S. and Quay, L.C. (1984) 'Crossracial Acceptance and Best Friend Choice', *Urban Education*, 19, pp. 215–225.

Kennedy, P. and Bruininks, R.H. (1974) 'Social Status of Hearing Impaired Children in Regular Classrooms', *Exceptional Children*, 40, pp. 336–342.

Kennedy, P., Northcott, W., McCauley, R. and Williams, S.M. (1976) 'Longitudinal Sociometric and

Cross-Sectional Data on Mainstreaming Hearing Impaired Children: Implications for Preschool Programming', *The Volta Review*, 78, pp. 71–81.

Kuhn, D., Nash, S.C. and Brucken, L. (1978) 'Sex Role Concepts of Two and Three Year Olds', *Child Development*, 49, pp. 445–451.

Kummer, H., Gotz, W. and Angst, W. (1974) 'Triadic Differentation: An Inhibiting Process Protecting Pair Bonds in Baboons', *Behavior*, 49, pp. 62–87.

LaFreniere, P., Strayer, F.F. and Gauthier, R. (1984) 'The Emergence of Same-Sex Preferences among Preschool Peers: A Developmental Ethological Perspective', *Child Development*, 55, pp. 1958–1965.

Lamb, M.E. (1976a) 'Effects of Stress and Cohort on Mother- and Father-Infant Interaction', *Developmental Psychology*, 12, pp. 435–443.

Lamb, M.E. (1976b) 'Twelve-Months-Olds and Their Parents: Integration in a Laboratory Playroom', *Developmental Psychology*, 12, pp. 237–244.

Lamb, M.E. (1977a) 'Father-Infant and Mother-Infant Interaction in the First Year of Life', *Child Development*, 48, pp. 167–181.

Lamb, M.E. (1977b) 'The Development of Mother-Infant and Father-Infant Attachments in the Second Year of Life', *Developmental Psychology*, 13, pp. 637–648.

Lamb, M.E., Easterbrooks, M.A. and Holden, G.W. (1980) 'Reinforcement and Punishment among Preschoolers: Characteristics, Effects, and Correlates', *Child Development*, 51, pp. 1230–1236.

Langlois, J.H. and Downs, A.C. (1980) 'Mothers, Fathers, and Peers as Socialization Agents of Sex-typed Play Behaviors in Young Children', *Child Development*, 51, pp. 1237–1247.

Lewis, M. (1987) 'Social Development in Infancy and Early Childhood', in J.D. Osofsky (Ed.), *Handbook of Infant Development*, 2nd ed., New York, John Wiley and Sons.

Lorenz, K. (1966) *On Aggression*, London, Methuen.

McCauley, R.W., Bruininks, R.H. and Kennedy, P. (1976) 'Behavioral Interactions of Hearing Impaired Children in Regular Classrooms', *The Journal of Special Education*, 10, pp. 277–284.

Maccoby, E.E. (1988) 'Gender as a Social Category', *Developmental Psychology*, 24, pp. 755–765.

Maccoby, E.E. (1990) 'Gender and Relationships: A Developmental Account', *American Psychologist*, 45, pp. 513–520.

Maccoby, E.E. and Jacklin, C.N. (1987) 'Gender Segregation in Childhood', in E.H. Reese (Ed.), *Advances in Child Development and Behavior* (Vol. 20), New York, Academic Press.

Milner, D. (1983) *Children and Race*, London, Sage Publications.

Patchen, M. (1982) *Black-White Contact in Schools*, West Lafayette, Ind., Purdue University Press.

Piaget, J. (1932) *The Moral Judgement of the Child*, Glencoe, Ill., Free Press.

Piaget, J. (1962) *Play, Dreams and Imitation in Childhood*, New York, Norton.

Plunkett, J.W., Klein, T. and Meisels, S.J. (1988) 'The Relationship of Preterm Infant-Mother Attachment to Stranger Sociability at 3 Years', *Infant Behavior and Development*, 11, pp. 83–96.

Porter, J.D.R. (1971) *Black Child, White Child*, Cambridge, Mass., Harvard University Press.

Rynders, J.E., Johnson, R.T., Johnson, D.W. and Schmidt, B. (1980) 'Producing Positive Interaction among Down Syndrome and Nonhandicapped Teenagers through Cooperative Goal Structuring', *American Journal of Mental Deficiency*, 85, pp. 268–273.

Schofield, J.W. (1979) 'The Impact of Positively Structured Contact in Intergroup Behavior: Does It Last under Adverse Conditions?' *Social Psychology Quarterly*, 42, pp. 280–284.

Schofield, J.W. (1982) *Black and White in School: Trust, Tension or Tolerance?* New York, Praeger.

Schofield, J.W. and Francis, W.D. (1982) 'An Observational Study of Peer Interaction in Racially-Mixed "Accelerated" Classrooms', *Journal of Educational Psychology*, 74, pp. 722–732.

Sherif, M. and Sherif, C.W. (1953) *Groups in Harmony and Tension*, New York, Harper.

Sherif, M., Harvey, O.J., White, B.J., Hood, W.R. and Sherif, C.W. (1961) *Intergroup Conflict and Cooperation: The Robbers Cave Experiment*, Norman, Okla., University of Oklahoma Book Exchange.

Shrum, W., Check, N.H. Jr. and Hunter, S.M. (1988) 'Friendship in School: Gender and Racial Homophily', *Sociology of Education*, 61, pp. 227–239.

Silverman, I. and Shaw, M.E. (1970) 'Effects of Sudden Mass School Desegregation on Interracial Interaction and Attitudes in One Southern City', *Journal of Social Issues*, 29, pp. 133–142.

Singleton, L.C. and Asher, S.R. (1977) 'Peer Preferences and Social Interaction among Third-Grade Children in an Integrated School District', *Journal of Educational Psychology*, 69, pp. 330–336.

Singleton, L.C. and Asher, S.R. (1979) 'Racial Integration and Children's Peer Preferences: An Investigation of Developmental and Cohort Differences', *Child Development*, 50, pp. 936–941.

Siperstein, G.N. and Chatillon, A.C. (1982) 'Importance of Perceived Similarity in Improving Children's Attitudes toward Mentally Retarded Peers', *American Journal of Mental Deficiency*, 86, pp. 453–458.

Siperstein, G.N., Bak, J.J. and O'Keefe, P. (1988) 'Relationship between Children's Attitudes toward and Their Social Acceptance of Mentally Retarded Peers', *American Journal of Mental Retardation*, 93, pp. 24–27.

Siperstein, G.N., Budoff, M. and Bak, J.J. (1980) 'Effects of the Labels "Mentally Retarded" and "Retard" on the Social Acceptability of Mentally Retarded Children', *American Journal of Mental Deficiency*, 84, pp. 596–601.

Sluckin, A.M. and Smith, P.K. (1977) 'Two Approaches to the Concept of Dominance in Preschool Children', *Child Development*, 48, pp. 917–923.

Stager, S.F. and Young, R.D. (1981) 'Intergroup Contact and Social Outcomes for Mainstream EMR Adolescents', *American Journal of Mental Deficiency*, 85, pp. 497–503.

Stevenson, H.W. and Stevenson, N.G. (1960) 'Social Interaction in an Interracial Nursery School', *Genetic Psychology Monographs*, 61, pp. 37–75.

Strain, P.S. (1985) 'Social and Nonsocial Determinants of Acceptability in Handicapped Preschool Children', *Topics in Early Childhood Special Education*, 4, pp. 47–58.

Strayer, F.F. and Trudel, M. (1984) 'Developmental Changes in the Nature and Function of Social Dominance among Young Children', *Ethnology and Sociobiology*, 5, pp. 279–295.

Tajfel, H. (1981) *Human Groups and Social Categories*, Cambridge, Cambridge University Press.

Van der Dennen, J.M.G. (1986) 'Ethnocentracism and In-group/Out-group Differentiation: A Review and Interpretation of the Literature', in V. Reynolds, V. Falger and I. Vine, *The Sociobiology of Ethnocentricism*, London, Croom Helm.

Vandall, D.L. and George, L.B. (1981) 'Social Interaction in Hearing and Deaf Preschoolers: Successes and Failures in Initiations', *Child Development*, 52, pp. 627–635.

Vandall, D.L., Anderson, L.D., Ehrhardt, G. and Wilson, K.S. (1982) 'Integrating Hearing and Deaf Preschoolers: An Attempt to Enhance Hearing Children's Interactions with Deaf Peers', *Child Development*, 53, pp. 1354–1363.

Voeltz, L.M. (1980) 'Children's Attitudes toward Handicapped Peers', *American Journal of Mental Deficiency*, 84, pp. 455–464.

Voeltz, L.M. (1982) 'Effects of Structured Interactions with Severely Handicapped Peers on Children's Attitudes', *American Journal of Mental Deficiency*, 86, pp. 380–390.

Watson, M.W. and Fischer, K.W. (1980) 'Development of Social Roles in Elicited and Spontaneous Behavior during the Preschool Years', *Developmental Psychology*, 16, pp. 483–494.

Williams, J. and Morland, K. (1976) *Race, Color, and the Young Child*, Chapel Hill, N.C., University of North Carolina Press.

# 3. The Roots of Racism

DAVID MILNER

In the most literal sense the roots of racism are grounded in the society, in the group and in the individual. This is not a platitude: each set of factors, each level of explanation, displays a part of the morphology of racism.

At the level of 'society' few would argue with the view that the development of racist beliefs has expedited the oppression and exploitation of human groups and their resources; perhaps the most compelling example of this has been the fate of the peoples of the African diaspora. Racist ideologies inferiorized Black people in order that their subhuman treatment be justified. And if these ideologies have no longer been employed in such neo-genocidal enterprises as the slave trade, nevertheless they have continued to assist the process of disprivileging those whose labour is to be extracted most cheaply. The economics, politics and history of racism are, therefore, a particularly intertangled root-system.

At the level of the group (and the individual within it) we can identify a nexus of socio-psychological processes and forces which also produce antipathy between groups, even in the absence of competition for material resources (and for that matter even in the absence of real differences between the groups). Tajfel and Turner's (1986) social identity theory suggests that the simple recognition of group membership (that is, social categorization) sets in motion a process of social comparison (between one's own and other groups), the aim of which is to establish a positive group identity. It follows from this that the negative qualities of other groups may be exaggerated (or indeed fabricated) for such comparisons to favour our own group.

This is not an alternative explanation of racism; rather, it highlights some fundamental human social dispositions which provide a 'natural' psychological context for racism, and continually reinforce it. Thus a human social propensity, it is argued, 'lay in wait' for Black people, or indeed other groups who were to be exploited: the propensity to devalue others in order to benefit self and group evaluation. In other words, racism was not conjured up from nowhere to provide rationalizations for the slave trade; it inflated, orchestrated and targeted some existing human dispositions.

Finally, at the level of individual differences we can identify a number of key motivational and personality factors which have been shown to influence the expression of racism in both attitudes and behaviour. The frustration-aggression hypothesis (Dollard *et al.*, 1939; Berkowitz, 1962) shows how frustration-induced aggression may be displaced and directed in the form of racial hatred against minority groups, whether that frustration is individually or socially occasioned. The authoritarian personality study (Adorno *et al.*, 1950) accounts for the development of a personality syndrome which is peculiarly vulnerable to the internalization of racist ideologies, in terms of harsh childrearing practices. Authoritarian parents beget authoritarian children, who not only need to despise 'inferiors' while obeying and idealizing higher authorities, but are also highly conformist and therefore more susceptible to racist ideology in and outside the family. In asking *where* those ideologies come from, the chicken begins to consume the egg, for the answer must be both 'society' and 'individual and group needs' as outlined here.

## CHILDREN AND RACISM

The other sense of 'the roots of racism' refers to its earliest origins in the child's consciousness and its developmental course through childhood and adolescence. Here we focus on a process of social learning and social construction over many years, for racist attitudes and behaviours do not appear suddenly at maturity.

Children's racial attitude development has been researched for a little over fifty years. This research is remarkable for the rather narrow range of methods employed and the consistency of empirical findings which have emerged, where similar methods have been used. Some would say that this is not a coincidence, and that the methodological tail has wagged the dog; different methods yield different data. However, half a century's effort by some eminent researchers has failed to deliver a satisfactory substitute for the use of figures representing different racial groups to which the young child can respond (in answer to questions), thus revealing his/her sentiments towards the groups that the figures represent (for a discussion of these issues of method see, for example, Teplin, 1977; Milner, 1983).

Mary Ellen Goodman (1952, 1964) was the first person to arrive at a schema describing the principal phases of racial attitude development. It was a simple three-stage affair: first, what she described as *racial awareness*, the ability to distinguish persons of one racial group from another (a facility which Ammons (1950) discovered in 20 per cent of his 2-year-old and 50 per cent of his 3-year-old subjects); second, *racial orientation*, or 'incipient attitude', the phase in which the first evidence of positive and negative feelings towards different racial groups is apparent, commonly between 4 and 5 years old; and finally, *true attitude*, when these rudimentary feelings have been elaborated with more complex information and stereotyped notions into something approximating an 'adult' attitude. This third phase begins between 7 and 9 years old.

Goodman's schema provides some of the broad brushstrokes, but is short on the detail which would help us to understand why and how the child progresses from one phase to the next, particularly the development of racial cognitions, in relation to general cognitive development processes. Phyllis Katz (1976) more than makes up for this deficiency in an eight-stage schema, as follows, in summary form, with approximate ages give in parentheses:

1  early observation of racial cues (skin, hair, etc.) [3];
2  formation of rudimentary concepts about Black people, labels for which may be provided by adults, often accompanied by evaluative information;
3  conceptual differentiation: refining of racial concepts through encountering positive and negative instances, testing grasp of defining characteristics of concepts against adult feedback;
4  recognition of irrevocability of cues;
5  consolidation of group concepts: further development of stages 3 and 4, such that the child understands the permanence of group membership and completes the functional interrelationship of perceptual and cognitive aspects together with the evaluative content [5+];
6  perceptual elaboration, proceeding from 'us' and 'them' categorizations of groups; greater intergroup differentiation, less intragroup differentiation, particularly in the case of the outgroup;
7  cognitive elaboration; 'the process by which concept attitudes become racial attitudes' (Katz, 1976), or in Goodman's terms, how incipient attitudes become true attitudes — through school experiences, contact with children of other races and contact with the attitudes of teachers and peers;
8  attitude crystallization: in which the child's attitudes fall increasingly into line with those in the immediate environment, thus becoming stable, socially supported and rather resistant to change. [8]

Katz's more cognitive approach corrects an emphasis in Goodman's schema which always seemed, intuitively, misleading. The notion that it was possible for the child to attain racial awareness within a society (i.e., the perceptual/cognitive element), without at the same time absorbing some notion of the way the society *valued* the groups that awareness focused upon (i.e., the affective dimension), was an unlikely one.

In a later review Katz (1987) maintains that attitudes 'may developmentally precede cognitions about ethnicity (Zajonc, 1980) or may occur at the same time' (Katz, 1983). We are moving away from the notion that attitudes might be some rational response to information if we are saying that feelings may even precede the simplest cognitions! The question that immediately presents itself is: what is the evidence? Can we demonstrate that it is the affective component which crystallizes first, or at least contiguous with the early awareness of racial differences? Lewis and Brooks (1975) present evidence which suggests that children as young as 10 months already exhibit same gender preferences. However we conceive of such inchoate gender dispositions, there appear to be no a priori reasons why racial dispositions should not also be identified at a similar stage, given that they depend on similar (or perhaps, in these androgynous times, *more* pronounced) visual cues. It is clear that, as in other aspects of child development, we have to look much earlier than we have done in the past for the onset of 'competences'.

How sophisticated do the child's perceptual and cognitive abilities have to be in order that an affective-cognitive link between feeling and target is made? In one sense the separation of the affective and the cognitive may be quite artificial. For many children, particularly those who are not in direct contact with other racial groups, the only sources of information about them are those which are overlaid with the source's attitudes towards them. It is most unlikely that parents can convey entirely neutral information to their children about other social groups, without any hint of their own feelings towards those groups colouring the picture.

It has been argued elsewhere that, conventionally, the complexity of the associative process has been exaggerated:

> At one level, the learning process is a simple marriage of two pairs of concepts: good-bad and black-white (as applied to people). The very simplicity of this scheme of things cuts directly through all the conventional objections to the idea that children can have racial attitudes (on the grounds that the issues are too complex for them to handle). The good-bad concept is one of the simplest (and one of the first) pairs of polar opposites that the child meets. Yes-no, positive-negative, smiling-frowning are all expressions of the same contrasting evaluations and are present in parent-child communication — in both directions — from the very beginning. One of the first things which parents try to teach their children is the concept of 'no' in relation to fires, cookers, stairs, electric plugs or valued objects of their own. Even earlier they may show disapproval of something the child does. All of this is a long time before the child has produced any speech, so it is done at an almost non-verbal level through facial expression and tone of voice. Thus children become very discriminating concerning their parents' affective tone and from early on can discern from these things alone what is approved of and what evokes disfavour. It is with this well-developed ability to grasp what is positive and what negative, what is liked and disliked, just from parental tone and gesture, that the child attends to parents' and others' information and comments about black people and white people. (Milner, 1983, pp. 111–112)

In other words, the information children receive about other racial groups will often be affectively tinged, reflecting their parents' and others' attitudes towards those groups; children can decode these messages (from their early sensitivity to parental affective tone) and tend to reproduce them as a part of their own rudimentary battery of social attitudes.

Although it has been argued that the racial categorization aspect of this process is in a sense a simple matter (because skin colour appears to be a clearcut defining attribute), others would take issue with this proposition. Aboud (1987), for example, raises the question of the 'constancy' of children's racial categorizations, suggesting that it is not fully established until the age of 7 or 8. She argues that in developing ethnic identification, the child proceeds from self-recognition, through perceiving his/her similarity with the own-group, categorizing other groups via perceptual cues, labelling them appropriately, and finally recognizing that these ethnic attributes (and ethnicity itself) are constant. According to this account, it is a largely cognitively driven process, which, while enjoying some empirical support, needs further clarification. While Aboud sequentially addresses the development of (a) ethnic self-identification and (b) ethnic attitudes, the two accounts do not completely marry. If the former were entirely cognitively driven, it would be difficult to explain the disparities between identity development in Black and White children so frequently reported in the past (e.g., Milner, 1983; Goodman, 1964). It is precisely the interaction between the development of identity and the development of attitudes which may well explain this disparity which we need to explore. As we shall see, social identity theory does precisely this; it recognizes the intimate relationship between attitudes and identity, and expresses them in terms of each other.

## SOURCES OF RACISM

Whatever the complexities of affective/perceptual/cognitive interaction, there remain some unsatisfactory aspects in the conventional account of the *sources* of these attitude elements, singly or together. Is an account which gives the paramount role to parental and social influence (in both directly teaching values and modelling others' behaviours) reinforced by a battery of cultural influences — books, comics, television, newspapers — really adequate? Is individual racism some stalagmite formed by accretion, the drip, drip of salts from many cultural fissures? Although the combination of parental, social and cultural influences appears to cover all the sources of information and attitudes available to children, all the things they *could* form their attitudes from, there remain some problems with this formulation.

1   The *variety* of children's experience with others, and with cultural products, does not square well with the relative homogeneity of their racial 'attitudes'. Despite its shortcomings, if the research on children's racial attitudes has established anything, it is a remarkably uniform pattern of development across childhood which seems to be *relatively* independent of local conditions. This empirical evidence supports the 'cultural' part of the account, but detracts from the role of parental and immediate social influence, where the greater variation in individual experience may occur.

2   When we 'unpack' the cultural products which are supposed to be the principal bearers of the racist message, we find that some of the media and forms of expression involved cannot be responsible (as far as young children's attitudes are concerned) for they are simply inaccessible to them. As adults we may squirm at the implicit racial biases of newspaper editorials, at the skewed and victim-blaming 'problem perspective' surrounding Black people in television documentary/discussion programmes; but these are the subtle nuances, the racist significance of which may well escape the majority of viewers, let alone their 5-year-olds. This is not to minimize the explicit racism of the all-too-accessible tabloids, but to pose the question whether the 'cultural' account can sustain the role we have given it, particularly since a number of watchdog bodies have begun to expunge the more obvious racism from some media, for example, children's literature.

3   Attributing children's developing racism to the press of domestic and cultural forces conveys a passive, tabula rasa view of children and their learning which is at odds with the last twenty-five years of theory and research. Children's *activity* in constructing a view of their social world must be acknowledged. In doing so we may begin to bridge some of the gaps in existing theory.

What is suggested here is that we have seen children as passively absorbing parental influences and cultural teaching, internalizing the racist ideas and feelings contained in these messages by some kind of slow permeation process: that children are immersed in a racist culture and these beliefs and sentiments are drawn through their 'skin' by an inevitable osmosis. Described in this way, it seems to be a slow affair, a matter of seepage, which the metaphor somehow defines in a way which implies uniformity among children. We can only allow for individual differences if we posit a greater concentration of racism in a particular environment, or a more permeable membrane. The osmosis metaphor appears to break down here, for that process involves the passage of solvent molecules from a less concentrated solution to a more concentrated one. However, it is retrieved if we see elements of racism as emanating from within the child and seeking out elements in the surrounding environment. This does not imply any 'instinct' for racism. Nor is it solely reducible to those psychopathological effects of an austerely authoritarian upbringing which might make the child more needful of, and therefore vulnerable to, ethnocentric or even fascist ideologies. Rather, it is an extrapolation of the central ideas of social identity theory back into childhood, beyond even the secondary school years whence it came (Tajfel *et al.*, 1971).

What is being suggested is a model of racial (and more general intergroup) attitude development which is altogether more 'driven' by the child than in previous conceptions of the process. Perhaps children actively seek out and initiate social categorization processes so that they can make social comparisons, and make their 'groups' and (by implication) themselves 'positively distinct' in the process. Much of what has been written about adults' social comparison and social identity needs applies to children with still more force: they are, *par excellence*, the people with the least established social identity, other than that often unsatisfactory (and generally powerless) one of 'child' in relation to countless powerful elders. Perhaps, then, it is precisely the need to construe and understand the complexity of the social world *and* locate oneself at an acceptable station within it that drives the child to seek 'knowledge' of existing social categorizations and ally him/herself with them. The notion that children were *actively* searching out precisely those elements of adult conversation and behaviour, or cultural products, which directly address groups and their status relations (i.e., how 'we' view them) would help to resolve the problem described in (2) above.

There may be a partial parallel in the area of gender relations. Here too there are powerful social norms and ideologies which influence children's alignment with gender groups, encourage identification with them, and prescribe appropriate behaviours. Children's passage from infancy, where play is relatively undifferentiated by gender, through to the early years of primary school, where it is increasingly segregated along gender lines, is open to a number of interpretations. Undeniably, the internalization of adult attitudes and values, and conformity with social norms provide a large part of the explanation for this transition. However, this account of the relatively passive absorption of social influences might be supplemented by a more active view of the child, based on identity needs. In other words, it is not only that a persuasive social climate guides the child towards 'appropriate' gender alignment; it is also that gender alignment brings with it increments of self-definition and positive identity that satisfy children's emerging needs to locate themselves in relation to others in their world and view themselves positively.

Given that children have a so much more restricted range of attributes and category memberships from which to construe their identity than do adults, those that are available assume relatively more importance. It is plausible that children will actively seek the few categorizations and alignments which are available to them with some energy, rather than simply acquiesce in the application of category labels to them and their behaviour. For young children there is security in the group, and security in seeing oneself as a category member. In the light of the needs thereby satisfied, it seems likely that the process is impelled from within the child, not simply imposed from without by society. The demonstration of a 'drive' towards categorization, based on identity needs, would enhance the explanation of the socialization of intergroup attitudes.

Such a demonstration would be hard to achieve empirically. It is not that it would be difficult to foment categorization among children: there have been countless illustrations of just how easy that process is, on the most spurious bases. Indeed, the enthusiasm with which child subjects have thrown themselves into experiments which have involved their categorization into groups on the basis of dot-judging, coin-flipping or preferences for Klee or Kandinsky is perhaps itself evidence of an appetite for categorization, quite as much as it reflects the power of the experimenter to call the shots. No, the difficulty resides in the interpretation of the categorization behaviour. Were a 'drive towards categorization' demonstrated, how could it be shown to originate unambiguously in the needs of the child, as opposed to an experimenter effect, or in simple modelling of divisions of older children and adults into teams, groups, etc., often for competitive purposes?

There may be a model for this 'investigation' in an earlier enterprise. It was Sherif and Sherif's (1953; Sherif *et al.*, 1961) meticulously detailed reporting of their classic boys' camps experiments which allowed Billig (1976) to discover aspects of the intergroup relations which had eluded the Sherifs themselves. The Sherifs had created a natural laboratory for the study of intergroup relations by the establishment of a summer camp over whose structure and activities they had control. In a typical study there were three or four phases: phase 1 in which activities were on a camp-wide basis, the boys constituting a single, large group; phase 2 in which the boys were separated into two groups (with friends separated) and activities were organized on a within-group basis; phase 3, the institutionalized competition phase, in which the groups competed with each other in most aspects of their activities, and which led to hostile intergroup attitudes and behaviour; and phase 4, the phase of institutionalized cooperation, in which matters were so arranged as to necessitate the boys working together to achieve 'superordinate goals', which resulted in more positive intergroup attitudes. The theoretical formulation which emerged from this work — that competition led to negative intergroup attitudes and behaviour, while cooperation fostered the reverse — did not appear to be a startling revelation. Rather, it was based on an elegant 'laboratory' demonstration of phenomena commonly observed in the relations between real-life human groups. However, truisms are usually true; the familiarity of the Sherifs' theory should be seen as enhancing rather than detracting from its validity.

Nevertheless, Billig (1976) detected an appetite for competition in the reports of the boy's behaviour in phase 2, *before* they were 'supposed' to be feeling competitive (i.e., before the competition was institutionalized in phase 3). This suggested that the mere fact of categorization into groups set in train a comparative and competitive process, a corollary of which was the development of negative intergroup attitudes and behaviours. Indeed, this is the central theme in the empirical and theoretical work embodied in social identity theory (Tajfel and Turner, 1986).

Perhaps it would be possible, following Billig's lead, to extrapolate back a stage further. Just as he identified a clamour for competition before it was officially institutionalized, it may also be possible to look in the first phase for an appetite for groupness, division and categorization before the fact, in phase 2. Certainly observers of young children, who found Billig's discovery only too plausible, would have little problem in validating a still earlier stage in the intergroup process: the active desire to divide into groups in the first place.

Unfortunately, Sherif (1966) provides a less detailed account of phase 1 than any other. There is little in the account which could fairly be represented as signifying an appetite for 'grouping', other than the survey of the boys' preferred activities, in which competitive team games predominate over other activities. However, when the richer account of phase 2 is considered, it is clear that the enthusiasm with which each group of boys threw themselves into the creation of the ingroup culture — in contradistinction to the other group — could not have been generated overnight, and probably not simply from the *fact* of division into groups.

In addition to developing a clear status hierarchy within each group, both developed strong ingroup feelings of loyalty and solidarity. Names were chosen to distinguish the groups: the Bull Dogs and the Red Devils. Members who inter-mingled with boys from the other group were branded 'traitors' and were threatened. Packages of food and candy sent by parents were shared with the ingroup, and their cabins were now referred to as 'home'. Boys were given nicknames within the group. Each group came to prefer and adopt their own songs, developed their own codes of behaviour and punishment, framed oaths of loyalty and secrecy (*vis-à-vis* the other group), allied themselves with group colours and used them in every way possible to affirm their groupness and distinguish themselves from the other group. In short, each developed its own characteristic culture. Even with little direct contact with the other group, 'they' were a constant referent in conversation. This reference was most usually com-parative ('we' versus 'they'), and competitive in that the comparisons were couched in terms of better/worse. There was soon a clamour for competition with the other group in which, each felt, their own group's superiority would be demonstrated. In other words, categorization/grouping provided a trigger, allowing the expression of group identity needs in habitual ways sanctioned by the wider society and therefore familiar through experience.

What is being argued is that categorization/grouping opens a door; what bursts through are some individual/group appetites for intergroup comparison, for the purposes of building self/group-esteem, and the arena or vehicle for their expression has already been socially defined and constructed: intergroup competition.

However, some caveats need to be inserted here. These central tenets of social identity theory have received much more widespread validation with male than female subjects, and 'cultural universals' need to satisfy all groups, home and away. Second, as highlighted earlier, we have some difficulty in distinguishing between an appetite for competition arising out of identity needs and competition based simply on habitual ways of organizing children's recreations via competitive team games. However, it seems unlikely that the enthusiasm for competition that was unleashed by the Sherifs (and commonly observed elsewhere) can be *solely* explained in terms of habit and experience. It becomes more plausible to look for explanation in terms of inner individual and social needs for identity that are thus satisfied.

It should also be clear that these considerations may interact: boys may be more disposed towards competitive self- and group-evaluation than girls are, and they are certainly directed more towards competitive sports. The era since the Sherifs made their seminal studies (and since the original Tajfel *et al.* (1971) 'minimal group studies') should allow us to see whether both feminism and the increasing emphasis on non-competitive games and sports in schools have made substantial inroads into the 'universality' of these phenomena. The truth may combine these elements: perhaps there exists a universal drive for positive identity, achieved through social comparison and social competition, but that drive is particularly enhanced in societies based upon competitive relations, and within them some groups (e.g., men cf. women) are socialized in ways which enhance such needs.

In some respects we should be happier if the furthest excesses of these processes do originate in specific socialization processes rather than in universal human drives. They remain, then, within our potential sphere of influence for change. 'Universal human drives' can, at least in the popular mind, stray into the realms of irresistible and irrevocable 'instincts'. At the same time the universality of these needs and drives, via reductionism, would seem to give them a conceptual priority over other social factors in explaining racism, which the authors of social identity theory quite explicitly disclaimed.

## ATTITUDES AND BEHAVIOUR

The time-worn issue of the relationship of attitudes to behaviour surfaces frequently in this area. Many school teachers responded with disbelief to the early findings demonstrating that young children harboured rudimentary hostile racial attitudes. Although it may have been a rose-tinted view, they saw their multiracial classes mixing and playing together and thus concluded that all was well. More recently, many school playgrounds and other areas of young children's social life seem to show a healthy degree of interracial contact, at least to the casual observer; and so the argument that interracial *behaviour* among children is as it should be appears to gain force. However, as the study of young children's *attitudes* paints a contrasting picture, of actual or incipient hostility, there is a problem. Are the attitudes studies wrong, are the behavioural impressions misleading, or are there separate, identifiable reasons for the discrepancy between the two? Each of these possibilities will be addressed in turn.

1   Even the harshest methodological criticisms of racial attitude testing in children cannot entirely dismiss the consistent findings of fifty years of these studies. It could certainly be said, however, that the business of eliciting racial attitudes by experimenters, in artificial circumstances, away from other people and from the social consequences of the choices, *may* disinhibit respondents to the point where their expressed sentiments are far in excess of anything they would say or practise in face-to-face racial interaction — thus increasing the discrepancy between elicited attitudes and observed behaviour. This is a real possibility, that in some sense the process of testing holds a magnifying glass to the attitudes; but equally,

others might argue that the situation simply allows the child's 'true' attitudes or sentiments to emerge, unconstrained by the niceties of social behaviour, so that it is a more, not less, valid indicator of the child's real orientation towards other racial groups than other measures, like observed behaviour.

2   Unstructured observation of racial interaction of children at play may well convey misleading impressions. There are very few structured observational studies (though see McCandless and Hoyt, 1961), so we have to rely more on what children *say* they do, in choosing friends and play companions, than direct observation of what they *actually* do. Sociometric studies requiring children to indicate the names of other children in their class/school/locality in order of preference for 'best friends', 'someone you would like to sit next to in class' and so on, provide a kind of compromise: they are more reality-based than attitude measures, though less so than direct observation of behaviour. The sociograms that are constructed from the children's choices reveal those who are most chosen, and those whose choices are not reciprocated, and these can be analyzed by ethnic group, among other things. Early work of this kind found little racial cleavage among very young children (Moreno, 1934), although Criswell (1937, 1939) found it increased through ages 9–11. Koch (1946) similarly demonstrated a slow withdrawal into own ethnic groups between ages 8 and 16, and this picture was broadly confirmed in the work of Loomis (1943) and Lundberg and Dickson (1952). Interestingly, more recent studies in the post-desegregation era by St John (1975) and McConahay (1978) show little if any improvements in interracial friendships.

British sociometric studies of interracial friendship parallel these findings. Rowley (1968), Kawwa (1963) and Saint (1963) all show the same picture of predominantly ingroup friendship choice, tending to increase with age. More recently, Davey and Mullin (1982) found that with a sample of nearly 4000 children in multiracial schools in London and Yorkshire, 'a significant degree of ingroup preference characterized the friendship patterns of all three ethnic groups' (English, Asian, Afro-Caribbean). Significantly, the operation of wider social pressures was evident here in the fact that the children were even less willing to take home friends from another ethnic group, or play with them in the playground, than they were to sit next to them in class.

3   Aside from the validity of our measures either of attitudes or of behaviour, there are many reasons why one does not translate directly into the other. Many factors intervene between what we feel, believe and would like to do, and how we actually behave. Wicker (1969) listed a number of examples of personal factors and situational factors which compete with or hinder such impulses, and they are best illustrated by example. Let us suppose that on conventional semi-projective attitude measures a 7-year-old evinces a very hostile reaction towards the Black figures she is shown. Will this hostility be evident in her behaviour towards her Black classmates? If not, why not? According to Wicker, the following factors influence the process:

*personal factors*, for example:

i    other attitudes ('you shouldn't be unfriendly to other people');

ii   competing motives (her needs for acceptance by a group which includes some Black girls);

iii  verbal, intellectual, social abilities (her ability to articulate, justify and defend her prejudice);

iv  activity levels (inertia restraining the active prosecution of her hostility through aggression);

*situational factors*, for example:

i    actual or considered presence of other people (what will other people — friends, teachers, parents — think of her behaviour, and how will they respond?);

ii   normative prescriptions of proper behaviour (school policy/ philosophy of 'harmony' and 'integration');

iii  alternative behaviour available (easier to dislike covertly, while outwardly falling in with the norm of mixing);

iv  specificity of attitude objects (while disliking 'Blacks', this or that Black girl may be made an exception);

v    unforeseen extraneous events (unsolicited gesture of friendship from Black girl);

vi  expected and/or actual consequences of various acts (will/does aggression call forth aggression from the target?).

The parenthetic examples are a few of many possible instances; together they aggregate into a formidable series of barriers to the basic hostility being realized in actual aggression, verbal or physical. Perhaps it is not until we spell it out in this way that we appreciate how *unlikely* it is that behaviour will directly mirror attitudes in every case.

## TWO KINDS OF RACIAL LEARNING?

The literature on children's racial attitudes and behaviour could be interpreted in yet another way. It is almost as though there are two kinds of racial learning process in childhood, one relating to what we have called attitudes and the other to behaviour. Although they appear to embody the same issue, 'race', there may be reasons why they are so apparently discrepant, *over and above* the familiar explanations of attitude-behaviour divergence.

First, the accumulation of research evidence on children's racial attitudes shows clearly how common it is to elicit preference choices for White over minority figures, hostile feelings towards racial minorities, and stereotyped notions of minority characteristics and social roles. These responses from majority White children seem to be relatively independent of local conditions (Milner, 1978; Davey, 1984), including the presence or concentration of racial minorities in the community. As this holds good in all-White areas, this is clearly not a case where Bem's (1967) self-perception theory holds good: children are not 'reading' their attitudes off their behaviour, because there is no interracial behaviour involved. This is a phenomenon that was recognized in one of the earliest studies in this field: Horowitz (1936) maintained that: 'Attitudes towards Negroes are now determined not by contact with Negroes but by contact with the prevalent attitude towards Negroes.'

This suggests an altogether more abstract kind of conceptualization of racial groups by children, where those in all-White areas only have a very limited concretization of racial categories through seeing Black people on television, in contrast to the daily contact with category-exemplars of children in multiracial areas. It is, therefore, doubly indicative of the power of the climate in instilling such attitudes that the children in the former areas reproduce them with all the alacrity of those in the latter. Daily experience of Black people, it seems, has very little to do with the process. This, of course, is not a new discovery. At the level of adult attitudes we have seen that people are quite prepared to voice disparaging attitudes towards 'groups' with whom they have no direct contact, but who actually do not exist (Hartley, 1946).

More directly relevant is Tajfel and Jahoda's (1966) investigation of the national attitudes of children: 6–7-year-olds had well developed preferences for a range of nations about whom they knew very little, with whom they had had no direct contact, and whose peoples were visually indistinguishable from themselves. Johnson (1966) and Johnson *et al.* (1970) showed how these preferences corresponded with the national alliances and enmities of World War II, and the degree of positive feeling for allies and negative feeling for enemies correlated with the boys' readership of war comics. This is not to suggest that the comics were the sole cause of their attitudes. What these studies do show, however, is that where there is a strong enough propaganda environment surrounding certain groups, this is made real to children and internalized by them, even where the groups concerned remain rather abstract notions. Clearly, 'race' is an easier criterion to categorize from than 'nationality', but the essential ingredient seems to be the affective climate, rather than the facility with which a group can be distinguished and categorized. Language facilitates the process by reifying the categorization: thus in Britain the term 'Pakis' (originating from Pakistanis) within a climate of racist hosility became a term of abuse rather than a category name, and was used widely beyond its original referents. This is a common feature of racist nomenclature. As a by-product, it allows children to absorb and use racist abuse (having identified the affective message) with little or no knowledge of the groups concerned. Language itself, then, provides a vehicle which facilitates racial attitude development, even in the absence of knowledge about attitude-objects.

In summary, racial attitude learning in childhood may be more abstract, affective, verbally mediated and related to parental/peer/cultural attitudes and teachings (as opposed to direct behavioural experience) than we have supposed.

Second, what kind of process is involved in the learning of racial behaviour, and is it indeed different from the process just described? An argument could be made for the process of learning social behaviour in interracial contexts having little to do with race at all. In other words, whereas children learn inter*group* attitudes, they learn inter*individual* behaviours, first and foremost, and race is of secondary importance. It is an approach from the other end of the issue, looking at the formation of friendship bonds between children who happen to be of different ethnic groups, but whose ethnicity is one of a whole array of attributes, and not necessarily the most important one in determining whether bonds are made.

Children are attracted to each other on many bases. For reasons discussed earlier, gender is a more critical determinant of childhood friendship than race. Intelligence and physical attractiveness have also been advanced as key variables, together with a range of personality factors. As soon as we begin to consider the full list of individual differences, it becomes clear that these choices are multi-determined, *and* that race would have to be of momentous importance to the child to outweigh all of them. Personality (hardly fairly represented as a single variable), sociability, sporting prowess, behaviour in class and a host of other features, singly or in combination, bear on the process. Some children will use these criteria to select friends on a basis of similarity, others for complementarity, many will do something of both in a very complex chemistry of needs and satisfactions. Nor are choices static or unilateral for very long.

Sociometric studies show us that, as a dynamic unfolds, children's choices are also affected (of course) by who chooses them. Given this complexity, it is easy to see how race is at least masked in the process, if not actually obscured. However, following the precedent of gender as the only single attribute demonstrated to be capable of outdistancing all others combined, is it not possible that there are circumstances in which race could be equally or more critical to friendship choice? It takes little imagination to be able to answer this affirmatively. Whereas South Africa has institutionalized segregation in apartheid, effectively limiting inter-racial friendship, other contexts show that even without such extreme oppressive laws, community norms and practices can effect the same racial cleavage, i.e., elevate the race criterion above all others in the business of friendship choice. In an early study in the American south, Horowitz and Horowitz (1938) investigated the issue and found that children in these communities did precisely that; using three separate tests, they found clear and consistent evidence that, for these children, 'the general order of importance of these attributes appears to be race first, then sex, age and socio-economic status.'

Nevertheless, these are extreme exceptions; we are more concerned with the salience of race to friendship choice where interracial choices are not rigidly proscribed by law or practice, indeed where they may be officially encouraged. However, it would be an overly optimistic view of the matter to see race as entirely *irrelevant* to friendship choice; that is not what is being argued. Rather, it may be that 'race' should simply be demoted down the hierarchy of criteria children bring to bear in choosing friends and playing companions. Two arguments would support this view:

1  if the view of racial attitude learning put forward here is substantially correct, then it would follow that children would be less likely to apply those rather abstract intergroup attitudes to specific individuals, about whom other attributes seem more important;

2  increasingly, in the school context, philosophies and policies of multiracial education have sought to create a norm of interracial acceptance, respect and interaction; These may be successful in changing or forming 'hearts and minds', but in any event they make very clear what kinds of overtly hostile behaviours are *not* acceptable.

**THE STORY SO FAR...**

The empirical evidence seems to point to the fact that young children develop rather hostile racial attitudes (insofar as we can measure these accurately) while for the most part displaying more accepting behaviour in interracial situations. It has been argued here both that the discrepancy may have been exaggerated by methodological factors and that in any event the relationship between attitudes and behaviour is a particularly tenuous one in this realm. Beyond the common-place finding of low correlations between the two, there is a question as to whether separate kinds of learning processes take place, with quite different cognitive and behavioural products, particularly as regards their respective affective tone.

Although this view promotes an expectation of discrepancy rather than similarity, and explains away some embarrassingly low attitude-behaviour correlations, it is also logically perverse. Are we really saying that attitudes and behaviour towards the same targets — Black people — need bear no relation to each other? While logical and psychological consistency can be very different things, we would nevertheless expect the individual to tend towards closer agreement between attitude and behaviour over time. Theory and research in social psychology have long suggested that where attitudes and behaviour conflict, the pressure is on to 'rationalize' away the conflict or change one of the elements in line with the other. This would offer an optimistic prognosis, in that the 'public' commitment to positive interracial behaviour is more reinforced, sanctioned and therefore resistant to change than privately held attitudes. In addition, the greater behavioural contact there is in equal status situations (Amir, 1969), the greater opportunity there is for stereotyped notions to be broken down and attitude change to take place in a more positive direction.

It is also true, however, that behaviour is much more variable across different situations. When we are talking about children's positive, accepting interracial behaviour, we may only be talking about friendship with particular children with whom they are thrown together in a particular place and time, who happen to be Black. They have formed bonds with these children, but can we generalize from their behaviour towards them, to other Black children, Black people in general, in any situation, or at any time? Again, while it is true that a positive relationship with one Black child *should* dispose an individual to be more positive towards others (or at least not negative), it does not necessarily follow. How far are our generalizations about positive interracial behaviour based upon the relative harmony of the junior school playground? Do these relationships even hold good outside the school gate and extend into the home? Of course there are thorough-going interracial friendships, but are we making them the basis for predictions about interindividual and intergroup relations?

These issues are thrown into fine focus at transitional points in the child's life and development: moving from junior to secondary school, from school to work or from place to place. These transitions often involve some breaking down of existing friendship networks and dyads. Specific friendships lapse, if only through separation. Faced with a new array of potential friends, the question whether a child is truly accepting of a whole ethnic group, and is as likely to choose friends from other groups as his/her own, it put to the test. Notwithstanding interracial friendship in the primary schools, the sociometric studies of secondary school students suggest a decline in cross-racial friendship choices.

Several factors are involved. Increasingly through adolescence, the individual's racial attitudes become both more integrated and more differentiated: integrated in the sense that the various components of the attitude and the relevant behaviour tend to become more consistent with each other; differentiated in the sense that the child can allow exceptions to the general rule whereby an individual is acceptable as a friend without this threatening the stereotyped and negative notion of the group as a whole. By portraying the individual as exceptionally different, not only is s/he liberated from the stereotype, but the stereotype is subtly confirmed. Thus are individuals' stereotypes inoculated against disconfirmation, at least until so many 'exceptions' are encountered that the general rule has to be rewritten. Even the younger child may count her Black friend as different from the 'Blacks' her father talks about disparagingly; and even she, entering secondary school without her friend, may only form cross-race friendships of the 'exceptional' kind.

Why should we place such a negative and pessimistic construction on the experience of children entering other schools and situations? Mostly because they are encountering strangers. Strangers are, by definition, unknown — and therefore uncategorized and unevaluated (to use the concepts of social identity theory). If that theory is correct, there will be a pressing need for individuals and groups in this situation of strangeness to categorize, compare and evaluate themselves against others to establish their own/group identity, and to do so in a way that favours their own group and themselves. The theory would anticipate this process happening in any situation of groups of strangers meeting. How much more predictable, then, is the outcome where the meeting involves groups who are visually distinguishable (i.e., easily categorized), and around whom there exists a powerful attitudinal climate which almost predicates the outcome of the comparative/evaluative part of the process. Where the child has already absorbed, to a degree, racist attitudes, the raw material for derogation and for establishing a feeling of superiority is only too available. Even were this not the case, the child could still arrive at the same destination, attitudinally, via a microcosm of White people's first contacts with Black people: imposing 'inferiority' by reading the superficial signs of racial difference as signifying more profound constitutional, characterological and cultural differences, and viewing those as deficits. In one manoeuvre, own-group identity is enhanced and the threat of the unknown is reduced.

This is not to say that there will not be flourishing, genuine interracial friendships among children and later as adults, but simply that the scales inevitably tip the other way, making them less likely. It does suggest, however, that we should not be misled by early appearances, and feel that the racial mixing of the primary school will continue as a template for the child's future social life.

## IN CONCLUSION

Revealing the roots of racism is, in the first instance, a theoretical and educational exercise. It should also be the first, necessary, phase in the process of their excavation. However, it would be naively utopian to believe that mere exposure to the light will undermine them, or cause them to wither or perish. For, as we have shown, racism not only grows from these roots but is also sustained by a climate of attitudes and practices which encourage its proliferation. If racism did not exist, then society would have to invent it, whenever it needed to facilitate the exploitation of others, inside or outside its boundaries. We cannot ignore the fact that racism fulfils an important function for dominant groups: it provides some of the essential raw material with which the structure of a competitive society is built. Efforts to root it out meet with resistance and countermeasures to reinforce it, in order to preserve the economic and political superstructure.

In one sense, the argument that a 'drive' to categorize and differentially evaluate other people, starting in childhood, appears to have pessimistic implications for our attempts to excise racism. A fundamental human disposition based on a need to see ourselves as superior seems to provide fertile ground in which ideologies like racism can flourish. Nevertheless, there are any number of human categorizations that are imbued with negligible significance or affect, and which do not lead to the wholesale oppression of other human groups. We do not systematically exploit and disprivilege left-handed, red-haired or obese people. It is society's teaching which targets particular groups, elaborates their difference, fabricates their inferiority (with the help of prostituted 'scientific' data), encourages hostility and rejection, enshrines discrimination within the law and institutional practice, locates them at the bottom of the social ladder (and places barriers to the higher rungs) and thus provides us with continuing 'objective' empirical evidence of their social worth. No serious opponent of racism can neglect this press of forces which shape our attitudes and behaviour towards other racial groups; nor can 'education' or 'attitude change' be held up as panaceas, as though a change in social consciousness were simply a matter of providing information or dispelling 'faulty generalizations'. Racism is not simply a matter of cognitive errors to be corrected, and while education must address such symptoms, only the political will for racial justice and social equality can begin to excavate its roots.

## REFERENCES

Aboud, F. (1987) 'The Development of Ethnic Self-Identification and Attitudes', in J.S. Phinney and M.J. Rotheram (Eds), *Children's Ethnic Socialisation*, Newbury Park, Sage Publications.

Adorno, T.W., Frenkel-Brunswik, E., Levinson, D.J. and Sanford, R.N. (1950) *The Authoritarian Personality*, New York, Harper and Row.

Amir, Y. (1969) 'Contact Hypothesis in Ethnic Relations', *Psychological Bulletin*, 71, 5, pp. 319–342.

Ammons, R.B. (1950) 'Reactions in a Projective Doll-Play Interview of White Males Two to Six Years of Age to Differences in Skin-Color and Facial Features', *Journal of Genetic Psychology*, 76, pp. 323–341.

Bem, D. (1967) 'Self-perception: An Alternative Interpretation of Cognitive Dissonance Phenomena', *Psychological Review*, 74, pp. 183–200.

Berkowitz, L. (1962) *Aggression: A Social Psychological Analysis*, New York, McGraw-Hill.

Billig, M. (1976) *Social Psychology and Inter-Group Relations*, London, Academic Press.

Criswell, J.H. (1937) 'Racial Cleavage in Negro-White Groups', *Sociometry*, 1, pp. 81–89.

Criswell, J.H. (1939) 'A Sociometric Study of Racial Cleavage in the Classroom', *Archives of Psychology*, 235.

Davey, A.G. (1984) *Learning to Be Prejudiced*, London, Arnold.

Davey, A.G. and Mullin, P.N. (1982) 'Inter-Ethnic Friendship in British Primary Schools', *Educational Research*, 24, 2, pp. 83–92.

Dollard, J., Miller, N.E., Doob, L.W., Mowrer, O.H. and Sears, R.R. (1939) *Frustration and Aggression*, New Haven, Conn., Yale University Press.

Goodman, M.E. (1952) *Race Awareness in Young Children*, Cambridge, Mass., Addison-Wesley.

Goodman, M.E. (1964) *Race Awareness in Young Children*, New York, Collier Books.

Hartley, E.L. (1946) *Problems in Prejudice*, New York, King's Crown Press.

Horowitz, E.L. (1936) 'Development of Attitudes towards Negroes', *Archives of Psychology*, 194.

Horowitz, E.L. and Horowitz, R.E. (1938) 'Development of Social Attitudes in Children', *Sociometry*, 3, pp. 321–341.

Johnson, N.B. (1966) 'What Do Children Learn from War Comics?' *New Society*, 7 July.

Johnson, N.B., Middleton, M.R. and Tajfel, H. (1970) 'The Relationship between Children's Preference for and Knowledge about Other Nations', *British Journal of Social and Clinical Psychology*, 9, pp. 232–240.

Katz, P.A. (1976) *Towards the Elimination of Racism*, New York, Pergamon Press.

Katz, P.A. (1983) 'Development of Racial and Sex-Role Attitudes', in R. Leahy (Ed.), *The Child's Construction of Social Inequality*, New York, Academic Press.

Katz, P.A. (1987) 'Developmental and Social Processes in Ethnic Attitudes and Self-Identification', in M.J. Rotheram and J.S. Phinney (Eds), *Children's Ethnic Socialisation*, Newbury Park, Sage Publications.

Kawwa, T. (1963) 'Ethnic Prejudice and Choice of Friends amongst English and Non-English Adolescents', Unpublished MA Dissertation, University of London.

Koch, H.L. (1946) 'The Social Distance between Certain Racial, Nationality and Skin-Pigmentation Groups in Selected Populations of American Schoolchildren', *Journal of Genetic Psychology*, 68, pp. 63–95.

Lewis, M. and Brooks, J. (1975) 'Infants' Social Perception: A Constructivist View', in L.Coven and P. Salapatek (Eds), *Infant Perception: From Sensation to Cognition*, New York, Academic Press.

Loomis, C.P. (1943) 'Ethnic Cleavage in the South West as Reflected in Two High Schools', *Sociometry*, 6, pp. 7–26.

Lundberg, G.A. and Dickson, L. (1952) 'Selective Association among Ethnic Groups in a High School Population', *American Sociological Review*, 17, pp. 22–35.

McCandless, B.R. and Hoyt, J.J. (1961) 'Sex, Ethnicity and Play Preference of Pre-School Children', *Journal of Abnormal and Social Psychology*, 62, pp. 683–685.

McConahay, J. (1978) 'The Effects of School Desegregation upon Students' Racial Attitudes and Behaviour: A Critical Review of the Literature and Prolegomenon to Future Research', *Law and Contemporary Problems*, 42, 3, pp. 77–107.

Milner, D. (1983) *Children and Race: Ten Years On*, London, Ward Lock Educational.

Moreno, J.L. (1934) *Who Shall Survive?* Washington, Nervous and Mental Disorders Publishing Co.

Rowley, K.G. (1968) 'Sociometric Study of Friendship Choices among English and Immigrant Children', *Educational Research*, 10, 2, pp. 145–148.

Saint, C.K. (1963) 'Scholastic and Sociological Adjustment Problems of the Punjabi-Speaking Children in Smethwick', Unpublished MEd dissertation, University of Birmingham.

St John (1975) *School Desegregation: Outcomes for Children*, New York, Wiley.

Sherif, M. (1966) *Group Conflict and Co-operation: Their Social Psychology*, London, Routledge and Kegan Paul.

Sherif, M. and Sherif, C. (1953) *Groups in Harmony and Tension*, New York, Harper and Row.

Sherif, M., Harvey, O.J., White, B.J., Hood, W.R. and Sherif, C. (1961) *Intergroup Conflict and Co-operation: The Robber's Cave Experiment*, Norman, Okla., University of Oklahoma Press.

Tajfel, H. and Jahoda, G. (1966) 'Development in Children of Concepts and Attitudes about Their Own and Other Nations: A Cross-National Study', *Proceedings of the Eighteenth International Congress in Psychology*, Moscow, Symposium 36, pp. 17–33.

Tajfel, H. and Turner, J. (1986) 'The Social Identity Theory of Intergroup Behaviour', in W.G. Austin and S.G. Worchel (Eds), *Psychology of Intergroup Relations*, Chicago, Ill., Nelson-Hall.

Tajfel, H., Flament, C., Billig, M. and Bundy, R. (1971) 'Social Categorisation and Intergroup Behaviour', *European Journal of Social Psychology*, 1, pp. 149–178.

Teplin, L.A. (1977) 'A Multi-Method Analysis of Children's Discrepant Racial Choices.' *Social Science Quarterly*, 58, 390–406.

Wicker, A.W. (1969) 'Attitudes vs. Actions: The Relation of Verbal and Overt Behavioural Responses to Attitude Objects', *Journal of Social Issues*, 25, pp. 41–78.

Zajonc, R.B. (1980) 'Feeling and Thinking: Preferences Need No Inferences', *American Psychologist*, 35, pp. 151–175.

# 4. The Development of Racial Attitudes in Children

MARCIA ALBERT AND BRENDA DERBY

There is a growing awareness in business and media that future prosperity requires an educated and effective workforce; but demographic patterns have changed — new entrants to the job market are more likely to be female and to be members of minority groups. The consequences of pervasive prejudice and discrimination are becoming more apparent, in terms of both the human cost of undeveloped potential and economic costs of recruiting and training employees, and ensuring that once in the door the new recruits are able to progress and contribute. While business and industry are seeking solutions within the workplace (e.g., training/programmes on managing diversity, active equal educational opportunities/affirmative action efforts, cooperative relationships with colleges, etc.), the deep-seated and sometimes unconscious prejudices that have contributed to the underutilization of females and minorities in the workplace and strained relations among diverse groups take form early in life.

Despite important gains made in civil rights during the 1960s and 1970s, racial prejudice persists in the United States. During the Reagan years, federal commitment to eradicating discrimination waned. Support for affirmative action and equal employment opportunity programmes diminished. There is little evidence that these setbacks will be turned around in the early 1990s, as the federal deficit and high profile programmes such as the war on drugs continue to predominate.

The racial attitudes of adults, in particular their racial prejudices, take form in early childhood. It may be easier and more effective to influence attitude development, enabling children to develop more positive attitudes about their own and other groups, than to change prejudiced attitudes that have been held for many years.

This chapter reviews the literature on the development of racial attitudes. The focus is on the development of racial awareness, racial preferences and, subsequently, racial attitudes, including prejudice, that develop during a child's first twelve years. Historical studies on racial attitudes among children focused on Black and White children; more recent research has broadened to include other groups under the rubric of ethnic attitudes. This parallels awareness and concern in schools and workplaces with relations among different ethnic groups that has arisen in response to the tremendous increase in ethnic diversity in major American cities. The lessons learned in studies of Black and White children provide a foundation for understanding ethnic diversity; but they also demonstrate the need for theories to take into account historical and cultural factors in understanding how children develop attitudes about their own and other groups.

## BACKGROUND

The early research on racial awareness and preference stemmed from a concern about the effect of widespread discrimination and segregation on Black children. Three research questions were studied: (1) at what age are children aware of racial differences; (2) how does racial awareness affect children's perception of themselves and others; and (3) how do children develop prejudice?

Early studies by Clark and Clark (1939, 1947) found young Black children preferred White over Black dolls. This was interpreted as demonstrating low self-esteem in Black children. These findings were incorporated into the landmark 1954 *Brown vs Board of Education* Supreme Court decision, which barred segregation in the schools. Subsequently, the civil rights movement of the 1960s, followed by the gradual desegregation of schools and the emphasis on educational equality by means of school integration, stimulated research on the effects of these social changes on children's racial attitudes.

## THEORETICAL PERSPECTIVE

The study of racial awareness focuses on young children in order to determine how and when they become aware of skin colour differences and develop the ability accurately to classify people by race. Racial preference refers to a preference for one racial group, without implying that the least preferred group is disliked. Therefore, this concept provides only an indirect measure of racial prejudice. Racial preference has also been studied in young children as well as in older children and adolescents. Although all children develop racial awareness and preferences, not all children become prejudiced. A greater understanding of racial awareness and preference may help social scientists to understand better the formation of racial prejudice in children.

### Explanations of Racial Awareness and Preference

Early studies on nursery school children's racial awareness (e.g., Clark and Clark, 1947; Goodman, 1952) were greeted with surprise by adults who thought young children were not aware of skin colour differences. Many studies of awareness have been concerned with the age at which the children notice differences based on racial cues. Three explanations have been proposed to explain children's development of racial awareness and preference.

Allport (1954) proposed that children negatively evaluate individuals of different races as an instance of a general fear of strange and unfamiliar things. Allport suggested that visual differences between people may influence the child to assume there are other differences between races as well. There has been little systematic investigation of Allport's 'strange person phenomenon' and its potential impact on racial attitude development. Williams and his colleagues (Williams, 1972; Williams and Morland, 1976) hypothesized that early racial awareness and racial preference of children reflect primitive feelings concerning day and night. Reactions to light and darkness are presumed to generalize to the colours white and black first, and subsequently to skin colours (Williams and Morland, 1976). Alternatively, Stabler *et al.* (1969) suggest that the colours white and black are used as symbolic references for positive and negative evaluations; i.e., if children learn that blackness is bad and in contrast whiteness is good, then through stimulus generalization children will categorize Black people as bad and White people as good.

## Studies of Racial Awareness

Early studies of children's racial awareness reported greater racial awareness among Black children than White children (e.g., Goodman, 1952; Horowitz, 1936), and some later research replicated these findings (e.g., Porter, 1972). Other researchers have reported earlier and greater awareness of racial differences among White children (e.g., Morland, 1958; Morland, 1966; Stevenson and Stewart, 1958). Black children have also been reported to 'misidentify' themselves in racial self-identification tasks. These findings raise questions about the methodologies used to study racial awareness and the potential role social desirability may play in explaining divergent results.

In their historic study Clark and Clark (1947) found that among a sample of 3–7-year-old southern Black children, two in three identified a White rather than a Black doll as the one that 'looks like you'. In a later study Clark and Clark (1950) reported that racial awareness emerges as early as age 3, with increasing awareness with age. Using photographs as stimulus materials, Morland (1958) found greater racial awareness among White preschoolers. In a later study comparing southern and northern children, Morland (1966) found highest recognition ability among southern White children. Northern Black children showed higher awareness than southern Black children.

To summarize, the research on racial awareness in young children suggests that awareness appears as early as the age of 3, increases quickly in the next few years, and is well established by early elementary school. Although significant differences in racial recognition ability of Black and White children have been found, the specific mechanisms by which children become aware of race, and factors that make race salient (e.g., geographical location, testing) have not been explored systematically.

## Studies of Racial Preference

Early studies concerning racial preference report that by the age of 5, both Black and White children report a preference for White playmates and White stimuli (e.g., Horowitz, 1936; Morland, 1962, 1966). By the 1970s studies reported a preference for Black among Black preschool and elementary school children (e.g., Fox and Jordan, 1973; Hraba and Grant, 1970). Several explanations have been offered for this change in preference among Black children (e.g., Black pride as a result of the civil rights movement: Hraba and Grant, 1970).

Clark and Clark (1947) looked at the racial preference of Black children, using a forced choice technique in which the children were shown a White or Black doll and asked to 'Give me the doll that is a nice doll' (p. 602). Of their 253 subjects 59 per cent selected the White doll and 38 per cent chose the Black doll.

Morland (1962) investigated whether Black and White children reared in a segregated community were willing to accept members of the other race as playmates and whether they had a preference for playmates of one race or the other. Acceptance of each race was high for both Black and White preschool children. When asked to choose between a White and Black playmate, most of the White subjects preferred to play with children of their own race (73 per cent), and a majority of Black subjects also preferred to play with White children (58 per cent). Age was significantly related to preference scores of White subjects, with the older White children showing higher levels of White preference.

Porter (1971) studied Black and White Bostonian preschoolers' preference for White or Black dolls in a television story game. Children of both races tended to reject the Black dolls and prefer the White dolls. By age 5 children were expressing strong preferences for the White doll and verbalizing reasons for their selections.

### Patterns of Black Preference

Crooks (1970), in a replication of Clark and Clark (1939), investigated sixty-eight Black and White 4–5-year-old lower status children. Black children in an interracial preschool programme demonstrated more own-colour preference than a Black control group, and White preschool participants showed less White preference than the White control group, suggesting that interracial preschool programmes may be effective in changing racial preferences.

Hraba and Grant (1970) studied 160 Black and White children aged 4–8 from Lincoln, Nebraska public schools. Using the Clark Doll Test, a clear majority of both Black and White children preferred playing with the doll of their own race. Unlike the Clarks' original study (1939), both light and dark Black children preferred the Black doll, and for all children same-race preference increased with age.

Koslin, Amarel and Ames (1970) interviewed first and second grade Black and White children attending integrated or segregated schools in a middle-sized eastern city. Using pairs of sketches of classroom scenes which varied in racial composition, White subjects clearly preferred predominantly White classrooms, while the Black children revealed no consistent pattern of preference regarding the racial composition of classes.

In sum, early research was consistent in finding both young Black and White children demonstrating a preference for White dolls and White people. Since the 1970s studies have not demonstrated this clearcut preference for White by Black children.

## Factors Influencing Children's Racial Awareness and Racial Preference

The findings on children's development of racial awareness and their racial and colour preferences are inconsistent. Factors which have been looked at to explain these inconsistencies include the racial environment the child lives in and the socio-economic status of the family.

*Child's Racial Environment.* Differences in the level of racial awareness and racial preferences of White and Black children may be a result of where they live in the United States (e.g., the south versus other regions) and whether they attend integrated or segregated schools. Morland (1966) found significantly greater racial awareness among southern White children than northern White children or among northern or southern Black children. Black and White children in the north were equally aware of racial cues. There was also greater own-race preference among northern than southern Black children (see also Fox and Jordan, 1973; Hraba and Grant, 1970). Some studies (e.g., Fox and Jordan, 1973; Koslin *et al.*, 1970) did not find evidence that Black children attending integrated schools had greater own-race preference than those attending segregated schools.

Crooks (1970) found an increase in Black preference among both Black and White preschoolers participating in a special interracial programme. Attending a desegregated school in and of itself does not increase the self-esteem of minority children, nor does it improve acceptance of the minority children by majority children, without explicit programmes or strategies within the school aimed at changing children's attitudes.

Several studies have demonstrated that a crucial variable is classroom racial composition, rather than just school desegregation. A study of White and Black third graders in a desegregated eastern school district found that if the racial composition of a classroom mirrored the school as a whole, there was a reduction in racial polarization and racial tension (Koslin *et al.*, 1972).

Goldstein *et al.* (1979) investigated the racial attitudes and preferences of 5- and 6-year-old White and Black children from an all-White, an all-Black and an integrated school in which the ratio of Blacks to Whites was one to one in both the school and the classroom. They reported that White children in interracial classrooms increased their acceptance of Blacks versus segregated Whites; they also emphasized that classroom integration alone may not overcome racial prejudice from the child's home environment. Black children in integrated classrooms also showed less White preference and more own-race preference than segregated Black children. These findings concur with other research reporting a shift toward own-race preference among Blacks in interracial settings (e.g., Hraba and Grant, 1970).

*Socio-Economic Status.* Often early studies of racial awareness and preference did not control for the socio-economic status (SES) of the children (e.g., Clark and Clark, 1939; Morland, 1966), or SES was only controlled for White children (Morland, 1958, 1962). Morland (1958) found no differences in racial recognition ability by SES, but lower status White children showed greater preference for White playmates than upper status children. Porter (1971) found no significant differences among White children at three SES levels, but middle-class Black children showed greater White preference than working-class or welfare Black children. Other researchers have not found SES differences (e.g., Asher and Allen, 1969).

## Development of Racial Attitudes

Studies of racial awareness demonstrated that children attend to racial cues and with age are more able accurately to classify people by race. Studies of racial preference looked at whether children preferred one racial group over another, without necessarily implying that the group least preferred was disliked. Much of the literature dealing with children's racial attitudes looks beyond racial awareness and preferences by studying racial prejudices, the child's rejection of others solely on the basis of race. Researchers have explored a number of mechanisms by which children acquire their racial attitudes: the home environment, reinforcement mechanisms and cognitive processes.

*Home Environment.* Factors researchers have examined to explain a child's racial attitudes include the parents' racial attitudes, and the child's exposure to other races via television and books. Horowitz and Horowitz (1938) found that parents were the primary source of their children's racial attitudes. Although the younger children were aware that their prejudice toward Blacks stemmed from their parents, older children were more likely to forget the source of their attitudes and rationalize them.

Observational learning and modelling, as well as the specific timing of instruction, may be the mechanisms by which parents inculcate their racial attitudes in children (e.g., Liebvert, Sobol and Copermann, 1972; Williams and Morland, 1976). Parents may heighten a child's awareness of different races by an increased preoccupation with racial differences. Williams and Morland (1976) suggest that with this type of influence, the child develops an earlier awareness of racial categories and views race as highly salient. This increased saliency may alert the child to cultural messages concerning race and lead to greater prejudice.

Television is increasingly being considered as a potentially important factor in influencing children's racial attitudes. As a socialization factor, television has often portrayed Black families as poor, fatherless and less important than other segments of American society (Zuckerman, Singer and Singer, 1980). Zuckerman and her colleagues reported that children's racial attitudes were not related to their demographic background or their family television viewing habits, but viewing programmes with Black characters predicted slightly more favourable attitudes towards Black children.

Although television may have the potential to modify evaluative perceptions of Black persons, it will not do so as long as race stereotyping is still present on television, and the proportion of Black characters on television is still very low.

Books, magazines and advertizing are also guilty of inaccurately portraying Blacks. Press coverage of Blacks has remained scanty and is generally negative (e.g., concentration upon crime news), which serves to reinforce negative stereotypes (Wirtenberg, 1978).

*Reinforcement Components.* The psychological concept of reinforcement has been offered as an alternative explanation of how children acquire negative intergroup attitudes. Williams and Morland (1976) hypothesized three determinants of children's responses to colour and race: 'the biologically-based early learning experiences of the child with light and darkness; the messages regarding color and race which the child receives from the general culture; and the amplification or suppression of the general cultural messages as a result of subcultural or family membership' (p. 20).

Boswell and Williams (1975) found children with the highest degree of pro-White bias also had the greatest degree of aversion to night darkness and thunderstorms. Racial bias scores were not significantly correlated with fear of the dark but did correlate significantly with the mother's racial attitude scores. They concluded that the degree of a child's White/Black colour bias and the mother's racial bias independently predict the child's racial bias. The mother's anxiety and authoritarianism were not related.

In essence, the reinforcement model suggests that children's early experiences with light and darkness predispose them toward a positive connotation toward the colour white and a negative connotation to the colour black that may then be generalized from colour to people. Williams and Morland (1976) offered three factors that may act to reinforce initial colour evaluations: (1) the parents' racial attitudes (e.g., frequency with which race is discussed and the importance attached to race); (2) exposure to people of other races (e.g., more often encountering Blacks in inferior positions and Whites in positions of power and prestige); and (3) general cultural and subcultural norms in the child's community (e.g., cultural symbolism of White as positive and Black as negative).

*Cognitive Processes.* The formation of racial attitudes can also be understood in terms of cognitive processes. Piaget (1928, 1951) suggested a parallel in the thinking of the young child and the prejudiced person. Piaget described a type of thinking called 'transductive reasoning', in which a person generalizes that because two people are alike in one aspect (such as race), they must also be similar in other attributes (e.g., intelligence). Transductive reasoning is characteristic of young children aged 3 or 4 who are in the 'pre-operational stage'. If Piagetian stages are used, children's attitudes toward other groups can be understood in terms of their level of cognitive development.

Katz and Seavey (1973) looked at the effect of labelling on the process of ethnic differentiation in a sample of Black and White 7- and 12-year-olds. The use of colour labels (purple or green faces) increased the perceptual differentiation of colour cues for White children, but Black children already perceived colour cues as salient prior to label training. In another study Katz (1973) found 3- to 5-year-old children took more trials to learn to discriminate pairs of faces of another race than their own, but no difference in trials needed when discriminating green faces from their own-race faces. Black children demonstrated superior performance on all the tasks, and younger children of both races learned more quickly when tested by an examiner of the other race. Katz suggests that 'racial labels may increase the perceptual similarity of faces of another race' (p. 298) and may also 'facilitate the subsequent learning of stereotypes and negative attitudes' (p. 298).

**Table 1.**  *Stages in the Development of Racial Attitudes*

| Allport (1954) | Goodman (1964) | Porter (1971) | Katz (1976b, 1981) |
|---|---|---|---|
| | | | Early observation of cues (0-3) |
| Pre-generalized learning | Ethnic awareness (3-4) | Awareness of colour differences (3) | Formation of rudimentary concepts (1-4) |
| | | Incipient racial attitudes | Recognition |
| Rejections | Ethnic orientation (4-8) | Strong social preferences with reasons | Consolidation of group concepts |
| Differentiation | | | Perceptual elaboration |
| | | | Cognitive elaboration |
| | | | Attitude crystallization |

Katz, Sohn and Zalk (1975) found that highly prejudiced White children were significantly more aware of racial cues in differentiating faces and, conversely, less attentive to non-racial cues such as eyeglasses. All Black children found colour and shade cues salient. The authors suggest that White society found colour and shade cues salient. The authors suggest that White society does not allow Blacks to ignore racial cues.

Semaj (1981) compared the development of racial attitudes with the child's mastery of Piagetian tasks. She found a significant relationship between the physical understanding of the conservation of mass and weight and the child's understanding of racial constancy. Her results suggested that children acquire physical conservation skills before racial constancy. Clark, Hocevar and Dembo (1980) found a similar pattern of results. Children's reasoning concerning race followed a developmental hierarchy that correlated significantly with measures of physical conservation. They also found positive White bias lower among children at a higher level of cognitive development.

**Developmental Stage Perspective on Attitude Development**

Several theorists have looked at acquisition of racial attitudes in terms of developmental stages. Allport (1954), Goodman (1964), Porter (1971) and Katz (1976b, 1981) propose stage models to explain the acquisition of ethnic identity and attitudes in children. Each stage is outlined and summarized in Table 1.

Although these theories vary, each theorist assumes a developmental model of change depending on the age of the child. For example, Goodman (1964) described a three-stage progression consisting of ethnic awareness, ethnic orientation, and ethnic attitude to explain children's acquisition of ethnic attitudes. These three stages are similar to those suggested by Allport (1954) in his description of racial prejudice, and recent research by Porter (1971) has been interpreted in terms of Allport's three stages of attitude development ('pre-generalized learning', 'rejection', and 'differentiation'). However, both Goodman (1964) and Porter (1971) neglect to mention how racial attitudes might be related to the concrete operational stage in which the child becomes aware of racial constancy. The stage at which the child's awareness of the physical constancy of cues involved in ethnoracial classification may represent the transition point between mere classification and later stages during which ethnoracial attitudes become crystallized and resistant to change (Semaj, 1981).

Katz's theoretical model of the acquisition of racial attitudes constitutes the best effort so far to place racial concepts within a general developmental perspective (Katz, 1976b, 1981). The eight stages take into account a Piagetian stage framework in which the child's racial attitude formation parallels cognitive development in other areas. This age progression covers the child's first ten years. Katz emphasizes that a number of determinants can influence a child's racial attitude formation. Her framework takes into account parents, peers, the school and interracial contacts, and suggests that opportunities for attitude modification are present when the child's young mind is still open to learning to see people as individuals rather than as members of a particular group or race. An implication of the stage model is that an older child's or an adult's racial prejudice is well established and not easily modifiable.

In sum, by developing a theoretical framework to understand the acquisition and development of racial attitudes in children, this knowledge about when and how children develop their attitudes can be applied to the development of age-appropriate strategies to reduce children's prejudiced attitudes and stereotyped thinking about others.

## MEASUREMENT ISSUES

The findings on children's development of racial awareness and preferences over the past half-century have been at times surprising, often ambiguous and many times conflicting. Some of this confusion can be attributed to research methods and measurement instruments. A detailed description of the many, often creative, approaches researchers have taken in the difficult task of assessing young children's perceptions and racial attitudes concerning race deserves a chapter of its own (see Albert, 1984, for a comprehensive overview of the major measurement techniques used to assess children's racial awareness, racial preference and racial attitudes). To make tests usable with preschool children, many instruments do not require reading (e.g., dolls, photographs, line drawings). Paper and pencil tests, verbalized attitudes, perceptual tests and disguised/ projective tests are also used. Issues related to methodology and measurement include:

> *geographical location:* some measurement instruments have been developed and used only by one researcher and his/her associates, usually in one or two geographical locations. This makes it more difficult to determine if results are

unique to particular populations or reflect general developmental trends. Children's knowledge and preferences are likely to be influenced by where they live and attend school as well as community mores.

*confounding stimulus characteristics:* the Clark Doll Test, and its modifications, have been widely used to measure self-identification, racial awareness and racial preference in children. Early studies confounded skin colour of the dolls with other cues. When Katz and Zalk (1974) controlled for eye and hair colour, children chose on the basis of sex rather than race. Also, Black children made fewer misidentifications when light and dark brown dolls were used as well as White ones (Greenwald and Oppenheim, 1968). Other stimulus materials (e.g., puppets, photographs) have also had the problem of differing in multiple aspects, not just skin colour.

*race of examiner:* early studies did not control for the race of the examiner. Katz (1976) found less prejudice expressed by young Black children with a White examiner, while White children seemed less susceptible to other-race examiner effects.

*social desirability:* related to the race of examiner issue is the concern that findings interpreted as a White preference by Black children may reflect social desirability rather than true preferences. Race is more salient to Black children, and questions about identification and preference can provoke anger or tears. The sensitivity of the topic suggests that social desirability may play a role in children's responses.

*inferred development trends:* most studies have been cross-sectional, not longitudinal, so that children's cognitive development over time is inferred from differences found with different age groups, rather than by actually following the process in a group of children. Cross-sectional studies also make it more difficult to tease out the influences of historical events on children's perceptions and attitudes.

*forced choice:* often children are asked to choose between a White and a Black figure. This response provides a relative evaluation of the stimuli, not an absolute evaluation. Such findings can imply greater differences than a continuous scale would provide. On the other hand, preschool children are prone to 'yea-saying' response sets that the forced choice procedure overcomes. Results based on forced choice need to be critically evaluated. For example, Banks (1976) did a statistical analysis of the frequencies reported in twenty-five studies of Black children's preferences. He reported a predominant pattern of chance responses rather than White preferences, as originally reported.

*paucity of behavioural measures:* most studies have not included behavioural measures in assessing children's racial attitudes. Studies that do so usually look at friendship choices and spontaneous play. Often non-racial factors (sex, personality, play style) are more critical determinants than race for preschoolers and early elementary school students (Hraba and Grant, 1970). To put children's attitudes in a fuller perspective, the relationship between their expressed preferences and their actual behaviour in interracial situations needs more attention.

## CONCLUSIONS AND RECOMMENDATIONS

Much of the research suggests that children develop racial awareness and racial preferences during preschool years, ages 3 through 6 (e.g., Katz, 1976b, 1981). It has not been established whether Black or White children develop racial awareness earlier. Since many of the early studies did not control for geographical location, socio-economic status, race of examiner and other factors, this dispute remains unresolved. There has been consistent preference for White by White children, while findings for Black children have been more variable. Recent reinterpretation (Banks, 1976; Banks *et al.*, 1979) and replications (e.g., Katz and Zalk, 1974; Semaj, 1981) have suggested that White preference among Black children has not been clearly demonstrated. In addition, some research has demonstrated that children may attend to other non-racial cues, especially gender, when stating preference choices of dolls or friends (e.g., Katz and Zalk, 1974; Semaj, 1981). Although there have been a number of explanations of racial attitude development, the perceptual and cognitive approach seems best to explain racial attitude formation (e.g., Katz, 1976b, 1981).

Another issue relates to the groups studied. Until recently, the large majority of racial/ethnic research has been on Black and White children (Milner, 1983). However, with increasing ethnic diversity in our society, more research has been emerging on other racial/ethnic groups, particularly Hispanics and Asians (Hofstede, 1984). There are limitations inherent to research based on only two groups. Researchers will need to continue to expand the range of groups studied to assess the differences and similarities among various ethnic groups.

While there have been many strides toward the elimination of racism, prejudice is still part of our society. The status of Blacks remains inferior to that of Whites. According to Ron Herbers, 'On measures of income, poverty and unemployment, wide disparities between Blacks and Whites have not lessened or have even worsened since 1960' (Herbers, 1983, p. A8). The civil rights laws enacted in the mid-1960s were seen as a means for minorities to gain access to the good life. No longer were minority students excluded from higher education; a system of financial aid for schools and students was implemented, and educational interventions (e.g., Head Start) were launched. 'By 1975, minority enrollment reached a plateau — one-third of the Black, White, and Hispanic 18-to-24-year-old populations were enrolled in college' (American Council of Education, 1989, p. 2).

The major emphasis of much of the research in the 1950s and 1960s was to assess and measure the development of racial awareness, racial preference and racial attitudes in children. A consistent trend noted in the research from the mid-1970s is the effort to apply this knowledge toward the task of modifying children's racial attitudes in various environments from the perspective of a multicultural society.

Although Katz and other social scientists have proposed theoretical models to explain attitude development, further development is needed. These models have been successful in explaining racial attitude development and modification of White children, while they have been less successful in accounting for the development of racial attitudes and modification among Blacks. Therefore, theories need to be developed that can explain the attitudes and behaviour of children from diverse ethnic/racial backgrounds.

In conclusion, the most serious concern for the social scientist is assessing and modifying racial attitudes, and facilitating harmonious interracial relationships in the schools and in the workplace. This concern requires a national commitment. The next decade will determine whether the United States will rekindle its level of commitment to ensure that minorities will participate in society in the fullest sense. This represents a tremendous challenge, and failure to pursue these worthy goals will perpetuate an unequal and a racially separate society.

## REFERENCES

Adair, A.V. and Savage, J. (1974) 'Sex and Race as Determinants of Preferences, Attitudes and Self Identify among Black Preschool Children: A Developmental Study', *Journal of Social and Behavioral Sciences*, 22, pp. 94–101.

Adorno, T.W., Frenkel-Brunswik, E., Levinson, D.J. and Sanford, R.N. (1950) *The Authoritarian Personality*, New York, Harper.

Albert, M.A. (1984) *The Development of Racial Attitudes in Children*. Unpublished manuscript, the Claremont Graduate School, Claremont, Ca.

Allport, G.W. (1954) *The Nature of Prejudice*, Reading, Mass., Addison-Wesley.

Allport, G.W. (1979) *The Nature of Prejudice*, Rev. Ed., Garden City, N.Y., Doubleday Anchor Books.

Asher, S.R. and Allen, V.L. (1969) 'Racial Preference and Social Comparison Processes', *Journal of Social Issues*, 25, pp. 157–166.

Baker, B. (1989) 'Toward Equality: Exploring a World of Difference', *Los Angeles Times*, 2, 13 February.

Banks, J.A. (1979) *Teaching Strategies for Ethnic Studies*, Boston, Mass., Allyn and Bacon.

Banks, W.C. (1976) 'White Preference in Blacks: A Paradigm in Search of a Phenomenon', *Psychological Bulletin*, 83, pp. 1179–1186.

Banks, W.C., McQuater, G. and Ross, J.A. (1979) 'On the Importance of White Preference and the Comparative Difference of Blacks and Others: Reply to Williams and Morland', *Psychological Bulletin*, 86, pp. 33–36.

Bird, C., Monachesi, E.D. and Burdick, H. (1952) 'Infiltration and the Attitudes of White and Negro Parents and Children', *Journal of Abnormal Social Psychology*, 47, pp. 688–699.

Boswell, D.A. and Williams, J.E. (1975) 'Correlates of Race and Color Bias among Preschool Children', *Psychological Reports*, 36, pp. 147–154.

Branch, C. and Newcombe, N. (1980) 'Racial Attitudes of Black Preschoolers as Related to Parental Civil Rights Activism', *Merrill-Palmer Quarterly*, 26, pp. 425–428.

Butler, R. (1976) 'Black Children's Racial Preference: A Selected View of the Literature', *Journal of Afro-American Issues*, 4, pp. 168–171.

Carithers, M.W. (1970) 'School Desegregation and Racial Cleavage, 1954–1970: A Review of the Literature', *Journal of Social Issues*, 26, pp. 25–47.

Chesler, M., Wiltes, S. and Radin, N. (1968) 'What Happens When Northern Schools Desegregate', *American Education*, 4, pp. 2–4.

Clark, A., Hocevar, D. and Dembo, M.H. (1980) 'The Role of Cognitive Development in Children's explanations and Preferences for Skin Color', *Developmental Psychology*, 16, pp. 332–339.

Clark, K.B. and Clark, M.P. (1939) 'The Development of Consciousness of Self and the Emergence of Racial Identification in Negro Preschool Children', *Journal of Social Psychology*, 10, pp. 591–599.

Clark, K.B. and Clark, M.P. (1947) 'Racial Self Identification and Preference in Negro Children', in T.M. Newcomb and E.L. Hartley (Eds), *Readings in Social Psychology*, New York, Henry Holt, pp. 169–178.

Clark, K.B. and Clark, M.P. (1950) 'Emotional Factors in Racial Identification and Preference of Negro Children', *Journal of Negro Education*, 19, pp. 341–350.

Coleman, J.S., Campbell, E.Q., Hobson, C.F., McPartland, J., Mood, A.M., Weinfield, F.D. and York, R.L. (1966) *Equality of Educational Opportunity* (US Department of Health, Education, and Welfare), Washington, D.C., US Government Printing Office.

Cook, S.W. (1975) 'Social Science and School Desegregation: Did We Mislead the Supreme Court?' *Personality and Social Psychology Bulletin*, 5, pp. 420–437.

Crooks, R.C. (1970) 'The Effects of an Interracial Preschool Program upon Racial Preferences, Knowledge of Racial Differences, and Racial Identification', *Journal of Social Issues*, 26, pp. 137–143.

Fox, D.J. and Jordan, V.B. (1973) 'Racial Preference and Identification of Black, American Chinese, and White Children', *Genetic Psychology Monographs*, 88, pp. 229–286.

Frenkel-Brunswik, E. (1948) 'A Study of Prejudice in Children', *Human Relations*, 1, pp. 295–306.

Goldstein, C.G., Koopman, E.J. and Goldstein, H.H. (1979) 'Racial Attitudes in Young Children as a Function of Interracial Contact in the Public Schools', *American Journal of Orthopsychiatry*, 49, pp. 89–99.

Goodman, M.E. (1952) *Race Awareness in Young Children*, Cambridge, Mass., Addison-Wesley.

Greenwald, H.J. and Oppenheim, D.B. (1968) 'Reported Magnitude of Self-Misidentification among Negro Children — Artifact?' *Journal of Personality and Social Psychology*, 8, pp. 49–52.

Harris, D., Gough, H. and Martin, W.E. (1950) 'Children's Ethnic Attitudes. II: Relationships to Parental Beliefs Concerning Child Training', *Child Development*, 21, pp. 169–181.

Herbers, R. (1983) 'Gap in Income between Blacks and Whites Is Large as 1960's, Study Finds', *New York Times*, 18 July, pp. A1, A8.

Hofstede, C. (1984) *Culture's Consequences: International Differences in Work-related Values*, Beverly Hills, Calif., Sage.

Horowitz, E.L. (1936) 'The Development of Attitude toward the Negro', *Archives of Psychology*, 194, pp. 91–99.

Horowitz, E.L. and Horowitz, R.E. (1938) 'Development of Social Attitudes in Children', *Sociometry*, 1, pp. 301–338.

Hraba, J. (1979) *American Ethnicity*, Itasca, Ill., F.S. Peacock.

Hraba, J. and Grant, G. (1970) 'Black Is Beautiful: A Reexamination of Racial Preference and Identification', *Journal of Personality and Social Psychology*, 16, pp. 398–402.

Katz, P.A. (1973) 'Perception of Racial Cues in Preschool Children: A New Look', *Developmental Psychology*, 8, pp. 295–299.

Katz, P.A. (1976a) 'Attitude Change in Children: Can the Twig Be Straightened?' in P.A. Katz (Ed.), *Towards the Elimination of Racism*, New York, Pergamon Press, pp. 213–241.

Katz, P.A. (1976b) 'The Acquisition of Racial Attitudes in Children', in P.A. Katz (Ed.), *Towards the Elimination of Racism*, New York: Pergamon Press, pp. 126–154.

Katz, P.A. (1982) 'Development of Children's Racial Awareness and Intergroup Attitudes', in L. Katz (Ed.), *Current Topics in Early Childhood Education, Vol. 4*, Washington, D.C., National Institute of Education, pp. 1–43.

Katz, P.A. and Seavey, C. (1973) 'Labels and Children's Perception of Faces', *Child Development*, 44, pp. 770–775.

Katz, P.A. and Zalk, S.R. (1974) 'Doll Preferences: An Index of Racial Attitudes', *Journal of Experimental Pyschology*, 66, pp. 663–668.

Kennedy, R. (1989) 'Civil Rights vs. Supreme Court: A New and Historic Battleground', *Los Angeles Times*, 25 June, p. 3.

Koslin, S., Koslin, B., Pargament, R. and Waxman, H. (1972) 'Classroom Racial Balance and Students' Interracial Attitudes', *Sociology of Education*, 45, pp. 386–407.

Lee, M. (1983) 'Multiculturalism: Educational Perspectives for the 1980s', *Education*, 103, pp. 405–409.

McPartland, J. (1969) 'The Relative Influence of School and of Classroom Desegregation on the Academic Achievement of Ninth Grade Negro Students', *Journal of Social Issues*, 25, pp. 93–102.

Milner, D. (1983) *Children and Race*, 2nd ed., Harmondsworth, Penguin.

Morland, J.K. (1958) 'Racial Recognition in Nursery School Children in Lynchburg, Virginia', *Social Forces*, 37, pp. 132–137.

Morland, J.K. (1962) 'Racial Acceptance and Preference in Nursey-School Children', *Merrill-Palmer Quarterly*, 8, pp. 271–280.

Morland, J.K. (1966) 'A Comparison of Race Awareness in Northern and Southern Children', *American Journal of Orthopsychiatry*, 36, pp. 22–31.

Piaget, J. (1928) *Judgment and Reasoning in the Child*, New York, Harcourt, Brace.

Piaget, J. (1951) *The Child's Conception of the World*, New York, Humanities Press.

Porter, J. (1971) *Black Child, White Child: The Development of Racial Attitudes*, Cambridge, Mass., Harvard University Press.

Radke, M.J. and Trager, H.G. (1950) 'Children's Perceptions of the Social Roles of Negroes and Whites', *Journal of Psychology*, 29, pp. 3–33.

Roper, L.D. and Sedlacek, W.E. (1982) 'Student Affairs Professionals in Academic Roles: A Course on Racism', *NASPA Journal*, 26, 1, pp. 27–31.

St John, N.H. (1975) *School Desegregation: Outcomes for Children*, New York, Wiley.

Semaj, L.T. (1981) 'The Development of Racial-Classification Abilities', *Journal of Negro Education*, 50, pp. 41–47.

Stabler, J.R., Johnson, E.E., Berke, M.A. and Baker, R.B. (1969) 'The Relationship between Race and Perception of Racially Related Stimuli in Preschool Children', *Child Development*, 40, pp. 1233–1239.

Stevenson, H.W. and Stewart, E.C. (1958) 'A Developmental Study of Racial Awareness in Young Children', *Child Development*, 29, pp. 399–409.

US Commission on Civil Rights (1967) *Racial Isolation in the Public Schools*, Washington, D.C., US Government Printing Office.

Weinberg, M. (1975) 'The Relationship between School Desegregation and Academic Achievement: A Review of Research', *Law and Contemporary Problems*, 39, pp. 240–269.

Williams, J.E. (1972) 'Racial Attitudes in Preschool Children: Modification via Operant Conditioning, and a Revised Measurement Procedure', Paper presented at the meeting of the American Psychological Association, Honolulu.

Williams, J.E. and Morland, J.K. (1976) *Race, Color, and the Young Child*, Chapel Hill, N.C., University of North Carolina Press.

Wirtenberg, J. (1978) 'Cultural Fairness in Materials Development', Paper presented at the skills workshop of the Women's Educational Equity Act program, Washington, D.C., April (abstract).

Zuckerman, D., Singer, D. and Singer, J. (1980) 'Children's Television Viewing, Racial and Sex-Role Attitudes', *Journal of Applied Social Psychology*, 10, pp. 281–294.

# 5. Gender Discrimination and Education

GENEVA GAY

Gender inequality in education is a well established fact. World-wide, females do not attend school as often, are not afforded the instructional opportunities, and do not derive educational outcomes and benefits comparable to males (Finn, Reis and Dulberg, 1982). The general patterns of these inequities have been documented by research in North America, Australia, Europe, the United Kingdom, Africa and Asia, and they are strikingly similar in kind and occurrence (Finn, Dulberg and Reis, 1979). The specific causes, magnitude, effect and solutions of gender discrimination are less unequivocal.

Some analysts attribute gender differences in school achievement to genetically determined ability, and others point to environmental conditions, cultural values, gender role socialization and the sexism that permeates societal and cultural systems. Some researchers have produced significant gender differences, some has revealed only nominal differences, some has found no differences at all, and some have reported conflicting results. However, consensus does exist across these studies on four major points. First, the specific character that gender discrimination in education takes is affected by many different variables including ethnicity, social class, experiences of students, the assessment measures used, and the contexts and skills that are being analyzed. Second, disparities in the processes of education are more informative indicators of gender discrimination than measures of female and male students' performance outcomes. Third, gender differences crystallize about the time students reach junior secondary school (approximately age 11) and persist thereafter through secondary, college and graduate school education. Fourth, successful gender equity efforts depend upon how well the structural dimensions and expressive dynamics of the inequities are understood. To these ends, this chapter explores some of the evidence, causes and effects of gender discrimination in education, and offers some suggestions for remediation.

## GENDER DISCRIMINATION DOES EXIST

Voluminous amounts of empirical, theoretical and anecdotal evidence have accumulated over the last two decades demonstrating unequivocally that females and males often do not have equal educational opportunities, experiences and outcomes. These inequities are mainfested in both the informal domains and the formal structures of education, including curricular designs, instructional materials and styles, course selections, classroom climates, and teachers' attitudes, expectations and interactions (Stanworth, 1983, Wilkinson and Marrett, 1985).

Two major avenues through which gender discrimination is conveyed are the gender distribution of school personnel, and the treatment of females and males in textbooks and other instructional materials. Teachers and textbooks are especially important in analyzing gender inequities in education because they are the most pervasively constant factors in the educational process. Seventy-five to 90 per cent of all classroom instruction is based on textbooks (Davis *et al.*, 1986), and the greater portion of all learning activities is determined, defined, directed and controlled by teachers (Goodlad, 1984). Too often, both of these commonly used conduits of education perpetuate in schooling gender inequities similar to those that exist in society at large. Thus, 'from the books they read, to the role models they see, to the way they are treated in classrooms, girls and boys continue to learn subtle yet powerful messages about separate and unequal opportunities based on gender' (Sadker, Sadker and Long, 1989, p. 106).

The overrepresentation of females among classroom teachers and their underrepresentation among school administrators are also testimony of gender discrimination. This disproportionality is most extreme among elementary teachers and school superintendents. According to Shakeshaft (1985), 28.3 per cent of school board members, 1.8 per cent of superintendents, 18 per cent of elementary principals and 7 per cent of secondary principals in the United States are females. Yet in 1986 females comprised 68.8 per cent of all teachers in the United States (National Center for Education Statistics, 1988). An international survey conducted by Shapiro and Dank (1980) indicates that females comprise approximately 98 per cent of all teachers in the primary grades across all of English-speaking North America. Davies (1988) reports similar trends in other Western countries like Australia, Canada and the United Kingdom, as well as in most Third World nations. His findings confirm that the apparent perception of educational administration as a masculine occupation, and the decline in the proportion of female teachers as the age and status of students, and the level of schooling increase are international phenomena.

The extent of these disproportionalities may have lessened somewhat recently, but equitable representation of females in all levels of school leadership is still far from being realized. When female and male teachers and administrators are compared on selected criteria, such as teaching exam scores, college grade point averages, sensitivity, caring and warmth, and interpersonal and human relations skills, females often perform better than males (Shakeshaft, 1986). Nevertheless, they are not selected for administrative positions as often as males, they spend more time in second order assistantship assignments, are not promoted as easily, and are more heavily represented among off-line, central office administrative positions, such as supervisors, coordinators, and/or directors of special programmes and instructional services. These conditions led Shakeshaft (1985, p. 125) to conclude that 'both gender and talent imbalances result when women are passed over for administrative positions.' They also convey the powerfully biased message that women are not as capable as men in providing educational leadership or as important to policy decision-making (Sadker, Sadker and Long, 1989).

In the other most commonly used conduit of education — textbooks — the presentation of females continues to be less than desirable. Admittedly, some significant gains have been made in how females are treated in the narrative, pictorial and illustrative content of texts and story books since the early 1970s, when the issue of sex discrimination in instructional materials became a serious educational issue. These changes include increased visibility and role versality; a greater proportion of female-related story problems in mathematics and science; less stereotypic images of females as docile, passive, subservient and helpless; and the elimination of the most glaring examples of sexist language. Yet gender biases and misrepresentations in instructional materials and activities remain. They are revealed more in the overall approaches to subject matter, questions asked, the tone of the content presented, and the cultural, valuative and philosophical assumptions which govern how textbook materials are designed than in the content per se (Rothschild, 1986).

Analyses of textbooks and story books in Australia, England, Europe, India and the United States indicate that males are still largely portrayed as ingenuous, independent, creative, brave, active, curious, conquering, assertive and skilful actors who are inclined to select military, medical, scientific, political and legal careers. Females are stereotyped as dependent, passive, quiet, compliant and acquiescent, who engage in helping and care-giving careers (Finn, Reis and Dulberg, 1982; Hahn and Powers *et al.*, 1985; Kalia, 1983; Sadker, Sadker and Long, 1989). Women in non-traditional roles are often qualified as 'the first', 'the only one', 'the exceptionally capable' doctor, lawyer, engineer, scientist, pilot or architect. These stereotypical treatments comprise a 'conspiracy of conditioning' (Trecker, 1973) in which gender inequities are perpetuated by portraying women as having negatively valued personality traits, and being capable of participating in only a narrow range of social and occupational roles that have low economic status and power potential (Finn, Dulberg and Reis, 1979; Finn, Reis and Dulberg, 1982).

Furthermore, discussions of female contributions in textbooks frequently are treated as unique or tangential occurrences isolated from any broader context, and women are depicted as interacting primarily among themselves. These distortions explain in part why some advocates of gender equity accuse textbooks of only telling 'his-story', and demand that greater attention be given to 'her-story' as well. They convey to students that females are cosmetic, optional and occasionally interesting afterthoughts that can be relegated to the sidelines of the human story. Misrepresentations like this belie scholarly accuracy, distort self-images and rob female and male students of role models that they need in order to develop healthy, well-balanced self-esteem.

Three other pervasive indicators of gender discrimination in education are the discrepancies in school enrolment and literacy rates, classroom interactions between teachers and students, and achievement outcomes. World-wide, the discrepancy gaps in female and male school attendance and literacy rates widen as the level of schooling increases and the context changes from urban to rural (Bowman and Anderson, 1982; Porras-Zuniga, 1988; Kurian, 1988b). Kurian (1988b) proposes that of all the inequities in educational opportunities related to gender, socio-economic status, ethnicity and geographic region, 'none is more glaring than discrimination based on gender' (p. xv).

Statistics reported in the *World Education Encyclopedia* (Kurian, 1988b) indicate that the world-wide literacy rate for females is 54 per cent compared to 67 per cent for males. In Western industrialized countries the overall literacy rates of males and females are comparable and far exceed this average at 98 and 97 per cent respectively. Although not quite as high, literacy in most of Latin America also exceeds the world-wide average, with 76 per cent for males and 70 per cent for females. In non-industrialized, non-Western nations the literacy rates are considerably lower, and the discrepancies between females and males are much higher. For the developing nations as a whole the literacy rate for males is 52 per cent and for females 32 per cent. In Asian countries (excluding Japan) it is slightly above this average, at 56 per cent for males and 34 per cent for females. African nations have much lower rates: about 33 per cent for males and 15 per cent for females (Kurian, 1988b).

Even where there is comparability in female and male school attendance and literacy rates, gender equality in educational opportunities is not assured. Discrimination still occurs in the quality of learning experiences, classroom interactions and curricular assignments availed to female and male students. Analyses of these aspects of schooling indicate that their gender differentiations are (1) consistent with traditional gender role socialization and perceptions; (2) more a function of students' initiations than teachers' solicitations; (3) observable in all levels and dimensions of education, preschool though graduate school; (4) not a function of teachers' gender, since both male and female teachers behave similarly; and (5) more supportive of males than females with respect to accessibility, efficacy, skill mastery, expectations, reinforcement and academic performance (Harlen, 1987; Lockheed and Klein, 1985; Organisation for Economic Cooperation and Development, 1986; Rychman and Peckham, 1987; Sadker and Sadker, 1986; Wilkinson and Marrett, 1985). For example, males interact more with teachers than females, receive more task mastery instructions, are asked higher order questions, and they outnumber females in computer courses, mathematics, physical and chemical sciences curricula. Because males also enrol at higher rates in special and gifted education programmes, they receive more remediation for academic problems and enrichment of special abilities than females (Holbrook, 1988; Sadker, Sadker and Long, 1989; Shakeshaft, 1986).

As might be expected, the gender differences that are apparent in the processes of teaching and learning cause inequities in educational outcomes and effects. Sadker, Sadker and Long (1989) summarize these in the form of a report card on the costs of sexism in schools. Although their particular focus is the United States, most of the costs they list are observable in other countries as well. The report card indicates that gender differences in school achievement are (1) quantitatively less than they were previously thought to be; (2) persistent across both subjects and skills within subject areas; (3) more evident as the levels of subjects and skills increase in academic complexity; (4) not only academic but sociological, psychological, vocational and personal as well; and (5) are more academically advantageous to males (Aiken, 1986–87; Emanuelsson and Fischbein, 1987; Fennema and Peterson, 1985; Lockheed and Klein, 1985; Linn and Petersen, 1985; Tohidi, Steinkamp and Maehr, 1986). The overall effect of these differences is that as females progress through school, the proportionality of their achievement declines while that of males increases (Sadker, Sadker and Long, 1989).

## CAUSES OF GENDER DISCRIMINATION

Several different explanations are advanced to account for gender differences in educational opportunities, experiences and outcomes. They extend the gambit from innate intellectual abilities, to brain lateralization, to socio-cultural conditioning; but the greatest amount of support favours environmental factors and social conditioning. Tinker and Bramsen (1975) attribute the causes to cultural attitudes which mediate against the full participation of females in educational institutions, the low value of females' education to local and national economies, and the teaching methods used in classrooms. Finn, Reis and Dulberg (1982) point to three related but different sets of influences that cause gender difference in school attainment. These are modelling of sex-appropriate behaviours, exposure to specific curricular content, and the academic support provided to students. Campbell (1986) adds that the relationship between sex and achievement is correlational, not causal.

The basic proposition of most explanations of gender discrimination in education is that schools are microcosms of the larger society. As such, they mirror the macro-culture in gender values, role expectations and sex biases; 'formal schooling is itself a significant agent in teaching and reinforcing cultural expectations for males and females' (Finn, Reis and Dulberg, 1982, p. 109). These general explanations are supported by others found in the differential fit between societal gender roles and the expected roles of students; the gender-typing of school subjects, skills and activities as feminine or masculine; and the gender role socialization and behaviours of students instead of their sex per se (Brophy, 1985).

Both students and teachers bring similarly biased gender role expectations to learning interactions, and behaviours which conform to these are reinforced and rewarded. Being assertive, active, individualistic, autonomous and self-confident places males at an advantage in schools. They are more initiating, persistent and efficacious in classroom activities. However, females who are taught to be social, subservient, dependent and accommodating are less likely to be as assertive, confident and persistent in their interactions with male peers and classroom teachers. Thus they get fewer chances to participate in instruction. This happens because (1) there is a high correlation between feelings of self-confidence, personal competence and persistence in learning; (2) teachers interact more frequently, at higher cognitive levels and in more efficacious ways with high achieving, confident students; and (3) the quality of education students receive is influenced significantly by the nature of their participation in interactions with teachers. The male advantage in these attitudes and behaviours tells boys that their actions can facilitate their learning and elicit individual assistance from the teacher in the process. At the same time the individual needs of female students are largely ignored, since they are 'invisible', immersed as they are among the better behaved, but less distinguished classroom crowd (Organisation for Economic Cooperation and Development, 1986).

Closely related to the sex role socialization and expectations in perpetuating gender discrimination in education is the gender image of school subjects and academic skills. Certain of these are gender-typed as feminine or masculine. Mathematics, science, problem-solving, mechanical tasks, decision-making and logical thinking are often perceived as masculine domains. Feminine perceptions are ascribed to reading, fine arts, literature, writing, human relations and creativity. Actual gender achievement patterns correlate positively with such subject/skill gender-typing (Campbell, 1986).

The gender image of school subjects and skills is persuasive enough to convince students that if their personal gender role socialization and that of different subjects are not compatible, they cannot perform successfully in those areas of learning. Thus a self-fulfilling prophecy is activated. It creates gender-based subject segregation within school curricula, since students self-select in or out of given subjects. These perceptions are reinforced by attributional and aspirational patterns found among female and male students. On both of these females have lower expectations across a wider variety of domains than males. Furthermore, they tend to attribute their academic successes and failures to effort, while males credit ability (Garber and Seligman, 1980; Rychman and Peckham, 1987).

Gender-based attribution patterns prevail even in the absence of any real sex differences in actual ability and achievement. When females perform as well as males in maths and science, they are still more likely to attribute their success to hard work or luck instead of intelligence and capability. These attributions may result from both the learned helplessness associated with traditional female socialization and the belief that being feminine and a high achiever in masculine subjects like maths and science are inherently contradictory.

The sex-biased messages transmitted through teaching styles form a third explanation for gender discrimination in education. The teaching processes used in most classrooms that emphasize student passivity, conformity and mental activity may be more similar to how females are socialized outside school than males. They experience less role conflict and social adjustment problems in school, and they are rewarded more for 'acting right'. However, this social rewards system does not facilitate females being as well prepared for academic competition and achievement as males. This may explain why they can receive better grades and have fewer behavioural problems yet perform lower on standardized achievement tests. Male students lose out in social skills, but they have greater access to academic substance, and subsequently better achievement performance. Harvey (1986, p. 510) provides some insights into this apparent contradiction. He says that 'what is perceived to be a supportive environment for girls is in reality one that ignores female learning deficits. What is perceived to be hostile to boys is really an emphasis on early identification of and attention to male learning deficits.'

Added to the gender differentiated competences and accessibility to learning opportunities created by how teachers teach is the role of teaching and testing materials in perpetuating gender inequities in education. The preferential treatment they give to male influences contributes significantly to the learned helplessness and lack of self-confidence observed among females, and the higher levels of mastery orientation, ability attribution and self-reliance exhibited by males. These attitudes and values are further extended through the underrepresentation of female teachers in powerful leadership positions in schools, the distribution of females and males across teaching assignments, the peripheral position of females in textbook content and the use of pro-male testing materials. These forms of gender bias limit motivation to learn and discourage students from pursuing non-stereotypical curricular programmes and educational options. They can lead to inaccurate diagnoses of individual needs and inappropriate remediation (Klein *et al.*, 1985). The students learn, through the examples and images provided in teaching and testing materials, to conform in schools to the gender caste structures that operate in society. Thus the chances for female and male students to receive educational experiences that are comparable in quality and in the celebration of both genders are severely constrained if not blocked entirely.

## ACHIEVING GENDER EQUITY

The persistence and pervasiveness of gender inequities in education require multi-dimensional strategies to counterbalance their causes, manifestations and effects. Educational laws, policies, practices, programmes, processes, personnel and materials must be reformed simultaneously. Research (Campbell, 1986; Finn, Reis and Dulberg, 1982; Klein, 1985; Sadker and Sadker, 1986; Wilkinson and Marrett, 1985) indicates that interventions deliberately designed to change specifically targeted gender discriminations produce positive results for female and male students, and for the overall quality of education.

Strategies for achieving gender equity should be organized according to school functions. Among the most critical ones where interventions are needed are school administration, instructional materials, classroom climate, teacher interactions and expectations, and curricular content areas. Reform in these aspects of schooling will generate revisions in all others. Each intervention should have five developmental phases: creating awareness of gender discrimination and inequities in general and specifically in the selected aspect of schooling; review and analysis of proposals for remediation; choosing and implementing the reform actions; monitoring and evaluating the reform efforts; and using the results of the intervention as feedback to develop or extend subsequent actions (Smith, 1988).

Administrative interventions for gender equity should differ according to whether they are intended for institutional or individual changes. Institutional changes include creating and monitoring equity policies, providing technical assistance to other efforts, making all educational opportunities in the classroom and the profession more accessible to females, offering gender-fair staff development for personnel, and developing and implementing criterial guidelines of accountability for gender equity (Cels-Offermans, 1987). Strategies directed toward individual change focus on creating awareness, acquiring information, establishing networks and developing the new skills required for gender equity (Klein, 1985). Many countries have created national commissions to develop awareness, design policies and increase gender recruitment of teachers. Among these are the sex quotas for teachers in Norway, the Netherlands and Finland; the Commission on Sex Roles and Education in Denmark; the 'Changing Attitudes' programme in Portugal; the 'Free Choice' action programmes in Sweden; and the 'Forder-programme' in the Federal Republic of Germany (Cels-Offermans, 1987).

The effects of discrimination in classroom interactions with teachers may have the most devastating effects upon educational opportunities. It is here where students either have or are denied equal access to high status knowledge. Teachers should be sensitized to how they differentiate their performance expectations, communication styles and evaluative feedback systems according to the gender of students, the effects this has on academic efforts and achievement, and how they can be changed to be more gender equitable. Some specific targets of remediation should be patterns of praise and criticism, response wait time, questioning strategies, encouragement and cues to facilitate performance, and the use of competitive and cooperative learning strategies. On the last issue Klein *et al*. (1985, p. 497) suggest that 'since competition appears to be a major component of classroom climate, we need to determine its role in continuing classroom inequity and the possible effects of a cooperative classroom environment on decreasing sex differences in teacher-student and student-student interactions.'

Changes in curriculum content to reflect more accurately female and male contributions have taken three major forms. First, areas within various subjects are identified to determine when, where and how the genders are treated differently, and then the required revisions are made. Initiatives for these efforts are often national, regional and/or local policy mandates against gender discrimination. For example, in Norway guidelines were issued in 1983 to bring equal status gender perspectives in curriculum designs, and to make domestic arts a compulsory part of primary and lower secondary curricula for all students (Cels-Offermans, 1987). Title IX regulations in the United States are national prohibitions against sex discrimination in employment, school enrolment and access to curricular options.

A second strategy to make school curricula more gender-fair is to give compensatory opportunities to the least advantaged sex to overcome its disadvantaged status. Early childhood gender education programmes, special recruitment programmes to increase female enrolment in maths and science courses, and presenting females role models in non-traditional careers are some of the specific ways in which gender compensatory education has been attempted. In France a parliamentary bill has been passed which gives preferential treatment to women-friendly instructional materials in order to accelerate the process of gender equity. The Dutch project, 'Girls in Technical Jobs', is designed to make male career training courses more accessible to females (Cels-Offermans, 1987).

In some countries which traditionally segregate students by sex a third gender equity strategy is being applied. Sex-integrated activities and coeducational settings are created to increase the possibility of female and male students being treated comparably. In addition to improving the likelihood of both genders having access to the same curricular programmes, gender integration helps female and male students to adopt the behaviours, values and personality traits of each other, and dissuade them from gravitating so easily toward traditional gender role expectations.

Each of these categorical interventions to achieve gender equity generates more specific strategies. Some of them that relate most directly to the causes and manifestations of gender discrimination discussed earlier include:

integrating scholarship on women and gender equity issues into school curricula and instructional activities for all students and subjects;

training teachers and school leaders in what gender equity means, how to analyze the various aspects of educational systems for gender bias, and how to make changes where needed to achieve gender equity;

diversifying gender representation of instructional and administrative staffs across the full spectrum of the educational system;

making students and teachers aware of the habitual ways in which gender discrimination is practised in classroom routine, participation styles and communication patterns;

increasing the enrolment of females in traditional 'masculine' and males in traditional 'feminine' subjects;

including classroom climate and interactional styles in teachers' performance appraisals on gender equity, and gender equity in their total performance evaluation;

confronting gender discrimination directly and unequivocally, to show how women's and girls' lives are circumscribed, and how they can be transformed (Stanworth, 1983);

changing the ethos of schools to diminish traditional sex role typing.

## CONCLUSION

These interventions facilitate gender equity as well as improve the overall quality of general education. As Klein *et al.* (1985, p. 499) explain, 'work toward achieving sex equity ... is congruent with some of the recent findings about how to create effective, high-quality educational experiences.' This reciprocity is indicative of two important premises of all efforts to achieve more educational equality for a wider variety of students from different backgrounds, whether those are gender, race, ethnicity, social class or national origin. First, the ultimate destiny of all factions of society is inextricably interwoven. To the extent that the educational opportunities of any group of students are constrained, those of all groups are limited. Conversely, to the degree that all subsets of society can maximize their academic and personal potential through comparable, high quality educational experiences, the total society benefits. Second, the educational excellence of female and male students, as measured by achievement outcomes, is a direct result of gender comparability in educational opportunities. Equality of educational opportunities has four interrelated aspects: accessibility, participation, results, and effects on life chances. Gender discrimination begins with access and compounds thereafter. To deny one sex access to and involvement in the full range of course content, programmes, adult role models, and the psychological and pedagogical benefits associated with the highest expectations of and support for performance is to deny them real chances for equality of outcomes and effects (Finn, Dulberg and Reis, 1979). Thus gender equity and excellence in education are two parts of the same process. They are inseparable. One cannot be accomplished without simultaneously facilitating the other.

## REFERENCES

Aiken, L. (1986–87) 'Sex Differences in Mathematical Ability', *Educational Research Quarterly*, 10, pp. 25–35.

Bowman, M.J. and Anderson, C.A. (1982) 'The Participation of Women in Education in the Third World', in G.P. Kelly and C.M. Elliot (Eds), *Women's Education in the Third World: Comparative Perspectives*, Albany, N.Y., State University of New York Press, pp. 11–30.

Brophy, J. (1985) 'Interactions of Male and Female Students with Male and Female Teachers', in L.C. Wilkinson and C.B. Marrett (Eds), *Gender Influences in Classroom Interaction*, New York, Academic Press, pp. 115–142.

Campbell, P.B. (1986) 'What's a Nice Girl Like You Doing in a Math Class?', *Phi Delta Kappan*, 67, pp. 516–520.

Cels-Offermans, A. (1987) 'Education and Equality of Opportunity for Girls and Women', *Western European Education*, 19, pp. 6–25.

Davies, L. (1988) 'Gender and Educational Management in Third World Countries', in T. Husen and T.N. Postlethwaite (Eds), *The International Encyclopedia of Education: Research and Studies*, Supplementary Vol. 1, New York, Pergamon Press, pp. 367–371.

Davis, O.L., Ponder, G., Burlbaw, L.M., Garza-Lubeck, M. and Moss, A. (1986) *Looking at History: A Review of Major US History Textbooks*, Washington, D.C., People for the American Way.

Emanuelsson, I. and Fischbein, S. (1987) 'Vive la Difference? A Study on Sex and Schooling', *Western European Education*, 19, pp. 31–49.

Fennema, E. and Peterson, P. (1985) 'Autonomous Learning Behavior: A Possible Explanation of Gender-related Differences in Mathematics', in L.C. Wilkinson and C.B. Marrett (Eds), *Gender Influences in Classroom Interaction*, New York, Academic Press, pp. 17–35.

Finn, J.D., Dulberg, L. and Reis, J. (1979) 'Sex Differences in Educational Attainment: A Cross-National Perspective', *Harvard Educational Review*, 49, pp. 477–503.

Finn, J.D., Reis, J. and Dulberg, L. (1982) 'Sex Differences in Educational Attainment: The Process', in G.P. Kelly and C.M. Elliot (Eds), *Women's Education in the Third World: Comparative Perspectives*, Albany, N.Y., State University of New York Press, pp. 107–126.

Garber, J. and Seligman (Eds) (1980) *Human Helplessness: Theory and Applications*, New York, Academic Press.

Goodlad, J.I. (1984) *A Place Called School: Prospects for the Future*, New York, McGraw-Hill.

Hahn, C.L. and Powers, J.B., *et al.* (1985) 'Sex Equity in Social Studies', in S.S. Klein (Ed.), *Handbook for Achieving Sex Equity through Education*, Baltimore, Md., The Johns Hopkins University Press, pp. 280–297.

Harlen, W. (1978) 'Girls and Primary-School Education: Sexism Stereotypes, and Remedies', *Western European Education*, 19, pp. 50–66.

Harvey, G. (1986) 'Finding Reality among the Myths: Why What You Thought about Sex Equity in Education Isn't So', *Phi Delta Kappan*, 67, pp. 509–512.

Holbrook, H.T. (1988) 'Sex Differences in Reading: Nature or Nurture?', *Journal of Reading*, 31, pp. 574–576.

Kalia, N.N. (1983) 'Images of Men and Women in Indian Textbooks', in G.P. Kelly and C.M. Elliot (Eds), *Women's Education in the Third World: Comparative Perspectives*, Albany, N.Y., State University of New York Press, pp. 173–187.

Klein, S.S. (Ed.) (1985) *Handbook for Achieving Sex Equity through Education*, Baltimore, Md., The Johns Hopkins University Press.

Klein, S.S., *et al.* (1985) 'Summary and Recommendations for the Continued Achievement of Sex Equity in and through Education', in S.S. Klein (Ed.), *Handbook for Achieving Sex Equity through Education*, Baltimore, Md., The Johns Hopkins University Press, pp. 489–519.

Kurian, G.T. (1988a) 'Introduction', in G.T. Kurian (Ed.), *World Education Encyclopedia*, Vol. 1, New York, Facts on File Publications, pp. xiii–xix.

Kurian, G.T. (Ed.) (1988b) *World Education Encyclopedia*, Vols 1 and 3, New York, Facts on File Publications.

Linn, M.C. and Petersen, A.C. (1985) 'Facts and Assumptions about the Nature of Sex Differences', in S.S. Klein (Ed.), *Handbook for Achieving Sex Equity through Education*, Baltimore, Md., The Johns Hopkins University Press, pp. 53–77.

Lockheed, M.E. and Klein, S.S. (1985) 'Sex Equity in Classroom Organization and Climate', in S.S. Klein (Ed.), *Handbook for Achieving Sex Equity through Education*, Baltimore, Md., The Johns Hopkins University Press, pp. 189–217.

National Center for Education Statistics (1988) *Digest of Education Statistics*, Washington, D.C., US Department of Education, Office of Educational Research and Improvement.

Organisation for Economic Cooperation and Development (1986) *Girls and Women in Education: A Cross-National Study of Sex Inequities in Upbringing and in Schools and College*, ERIC Document, ED 278 583.

Porras-Zuniga, P. (1988) 'Comparative Statistics in Education', in T.N. Postlethwaite (Ed.), *The Encyclopedia of Comparative Education and National Systems of Education*, Oxford, Pergamon Press, pp. 21–28.

Rothschild, J. (1986) 'Turing's Man, Turing's Woman, or Turing's Person?: Gender, Language, and Computers', Working Paper No. 166, ERIC Document, ED 298 946.

Rychman, D.B. and Peckham, P. (1987) 'Gender Differences in Attributions for Success and Failure Situations across Subject Areas', *Journal of Educational Research*, 81, pp. 120–125.

Sadker, D. and Sadker, M. (1986) 'Sexism in the Classroom from Grade School to Graduate School', *Phi Delta Kappan*, 67, pp. 512–515.

Sadker, M., Sadker, D. and Long, L. (1989) 'Gender and Educational Equality', in J.A. Banks and C.A.M. Banks (Eds), *Multicultural Education: Issues and Perspectives*, Boston, Mass., Allyn and Bacon, pp. 106–123.

Shakeshaft, C. (1985) 'Strategies for Overcoming the Barriers to Women in Educational Administration', in S.S. Klein (Ed.), *Handbook for Achieving Sex Equity through Education*, Baltimore, Md., The Johns Hopkins University Press, pp. 124–144.

Shakeshaft, C. (1986) 'A Gender at Risk', *Phi Delta Kappan*, 67, pp. 499–508.

Shapiro, J.E. and Dank, H. (1980) 'The Feminized School: A Status Report', *Education*, 100, pp. 254–259.

Smith, J. (1988) *Gender Equality: Strategies from the Second Transition Programme*, Working Document, Transition of Young People from Education to Adult and Working Life, ERIC Document, ED 297 097.

Stanworth, M. (1983) *Gender and Schooling*, London, Hutchinson and Company.

Tinker, I. and Bramsen, B.M. (1975) 'Proceedings of the Seminar on Women in Development', in I. Tinker and B.M. Bramsen (Eds), *Women and World Development*, Washington, D.C., American Association for the Advancement of Science, pp. 138–218.

Tohidi, N.E., Steinkamp, M.W. and Maehr, M.L. (1986) 'Gender Differences in Performance of Tests of Cognitive Functioning: A Meta-Analysis of Research Findings', ERIC Document, ED 302 452.

Trecker, J.L. (1973) 'Women in United States History in High School Textbooks', *International Review of Education*, 19, pp. 133–139.

Wilkinson, L.C. and Marrett, C.B. (Eds) (1985) *Gender Influences in Classroom Interaction*, New York, Academic Press.

# 6. Cultural Diversity and Prejudice in Non-Verbal Communication*

RAPHAEL SCHNELLER

## INTRODUCTION

Human relations are primarily based on 'communication', i.e., on mutual under-standing. Every understanding is based on shared communicational behaviour with shared messages. The transmission of messages is generally performed by overt language signs which are received by the physical senses of the addressee. But the final understanding is the outcome of a two-step process. The first step requires that an aural or visual sign is acknowledged as a language-sign. The second step requires that a certain meaning is attributed to the observed sign.

In intergroup communication, certain language signs bear certain meanings shared by both communication partners because of previously shared socialization patterns and experience. However, a different situation obtains in an outgroup, and especially with outculture partners. Every group develops a way of living with characteristic standards, beliefs and codes (Allport, 1954). These codes become explicit in the social behaviour of the group's members and represent the likeness and uniformity of beliefs, standards and norms, supporting and strengthening group identity. Unshared experience leads to communication barriers rooted in non- or even misunderstanding (Schneller, 1989a). According to Smith (1973), persons unable to arouse shared experience within others are considered abnor-mal. Man in most societies responds to the same realities; the *perception* of those, however, manifests itself in various manners.

Correct understanding of outgroup messages results in fact-based judgment, while failed or false interpretation leads to misjudgment and to a distorted perception of underlying behavioural standards as well as personal values, beliefs and attitudes. In the process of generalized transfer of this misinterpretation from the single person to all other members of his ethnic group, it becomes ethnic prejudice (Ehrlich, 1973). Similarly, already existing prejudice towards an out-group may cause the misinterpretation of the language-sign presented by its

* The author thanks Dr Joseph Sherman, of WITS University, Johannesburg, for his valuable assistance with the final version of this chapter.

individual member, in order to fit into the predisposed attitude to his group, which is then projected onto the individual communication partner. Consequently, to develop correct and undistorted intercultural judgments it is essential to understand how people send and receive messages from other persons who do not share similar heritage and culture (Smith, 1973).

Different groups are known to have different languages. People generally are well aware of lingual differences and therefore are careful about making judgments about their outgroup interactants as long as they are not sure of their correct interpretation. But this awareness usually holds for verbal language only. The term 'language' is closely associated, at least for human interaction, with the spoken or the written word. In the past, and in current Western thinking, the basic concepts of and research on communication have dealt with verbal language only, portraying the dignity of man (Harrison, 1974; Nolan, 1975). However, since the 1950s, a wide range of empirical evidence has demonstrated that verbal language is only one of the various human communication channels, and not always the strongest or dominant one (Harrison, 1974; Fonagy, 1980; Raffler-Engel, 1980; Druckman, 1982; Poyatos, 1983). Non-verbal communication (NVC) includes in its broadest definition all communication vehicles except words (Eisenberg and Smith, 1971; Rich, 1974). The main source for NVC signs and messages is human behaviour in front of others (Watzlawick, 1976). Since man cannot not behave, man cannot not communicate, although widely unconsciously (Watzlawick *et al.*, 1968; Knapp, 1978; Siegman and Feldstein, 1987). NVC may be categorized according to the participating parts of the human body, and according to their combination with verbal expression or their communicational independence.

The acquisition of verbal language is quite simple. It develops from early childhood followed by formal education up to the adult's needs in his society. Additional verbal languages also may easily be learnt; there are dictionaries, grammatical and syntactical rules, language schools and literature. The limited number of main language groups in human society makes possible sufficient communication skills even with a variety of foreign languages.

By contrast, NVL (non-verbal language) has been found to be much more culture-bound; not only along the verbal language groups but also widely in the boundaries of each of them (Argyle, 1975; Leach, 1972; Raffler-Engel, 1980; Schneller, 1985). In fact, each culture has its different unwritten 'vocabulary' (Eckman, 1983). Non-verbal behaviour (NVB) as cultural heritage is acquired, informally only, in the early stages of the socialization process. It has no written rules or grammar. The communicants (the 'behavers') are hardly aware of it, and — except for some limited and mainly explorative cultural inventories — no adequate outgroup NVL sources are available (for an evaluation of those, see Poyatos, 1981).

While verbal language usually serves for the transmission of cognitive and impersonal messages, NVL — initiated by its sender or sent as feedback on the verbal stimulation of the partner — offers the observer consciously or unconsciously sent information about personal emotions and feelings, thoughts, attitudes, interpersonal relations and even about personal and cultural values. This information is perceived, processed and judged according to the meaning which would be attributed to the observed NVL signs by the recipient's culture and personal life experience (Samovar *et al.*, 1981; Salomon, 1981). However, the widely existent cultural differences of meaning make it highly plausible that misinterpretation will be more the rule than the exception, as has been stated already by Ichheiser (1949) and also found by other empirical studies (Shuter, 1979; Ben-Ezer, 1987; Schneller, 1988a).

Although it may be assumed that extensive crosscultural contact and learning could by itself decrease misinterpretation, it may be that this contact *provides* the basic condition for initial misjudgment and its occurrence and impact will depend on the dimensions of cultural divergence (Hall, 1966; Prosser, 1978); the greater the diversity, the greater will be the probability of ethnic prejudice.

This chapter provides descriptive and empirical evidence for, and demonstration of cultural divergence of NVC. The findings are evaluated for their relevance and importance for the understanding of the causes and the processes of prejudice. Taking into account the still largely unknown factors of culture-bound NVB, the following section introduces some basic theories, facts and processes of NVC in human society.

## THE TRIPLE STRUCTURE OF LANGUAGE

Man has been regarded since ancient times as 'the speaking animal'. Indeed, it is the symbol and abstract verbal sign, called 'word', which enables man — and, as far as we know, man only — to convey thoughts, ideas and general 'mentation' to other human beings (Dance and Larsen, 1967). In order to overcome limitations of distance and time, from his earliest stages man developed the art of expressing and conveying messages graphically, from pictorial drawings through symbolic signs to the present non-symbolic phonetical letters.

Nevertheless, in oral face-to-face communication man simultaneously emits non-verbal (NV) messages for linking and regulating human behaviour and various other interpersonal needs (Heslin and Patterson, 1982). Such NV messages are widely found in animal social life (Davis, 1971; Argyle, 1975); and according to Harrison and Crouch (1975) they stayed on and served man also in his early stages of social development.[1] In the ontogenic development of man as well, NV precedes verbal expression (Knapp, 1978; Fonagy, 1986) and it remains for the duration of his life.

Social functions, categories and channels of human NVC have been systematically explored only in the second half of the twentieth century, and broad and extensive research is still going on.[2] Man communicates in face-to-face interaction through a 'triple-language' system: the verbal, the vocal and the motoric (Birdwhistell, 1967; Wolfgang, 1979; Poyatos, 1983, 1984). The vocal usually accompanies the spoken word, contributes to its meaning and impact, emphasizes it and sometimes also reveals the mental state of the sender. This 'voice quality', which has been termed 'paralanguage' (Trager, 1958; Abercrombie, 1968), often determines the impact and meaning of the spoken word. Moreover, the voice channel may even be used for the sending of messages of its own, by certain vocal signs with shared meaning, independently of words, e.g., 'Hmm ...', 'Oho!', 'Ahah!', etc., representing the prosodic messages (Argyle, 1975).

The third component of the combined threefold communication process is non-verbal as well as non-vocal. It is the 'silent language' (Hall, 1959), or the source for 'silent messages' (Mehrabian, 1971), sent by muscular body movement, and perceived mainly by the visual senses, often by the tactile senses and sometimes even conveyed unconsciously by glandular activity and received by the sense of smell. These exclusively sensuous communication channels include all kinds of conscious or unconscious human behaviour which may be interpreted by the co-communicant as information. They encompass a great variety of 'languages', some of which will be presented below.

The first is the 'language of space', termed 'proxemics' (Hall, 1963). It presents the 'personal bubble' which every person bears with him in order to protect his individual territory (Horowitz *et al.*, 1964; Sommer, 1969). In the boundaries of this space or immediate territory around the individual, changing its dimensions according to the interpersonal and social situation, most of human interaction occurs. It is of great socio-psychological importance and may serve as a criterion for the quality of interpersonal relations (Hall, 1963). This language 'speaks' not only through the distances between human bodies but also through the arrangement of furniture, particularly in living rooms, offices and other meeting rooms, and even by the design of houses and their environment (Sommer, 1969; Ruesh and Kees, 1972; Knapp, 1978; Condon and Yousef, 1981). Closely related to space are the communicational functions of interpersonal touch or 'tactility' and also those of olfactory messages (Montagu, 1971; Knapp, 1978; Shuter, 1979).

Another source of information is the posture of the whole body, while standing, sitting or lying down. It conveys messages by the combined position of the legs, the trunk, the arms and hands and the head (Lamb and Watson, 1979). The relative position of all these body parts offers to the interaction partner a general expression of the intra- or interpersonal physical or emotional feelings, as they really are, or as they are intended to impress the partner (Ichheiser, 1949; Goffman, 1959; Scheflen, 1972).

A particularly rich source of information is provided by the kinetic movement of the various parts of the body (Birdwhistell, 1971), especially by the manifold uses of hands and arms. These movements, while conveying any message, are called gestures. They have been systematically studied by Efron (1972 [1941]) and were further widely explored (e.g., Argyle, 1975; Knapp, 1978; Raffler-Engel, 1980; Eckman and Friesen, 1981; Kendon, 1981; Schneller, 1985, 1988b, 1989a).

Gestures may accompany words, emphasizing, complementing and explaining. However, many gestures bear visual messages without words. When these messages might also have been conveyed by words, but were actually sent without them, they are called emblems (Eckman, 1980). Some gestures even convey messages beyond words by signs shared by other members of the group. These usually express emotions, i.e., admiration, desperation, excitement, but also attention, concentration, etc. They are particularly common and important as feedback to verbal messages (Eisenberg and Smith, 1971; McQuail, 1975).

A further silent source of information is the face expression. The rich face muscularity offers uncounted versions of expression and impression, particularly around the lips, the brows, the forehead and the nose. All of these convey expanses of emotional feelings and expressions, positive as well as negative attitudes or responses, cognitive acceptance or rejection and more (Mehrabian, 1971; Eckman and Friesen, 1975; Argyle *et al.*, 1981; Eckman, 1983). Their specific importance in human communication lies in the fact that they are observed by the co-communicant more than all other NV sources of the human body. Moreover, their reliability — but hence also their function of deceit — is regarded as the highest among all other communication channels, including even verbal ones (Mehrabian and Wiener, 1967; Eckman, 1986).

A special place in face expression is the eye-gaze (Hall, 1966; Eckman and Friesen, 1975; Knapp, 1978; Argyle *et al.*, 1981; Eckman, 1983). It may be regarded as one of the basic conditions for face-to-face communication. Eye-gaze expresses a great variety of messages and serves as a most reliable 'mirror of thoughts'. Like face expression in general, this reliability makes it also the strongest vehicle for deceiving (Eckman and Friesen, 1969; Eckman, 1986).

Further branches of NVC are the language of time, demonstrated extensively by Hall (1959, 1966, 1984); Samovar *et al.* (1981), and that of silence (Jensen, 1973; Harrison, 1974; Poyatos, 1983), physical reaction to external and other stimuli.

It would be misleading to refer separately to each one of the presented 'languages' as independent bearers of messages and particularly those of the proxemic and kinetic channels. Hardly any single movement or 'language' communicates on its own. It is the combined impression of most — or even all — of the kinetic components which makes the message (Lamb and Watson, 1979; Wolfgang, 1979; Poyatos, 1983).

## THE FUNCTIONS OF NVC

The wide range of communication channels provides the sender with a great variety of vehicles and tactics for conscious transmitting, while the richness of available extra-verbal information for the receiver is even greater (Eckman and Friesen, 1975; Eckman, 1980). One may ask why all these channels still exist subsequent to man's ability to communicate verbally and to express himself also over time and spatial distances. Not only have NVC channels failed to vanish or even been reduced to secondary importance in human interaction, but rather they are still found to dominate functionally in certain situations of face-to-face interaction, particularly nowadays in the 'language of the screen' transmitted by television and video.

The answer may be derived from the recognition that former means do not cease to serve us as long as their functions are not completely displaced by new ones (Himmelweit *et al.*, 1958; Brown *et al.*, 1974). A functional analysis of NVL use will support this assumption. As cited from Dance and Larsen (1967), only 'mentation' classifies the uniqueness of human speech, while linking and regulating are shared with non-human communication channels. A broader view on NVL was presented by Heslin and Patterson (1982) by a multistage functional model including twelve NVC behaviours and six different communication functions. Even though in human interaction many of these may basically also be achieved through words, it has been found that NVLs may be more successful in their task: they are instantaneous and save time; they are mentally more easily perceived than vocal-verbal information; and they even function in a voice-full environment (Argyle, 1975; Druckman, 1982). Moreover, there are some further functions which are either not covered completely or only partially by verbal language:

making contact solely by words would be uncomfortable, and the regulation of the communication process — starting, maintaining and terminating — with words only is almost unthinkable. For certain needs NVL is much richer than a verbal vocabulary: only a very limited range of words is available for the expression of feelings and emotions. A person will hardly ever announce his physical or mental well-being verbally. As noted, there even exist some communicative NV expressions without sufficient verbal substitute.

One may conclude that NVC serves as the dominant, sometimes even sole, channel not only for regulating the interaction but particularly for the expression of attitudes, feelings, acceptance and rejection in the social and non-formal context. Paralingual NV signs also indicate the involvement attitudes and seriousness of the speaker and of his spoken words (Argyle, 1975; Knapp, 1978; Wolfgang, 1979; Argyle and Tower, 1979; Schneller, 1989b). A variety of particular functions has been offered by Argyle *et al.* (1981) also for gaze. No less does NVL contribute directly to verbal language by emphasizing, illustrating, complementing and sometimes even by contradicting the verbal message (Mehrabian and Wiener, 1967; Mehrabian, 1971).

A specific function, usually solely by combined NV signs, is immediate and even simultaneous feedback, emotional and cognitive alike. Feedback is most essential for the sender as a control of the effect of his words, or his own NV behaviour, in order to organize himself for the next stage of interaction (Lederman, 1977; Knapp, 1978; Poyatos, 1983). Man can scarcely not send feedback, although usually he is unaware of it, as Argyle and Tower (1979) put it generally for NV interaction: 'We are only partly aware of NV signs from others; we are hardly aware of those we are sending by ourselves.' This unawareness of sending NV signs bears high reliability (Argyle, 1975). As Eckman and Friesen (1975) state: while the message provided by the emblem is given, the knowledge joined from 'body-manipulation' is stolen. Thus it is the combined impact of verbal and non-verbal human language which makes human face-to-face interaction highly effective: 'We speak with our vocal mechanism, but we talk with our whole body' (Abercrombie, 1968).

According to available evidence, the NV part in conversation is superior to the verbal, both quantitatively and qualitatively. The verbal message occupies only a small part of social interaction, while the NV one proceeds during the complete encounter, from the first contact until its breaking off; verbal expression is limited by turn-taking, and only one of the partners can speak at a time, while NV interaction goes on between both — or even all — participants; verbal expression may temporarily turn off, while visual will not (Nolan, 1975; Eckman and Friesen, 1975; Key, 1980; Kendon, 1984; and see also Kendon, 1983), and the same holds for silence as one of the non-verbal-non-vocal communication channels (Jensen, 1973; Poyatos, 1983).

Measurable (quantitative) data show that the ratio between verbal-non-verbal in a regular sentence reaches 1:35 (Birdwhistell, 1971). Hall (1959) found that out of ten identified primary message systems only one also included words. In classroom interaction, Grant and Henning (1971) observed that 82 per cent of the teacher's messages are on the NV channel, particularly in the expression of feelings. Lamb and Watson (1979) concluded that the majority of our talk is done without speaking.

This superiority also holds qualitatively. Mehrabian (1971) found in his studies that even when a NV message contradicts the spoken word — e.g., a hardly hidden yawn while declaring: 'Very interesting! Fascinating!', or a frequent looking at the watch while affecting to have plenty of time — the combined final impact is mainly determined by the NV components; face expression being the main indicator and the paralingual signs, or 'voice quality', the other, and both of them outweigh the spoken word (Mehrabian and Wiener, 1967).[3]

One may conclude this introductory presentation of the triple structure of language with the statement of Birdwhistell, one of the founders of the NVC discipline (in Davis, 1971): '... Now I ask when is it appropriate to use words? ... apparently to teach or to talk on the telephone. These days I put it: Man is a multisensual being; occasionally he verbalises.'

## THE CULTURAL CONTEXT OF NVB

The cultural origin and diversity of verbal communication are generally recognized as basic social facts. This diversity is represented by quite a limited number of larger language groups and by a very great number of local or regional languages and dialects. People are aware of these differences, and it is taken for granted that each partner has to understand the other's language. Without this knowledge, even a passive one only, no communication can be expected.

Concerning the NV languages in all their channels and functions, one should consider the following plausibilities.

> They are bodily-rooted physiological phenomena, and therefore they may be universals, similarly understood by the speakers of all languages, thus offering an intercultural language bridge.

> Since different cultures have different language needs, they may not be universal but pancultural, i.e., they may basically exist as NV language groups, comparable to those of verbal language.

> These NV language groups may be linked to those of specific verbal languages, raising expectation for NV as well as for verbal divergence.

> NVL is culture-bound by itself within the verbal language boundaries or even without any links to verbal diversity.

The last mentioned state, if found to exist, consequently raises certain questions.

> Are people aware of culture-specific differences?

> Is NVL usually acquired along with verbal language by study or continued interaction with outcultures?

> If generally outculture NVL is not sufficiently acquired for *active* use ('sending'), is it at least understood *passively* ('reading')?

Some of the possibilities have already been mentioned in the introductory section. Those and others will now be discussed more extensively.

To understand the cultural context of NVC diversity, one has to bear in mind that behaviour is determined by certain concepts, attitudes and values. Its structure and performance are based on certain thought patterns, perceptions and social patterns. It has already been stated as a general assumption that any behaviour in front of others bears with it messages which can be interpreted by other interactants. Summarizing many writings and findings about existing cultural differences, Prosser (1978) generalizes that every culture develops its own sign-action and object language, and corresponding uses of body motions, including kinetic behaviour, physical characteristics and also touching, space behaviour, objects, environmental factors as well as paralanguage. He concludes that cultural differences in non-verbal codes may be considerable, following the culture's perceptions, thought patterning attitudes, values and role systems, as is also found with verbal communication codes. This highly culture-bound diversity is the rule for most of the NV expressions (Efron, 1972 [1941]; Argyle, 1975; Raffler-Engel, 1980; Heslin and Patterson, 1982; Eckman, 1983; Schneller, 1987, 1988a, and others).

Universality, or at least broad pancultural similarity, has been found only for some basic face expressions, some contact signs and a few used in mother-child and other intrafamily relations (Eckman and Friesen, 1975; Eibl-Eibesfeldt, 1979; Eckman, 1983). On the other hand, wide empirical evidence is available for the unawareness of the existing differences (Smith, 1973; Prosser, 1978; Shuter, 1979; Samovar *et al.*, 1981; Schneller, 1985, 1988b, 1989a). The explanation for this remarkable contrast between the high cultural diversity of NVC and people's general unawareness of it must be derived from the observable fact that most people in most cultures present similar behaviour patterns and perform basically similar body movements. Visually one may recognize the same patterns of face expressions, eye-gazing, kinetic use of limbs and hands, sitting and standing around in various distances in many different cultures. In the same way one may listen to similar voices of shouting, crying, laughing and other paralingual expressions. If there exists such a broad conformity of NV signs, one can hardly be surprised at communicational diversity!

However, these differences do exist and they arise from the cultural diversity of the specific semantic meaning attributed to phenomenal similar NV signs. Kendon (1984), discussing the diversity of gestures, concludes that the principles which govern the form of the gestures, as observed kinetic movements, are very similar across cultures. It may be that their basic meanings are universal, while their precise meaning changes according to cultural and situational circumstances.

Kluckhohn and Strodtbeck (1961) mention five orientations in which cultures are seen to differ significantly: orientation to self, to others, to environment, to activity and to time. Samovar and Porter (1976) specified thought patterns, organization of space and concepts of time as cultural variables. Prosser (1978) pointed to the cultural differences in perception, thought patterning attitudes and other socio-cultural characteristics as the underlying roots for the crosscultural diversity of NVC. Thus it is necessary to gain some insight into these characteristics to understand NV diversity and to relate it to its roots.

### Diversity of Perception, Attitudes and General Behaviour

The basic assumption states that we perceive every situation in a manner determined by our past cultural experiences (Prosser, 1978). People differ individually and culturally in their orientation to given realities. The peculiar perceptions of reality may affect transcultural communication (Smith, 1973). These culture-derived perceptions account widely for the individual's consistency of behaviour and communication. Non-verbal codes play a significant role in culture, and they serve as one of the obvious indicators for self- and group identity. Some examples of crosscultural differences of perception will be detailed below. The following characteristics are mainly developed from the writings of Kluckhohn and Strodt-beck, 1961; Patai, 1970; Stewart, 1971; Smith, 1973; Prosser, 1978; Hopes and Ventura, 1979; Gowlett, 1986; Rosen, 1987; Ben-Ezer, 1987; Schneller, 1987; Safadi and Valentine (n.d.).

*The Perception of the Self.*   The perception of the self in North American culture is identified with the individual, and behaviour is aimed at individual goals. Consequently, personal achievement is a central motivation in his efforts. Personal status is achieved and mainly measured by material wealth. Physical comfort serves as an important value. Since achievement demands doing to satisfy private needs as well, the North American lives in a dichotomy of work and play.

By contrast it was found that Filipinos perceive themselves in the context of family. Behaviour is aimed at group affiliations and interpersonal relationships. The status of the individual is ascribed, and therefore his motivation is towards smooth relationships with others. Decisions are to be made by authorities or by the group. One is expected to take it easy in one's work, and not separate it from one's social life.

Ethiopian Jews are individualistically oriented; guarding one's personal interest while developing continuous competition are central values. As in Arab cultures, honour outweighs money and wealth, and intellectual rather than material achievement is rated higher. Mastering of emotion, patience and understanding, as well as correct and sufficient acting, are basic concepts of the self.

Arabs work for their maintenance, and find no need for overwork to achieve materially. The same holds true for North African Jews. Work is regarded as a burden, and the worker is an artisan. All work should be done carefully and be pleasing to see. Man should be self-reliant and not dependent on others or on sophisticated technology.

African and American Blacks have highly ethnocentric and self-oriented perceptions. Recent findings by Grove (1988) showed a surprising disinterest in other cultures, rooted in a high and proud absorption in their own culture and heritage. The same has been reported for Arabs and Japanese (Grove, 1988; Prosser, 1978). Work demands efficiency, and finishing a task outweighs finishing on time.

*Perception of Environment, Time and Space.*   In North American culture man has to change and master the environment. Time moves fast, and one must keep up with it. This world's achievements are the responsibility of each individual. Life is future oriented, and work has to serve the future.

In Filipino culture man must integrate himself with the environment and adapt it, rather than change it. The stress lies on present and past and life goes on with a 'day-to-day' orientation. Arabs are highly past oriented, with much nostalgia for a glorious past. The will of God controls the world, and public opinion is what determines one's 'face'.

African Blacks, and some other non-Western cultures, are closely adjoined to the present, while past and future are generally mainly orientative: what has been and what will be, without interval or even ordinal measurement; and a similar approach has been found for the spatial concepts of here and there.

*Perception of Others.* Social perception also differs obviously between the cultures. North Americans avoid social obligations, and no deep or permanent friendships outside their nuclear family are needed for the individual's well feeling. Social contact is mainly informal and direct, and social roles are distributed among the members of the group. In interpersonal tension, vocal aggression may imply the degree of violent action which may follow. By contrast, vocal aggression in Arab culture may serve to diffuse passions and prevent physical violence. In this culture, extended family and community allegiance outweigh personal interests.

Japanese, on the other hand, are selective in choosing a friend, but develop deep bonds with the chosen, and are concerned about the other's feelings. They pay attention to age and seniority no less than to ability and talent. Their social relationships are lubricated by a gift-giving custom as part of the social life, and they pay more attention to 'how' rather than to 'what' to say.

Social interaction of Filipinos is more structured than that of North Americans and is more formal in a social obligation network, while all social functions are vested in the leader. Black Americans socialize in the context of wider extended families. As Smith (1973) states, to be Black in America is to have the largest family in the world, with many — functional — mothers and brothers. Gowlett (1986) reports the same for African Blacks, where the older women assume the role of the biological mothers who usually work far away from their families. The concern of this population about pleasing others may cause answers which out of this noble intention would lead to 'lying' as it is perceived by the outsider. Similar trends have been found among Ethiopian newcomers to Israel.

*Thought Pattern.* A further basic factor in cultural diversity is the thought patterning which determines the way that perception operates individually. Kaplan (1970) offers a graphic demonstration of different thought patterns of English, Romance, Russian, Semitic and Oriental cultures. Recent findings of differential functions of the brain hemispheres (Springer and Deutsch, 1981; Sonnenfeld, 1982) raise the issue of hemispherical dominance, or at least of its style (Stacks and Sellers, 1986), which may be related also to cultural groups. Different ways of thinking affect NVB not less than verbal communication. In 1949 Pribram isolated four distinctive patterns of thought that are common to most Western cultures: universalistic reasoning, in which reason is assumed to gain the truth with the aid of given concepts, attributed to French, Mediterranean and largely Romance language societies, including most of Latin America; the nominalistic or hypothetical reasoning, which is distrustful of pure reason and broad categories, but emphasizes inductive and empirical reasoning, and owes much of its force to the impact of technology. This type of reasoning is attributed to Anglo-American thought. Prevalent for German and Slavic Central Europe as well as for Eastern cultures like those of China and Japan is intuitional or organismic reasoning, which stresses the organic harmony between the whole and its parts, and utilizes arguments from analogy and authority. A further type, dialectic reasoning, is used in some of the philosophical literature. Prosser (1978) stresses that if members of one culture think in an entirely different fashion from members of other cultures, the influence of these contrasting thought patterns has a significant effect on the perceptual experiences of the members of each culture.

Arabs learn by memorizing and retaining, and rote learning is generally still dominant in this culture (Safadi and Valentine, n.d.). Black Africans put much emphasis on 'thinking'. Understanding is important; however, often it is not checked in its context, mainly because Blacks regard it as disrespectful to ask twice and therefore action is undertaken according to the 'subjective understanding' of the performer. Black Africans generally tend to avoid controversies and discussion; and trouble at work is avoided by 'going out of work', even by fleeing for good at night. Their thinking is practical and pragmatic, rather than logical and abstract. Some subgroups have developed a depersonalized mode of thinking, e.g., things 'got' broken or lost — by a non-identifiable external agency (Gowlett, 1986).

*Diverse Behaviour in Time and Space: The Language of Action.*   Cultural differences in perception and thought patterning cause different behaviour patterns. Distinctive behaviour interpreted and judged on its own is easily misleading, but it may become much more perplexing when this divergent behaviour is accompanied by verbal terms which raise radically contradictory expectations. This is the case with the use of 'time' and 'space'.

*Time* is one of the central factors in the regulation of human action and interaction. Contradictory concepts of time or different interpretation of time-signs make social life and cooperation more than difficult.

The complexity of crosscultural language of time has been extensively highlighted by Hall (1959, 1966, 1984), who noted that 'time speaks more plainly than words' (see also Gowlett, 1986). The conceptions and use of time do not differ signally between single cultures but generally between regional cultural groups. Hall defined three basic cultural perceptions of time. The first is monochronic versus polychronic. In the former people expect that things should be done one after the other, lineally in terms of speaking, thinking, dealing with and working. In the latter many mental and physical activities may be performed multioriented-ly and simultaneously. The second is time as accurate regulator of interpersonal meeting and interaction versus time as approximated intention. The third is time as a measurable unit versus time as orientation for past-present-future, or for length and shortness of a period. Some examples will illustrate the cultural diversity of time.

Most Western countries in central and northern Europe, and North America in particular, are highly monochronic. Smith (1973) presents verbal evidence for the importance of time in American life: time is money; one gains or loses time; industry offers a variety of 'time savers'. Coming, working and finishing on time are basic foundations of American lifestyle and expectations. Being late is highly annoying, and in conversation one has immediately to come to the point. Sentences have to be short and topic-centred, and personal matters and relations must not interfere with the formal meeting. This approach to time may be found, though not in so demanding and extreme a form, in many other Western countries.

The Arab concept of time is 'non-exact'. Time is generally orientation only, and is used polychronically (Hall, 1984; Safadi and Valentine, n.d.). A similar approach to time has been identified in Latin America. Black Americans have also a 'hang loose' attitude to time (Smith, 1973). Appointments are just a hint for the approximated time, and 'important' things like the meeting of a friend or feeding the family will be given priority and do not require apology. Similar observations have been made of Ethiopian newcomers to Israel (Ben-Ezer, 1987). Moreover, to appear just on time is an indicator of low status; to receive attention, one must arrive late! In work, well-done generally takes precedence over done-on-time.

Kluckhohn and Strodtbeck (1961) showed that since all cultures and societies must deal with time problems, they all have conceptions of past, present and future. Nevertheless, the *priority* of these differs: Spanish-Americans, Filipinos and Latin Americans place the present in the first rank, while ancient China gave first-order value preference to past time orientation. Even British and other industrially advanced societies have relatively strong past orientation, compared with the obvious future orientation of the North American.

Smith (1973) emphasizes that one concept of time is not more 'correct' or right than another, and each one has its base and utility. However, when the same terms, e.g., 'immediately', 'soon', 'later', 'tomorrow', 'next week', etc., are used crossculturally, each of the partners will expect the actual timing of the action according to his own, or 'self-cultural', interpretation.

These differences, in all the mentioned dimensions, may be crucial to human interaction, cooperation and consensus. Although they are highly diverse in their meaning, the crosscultural vocabulary does not differ between these contradictory perceptions and conceptions of time; and this fact obviously contributes to further misinterpretation. A concrete example for the political outcome of different concepts of time has been demonstrated by Merriam (1983), comparing conflicting American and Iranian chronemics and their impact on the diplomatic tension that developed between Teheran and Washington during the seizure of fifty Americans at the US Embassy in November 1979.

Another language of action (Ruesch and Kees, 1972/1954) is the *spatial behaviour* of man, as well as of animals, which Hall (1959, 1963) explored across many different cultures (see also Rich, 1974; Knapp, 1978; Shuter, 1979). He sees in personal space, or 'the organism's territory', a socio-cultural phenomenon which Sommer (1969) regards as the person's human world and natural centre for himself and for any relationship from and towards himself. This 'personal bubble' is not of a fixed size, but shrinks and expands in relation to individual personal factors and to the stimuli of his social situation. It is no less determined by demographic factors, thus making for difference in the same interactive situation between distinct cultures (Horowitz, 1966; Ducke and Nowicki, 1972). Accordingly, the 'distant table' for public-official-social and intimate interaction set up by Hall — and which is universally cited — has relevance only for the North American culture in which it was developed; different tables have to be set up for other cultures.

By contrast with the dichotomy of time, the culturally defined dimensions of *space* may be found in many regions on a highly contact to extremely non-contact continuum. While Central Europe and many Oriental countries present extremely non-contact cultures, North America and Northern European countries lagging behind, Arab countries, Mediterranean peoples and Latin Americans are on the opposite pole. Among them, contact is as close as possible, with much mutual touching, the most extreme form of which is practised by the Eskimos. Moderate contact culture may be found in Eastern Europe and the Balkans.

These culturally defined personal distances exist not only as dynamic personal bubbles, but also as a basic factor in city planning, home architecture, division of living space and the arrangement of furniture (Hall, 1966; Mehrabian, 1971; Knapp, 1978). The individualistic orientation of North Americans and Europeans demands wide space, separated rooms, closed doors, distant seating and standing. Disregard of these standards of space will be adjudged highly offending and as an invasion of another's personal territory. On the other hand, Arab and Latin American cultures locate their personal self inside the individual, so that even touching another's skin is in no way offensive. Crowding is a normal — and even demanded — condition for well feeling.

Consequently, high contact cultures are often also 'touch cultures', making use not only of the visual senses but also of the tactile ones — and often, as in Arab culture, also that of smell: closeness means 'breathing distance'. As Prosser (1978) states: 'The ratio of senses almost defines the culture in its entirety.' Montagu (1971) shows that national and cultural differences in tactility, like those relating to space, run the full gamut from the absolute non-touchability dominant in Anglo-Saxon and even more German-derived language countries, to that of Latin peoples who are located at the opposite pole of the tactility continuum. This unique location holds not only for intracultural relations but also for intrafamily ones (Prosser, 1978).

Inconsistent chronemic behaviour and use of time, particularly that accompanied by shared terms, is harmful for social and economic cooperation, but it generally does not affect physical and emotional interpersonal relations. In contradistinction, proxemic disaccordance causes immediate emotional physical and social discomfort. This holds not only for the member of a 'distant culture' who is insulted by the rude invasion into his personal self and discomfited by the physical nearness of a stranger, but also conversely, for the touch-cultural person who finds himself rejected and alienated by the incomprehensible distant behaviour of his interactant.

While the language of time is connected to a very limited set of situations and occasions, space, contact and touch are omnipresent factors in face-to-face communication. It is needless to emphasize the complications, disappointments, frustrations and misjudgments which emerge from the divergent patterns of these two action languages in the crosscultural encounter.

*Shared Kinetic Behaviour with Diverse Meanings.* Crosscultural emblemic patterns in respect of thought patterns relating to time and space are not distributed according to regional grouping. Although the kinetic movements — gestures and facial expression — are basically alike and shared panculturally, it has been proved that most of their semantic meanings — their 'messages' — differ from culture to culture. Moreover, emblemic diversity exists not only interculturally but even intraculturally, according to environmental or personal life experience (Argyle, 1975; Condon and Yousef, 1981; Shuter, 1979; Prosser, 1978; Schneller, 1988a).

Nevertheless, there are detectable similar trends for the *relative* function of kinetic NVL in the overall face-to-face communication act. Hall (1984) distinguishes between 'high context' cultures in which NVL plays only a secondary role, as in North America, Germany and England, and 'low context' cultures which use NVL extensively and expressively. This group includes East European, Mediterranean and Latin American cultures.

However, NVL as such exists in all kinds and groups of human — and animal — societies, and its different culture-bound functions, expressions, components and relationship to verbal language have already been shown. Some empirical findings for this inter- and intracultural diversity will be offered below.

Morris *et al.* (1981) presented a number of identical gestures to people of different verbal language groups in forty different locations across Europe (including one in Tunisia), and found a remarkable diversity in their emblemic interpretation. Some of these gestures were decoded in up to five different meanings, some even contradictory. Safadi and Valentine (n.d.) analyzed the interpretation of eighty gestures by Arabs and Americans. Thirteen per cent were found to be contradictory, 22 per cent were not recognized at all by the Americans and a few by the Arabs, bringing the total of non-shared meaning to 41 per cent. Schneller (1988b) presented twenty-six gestures common to Ethiopian newcomers to Israeli respondents belonging to fourteen different cultural origins. General misinterpretation of the gestures reached 39 per cent, including 27 per cent of antithetical decoding; with some Israeli subgroups, such as European, North African and Yemen, the variation moved up to 39 per cent.

Similar NV diversity has been found between national subgroups of a common verbal language group: Barakat (1973) compared the emblemic interpretation of 247 gestures by the respondents of seven Arab countries: Egypt, Jordan, Lebanon, Kuwait, Saudi Arabia, Syria and Libya. Only a few were similarly decoded by all of these subgroups. Schneller (1985) tested nine selected and commonly used Israeli emblemic gestures on 395 respondents, all speaking fluent Hebrew. Interpretation consensus varied between 30 and 33 per cent even with second- and third-generation Israelis.

Evidence for some intracultural diversity has also been reported. A verification test of shared decoding of approximately 150 Iranian emblems was conducted by Sparhawk (1981) with the Iranian population itself. About fifty of them were found to be ambiguous, divergent or low-shared. A similar test was conducted by Johnson *et al.* (1981) for a WASP population. Only 38 per cent were found to be probable or analogously interpreted.

The qualitative dimensions of this inter- and intracultural diversity have recently been tested by Schneller (1988b). One hundred out of a broader list of common Israeli emblems were grouped according to five situations of communicative interaction. They were presented to 200 respondents from nine Israeli subgroups in order to analyze the different grades of unshared decoding for each situation. The results are shown in Table 1. This table shows that the highest degree of misinterpretation occurs in the three last situations in which communication goes on almost exclusively in NVL. In the first of them, unshared decoding will harm the interaction fluency, while in the last situations it will mislead the communicant in his judgment of the intra- and interpersonal feelings of his partner.

The broadly cumulated empirical evidence for cultural diversity finally also

**Table 1.** *Total of Unshared Decoding of Israeli Emblems in Five Situations (percentages)*

| Situation | Number of emblems | Generally shared | Partly shared | Different meaning | Total of unshared |
|---|---|---|---|---|---|
| Contact | 11 | 36.4 | — | 63.6 | 63.6 |
| Information | 28 | 46.4 | 21.4 | 32.2 | 53.6 |
| Feedback | 28 | 17.9 | 14.3 | 67.8 | 82.1 |
| Intrapersonal feelings | 23 | 13.0 | 43.5 | 43.5 | 87.0 |
| Interpersonal attitudes | 10 | — | 40.0 | 60.0 | 100.0 |
| Total | 100 | 22.7 | 23.9 | 53.4 | 77.3 |

*Note*: Total decoding numbers present the mean of percentages. The data in this table are part of a research project sponsored by the Smart Family Foundation, the Communication Institute, Hebrew University, Jerusalem.

supplies the answer to the last of our questions, posed at the beginning of this section: people differ significantly and extensively not only in their *active* NVL, as 'senders', but also widely in their interpretive decoding as 'readers' of outcultural NV behaviour. It has also been proved that this misinterpretation persists even after extended common social life and crosscultural contacts.

A wide range of anecdotal examples for intercultural gesture misinterpretation may be found in many works (e.g., Asante *et al*., 1979; Argyle and Tower, 1979; Shuter, 1979; Landis and Brislin, 1979; Samovar *et al*., 1981; Condon and Yousef, 1981). Other writers offer inventories of the unique patterns of emblemic gestures in different cultures, some of them even pictorially.[4] All these are important efforts to supply sources for systematically learning how to 'read' correctly the gestural message of an outculture co-communicant. However much this aids the communication fluency with specific outcultures, it is hardly sufficient for the mutual understanding of man in our contemporary multicultural human society.

To this wide range of *meanings* one has to add the sometimes remarkable number of culture-unique *gestures* (movements), reported by most of the researchers and particularly by the authors of inventories that are completely unknown to the decoder. At best, they are not transmitting any message, or, more commonly, they are decoded by failed attribution of meaning through guessed analogical or 'iconic' interpretation, as demonstrated in various studies by Schneller (1985, 1987, 1988a, 1988b, 1989a).

To the diversity of gestures one has to add that of face expression, which bears a great amount of conscious and unconscious information as well. While a few face expressions are pancultural, one of the most commonly used, the smile, has different functions and meanings in certain cultures (Birdwhistell, 1971). It may cause severe damage to, and even complete breakdown of, intercultural communication, as demonstrated by Howell (1979) for Japanese-American interaction.

The last source for widespread NV misinterpretation which will be mentioned is the eye-gaze: should one look or not look at one's partner's eyes? Should one fix a steady gaze or simply glance 'for control'? While sending messages or while 'receiving' them as well? Answers will differ mainly in the interaction of Blacks and Whites in the US (Erickson, 1979), as well as in South and East Africa (Gowlett, 1986; Rosen, 1987), but also in the interaction of Arabs and Americans, and between some European countries (Hall, 1966; Siegman and Feldstein, 1987).

Thus one may generalize with Prosser (1978) that every culture develops its own sign action and object language and corresponding uses of body motion or kinetic behaviour, physical characteristics, touching behaviour, paralanguage, proxemics, artefacts and environmental factors which help to set that culture apart from others.

Concluding the presentation of existing widespread cultural NVB diversity, and considering its high dominance particularly in cases of non-shared verbal language, one may wonder if there exists a reliable channel in crosscultural communication at all. The contemporary human race is a multilingual society in which cultural NV diversity considerably outweighs verbal diversity.

## CROSSETHNIC COMMUNICATION AND THE PROCESS OF PREJUDICE

This final section discusses some characteristics of crosscultural misinterpretations and their impact on the creating and/or maintaining of ethnocentric prejudice.

Most cultures attribute to other cultures certain qualities and characteristics, distinct from their own. Different behaviour is usually evaluated as strange, queer and often as inferior or even primitive. These attributes are misjudgments of distinct behaviour, based on unsubstantiated prejudgment of an individual or a group. While some earlier authors hold that these prejudgments are of favourable or unfavourable character (Saenger, 1953; Klineberg, 1954; Sills, 1968), others connect them with only a negative orientation, even as antipathy (Allport, 1954; Ehrlich, 1973; Aboud, 1988). When a prejudgment becomes so consistent that it is not reversible, even if it is exposed to new knowledge, it becomes prejudice, defined also as social attitudes which are developed before, in lieu of or despite objective evidence (Allport, 1954; Cooper and Gaugh, 1963).

Ehrlich (1973) emphasizes the inflexible generalization as an essential characteristic of prejudice. To reinforce prejudice with its beliefs and disbeliefs of its users against possible contradictory evidence and experience, the related attributes are presented as stereotypes of the outculture. According to Smith (1973), stereotypes are shortcuts not only of our thinking but also of our judging, because they rob a single person of his individuality. Generally preconceived and generalized notions blind us to the individuality of those with whom we interact (Rich, 1974).

Stereotype assignments also provide a rich vocabulary of motives for the creation and maintenance of solidarity of prejudiced persons. In Ehrlich's (1973) list of 123 major stereotype terms for American ethnic groups only 18 per cent show positive stereotyping, while 41 per cent are negative. Further lists have been presented by Rich (1974). As Smith (1973) stressed, these stereotype attributes prejudice the communicants long before the interaction.

The following discussion of the mutual relationship of prejudice and communication deals with two situations: the maintenance and reinforcement of prejudice, and the emergence of primary misjudgment leading to ethnocentric prejudice, both as a result of intercultural communication diversity.


*The Reinforcement of Prejudice by Cultural NVL Diversity.* The crosscultural encounter bears a wide range of potential misinterpretation of NVL signs. NVC diversity hardly affects the overt performance of the bodily communication *signs*, but is found as vastly different in their intentional *meanings*. These misinterpretations are not only based on the actual differences between the interactants as individuals, but are also not limited to cognitive relations and misunderstanding. Each partner brings with him a set of emblems, expressive of emotions, attitudes and other NVC messages based on his self-culture and rooted in its specific values, perceptions, thought patterning and social models. To transfer his messages, he also brings to the interaction the communication signs he has acquired for active use during the early stages of his socialization, i.e., actively 'encoding', and passively 'reading', i.e., interpreting or 'decoding' them accordingly. His outculture partner likewise brings with him not only his own perceptions and patterns, but also his previous experiences and/or prejudices towards the cultural group represented by his co-communicant.

The developing NV interaction may issue in different possibilities. First, there may exist a *likeness* of NVL *signs* combined with a crosscultural constancy of their meanings — as is generally and erroneously assumed by laymen to be the case — which would make NVL an international and pancultural language, possibly bridging differences and reducing social distance. Contrarily, the *lack* of similar NVL *signs* would probably make the communicants aware of existing cultural differences of communication patterns, thus fostering and broadening social distance. This awareness also may have positive consequences, when such awareness contributes to further efforts for better understanding and judging (Watzlawick, 1976), as Schneller has also shown (1989a). This probability holds mainly in the case of first encounter, not preceded by prejudice. The third and most problematic situation as main source for maintaining or creating misunderstanding, misjudgment and prejudice is the similarity of the *signs* and the high divergence of their *meanings*, as has previously been demonstrated.

In the case of unpredisposed attitudes, differences and social distance by themselves may still be acceptable as a legitimate fact of cultural pluralism, which regards dissimilarities as expected crosscultural characteristics, existing with equal status side by side. However, if one of the communication partners belongs to an ethnocentric culture, he has grown up from early childhood to evaluate members of outcultures not solely as different, permitting also positive attitudes towards them, but chiefly as strange, queer, inferior and even 'primitive', glorifying the ingroup while denigrating outgroups (Bettelheim, 1985). This approach is accompanied with intolerance and disapproval, and a rigidity which prevents shifting from one line of thought or hypothesis to another (Sills, 1968; Rich, 1974). Moreover, the ethnocentric culture maintains its misjudgment by categorical, stereotyped thinking that systematically misinterprets facts (Simpson and Yinger, 1965). Ethnocentrism, as 'absolute culturism', puts outculture on a continuum of like-unlike its own cultural patterns and accompanies this placement with an accordant evaluation, which might be positive. However, different behaviour is regarded as 'nonconformity', as a deviance from 'normative' cultural behaviour.

The basic concept of ethnocentrism contributes to a high degree of overlooking or even ignoring cultural diversity. As Saenger (1953) has noted, ethnocentrists tend to consider *their* own motives and values, *their* way of looking upon things — and, one might add, *their* ways of bodily expressions and connected meanings — as part of basic human nature; they regard those having a different outlook on life as unnatural and misguided. Such a self-culture-determined concept of social reality has been criticized by Watzlawick (1976): 'the belief that one's own view of reality is the only reality, is the most dangerous of all illusions!'

It has been widely supposed that this ethnocultural approach chiefly characterizes cultural empires such as the US, Western and Central European nations. Asante (1980) found that most of the intercultural theories have a Eurocentric rather than an Afro- or Asiocentric bias. However, a wide range of literature supplies evidence that ethnocentrism exists to no less a degree in many of the 'non-Western' nations and cultures: the Japanese (Prosser, 1978; Grove, 1989), the Arab nations (Grove, 1988), African Blacks, and certain minority groups in the US (Grove, 1989). Like the Western cultures, the Eastern, Southern and Mediterranean cultures are equally proud of their self-culture and do not find it necessary or even justifiable to make any effort to acquire further knowledge in order to understand outcultures (Prosser, 1978; Grove, 1988).

This evidently widely existent ethnocentrism, accompanied by strong stereotyping, makes understanding even less probable. Since each of the communicants perceives and judges — and usually misjudges and prejudges — his partner through his own cultural prism, none of them will make any serious effort to change his stereotyped attitude in order to understand the other even as a unique individual. In the case of recognized NVL signs performed by the outculture partner, the ethnocentric communicator tends to translate the signs of the other's behaviour into his own signal system, usually experiencing a 'signal discontinuity' when he discovers that the signs do not mean what he thought they should (Smith, 1973). This discrepancy is part of an 'internal monologue' of the decoder which exists in any communication process, but is of particular complexity in crosscultural interaction (Howell, 1979). The first stage is sign recognition and self-cultural interpretive attribution. If this 'decoding' is consensual with the situational and verbal context, no further monologue takes place and action or interaction proceeds according to the sender's expectations. If it contradicts contextual evidence or the decoder's expectations, it will arouse a state of cognitive dissonance which may activate the following assumed thinking of the prejudiced decoder: 'My partner belongs to group $Y$. According to my existing attitudes towards this group, I judge his gesture as an expression of the attributed perception or values of his group.' Consequently, it will be distortedly adjusted to existing prejudice. When this adjustment is incompatible with the ongoing interaction, he will blame his partner for its final breakdown.

A similar monologue will take place even when the gesture or other expression is not recognized at all as a language sign: 'I have never seen such a gesture. Since my partner belongs to group $Y$, this expression obviously represents his group, which is judged by me to have these or those characteristics. The gesture, therefore, expresses those characteristics, and I have to decode it accordingly!' Thus the unknown gesture will be interpreted — by contextual guessing or by analogical association — to fit into the conceptual prejudiced framework of the decoder (see also Festinger in Emmert and Donaghy, 1981). This adding of new reasoning in order 'to fit in' not only solves its dissonance, but also serves to reinforce his prejudice and adds to its stereotype vocabulary new NV evidence which will be used in the future. According to Watzlawick (1976), however, this situation is often the first occurrence of the basic awareness for crosscultural NVC diversity.

*The Emergence of Misjudgment as Pre-state of Prejudice.* Cultural diversity and the ensuing internal monologue are responsible not only for establishing existing prejudice, but also for fostering the initial development of misjudgment. Gestures, which are recognized as language signs but are inconsistent in their contextual interpretation with previous experience, raise in the decoder another direction of internal monologue. 'He is a stranger. He doesn't communicate like my group. He behaves like me, but means other things. Apparently it comes from different perceptions, attitudes, social norms, and so on. Since my culture is the right and only normative one, my partner is strange, not possessed of normal values, and is thus inferior, or even primitive. My partner represents his group. Hence his group as a whole is backward, inferior. When I meet other representatives of his group in future, I will have to take his backwardness into account in advance.' Further details of these attitudes towards the non-cultural group will be elaborated and fixed by the reinterpretation of the sender's inconsistent gestures.

In the case of non-recognized gestures, the monologue will contribute to an even more negative evaluation of the partner's group and accordingly of that group's value system, perception and social norms. While in the former case the partner at least behaved like the decoder, i.e., like a 'cultured person', in the case of non-recognition the sender and his group may even be regarded and judged as 'out of culture'.

## CONCLUSIONS

This chapter has presented and demonstrated a diversity of cultural NVC in various socio-cultural domains. We have shown that this diversity bears a high potentiality for the emergence or the reinforcement and justification of existing ethnic prejudices. The differences between intentional and attributed meanings give way to or even invite misunderstandings, which by themselves may be harmful for the specific phase of interaction. They easily lead to misjudgment, which affects the outcultural partner's whole personality and may, through generalization, turn into ethnic prejudice. Where previous prejudice exists, misinterpretation will be adjusted and fitted into fixed attitudes towards the communication partner and his group. This process is particularly probable in cases of 'inconsistent signs', when these shared signs bear different and often contradictory meanings. Their misinterpretation will soon lead to misjudgment of the values, norms and social patterns of their senders. Extensive evidence for the cultural divergence of NVL has been offered in the section on cultural diversity. Their relevance for the formation and maintenance of misjudgments will be demonstrated below by only a few examples of already reported differences.

The 'hands purse' gesture, performed by outstretched concave palm or joint palms is generally recognized as a 'begging' gesture; however, it is used by South African Blacks for the expression of thanks and gratitude after receiving something. For Westerners, that would say: 'I still beg for more', consequently arousing a negative attitude of ingratitude, while exactly the opposite was intended. Similarly, avoidance of eye-gaze during conversation or in the class session is intended by this population, as well as by American Blacks, to express obedience and respect. The Western decoder will easily attribute to this behaviour disrespect, psychological disturbance or a bad conscience; and the class teacher may severely misjudge it as disinterest or lack of concentration.

As a typical example for other cultures we may mention the universally used act of smiling. A broad smile performed by European or Near Eastern people is usually intended to express or transmit happiness and a positive acceptance of the partner's message. However, it may be misdecoded by a North American as a 'professional' or socially expected introductory gesture, completely non-evident of the sender's mood or attitude. Even worse, a Japanese would attribute to this smile the entirely antithetical state of deep anger and upset — each one according to his self-cultural interpretation. Little effort is required to imagine the negative — or occasionally positive — misjudgments and attributes for the outcultural interactant. One may add the many occasions of total misjudgment of spatial and chronemic behaviour, not to speak of that representing the different perceptions of the self and the world. These examples illustrate the contribution of cultural NVL diversity to misjudgment and prejudice.

It is beyond the scope of this chapter to investigate the strategies and tactics of crosscultural training. A broad literature is already available, and this challenge is dealt with in depth by other contributors to this volume. However, some relevant basic assumptions and conceptions for the reduction of crosscultural misunderstanding and its outcome should be summarized.

One must acknowledge perceptual and conceptual cultural differences as existent and consistent facts. The same holds for cultural NVL diversity. In Hall's words: 'No matter how hard man tries, it is impossible for him to divest himself of his own culture (even while living for many years with people of out-cultures); for it has penetrated to the roots of his nervous system and determines how he perceives the world' (1966). The same has been proved by many other studies.

Further, one must recognize that ethnocentrism has already ceased to be the monopoly only of the well-established nations and superpowers and that must be expected to develop into a common cultural trend. While members of most cultures tend to become ethnocentrists, mutual adjustment of perceptions and conceptions will be inevitable. The conclusion must be a basic awareness of cultural equality, in spite of its dissimilarity and unlikeness. Differences should not be blurred or ignored, but, on the contrary, recognized, acknowledged and respected.

Nevertheless, differences should by no means be thought of as unbridgeable. The main human link is to be the mutual understanding based on crosscultural communication fluency. However, sign inconsistency may turn efforts towards objective understanding into misunderstanding with all its undesirable consequences. Therefore, at least for the initial crossculture communication encounter, the basic rule should be the deep understanding that for cultural reasons it is highly probable that often we not only fail to understand our crosscultural communication partner in congruence with his intention, but that he also may fail. to understand us as well.


## NOTES

1   A literary portrayal of this preverbal stage of mankind can be found in F.M. Auell's series, *The Clan of the Bear Cave* (1981); *The Valley of the Houses* (1982), etc.
2   For comprehensive lists of relevant literature, see Key (1977), Davis and Skupien (1982), and Wolfgang and Bhardwaj (1984).
3   This conclusion is known as 'the Mehrabian rule' and has also been developed by him as a mathematical formula. For an extended list of verbal-non-verbal dichotomy, see Harrison (1984).
4   Exploratory or systematic inventories have been published for East Africa, Ethiopian Jews, France, Iran, Israel, Japan, Spain, the US and probably for others. Comparative inventories may be found for US-Colombia; US-Arab countries; US-Japan.


## REFERENCES

Abercrombie, D. (1968) 'Paralanguage', *British Journal of Disorders of Communication*, 3, pp. 55–59.
Aboud, F. (1988) *Children and Prejudice*, Oxford, Blackwell.
Allport, G.W. (1954) *The Nature of Prejudice*, Boston, Mass., Beacon Press.
Argyle, M. (1975) *Bodily Communication*, New York, International University.
Argyle, M. and Tower, P. (1979) *Person to Person: Ways of Communication*, New York, Harper and Row.
Argyle, M., Ingham, R., Alkema, F. and McCallin, M. (1981) 'Different Functions of Gaze', in A. Kendon (Ed.), *Nonverbal Communication, Interaction and Gesture*, The Hague, Mouton.
Asante, M.K. (1980) 'Intercultural Communication: An Inquiry into Research Directions', in D. Nimmo (Ed.), *Communication Yearbook*, 4, New Brunswick, N.Y., Transaction Books.
Asante, M.K., Newmark, E. and Blake, A. (Eds) (1979) *Handbook of Intercultural Communication*, Beverly Hills, Calif., Sage.
Auell, F.M. (1981) *The Clan of the Cave Bear*, London, Hodder and Stoughton.
Auell, F.M. (1982) *The Valley of the Horses*, New York, Crown.
Barakat, R.A. (1973) 'Arabic Gestures', *Journal of Popular Culture*, 7, pp. 749–787.
Ben-Ezer, G. (1987) 'Cross-Cultural Misunderstandings: The Case of Ethiopian Immigrant Jews in Israeli Society', in M. Ashkenazi and A. Weingrod (Eds), *Ethiopian Jews and Israel*, New Brunswick, N.Y., Transaction Books.
Bettelheim, D.W. (1985) *A Social Psychology of Prejudice*, London, Croom Helm.
Birdwhistell, R.L. (1967) 'Some Body Motion Elements Accompanying Spoken American English', in I. Thayer (Ed.), *Communication: Concepts and Perspectives*, Washington, D.C., Spartan Books.
Birdwhistell, R.L. (1971) *Kinesis and Context*, London, Allen Lane.
Brown, J.R., Cramond, J.K. and Wilde, R.J. (1974) 'Displacement Effects of Television and the Child's Functional Orientation to Media', in J. Blumler and E. Katz (Eds), *The Uses of Mass Communication: Current Perspectives on Gratification Research*, Beverly Hills, Calif., Sage.
Condon, J.C. and Yousef, E. (1981) *An Introduction to Intercultural Communication*, Beverly Hills, Calif., Sage.
Cooper, J.B. and Gaugh, M.C. (1963) *Integrative Principles of Social Psychology*, Cambridge, Mass., Schenkman.
Dance, F.E.X. and Larsen, L.E. (1967) *The Function of Human Communication: A Theoretical Approach*, New York, Rinehart and Winston.
Davis, F. (1971) *Inside Intuition: What We Know about Nonverbal Communication*, New York, Melgrand.

Davis, M. and Skupien, Y. (Eds) (1982) *Nonverbal Communication and Body Movement 1971–1981: An Annotated Bibliography*, Bloomington, Ind., Indiana University Press.

Druckman, D. (1982) *Nonverbal Communication: Survey, Theory and Research*, Beverly Hills, Calif., Sage.

Ducke, M.P. and Nowicki, S.F. (1972) 'A New Measure and Social Learning Model for Interpersonal Distance', *Journal of Experimental Research in Personality*, 6, pp. 119–132.

Eckman, P. (1980) 'Three Classes of Nonverbal Behaviour', in von Raffler-Engel, W. (Ed.), *Aspects of Nonverbal Behaviour*, Lisse, Swets and Zeitlinger.

Eckman, P. (1983) *Emotion in the Human Face*, Cambridge, Cambridge University Press.

Eckman, P. (1986) *Telling Lies*, Berkeley, Calif., Berkeley.

Eckman, P. and Friesen, W.V. (1969) 'Nonverbal Leakage and Clues Deception', *Psychiatry*, 32, pp. 88–105.

Eckman, P. and Friesen, W.V. (1975) *Unmasking the Face*, Englewood Cliffs, N.J., Prentice-Hall.

Eckman, P. and Friesen, W.V. (1981) 'The Repertoire of Nonverbal Behaviour', in A. Kendon (Ed.), *Nonverbal Communication, Interaction and Gesture*, The Hague, Mouton.

Efron, D. (1972 [1941]) *Gesture, Race and Culture*, The Hague, Mouton.

Ehrlich, H.J. (1973) *The Social Psychology of Prejudice*, New York, Wiley.

Eibl-Eibesfeldt, I. (1979) 'Universals in Human Expressive Behaviour', in A. Wolfgang (Ed.), *Nonverbal Behaviour: Applications and Cultural Implications*, New York, Academic Press.

Eisenberg, A.M. and Smith, R.R. (1971) *Nonverbal Communication*, Indianapolis, Ind., Bobbs-Merrill.

Emmert, P. and Donaghy, W.D. (1981) *Human Communication: Elements and Contexts*, Reading, Mass., Addison-Wesley.

Erickson, F. (1979) 'Talking Down: Some Cultural Sources for Misunderstanding in Interpersonal Interview', in A. Wolfgang (Ed.), *Nonverbal Behaviour: Applications and Cultural Implications*, New York, Academic Press.

Fonagy, I. (1986) 'Preverbal Communication and Language Evolution', in M.R. Key, *The Relation of Verbal-Nonverbal Communication*, The Hague, Mouton.

Goffman, E. (1959) *The Presentation of Self in Everyday Life*, Garden City, N.Y., Doubleday.

Gowlett, D.F. (1986) *Towards Black-White Understanding in South Africa*, Johannesburg, Society for the Study of Man in Africa.

Grant, B.M. and Henning, D.S. (1971) *The Teacher Moves: An Analysis of Nonverbal Activity*, New York, Teachers College.

Grove, N. (1988) 'To Search Again and Repeatedly', *SIETAR Communique*, 18, 4, p. 4; 18, 6, p. 4; 19, 3, p. 3; 19, 2, p. 6.

Grove, N. (1989) 'To Search Again and Repeatedly', *SIETAR Communique*, 19, 2, p. 3; 19, 3, p. 6.

Hall, E.T. (1959) *The Silent Language*, New York, Doubleday.

Hall, E.T. (1963) 'Proxemics — The Study of Man's Spatial Relations', in I. Goldstone (Ed.), *Man's Image in Medicine and Anthropology*, New York, International University.

Hall, E.T. (1966) *Hidden Dimensions*, New York, Doubleday.

Hall, E.T. (1984) *The Dance of Life: The Other Dimensions of Time*, New York, Anchor.

Harrison, R.P. (1974) *Beyond Words: An Introduction to Nonverbal Communication*, Englewood Cliffs, N.J., Prentice-Hall.

Harrison, R. (1984) 'Past Problems and Future Directions in Nonverbal Research', in A. Wolfgang (Ed.), *Nonverbal Behaviour: Perspectives, Applications, Intercultural Insight*, Toronto, Hogrefe.

Harrison, R.P. and Crouch, W.W. (1975) 'Nonverbal Communication: Theory and Research', in G.E. Hanneman and J.W. McEwan (Eds), *Communication and Behaviour*, Reading, Mass., Addison-Wesley.

Heslin, R. and Patterson, M.L. (1982) *Nonverbal Behaviour and Social Psychology*, New York, Plenum Press.

Himmelweit, H.T., Oppenheim, A.P. and Vince, P. (1958) *Television and the Child*, London, Oxford Press.

Hopes, D.S. and Ventura, P. (1979) *Intercultural Sourcebook: Cross-Cultural Training Methodology*, Chicago, Ill., International Press.

Horowitz, M.F. (1966) 'Body Image', *Archives of General Psychiatry*, 14, pp. 456–460.

Horowitz, M.F., Duff, D. and Stratton, L. (1964) 'The Buffer Zone: An Exploration of Personal Space', *Archives of General Psychiatry*, 11, pp. 651–656.

Howell, W. (1979) 'The Theoretical Directions of Intercultural Communication', in M. Asante *et al.*, *Handbook of Intercultural Communication*, Beverly Hills, Calif., Sage.

Ichheiser, G. (1949) 'Misunderstanding in Human Relations — A Study in False Perception', in *American Journal of Society*, 55, Supplement.

Jensen, E.V. (1973) 'Communicative Functions of Silence', *Review of General Semantics*, 30, pp. 249–257.

Johnson, H.G., Eckman, P. and Friesen, W.V. (1981) 'Communicative Body Movements: American Emblems', in A. Kendon (Ed.), *Nonverbal Communication, Interaction and Gesture*, The Hague, Mouton.

Kaplan, R. (1970) 'Cultural Thought Patterns in Intercultural Education', *Language and Learning*, 16, pp. 1–20.

Kendon, A. (Ed.) (1981) *Nonverbal Communication, Interaction and Gestures*, The Hague, Mouton.

Kendon, A. (1983) 'Gesture and Speech: How They Interact', in J.M. Wieman and R.P. Harrison (Eds), *Nonverbal Communication*, Beverly Hills, Calif., Sage.

Kendon, A. (1984) 'Did Gestures Have the Happiness to Escape the Curse of Babel', in A. Wolfgang (Ed.), *Nonverbal Behaviour: Perspectives, Applications, Intercultural Insights*, Toronto, Hogrefe.

Key, M.R. (1977) *Nonverbal Communication: A Research Guide and Bibliography*, Metnuen, N.J., Scarecrow Press.

Key, M.R. (1980) *The Relationship of Verbal and Nonverbal Communication*, The Hague, Mouton.

Klineberg, O. (1954) *Social Psychology*, New York, Holt Rinehart and Winston.

Kluckhohn, F. and Strodtbeck, F.L. (1961) *Variations in Value Orientation*, Evanston, Ill., Row and Paterson.

Knapp, M.L. (1978) *Nonverbal Communication in Human Interaction*, 2nd ed., New York, Holt Rinehart and Winston.

Lamb, W. and Watson, E. (Eds) (1979) *Body Code: The Meaning of the Movement*, London, Routledge and Kegan Paul.

Landis, D. and Brislin, G. (Eds) (1979) *Handbook of Intercultural Training*, Vols 1–3, New York, Pergamon Press.

Leach, E. (1972) 'The Importance of Context for Nonverbal Communication' in R. Hinde (Ed.), *Nonverbal Communication*, Cambridge, Cambridge University Press.

Lederman, L.C. (1977) *New Dimensions: An Introduction to Human Communication*, Dubuque, Iowa, WMC Brown Co.

McQuail, D. (1975) *Communication*, London, Longman.

Mehrabian, A. (1971) *Silent Messages*, Belmont, Calif., Wadsworth.

Mehrabian, A. and Wiener, M. (1967) 'Decoding of Inconsistent Communication', *Journal of Personality and Social Psychology*, 6, pp. 109–114.

Merriam, A.H. (1983) 'Comparative Chronemics and International Communication: American and Iranian Perspectives on Time', in R.N. Bostrous and B.H. Westley (Eds), *Communication Yearbook*, 7, Beverly Hills, Calif., Sage.

Montagu, A. (1971) *Touching: The Human Significance of the Skin*, New York, Columbia.

Morris, D., Collet, P. and O'Shaughnessy, M. (1981) *Gestures: Their Origin and Distribution*, London, Triad/Granada.

Nolan, M.J. (1975) 'The Relationship between Verbal and Nonverbal Communication', in G.H. Hanneman and W.J. McEwan (Eds), *Communication and Behaviour*, Reading, Mass., Addison-Wesley.

Patai, R. (1970) *Israel between East and West*, Westport, Conn., Greenwood Press.

Poyatos, F. (1981) 'Gesture Inventories', in A. Kendon (Ed.), *Nonverbal Communication: Interaction and Gesture*, The Hague, Mouton.

Poyatos, F. (1983) *New Perspectives in Nonverbal Communication*, Oxford, Pergamon Press.

Poyatos, F. (1984) 'Linguistic Fluency and Nonverbal Fluency', in A. Wolfgang (Ed.), *Nonverbal Behaviour: Perspectives, Applications, Intercultural Insights*, Toronto, Hogrefe.

Pribram, K. (1949) *Conflicting Patterns of Thought*, Washington D.C., Public Affairs.

Prosser, M.H. (1978) *The Cultural Dialogue: An Introduction to Intercultural Communication*, Boston, Mass., Houghton-Mifflin.

Raffler-Engel, W. von (1980) 'Development Kinesis: The Acquisition of Conversational Nonverbal Behaviour', in W. von Raffler-Engel (Ed.), *Aspects of Nonverbal Behaviour*, Lisse, Swets and Zeitlinger.

Rich, A.L. (1974) *Interracial Communication*, New York, Harper and Row.

Rosen, C. (1987) 'Core Symbols of Ethiopian Identity, and Their Role in Understanding the Beta-Israel Jews and Israel,' in M. Ashkenazi and A. Weingrod (Eds), *Ethiopian Jews and Israel*, New Brunswick, Transaction Books.

Ruesch, F. and Kees, W. (1972/1954) *Nonverbal Behaviour*, Los Angeles, Calif., University of California Press.

Saenger, G. (1953) *The Social Psychology of Prejudice*, New York, Harper and Brother.

Safadi, M. and Valentine, C.A. (n.d.) *Contrastive Analysis of American and Arab Nonverbal and Paralinguistic Communication*, Arizona State University, Department of Education.

Salomon, G. (1981) *Communication and Education*: *Social and Psychological Interaction*, Beverly Hills, Calif., Sage.

Samovar, L. and Porter, R. (Eds) (1976) *Intercultural Communication*: *A Reader*, Belmont, Calif., Wadsworth.

Samovar, L.A., Porter, R. and Tain, N.L. (1981) *Understanding Intercultural Communication*, Belmont, Calif., Wadsworth.

Scheflen, A.E. (1972) *Body Language and Social Order*, New York, Prentice-Hall.

Schneller, R. (1985) 'Changes in the Understanding and Use of Culture-Bound Nonverbal Messages', *16th Conference of the Israeli Sociological Association*, Tel-Aviv.

Schneller, R. (1987) 'Heritage and Changes in the Nonverbal Language of Ethiopian Newcomers to Israel', in M. Ashkenazi and A. Weingrod (Eds), *Ethiopian Jews and Israel*, New Brunswick, Transaction Books.

Schneller, R. (1988a) 'The Israeli Experience in Cross-Cultural Misunderstanding: Insights and Lessons', in F. Poyatos (Ed.), *Cross-cultural Perspectives in Nonverbal Communication*, Toronto, Hogrefe.

Schneller, R. (1988b) 'Mutual Nonverbal Communication Barriers between Ethiopian Newcomers and Veteran Israelis', *Research Report*, Jerusalem, The Hebrew University, Communication Institute.

Schneller, R. (1989a) 'Intercultural and Intrapersonal Processes and Factors of Misunderstanding: Implications to Multicultural Training', *International Journal of Intercultural Relations*, Vol. 13, pp. 465–488.

Schneller, R. (1989b) 'The Forgotten Languages', in *Ijunim Be'hinuch (Studies in Education)*, University of Haifa, School of Education.

Shuter, R. (1979) *Understanding Misunderstandings*, New York, Harper and Row.

Siegman, A.W. and Feldstein, S. (Eds) (1987) *Nonverbal Behaviour and Communication*, Hillsdale, N.Y., Lawrence Elbaum Associates.

Sills, D.D. (Ed.) (1968) *Encyclopaedia of the Social Sciences*, New York, Macmillan and Free Press.

Simpson, G.E. and Yinger, F.M. (1965) *Racial and Cultural Minorities*, New York, Harper and Row.

Smith, A.L. (1973) *Transracial Communication*, Englewood Cliffs, N.J., Prentice-Hill.

Sommer, R. (1969) *Personal Space*: *The Behavioural Basis of Design*, Englewood Cliffs, N.J., Prentice-Hall.

Sonnenfeld, J. (1982) 'The Communication of Environmental Meaning', in M.R. Key (Ed.), *Nonverbal Communication Today: Current Research*. The Hague, Mouton.

Sparhawk, C.M. (1981) 'Features of Persian Gestures', in A. Kendon (Ed.), *Nonverbal Communication*, Interaction and Gesture, The Hague, Mouton.

Springer, S.P. and Deutsch, S. (1981) *Left Brain, Right Brain*, San Francisco, Calif., Freeman.

Stacks, D.W. and Sellers, D.E. (1986) 'Towards a Holistic Approach to Communication: The Effect of "Pure" Hemisphere Reception on Message Acceptance', *Communication Quarterly*, 34, 3, pp. 226–285.

Stewart, E.C. (1971) *American Cultural Patterns: A Cross-cultural Perspective*, Washington, D.C., SIETAR.

Trager, C.L. (1958) 'Paralinguistics — A First Approximation', *Studies in Linguistics*, 13, pp. 1–12.

Watzlawick, P. (1976) *How Real Is Real*, New York, Random House.

Watzlawick, P., Beavin, J.H. and Jackson, D.D. (1968) *Pragmatics of Human Communication*, London, Faber and Faber.

Wolfgang, A. (1979) 'The Teacher and Nonverbal Behaviour in the Multicultural Classroom', in A. Wolfgang (Ed.), *Nonverbal Behaviour: Application and Cultural Implications*, New York, Academic Press.

Wolfgang, A. and Bhardwaj (1984) 'Hundred Years of Nonverbal Study', in A. Wolfgang (Ed.), *Nonverbal Behaviour: Perspectives, Application and Intercultural Insights*, Toronto, Hogrefe.

# Part Two: Intergroup Relations and Prejudice Reduction

# 7. Intergroup Anxiety and Intergroup Interaction

COOKIE WHITE STEPHAN

In recent years a number of social psychologists have criticized the discipline's overreliance on cognitive explanations of prejudice (Billig, 1985) and called for increased attention to the neglected role of affect in intergroup relations (Dijker, 1987; Pettigrew, 1981, 1986) and in social inference (Zajonc, 1980). As a partial remedy for this neglect, this chapter focuses on the role of anxiety in the creation and maintenance of the affect, cognitions and behaviour stemming from intergroup interaction.

What is meant by anxiety? Stress combined with the perception of a situation as personally dangerous or threatening to an individual produces anxiety. Anxiety is experienced as feelings of tension, apprehension, nervousness and worry; heightened autonomic nervous system activity accompanies these feelings. Anxiety can be distinguished from fear, in that fear involves a real, objective danger, while anxiety is either objectless, or the intensity of the negative feelings is disproportionate to the objective reality (Spielberger, 1976).

## ANXIETY AND INTERGROUP INTERACTION

For many years, social observers have noted that interaction with members of outgroups is anxiety-provoking. Park (1928/1950) stated that when races meet, 'The first effect is to provoke in us a state of tension ...' (p. 238). Myrdal (1944) believed that the contradiction between American racism and the egalitarianism of the American creed created strain. In speaking of the Black presence in America, he wrote:

> ... his entire biological, historical, and social existence as a participant American represent to the ordinary white man in the North as well as in the South an anomaly in the very structure of American society. To many, this takes on the proportion of a menace — biological, economic, social, and at times, political. This anxiety may be mingled with a feeling of individual and collective guilt. (p. lxix)

**145**

Of the contradiction, he wrote:

> ... most people, most of the time, suppress such threats to their moral integrity together with all the confusion, the ambiguity, and the inconsistency which lurks in the basement of man's soul. This, however, is rarely accomplished without mental strain. Out of the strain comes a sense of uneasiness and awkwardness which always seems attached to the Negro problem. (p. lxix)

This chapter reviews empirical studies linking anxiety and intergroup interaction, and presents a model of intergroup anxiety. Finally, support for the model of intergroup anxiety, the relationship of this model to current models of racism, the importance of the focus on anxiety, and interventions to reduce anxiety are discussed.


## ANXIETY AND INTERGROUP RELATIONS


Anxiety is widely thought to exist in crosscultural interaction (Barna, 1983; Landis *et al.*, 1985; O'Berg, 1960; Smalley, 1963) and, as a result, intervention programmes have been devised to mitigate this anxiety (Brislin *et al.*, 1983, 1986; Brislin and Petersen, 1976).

Anxiety also has been observed in interactions among groups within a single culture. First, empirical studies have demonstrated the existence of anxiety in interracial interaction. Early studies demonstrated physiological responses associated with anxiety to contact (Porier and Lott, 1967; Rankin and Campbell, 1955) and anticipated contact (Vander Kolk, 1978) with racial minorities. Physiological reactions of anxiety have even been measured in response to visual presentations of Blacks to White subjects (Westie and DeFleur, 1959) and have been shown to be associated with degree of prejudice (Vidulich and Krevanick, 1966). Similarly, greater physiological reactions were shown to other racial and ethnic minorities for whom subjects had indicated negative attitudes (Cooper and Siegal, 1956; Cooper and Singer, 1956). Other reactions to contact with Blacks compared to Whites include greater seating distance and more and sooner discomfort when approached (Hendricks and Bootzin, 1976).

More recently, anxiety stemming from interracial interaction has been demonstrated in several laboratory experiments. In one study Dutch majority group members reported experiencing anxiety in interaction with three ethnic minorities in the Netherlands; further, anxiety was strongly related to negative ethnic attitudes towards the minority groups (Dijker, 1987). Ickes (1984) classified White males as 'approachers' or 'avoiders' on the basis of their responses to questions about interracial social contact. In unstructured interracial interactions, both Blacks and Whites experienced more stress and discomfort in dyads in which the White was classified as an 'avoider'. This experience was particularly uncomfortable for Whites when the experimenter was also Black. Overall, Whites experienced the interactions as more stressful than did the Blacks, probably because Whites are less accustomed than Blacks to interracial contacts. Feinman (1980) found that White infants between 4 and 24 months were less receptive to the approach of Black than White strangers, particularly infants in the stage in which 'stranger anxiety' is prominent.

Second, anxiety has been demonstrated in interaction with other outgroups. In one study subjects were more anxious when approached by a young woman dressed as a punk rocker than a conventionally dressed young woman, and were less likely to comply with her request to complete a short questionnaire when the request was made at close range (Glick, DeMorest and Hotze, 1988). Anxiety has also been demonstrated in interaction between competitive outgroups (Heiss and Nash, 1967; Nash and Wolfe, 1957). For example, using work groups that were either cooperative or competitive in orientation, Wilder and Shapiro (1989) found that, particularly in a competitive context, the prospect of interaction with an outgroup member induces anxiety. This anxiety thwarted the impact of the positive gestures of the outgroup member. Anxiety was associated with poor differentiation among outgroup members and greater reliance on negative expectations about the outgroup.

In short, anxiety is produced any time an individual interacts with others who may have different world-views. In such circumstances, ambiguity, uncertainty and unpredictability reign (Barna, 1983). In intergroup interaction, one's experiences may no longer be useful, and one's customary actions, beliefs and values may not be accepted. The predominant feelings can be lack of control and a sense of general threat.

## ANXIETY AS A MEDIATOR OF INTERGROUP RELATIONS

Stephan and Stephan (1985) have proposed a model of intergroup relations which focuses on intergroup anxiety, anxiety stemming from actual or anticipated contact with outgroup members. While this model stresses the role of affect in intergroup interaction, it also acknowledges the important roles of cognition and motivation as well.

Intergroup anxiety stems from four types of feared negative consequences of intergroup contact: (1) negative psychological consequences for the self (e.g., confusion, frustration, incompetence, loss of control, embarrassment, frustration, guilt, loss of self-esteem); (2) negative behavioural consequences for the self (e.g., exploitation, domination, discrimination, physical harm, verbal derogation); (3) negative evaluations by outgroup members (e.g., disapproval, negative evaluations by outgroup members (e.g., disapproval, negative stereotyping, scorn, distain, judgments of inferiority); and (4) negative evaluations by ingroup members (e.g., disapproval or rejection for having contact with the outgroup, identification with the outgroup).

Anxiety resulting from intergroup contact is posited to be a mediator between the factors antecedent to the contact and the consequences of the contact. Three categories of antecedents of contact are important: (1) prior intergroup relations (e.g., amount and conditions of contact, status differences between groups, attitudes of significant others); (2) prior intergroup cognitions (e.g., knowledge of the subjective culture of the outgroup, stereotyping and prejudice, ethnocentrism, expectations, perceptions of ingroup-outgroup differences); (3) situational factors (e.g., degree of structure, type of interdependence, group composition, relative status of the groups).

The consequences of anxiety induced by intergroup contact are amplified behavioural, cognitive and affective responses. Amplification results from the arousal generated from one source being transferred to and amplifying other emotional states (Hull, 1951; Zillman, 1978).


*Behavioural Responses.*   Drive increases the intensity of habitual responses to situations. Since anxiety elevates drive levels, it energizes dominant responses. The dominant behavioural response to many forms of anxiety is avoidance, because it is effective in terminating the anxiety. Thus avoidance of contact may be the most frequent response to intergroup anxiety. If contact is unavoidable, normative behavioural responses to the group will be amplified as anxiety increases. If no such normative responses exist, cultural norms regarding the treatment of strangers (e.g., suspicion, rejection, aloofness) will be amplified with increased anxiety.

High status groups may have norms prescribing or condoning discrimination against members of low status groups. Since anxiety amplifies normative behaviour, high levels of anxiety can lead members of high status groups to behave in extremely arrogant or condescending ways. The most extreme forms of discrimination should occur when the ingroup's superior status is threatened by the outgroup. The dominant response of members of low status groups is likely to be submission or ingratiation.

Individuals' acceptance of the ingroup's perceptions of its own and the other group mediate the effects of the relationship between the groups. Positive outgroup perceptions, whether acquired on the basis of positive intergroup contact or some other means, should lessen the likelihood that ingroup norms regarding the treatment of the outgroup will be accepted. The perceptions of significant others should also be important in determining the individuals' views of each group.

In intergroup interactions that provoke high levels of anxiety, the members of each group are likely to observe members of the other group behaving in stereotype-consistent ways due to the amplification of each group's normative responses. Since the members of each group are not likely to be aware of the degree to which the behaviour they observe is caused by the anxiety generated by their presence, they are likely to use these behaviours to make stereotypical trait inferences about members of the other group.


*Cognitive Responses.*   Intergroup anxiety should increase schematic processing and promote simplified information processing. Under the best of circumstances, biases exist in the attention, encoding and retrieval domains of cognitive information processing. As anxiety increases, these biases should become more pronounced. Such factors as categorization, narrowed focus of attention, perceptual assimilation and contrast, the principle of least effort, the ultimate attribution error, ethnocentrism and stereotyping, dependence on scripts, schemata and prototypes, and expectancy confirmation should result in more amplified thoughts regarding outgroup relative to ingroup members (see also Hamilton, 1981; Stephan, 1985; Wilder, 1986).

Heightened anxiety should also lead to increased concerns regarding self-esteem and self-identity. These increased concerns may lead ingroup members to make more extreme ego-defensive and ego-enhancing attributions for their behaviour than is usual. Perception of threats to self-identity may increase the tendency toward ingroup-outgroup bias in the evaluation of group differences.

*Affective Responses.* Emotional and evaluative responses should be amplified. When intergroup anxiety raises arousal, this arousal may be transferred to other emotions experienced during or immediately after the interaction (Zillman, 1978). Thus positive interactions with an outgroup member lead to strong positive emotions during the interaction and amplified positive evaluations afterwards relative to contact with an ingroup member, while negative interactions with an outgroup member will lead to comparatively strong negative emotions and evaluations.

## SUPPORT FOR THE INTERGROUP ANXIETY MODEL

Construct validity for the concept of intergroup anxiety was partially assessed by surveying a sample of Hispanic-American college students about their intergroup anxiety in positive voluntary contact with Caucasians (Stephan and Stephan, 1985). In addition, five antecedent variables were measured: ethnocentrism, contact with Caucasians, knowledge of the subjective culture of Caucasians, stereotyping of Caucasians, and perceived similarity to Caucasians. A regression analysis showed low contact with Caucacians, perceived dissimilarity to Caucasians, and stereotyping of Caucasians were associated with high levels of intergroup anxiety.

Several tests of the model of intergroup anxiety have been completed. A partial test of the antecedents of intergroup anxiety has been made in a study of contact with Caucasian-Americans among two minority groups, Japanese-Americans in Hawaii and Hispanic-Americans in New Mexico (Stephan and Stephan, 1989b). In our model we suggest that the principal antecedents of intergroup anxiety can be divided into three categories: prior intergroup relations, prior intergroup cognitions, and the characteristics of the situation. In this study we examined prior intergroup relations and prior intergroup cognitions. Five aspects of prior intergroup relations were examined: the perceived relations between their group and Caucasians, perceptions of the warmth/hostility of the intergroup interaction norms, the extent of the subject's voluntary positive contact with Caucasians, the perceived attitudes of the subject's significant others toward Caucasians, and the relative status of their group and Caucasians. Four prior intergroup cognitions were measured: the subject's stereotype of Caucasians, ethnocentrism, perceived dissimilarity of their group to Caucasians, and knowledge of Caucasian values.

College students from these groups completed a questionnaire concerning prior intergroup relations, prior intergroup cognitions, and a measure of anxiety which asked subjects to report the degree to which they would experience a variety of emotions during a future hypothetical work interaction with Caucasians. Asian-Americans expressed more anxiety about interacting with Caucasians than Hispanic-Americans. Asian-Americans also reported more negative attitudes toward Caucasians, perceived less positive relations between the groups, and reported fewer positive contacts with Caucasians than did Hispanic-Americans.

The results of a regression analysis showed that low levels of positive, voluntary contact were associated with high levels of intergroup anxiety in both groups. Perceived negative relations between the groups and high ethnocentrism were associated with high levels of intergroup anxiety in Asian-Americans. For Hispanic-Americans, low perceived relative status and negative stereotyping were associated with high levels of intergroup anxiety. These ethnic group differences were related to differences between the groups in their historical and contemporary relations with Caucasians. Thus for different groups in varying settings, different variables seem to be important in contributing to intergroup anxiety.

In a laboratory examination of the amplification of emotion hypothesis, race of partner, achievement outcome and level of public self-awareness were varied (Stephan and Stephan, 1989a). College student subjects interacted with a Black or White partner on an achievement task, at which they either succeeded or failed. Half of the subjects in each condition were in a heightened state of public self-awareness. As anticipated, emotional reactions to success were more positive with a Black partner than with a White partner, while emotional reactions to failure were more negative with a Black partner than with a White partner. Under conditions of low public self-awareness, Black partners were given less credit for success and were blamed more for failure than White partners. This prejudicial pattern of attributions disappeared under conditions of high public self-awareness. It seems likely that public self-awareness increased the salience of norms prescribing egalitarian, non-prejudiced behaviour.

In this study subjects did not report feeling more anxious when working with a Black than with a White partner. We believe the subjects were in fact experiencing anxiety, but were reluctant to admit it for fear of appearing prejudiced. Thus we cannot be certain that anxiety mediated the amplified emotional reactions. Because students are typically reluctant to display behaviour or attitudes that could be interpreted as prejudice (Crosby, Bromley and Saxe, 1980; Donnerstein and Donnerstein, 1973, 1976; Gaertner and Dovidio, 1986), we hoped to be able to demonstrate that anxiety is the mediator of subsequent effects through psycho-physiological measurements. The research in our laboratory has employed a measure of vocal stress, fundamental frequency (Sherer, 1986; Scherer and Ekman, 1982), as well as measures of blood pressure and heart rate but found no significant associations of the measures with anxiety.

In a laboratory test of the response amplification hypothesis, self-awareness and group of partner were varied in a self-disclosure paradigm (Stephan and Stephan, 1990). The experimental task required the subject and the partner to engage in structured interactions. Self-awareness was measured by the presence or absence of a video camera taping the conversations. The outgroup partner was handicapped (in a wheelchair), while the ingroup partner was not.

As anticipated, subjects disclosed more positive and neutral information in the non-handicapped than in the handicapped condition. Both public and private self-awareness increased in the handicapped conditions, suggesting that interaction with a handicapped person narrowed the focus of attention and thus interfered with focusing attention on the self. The analysis of the anxiety measure showed a marginal two-way interaction. Subjects in the handicapped/video condition reported the highest level of anxiety, while subjects in the handicapped/no video condition reported the lowest level of anxiety.

In a second laboratory test of the response amplification hypothesis using a self-disclosure paradigm, race of partner and similarity to partner were varied (Stephan and Stephan, 1990). Female Caucasian subjects were paired with a Caucasian or Black female partner; similarity was manipulated with false feedback on a questionnaire regarding personal values. The subject and the partner were asked to make a series of increasingly intimate self-disclosures in response to topics presented to them. The partner's responses were of course scripted. Since the anxiety model predicts that intergroup interactions elicit a norm of politeness and reserve plus a desire for avoidance, we expected subjects to disclose less intimate information to the outgroup than the ingroup member, particularly when she was dissimilar to the subject.

We found a significant interaction on the measure of number of references to the self and others and a marginal similarity by number of self and other references interaction on the measure of intimacy of self-disclosure. Subjects made significantly more references to the self and others in the Caucasian/similar partner condition and significantly fewer references to the self and others in the Black/dissimilar partner condition. The marginal similarity interaction is due to subjects in the similar condition making somewhat more intimate disclosures about the self than subjects in the dissimilar condition.

The self-disclosure sessions were tape recorded, and were analyzed for fundamental frequency. We anticipated higher voice stress levels in the outgroup than in the ingroup conditions, particularly when the partner was dissimilar, but found no significant differences across conditions.

Ample evidence exists that response amplification is a consequence of intergroup interaction. Amplified responses have been shown after interaction with minority group members (Dienstbier, 1970; Katz, Cohen and Glass, 1975; Katz *et al.*, 1979), as well as with the stigmatized (Kleck, 1966, 1968; Kleck *et al.*, 1966, 1968). This amplification has been attributed to cognitive complexity (Linville and Jones, 1980), ambivalence stemming from the elicitation of positive and negative cognitions about outgroup individuals (feelings of friendliness and aversion toward the handicapped, feelings that minorities are both unfairly disadvantaged and deviant) (Katz, Wachenhut and Hass, 1986). This latter explanation is similar to that of aversive racism (Gaertner and Dovidio, 1981, 1986), modern racism (McConahay, 1986; McConahay and Hough, 1976) and symbolic racism (Sears, 1988; Sears and Kinder, 1971). We turn next to a discussion of these models of racism.

## COMPARISON WITH OTHER MODELS

Myrdal's contradiction theme has been iterated by theorists who argue that current racism, whether called racial ambivalence (Katz, Glass and Cohen, 1973; Katz *et al.*, 1979; Katz, Wachenhut and Glass, 1988), or modern (McConahay, 1986; McConahay and Hough, 1976), aversive (Gaertner and Dovidio, 1981, 1986) or symbolic racism (Sears, 1988; Sears and Kinder, 1971), is less direct and overt than past racism. In aversive racism theory this new racism is said to stem from the contradiction between egalitarian values and unacknowledged feelings and beliefs regarding Blacks (Gaertner and Dovidio, 1981, 1986). In modern racism theory it is thought to arise from the contradiction between the belief that recent gains by Blacks are undeserved and values embodied in the Protestant ethic (McConahay, 1986; McConahay and Hough, 1976). In response amplification this racism is believed to arise from the contradiction between both positive and negative feelings held simultaneously about minorities (Katz *et al.*, 1973, 1979, 1988).

Due to the contradiction in values, beliefs or feelings, all these models suggest that the 'new racists' experience discomfort, uneasiness or diffuse negative feelings with respect to Blacks and other disliked minorities. For instance, Katz (1981) states that the existence of both positive and negative feelings towards Blacks 'creates in the person a high vulnerability to emotional tension in situations of contact with the attitudinal object' (p. 25).

The theory of intergroup anxiety has points in common with all these theories. The theories of racial ambivalence, aversive racism, modern racism and symbolic racism all suggest that some negative affect is associated with racism, and the theorists' description of this affect bears much in common with anxiety. In addition, all suggest the negative affect, cognitions or behaviour are amplified in the presence of outgroup members. In addition, all but symbolic racism theory have predicted amplified positive affect, cognitions, or behaviour in some circumstances.

The two theories that most clearly predict positive amplification, racial amplification and intergroup anxiety, differ in their explanation for the amplification. In ambivalence theory, contradictory attitudes about minorities are said to create ambivalence in interethnic contact situations. The result is a threat to the individual's self-image as a non-prejudiced yet discerning person. In contrast, intergroup anxiety is believed to be the cause of the amplification in the intergroup anxiety model. Another difference between these two models is that the racial ambivalence model does not posit affective consequences of intergroup interaction, as does intergroup anxiety.

A major distinction between intergroup anxiety and response amplification and of the two remaining models of racism is that these other models apply only to individuals with particular types of values, beliefs or attitudes. Modern and symbolic racism were initially conceptualized to account for the behaviours of the political right, while aversive racism was developed to account for the behaviours of the political left. By contrast, response amplification and intergroup anxiety are thought to exist to a greater or lesser extent in all intergroup interactions. In intergroup anxiety theory the degree of anxiety is dependent upon the characteristics of the individual and the situation and the prior relations between the groups, but even the simple categorization of people into the ingroup and the outgroup is likely to create some degree of intergroup anxiety.

Thus intergroup anxiety applies to all intergroup interactions, whether cross-cultural or between members of differing racial or ethnic groups or between 'normals' and stigmatized individuals, or between people of different generations, lifestyles or sexes within a single culture, whereas applications of the other theories have been more limited in scope. Symbolic racism has been applied exclusively to Whites' political responses and modern racism only to other attitudes of Whites toward Blacks. Aversive racism has been applied to male-female relations, and ambivalence theory to other stigmatized groups.

In addition, the intergroup anxiety model incorporates affect and arousal as well as cognition into the concept of intergroup relations. By contrast, the other theories rely heavily on cognitive factors. As a result, the intergroup anxiety model is able to specify a greater range of consequences than the other models.

However, it could be argued that any of these theories could be applied to other types of intergroup interaction then those for which they were proposed. Similarly, it could be argued that these theories may have other consequences not initially specified by their authors. Therefore, the data amassed for the negative amplification of attitudes, affect and behaviours may be viewed as supporting all of these theories. In addition, the positive amplification data support both intergroup anxiety and ambivalence. The task for the future is to achieve some theoretical clarity by experimental work that tests these models against each other.

## THE IMPORTANCE OF THE FOCUS ON ANXIETY

The focus on anxiety as a mediator of the consequences of intergroup contact is important for several reasons. First, it places attention directly on the neglected role of affect in intergroup relations. Mere cognition does not a racist make; the strength of feeling is the predominant characteristic of racism (Pettigrew, 1986).

Second, the focus on anxiety provides an explanatory mechanism for many otherwise confusing intergroup interaction findings. For example, intergroup contact under specified conditions (contact is equal status, pleasant, intimate, cooperative and supported by social norms) has long been thought to mitigate prejudice (Allport, 1954; Cook, 1978; Pettigrew, 1981). Such contact can be thought of as a desensitization technique for anxiety. Conceptualized in this manner, it becomes apparent why the specific conditions stated above are so important — these conditions lower anxiety — and why contact has failed to mitigate prejudice in some circumstances, provoking higher levels of anxiety.

Further, the model explains why cooperative contact improves intergroup relations primarily when the outcomes are favourable (Kennedy and Stephan, 1977; Worchel and Norvel, 1980). The amplified positive emotions experienced after success may directly contribute to improved relations, since, as reinforcement-affect theory suggests, people are attracted to those who are associated with positive experiences (Clore and Byrne, 1974). When the outcome of the cooperative contact is negative, the amplified negative emotions are likely to contribute directly to deteriorated relations, for the same reason.

Third, it suggests interventions for negative affect, cognitions and responses that are parallel to interventions for other types of anxiety. Desensitization is one highly successful intervention for anxiety (Agras, 1985; Heinrich, 1984), and has been shown to reduce prejudice (Sappington, 1976). Other behavioural therapies such as behavioural rehearsal, cognitive relabelling and reinforcement may be useful in some instances (Goldfried and Davison, 1976; Heinrich, 1984; Rimm and Masters, 1974). Even simple relaxation exercises to lower autonomic nervous system arousal may reduce intergroup anxiety.

## REDUCING INTERGROUP ANXIETY

Any technique that mitigates negative prior intergroup cognitions should reduce anxiety. The use of the cultural assimilator for ethnic groups within a country (Stephan and Stephan, 1985; Triandis, 1972, 1976) and the use of altered negative expectations for an individual (Cohen, 1980, 1982, 1984) demonstrate the efficacy of this approach in reducing prejudice toward an entire group and toward a single individual within a group, respectively.

When directing change toward an entire group, one question has been whether to use materials that stress intergroup similarities or those that stress intergroup differences. While an emphasis on intergroup similarities may mitigate the effects of cognitive information biases such as categorization, perceptual assimilation and contrast, the principle of least effort, and the norm of ingroup/outgroup bias (Stephan and Stephan, 1985), obviously dismissing fundamental differences would be harmful (Hewstone and Brown, 1986). Thus both differences and similarities need to be addressed. Discussing differences in a non-evaluative format (such as the cultural assimilator) is best accompanied by stress on intergroup similarities as well (Hewstone and Brown, 1986; Stephan and Stephan, 1985).

A similar question has arisen when addressing prejudice directed at individuals. Several researchers have noted the importance of the distinction between interpersonal behaviour (actions of individuals evaluated as individuals) and intergroup behaviour (actions of individuals evaluated as group members) in altering intergroup cognitions (Tajfel, 1978; Brown and Turner, 1981). Brown and Turner (1981) and Hewstone and Brown (1986) argue that intergroup contact reduces prejudice only when it changes the nature of the intergroup relations, not of interpersonal relations. In contrast, Brewer and Miller (1984; Miller and Brewer, 1986) argue that social categorization as the primary basis for organizing information about others must be abandoned and replaced by a more personalized view before prejudice reduction can occur. This interpersonal orientation can result from the assignment of non-category-based or cross-cutting roles, status and functions to participants in intergroup interactions.

Since these models address different aspects of cognitive processing biases during contact, they make complementary rather than contradictory recommendations for intergroup relations (Pettigrew, 1986). Hewstone and Brown are concerned with generalization of positive consequences from specific individuals to the group, while Brewer and Miller address the problem of rigid categorization of individuals within groups. For the purposes of reducing anxiety, guarding against both biases is important.

## SUMMARY

It has been argued that anxiety created by intergroup contact creates amplified affect, cognitions and behaviours. Factors antecedent to the contact include prior intergroup relations, prior intergroup cognitions and the structure of the situation. The interaction of these antecedent factors determines whether the amplified consequences are positive or negative.

Data in support of the model of intergroup anxiety were reported, and the suggestion was made that future work must better distinguish between the predictions made by a series of related models of intergroup relations. Finally, it was argued that consideration of the role of anxiety has several positive consequences for the conceptualization of intergroup relations.

## REFERENCES

Agras, S. (1985) *Panic: Facing Fears, Phobias, and Anxiety*, New York, Freeman.

Allport, G.W. (1954) *The Nature of Prejudice*, Cambridge, Addison-Wesley.

Barna, L.R. (1983) 'The Stress Factor in Intercultural Relations', in D. Landis and R.W. Brislin, *Handbook of Intercultural Training*, Vol. 2, New York, Pergamon Press.

Billig, M. (1985) 'Prejudice, Categorization, and Particularization: From a Perceptual to a Rhetorical Approach', *European Journal of Social Psychology*, 15, pp. 79–103.

Brewer, M.B. and Miller, N. (1984) 'Beyond the Contact Hypothesis: Theoretical Perspectives on Desegregation', in N. Miller and M.B. Brewer (Eds), *Groups in Contact: The Psychology of Desegregation*, New York, Academic Press.

Brislin, R.W. and Petersen, P. (1976) *Cross Cultural Orientation Programs*, New York, Gardner.

Brislin, R.W., Cushner, K., Cherrie, C. and Yong, M. (1986) *Intercultural Interactions*, Beverly Hills, Calif., Sage.

Brislin, R.W., Landis, D. and Brant, M.E. (1983) 'Conceptualizations of Intercultural Behavior and Training', in D. Landis and R.W. Brislin (Eds), *Handbook of Intercultural Training*, Vol. 1, New York, Pergamon Press.

Brown, R.J. and Turner, J.C. (1981) 'Interpersonal and Intergroup Behavior', in J. Turner and H. Giles (Eds), *Intergroup Behavior*, Oxford, Basil Blackwell.

Clore, G.L. and Byrne, D. (1974) 'A Reinforcement-Affect Model of Attraction', in T. Huston (Ed.), *Foundations of Interpersonal Attraction*, New York, Academic Press.

Cohen, E. (1980) 'Design and Redesign of the Desegregated School: Problem of the Status, Power, and Conflict, in W.G. Stephan and J.R. Feagin (Eds), *School Desegregation: Past, Present, and Future*, New York, Plenum Press.

Cohen, E. (1982) 'Expectation States and Interracial Interaction in School Settings', *Annual Review of Sociology*, 8, pp. 209–235.

Cohen, E. (1984) 'The Desegregated School: Problems in Status Power and Interethnic Climate', in N. Miller and M.B. Brewer (Eds), *Groups in Contact: The Psychology of Desegregation*, New York, Academic Press.

Cook, S.W. (1978) 'Interpersonal and Attitudinal Outcomes in Cooperating Interracial Groups', *Journal of Research and Development in Education*, 12, pp. 97–113.

Cooper, J.B. and Siegel, H.E. (1956) 'The Galvanic Skin Response as a Measure of Emotion in Prejudice, *Journal of Psychology*, 42, pp. 149–155.

Cooper, J.B. and Singer, D.N. (1956) 'The Role of Emotion in Prejudice', *Journal of Social Psychology*, 44, pp. 241–247.

Crosby, F.S., Bromley, K. and Saxe, L. (1980) 'Recent Unobtrusive Studies of Black and White Discrimination and Prejudice: A Literature Review', *Psychological Bulletin*, 87, pp. 546–563.

Dienstbier, R.A. (1970) 'Positive and Negative Prejudice: Interactions of Prejudice with Race and Social Desirability', *Journal of Personality*, 38, pp. 198–215.

Dijker, A.J.M. (1987) 'Emotional Reactions to Ethnic Minorities', *European Journal of Social Psychology*, 17, pp. 305–325.

Donnerstein, E.M. and Donnerstein, M. (1973) 'Variables in Interracial Aggresion: Potential Ingroup Censure', *Journal of Personality and Social Psychology*, 27, pp. 143–150.

Donnerstein, M. and Donnerstein, E. (1976) 'Research in the Control of Interracial Aggression', in R.G. Geen and G. O'Neal (Eds), *Perspectives on Aggression*, New York, Academic Press.

Feinman, S. (1980) 'Infant Response to Race, Size, Proximity, and Movement of Strangers', *Infant Behavior and Development*, 3, pp. 187–204.

Gaertner, S.L. and Dovidio, J.F. (1981) 'Racism among the Well-Intentioned', in E.G. Clausen and J. Bermingham (Eds), *Pluralism, Racism, and Public Policy: The Search for Equality*, Boston, Mass., G.K. Hall.

Gaertner, S.L. and Dovidio, J.F. (1986) 'The Aversive Form of Racism', in J.F. Dovidio and S.L. Gaertner (Eds), *Prejudice, Discrimination, and Racism*, Orlando, Fla., Academic Press.

Glick, P., DeMorest, J.A. and Hotze, C.A. (1988) 'Keeping Your Distance: Group Membership, Personal Space, and Requests for Small Favors', *Journal of Applied Social Psychology*, 28, pp. 315–330.

Goldfried, M.R. and Davison, G.C. (1976) *Clinical Behavior Therapy*, New York, Holt, Rinehart and Winston.

Hamilton, D.L. (Ed.) (1981) *Cognitive Processes in Stereotyping and Intergroup Behavior*, Hillsdale, N.J., Lawrence Erlbaum Associates.

Heinrich, R.L. (1984) 'Behavioral Approaches to the Evaluation and Treatment of Anxiety Disorders', in R.O. Pasnau (Ed.), *Diagnosis and Treatment of Anxiety Disorders*, Washington, D.C., American Psychiatric Press.

Heiss, J. and Nash, D. (1967) 'The Stranger in Laboratory Culture Revisited', *Human Organization*, 26, pp. 47–51.

Hendricks, M. and Bootzin, R. (1976) 'Race and Sex as Stimuli for Negative Affect and Physical Avoidance', *Journal of Social Psychology*, 98, pp. 111–120.

Hewstone, M. and Brown, R. (1986) 'Contact Is Not Enough: An Intergroup Perspective on the "Contact Hypothesis"', in M. Hewstone and R. Brown (Eds), *Contact and Conflict in Intergroup Encounters*, Oxford, Basil Blackwell.

Hull, C.L. (1951) *Essentials of Behavior*, New Haven, Conn., Yale University Press.

Ickes, W. (1984) 'Compositions in Black and White: Determinants of Interaction in Interracial Dyads', *Journal of Personality and Social Psychology*, 47, pp. 330–341.

Katz, I. (1981) *Stigma: A Social Psychological Analysis*, Hillsdale, N.J., Lawrence Erlbaum Associates.

Katz, I., Cohen, S. and Glass, D.C. (1975) 'Some Determinants of Cross-Racial Helping Behavior', *Journal of Personality and Social Psychology*, 32, pp. 964–970.

Katz, I., Glass, D.C. and Cohen, S. (1973) 'Ambivalence, Guilt, and the Scapegoating of Minority Group Victims', *Journal of Experimental Social Psychology*, 9, pp. 423–436.

Katz, I., Wachenhut, J. and Glass, D.C. (1988) 'An Ambivalence-Amplification Theory of Behavior toward the Stigmatized', in S. Worchel and W.G. Austin (Eds), *Psychology of Intergroup Relations*, 2nd ed., Chicago, Ill., Nelson-Hall.

Katz, I., Glass, D.C., Lucido, D.J. and Farber, J. (1979) 'Harm-doing and Victim's Racial or Orthopedic Stigma as Determinants of Helping Behavior', *Journal of Personality*, 45, pp. 419–429.

Katz, I., Wachenhut, J. and Hass, R.G. (1986) 'Racial Ambivalence, Value Duality, and Behavior', in J.F. Dovidio and S.L. Gaertner (Eds), *Prejudice, Discrimination, and Racism*, Orlando, Fla., Academic Press.

Kennedy, J. and Stephan, W.G. (1977) 'The Effects of Cooperation and Competition on Ingroup-Outgroup Bias', *Journal of Applied Social Psychology*, 2, pp. 115–130.

Kleck, R. (1966) 'Emotional Arousal in Interactions with Stigmatized Persons', *Psychological Reports*, 19, pp. 12–26.

Kleck, R. (1968) 'Physical Stigma and Nonverbal Cues Emitted in Face-to-Face Interaction', *Human Relations*, 21, pp. 19–28.

Kleck, R., Buck, P.L., Goller, W.I., London, R.S., Pfeiffer, J.R. and Vukcevic, D.P. (1968) 'Effect of Stigmatizing Conditions on the Use of Personal Space', *Psychological Reports*, 23, pp. 111–118.

Kleck, R., Hastorf, A.H. and Ono, H. (1966) 'The Effects of Physical Deviance upon Face-to-Face Interaction', *Human Relations*, 19, pp. 425–436.

Landis, D., Brislin, R.W. and Hulgus, J.F. (1985) 'Attributional Training versus Contact in Acculturative Learning: A Laboratory Study', *Journal of Applied Social Psychology*, 15, pp. 466–482.

Linville, P.W. and Jones, E.E. (1980) 'Polarized Appraisals of Outgroup Members', *Journal of Personality and Social Psychology*, 42, pp. 193–211.

McConahay, J.B. (1986) 'Modern Racism, Ambivalence, and the Modern Racism Scale', in J.F. Dovidio and S.L. Gaertner (Eds), *Prejudice, Discrimination, and Racism*, Orlando, Fla., Academic Press.

McConahay, J.B. and Hough, J.C. (1976) 'Symbolic Racism', *Journal of Social Issues*, 32, pp. 23–45.

Miller, N. and Brewer, M.B. (1986) 'Categorization Effects on Ingroup and Outgroup Perception', in J.F. Dovidio and S.L. Gaertner (Eds), *Prejudice, Discrimination, and Racism*, Orlando, Fla., Academic Press.

Myrdal, G. (1944) *An American Dilemma*, New York, Harper.

Nash, D. and Wolfe, A. (1957) 'The Stranger in Laboratory Culture', *American Sociological Review*, 22, pp. 400–405.

O'Berg, K. (1960) 'Culture Shock: Adjustment to New Cultural Environments', *Practical Anthropology*, 7, pp. 177–182.

Park, R.E. (1928/1950) *Race and Culture*, Glencoe, Ill., Free Press.

Pettigrew, T.F. (1981) 'Extending the Stereotype Concept', in D.L. Hamilton (Ed.), *Cognitive Processes in Stereotyping and Intergroup Behavior*, Hillsdale, N.J., Lawrence Erlbaum Associates.

Pettigrew, T.F. (1986) 'The Intergroup Contract Hypothesis Reconsidered', in M. Hewstone and R. Brown (Eds), *Contact and Conflict in Intergroup Encounters*, Oxford, Basil Blackwell.

Porier, G.W. and Lott, A.J. (1967) 'Galvanic Skin Response and Prejudice', *Journal of Personality and Social Psychology*, 5, pp. 253–259.

Rankin, R.E. and Campbell, D.T. (1955) 'Galvanic Skin Response to Negro and White Experimenters', *Journal of Abnormal and Social Psychology*, 51, pp. 30–33.

Rimm, D.C. and Masters, J.C. (1974) *Behavior Therapy: Techniques and Empirical Findings*, New York, Academic Press.

Sappington, A.A. (1976) 'Effects of Desensitization of Prejudiced Whites to Blacks upon Subjects' Stereotypes of Blacks', *Perceptual and Motor Skills*, 43, pp. 311–411.

Sears, D.O. (1988) 'Symbolic Racism', in P.A. Katz and D.A. Taylor (Eds), *Eliminating Racism*, New York, Plenum Press.

Sears, D.O. and Kinder, D.R. (1971) 'Racial Tensions and Voting in Los Angeles', in W.Z. Hirsch (Ed.), *Los Angeles: Viability and Prospects for Metropolitan Leadership*, New York, Praeger.

Sherer, K.R. (1986) 'Vocal Affect Expression: A Review and a Model for Future Research', *Psychological Bulletin*, 99, pp. 143–165.

Sherer, K.R. and Ekman, P. (1982) 'Methodological Issues in Studying Nonverbal Behavior', in K.R. Scherer and P. Ekman (Eds), *Handbook of Methods in Nonverbal Behavior Research*, Cambridge, Cambridge University Press.

Smalley, W. (1963) 'Culture Shock, Language Shock, and the Shock of Self-Discovery', *Practical Anthropology*, 10, pp. 49–56.

Spielberger, C.D. (1976) 'The Nature and Measurement of Anxiety', in C.D. Spielberger and R. Diaz-Guerrero (Eds), *Cross-Cultural Activity*, Washington, D.C., Hemisphere.

Stephan, W.G. (1985) 'Intergroup Relations', in G. Lindzey and E. Aronson (Eds), *Handbook of Social Psychology*, Vol. 3, New York, Addison-Wesley.

Stephan, W.G. and Stephan, C.W. (1985) 'Intergroup Anxiety', *Journal of Social Issues*, 41, pp. 157–175.

Stephan, W.G. and Stephan, C.W. (1989a) 'Emotional Reactions to Interracial Achievement Outcomes', *Journal of Applied Social Psychology*, 19, pp. 608–621.

Stephan, W.G. and Stephan, C.W. (1989b) 'Antecedents of Intergroup Anxiety in Asian-Americans and Hispanic-Americans', *International Journal of Intercultural Relations*, 13, pp. 203–219.

Stephan, W.G., Stephan, C.W., Wenzel, B. and Cornelius, J. (1991) 'Intergroup Interaction and Self-Disclosure', *Journal of Applied Social Psychology*, 21, pp. 1370–1378.

Tajfel, H. (1978) 'Interindividual Behaviour and Intergroup Behaviour', in H. Tajfel (Ed.), *Differentiation between Social Groups*, London, Academic Press.

Triandis, H.C. (1972) *The Analysis of Subjective Culture*, New York, Wiley.

Triandis, H.C. (1976) *Variations in Black and White Perceptions of the Social Environment*, Urbana, Ill., University of Illinois Press.

Vander Kolk, C.J. (1978) 'Physiological Reactions of Black, Puerto Rican, and White Students in Suggested Ethnic Encounters', *Journal of Social Psychology*, 104, pp. 107–114.

Vidulich, R.N. and Krevanick, F.W. (1966) 'Racial Attitudes and Emotional Response to Visual Representation of the Negro', *Journal of Social Psychology*, 68, pp. 82–93.

Weitz, S. (1972) 'Attitude, Voice, and Behavior: A Repressed Affect Model of Interracial Interaction', *Journal of Personality and Social Psychology*, 24, pp. 14–21.

Westie, F.R. and DeFleur, M. (1959) 'Autonomic Responses and Their Relationship to Race Attitudes', *Journal of Abnormal and Social Psychology*, 58, pp. 340–347.

Wilder, D.A. (1986) 'Cognitive Factors Affecting the Success of Intergroup Contract', in S. Worchel and W.G. Austin (Eds), *Psychology of Intergroup Relations*, 2nd ed., Chicago, Ill., Nelson-Hall.

Wilder, D.A. and Shapiro, P.N. (1989) 'Role of Competition-induced Anxiety in Limiting the

Beneficial Impact of Positive Behavior by an Out-Group Member', *Journal of Personality and Social Psychology*, 56, pp. 60–69.

Worchel, S. and Norvel, N. (1980) 'Effects of Perceived Environmental Conditions during Cooperation on Intergroup Attraction', *Journal of Personality and Social Psychology*, 38, pp. 764–772.

Zajonc, R.B. (1980) 'Feeling and Thinking: Preferences Need No Inferences', *American Psychologist*, 35, pp. 151–175.

Zillman, D. (1978) 'Attribution and Misattribution of Excitatory Arousal', in J.H. Harvey, W. Ickes and R.F. Kidd (Eds), *New Directions in Attribution Research*, Hillsdale, N.J., Lawrence Erlbaum Associates.

# 8. Research and Theory in Intergroup Relations: Issues of Consensus and Controversy

HUGH JORDAN HARRINGTON AND
NORMAN MILLER

The contact hypothesis (Allport, 1954), published the same year the US Supreme Court ruled that segregated schools violated the principles of the Constitution, argued that previously segregated groups would benefit from mutual contact. Not assuming that mere contact is sufficient to promote intergroup harmony, a number of contingencies that qualify the nature of contact were suggested as important. As summarized by Cook (1978), they stipulate: (1) cooperative activity towards a common goal; (2) equal status contact; (3) opportunity to disconfirm stereotypes; (4) normative support from authority figures; and (5) high acquaintance potential.

## REVISITING THE CONTACT HYPOTHESIS

The expanded contact hypothesis was important in at least two respects. First, it focused on conditions that promote harmony and, therefore, had implications for intervention strategies. Second, it articulated an array of variables that influence the intergroup setting. We use these contingencies as a framework for organizing our discussion of intergroup work and for focusing on issues of controversy, particularly as they relate to educational settings.

### Cooperative Interdependence

One of the earliest approaches to understanding intergroup conflict, dating back at least to Sumner (1906), has been labelled by Campbell (1965) as realistic conflict theory (RCT). According to RCT, one can expect conflict whenever two or more groups must compete for scarce resources. This is readily apparent with survival resources such as food or jobs, but is just as applicable to such limited resources as top grades or a teacher's attention in the school setting. Even in one-to-one interactions wherein cooperative or competitive choices may be made, people tend to adopt a competitive orientation (Deutsch and Krauss, 1962). Merely performing in a group and being aware that another group is performing the same task is sufficient to engender a competitive orientation (Ferguson and Kelley, 1964). Interaction among multiple members of an ingroup and outgroup, in comparison to individual interaction, heightens this competitive orientation, makes social categories more salient, and ingroup favouritism more evident (Dustin and Davis, 1970).

Within a group, perceived similarity to others increases cohesion and cooperative actions in the Prisoner's Dilemma Game (Dion, 1973). Competition between groups can also heighten ingroup cohesion (Ryen and Kahn, 1975). Even the mere anticipation of interaction with another group will heighten group solidarity and arouse a competitive orientation whether reward structures are explicitly competitive or independent (Kahn and Ryen, 1972; Rabbie and Wilkens, 1971). For groups with a past history of competition then, conflict seems inevitable. Indeed, perceived conflict is a reliable predictor of intergroup discrimination (Brown and Williams, 1984). Even when induced to categorize self and others arbitrarily into different groups, subjects expect and recall more negative behaviours of outgroup members (Howard and Rothbart, 1980), maximize the differences in rewards allocated to ingroup versus outgroup members rather than maximize ingroup rewards (Tajfel, 1978), attribute more negative qualities to and express less desire to interact with outgroup members (Rabbie and Horowitz, 1969) and evaluate outgroup performance less favourably than ingroup performance (Ferguson and Kelley, 1964). Thus mere categorization is sufficient to engender the type of hostility expressed by naturally occurring groups with a history of conflict. This suggests that despite cultural and subcultural differences in the extent to which groups are competitive and biased (Shapiro and Madsen, 1969), there are processes more basic than (and in addition to) those based on realistic conflict of interest that contribute to intergroup conflict. It is not surprising, therefore, that most agree that interventions are needed to reduce the antagonism associated with a competitive orientation.

*Variations of Interdependence.*   Cooperative interdependence has been one of the most frequently mentioned conditions for successful contact. Condor and Brown (1988) note that cooperation is usually imposed on groups rather than being a solution developed by them. There are actually several distinct meanings of cooperative interdependence. First, it may mean that there is a superordinate or *shared goal* that both groups find important and desire (Worchel, 1979). This intergroup outcome or common fate (Campbell, 1958) may also involve a *shared threat*. Second, cooperative interdependence can refer to *shared rewards*, as when each team member (or each group) receives the same outcome or the same magnitude of reward. It is not always the case (e.g., management and labour) that achievement of a shared goal results in equal distribution of reward. Third, this condition may mean that a superordinate identity has been formed, in which case a new and *shared social identity* is created and the salience of the former intergroup distinction has been diminished (Gaertner *et al.*, 1989). Fourth, it may imply that neither group can accomplish the goal on its own, such as the conditions involved in the Sherif studies (1967). This *shared need* constitutes intergroup dependence but is rarely a condition in either laboratory or classroom studies. This condition would occur when a task requires a certain number of persons, more ingroup members are not available, and outgroup members are the only available persons to help meet this need. *Task interdependence* is a fifth interpretation of cooperation. Task completion may require that individuals be dependent on the actions of each other and, consequently, interact with one another (as opposed to the preceding dependence in which groups may operate together but maintain their group boundaries). In this case there is a sense of *shared responsibility*. Finally, cooperative interdependence can be applied to shared rewards to the intergroup teams as a whole, that is, to both groups equally.

Any single type of cooperative interdependence may be insufficient to promote intergroup harmony. A superordinate goal, in and of itself, is not always effective in reducing intergroup conflict (Blake, Shepard and Moulton, 1964). A superordinate identity may threaten a group's identity (Brown and Abrams, 1986). In addition to social identity needs, there are personal identity needs. Under conditions of anonymity in which one's individual contributions cannot be recognized, there may be a decrease in sense of responsibility, leading to the social loafing effect (Latane and Nida, 1980). Thus task interdependence may not be sufficient to promote positive interaction. Similarly, rewards to the team as a whole may obscure needs for group or individual recognition.

*Effects of Outcome.* The outcome of interaction has significant and similar effects within a group and between groups in a cooperative endeavour. Members are more attracted toward their own group when either the group as a whole (Hoffman, 1958) or they individually (Lott and Lott, 1968) succeed, whereas group failure can lower attraction to the group (Worchel, Lind and Kaufman, 1975). Within groups that fail, members with high self-esteem maintain higher group liking than those with low self-esteem (Stotland, 1959). It has been argued that it is the perceived likelihood of success which determines whether ingroup cohesion is greater in intergroup cooperation or competition — increased ingroup attraction can occur if members expect to succeed in competition ('we're better') or fail in cooperation ('they'll make us lose') with an outgroup (Rabbie *et al.*, 1974). Many of these results can be interpreted within reinforcement theory, since people like those who do or can reward them (Lott, 1961). Similarly, social exchange theory (Homans, 1961) underscores the value of the group in providing social approval for cooperation and other group-supporting behaviours. Because intergroup competition requires dependence on the ingroup, it may foster attraction to the ingroup (Thibaut and Kelley, 1959), perhaps as part of the general phenomenon of increased liking of those with whom one expects to interact (Rabbie and Wilkens, 1971).

Attributions can moderate the effect of outcomes in intragroup situations. If self is blamed for group failure, it will result in increased attraction to the group, whereas if the group is blamed, it will lower attraction to the group (Lerner, 1965). In intergroup situations, successful interaction can promote outgroup acceptance, even for groups who have previously competed (Worchel, Andreoli and Folger, 1977). Cooperative intergroup failure, on the other hand, can lead to outgroup rejection if the outgroup is seen as its cause, but they will not be derogated if there is a salient external cause of the failure (Worchel and Norvell,

1980). One study tested the generalization of intergroup interaction following outcome information (Miller and Harrington, 1990b). For own heterogeneous (intergroup) team, success increased and failure decreased both ingroup and outgroup member attraction. Outcome had no effect on generalized bias toward the outgroup members of another heterogeneous team; however, own-team success led to more favourable evaluations of the ingroup members of that other team. This differential effect resulted in a generalized bias of increase in ingroup favoritism. Own-team failure, on the other hand, lowered generalized evaluations of the ingroup, and thus no bias was expressed. Therefore, successful interaction in itself is not more positive than failure in terms of generalized effects.

*Issues of Reward.*    The issue of reward structure has raised two points of controversy. The first is whether rewards should be allocated to the individual or to the intergroup team. Steiner (1972) argues that outcomes which are dependent on either the contributions of all members or on the least skilled members benefit most from team level rewards, whereas when outcomes are dependent on contributions from the most skilled members, individual level rewards are superior. In a study with children, rewards based on the performance of the least skilled members more effectively promoted cooperative behaviours (Wodarski *et al.*, 1973). Cooperative team learning (CTL) methods, such as Jigsaw (Aronson *et al.*, 1978) address personal identity needs by providing recognition for individual contributions yet reinforce team identity by providing rewards (points toward a final grade) to the team. In any event, some standard of comparison must be used, whether it is an absolute standard, relative to the class or other teams, or based on own past performance. The latter (gain-scores) helps to reinforce students' efforts and to equalize pre-existing ability differences which may converge with social category membership. Several CTL methods use just such an approach. A related issue that has not engendered much discussion is 'what to reward'. It may seem obvious, particularly in a school setting, that one should reward task outcomes (academic learning), but it may be equally valid to reward acquired skills. Social skills (interpersonal interaction, communication, teamwork) should be equally valued and rewarded as academic skills, if the school is regarded as the formal institution of socialization.

*Interteam Competition.*    The second issue that has been debated concerns the use of interteam competition in CTL. Slavin (1985) argues that interteam competition produces positive results, whereas others (Johnson, Johnson and Maruyama, 1983) argue that methods which avoid it generally produce greater benefit. On theoretical grounds we have argued (Miller, Brewer and Edwards, 1985) that competitive structures tend to produce task orientations as opposed to interpersonal orientations. These two orientations result in outcomes that parallel competition and cooperation, respectively. A final concern about rewards within the context of cooperation is that they are typically extrinsic, which results in lowered future motivation to engage in the antecedent actions, namely, cooperative behaviour (Deci, 1975). That is, participants can easily overlook the intrinsic rewards of cooperative experience. If students have the opportunity to establish a positive identity and to develop friendships, then the cooperative activity itself can be a rewarding experience. Task interdependence contributes more to intergroup acceptance than does an interdependence defined in terms of the external reward structure (Miller and Davidson-Podgorny, 1987).

## Equal Status Contact

A second frequently mentioned condition of a successful contact situation is equal status, which is typically interpreted as equality within the cooperative setting (Cook, 1978). Cohen (1982) has emphasized the difference between external (social) status characteristics of the participants and status in the situation, which is usually induced by equal or equivalent roles and responsibilities. According to expectation status theory, the social status of a given characteristic, for example, gender, ethnicity or age, is a function of the cultural evaluation of that characteristic (Berger and Zelditch, 1985). Status characteristics then serve as a basis for expectations that people have toward themselves and others in social interaction. When status is salient, group members behave as if the status characteristic is a relevant indicator of the skills involved in the task, even when there is no logical connection between the status characteristic and competence on the task (Cohen, 1982). Thus equal status roles as team members, at the structural level, are not likely to be paralleled by equal status at the psychological level.

*Attributional Biases.* External status can have a profound impact on behaviour in the interaction setting. Typically, high status members are more assertive and display the most ingroup bias, whereas low status members tend to behave deferentially (Cohen, 1972; Sachdev and Bourhis, 1987). These patterns of behaviour are to some extent paralleled by patterns of attributions. High status groups assume more credit for success and less blame for failure than low status groups (Hewstone and Ward, 1985). Thus the self-serving bias for own performance is similar to an ethnocentric bias or what Pettigrew (1979) has labelled the ultimate attribution error. Whereas high status groups tend to blame the victim, low status groups engage in defensive attribution (Furnham, 1982). Blaming the system for the ingroup's low social status protects the self-esteem of its members (Simmons, 1978), whereas attributing negative outcomes to internal and stable factors could result in feelings of helplessness (Weiner, 1982). Furthermore, the outgroup can be perceived as the cause of the ingroup's condition (Campbell, 1967). When there are status differences on evaluative dimensions, members can judge those dimensions on which they are superior to be more important, invent new dimensions or change the value of existing evaluative dimensions (Skevington, 1981).

Cohen (1982) proposes that if the contact is to be promotive of intergroup acceptance, the expectations for competency that are derived from external status must be altered prior to the contact setting — for members of both the high and the low status group. Otherwise, the patterns of interaction will serve to reinforce existing expectancies. Slavin (1985) contests these arguments on the basis of data from studies of CTL which demonstrate positive results without such pretreatment. Research from the two employs different measures. Cohen's studies use judges' one-time observations of behaviour patterns, whereas Slavin measures longer-term liking (friendships) and not status perceptions or observations of behaviour. In addition, Norvell and Worchel (1981) caution that groups will resist attempts to redress status differences if these attempts are perceived as unfair. We have proposed that behaviour within the interaction setting can be altered and that this, in turn, will modify attitudes, namely, by personalizing interaction, which is discussed in a later section.

*Assignment to Teams.*   One issue related to equal status concerns the method of assignment to heterogeneous teams. Several CTL procedures deliberately use social category membership in the formation of teams. Although this has the potential benefit of conveying the teacher's normative support for interracial interaction, it has the disadvantage of making race (or other social category) the salient feature of interactants. This, in turn, can provoke information processing in terms of category membership, thereby reinforcing expectancies.

   Additionally, assignment should consider numeric status of the categories represented within the team because a minority will be more salient (Duval and Duval, 1983). Therefore, we have recommended that attempts be made to compose teams that have roughly equal numbers of high and low status persons within a particular team, even if other teams remain homogeneous (Miller and Harrington, 1990a). By frequently recomposing teams, eventually all students within the classroom will have heterogeneous team experience. This approach argues against interteam competition because homogeneous teams may derogate heterogeneous teams, that is, use category membership as a basis for negative social comparison. The use of multiple or crosscutting categories can be an additional means of reducing the salience of category memberships (Vanbeselaare, 1987). One method of team assignment that was effective in a laboratory simulation is the use of individuals' unique characteristics (Miller *et al.*, 1985). Equally heterogeneous teams were created by explicit use of category membership or on the basis of the unique attributes of individuals. Ingroup bias was strong in the former, but eliminated in the latter condition.

*Role Assignment.*   Teams in which members perform identical functions may be outcome dependent but are not necessarily interactively dependent — outcome may be simply the sum of members' output. In contrast, teams with more task complexity often require role differentiation and division of labour. Task roles may differ in status; therefore, it is possible for role status either to converge with or to crosscut the external status of social categories. Furthermore, emergent leadership can develop and high status members will often assume such roles. Whereas Cook (1969) has argued that roles should convey equal opportunity to participate and contribute to the team product, others have argued that similar roles will lead to intergroup bias and that distinctive roles will diminish bias (Brown and Turner, 1979). Brown (1988) proposes that there is a 'threshold of similarity' beyond which social identity becomes threatened and that intergroup bias will restore positive identity. We suggest that in situations analogous to the minimal group paradigm, that is, in which the group member is anonymous and initially indistinguishable from others, and individual contributions are unrecognizable, then the only source of identity is the group and, therefore, social identity is salient. There is no opportunity for personal identity needs to be positively established, and in this restricted case intergroup bias can be expected.

In contrast, in situations in which the salience of social identity is minimized and where personal identity can be positively valued and individual contributions recognized, we propose that crosscutting rather than convergent role assignments will be more positive.

*Bias and Status Differences.*   Although we have discussed status as an evaluative dimension, there are also status differences due to numerosity (majority and minority) in the population (Sachdev and Bourhis, 1984) or the contact setting (Rogers, Hennigan, Bowman and Miller, 1984). Status is also related to differences in power, and these differences can threaten group identity and enhance competition (Tjosvold, 1981). Although bias increases with power, when power becomes extreme there is some moderation of this relationship (Sachdev and Bourhis, 1985). Additionally, status stability will influence group differentiation. Tajfel and Turner (1985) propose that low status groups will seek to change the basis of status assignment when the present basis is perceived as illegitimate (Caddick, 1982) or unstable (Turner and Brown, 1978). In contrast to unequal status groups, Turner (1978) has shown the equal status groups will display more bias when the basis of status is perceived as stable. That is, equal status groups, with no objective basis on which to assert their relative superiority, will seek positive differentiation through biased evaluations. They should be less inclined to do so, however, if members could augment self-esteem via the personal identity dimension.

## Stereotype Disconfirmation

Categorization of physical and social objects is a natural process and a useful means of simplifying and ordering the world. It facilitates the processing of information quickly and efficiently. Nevertheless, there is a cost for such efficiency due to inherent biases in the categorization process. Moreover, social categories such as race, gender, age and occupation become associated within a given culture with physical features, personality traits, preferences, values and behaviours (Brewer, Dull and Lui, 1981). The specific content of these associations constitutes the stereotypes of a social group.

*Undifferentiated Perceptions.*   Following categorization, both the perceived similarity within groups and the dissimilarity between groups is exaggerated (Dion, 1973). There is also greater perceived similarity within groups among stereotype-relevant attributes than among those attributes that are not category-relevant (Tajfel, Sheikh and Gardner, 1964). This assimilation-contrast effect blurs individual distinctiveness. Group members are seen as relatively interchangeable, and people are prone to more within-group errors in identification whereas they are more accurate in between-group identification (Taylor *et al.*, 1978). In comparison to the ingroup, the outgroup is seen as relatively more homogeneous. This is due in part to greater familiarity with ingroup members and more complex schemas for them. Consequently, evaluations of an undifferentiated outgroup tend to be more polarized (Linville and Jones, 1980). Furthermore, this perceive homogeneity deindividuates members of the outgroup, making them easier targets for hostility (Wilder, 1978). The exception to the outgroup homogeneity effect is that minorities often tend to see their ingroup as more homogeneous, which can be a means of enhancing cohesion and identity (Simon and Brown, 1987).

Categorization also influences the expectations of others' behaviour as well as the perceiver's interpretation of that behaviour. Favourable expectations for ingroup members and unfavourable expectations for outgroup members in turn affect causal attributions for actions and outcomes. Stereotypes exacerbate these attributional biases (Deaux and Emswiller, 1974), in part because they imply particular dispositional traits (Pyszczynski and Greenberg, 1981) and because it is easier to recall impressions that are based on atrributions to dispositions as opposed to attributions to situations (Crocker, Hannah and Weber, 1983). Not only are negative traits easier to confirm than to disconfirm (Rothbart and John, 1985), but there is greater recall of negative information about the outgroup, whereas disconfirming information is not well remembered (Rothbart, Evans and Fulero, 1979). This bias in differential processing of information is compounded by the tendency to seek confirmation of hypotheses (Pyszczynski and Greenberg, 1987), to prefer information that reinforces the assumption that ingroup members are similar to self and outgroup members dissimilar to self (Allen and Wilder, 1975), to perceive stereotype-consistent behaviour even when it does not occur (Cantor and Mischel, 1977), and to behave in self-fulfilling ways (Snyder and Swann, 1978). Impersonal treatment of outgroup members actually inhibits their performance (Word, Zanna and Cooper, 1974).

The distinctiveness of a stimulus, that is, its novelty or salience, influences attention and can distort perceptions. People are prone to illusory correlation, the tendency to overestimate the number of socially undesirable traits associated with minorities because both are relatively infrequent (Hamilton and Rose, 1980). Solo status in a group can produce a number of undesirable effects, particularly for those who have lower social status (Kanter, 1977).

*Extent of Disconfirmation.*   Prejudice, the treatment of an individual on the basis of group membership, has been interpreted as being due to perceived dissimilarity of beliefs (Rokeach, 1960). Just as perceived dissimilarity leads to rejection (Rosenbaum, 1986), perceived similarity leads to attraction (Byrne, 1971; Smeaton, Byrne and Murnen, 1989). Many have argued some form of the 'ignorance causes prejudice' model and propose that knowledge of similarity between self and the outgroup should lead to positive change (Myrdal, 1944; Stephan and Stephan, 1984). Thus an additional condition of positive contact situations is the opportunity for interactants to disconfirm existing stereotypes. However, the development of a model for stereotype change has led to some disagreement. Should multiple disconfirmations be concentrated in one person or be distributed across multiple outgroup members? Rose (1981) has argued that individual interaction is likely to be more effective in generating change because it is more personal, and this intimacy will in turn reveal more information that disconfirms the stereotype. Others (Whitley, Schofield and Snyder, 1984) have also proposed that individuation is more effectively induced by dyadic interaction. On the other hand, Rothbart and John (1985) contend that individuation will not lead to generalization to the group, presumably because the individuated member is no longer perceived as representative of the group. Perhaps this is a straw man issue.

We concur that individualization not only allows more disconfirming information to be encountered but has other positive effects as well, described in a later section. We propose that multiple contacts that allow for personalization, either in dyads or small groups, can be developed over time by recomposing teams. In this manner, there will be both intimate disconfirmations that are encountered across a wide spectrum of outgroup members, not only personalizing the members but differentiating the outgroup.

*Typicality of Outgroup Members.* Another issue concerns the typicality of outgroup members. It is argued that, if typical, then the possibility for stimulus generalization exists, whereas an atypical outgroup member will be discounted as an exception and generalization will not occur (Rothbart and John, 1985). Alternatively, others propose that the outgroup member needs to disconfirm the stereotype and, as such, must be countertypical (Cook, 1978). Thus Amir (1969) suggests that contact with a high as opposed to low status minority member is more promotive of attitude change. This seems to us to be a Scylla and Charybdis issue: if the outgroup member is seen as typical, then responses will.be biased toward expectancy confirmation (Cantor and Mischel, 1977); on the other hand, the outgroup member who disconfirms the group stereotype can be subtyped (Weber and Crocker, 1983) and discounted as an exception. We propose a solution to this dilemma later under the section on acquaintance potential.

*Group Similarities and Differences.* Debate about stereotype disconfirmation also centres on appropriate topics for classroom discussion. Should they focus on fundamental similarities between groups, group-specific and valued differences, both, or neither? Consistent with the similarity-attraction hypothesis, some have proposed a focus on group similarities, whereas others have suggested that both are necessary foci of discussion (Hewstone and Brown, 1986). A focus on positive group differences can acknowledge real differences that may exist and simultaneously demythologize misconceptions of differences. This begs the question, however, of what stereotypes each social group holds toward other social groups. This is particularly problematic when a large variety of social groups exists within a single setting. In the Los Angeles County (California) School District, for example, there are more than seventy-five languages spoken by its students. Proponents of the group differences approach fail to articulate what those real differences are, the extent to which they are valued by members of the target group, and the extent to which they are relevant to the stereotype held of that group. Furthermore, we contend that a focus on group level information, whether similarities or dissimilarities, reinforces the salience of category membership and promotes categorization effects. Indeed, such a focus falls victim to one of the hallmarks of stereotyping — it makes the assumption that all group members share that characteristic.

## Normative Support

It may be quite natural, at least in many Western cultures, that tasks and teams elicit competitive norms. Moreover, group developed norms can exacerbate this tendency and can be expected to be stronger with greater identification with and conformity to the group. Normative support of authority figures, another condition espoused as necessary to obtain positive contact effects, has received the least systematic research. Some evidence suggests that teachers' attitudes towards interracial contact have a significant impact on the quality of students' interaction. In particular, Epstein (1985) illustrates how teachers' attitudes affect how students are organized for learning, which in turn affects the extent of their interaction patterns. Teachers who are not favourably disposed to interracial interaction tend to use some form of academic tracking which has the frequent consequence of segregating students (Oakes, 1985), whereas those favourably disposed are more likely to use cooperative learning methods. Weigel and Howes (1985) also point out that those students who have the most negative attitudes toward interracial contact are the ones most susceptible to the influence of authority figures — the very persons who can prescribe or proscribe certain behaviours within the class. Teachers have the opportunity to reinforce desired behaviours. Even 4-year-olds will demonstrate greater sharing when reinforced (Fischer, 1963). Teachers must also model the desired behaviours. Experimental studies have shown that the more powerful influence on children is the behaviour exhibited by the adult rather than the values espoused (Bryan and Walbek, 1970), although even espousing proper behaviours and explaining the rationale for them can be effective (Anderson and Perlman, 1973).

*Peer Norms.*   In addition to the social, cultural and familial norms regarding intergroup contact outside the school setting and the norms espoused by administrators and teachers within it, students are also exposed to peer norms. Subjects who express ingroup preference also expect others to exhibit the same bias (Allen and Wilder, 1975). Although ingroup favouritism is a robust phenomenon, it is seldom extreme. Further, norms for equality and fairness, when invoked, will act to counter bias. Stephan and Stephan (1984) have drawn attention to the significant influence of peers on intergroup contact. In their review of CTL, Johnson, Johnson and Maruyama (1983) indicated that the most significant feature of these methods is the within-team peer tutoring that can occur. There has been little, if any, attempt to understand the conditions which foster the development of team norms for equity and respect. We suspect that a crucial area for investigation is the values of cooperation, diversity, fairness and interracial contact, as well as how these are learned. Fortunately, these issues are discussed at length in other chapters.

**Acquaintance Potential**

A final condition that was part of Allport's (1954) initial contact hypothesis as well as the social science statement to the Supreme Court in the *Brown* case (1954) is the opportunity to come to know members of the other group as individuals — what Cook (1978) has referred to as acquaintance potential. We submit that this may be one of the most critical and least investigated avenues in intergroup research. We first review a model of decategorization (Brewer and Miller, 1984) and discuss the roles of similarity, anxiety, esteem and self-disclosure as they relate to this model. Then we discuss two related issues in the next section that have engendered some controversy: the distinction between interpersonal and intergroup interaction, and whether or not category salience should be high in the contact setting.

*Decategorization.* Brewer and Miller (1984) propose that intergroup conflict and prejudice can be reduced if attempts are made to decategorize the outgroup and its members, that is, to reverse the assimilation-contrast effects of categorization described earlier. According to this model, differentiation of the outgroup is one aspect of the intervention — to facilitate the recognition of individual differences within the otherwise undifferentiated group. The second aspect, personalization, is the process of discovering the uniqueness of individual members — knowledge of the personal attributes of the other. Part of the rationale for this approach is based on the similarity-attraction hypothesis (Byrne, 1971). In addition to liking those who are similar, there is a tendency to see similarity in people we like and to believe that other's likeable characteristics are also descriptive of self (Marks, Miller and Maruyama, 1981). Individuals tend to be responded to more positively than a group (Sears, 1983), and personal aspects of identity appear to be more central than social memberships. Taylor and Dubé (1986) claim that, at least among North Americans, people 'believe there is something inherently wrong about having *any* judgment about themselves based on their membership in a social category' (p. 92). There is also a need for individuals to differentiate self from the ingroup (Wilder, 1986). Thus we believe a critical feature of positive interaction is that aspects of personal identity be disclosed.

It has been proposed that outgroup avoidance is mediated by anxiety and lack of familiarity with outgroup members (Stephan and Stephan, 1984). Contact which promotes anxiety amplifies behavioural responses, increases information processing biases, increases self-awareness and augments emotional reactions (Stephan and Stephan, 1985). Intergroup competition augments anxiety (Wilder and Shapiro, 1989). A series of individual level contacts may be less stressful and anxiety provoking than contact among multiple members of groups. Individuating members helps to differentiate the group (Brigham and Malpas, 1985) and simultaneously allows the individual to maintain his or her unique identity.

*Reciprocal Disclosure.* We have elaborated the initial decategorization model (Miller and Harrington, 1990a) to emphasize the reciprocal nature of this process. The initial model (Brewer and Miller, 1984) stressed the role of the interactants as outgroup perceivers and the importance of changes in how the other is viewed. Instructions to form an accurate impression of outgroup members, as opposed to forming an evaluation of them, produce individualization and more positive reactions. Furthermore, these instructional sets parallel results for cooperation (positive outcome dependency) and competition, respectively (Fiske and Neuberg, 1990; Miller *et al.*, 1985). Our elaboration addresses the role of self-disclosure in the individualization process and in distinguishing self from the ingroup. Hostility towards outgroup members is as much a function of deindividuation of the perceiver (Zimbardo, 1969) as it is of the lack of differentiation among targets. Although Hewstone and Brown (1986) have referred to the process of personalization as a 'chimera', we believe that, as described, it is just what was implied in Allport's (1954) condition for favourable contact effects. Of importance is not only how one perceives and categorizes others, but the knowledge that they too do the same with us. The teacher (or other interventionist) can play an important role in adding value to the other's perception of self.

## INTEGRATING THE RESEARCH

### Levels of Processes

It has been contended (Brown and Turner, 1981) that contacts between members of different social groups on an interpersonal basis as opposed to an intergroup basis represent two different domains that are controlled by different psychological processes. These authors argue further that contact at an interpersonal level is not likely to change relationships at an intergroup level. Moreover, they propose that interpersonal changes are an effect and not a cause of changes at the intergroup level. Clearly, this line of argument begs the question of how interpersonal and intergroup processes differ. We suggest that the characteristics of positive intergroup interactions are identical to characteristics of positive interpersonal interactions. If the contact contingencies discussed above are regarded as outcomes rather than conditions to be manipulated, namely, cooperative behaviours, shared roles and responsibilities, perceived similarities, peer-developed norms for equity, and discovery and treatment of the other as an individual, then the social skills and values involved in positive interpersonal interactions are the same as those involved in positive intergroup interaction. Therefore, conditions that promote the latter are related to those that promote positive interaction among ingroup and outgroup members.

Social identity theory is premised on the assumption that individuals seek to establish and maintain positive identity and that identity is composed both of personal characteristics and social category memberships. We suggest that whether the situation is best defined as interpersonal or intergroup is not determined by the numbers of members or categories present (Hewstone and Brown, 1986) but rather by the basis of the responses to one another. To the extent that one's attention is focused on personal aspects of identity, such a relationship is interpersonal; to the extent that it is focused on social aspects of identity, the relationship is intergroup. Because responding to others is, in part, a function of the dominance of different cues on attention, over the course of interaction, whether a relationship is interpersonal or intergroup is proportional rather than dichotomous. Lest the reader misinterpret us, we are not assuming that interpersonal responding is, by definition, positive and intergroup responding negative (nor the reverse). Interpersonal hostility and intergroup harmony are real states.

In the manner in which we define the terms, it is indeed possible for two (or more) members of different groups to be interacting such that one is responding interpersonally and the other in terms of category membership and, furthermore, that responding can shift rapidly in the situation for either party. Our 'proportional attention' criterion makes this a continuum and, therefore, probabilistic rather than discrete. Not only have some theorists (Tajfel, 1981) argued for the discontinuity of interpersonal and intergroup situations; they have also proposed that personal and social components of identity are discontinuous. Because stereotypes are the association of personal characteristics with social category memberships, the two domains are not as distinctive as some would argue. Furthermore, personal identity is not a fixed image that one carries into each situation; it is often derived in context from intragroup comparisons that serve to differentiate self from the group. In addition, aspects of identity interweave the personal-social dimension with two other dimensions: the extent to which characteristics are consistent with stereotypes and the extent to which they are similar to self. These features can best be understood, we argue, as continuous rather than discrete.

Identity is not a given but is negotiated in a social context, it is relational — who we are *vis-à-vis* others; and it is principally affective. Most of the research we have reviewed thus far can be interpreted in the light of these premises. If we assume that most people, particularly students, have fragile egos, then it is not surprising that competition, failure, status relations and the like can be threatening to one's esteem. Threat will increase task-focus, tension and non-cooperative behaviours (Deutsch and Krauss, 1962). The value of stereotypes, we believe, is less in how they help guide interactions than in how they shore up one's esteem. Self-esteem can be restored by the opportunity to discriminate against another group (Lemyre and Smith, 1985). A consistent theme of our recommendations has been to minimize threats to social esteem, while providing opportunities for personal esteem to be positively expressed without being at the expense of outgroup derogation.

We use a simple input-output model in which attention is the channel for inputs that can be perceptual, cognitive or motivational, and in which responding, the output, can be either internal (such as assumptions or affect) or external (such as verbal and non-verbal behaviour). By process, then, we mean an explanatory construct that systematically relates input to output in a predictable manner. We agree that there are often important differences in response, depending upon whether the other is categorized as the same as or different from the perceiver, but the process of categorization is similar in both cases. To avoid the problem of defining a situation by the response (post hoc), we focus instead on the situational demands on attention in order to develop a predictive model.

The criticism introduced at the beginning of this section referred again to the central problem of generalization that we have mentioned in the context of other issues. The argument was that changes at an interpersonal level will not affect changes at an intergroup level. That is, a friendship that develops between an ingroup and an outgroup member will not affect attitudes toward other outgroup members. However, as Slavin (1985) has demonstrated, friendships come to extend beyond one's immediate teammates in CTL and across category boundaries. Because of social networks, one comes to know and be accepted by the prior friends of one's new friends. We propose that the acquisition of the social skills and values we have discussed can serve to generalize across diverse social categories.

## Category Salience

Similar to the issues raised earlier with respect to the focus on classroom discussions of group level information and the typicality of outgroup members, some have proposed that it is critical for generalization that category salience remain high in the contact setting (Rothbart and John, 1985), whereas we have proposed that it be minimized during interaction (Brewer and Miller, 1984). Recognizing the merits of both sides of this debate, Pettigrew (1986) has asked instead when in the contact setting should category salience be reduced or enhanced. We proposed that initially category salience is typically high with respect to social categories such as gender or race and that outgroup members are perceived as representatives of their social category. The interaction itself, however, should minimize category salience in order to promote personalization of the individuals involved. That is, participants should have the opportunity to come to know each other as individuals. When formal evaluations of one another are utilized (as when dependent measures are collected in experimental studies, or when explicitly incorporated in a CTL procedure), then category salience can be enhanced to remind participants that the outgroup members they have come to know are typical of their respective groups. The purpose of enhanced salience at this point is to facilitate generalization of the positive affect associated with the personalized interaction to the outgroup. This model has been experimentally tested (Miller and Harrington, 1990b) and shown to be effective, not only in promoting positive interaction among participants but in promoting generalization to outgroup strangers with whom participants have not interacted. Now the model needs to be validated with real social categories.

## SUMMARY OF RECOMMENDATIONS

We have made a number of recommendations throughout this chapter for the use of teams in the classroom. These have been elaborated elsewhere (Miller and Harrington, 1990b), so we will summarize them here. We propose that when teams are formed, teachers use the unique characteristics of students for assignment. For example, those with common interests in particular aspects of a subject matter or those with different but complementary skills may form the basis of assignment. We propose that teams be frequently recomposed and that, whenever possible, students have opportunities to interact in less threatening dyads. We advocate the use of multiple or crosscutting categories, and caution teachers about assignments of task roles that converge with social category membership. Leadership roles can deliberately be varied so that all students have the opportunity to develop these skills. Caution is also suggested with respect to numerical composition of teams, even if this means that there will be some homogeneous teams along with equally balanced heterogeneous teams. We argue for a balance between the traditional task-focused orientation and an interpersonal orientation such that members are encouraged to come to know one another as individuals. To satisfy personal identity needs, we recommend some form of recognition for individual contributions as well as the use of team rewards to encourage cooperative behaviours. It is important to be sensitive to and minimize threats to social identity. The use of gain-scores is one way in which to minimize the threat of failure. We stress a focus on commonalities among students — the similarity of their problems and aspirations in the face of their tangible physical and cultural differences. Most important, we feel that the development of reciprocal disclosure is the foundation of mutual trust and respect.

Certainly, many of these recommendations require attention to the development of social skills. This will require special training and attention to group process, as well as modelling of these behaviours by teachers. These behaviours need to be reinforced. Therefore, rewards sufficient to induce cooperation, sharing, helping, asking for help and respecting other viewpoints should be an integral part of the reward system. Clearly, the teacher plays a critical role in the character development of students — in modelling, training and reinforcing the desired behaviours. Although teachers may be intrinsically motivated for this approach, in many cases it will be imperative that the school provide specialized training in the use of cooperative learning methods, training in modelling the skills that students would be expected to learn, and knowledge of the intricacies of intergroup relations, some of which have been articulated in this chapter. Furthermore, schools, if they value cooperative interracial interaction, must provide incentives and rewards to teachers to excel in these areas. Finally, we advocate a participative teaching style that involves students in the learning process and enables them to share with each other a responsibility for the selection and mastery of subject matter.

# REFERENCES

Allen, V.L. and Wilder, D.A. (1975) 'Categorization, Beliefs, Similarity, and Intergroup Discrimination', *Journal of Personality and Social Psychology*, 32, pp. 971–977.

Allport, G.W. (1954) *The Nature of Prejudice*, Reading, Mass., Addison-Wesley.

Amir, Y. (1969) 'Contact Hypothesis in Ethnic Relations', *Psychological Bulletin*, 71, pp. 319–341.

Anderson, J.P. and Perlman, D. (1973) 'Effects of an Adult's Preaching and Responsibility for Hypocritical Behavior on Children's Altruism', *Proceedings of the 81st Annual Convention, American Psychological Association*, 8, pp. 291–292.

Aronson, E., Blaney, N., Stephan, C., Sikes, J. and Snapp, M. (1978) *The Jigsaw Classroom*, Newbury Park, Calif., Sage.

Berger, J. and Zelditch, M., Jr (1985) *Status, Rewards, and Influence: How Expectations Organize Behavior*, San Francisco, Calif., Jossey-Bass.

Blake, R.R., Shepard, H.A. and Moulton, J.S. (1964) *Managing Intergroup Conflict in Industry*, Houston, Tex., Gulf Publications.

Brewer, M.B. and Miller, N. (1984) 'Beyond the Contact Hypothesis: Theoretical Perspectives on Desegregation', in N. Miller and M.B. Brewer (Eds), *Groups in Contact: The Psychology of Desegregation*, New York, Academic Press, pp. 281–302.

Brewer, M.B., Dull, V. and Lui, L. (1981) 'Perceptions of the Elderly: Stereotypes as Prototypes', *Journal of Personality and Social Psychology*, 41, pp. 656–670.

Brigham, J.C. and Malpas, R.S. (1985) 'The Role of Experience and Contact in the Recognition of Faces of Own and Other Race Persons', *Journal of Social Issues*, 41, pp. 139–155.

*Brown vs Board of Education* (1954) 347 US 483.

Brown, R. (1988) *Group Processes: Dynamics within and between Groups*, Oxford, Blackwell.

Brown, R. and Abrams, D. (1986) 'The Effects of Intergroup Similarity and Goal Interdependence on Intergroup Attitudes and Task Performance', *Journal of Experimental Social Psychology*, 22, pp. 78–92.

Brown, R.J. and Turner, J.C. (1979) 'The Criss-cross Categorization Effect in Intergroup Discrimination', *British Journal of Social and Clinical Psychology*, 18, pp. 371–383.

Brown, R.J. and Turner, J.C. (1981) 'Interpersonal and Intergroup Behavior', in J.C. Turner and H. Giles (Eds), *Intergroup Behaviour*, Oxford, Blackwell.

Brown, R.J. and Williams, J. (1984) 'Group Identifications: The Same Thing to All People?' *Human Relations*, 37, pp. 547–564.

Bryan, J.H. and Walbek, N. (1970) 'The Impact of Words and Deeds Concerning Altruism upon Children', *Child Development*, 41, pp. 747–757.

Byrne, D. (1971) *The Attraction Paradigm*, New York, Academic Press.

Caddick, B. (1982) 'Perceived Illegitimacy and Intergroup Relations', in H. Tajfel (Ed.), *Social Identity and Intergroup Relations*, Cambridge, Cambridge University Press.

Campbell, D.T. (1958) 'Common Fate, Similarity, and Other Indices of the Stress of Aggregates of Persons as Social Entities', *Behavioral Science*, 3, pp. 14–25.

Campbell, D.T. (1965) 'Ethnocentric and Other Altruistic Motives', in D. Levine (Ed.), *Nebraska Symposium on Motivation*, Vol. 13, Lincoln, Neb., University of Nebraska Press, pp. 283–311.

Campbell, D.T. (1967) 'Stereotypes and Perceptions of Group Differences', *American Psychologist*, 22, pp. 812–829.

Cantor, N. and Mischel, W. (1977) 'Traits as Prototypes: Effects on Recognition Memory', *Journal of Personality and Social Psychology*, 35, pp. 38–48.

Cohen, E.G. (1972) 'Interracial Interaction Disability', *Human Relations*, 25, pp. 9–24.

Cohen, E.G. (1982) 'Expectation States and Interracial Interaction in School Settings', *Annual Review of Sociology*, 8, pp. 209–235.

Condor, S. and Brown, R. (1988) 'Psychological Processes in Intergroup Conflict', in W. Stroebe, A. Kruglanski, D. Bar-Tal and M. Hewstone (Eds), *The Social Psychology of Intergroup Conflict*, New York, Springer-Verlag, pp. 3–26.

Cook, S.W. (1969) 'Motives in a Conceptual Analysis of Attitude-Related Behavior', in W.J. Arnold and D. Levine (Eds), *Nebraska Symposium on Motivation*, Vol. 18, Lincoln, Neb., University of Nebraska Press.

Cook, S.W. (1978) 'Interpersonal and Attitudinal Outcomes in Cooperating Interracial Groups', *Journal of Research and Development in Education*, 12, pp. 97–113.

Cook, S.W. (1984) 'Cooperative Interaction in Multiethnic Contexts', in N. Miller and M. Brewer (Eds), *Groups in Contact: The Psychology of School Desegregation*, Orlando, Fla., Academic Press, pp. 156–185.

Crocker, J., Hannah, D.B. and Weber, R. (1983) 'Person Memory and Causal Attribution', *Journal of Personality and Social Psychology*, 44, pp. 55–66.

Deaux, K. and Emswiller, T. (1974) 'Explanations of Successful Performance on Sex-linked Tasks: What Is Skill for the Male Is Luck for the Female', *Journal of Social Psychology*, 29, pp. 80–85.

Deci, E.L. (1975) *Intrinsic Motivation*, New York, Plenum.

Deutsch, M. and Krauss, R.M. (1962) 'Studies of Interpersonal Bargaining', *Journal of Conflict Resolution*, 6, pp. 52–76.

DeVries, D., Edwards, K. and Slavin, R. (1978) 'Biracial Learning Teams and Race Relations in the Classroom: Four Field Experiments in Teams-Games-Tournament', *Journal of Educational Psychology*, 70, pp. 356–362.

Dion, K.L. (1973) 'Cohesiveness as a Determinant of Ingroup-Outgroup Bias', *Journal of Personality and Social Psychology*, 28, pp. 163–171.

Dustin, D.W. and Davis, H.P. (1970) 'Evaluative Bias in Group and Individual Competition', *Journal of Social Psychology*, 80, pp. 103–108.

Duval, S. and Duval, V.H. (1983) *Consistency and Cognition: A Theory of Causal Attribution*, Hillsdale, N.J., Lawrence Erlbaum Associates.

Epstein, J.L. (1985) 'After the Bus Arrives: Resegregation in Desegregated Schools', *Journal of Social Issues*, 41, pp. 23–43.

Ferguson, C.K. and Kelley, H.H. (1964) 'Significant Factors in Overevaluation of Own Group's Product', *Journal of Abnormal and Social Psychology*, 69, pp. 223–228.

Fischer, W.F. (1963) 'Sharing in Preschool Children as a Function of Amount and Type of Reinforcement', *Genetic Psychology Monographs*, 68, pp. 215–245.

Fiske, S.T. and Neuberg, S.L. (1990) 'A Continuum of Impression Formation, from Category-based to Individuating Processes: Influences of Information and Motivation on Attention and Interpretation', in M.P. Zanna (Ed.), *Advances in Experimental Social Psychology*, 23, New York, Academic Press, pp. 1–74.

Furnham, A. (1982) 'Explanations for Unemployment in Britain', *European Journal of Social Psychology*, 12, pp. 335–352.

Gaertner, S.L., Mann, J., Murrell, A. and Dovidio, J.F. (1989) 'Reducing Intergroup Bias: The Benefits of Recategorization', *Journal of Personality and Social Psychology*, 57, pp. 239–249.

Hamilton, D.L. and Rose, T.L. (1980) 'Illusory Correlation and the Maintenance of Stereotypic Beliefs', *Journal of Personality and Social Psychology*, 39, pp. 832–845.

Hewstone, M. and Brown, R. (1986) 'Contact Is Not Enough: An Intergroup Perspective on the "Contact Hypothesis",' in M. Hewstone and R. Brown (Eds), *Contact and Conflict in Intergroup Encounters*, New York, Basil Blackwell, pp. 1–44.

Hewstone, M. and Ward, C. (1985) 'Ethnocentrism and Causal Attribution in Southeast Asia', *Journal of Personality and Social Psychology*, 48, pp. 614–623.

Hoffman, M.L. (1958) 'Similarity of Personality: A Basis for Interpersonal Attraction?' *Sociometry*, 21, pp. 300–308.

Homans, G.C. (1961) *Social Behavior*, New York, Harcourt, Brace.

Howard, J.W. and Rothbart, M. (1980) 'Social Categorization and Memory for In-group and Out-group Behavior', *Journal of Personality and Social Psychology*, 38, pp. 301–310.

Johnson, D.W., Johnson, R. and Maruyama, G. (1983) 'Interdependence and Interpersonal Attraction among Heterogeneous and Homogeneous Individuals: A Theoretical Formulation and Meta-analysis of the Research', *Review of Educational Research*, 52, pp. 5–54.

Kahn, A.S. and Ryen, A.H. (1972) 'Factors Influencing the Bias toward One's Own Group, *International Journal of Group Tensions*, 2, pp. 33–50.

Kanter, R.M. (1977) 'Some Effects of Proportions on Group Life: Skewed Sex Ratios and Responses to Token Women', *American Journal of Sociology*, 82, pp. 965–991.

Latane, B. and Nida, S. (1980) 'Social Impact Theory and Group Influence: A Social Engineering Perspective', in P. Paulus (Ed.), *Psychology of Group Influences*, New York, Lawrence Erlbaum, pp. 3–34.

Lemyre, L. and Smith, P.M. (1985) 'Intergroup Discrimination and Self-Esteem in the Minimal Group Paradigm', *Journal of Personality and Social Psychology*, 49, pp. 660–670.

Lerner, M.J. (1965) 'Evaluation of Performance as a Function of Performance Reward and Attractiveness', *Journal of Personality and Social Psychology*, 1, pp. 355–360.

Linville, P.W. and Jones, E.E. (1980) 'Polarized Appraisal of Out-group Members', *Journal of Personality and Social Psychology*, 38, pp. 689–703.

Lott, A.J. and Lott, B.E. (1965) 'Group Cohesiveness as Interpersonal Attraction: A Review of Relationships with Antecedent and Consequent Variables', *Psychological Bulletin*, 64, pp. 259–309.

Lott, A. and Lott, B. (1968) 'A Learning Theory Approach to Interpersonal Attitudes', in A. Greenwald, T. Brock and T. Ostrom (Eds), *Psychological Foundations of Attitudes*, New York, Academic Press.

Lott, A.J. (1961) 'Group Cohesiveness: A Learning Phenomenon', *The Journal of Social Psychology*, 55, pp. 275–286.

Marks, G., Miller, N. and Maruyama, G. (1981) 'The Effect of Physical Attractiveness on Assumptions of Similarity', *Journal of Personality and Social Psychology*, 41, pp. 198–212.

Miller, N. and Davidson-Podgorny, G. (1987) 'Theoretical Models of Intergroup Relations and the Use of Cooperative Teams as an Intervention for Desegregated Settings', in C. Hendrick (Ed.), *Group Processes and Intergroup Relations*, Beverly Hills, Calif., Sage, pp. 41–67.

Miller, N. and Harrington, H.J. (1990a) A Situational Identity Perspective on Cultural Diversity and Teamwork in the Classroom', in S. Sharan (Ed.), *Cooperative Learning: Theory and Application*, New York, Praeger Press, pp. 39–75.

Miller, N. and Harrington, H.J. (1990b) 'A Model of Social Category Salience for Intergroup Relations: Empirical Tests of Relevant Variables', in P. Drenth, J. Sergeant and R. Takens (Eds), *European Perspectives in Psychology*, Vol. 3, Chichester, Wiley, pp. 205–220.

Miller, N., Brewer, M.B. and Edwards, K. (1985) 'Cooperative Interaction in Desegregated Settings: A Laboratory Analogue', *Journal of Social Issues*, 41, pp. 63–81.

Miller, N., Rogers, M. and Hennigan, K. (1983) 'Increasing Interracial Acceptance: Using Cooperative Games in Desegregated Elementary Schools', in L. Bickman (Ed.), *Applied Social Psychology Annual*, 4. Beverly Hills, Calif., Sage, pp. 199–216.

Myrdal, G. (1944) *An American Dilemma: The Negro Problem and American Democracy*, 2 vols, New York, Random House.

Norvell, N. and Worchel, S. (1981) 'A Reexamination of the Relation between Equal Status Contact and Intergroup Attraction', *Journal of Personality and Social Psychology*, 41, pp. 902–908.

Oakes, J. (1985) *Keeping Track: How Schools Structure Inequality*, New Haven, Conn., Yale University Press.

Oakes, P.J. and Turner, J.C. (1980) 'Social Categorization and Intergroup Behaviour: Does the Minimal Intergroup Discrimination Make Social Identity More Positive?', *European Journal of Social Psychology*, 10, pp. 295–301.

Pettigrew, T.F. (1979) 'The Ultimate Attribution Error: Extending Allport's Cognitive Analysis of Prejudice', *Personality and Social Psychology Bulletin*, 5, pp. 461–476.

Pettigrew, T.F. (1986) 'The Intergroup Contact Hypothesis Reconsidered', in M. Hewstone and R. Brown (Eds), *Contact, Conflict, and Intergroup Relations*, Oxford, Blackwell, pp. 169–195.

Pyszczynski, T.A. and Greenberg, J. (1981) 'Role of Disconfirmed Expectancies in the Instigation of Attributional Processing', *Journal of Personality and Social Psychology*, 40, pp. 31–38.

Pyszcznski, T. and Greenberg, J. (1987) 'Toward an Integration of Cognitive and Motivational Perspectives on Social Inference: A Biased Hypothesis Testing Model', in L. Berkowitz (Ed.), *Advances in Experimental Social Psychology*, New York, Academic Press.

Rabbie, J.M. and Horowitz, M. (1969) 'Arousal of Ingroup-Outgroup Bias by a Chance Win or Loss', *Journal of Personality and Social Psychology*, 13, pp. 269–277.

Rabbie, J.M. and Wilkens, G. (1971) 'Intergroup Competition and Its Effect in Intragroup and Intergroup Relations', *European Journal of Social Psychology*, 1, pp. 215–234.

Rabbie, J.M., Benoist, F., Osterbaan, H. and Visser, L. (1974) 'Differential Power and Effects of Expected Competitive and Cooperative Intergroup Interaction upon Intragroup and Outgroup Attitudes', *Journal of Personality and Social Psychology*, 30, pp. 46–56.

Rogers, M., Hennigan, K., Bowman, C. and Miller, N. (1984) 'Intergroup Acceptance in Classroom and Playground Settings,' in N. Miller and M. Brewer (Eds), *Groups in Contact: The Psychology of Desegregation*, New York, Academic Press, pp. 214–227.

Rokeach, M. (1960) *The Open and Closed Mind: Investigations into the Nature of Belief Systems and Personality Systems*, New York, Basic Books.

Rose, T.L. (1981) 'Cognitive and Dyadic Processes in Intergroup Contact', in D. Hamilton (Ed.), *Cognitive Processes in Stereotyping and Intergroup Behavior*, Hillsdale, N.J., Lawrence Erlbaum Associates.

Rosenbaum, M.E. (1986) 'The Repulsion Hypothesis: On the Non-Development of Relationships', *Journal of Personality and Social Psychology*, 51, pp. 1156–1166.

Rothbart, M. and John, O.P. (1985) 'Social Categorization and Behavioral Episodes: A Cognitive Analysis of the Effects of Intergroup Contact', *Journal of Social Issues*, 41, pp. 81–104.

Rothbart, M., Evans, M. and Fulero, S. (1979) 'Recall for Confirming Events: Memory Processes and the Maintenance of Social Stereotypes', *Journal of Experimental Social Psychology*, 15, pp. 343–355.

Ryen, A.H. and Kahn, A.S. (1975) 'The Effects of Intergroup Orientation on Group Attitudes and Proxemic Behavior: A Test of Two Models', *Journal of Personality and Social Psychology*, 31, pp. 302–310.

Sachdev, I. and Bourhis, R.Y. (1984) 'Minimal Majorities and Minorities', *European Journal of Social Psychology*, 14, pp. 35–52.

Sachdev, I. and Bourhis, R.Y. (1985) 'Social Categorization and Power Differentials in Group Relations', *European Journal of Social Psychology*, 15, pp. 415–434.

Sachdev, I. and Bourhis, R.Y. (1987) 'Status Differentials and Intergroup Behavior', *European Journal of Social Psychology*, 17, pp. 277–293.

Scanlan, T. and Lewthwaite, R. (1984) 'Social Psychological Aspects of Competition for Male Youth Sport Participants: I. Predictors of Competitive Stress', *Journal of Sport Psychology*, 6, pp. 208–226.

Sears, D.O. (1983) 'The Person-Positivity Bias', *Journal of Personality and Social Psychology*, 44, pp. 233–250.

Shapiro, A. and Madsen, M.C. (1969) 'Cooperative and Competitive Behavior of Kibbutz and Urban Children in Israel', *Child Development*, 40, pp. 609–617.

Sherif, M. (1967) *Group Conflict and Cooperation*, London, Routledge and Kegan Paul.

Simmons, R. (1978) 'Blacks and High Self-Esteem: A Puzzle', *Social Psychology*, 41, pp. 54–57.

Simon, B. and Brown, R.J. (1987) 'Perceived Intragroup Homogeneity in Minority-Majority Contexts', *Journal of Personality and Social Psychology*, 56, pp. 54–59.

Skevington, S. (1981) 'Intergroup Relations and Nursing', *European Journal of Social Psychology*, 11, pp. 43–59.

Slavin, R.E. (1985) 'Cooperative Learning: Applying Contact Theory in Desgregated Schools', *Journal of Social Issues*, 41, pp. 45–62.

Smeaton, G., Byrne, D. and Murnen, S.K. (1989) 'The Repulsion Hypothesis Revisited: Similarity Irrelevance or Dissimilarity Bias', *Journal of Personality and Social Psychology*, 56, pp. 54–59.

Snyder, C.R. and Fromkin, H.L. (1980) *Uniqueness: The Pursuit of Human Difference*, New York, Plenum Press.

Snyder, M. and Swann, W.B. (1978) 'Behavioral Confirmation in Social Interaction: From Social Perception to Social Reality', *Journal of Experimental Social Psychology*, 14, pp. 148–162.

Steiner, I.D. (1972) *Group Process and Productivity*, New York, Academic Press.

Stephan, W.G. and Stephan, C.W. (1984) 'Intergroup Anxiety', in N. Miller and M.B. Brewer (Eds), *Groups in Contact: The Psychology of Desegregation*, New York, Academic Press, pp. 229–255.

Stephan, W.G. and Stephan, C.W. (1985) 'Intergroup Anxiety', *Journal of Social Issues*, 41, pp. 157–175.

Stotland, E. (1959) 'Peer Groups and Reactions to Power Figures', in D. Cartwright (Ed.), *Studies in Social Power*, Ann Arbor, Mich., University of Michigan Press.

Sumner, W.G. (1906) *Folkways*, New York, Ginn.

Tajfel, H. (1978) *Differentiation between Social Groups: Studies in the Social Psychology of Intergroup Relations*, London, Academic Press.

Tajfel, H. (1981) *Human Groups and Social Categories*, Cambridge, Cambridge University Press.

Tajfel, H. and Turner, J.C. (1985) 'The Social Identity Theory of Intergroup Behavior', in S. Worchel and W.G. Austin (Ed.), *Psychology of Intergroup Relations*, Chicago, Ill., Nelson-Hall, pp. 7–24.

Tajfel, H., Sheikh, A.A. and Gardner, R.C. (1964) 'Content of Stereotypes and the Inferences of Similarity between Members of Stereotyped Groups', *Acta Psychologica*, 22, pp. 191–201.

Taylor, D.M. and Dubé, L. (1986) 'Two Faces of Identity: The "I" and the "We"', *Journal of Social Issues*, 42, pp. 81–98.

Taylor, S.E., Fiske, S.T., Etcoff, N.L. and Rinderman, A.J. (1978) 'Categorical Bases of Person Memory and Stereotyping', *Journal of Personality and Social Psychology*, 36, pp. 778–793.

Thibaut, J.W. and Kelley, H.H. (1959) *The Social Psychology of Groups*, New York, Wiley.

Tjosvold, D. (1981) 'Unequal Power Relationships within a Cooperative or Competitive Context', *Journal of Applied Social Psychology*, 11, pp. 137–150.

Turner, J.C. (1975) 'Social Comparison and Social Identity: Some Perspectives for Intergroup Behavior', *European Journal of Social Psychology*, 5, pp. 5–34.

Turner, J.C. (1978) 'Social Comparison, Similarity and Ingroup Favoritism', in H. Tajfel (Ed.), *Differentiation between Social Groups*, London, Academic Press.

Turner, J.C. (1981) 'The Experimental Social Psychology of Intergroup Behavior', in J.C. Turner and H. Giles (Eds), *Intergroup Behavior*, Chicago, Ill., University of Chicago Press.

Turner, J.C. (1982) 'Towards a Cognitive Redefinition of the Social Group', in H. Tajfel (Ed.), *Social Identity and Intergroup Relations*, Cambridge, Cambridge University Press, pp. 15–40.

Turner, J.C. and Brown, R. (1978) 'Social Status, Cognitive Alternatives and Intergroup Relations', in H. Tajfel (Ed.), *Differentiation between Social Groups*, London, Academic Press.

Vanbeselaere, N. (1987) 'The Effects of Dichotomous and Crossed Social Categorization upon Intergroup Discrimination', *European Journal of Social Psychology*, 17, pp. 143–156.

Weber, R. and Crocker, J. (1983) 'Cognitive Processes in the Revision of Stereotypic Beliefs', *Journal of Personality and Social Psychology*, 45, pp. 961–977.

Weigel, R.H. and Howes, P.W. (1985) 'Conceptions of Racial Prejudice: Symbolic Racism Reconsidered', *Journal of Social Issues*, 41, pp. 117–138.

Weiner, B. (1982) 'The Emotional Consequences of Causal Attributions', in M. Clark and S.T. Fiske (Eds), *Affect and Cognition: The 17the Annual Carnegie Symposium on Cognition*, Hillsdale, N.J., Lawrence Erlbaum Associates.

Whitley, B.E., Schofield, J.W. and Snyder, H.N. (1984) 'Peer Preferences in a Desegregated School: A Round Robin Analysis', *Journal of Personality and Social Psychology*, 46, pp. 799–810.

Wilder, D.A. (1978) 'Perceiving Persons as a Group: Effects on Attributions of Causality and Beliefs', *Social Psychology*, 1, pp. 13–23.

Wilder, D.A. (1984) 'Intergroup Contact: The Typical Member and the Exception to the Rule', *Journal of Experimental Social Psychology*, 20, pp. 177–194.

Wilder, D.A. (1986) 'Social Categorization: Implications for Creation and Reduction of Intergroup Bias', in L. Berkowitz (Ed.), *Advances in Experimental Social Psychology*, New York, Academic Press, 19, pp. 291–355.

Wilder, D.A. and Allen, V.L. (1978) 'Group Membership and Preference for Information about Other Persons', *Personality and Social Psychology Bulletin*, 4, pp. 106–110.

Wilder, D.A. and Shapiro, P. (1989) 'The Role of Competition-Induced Anxiety in Limiting the Beneficial Impact of Positive Behavior to an Out-group Member', *Journal of Personality and Social Psychology*, 56, pp. 60–69.

Wodarski, J.S., Hamblin, R.L., Buckholdt, D.R. and Ferritor, P.E. (1973) 'Individual Consequences versus Different Social Consequences Contingent on the Performance of Low-Achieving Group Members', *Journal of Applied Psychology*, 3, pp. 276–290.

Worchel, S. (1979) 'Intergroup Cooperation', in W. Austin and S. Worchel (Eds), *The Social Psychology of Intergroup Relations*, Monterey, Calif., Brooks/Cole., pp. 288–304.

Worchel, S. and Norvell, N. (1980) 'Effect of Perceived Environmental Conditions during Cooperation on Intergroup Attraction', *Journal of Personality and Social Psychology*, 38, pp. 764–772.

Worchel, S., Andreoli, V.A. and Folger, R. (1977) 'Intergroup Cooperation and Intergroup Attraction: The Effect of Previous Interaction and Outcome of Combined Effort', *Journal of Experimental Social Psychology*, 13, pp. 131–140.

Worchel, S., Lind, A. and Kaufman, K. (1975) 'Evaluations of Group Products as a Function of Expectations of Group Longevity, Outcome of Competition, and Publicity of Evaluations', *Journal of Personality and Social Psychology*, 31, pp. 1089–1097.

Word, C.O., Zanna, M.P. and Cooper, J. (1974) 'The Nonverbal Mediation of Self-Fulfilling Prophecies in Interracial Interaction', *Journal of Experimental Social Psychology*, 10, pp. 109–120.

Zimbardo, P. (1969) 'The Human Choice: Individuation, Reason, and Order versus Deindividuation, Impulse, and Chaos', in W. Arnold and D. Levine (Eds), *Nebraska Symposium on Motivation*, Vol. 17, Lincoln, Neb., University of Nebraska Press.

# 9. Social Interdependence and Crossethnic Relationships

DAVID W. JOHNSON AND ROGER T. JOHNSON

To understand the relationship between social interdependence and ethnic relationships, theory, research and practice are all needed. For the past twenty years we have formulated a basic theoretical model of crossethnic relationships, conducted a series of controlled experimental studies to validate the theory, and applied the results in schools throughout North America, Europe and other countries. We have attempted to follow a process of theorizing to summarize and guide research on social interdependence, conducting research to validate or disconfirm the theory, and applying cooperative learning in classrooms and schools to reveal inadequacies that, in turn, lead to refinement of the theory, a new set of research studies and additional fine-tuning of cooperative learning.

In this chapter we present our theoretical model of the processes of acceptance and rejection. We then present the results of our research programme to validate the theoretical model. Finally, we present the results of a meta-analysis that summarizes the findings of *all* studies that have been conducted on social interdependence and crossethnic relationships.

## FORMING AND MAINTAINING POSITIVE CROSSETHNIC RELATIONSHIPS

A prerequisite for studying the relationship between social interdependence and crossethnic relationships is the formulation of a theoretical model explaining why a relationship should exist and detailing the mediating variables. An explanation of the antecedents and causes of positive crossethnic relationships may be found in the examination of three factors: preinteraction attitudes, physical proximity, and actual interaction (Johnson and Johnson, 1980, 1989; Johnson, Johnson and Maruyama, 1983, 1984). It may be posited (for the specific research studies on which our theorizing is based see Johnson and Johnson, 1989):

1   Preinteraction attitudes influence interpersonal attraction. Individuals
    from different ethnic groups meet each other with impressions of what
    each other is like. Although preinteraction attitudes may be either posi-
    tive or negative, frequently crossethnic impressions are negative.
2   Physical proximity is a necessary but not sufficient condition for the
    formation of caring and committed relationships. If physical proximity
    were sufficient to create positive crossethnic relationships, all theorizing
    could end at this point. It is not. Physical proximity among ethnically
    heterogeneous individuals is the beginning of an opportunity, but like all
    opportunities, it carries a risk of making things worse as well as the
    possibility of making things better. Physical proximity does not mean that
    minority and majority individuals will like and accept each other *or* that
    they will automatically stigmatize, stereotype and reject each other.
3   Whether positive relationship results from proximity depends on whether
    crossethnic interaction takes place within a cooperative, competitive or
    individualistic context. A cooperative context promotes a process of
    acceptance while competitive and individualistic contexts promote a pro-
    cess of rejection.

## SOCIAL JUDGMENT THEORY

A process of acceptance or rejection takes place depending on whether interaction occurs within a context of positive, negative or no interdependence (Johnson and Johnson, 1980, 1989; Johnson, Johnson and Maruyama, 1983, 1984). The
process of acceptance may be defined as relationships becoming more and more
positive and committed as interaction continues (see Figure 1). The process of acceptance begins with positive interdependence — the perception that either all gain
or all lose on the basis of joint efforts, that is, 'you sink or swim together.' Striving for
mutual benefits requires promotive interaction — assisting, helping, sharing and
encouraging each other's efforts to achieve. Promotive interaction may be contrasted with oppositional interaction (individuals attempting to obstruct and
frustrate each other's efforts to achieve), and no interaction (individuals ignoring
— neither facilitating nor frustrating — each other's efforts to achieve). It may be
posited that positive interdependence leads to promotive interaction, which in
turn leads to interpersonal attraction via a number of mediating variables. More
specifically, the following propositions may be made.

*The relationship between cooperative experiences and interpersonal attraction*
*may be partially caused by the frequent and accurate communication occurring*
*among collaborators.* Frequent, accurate and open communication is (1) required
to coordinate efforts to maximize mutual benefit and gain; (2) involves giving and
receiving help, assistance, encouragement and support; and (3) results in understanding each other's needs, interests, perspectives, abilities and reasoning processes. To coordinate efforts to achieve, collaborators communicate as they
encourage, support, help and assist each other's efforts to achieve. Effective
coordination and communication requires understanding each other's needs,
interests, perspectives, abilities and reasoning processes. Doing so results in
realistically (1) knowing each other on a personal level and (2) seeing each other

*Figure 1. Process of Acceptance*

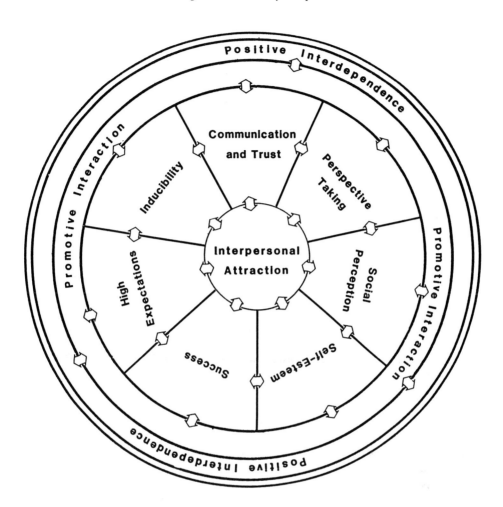

as complexes of qualities (who persons are) rather than as complexes of perform-ances (what persons do). The coordination, mutual helping and personal rela-tionships result in interpersonal attraction among group members. Thus the more frequent, accurate and open the communication aimed at facilitating each other's success, the greater the interpersonal attraction.

*The relationship between cooperative experiences and interpersonal attraction may be partially caused by the accuracy with which collaborators are able to understand each other's perspectives.* Social perspective-taking is the ability to understand how a situation appears to another person and how that person is reacting cognitively and emotionally to the situation. The opposite of per-spective-taking is egocentrism, the embeddedness in one's own viewpoint to the extent that one is unaware of other points of view. Egocentrism has been found to be related to competitive and individualistic attitudes and efforts, while perspective-taking accuracy and ability have been found to be related to coopera-tive attitudes and efforts. Mutual understanding resulting from efforts to enhance mutual benefit increases liking. Thus, within a cooperative context, the more accurate the understanding of others' perspectives, the greater the interpersonal attraction.

*The relationship between cooperative experiences and interpersonal attraction may be partially caused by the mutual influence that occurs among collaborators.* Inducibility exists when individuals are receptive to the influence attempts of others. Cooperation tends to increase openness to be influenced by others, while competitive and individualistic experiences tend to create resistance to others' influence. Being influenced to engage in more effective and efficient actions (thereby being more successful) creates appreciation and liking. Within a cooperative context, therefore, the greater the inducibility among individuals, the greater the interpersonal attraction.

*The relationship between cooperative experiences and interpersonal attraction may be partially caused by the differentiated and multidimensional views of each other held by collaborators.* The more differentiated (taking into account many different characteristics), dynamic (being modified from situation to situation) and realistic (accurate) one's views of collaborators, the more one likes and identifies with them and the greater the group cohesion. The more monopolistic (single-dimensional) and static (unchanging from situation to situation) the views of others, the less they will be liked. In competitive and individualistic situations, individuals tend to organize information about others on the basis of the few characteristics most salient for individual high performance. The perceived distribution of ability becomes polarized and shared. A person is a winner or a loser, but not in between. Within cooperative situations, a multidimensional, dynamic and realistic view of others is generated. Negative stereotypes tend to lose their primary potency and to be reduced when interactions reveal enough detail that group members are seen as individuals rather than as members of an ethnic group. All collaborators become 'one of us'. In other words, cooperation widens the sense of who is in the group, and 'they' become 'we'.

*The relationship between cooperative experiences and interpersonal attraction may be partially caused by the higher self-esteem of collaborators.* The better one is known, liked and supported, the higher one's self-esteem tends to be. The higher one's self-esteem, the higher one's acceptance of and liking for others and the lower one's prejudices against others. Cooperation promotes higher self-esteem and more healthy procedures for deriving self-esteem than do competitive and individualistic experiences.

*The relationship between cooperative experiences and interpersonal attraction may be partially caused by the greater productivity of collaborators.* The greater one's psychological success, the more one likes those who have contributed to and facilitated that success. Cooperation tends to produce higher achievement and greater productivity than do competitive or individualistic efforts.

*Finally, the relationship between cooperative experiences and interpersonal attraction may be partially caused by the expectations for enjoyable and productive interactions in the future.* The more one expects future interactions to be positive and productive, the more one likes others.

The process of rejection may be defined as relationships becoming more and more negative as proximity and interaction continue (see Figure 2). It results from interaction within a context of negative or no goal interdependence. Negative goal interdependence promotes oppositional interaction, and no goal interaction results in no interaction with peers. Both lead to an avoidance of and/or inaccurate

*Figure 2.  Process of Rejection*

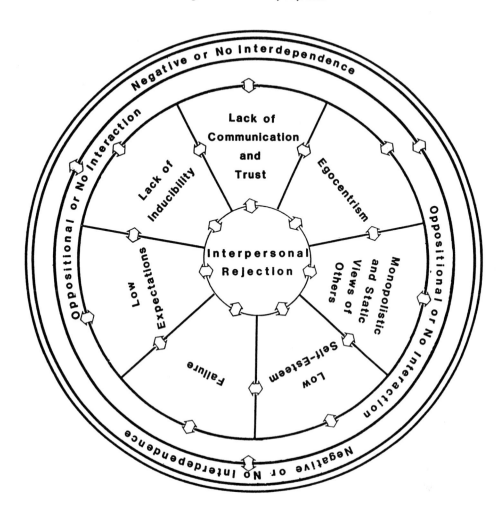

communication, egocentrism, resistance to influence, monopolistic, static and stereotyped views of others, feelings of psychological rejection and low self-esteem, psychological failure, and expectations of distasteful and unpleasant interactions with others. All of these factors promote dislike and rejection among individuals.

The factors involved in the processes of acceptance and rejection are interdependent and each influences the others. Deutsch (1985), for example, states that positive interdependence creates a variety of interrelated and interdependent outcomes, which in turn create greater positive interdependence. Any part of the process elicits all other parts of the process. Frequent and open communication results in better understanding of each other's perspectives, and increased understanding of each other's perspectives leads to more frequent and open communication. The more multidimensional and dynamic the perception of each other, the higher the self-esteem of everyone involved, which in turn makes it easier to have multidimensional and dynamic views of each other. The many variables related to positive interdependence are interconnected so that they can influence/cause each other as well as further positive interdependence. The variables are a 'gestalt', with each variable being a door into the whole process.

## OUR RESEARCH ON SOCIAL INTERDEPENDENCE AND CROSSETHNIC RELATIONSHIPS

To confirm or disconfirm our model of the processes of acceptance and rejection, we have conducted a twenty-year programme of research consisting of over eighty studies (see Johnson and Johnson, 1989). Several of those studies were highly controlled field-experimental studies of crossethnic relationships. The measures of interpersonal attraction used included (1) an observation system that classified student-student interactions into task, maintenance and social statements; (2) an observation system that classified student-student interactions during classroom free time; (3) a social-schema, figure-placement measure consisting of having students position all class members on a classroom diagram according to where they would be during classroom free time; and (4) a sociometric measure of interpersonal attraction consisting of having students write down the names of three students they would like to work with in a future learning group. Our studies addressed five questions.

The first question we addressed was whether cooperative, competitive and individualistic experiences differentially affect crossethnic interaction and relationships. Cooper *et al.* (1980) compared the effects of cooperative, competitive and individualistic experiences on crossethnic relationships. Sixty students were randomly assigned to conditions stratifying for sex, ethnic membership and ability. The students were lower- and working-class students from an inner-city junior high school. The same curriculum was used in and teachers were rotated across all conditions. Students participated in the study for three hours a day (English, geography and science classes) for fifteen instructional days. The results indicated that cooperation promoted more positive crossethnic relationships than did competitive or individualistic experiences. In a similar study Johnson and Johnson (1982) randomly assigned seventy-six students to cooperative, competitive and individualistic conditions on a stratified random basis, controlling for ethnic membership, ability and sex. The same curriculum was used in and teachers were rotated across all conditions. Both behavioural and sociometric measures of interpersonal attraction were used. Students participated in two instructional units for forty-five minutes a day for fifteen instructional days. Behavioural and attitudinal measures were taken for crossethnic interaction during the instructional sessions and during daily free-time periods. They found that cooperative learning promoted more crossethnic interaction and more positive crossethnic attitudes and relationships than did competitive or individualistic learning.

The second question was whether or not intergroup competition increased or decreased positive crossethnic relationships. Two studies were conducted comparing intergroup competition and intergroup cooperation. Johnson, Johnson, Tiffany and Zaidman (1984) randomly assigned fifty-one fourth-grade students to intergroup competition and cooperation conditions, stratifying for minority status and sex. The same curriculum was used in all conditions and teachers were rotated across conditions. Students participated in the study for fifty-five minutes a day for ten instructional days. Both behavioural and sociometric measures of interpersonal liking were used. While there were no differences for within-group crossethnic liking, there was more inclusion of minority students and greater crossethnic liking for members of different cooperating groups within the intergroup cooperation condition. In other words, the positive crossethnic relationship established in the cooperative groups tended to generalize to other crossethnic relationships more within the intergroup cooperation than within the intergroup competition condition. In a follow-up study Johnson and Johnson (1985) randomly assigned forty-eight sixth-grade students to intergroup cooperation and competition conditions, stratifying for minority status, ability and sex. The same curriculum was used in and teachers were rotated across all conditions. The students participated in the study for fifty-five minutes a day for ten days. Both behavioural and paper-and-pencil measures of interpersonal attraction were used. More positive crossethnic relationships within and between groups were promoted by intergroup cooperation than by intergroup competition.

The third question was whether or not minority students who achieved at a lower level than their majority classmates would be liked. When minority students achieve at a lower level than their majority classmates, they have, in essence, two strikes against them. They may be disliked because they are from a low status minority, and, additionally, they may be disliked because their low achievement decreases the likelihood of the group winning. Johnson, Johnson, Tiffany and Zaidman (1983) compared the effects of cooperative and individualistic learning experiences on the relationship between majority students and lower achieving minority peers. Forty-eight students (twenty minority and twenty-eight majority) were assigned to conditions on a stratified random basis, controlling for ethnic membership, sex, social class and ability level. They participated in the study for fifty-five minutes a day for fifteen instructional days. The same curriculum was used in and teachers were rotated across all conditions. Both behavioural and sociometric measures of interpersonal attraction were used. Minority students did in fact achieve at lower levels than did their majority peers. Yet more positive crossethnic interaction and relationships were found in the cooperative than in the individualistic condition. Johnson, Johnson, Tiffany and Zaidman (1984) found that intergroup competition accentuates the salience of ability and status within cooperative learning groups. Intergroup cooperation produced more participation and more inclusion of minority students than did intergroup cooperation. Although minority students achieved at a lower level than majority students, perceived themselves to be less able as students, and were perceived as needing more academic help, they were viewed as being equally valuable members of the learning groups in the intergroup cooperation condition. In the intergroup competition condition they were viewed as being less valuable members.

The fourth question was whether or not the presence of conflict within cooperative groups would create divisive crossethnic relationships. Within cooperative groups disagreements and intellectual challenges occur frequently. Such conflicts are 'moments of truth' that strengthen relationships or create divisiveness and hostility. Low achieving students may be at a disadvantage in academic conflicts. When low achievers are minority students, academic conflicts could (1) increase crossethnic hostility and rejection and (2) lower the academic self-esteem of minority students. Johnson, Johnson and Tiffany (1984) compared the effects of controversy, debate and individualistic learning on crossethnic relationships. Seventy-two sixth-grade students were randomly assigned to conditions on a stratified random basis controlling for sex, reading ability and ethnic membership. The same curriculum was used in and teachers were rotated across all conditions. Both behavioural and sociometric measures of interpersonal attraction were used. In all three conditions students studied a controversial issue with materials representing both pro and con views. In the controversy condition each learning group was divided into two pairs representing the pro and con sides. In the debate condition each member of a learning group was assigned a pro or con position to represent in a competition to see who could make the best presentation. In the individualistic condition subjects were given all the pro and con materials and told to learn the material without interacting with other students. Controversy promoted the most crossethnic interaction, the most supportive crossethnic relationships and the greatest crossethnic liking. It seems that despite the existing prejudices and hostility between majority and minority students, structured academic conflicts characterized by high positive interdependence promote considerable crossethnic liking. Minority students, furthermore, felt more successful in the controversy condition than in the debate and individualistic conditions.

The fifth question was whether or not the crossethnic relationships formed within cooperative groups generalize to post-instructional situations. Even though individuals interacted constructively with peers from other ethnic groups and expressed liking for them during achievement oriented situations, there is a need to determine whether these relationships and interaction patterns will generalize to free-choice situations in which individuals can interact with whomever they wish. A number of our studies demonstrated that when individuals were placed in post-instructional, free-choice situations, there was more crossethnic interaction when individuals had been in a cooperative rather than a competitive or individualistic situation (Johnson and Johnson, 1981, 1982; Johnson, Johnson, Tiffany and Zaidman, 1983). Warring *et al.* (1985) surveyed seventy-four sixth-grade and fifty-one fourth-grade students in an ethnically integrated, inner-city elementary school as to the crossethnic interactions they had engaged in during the academic year. An Activity Report Scale was given to students to determine with whom they interacted in structured class activities, unstructured class activities, school activities outside class and activities in their homes. They found that individuals who participated in cooperative learning groups had more non-instructional ethnic interactions within the classroom and school and more out-of-school interactions than did individuals who participated in individualistic learning situations.

The results of our research indicate that cooperative efforts promote more positive crossethnic relationships than do competitive or individualistic efforts, that intergroup cooperation increases the frequency of positive crossethnic relationships within a class, while intergroup competition may reduce them, that positive crossethnic relationships form within cooperative efforts even when the minority students achieve at lower levels than do the majority students, that intellectual conflicts between majority and minority students can increase crossethnic liking within cooperative groups, and that the crossethnic relationships formed within cooperative groups generalize to free-time, school and out-of-school situations.

**Table 1.**   *Impact of Social Interdependence on Crossethnic Relationships: Mean Effect Sizes*

|                              | Mean  | Standard deviation | N   |
|------------------------------|-------|--------------------|-----|
| Cooperative/Competitive      | 0.54  | 0.50               | 38  |
| Cooperative/Individualistic  | 0.44  | 0.51               | 11  |
| Competitive/Individualistic  | −0.65 | 0.40               | 3   |

## CROSSETHNIC RELATIONSHIPS

In addition to our own programme of research, we conducted a meta-analysis of all available studies on social interdependence and interpersonal attraction (Johnson and Johnson, 1989). Fifty-three studies were found and reviewed comparing the relative effects of two or more goal structures on interpersonal attraction between majority and minority individuals. From Table 1 it may be seen that cooperative experiences promoted significantly better relationships between majority and minority students than did competitive (effect size = 0.54) or individualistic efforts (effect size = 0.44). Individualistic efforts promoted more positive crossethnic relationships than did competition (effect size = −0.65), but the small number of studies makes this finding suggestive only. Each of the studies reviewed was rated in terms of its methodological quality. When only the high quality studies were included in the analysis, the advantage of cooperative over competitive and individualistic efforts was even more apparent (effect sizes = 0.68 and 0.53 respectively).

A number of the studies conducted operationally defined cooperation in a way that included elements of competition and individualistic work. The original Jigsaw studies, for example, operationalized cooperative learning as a combination of positive resource interdependence and an individualistic reward structure (Aronson, 1978). Teams-Games-Tournament (TGT) (DeVries and Edwards, 1974) and Student Teams Achievement Divisions (STAD) (Slavin, 1986) operationalized cooperative learning as a combination of ingroup cooperation and intergroup competition, and Team-Assisted Individualization (TAI) (Slavin, 1986) is a mixture of cooperative and individualistic learning. When such 'mixed' operationalizations were compared with 'pure' operationalizations, the effect sizes for the cooperative versus competitive comparison were 0.45 and 0.74 respectively, $t(37) = 1.60$, $p < 0.06$. The effect sizes for the cooperative versus individualistic comparisons were 0.13 and 0.61 respectively, $t(10) = 1.64$, $p < 0.07$.

Since the most credible studies (due to their high quality methodologically) and the 'pure' operationalizations of cooperative learning produced stronger effects, considerable confidence can be placed in the conclusion that cooperative efforts promote more positive crossethnic relationships than do competitive or individualistic efforts.

## APPLICATIONS OF COOPERATIVE LEARNING

On the basis of the theory and research on cooperation, we have trained tens of thousands of teachers and school administrators in many different countries in how to use cooperative learning. In helping teachers adapt cooperative procedures to their specific students, subject areas and instructional needs, the shortcomings of the present theory have been highlighted, thus enriching our theorizing and generating new research studies. This dynamic system of theory, research and practice increases the credibility of the conclusion that if teachers wish to promote positive crossethnic relationships and attitudes, the use of cooperative learning is required.

## CONCLUSIONS

Relationships are built on interdependence (Johnson, 1990). People reach out to others because they have goals they wish to pursue that other people share and/or require the participation of other people as well as themselves. The results of our research indicate that (1) cooperative experiences promote more positive crossethnic relationships than do competitive or individualistic experiences; (2) more positive crossethnic relationships, including relationships between members of different groups, will develop when groups cooperate than when groups compete; (3) low-performing minority members in cooperative groups are not disliked if they are perceived to be exerting effort and doing the best they can; (4) when crossethnic conflicts occur in cooperative groups within a structured controversy format, they increase positive crossethnic relationships; and (5) the crossethnic relationships formed within cooperative groups will continue voluntarily in subsequent non-task situations. In addition, a meta-analysis of the fifty-three available studies indicated that cooperative experiences, compared with competitive and individualistic ones, promote more positive crossethnic interpersonal relationships. The high quality studies tended to find stronger effects than the lower quality studies, and the 'pure' operationalizations of cooperation tended to find stronger effects than did the 'mixed' operationalizations.

The reason that cooperative experiences promote more positive crossethnic relationships than do competitive or individualistic experiences may be that cooperation promotes a process of acceptance rather than a process of rejection. Social judgment theory states that individuals become involved in a process of acceptance or rejection that determines whether they like or dislike each other. The processes of acceptance or rejection are a gestalt within which any part of the process tends to elicit all other parts of the process. When individuals cooperate with each other, the positive interdependence and promotive interaction result in frequent and accurate communication, accurate perspective-taking, inducibility, multidimensional views of each other, feelings of psychological acceptance and self-esteem, psychological success, and expectations of rewarding and productive future interaction. When individuals compete or work individualistically, the negative and no interdependence and oppositional or no interaction result in an absence of or inaccurate communication, egocentrism, resistance to influence, monopolistic and static views of each other, feelings of psychological rejection and low self-esteem, psychological failure, and expectations for oppositional interaction in the future.

The results of this research have important implications not only for future theorizing and research, but also for educators who are struggling with ethnic desegregation. In many classrooms throughout North America and other countries highly individualistic and competitive learning procedures are being used in desegregated classrooms. Students work on their own, on individualized materials, sitting in a row-by-column room arrangement, listening to lectures, with a minimum of interaction with their classmates. The results reported in this chapter provide some indication that such competitive/individualistic instructional procedures should be changed to cooperative ones.

# REFERENCES

Aronson, E. (1978) *The Jigsaw Classroom*, Beverly Hills, Calif., Sage Publications.

Cooper, L., Johnson, D.W., Johnson, R. and Wilderson, F. (1980) 'The Effects of Cooperative, Competitive, and Individualistic Experiences on Interpersonal Attraction among Heterogeneous Peers', *Journal of Social Psychology*, III, pp. 243–253.

Deutsch, M. (1985) *Distributive Justice: A Social Psychological Perspective*, New Haven, Conn., Yale University Press.

DeVries, D. and Edwards, K. (1974) 'Cooperation in the Classroom: Towards a Theory of Alternative Reward-Task Classroom Structures', Paper presented at the meeting of the American Educational Research Association, Chicago, April.

Johnson, D.W. (1990) *Reaching Out: Interpersonal Effectiveness and Self-Actualization*, 4th ed., Englewood Cliffs, N.J., Prentice-Hall.

Johnson, D.W. and Johnson, R. (1980) 'Integrating Handicapped Students into the Mainstream', *Exceptional Children*, 46, pp. 89–98.

Johnson, D.W. and Johnson, R. (1981) 'Effects of Cooperative and Individualistic Learning Experiences on Interethnic Interaction', *Jounral of Educational Psychology*, 73, pp. 454–459.

Johnson, D.W. and Johnson, R. (1982) 'Effects of Cooperative, Competitive, and Individualistic Learning Experiences on Cross-Ethnic Interaction and Friendships', *Journal of Social Psychology*, 118, pp. 47–58.

Johnson, D.W. and Johnson, R. (1985) 'Relationships between Black and White Students in Intergroup Cooperation and Competition', *Journal of Social Psychology*, 125, pp. 421–428.

Johnson, D.W. and Johnson, R. (1989) *Cooperation and Competition: Theory and Research*, Edina, Minn., Interaction Book Company.

Johnson, D.W., Johnson, R. and Maruyama, G. (1983) 'Interdependence and Interpersonal Attraction among Heterogeneous and Homogeneous Individuals: A Theoretical Formulation and a Meta-analysis of the Research', *Review of Educational Research*, 53, pp. 5–54.

Johnson, D.W., Johnson, R. and Maruyama, G. (1984) 'Goal Interdependence and Interpersonal Attraction among Members of Different Ethnic Groups and between Handicapped and Non-handicapped Individuals: A Meta-analysis', in N. Miller and M. Brewer (Eds), *Groups in Contact: The Psychology of Desegregation*, New York, Academic Press, pp. 187–212.

Johnson, D.W., Johnson, R. and Tiffany, M. (1984) 'Structuring Academic Conflicts between Majority and Minority Students: Hindrance or Help to Integration', *Contemporary Educational Psychology*, 9, pp. 61–73.

Johnson, D.W., Johnson, R., Tiffany, M. and Zaidman, B. (1983) 'Are Low Achievers Disliked in a Cooperative Situation? A Test of Rival Theories in a Mixed Ethnic Situation', *Contemporary Educational Psychology*, 8, pp. 189–200.

Johnson, D.W., Johnson, R., Tiffany, M. and Zaidman, B. (1984) 'Cross-ethnic Relationships: The Impact of Intergroup Cooperation and Intergroup Competition', *Journal of Educational Research*, 78, pp. 75–79.

Slavin, R. (1986) *Using Student Team Learning*, Baltimore, Md., Johns Hopkins University, Center for Research on Elementary and Middle Schools.

Warring, D., Johnson, D.W., Maruyama, G. and Johnson, R. (1985) 'Impact of Different Types of Cooperative Learning on Cross-Ethnic and Cross-Sex Relationships', *Journal of Educational Psychology*, 77, pp. 53–59.

# 10. Crosscultural Psychology and Teacher Training

PIERRE R. DASEN

Education for cultural diversity is more than a passing fad, it is possibly the most important issue facing educators today. All societies have become multicultural, and it is vital to prevent social conflict through an education that fosters understanding and respect for cultural diversity, as well as communication and cooperation between persons of different origins. This implies specific changes in teacher education. In the francophone world the various issues linked to 'intercultural' education and teacher training towards this goal have been hotly debated in the last decade, and several volumes have provided printed information over the years (e.g., Lorreyte, 1984; Rey, 1984; Abdallah-Pretceille, 1986; Dinello and Perret-Clermont, 1987; CERI, 1987; Ouellet, 1988, 1991; Gardou, 1990). But the debate is far from closed; in this chapter I would like to make a modest contribution to it, on the specific issue of the usefulness of including crosscultural psychology in the training of teachers.

In the course of the argument I will provide a definition of crosscultural psychology, and put it in perspective relative to several other approaches for which the relevance to teacher training is possibly more obvious. A general framework for crosscultural psychology will be outlined, and the interest of some of the findings will be illustrated in the area of developmental psychology, especially in relation to the concepts of enculturation, socialization and ethnocentrism. As a method, comparative crosscultural psychology offers an opportunity to unconfound variables that cannot be distinguished in monocultural studies; it leads to the discovery of previously unrecognized psychological phenomena; and it allows an empirical distinction between those aspects of human behaviour that are universal and those that are culturally specific. While these advantages may be mainly of theoretical interest, I will argue that they are also relevant to the design of curriculum and teaching practice. By giving teachers a general theoretical

* A previous version of this paper was presented to the Third International Congress of ARIC (Association pour la Recherche Interculturelle), University of Sherbrooke, Quebec, 16–18 August 1989, and will be published in French in the proceedings. The author thanks colleagues who provided critical comments, especially M. Abdallah-Pretceille, N. Berthoud-Aghili and M. Lavallée-Pons.

**191**

framework, an attitude of respect for cultural diversity and an understanding of the unity of mankind, one could hope that they will have the necessary guidelines enabling them to develop those educational structures and practices that are most appropriate in their specific context.

## CROSSCULTURAL PSYCHOLOGY DEFINED

In its simplest definition, crosscultural psychology is the study of the influence of culture on human behaviour. In other words, the crosscultural approach in psychology studies individuals (and variation across individuals), while taking into account variables at the societal level. Thus crosscultural psychology necessarily relies on information provided by other human sciences that study social phenomena at the 'macro' rather than 'micro' level: history, demography, sociology, and especially, anthropology. A crosscultural approach is possible only within a multidisciplinary paradigm.

Of course, other definitions of crosscultural psychology have been provided over the years, among them the following four:

> Cross-cultural psychology is the empirical study of members of various culture groups who have had different experiences that lead to predictable and significant differences in behavior. (Brislin, Lonner and Thorndike, 1973, p. 5)

> Cross-cultural psychology is concerned with the systematic study of behavior and experience as it occurs in different cultures, is influenced by culture, or results in changes in existing cultures. (Triandis, 1980, p. 1)

> Cross-cultural psychology [is] defined as the scientific study of the ways in which social and cultural forces shape human behavior. (Segall *et al.*, 1990, p. 3)

> Cross-cultural psychology is the study of similarities and differences in individual psychological functioning in various cultural and ethnic groups, and of the relationships between psychological variables and socio-cultural, ecological and biological variables, as well as ongoing changes in these variables. (Berry *et al.*, in press)

What all these definitions have in common is the reference to culture, cultural diversity and cultural change. This implies a definition of culture itself, by no means an easy task; there is, in fact, quite a controversy on the status of culture in crosscultural psychology, but we will not deal with it here. Among the many definitions of culture gathered by Kroeber and Kluckhohn (1952), the advantage of simplicity marks that of Herskovits (1948, p. 17): 'Culture is the man-made part of the human environment', a formula that applies to the physical, social and symbolic aspects of the milieu. It is important to note the difference between society, a collectivity of individuals, and their culture. It is also important to note that culture is never static but is subject to change, especially when individuals of different societies come into close contact.

The impact of social and cultural change on individuals — psychological acculturation, as Berry (1990) defines it — is itself a major area of study within crosscultural psychology, as are all the phenomena of interaction between individuals of different cultural backgrounds. According to a UNESCO (1984) document listing institutions dealing with crosscultural research, the latter follows two main orientations: 'either the comparison between different cultures (the comparative study of cultural phenomena), or the interaction between cultures (the study of the processes of interaction between individuals or groups having different cultural roots)' (p. 3, my translation). Berry (1985) has used respectively cultural psychology and ethnic psychology to refer to these two orientations, while keeping crosscultural psychology as the generic term. Others like Cole (1989), Camilleri (1985) and Boesch (1991) argue for a 'cultural psychology', while in French a problem arises with the term 'intercultural', which often refers to the social policies related to migrants without any reference to scientific research.

Beyond the quarrel of words, there exist different epistemological outlooks in these various orientations, but the main trend seems to be towards a unified field of enquiry and action based upon it. While the comparative method remains important, as we shall see later in this chapter, it is no longer a necessary hallmark of crosscultural studies, many of which take place within a single society.[1] Thus the two orientations defined above progressively blur into a single field; most crosscultural research now occurs wihtin large, industrialized and urbanized multicultural societies. This trend is quite obvious in the proceedings of the conferences of the two professional associations, the International Association for Cross-Cultural Psychology (IACCP) (e.g., Reyes Lagunes and Poortinga, 1985; Berry and Annis, 1988; Kagitcibasi, 1987) and the francophone Association pour la Recherche Interculturelle (ARIC) (e.g., Clanet, 1989; Retschitzki, Bossel-Lagos and Dasen, 1989).

In this chapter, however, I will concentrate on crosscultural psychology as the study of behaviour in various societies, whether the latter are in contact with each other or not, leaving aside the study of communication across cultures (whether verbal or non-verbal) and the phenomena usually studied by social pyschology (cultural identity, attitudes and stereotypes, racism, etc.). These last topics are of obvious importance to teacher training in multicultural societies: teachers are increasingly faced with multicultural classrooms, have to communicate with pupils and parents of different cultural origins, they are constantly confronted with intergroup dynamics, and are themselves agents of acculturation. Thus teachers should be trained to understand all the phenomena linked to migration, and they should be trained in crosscultural communication and in social psychology. Indeed, many teacher training courses already include these aspects. What I will argue in this chapter is that these are essential, but not sufficient, in the training of teachers in education for cultural diversity.

## THE ECO-CULTURAL FRAMEWORK

A general framework for crosscultural psychology is presented in Figure 1. Derived from previous versions developed by Berry (1976), and partly inspired by Whiting and Whiting's (1978) psycho-cultural model, it is the backbone of the recent textbooks of crosscultural psychology produced by Segall *et al.* (1990) and Berry *et al.* (in press).

It is not possible to develop here all the aspects of this theoretical framework, so I will only explicate the main features. The basic idea is that individual behaviour (to the right of the figure) is determined at least partly by culture, that is

*Figure 1.   A Conceptual Framework for Crosscultural Psychology*

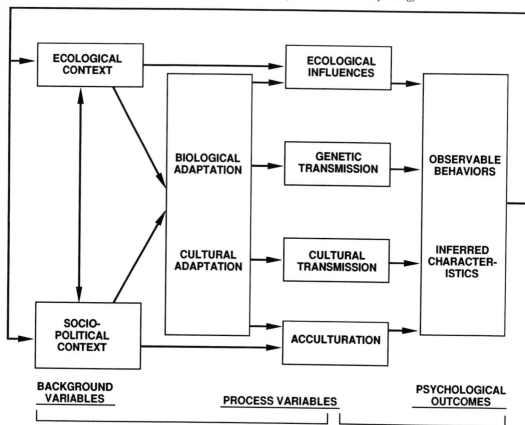

*Reprinted with permission from M.H. Segall, P.R. Dasen, J.W. Berry and Y.H. Poortinga (1990)*
*Human Behavior in Global Perspective: An Introduction to Cross-Cultural Psychology, New York,*
*Pergamon Press, p. 19.*

itself an adaptive response at the social level (left-hand side of the figure) to
ecological, socio-economic and historical conditions. The links between the elements at the group level and those at the individual level occur through processes,
of which acculturation and cultural transmission are those we are particularly
interested in. The latter occurs through enculturation and socialization; through
these two processes the individual is gradually led to restrict his behaviour to that
which is judged adequate by the surrounding society; in other words, among the
set of biologically possible behaviours only a small subset is socially acceptable.
This subset varies from one society to the next. Socialization corresponds to the
voluntary and conscious attempts to influence the individual to conform to group
norms, while enculturation also comprises all the unconscious influences.[2] For
someone born and raised in a particular society without ever leaving it, and
without having any contacts with people from outside, it would be impossible to
realize that the behaviours, role models and values available in the surrounding

social environment are not the only possible ones. Enculturation and socialization are therefore adaptive; they ensure a harmonious life within a social group, make the behaviour of others understandable and predictable, but at the same time these processes are at the roots of the ethnocentrism that characterizes all human individuals and groups.

Triandis (1990), commenting on the usefulness of the eco-cultural framework for overcoming ethnocentrism, said:

> It is very difficult to think about behaviors that are different from the ones we are used to and not judge them as wrong. Difference invites comparison and evaluation. Yet, if we see that the ecology of the other culture is different from our ecology (e.g., a difference in population density), we can find the difference understandable and even say to ourselves: 'If I lived in that ecology I probably would do exactly the same'. That can lead to tolerance for other cultures. (p. 36)

## THE DEVELOPMENTAL NICHE

Another useful theoretical framework, totally compatible with the eco-cultural framework presented above, is the 'developmental niche' proposed by Super and Harkness (1986). This framework allows for an integration between developmental psychology and cultural anthropology: while psychology has a tendency to study the individual out of the socio-cultural context, and anthropology deals only with macro-social phenomena, Super and Harkness consider the individual in cultural context to be the appropriate unit of analysis. The developmental niche has three components, all of which are culturally constituted:

1 the physical and social contexts in which the child lives and grows up;
2 the caretakers' childrearing and educational practices;
3 what Super and Harkness call the psychology of the caretakers, especially the latter's social representations of development and education.

These three parts are in constant interaction, and are composing a system open to the outside, in particular a system that adapts to the changing ecological and socio-historical conditions. Just like the eco-cultural framework, this model includes the processes of enculturation and socialization.

B. Whiting (1980) was first to draw attention to an important process through which culture influences child development: the selection of contexts, which corresponds to the first component of the developmental niche. The school, for example, is a very peculiar context: homogeneous age-groups, rigid institutional rules, formalized curricula, out-of-context learning, etc. To most of us these constitute unquestioned aspects of the learning environment because they have become so familiar through years of schooling and teaching. Learning contexts and educational practices vary to a large extent from one culture to another, as do the social representations, the so-called naïve theories or parental ethnotheories (Bril and Lehalle, 1988; Zack and Bril, 1989), that adults have concerning the development and education of children. What is due to nature and what to nurture? and what is the role of the sacred? which aspects of development are malleable? what are the skills that are expected? and at what age and what level of expertise? how is the end-stage of development defined? These are some of the items for which at least an implicit theory exists in each social group, and which Super and Harkness call the psychology of the caretakers.

This very brief presentation of two theoretical frameworks in crosscultural psychology is too sketchy and too abstract; in particular I should have liked to illustrate them with examples from empirical research. The interested reader will easily find these in the several volumes and journals devoted to crosscultural psychology, in the handbook edited by Munroe, Munroe and Whiting (1981) and in the two textbooks mentioned above.

I now come to a key question in this chapter: in what way is all this relevant to the training of teachers towards an education for cultural diversity? Before I attempt to answer this question, it may be useful to share some of my ideas about the latter, if only to avoid misunderstanding.

## EDUCATION FOR CULTURAL DIVERSITY

In French the expression 'intercultural' education is used most often, rather than 'multicultural', to indicate that there is a real interaction between people of different cultures, not only the juxtaposition of different cultural groups. Intercultural education is necessarily addressed to the whole class, i.e., to indigenous as well as to migrant pupils. It seeks to sensitize them to the respect of diversity, to tolerance and solidarity. Thus intercultural education corresponds to an ideological and political option, which, far from the absence of a clear choice of a system of values (an absence that is often deplored in relation to present-day education systems), is designed to prepare future citizens for a harmonious life in multicultural societies.

This definition may be very general and somewhat vague, but much has been written in more detail about education for cultural diversity in this series of volumes. What I would briefly like to do here is to draw attention to what intercultural education is not.

First, it is not compensatory education for minority groups (what is called 'Ausländerpädagogik' in German), seeking to solve the 'problems of migrant children'. In an intercultural perspective it is not so much the migrant children who have problems, but the school as an institution, faced with the difficulty of adapting to cultural diversity. This having been said, it is obvious that immediate needs have to be met; for example, the migrant children have to be helped in learning the host country's language, and in conforming to the local school norms, if only to give them a better chance of educational and professional success.

Crosscultural psychology takes a clear stand in relation to compensatory education: it refuses the 'deficiency model' in favour of a 'difference model'. This means that the cultural differences in performance (in school, or on psychological tests) are not automatically interpreted as deficiencies against some dominant norm, but are seen as just that, cultural differences reflecting an adaptation to different context. Similarly, crosscultural psychology is suspicious of the concept of 'cultural deprivation', which most often reflects an ethnocentric value judgment.

Second, intercultural education is not to be confused with the teaching of the language and culture of the migrants' country of origin. Such courses are very important. It is well known that a second language is acquired more easily if the first language has been well established, and a strong cultural identity may facilitate integration into a new society. The problem with these courses is that they are often devalued by the school system: they are not part of the normal school schedule, are often not taught in the ordinary classrooms but are confined to inadequate premises, they often take place when other pupils are out of school, thus becoming a punishment rather than a joy. The teachers of these courses are usually supplied by the various embassies, they are not well integrated into the local school systems, and are considered to have a lower status; in Switzerland, at least, they are most often not even paid by the local ministries of education but by the countries of origin. All these features carry with them an inherent devalorization of the minority languages and cultures, and may thus be even counterproductive. Such courses could be a part of intercultural education if they were offered to all pupils, irrespective of origin and nationality.

Third, intercultural education is not a new school subject, an addition to the curriculum designed to teach about other cultures. In any case it is difficult to teach the culture of others.[3] In no case should intercultural education be a folklorization, a stigmatization encapsulating children in an imposed, fixed cultural identity. The teachers who practise intercultural education will, in effect, take advantage of the presence of children from diverse cultural origins, in order to (re)value their cultural background and to sensitize others to cultural diversity, but they will avoid any stereotyping, and will not present any culture as an immutable entity.

For an intercultural education, what counts is the attitudes of the teachers in all of their behaviour, as well as in the structural features of the school system. These attitudes should pervade extracurricular activities as well as classroom teaching. If intercultural education is not a school subject in itself, each subject can be taught with an intercultural perspective, not only the obvious ones such as geography and history, but also the language subjects and even mathematics and science.

Intercultural education is also akin to a differentiated, individualized teaching that takes into account the specificities of each child. In particular, migrant children come to the new setting rich with knowledge and experience that can be recognized as such, and valued by the teacher, even if it is not the knowledge that is the normative prerequisite. The teacher can attempt to build on existing skills instead of considering them to be irrelevant.

At the institutional level an intercultural orientation implies a clear choice of an integration rather than an assimilation model. This means that people of different cultural backgrounds are given equal rights and as much as possible equal access to rewards, but they are not expected or required to relinquish any of the features of their own culture if they do not wish to do so.

## THE RELEVANCE OF CROSSCULTURAL PSYCHOLOGY TO TEACHER TRAINING

Crosscultural psychology provides a rationale for the acceptance of cultural diversity. It takes from cultural anthropology the paradigm of cultural relativity:

each society has designed its culture as an adaptive response to ecological and socio-historical conditions; there is, therefore, no reason to evaluate different cultures, especially not in comparison to one particular culture construed as a model. This respect for diversity does not prevent each individual from identifying with one specific social group, or from accepting its particular system of values, but it does keep one from imposing it on others.

The relevance of present-day cultural anthropology for intercultural education has been well demonstrated by Erny (1981) and by Camilleri (1986, 1988). Classical ethnography, of course, born in the colonial era and marked by it, has had a tendency to provide a stilted and stereotyped picture of the cultures under study, which has sometimes led to its rejection as a theoretical basis for intercultural education (Abdallah-Pretceille, 1986, 1988). However, these concerns are outdated. For quite some time now cultural anthropology has turned to the study of ethnic groups and minorities in multicultural societies, and to the study of culture change. It has also incorporated some of the methods of sociology and psychology. While cultural anthropology in the past has often neglected intracultural variations, the existence of individual differences is now widely recognized. The same trend has occurred within crosscultural psychology itself; in the beginning studies often reported and compared only group means, while now the tendency is to take variation and individual strategies into account, and to move towards more qualitative descriptions.

One of the most difficult tasks for a teacher, or indeed anyone dealing with intercultural education, is to overcome one's own ethnocentrism. The understanding of one's own enculturation hence plays a fundamental role in this respect. But, as I have mentioned before, it is only through contact with the outside, through struggling with what appears as foreign and strange, that it becomes possible to look back on one's own society, its institutions and one's own personal prejudices. The main contribution of crosscultural psychology is to facilitate this decentration, which is otherwise so difficult to achieve.

## THE ENCULTURATION OF SOCIAL SCIENCES

It is not only individuals who are enculturated, and hence need to seek decentration; just as each individual is born and raised in a particular society, the social sciences, and psychology in particular, were born in Europe, and have grown up there and in North America. Thus they are enculturated in a particular, Western, urbanized, industrialized society, with its particular system of values, for example the stress on individuality. Mainstream psychology usually claims to establish general laws of human behaviour, which it assumes to be universal, while they have in fact been established on a very narrow empirical basis, with very restricted and largely non-representative samples (often undergraduate university students). Even the choice of topics that are studied reflects the dominant values of Western society. This may be true especially of social psychology (Bond, 1988), where, furthermore, the methods of the experimental laboratory are particularly difficult to adapt to other cultural contexts (Jahoda, 1988), but it is also true of all other areas of psychology, for example developmental psychology, as we shall see below.

Crosscultural psychology, in addition to documenting cultural variation, also searches for general or even universal laws; however, it is not satisfied with universality as a postulate, but asks for it to be empirically demonstrated. It requires of psychology that it become a global science, one that deals with all of humankind, not only with a tiny part of it.

A large proportion of the education sciences and of teacher training is based on the social sciences, and on psychology in particular. Hence to train teachers in intercultural education, it is essential to bring about a decentration from the inherent ethnocentrism of the social sciences on which it is based. To illustrate this argument, I now turn to some examples in developmental psychology.

## THE POSTULATED UNIVERSALITY OF DEVELOPMENTAL PSYCHOLOGY

Jean Piaget, while calling for empirical crosscultural studies (Piaget, 1966) and paying lip-service to cultural variables, really considered his theory to be universal, considering that individual and cultural differences were only minor variations on the basic theme. The theory of stages implies the notion of levels of development, i.e., the possibility of attributing a unitary measure to an individual's position in cognitive development. This type of reasoning is not far removed from the psychometric definition of intelligence which allows the attribution to an individual of a single score such as an IQ. Yet crosscultural studies (Dasen and Heron, 1981), as well as individual differences studies (Dasen and de Ribaupierre, 1987), have demonstrated that, if indeed the hierarchical sequence of stages has proved to be universal, the concept of a unitary stage cannot be upheld, given the available empirical data. In particular, the rates of development in different conceptual areas are linked to specific cultural values and practices, which are themselves determined by the ecological demands linked to the means of production (Dasen, 1975). Furthermore, the very definitions of intelligence vary from one society to another (Berry, 1984; Dasen, 1984; Dasen *et al.*, 1985), which logically precludes the possibility of measuring it with a single instrument, and also destroys the hope of ever finding a culture-free or culture-fair intelligence test.

If crosscultural psychology thus questions some of the absolutist claims of mainstream psychology, it allows for the empirical demonstration of universal laws of behaviour.[4] To take again the example of Piagetian psychology, crosscultural research has repeatedly demonstrated that the qualitative aspects of the reasoning elicited by so-called Piagetian tasks are the same everywhere (Dasen and Heron, 1981). In a study in the Ivory Coast, West Africa, Dasen (1984) was also able to ascertain the internal and external validity of a battery of Piagetian tasks. More generally, the present consensus gained in crosscultural studies of cognition is that the basic cognitive processes are indeed universal, their application to particular contexts being what is culturally determined (Cole and Scribner, 1974; Segall *et al.*, 1990).

It will be useful for teachers to know that children from different cultural origins are not only diverse, but that they are also, in some and even many respects, similar. Education for cultural diversity includes this focus on the psychic unity of mankind, a concept first developed in cultural anthropology, but crosscultural research allows this unity to be based on empirical facts rather than on a simple assumption.

## THE UNCONFOUNDING OF VARIABLES

Research carried out within the confines of a single society cannot always separate variables that are confounded; a single society is often too homogeneous, i.e., it does not present within its subgroups the variability that would allow the necessary unconfounding. I shall take only one example: developmental psychology often attributes to chronological age the various changes that occur in children's behaviour. Now, age is always a confound between maturation and the various experiences acquired over time, particularly school. In Western societies age is stricly linked to schooling, since (with a few exceptions) all children go to school and follow much the same age-grading. To unconfound age and schooling, research has to be done in those settings where a large proportion of the children do not go to school. If this is done (for reviews, see Nerlove and Snipper, 1981; Rogoff, 1981), it is found that the development of some skills previously attributed to age (maturation) are really linked to the amount (and type) of schooling. This is the case, for example, of the use of certain mnemonic strategies (Wagner, 1981, Scribner and Cole, 1981), or formal operational reasoning on Piagetian tasks (Dasen and Heron, 1981).

The unconfounding function of crosscultural research is, of course, mainly of theoretical interest; cultural variation is used as a method, to complement laboratory research. However, the example quoted above, and similar ones like it, do have some practical implications, especially for teachers dealing with pupils from different cultural origins: instead of immediately attributing the lack of a specific skill to maturation (i.e., mental retardation), it may be linked to different environmental circumstances in the child's history. This is obviously a very banal statement, yet if one looks at special education classes in Switzerland (and, I suppose, elsewhere), why is it that they are mainly composed of pupils of foreign origin?

## THE SEARCH FOR NEW VARIABLES

Another function of crosscultural psychology is to draw attention to variables that may not be important within Western societies, but are so elsewhere. Variations in the amount and level of schooling have already been mentioned; the influence of malnutrition on psychological development would be another example (Dasen and Super, 1988). Thus whole new fields of research have been opened under the impetus of crosscultural psychology, for example, the dimension of collectivism versus individualism (Triandis, 1985, 1987, 1990; Bond, 1988; Kagitcibasi, 1988), and everyday cognition (Rogoff and Lave, 1984; Chamoux, 1986; Dasen and Bossel-Lagos, 1989), both of which will no doubt prove to be of practical as well as theoretical importance.

## CONCLUSION

In this chapter I have reviewed some of the contributions that crosscultural psychology should be able to make if it were included in teacher training, or at least in the training of teacher trainers. Crosscultural psychology provides a general theoretical framework that helps in understanding one's own enculturation, provides the means of decentration from one's ethnocentrism, and helps to understand and interpret the behaviour of others. It provides empirical evidence of psychological universals, and an explanation of cultural diversity in non-evaluative terms. It therefore fosters attitudes of tolerance and understanding of cultural diversity.

Given these general principles, teachers should be able to derive the educational implications appropriate to their particular context, more usefully than if offered recipes that tend to be situationally specific. If all schools tend to become multicultural, each particular situation has its own characteristics and calls for specific educational strategies. Therefore, it seems most useful to give teachers, during their initial or in-service training, a solid general framework that is likely to be applicable for a long time to come, even under rapidly changing circumstances.

## NOTES

1  For example, Schurmans and Dasen (1991) report a study on the social representations of intelligence that comprises three parts: (1) a comparison between a study among the Baoulé of the Ivory Coast, West Africa, and a subsequent study in the Swiss mountains; (2) a comparison between farmers and non-farmers within the Swiss mountain community; (3) independently of the socio-professional characteristics, the position of the families on a dimension of social change. In my opinion, not only the first, explicitly comparative part of the study should be labelled 'crosscultural', but so should all three aspects of the study.

2  For example, a child can be enculturated to value reading simply through the presence in the environment of many books; but the parents can also incite the child to read instead of watching television, in which case one would speak of socialization. The school teacher's official role is to socialize, but many aspects of the teacher's behaviour and of the school's structure remain unconscious, and therefore contribute to the children's enculturation.

3  Take the example of the schooling of first nations' children in Canada: there is no point in developing an Amerindian curriculum without at the same time training indigenous teachers, because Amerindian culture taught by White teachers just does not make sense (Larose, 1988).

4  The empirical testing of general laws of human behaviour is the specific endeavour of one branch of crosscultural psychology, the so-called hologeistic research, using the ethnographic data bank of the Human Relations Area Files (HRAF). Representative samples of all existing human societies, past and present, are used in mainly correlational hypotheses testing (Barry, 1980; Naroll, Michik and Naroll, 1980).

# REFERENCES

Abdallah-Pretceille, M. (1986) *Vers une Pédagogie interculturelle*, Paris, Publications de la Sorbonne.

Abdallah-Pretceille, M. (1988) 'Quelques Points d'Appui pour une Formation des Enseignants dans une Perspective interculturelle', in F. Ouellet (Ed.), *Pluralisme et École*, Québec, Institut québécois de Recherche sur la Culture, pp. 495–510.

Barry III, H. (1980) 'Description and Uses of the Human Relations Area Files', in H. Triandis and J.W. Berry (Eds), *Handbook of Cross-Cultural Psychology. Vol. 2: Methodology*, Boston, Mass., Allyn and Bacon, pp. 445–478.

Berry, J.W. (1976) *Human Ecology and Cognitive Style*, New York, Sage/Halsted/Wiley.

Berry, J.W. (1984) 'Towards a Universal Psychology of Cognitive Competence', *International Journal of Psychology*, 19, pp. 335–361.

Berry, J.W. (1985) 'Cultural Psychology and Ethnic Psychology: A Comparative Analysis', in I. Reyes Lagunes and Y.H. Poortinga (Eds), *From a Different Perspective: Studies of Behavior across Cultures*, Lisse, Swets and Zeitlinger, pp. 3–15.

Berry, J.W. (1990) 'Psychology of Acculturation: Understanding Individuals Moving between Cultures', in R.W. Brislin (Ed.), *Applied Cross-Cultural Psychology*, Newbury Park, Calif., Sage, pp. 232–253.

Berry, J.W. and Annis, R.C. (Eds) (1988) *Ethnic Psychology: Research and Practice with Immigrants, Refugees, Native Peoples, Ethnic Groups and Sojourners*, Amsterdam, Swets and Zeitlinger.

Berry, J.W., Poortinga, Y.H., Segall, M. and Dasen, P.R. (in press) *Cross-cultural Psychology: Research and Applications*, Cambridge, Cambridge University Press.

Boesch, E. (1980) *Kultur und Handlung. Eine Einfuerung in die Kultur-psychologie*, Bern, Huber.

Boesch, E.E. (1991) *Symbolic Action Theory for Cultural Psychology*, Berlin, Springer.

Bond, M.H. (Ed.) (1988) *The Cross-Cultural Challenge to Social Psychology*, Newbury Park, Calif, Sage.

Bril, B, and Lehalle, H. (1988) *Le Développement psychologique Est-Il universel? Approches interculturelles*, Paris, Presses Universitaires de France.

Brislin, R.W., Lonner, W.J. and Thorndike, R.M. (1973) *Cross-Cultural Research Methods*, New York, Wiley.

Camilleri, C. (1985) 'La Psychologie culturelle', *Psychologie française*, 30, pp. 147–151.

Camilleri, C. (1986) *Anthropologie culturelle et Éducation*, Lausanne, Delachaux et Niestlé.

Camilleri, C. (1988) 'Pertinence d'une Approche scientifique de la Culture pour une Formation par l'éducation interculturelle', in F. Ouellet (Ed.), *Pluralisme et École*, Québec, Institut québécois de Recherche sur la Culture, pp. 565–594.

CERI (Ed.) (1987) *L'Éducation multiculturelle*, Paris, Organisation for Economic Cooperation and Development.

Chamoux, M.N. (1986) 'Apprendre autrement: Aspects des Pédagogies dites informelles chez les Indiens du Mexique', in P. Rossel (Ed.), *Demain l'Artisanat?* Paris, Presses Universitaires de France, pp. 211–335.

Clanet, C. (Ed.) (1989) *Socialisations et Cultures*, Actes du premier colloque de l'ARIC, Toulouse, Presses Universitaires du Mirail.

Cole, M. (1989) 'Cultural Psychology: A Once and Future Discipline?' in J. Berman (Ed.), *Nebraska Symposium on Motivation: Cross-Cultural Perspectives*, Lincoln, Neb., University of Nebraska Press, pp. 279–335.

Cole, M. and Scribner, S. (1974) *Culture and Thought: A Psychological Introduction*, New York, John Wiley.

Dasen, P.R. (1975) 'Concrete Operational Development in Three Cultures', *Journal of Cross-Cultural Psychology*, 6, pp. 156–172.

Dasen, P.R. (1984) 'The Cross-Cultural Study of Intelligence: Piaget and the Baoulé', *International Journal of Psychology*, 19, pp. 407–434.

Dasen, P.R. and Bossel-Lagos, M. (1989) 'L'Étude interculturelle des Savoirs quotidiens: Revue de la Littérature', in J. Retschitzki, M. Bossel-Lagos and P. Dasen (Eds), *La Recherche interculturelle*, Vol. 2, Paris, L'Harmattan, pp. 98–114.

Dasen, P.R. and Heron, A. (1981) 'Cross-Cultural Tests of Piaget's Theory', in H.C. Triandis and A. Heron (Eds), *Handbook of Cross-Cultural Psychology. Vol. 4: Developmental Psychology*, Boston, Mass., Allyn and Bacon, pp. 295–342.

Dasen, P.R. and de Ribaupierre, A. (1987) 'Neo-Piagetian Theories: Cross-Cultural and Differential Perspectives', *International Journal of Psychology*, 22, pp. 793–832.

Dasen, P.R. and Super, C.M. (1988) 'The Usefulness of a Cross-Cultural Approach in Studies of Malnutrition and Psychological Development', in P.R. Dasen, J.W. Berry and N. Sartorius (Eds), *Health and Cross-Cultural Psychology: Towards Applications*, London, Sage, pp. 112–138.

Dasen, P.R., Dembélé, B., Ettien, K., Kabran, K., Kamagaté, D., Koffi, D.A. and N'Guessan, A. (1985) 'N'glouèlê, l'Intelligence chez les Baoulé', *Archives de Psychologie*, 53, pp. 293–324.

Dinello, R. and Perret-Clermont, A.N. (Eds) (1987) *Psychopédagogie interculturelle*, Cousset, Delval.

Erny, P. (1981) *Ethnologie de l'Éducation*, Paris, Presses Universitaires de France.

Gardou, C. (Ed.) (1990) 'Société interculturelle et éducative. Numéro spécial', *Le Binet Simon, Bulletin de la Société A. Binet et T. Simon*, 90, 622.

Herskovits, M.J. (1948) *Man and His Works: The Science of Cultural Anthropology*, New York, Knopf.

Jahoda, G. (1988) 'J'accuse', in M.H. Bond (Ed.), *The Cross-Cultural Challenge to Social Psychology*, Newbury Park, Calif., Sage, pp. 86–95.

Kagitcibasi, C. (Ed.) (1987) *Growth and Progress in Cross-Cultural Psychology*, Lisse, Swets and Zeitlinger.

Kagitcibasi, C. (1988) 'Diversity of Socialization and Social Change', in P. Dasen, J. Berry and N. Sartorius (Eds), *Health and Cross-Cultural Psychology: Towards Applications*, Newbury Park, Calif., Sage, pp. 25–47.

Kroeber, A.L. and Kluckhohn, C. (1952) *Culture: A Critical Review of Concepts and Definitions*, New York, Vintage Books/Random House.

Larose, F. (1988) 'Education indienne au Québec et Prise en Charge scolaire: De l'Assimilation à la Souveraineté économique et culturelle', Unpublished thesis, Université de Genève, FPSE.

Lorreyte, B. (Ed.) (1984) 'Les Transferts de Connaissances: Vers une Pédagogie interculturelle. Numéro spécial', *Education Permanente*, 75.

Munroe, R.L., Munroe, R.H. and Whiting, J.W.M. (Eds) (1981) *Handbook of Cross-Cultural Human Development*, New York, Garland STPM.

Naroll, R., Michik, G.L. and Naroll, F. (1980) 'Holocultural Research Method', in H. Triandis and J.W. Berry (Eds), *Handbook of Cross-Cultural Psychology. Vol. 2: Methodology*, Boston, Mass., Allyn and Bacon, pp. 445–522.

Nerlove, S.B. and Snipper, A.S. (1981) 'Cognitive Consequences of Cultural Opportunity', in R. Munroe, R. Munroe and B. Whiting (Eds), *Handbook of Cross-Cultural Human Development*, New York, Garland STPM, pp. 423–474.

Ouellet, F. (Ed.) (1988) *Pluralisme et École*, Québec, Institut québécois de Recherche sur la Culture.

Ouellet, F. (1991) *L'Éducation interculturelle a-t-elle une Spécificité? Essai sur le Contenu de la Formation des Maîtres*, Paris, L'Harmattan.

Piaget, J. (1966) 'Nécessité et Signification des Recherches comparatives en Psychologie génétique', *Journal International de Psychologie*, 1, pp. 3–13.

Retschitzki, J., Bossel-Lagos, M. and Dasen, P. (Eds) (1989) *La Recherche interculturelle*. Actes du deuxième Colloque de l'ARIC, 2 vols, Paris, L'Harmattan.

Rey, M. (Ed.) (1984) *Une Pédagogie interculturelle*. Actes des Journées de formation de Maîtres, Berne, Commission Nationale Suisse pour l'UNESCO.

Rey, M. (1986) *Former les Enseignants à l'Éducation interculturelle?* Les Travaux du Conseil de la Coopération culturelle (1977–1983), Strasbourg, Conseil de l'Europe.

Reyes Lagunes, I. and Poortinga, Y.H. (Eds) (1985) *From a Different Perspective: Studies of Behavior across Cultures*, Lisse, Swets and Zeitlinger.

Rogoff, B. (1981) 'Schooling and the Development of Cognitive Skills', in H. Triandis and A. Heron (Eds), *Handbook of Cross-Cultural Psychology, Vol. 4*, Boston, Mass., Allyn and Bacon, pp. 233–294.

Rogoff, B. and Lave, J. (Eds) (1984) *Everyday Cognition: Its Development in Social Context*, Cambridge, Mass., Harvard University Press.

Schurmans, M.N. and Dasen, P.R. (1991) 'Social Representations of Intelligence: Côte d'Ivoire and Switzerland', in M. von Cranach, W. Doise and G. Mugny (Eds), *Social Representations and Social Bases of Knowledge*, Berne, Huber.

Scribner, S. and Cole, M. (1981) *The Psychology of Literacy*, Cambridge, Mass., Harvard University Press.

Segall, M.H., Dasen, P.R. Berry, J.W. and Poortinga, Y.H. (1990) *Human Behavior in Global Perspective: An Introduction to Cross-Cultural Psychology*, New York, Pergamon Press.

Super, C. and Harkness, S. (1986) 'The Developmental Niche: A Conceptualization at the Interface of Child and Culture', *International Journal of Behavioral Development*, 9, 4, pp. 545–570.

Triandis, H.C. (1980) 'Introduction', in H.C. Triandis and W.W. Lambert (Eds), *Handbook of Cross-Cultural Psychology, Vol. 1: Perspectives*, Boston, Mass., Allyn and Bacon, pp. 1–15.

Triandis, H.C. (1985) 'Collectivism vs. Individualism: A Reconceptualization of a Basic Concept in Cross-Cultural Social Psychology', in C. Bagley and G.K. Verma (Eds), *Personality, Cognition and Values*, London, Macmillan.

Triandis, H.C. (1987) 'Individualism and Social Psychological Theory', in C. Kagitcibasi (Ed.), *Growth and Progress in Cross-Cultural Psychology*, Lisse, Swets and Zeitlinger, pp. 78–83.

Triandis, H.C. (1990) 'Theoretical Concepts That Are Applicable to the Analysis of Ethnocentrism', in R.W. Brislin (Ed.), *Applied Cross-Cultural Psychology*, Newbury Park, Calif., Sage, pp. 34–55.

UNESCO (1984) *Répertoire des Institutions d'Études interculturelles*, Paris, UNESCO.

Wagner, D.A. (1981) 'Culture and Memory Development', in H.C. Triandis and A. Heron (Eds), *Handbook of Cross-Cultural Psychology. Vol. 4: Developmental Psychology*, Boston, Mass., Allyn and Bacon, pp. 187–232.

Whiting, B.B. (1980) 'Culture and Social Behavior: A Model for the Development of Social Behavior', *Ethos*, 8, pp. 95–116.

Whiting, J.W.M. and Whiting, B.B. (1978) 'A Strategy for Psychocultural Research', in G.D. Spindler (Ed.), *The Making of Psychological Anthropology*, Berkeley, Calif., University of California Press, pp. 41–61.

Zack, M. and Bril, B. (1989) 'Comment les Mères françaises et bambara du Mali se Représentent-Elles le Développement de Leur Enfant?' in J. Retschitzki, M. Bossel-Lagos and P. Dasen (Eds), *La Recherche interculturelle*, Vol. 2, Paris, L'Harmattan, pp. 7–17.

# Part Three: Educational Approaches to Reduce Prejudice

# 11. Teaching Methods that Enhance Human Dignity, Self-Respect and Academic Achievement*

BASIL R. SINGH

> When schools are fair and compassionate, teachers and administrators will not simply teach values — they will live by them. (Joseph, 1986, p. 46)

## EDUCATION AND COMMITMENT TO VALUES

Few would doubt that schools, even when they make no attempt to instil moral values, affect the child's perception of right and wrong and of acceptable and unacceptable conduct. Even at the preschool level, classroom rules and procedures, as well as other indications of teacher and peer approval and disapproval, influence students. The orderly functioning of the classroom depends, in part, on the acceptance and internalization of certain values. Punctuality, courtesy, cooperation and honesty are fundamental. Teacher interventions at many levels, whether in fighting or in correcting incorrect academic responses, reveal certain values the teacher holds and is trying to transmit (Pyszkowski 1986, p. 42).

If the teacher accepts every kind of behaviour without showing some sign of approval or disapproval, is the student to conclude that all values are relative and that there is no such thing as truth, right, wrong, good and bad? Surely the teacher must, at least, give the impression that all answers or behavioural responses to others, or all views or opinions are not of equal value. The teacher, of course, can stand aside and ignore students' responses which are insulting to particular sex, racial, ethnic or religious groups, but what the teacher cannot do is to justify such action in terms of morality. As teachers and educators, we must be aware that if students deliberately and continuously cause harm to others without experiencing any kind of social disapproval, they impair not only the personality

---

* The author expresses his deepest gratitude to the authors and publishers cited in the references on which he drew for this chapter.

of the injured person, but also their own personality. Wrong-doing or injury is in a way an infringement of the rights of others to be free from wilful injury. It is also to deny that the injured person is a moral agent with moral rights, and a member of one's moral community.

Harmful acts to others, therefore, must be ruled out of court in a civilized classroom situation, for it goes without saying that in almost every civilized society there are 'absolute prohibitions' against wrong-doing, without which the society cannot exist (McIntyre, 1982, p. 159). In every society, and indeed in almost every social institution, the good of the individual is somehow bound up with the well-being of others. If this is true, then the claim of this chapter is that the central task of education is to strengthen the student's desire to promote his/her own good as well as promoting the good of others. Education, according to this view, would attempt to develop both cognitive and affective qualities in individuals. Among other things education must attempt to guide and shape individuals, and steer them toward feelings of concern for others, that is, towards a life in which shared moral values predominate. It is for these and other reasons that the teacher cannot stand aside and let wrong-doing against others go unchecked. It is for these reasons that the teacher cannot let sexism, racism, fascism or any kind of wilful discrimination or abuse go unchecked because they form part of the stock of views of some students, some parents, some peer groups or some pupils' culture or religious inheritance (Walkling and Brannigan, 1986, pp. 16–25). Accordingly, the aim of education emerging from these general postulates would be to get students to see their own good as inextricably bound up with the good of others. For, as Callan warns us: 'A child who has learnt always to advance his own interests at the expense of others will hardly achieve much fulfilment in a world where success depends so much on the goodwill and co-operation of others' (1985, p. 15).

More importantly, discriminating against some people on the basis of race, class or sex is a way of depriving them of their moral right as members of a moral community.

In teaching one tries to bring about the development of worthwhile states of mind and character of students. Consequently, in teaching one intends to bring about some results, one evolves methods of teaching and procedures of assessment. It follows, therefore, that teaching is an intentional act designed to bring about some desirable states of mind. It is the claim of this chapter that in teaching in a multicultural, multiracial setting, especially where racial or ethnic relationship is negative or strained, the teacher cannot teach effectively unless he or she frames his or her intentions, adopts appropriate procedures which are committed toward the eradication of such negative or strained relationship. Of course, there will be people who will object to the teacher's intervention in the education process to bring about certain forms of socially or morally acceptance relationships between students of different ethnic or racial origin. But the teacher need not worry, for he or she can appeal to the existence of moral or ethical standards which most people claim to live by. It is the existence of these standards that enables the teacher to demonstrate the superiority of reasonableness over unreasonableness, of justice over injustice, of respect for others over disrespect.

It is the duty of every teacher to instruct, create certain situations or initiate students into certain moral standards which have to do with promoting human good and avoiding human harm. Consequently, the teacher must take a stand against wrong-doing, or sexism or racism or certain other forms of prejudice based on, say, students' class, culture, or religion. A teacher who is committed to the eradication of, say, racial prejudice is concerned above all to establish the rightness or wrongness of behaving in certain ways. The wrongness of actions acquires significance in the core of values enshrined and intrinsic to the shared value framework laid down within a democratic form of life. Within such a framework the teacher will be concerned to develop students' cognitive as well as affective qualities. The teacher who is concerned with students' right thinking, as well as with right action, cannot leave the development of such qualities to chance. Students must be taught what it is to act justly, fairly, what it is to discriminate against others and to hurt others. The teacher must deliberately teach these qualities by example and by precept.

Well chosen aims, content and teaching strategies which engage students' minds and relationships to each other could help to bring about the development of desirable states of mind and character. It is not the intention here to suggest that these qualities of mind and character can be developed in the abstract in non-concrete situations. Indeed, since many of these qualities are 'picked up' rather than learnt, it is imperative that the student's environment be congenial to the acquisition of these virtues. Above all, classroom procedures and especially teaching techniques and reward structures must be deliberately designed to bring about these worthwhile states of mind and appropriate dispositions, i.e., morally and socially interpersonal relationships. The whole education process must constitute an abiding ongoing moral experience for every child, whatever his/her colour, creed or sex.

Many of the cooperative learning techniques described below are designed to take these into account. They are concerned to develop the mind as well as mutual concerns. The pedagogic approach the teacher adopts is of vital importance in the realization of objectives such as academic development within the framework of mutual concerns.

One of the main assumptions here is that denial of positive self-esteem or moral worth to others diminishes one's own worth as a rational, moral, self-forming being. Consequently, it is for the good of everyone that teachers and others should declare such (discriminatory) acts against others as invalid. The school community must express its denial of validity to the injurious discriminatory acts, uphold the rights of the injured and thereby uphold the rights of all others as well (Charvet, 1981, pp. 155–167). For the ultimate moral ground for the existence of any community of individuals is constituted by a collection of specific individuals valuing each other as ends and as members having rights in civic society. In such a society individuals' values consist of their common will and mutual valuing (Charvet, 1981, p. 192).

With regard to the place the individual occupies within a moral framework, Charvet argues that individuals who are already members of a particular society already participate in relations of interdependence. Interdependence of particular lives in actual societies means that the shape and content of such lives are formed by their development within a structure of relations to others, i.e., a social structure. This structure necessarily places a value on particular lives insofar as they conform to it by acting out the roles specified in the structure. To say that the individual's particular life is determined by his/her social structure is not, according to Charvet, to say that he/she does not participate in his/her own formation as an occupant of a role in that structure, for he/she must acquire the capacity to direct himself/herself in accordance with his/her society's values; nor does it deny the individual's capacity to manipulate, modify or change that structure to suit himself/herself. The individual is 'formed' and 'determined' by his/her place in the social whole. Social value is upheld only through the willing adherence of members of one's institution. Each member of one's institution is a co-determiner of each other's worth. It is this moral attitude implicit in an institution that helps to shape the consciousness and perceptions and quality of relationships among its participants. It follows that an educator who seriously wants to educate cannot stand aside and let wrong-doing go unchallenged without committing an offence against morality.

Moral attitudes come into being in the process of mutual valuing of individuals as members of a community. The standpoint of this community's values is the basis of the rights that ethnic minorities and others claim (Charvet, 1981, p. 172). In his/her daily activity the individual is dependent on other individuals; consequently, no individual within a community is completely self-determined, but is determined as part of a larger whole. Every individual must accommodate himself/herself to the fact that while he/she can think of his/her life apart from the whole, it is nevertheless true that his/her life is determined and completed by others as parts of a whole. The first element can be satisfied only if the individual has the opportunity to make decisions regarding his/her own particular life, chooses his/her occupation and engages in activities by himself/herself or with others, and these activities must not harm others. Within the existing structure of rights one has the right to pursue one's own good for oneself, but one is required to think of the possible harm it may do to others (Charvet, 1981, p. 180).

It follows from the above that schools should be concerned not only with intellectual development but also with character formation. Education is an intellectual and a moral enterprise. Parents expect the school to be an environment that cultivates intellectual growth as well as appropriate moral and caring dispositions. The school must become a nursery in which psychologically and morally healthy individuals develop. To achieve these objectives, it is necessary that the school community comes to share these values, articulate and disseminate them among all its participants. Some of the values that will help to make the school into an effective community will include a belief in the importance of rewarding success over a range of academic and non-academic performances, and a commitment to helping those who fail to come up to certain standards.

If, as Wright (1986) argues, concern for others is to develop in schools and become a consciously planned aspect of teachers' professional concerns, it is necessary to evolve a clear, simple and adequate conception of what it entails. Such a conception must involve what it is to be concerned for others and how this attribute develops within the young student within an organizational structure and, more particularly, how such concerns can be nurtured, strengthened and extended by the experience of schooling (Wright, 1986, p. 45). Since every individual is supposed to be of equal value, then it is unacceptable that one individual should have greater opportunities than another simply because of his/her particular location in the world. Charvet adds that the value of the individual is partly derivable from his/her membership of a community. Consequently, teachers must be conscious of the fact that they and their students are moral persons whose worth, as persons, is not derivable from their ability to perform or excel in any particular way on academic tasks.

Individuals are conscious beings who necessarily have intentions and purposes. They are conscious of themselves and the world they live in; but this does not imply that individuals are equally conscious of themselves and of their situations. Yet we know that such consciousness can be increased or decreased by social actions and by the environment in which one lives or learns. Individual consciousness is determined by one's role in society and in institutions, and this role with its attendant status is the product of social arrangements (Williams, 1962, p. 116).

Since people grow and develop in relationship to each other, the quality of such relationships will influence how they grow and develop, the moral values they share and their views of themselves and of others. As such, moral values govern the quality of human relationships, establishing what are acceptable and unacceptable patterns of behaviour between individuals. Morality in this sense is a public and not a private affair and, as Wright (1986) argues, 'the morality of others is . . . as much, though not more our concern as is our own' (Wright, 1986, p. 47). Wright points out that in the most general sense morality might be defined as the emergent, regulative equilibrium between people related to each other on the basis of reciprocal respect for each other's autonomy as moral agents who are capable of human actions, i.e., originating their own judgments and who are on that basis on an equal footing with other individuals.

As moral agents, therefore, we are answerable for our moral judgments. Consequently, the education system and its attendant processes should be concerned with helping students to acquire self-knowledge, acquired in the course of their acquiring knowledge of the world and about others. It is this knowledge of others, acquired through involvement and participation with others in interpersonal human relationships, that serves as the defining characteristic of oneself. Seeing ourselves as persons, or initiators of goals or purposes in a world with other persons like ourselves, we come to develop a conception of ourselves as moral persons too, entitled to a degree of forbearance from any other persons conceptually capable of grasping the nature of our self-perception. Thus, claiming respect — as moral persons — we are then committed to extend it to anyone else satisfying the same conditions. By so doing we show respect for persons. Consequently, if one proposes to thwart someone or reduce his/her options in some way, then it is not enough to justify such acts in terms of one's own wants or interests. For the priniciple demands that one takes the interests or wants of others into account as well (Benn, 1975–76, pp. 120–121). In failing to take the perspective of others, or failing to take account of their feelings, their wants or interests, or to judge their interests in terms of some negative characteristics based on race, class or sex would be to discriminate against them. Pre-judging others on the the basis of their race is what this chapter is partly about.

## ON PREJUDICE

Racial prejudice is one of the greatest social problems of the second half of the twentieth century. It has been described as a social disease of epidemic proportions and, unlike some other equally important social problems such as child abuse, aids or drug addiction, there has not yet been any unified, national effort in Britain to counteract its negative, all-pervading, damaging effects.

Prejudice is an attitude defined in varying ways. Secord and Backman (1974) defined it as a positive or negative attitude toward a person or a group. The notion of prejudice used here is of an attitude that is wrong, especially when it so frequently departs from ideal norms such as rationality, justice and human rights (McDougall, 1983, p. 4). Prejudice is thus conceived here as a bias or preconception (for or) against, for example, a particular group of people. As preconceptions, prejudices tend to be fairly stable and rigid, but potentially reversible. As a pre-judgment, prejudice results in evaluating, say, a group of people on assumed characteristics in advance of correct information about that group. In this sense it is an irrational pre-judgment which establishes fairly pre-set ways of perceiving and evaluating others who are different. Such irrational prejudgments are difficult to remove or modify by education, but, given the will and particularly the political and educational will, much could be done to halt the adverse social consequences that flow from such prejudices. However, not all prejudices are irrational. Consequently, education through its rational procedures and processes has an important place to play in helping to remove rational prejudices based, for example, on incorrect information, assumptions or 'evidence'.

In essence, prejudice is irrational, unjust and often leads to intolerant behaviour towards other groups. It is often accompanied by stereotyping, i.e., attributing certain supposed qualities or characteristics of a whole group to all its individual members. Such stereotyping or attributions of characteristics to others has the effect of exaggerating the uniformity within a group and its distinctions from others. As Milner (1975) puts it: 'The entire group is tarred with the same brush, obscuring individual differences.' Milner adds that the process is made easier where there are visible physical differences between groups; these can be convincingly depicted as signifying other, more profound differences and hence a 'reason' for differential treatment. In this way prejudiced attitudes have expedited the oppression of groups of people throughout history, and when there have been differences in skin colour, the most obvious and intractable of physical differences, the process has been facilitated (Milner, 1975, p. 9).

The assumption here is that in accordance with the norm of justice and rationality, people should seek correct information about others, for example, and should be cautious in drawing conclusions about them. Stereotypic thinking is an example of the kind of thinking that will deviate from the norms of justice or rationality. Stereotypes and prejudice not only deviate from the norms of rationality and justice in society but they cause untold suffering among innocent groups of people, including school children. Consequently, the school (and society) must endeavour to remove them. All prejudice in this sense is an offence against human decency and human rights, and any method that will remove it will help to advance human dignity and human rights. The claim of this chapter is that human rights may be the best overall policy for all schools, and this may be achieved by a variety of methods used simultaneously throughout the school. These would include a whole school's policy; changes in the curriculum such as elimination of prejudiced tests; and alteration in pupil-teacher relationships and methods of instruction. However, there is no single solution that is best in all situations, and a combined 'universal' approach will probably be most successful.

One method that has been extensively studies in recent years is cooperative learning; it is to a small sample of the exemplary pedagogical work which has attempted to address the task of academic achievement and prejudice reduction that we turn for some guiding principles for teachers at the chalk-face. Evidence examined below suggests that we already have the means whereby teachers and schools may address successfully the tasks of prejudice reduction and enhancement of academic achievement and human dignity.

Cumulatively, the force of such research and writing is sufficient to persuade us that a school can develop a good ethos, serving both intellectual and social dimensions of its work. Consequently, academic or intellectual work could improve social relations and attitudes. Academic attainment does not have to take a 'back seat' to improve social relations and attitudes (Crain *et al.*, 1982; Slavin, 1985). Prejudice reduction can give a double bonus in schools and classrooms, provided that they are organized according to the principles outlined below.

## IDEOLOGY, CULTURE AND RACE RELATIONS

Ideology and culture are important determinants in shaping race relations in schooling. Ideology, beliefs or values manifest themselves in educational structures and in the formal and informal practices of school life. School programmes, curricula, aims, teaching strategies that seek to address racial problems or discrimination based on sex, class or physical handicaps must take account of these beliefs, attitudes and values. They must also take into account the covert use of racial, gender or class evaluations which are encoded in both the rhetoric and criteria by which these groups are discussed, evaluated and treated. Thus if the roots of discrimination are to be found in normative and structural properties of institutions, it is to these that strategies aiming to eradicate discrimination must be directed (McCarthy, 1988, pp. 266–267).

## PREJUDICE AND EQUAL STATUS CONTACT

Some of the most important questions that researchers have been trying to answer in relation to prejudice and education in the last fifty years or so have been: what happens when Black and White students work on a cooperative task? Does one racial group tend to dominate the task situation, or will conditions of equality emerge? If there is a pattern of systematic domination by one racial group over another, then what type of intervention will be effective in altering this repeated pattern of single race domination? The complex answers to these difficult questions, as Lohman pointed out as early as 1972, have broad implications for many schools and work situations that require interaction and cooperation among group members who differ in racial backgrounds. The research considered here offers important insights into some crucial issues raised by the above questions.

As far back as 1954, Gordon Allport cited research indicating that superficial contact could be detrimental to race relations, as could competitive contact between individuals of markedly different status. However, he also cited evidence that when individuals of different racial or ethnic groups worked to achieve common goals, when they had opportunities to get to know one another as individuals, and when they worked with one another on an equal footing, they became friends and did not continue to hold prejudices against one another. Allport (1954) sums up the essence of his contact theory as follows:

> Prejudice may be reduced by equal status contact between majority and minority groups in the pursuit of common goals. The effect is greatly enhanced if this contact is sanctioned by institutional support ... and if it is of a sort that leads to the perception of common interests and common humanity between members of the two groups. (Allport, 1954, p. 281)

## CONTACT THEORY AND COOPERATIVE LEARNING THEORY

Since Allport's work over thirty years ago, there has been much research on the development and refinement of group techniques in the classroom to encourage good relations among children. Some of the techniques have been concerned with instructional methods designed to operationalize the principal elements of Allport's (1954) contact theory of intergroup relations. Basically, the 'contact hypothesis' posits that one's behaviour and attitudes toward members of a disliked social category will become more positive after direct interpersonal interactions, but only under certain conditions, that is:

1   that contact must occur in circumstances that define the status of the participants from the two social groups as equal;
2   that the attributes of the disliked group members with whom the contact occurs must disconfirm the prevailing stereotyped beliefs about them;
3   that the contact situation must encourage, or perhaps require, mutually interdependent relations, that is, cooperation in the achievement of a joint goal;
4   that the contact situation must have high acquaintance potential, that is, it must promote association of a sort that reveals enough detail about the members of a disliked group to encourage them as individuals rather than as persons with stereotyped group characteristics; and
5   that the social norms of the contact situation must favour group equality and egalitarian intergroup association (see Cook, 1978).

A review of the literature by Allport (1954) and by Amir (1969) led to the proposal that contact between ethnic groups is most likely to reduce prejudice when members of the majority encounter members of the minority who are at least equal in status to themselves. This sparked off a number of research proposals, a few of which are described below.

## THE NEED FOR EGALITARIAN STRUCTURE

Many attempts to bring Black and White students together in the same classroom in the hope of lessening crossracial hostility, eliminating racial stereotyping and increasing crossracial understanding have met with little success. These failures may have occurred, according to Cohen (1975), because the typical school mirrors the status order of the larger society that confirms the racial stereotypes.

Evidence of the existence of such stereotypes had been brought to our attention as early as the 1930s. In a study by Katz and Braly (1933), for instance, 100 White undergraduates were asked to give the traits selected from a list of eighty-four adjectives they considered most characteristic of each of ten groups (Germans, Italians, Negroes, Irish, English, Jews, Americans, Chinese, Japanese and Turks). After completing the tasks subjects were asked to select the five traits *most* typical of each group. It was found that the five traits most frequently chosen as typical of Negroes were 'superstitious', 'lazy', 'happy-go-lucky', 'ignorant' and 'musical'. The five most frequently chosen as typical for White Americans were 'industrious', 'intelligent', 'materialistic', 'ambitious' and 'progressive'. Bayton (1941) repeated the Katz and Braly investigation with a sample of 100 Black undergraduates and found similar stereotypes. Although Blacks included 'intelligent' among the first ten traits attributed to Negroes, they were more agreed on the intelligence of Whites. In 1956 Bayton *et al.*, found that the traits assigned to Whites by both Blacks and Whites were more favourable than those assigned to Blacks. Subsequent research provides evidence that race is a status characteristic and has profound consequences for education. These status characteristics provide the basis of evaluation and beliefs about actors in a participatory relationship. According to Berger *et al.* (1980), they are the centre around which evaluations and beliefs about others come to be organized. They provide the basis of performance expectations, i.e., the stabilized beliefs about how an individual possessing a particular characteristic will perform or behave (Berger *et al.*, 1980).

## IMPLICATIONS OF RACE AS A STATUS CHARACTERISTIC

Because race is seen as a status characteristic, researchers have found that in any given situation where Blacks and Whites participate, Whites are both given and take more opportunities to perform and are evaluated as performing better (for the same performance), and have more influence than Blacks. Katz, Goldstone and Benjamin (1958) found that in biracial groups performing problem-solving tasks, Whites initiated more interaction than Blacks, and both Whites and Blacks talked more to Whites than to Blacks, even though subjects were matched for intelligence and made to display equal ability at the task. Later work by Katz and Benjamin (1960) indicates that the relationship between Black and White pupils, when they are engaged cooperatively in problem-solving tasks, will be biased in the same direction as in the wider society. That is, the Whites will be more active and influential than the Blacks. The concept of 'interracial interaction disability' was coined to represent this state of affairs. In 1962 Katz devised an 'assertion training method' which attempted to reverse the status position of Black students by allowing them to have as many correct answers or responses to a series of mathematical problems as White students. In pre- and post-test tasks Katz asked the interracial pairs to solve an unambiguous task that involved influence and judgment. Comparing Blacks who had received assertion training to Blacks who had not, Katz reported a more aggressive pattern of behaviour in the post-test situation for the former group (Katz and Cohen, 1962). Thus the work of Katz (and later work by others) indicates that race is a powerful predictor of the power and prestige order in interracial task oriented group work. Berger *et al.* (1966), for example, show that initial differences in social status produce a power and prestige order resembling the ranking in status on new group tasks where competence at the task has no rational relationship to the state of the status characteristic.

## EXPECTATION TRAINING INTERVENTIONS

Intervention techniques have been devised to reverse the ranking of status characteristics between ethnically different groups. Cohen's (1972) early work was based on the assumptions and guidelines of status characteristic theory, whose main elements of expectation training interventions were as follows:

1   Blacks received a training procedure that taught them highly competent behaviour for a specific task;
2   Whites received a neutral training procedure which neither hindered nor helped their performance for the same specific task;
3   Blacks and Whites worked together on a specific task with the expectation that the superior training of the Blacks would be visibly demonstrated. Independent observation was made to determine the relative competence of each participant.

In her investigation of 'interracial interaction disability' Cohen (1972) found that White subjects were more active and influential than Black subjects. Also, influence and initiation rates of decision-making were positively correlated. White subjects had a higher rate of interrelation than Black subjects, and consequently they had more influence over decisions made by the group than Black subjects. Thus race was strongly associated with differences in rank order on the number of acts initiated, with the Whites much more likely to have a higher rank in the group than the Blacks. When the number of times a person's suggestion became the group's decision is taken into account, Whites were much more influential than Blacks, especially when decisions were contested. As indicated above, the indices of influence and rate of influence and the rate of initiation were strongly positively related (Cohen, 1972, pp. 23–24).

In using junior high school boys and controlling for height, socio-economic status (SES) and attitude toward school, Cohen found that Whites initiated more interaction, exerted more influence and were evaluated as having the best ideas, being most able to guide and direct the group and being the best leaders more often than Blacks.

In the same year Cohen and Roper (1972) attempted to produce equal status interaction among four-person interracial groups of junior high school boys by assigning a high level of competence to the Black subjects on two related tasks. Each treated group played a criterion game where the probabilities of Whites and Blacks being active and influential could be measured. The results show that unless the expectations for Black competence held by both Whites and Blacks are treated, Whites will dominate the interaction in the criterion game. In the experiment cited above, when expectations of Whites were treated by having Whites as students of a Black teacher, behaviour on the game approximated an equal status pattern (Cohen *et al.*, 1972, p. 643).

The evidence of Cohen and Roper (1972) suggests that assigning a high degree of competence to lower status subjects on a general performance characteristic will modify the effects of that status characteristic on a criterion task, i.e., that having high competence on the training task will raise expectations for competence on another task. But this was only so when both Black and White expectations for Black performance were treated. Thus providing Black subjects with success experience was not enough to change the interaction balance of Blacks and Whites. A positive balance was achieved when both Black and White expectations were treated. The results show 'that the effect of the diffuse status characteristic may be modified by assigning low status members a high rating on competence on a general performance characteristic' (Cohen *et al.*, 1972, p. 655).

A decade later Cohen (1982) studied ethnicity as a status characteristic among nineteen groups of Mexican-American and Anglo junior high school boys rated on age, height and a combined index of socio-economic status (SES) and attitude toward school. Secondary analysis of the data showed that Mexican-Americans who were more clearly identifiable as ethnic group members had lower rates of initiation and influence than other group members. Under conditions involving a visible status characteristic (say, skin colour) Anglos were markedly more active and influential than Mexican-Americans. Cohen suggests that participants were acting as if race or ethnicity were directly relevant to success on the collective task. They gave more action opportunities to those who belonged to the high status group; high status members talked more and their suggestions were treated as if they were more competent. High status members were seen as having better ideas and as having done more to guide the group. This occurred despite the fact that there was no logical connection between the status characteristic and competence on the task (Cohen, 1982, pp. 212–213). The actors, according to Cohen, behaved as if the status elements were relevant indicators of task skills, thus putting the burden of proof on anyone who would show otherwise. Thus Cohen infers that: 'When a racial status characteristic becomes salient in the situation, the prestige and power order of the small group working on a collective task comes to reflect the broader social status ranking of the races in a kind of self-fulfilling prophecy' (Cohen, 1982, p. 213).

Cohen maintains that there is ample evidence that in contemporary society, when interracial groups work on a collective task, Whites are more active and influential than Blacks and Browns. This occurs even though the task has nothing intrinsically to do with race (Cohen, 1982, p. 210). Elsewhere Cohen (1984) argues that if reading ability, for example, is seen as a 'specific status characteristic', this status characteristic can spread to new and irrelevant tasks within the school. Consequently, if White students are seen to be better at reading skills, they may come to dominate discussions in an interracial group, which may come to confirm the pre-existing beliefs concerning lesser intellectual competence of Blacks and Browns. Cohen warns us that if students who are poor readers, for example, expect to be and are expected to be incompetent at intellectual tasks, they will withdraw, refuse to work on learning tasks and even become what is known as 'difficult' students, regardless of the challenge or intrinsic interest of the task at hand (Cohen, 1984, p. 79).


## INTERRACIAL INTERACTION DISABILITY UNDER CLASSROOM CONDITIONS

The next question to be answered by researchers working within the interracial interaction disability framework was whether the findings obtained under experimental conditions could have validity within a classroom situation. Cohen and her colleagues (1976) set out to investigate this question. They wanted to know if equal status behaviour produced by experimental intervention could last over an extended period of classroom interaction. They created a special summer school, using the same school that the students regularly attended. This junior high school had experienced marked difficulty in race relations. Black and White parents complained of little learning and too much fighting. Although the students were drawn from this junior high school, they did not know each other. Staff members observed distrust, fear and stereotypical views held by students from the first day (Cohen *et al.*, 1976, p. 49).

The researchers reasoned that if they wished to foster equal status behaviour on the part of students of different races, they would have to distribute power and authority equally between Black and White personnel. Thus administrative, research and teaching posts were filled by interracial teams. The most visible role models for the children were the Black and White co-directors and the interracial teaching teams. Girls were also included in this study. The 145 children were 10–13 years old, racially mixed and from different socio-economic classes.

This study followed the same method as previous studies, except for the Black student becoming a teacher of a White student on four (instead of one) different tasks. Each task involved one lesson each morning for four mornings. Two tasks were academic — building plastic polygons and learning the Malay language and culture — and two were non-academic — a spatial problem-solving task and the building of a radio transmitter. Each Black child was taught all four tasks and was given preparation for his/her role as a teacher of a White child. The Black children went to school a week earlier for expectation training purposes. Videotape reinforcement of Black competence was provided as in previous research, and, as in previous research, students were formed into four-person single-sex interracial groups within treatment conditions. All students played the game called 'Kill the Bull', which required the team to make successive decisions as to which way to proceed on a game board. Children were encouraged to work cooperatively.

The results show that in no treatment sex category were Blacks markedly less active than Whites. There was a tendency for Black male dominance in male expectation training treatment. Furthermore, classroom interaction scores on both male and female expectation training show the Blacks participating more than would have been expected on an equal status basis. Students reported enjoying the curricula and their experiences at school. There was little evidence of the interracial conflict so characteristic of the same school during the regular term. The researchers concluded that 'the production of equal-status conditions is a necessary but not a sufficient condition for the improvement of black achievement ...' (Cohen *et al.*, 1976, p. 57).

## REDESIGNING THE TASK AND EVALUATIVE STRUCTURE TO ACHIEVE MUTUAL ADVANTAGE

Much of what has been said above in relation to status characteristics received evidential support in later studies. In a two-year study by Cohen (1984), for example, including a large-scale field experiment involving three schools which participated in a status equalization project involving interracial groups from a wide social class range, Cohen found that even in purely cooperative interracial groups there was a strong probability that White students who were seen as better readers would dominate minority students who were seen as poorer readers. This, according to Cohen, occurred with a task that did not require reading or other conventional academic skills. Cohen concluded that if an interracial school setting does not have adults of minority background in positions of authority, if the proportion of minority students is small and if the minority students are likely to be weaker in academic skills because of their socio-economic backgrounds, the stage is set for the unchecked operation of an academic status characteristic. For Cohen, attempts to produce interracial intergroup feeling and friendliness through such interventions as cooperative grouping may fail, since students who are low on academic status characteristics will exhibit depressed rates of interaction on academic tasks. Lower rates of task-related peer interaction in turn affect learning outcomes. Schools should, therefore, aim to redesign the task and evaluation structure so as to alter the status of those who are low in academic status. If the goal of the school is to improve academic performance as well as to improve mutual cooperation and race relations, then teaching techniques and curriculum content, for example, will have to change to provide appropriate and challenging learning experiences for classrooms with a wide range of academic achievement. These changes should be seen as supplementary to the introduction of cooperative task groups that have demonstrated a positive effect on intergroup reactions. However, Cohen does not think that the introduction of cooperative group techniques, for example, will produce the desired results for schools of mixed races (or classes). These results are attainable, but only if we start facing the complexity of the social structure of the school in which recommended changes must operate (Cohen, 1984, pp. 93–95).

## RACE, STATUS AND ABILITY ON HELPING BEHAVIOUR

Much of what Cohen reported found increasing support by researchers working in the same area. In their work on the effect of race, status and ability on helping behaviour, for instance, Dovidio and Gaertner (1981) found that status and not ability seemed to be the primary factor influencing subjects' helping behaviour to Black partners, but White ability, not status, seemed to be the dominant factor determining subjects' helping behaviour toward White partners. The evidence indicates more positive White reactions to Black subordinates relative to Black supervisors, which may reflect greater attraction to Blacks in subordinate positions. This helps to explain one factor that reinforces and helps to perpetuate the dependent and subordinate positions of Blacks. Furthermore, although subjects evaluated Black and White high ability partners as being quite intelligent and as being more intelligent than low ability partners, discrimination occurred when subjects compared highly competent Blacks to themselves. Dovidio and Gaertner point out that although subjects accepted high cognitive ability partners as being more intelligent than themselves, high ability Black partners were rated as significantly less intelligent than themselves. Thus high ability among Whites may be regarded as desirable, while among Black it may not be fully appreciated.

It appears that subjects were not only reluctant to accept that a Black person was more intelligent, but that they were even unwilling to acknowledge that a Black partner was equal in intelligence to themselves. Thus both high and low ability Blacks were regarded by White subjects as relatively less competent than themselves (Dovidio and Gaertner, 1981, pp. 199–200). Similar results were found in earlier work by Rubovits and Maehr (1973), who assessed differential teacher expectations for Black and White students. In an attempt to replicate the Rosenthal and Jacobson (1968) 'Pygmalion' technique, student teachers interacted with groups of two Black and two White students. One child of each race was labelled in advance as 'gifted'. In actuality, all children were matched for intellectual achievement. These investigators found that White student teachers responded quite differently to the White and Black junior high school students who were labelled gifted. Blacks were ignored more, criticized more and praised less. White student teachers' attitudes towards Black students who were equally gifted as White students were certainly less positive.

## RACISM AND THE SIGNIFICANCE OF INSTITUTIONAL NORMS

The role relationship between Blacks and Whites has traditionally been characterized by dependence, subordination and assumed inferiority of Blacks. Nevertheless, because racists are usually very sensitive about their egalitarian self-image, they are especially concerned with avoiding unfavourable or normatively inappropriate behaviour in interracial situations so as to avoid threatening their non-prejudiced self-concepts. Consequently, as Dovidio and Gaertner (1983) argued, discrimination against Blacks is relatively unlikely to occur in situations with salient normative structures. That is, in situations in which norms prescribing appropriate behaviour are clear and unambiguous, Blacks would not be treated less favourably than Whites because 'wrong-doing' would be obvious and would challenge the egalitarian self-image. The researchers continued that, when normative structures are strong, Whites may even respond more favourably to Blacks than to Whites, given this added threat to their self-image. However, when norms are weak, ambiguous or conflicting, rendering the concepts of right and wrong less applicable, Blacks may be treated differently and in a manner that disadvantages them. This discrimination will typically be expressed subtly and indirectly, in ways in which the person can rationalize his or her response without threatening a non-bigoted self-image (Gaertner and Dovidio, 1977).

A threat to self-esteem, according to Wills (1983), motivates people to enhance their self-image. One way to enhance one's self-image is by engaging in downward comparison and social comparison with less fortunate others. When downward comparison is not possible, another way of alleviating this threat may involve inflating one's self-evaluation to maintain feelings of relative efficacy. Dovidio and Gaertner (1981) also suggest that for many Whites the needs for relative status and for feelings of control and superiority are particularly salient in interracial interaction. If this is so, then prejudice may be particularly resistant to change, even after an apparently positive interaction between the groups.

## RESEARCH RELATING TO STATUS CHARACTERISTICS IN ANOTHER SOCIO-CULTURAL CONTEXT

Research carried out in other socio-cultural contexts seems to support the findings of Cohen and others. The social context of ethnic relations in Israel, for example, provides some marked contrasts to conditions in, say, the United States. Yet the study of academic status, differentiation and ethnic perceptions and preferences of Israeli youths by Amir *et al.* (1978), where the Jewish population consisted of two major ethnic groups, those from the Muslim countries of the Middle East and North Africa, and those from Western countries of Europe, South Africa and America, came to the same results found in America.

The lower social status of the Middle Eastern Jews in comparison with the Western group in Israel, according to Amir *et al.* parallels the social gap between Blacks and Whites in the United States. Some of the components of the social gap include academic achievement, professional, managerial and technical positions in employment, and leadership in society. Their study showed asymmetrical relations in which Western Jews preferred themselves and were preferred by the Middle Eastern group. Also, students of high academic status from both ethnic groups perceived less of a gap between the two groups than did students of lower academic status. However, higher ability students from both groups preferred members of the Western group more than did low ability students.

Thus the evidence obtained by Amir and his colleagues about preferential attitudes toward Western groups among members of both ethnic groups in Israel confirms results reported by previous investigators and is consistent with the asymmetrical ethnic relations reported in the USA. Amir *et al.* generalized from their findings that members of the Middle Eastern group who achieved a relatively high level of academic or socio-economic status displayed the same kind of positive attitude toward their own group as did members of the Western group toward their group. Equal socio-economic or academic status between ethnic groups thus exerts a particularly marked influence on attitudes towards one's own group.

The researchers added that high achieving students from both ethnic groups perceived less of a difference between themselves and members of the other ethnic group than did low achieving students. Nevertheless, the asymmetrical pattern of ethnic attitudes did not disappear altogether, even among the high achieving students. The sociometric questions revealed that high and low ability students from both ethnic groups preferred the Western to the Middle Eastern students, but this tendency was particularly marked among the high ability groups (Amir *et al.*, 1978, pp. 110–111).

A later study (Amir *et al.*, 1979) was designed to examine systematically the effects of both individual and group status on change in attitudes following ethnic contact in the classroom and the applications of these changes in attitude separately for the majority and minority ethnic groups from Western and Middle Eastern ethnic background in thirty classrooms, of 1033 students located in different parts of Israel. It was found that classrooms with equal status composition proved most salutary for attitude change of Western students (majority) toward Middle Eastern students (minority). Classrooms where the latter group excelled were also associated with positive change in the ethnic attitudes of Western towards Middle Eastern students. However, different outcomes emerged among Middle Eastern students. When their group occupied equal status in the classroom, or when the Middle Eastern group occupied a much lower status than the Western group, changes in attitude among the Middle Eastern group were not salutary. Only when the Middle Eastern group enjoyed superior status in the classroom did its members reveal positive changes in attitude. No change occurred in Middle Eastern students' attitude when the Western group was of moderately superior status (Amir *et al.*, 1979, p. 147). The researchers suggest that ethnic attitude change is a function of ethnic group status and not a function of individual status in the classroom.

The work of Amir *et al.* supports the work of Cohen *et al.*, who have shown that changes in the academic status of students could change ethnic attitudes. The Amir *et al.* (1979) findings suggest that group status in the classroom significantly affects change in ethnic attitudes, and this highlights the influence of status characteristics prevailing within the social settings where ethnic contact occurs, independent of that group's status in the macro-society.

## SIGNIFICANCE OF GROUP STATUS

These studies show that by defining equal status according to one or two important variables, such as academic achievement or popularity, one does not eradicate inequality on a host of other, perhaps equally important, variables such as the general status of one's ethnic group in society. Partial equalization of status does not appear to provide adequately positive features for minority group members who feel that they are of equal status in ability in their peer group with the majority members, but nevertheless remain disadvantaged. Perhaps, as Amir *et al.* (1979) add, only the attribution of higher status to the minority group can provide sufficient compensation for their relatively low status in society. But such attribution of superior status requires the intervention of powerful means to diminish the large status gap between minority and majority.

It is clear from the above studies that the problem of low status does not reside in the individual. White dominance is seen as a social product of the evaluation of self and others transmitted through cultural beliefs about the competence of Black and Whites, often reinforced in social interaction. Hence Cohen and her colleagues concluded that treating expectations of low status individuals only will not be effective. One must also treat the expectations of performance held by high status members.

Situations both inside and outside the classroom could be created where Black and White students could be put through a series of problem-solving sessions, and where the goal is to teach students how to work with people who are ethnically different. Expectation training could take place before members of different races, sexes, abilities were allowed to interact with and evaluate each other. In the overall design, expectation training could figure as a necessary, though probably insufficient, condition for long-term harmonious relations. Working in cooperative small group situations might help to treat the problems caused by status differences (Cohen *et al.*, 1982, p. 656). According to Cohen (1982), one cannot avoid the issue of academic status structure when dealing with race as a status characteristic in school settings. Moreover, in a school setting with wide variation in academic skills and competence, academic status structure could operate in the same direction as the diffuse status characteristic of race or ethnicity.

The main task of future research is to focus attention on the problem of how the task and evaluation structure of the classroom might be altered to produce a mixed set of expectations for intellectual competence held by everyone. For Cohen, although interaction is increased by the use of cooperative tasks, status factors will continue to depress the relative participation of low status children within the interacting group. Therefore, learning should be more favourable when both task structure and competence expectations are altered than when task structure alone is changed (1982, p. 232).

Successful interethnic relations depend upon a host of factors including equal status, interpersonal intimacy, social and institutional support, balanced representation of different cultures and an atmosphere of cooperation and mutual respect. Institutional support, both inside and outside the school, is of vital importance if any of the factors listed above are to be of any significance.

## TEACHER EXPECTATIONS AND STATUS CHARACTERISTICS

Expectations that teachers hold for their students may be potent determinants of students' performance because teachers translate their expectations into responses that affect the child's own expectations (Entwisle and Webster, 1974, p. 304). There is evidence (Coates, 1972) that White evaluations of Black performance are determined by race independently of actual performance. Coates (1972) found that White adults were significantly more likely to evaluate the performance of a Black child negatively than they were to evaluate an equivalent performance of a White child. The same effects were not found for White female adults. However, both male and female adults rated the personality traits of Black children more negatively than those of White children, despite the absence of behavioural differences between the two. Other studies by Entwisle and Webster (1974, 1977), offer some support to Coates' findings. In their 1974 research Entwisle and Webster attempted to find out what an adult can do to raise a child's expectations. Their other aim was to see how status characteristics of adults and of children affect expectation raising. They wanted to find out whether a Black adult would be more or less effective than a White adult in raising a Black child's expectations, and whether a child would volunteer more often in a mixed racial group than in a group where everyone's race matched his/her own.

The researchers set out to find what characteristics must be possessed by an adult to function as an effective raiser of children's expectations. One possible answer was that an effective expectation raiser should possess the characteristic of a 'significant other', i.e., he/she should be warm and trustworthy and should have the potential for affective ties to the children; he/she should also be perceived as highly competent to evaluate. In summary, Entwisle and Webster's (1974) research focused on social events or processes that led to small changes in children's behaviour or self-view and on what specific behaviour *by whom* brought about those changes. This led them to look at how adults interacting with children can raise the child's expectations, and how social factors affected the process. This study provides evidence that Black children who live in all-Black neighbourhoods and who attend all-Black schools have high self-esteem and high self-expectations. In this relatively 'insulated' context, Black adults are more effective at raising expectations of Black children, while White adults are not (Entwisle and Webster, 1974, p. 303). The explanation is that a child who is dependent upon other people like himself/herself for evaluation may be in a cocoon where the larger society is almost irrelevant.

Entwisle and Webster support the view that children from low socio-economic status (SES) relative to others of their own racial group — Whites from integrated neighbourhoods or inner-city Blacks living in the ghetto — may perceive adults of the opposite race as hostile, and constantly opposite-race adults who are perceived as hostile would not be accepted as expectation-raisers by such children. The second explanation is that social distance between adults and children could affect expectations of children. The Black experimenters who were ineffective with White Children in mixed groups happened to be upper-middle-class Blacks, so that race and class were strong points of difference between adults and children.

In their review of the literature regarding racial matching, they found that in general children perform better, faster or more effectively when the adult administering the reinforcement is of the same race as their own. The researchers were at pains to point out that the Black children in their study came from an integrated background, and apparently neither they nor their White classmates held low expectations for Blacks' performance (Entwisle and Webster, 1974, p. 316).

The implication for the classroom teacher is that he/she should aim to make race non-relevant as a sufficient basis for forming performance expectations. Sustained effort can break down the use of race as a basis for performance expectations. If a child holds low self-expectations, it is because he/she has been unable to perform well or received negative evaluations at a particular task, or because the child is in a group of others whom he/she has reason to suppose can perform better than he/she. Experiences of past successes and failures by comparison with others in a group determine expectation states. The teacher can overcome these outcomes by ensuring early and regular successes for every child. The school or classroom can be organized to prevent children perceiving race as a relevant status characteristic, thereby preventing them from forming expectations for each other based upon their respective race (or sex or class).

## OTHER DIRECTIONS IN COOPERATIVE LEARNING

Research on multiethnic cooperative learning groups shows that task interdependence induces cooperative, friendly behaviour and develops liking and respect for one's own groupmates. Cooperative learning interracial groups may also have the potential to bring about generalized intergroup attitude change. The research described above suggests avenues by which this potential may be realized. Adoption of an egalitarian (school policy and) teaching strategy would make it more difficult for prejudice and discrimination to flourish in teaching institutions.

In their review of over ninety studies comparing the relative effects of two or more goal structures on interpersonal attraction between majority and minority students, Johnson et al. (1984) found that (1) intergroup cooperation without intergroup competition tends to promote more positive attitudes and relationships between majority and minority students than either interpersonal competition or individualistic effects; and (2) intragroup cooperation with intergroup competition promotes more positive attitudes and relationships between majority and minority students than does either interpersonal competition or individualistic efforts.

In their 1983 study Johnson et al. explain that cooperative experiences may promote more interpersonal attraction among heterogeneous groups of individuals than do competitive or individualistic experiences because within cooperative situations participants benefit from encouraging others to achieve, whereas in competitive situations participants benefit from obstructing others' efforts to achieve, and in individualistic situations the success of others is irrelevant. Promotive interaction tends to be greater within cooperative situations than in competitive and individualistic ones (Johnson et al., 1983). They claim that:

1   there is more crossethnic and crosshandicap helping in cooperative than in competitive situations;
2   cooperative learning experiences, compared with competitive and individualistic ones, result in stronger beliefs that one is personally liked, supported and accepted by other students, with greater willingness to do homework with other students; and
3   students within cooperative learning situations perceive teachers as being more supportive and accepting both academically and personally than do students in competitive or individualistic learning situations.

The researchers indicate that cooperation promotes a lower fear of failure and higher feeling of safety than do the other two goal structures (Johnson et al., 1975). Some studies cited by the researchers show that cooperation is positively related to the ability to take the emotional perspectives of others.

If self-esteem and prejudice are negatively related, then an increase in self-esteem would result in a decrease in prejudice. According to Johnson et al. (1983), cooperative learning situations, compared with competitive and individualistic ones, promote higher levels of self-esteem and healthier processes for deriving conclusions about one's self-worth. In addition to positive peer evaluations, cooperative learning situations promote higher academic achievement for all.

Similarly, Slavin's (1983) survey showed that of forty-six studies, twenty-nine (63 per cent) showed cooperative learning methods to have significantly positive (or in one case marginally positive) effects on student achievement; fifteen (33 per cent) found no differences, and two (4 per cent) found significantly higher achievement for a control group than for a cooperative treatment (Slavin, 1983, p. 434). Of twenty-seven studies that used group study and group rewards for individual learning, twenty-four (89 per cent) found positive effects on student achievement, whereas three (11 per cent) found no differences! In contrast, none of the nine studies of group study methods that did not use group rewards for individual learning found positive effects on student achievement.

The basic assumption underlying cooperative learning is that in a cooperative situation individuals experience the same outcomes (Deutsch, 1949). If one person obtains his/her goal, then the others in the cooperative group obtain their goals as well. Competition is the reverse. It is interaction in which individuals have different outcomes. If one person obtains his/her goal, the others in the competitive group are prevented from obtaining their goals.

## THE MORAL MESSAGE

The school must avoid conveying the message that those who succeed academically in school, who belong to a particular race or group, are somehow better people for being so or doing this. It must possess a clear set of articulated values which the organization aspires to achieve in every sphere of its activities, including its teaching techniques. The values the school seeks to transmit should include:

1  fair treatment for all students: the school should treat *all* students with respect and appreciate their individual differences;
2  teachers and other adults working within the institution should be good models for students;
3  the goal of discipline should be to help students to learn cognitively and affectively, and to provide various means of success for a variety of students;
4  students should have opportunities for responsible and altruistic behaviour: schools should help pupils to appreciate each other and to understand what it is like to be in someone else's shoes, i.e., what it is to be disadvantaged or handicapped.

The school should give public recognition to students and teachers who display, in a special way, the values the school wishes to encourage. Special recognition should be given to students who demonstrate exceptional ability or scholarship, or particularly valuable community service, or a special performance in the arts, home economics, woodwork, or show particular caring attitudes to others. In this way it would made clear to the school population not only what the school cares about but that it values success in a number of domains in which a large number of students with varying abilities and aptitudes can attain. In other words, the school will allow each child all he/she is capable of becoming within a morally acceptable framework. It is important for such a school that goals should be set so that a lot of students can attain them. Rewards for excellence in a variety of areas should be given frequently to provide regular feedback to encourage motivation (Joseph, 1986, p. 85). The teaching techniques described above will help the school to encourage academic excellence within a caring, altruistic environment: an environment where status characteristics based on race will be invalid and ruled out of court.

# REFERENCES

Allport, G. (1954) *The Nature of Prejudice*, Cambridge, Mass., Addison-Wesley.

Amir, Y. (1969) 'Contact Hypothesis in Ethnic Relations', *Psychological Bulletin*, 71, pp. 319–342.

Amir, Y. and Garti, C. (1977) 'Situational and Personal Influence on Attitude Change Following Ethnic Contact', *International Journal of Intercultural Relations*, 1, pp. 58–75.

Amir, Y., Ahron, S., Ben-Ari, R., Bezman, A. and Riber, M. (1978) 'Asymmetry, Academic Status, Differentiation and the Ethnic Perceptions and Preferences of Israeli Youths', *Human Relations*, 31, 2, pp. 99–116.

Amir, Y., Charon, S., Rivner, M., Ben-Ari, R. and Bizman, A. (1979) 'Group Status and Attitude Change in Desegregated Classrooms', *International Journal of Intercultural Relations*, 3, pp. 137–152.

Bayton, J.A. (1941) 'The Racial Stereotypes of Negro College Students', *Journal of Abnormal Social Psychology*, 36, pp. 97–102.

Bayton, J.A., McAlister, L.B. and Hamer, J. (1956) *Section B. Race — Class — Stereotypes*, Washington, D.C., Howard University, Department of Psychology.

Benn, S.I. (1975–76) 'Freedom, Autonomy and the Concept of a Person', *Proceedings of the Aristotelian Society*, 76, New Series, pp. 89–109.

Berger, J.B.P., Cohen, E.G. and Zelditch, M. (1966) 'Status Characteristics and Expectation States', in J. Berger, M. Zelditch and B. Anderson (Eds), *Sociological Theories in Progress*, Boston, Mass., Houghton-Mifflin, pp. 29–46.

Berger, J., Rosenholtz, S.J. and Zelditch, M., Jr (1980) 'Status Organising Process', *Annual Review of Sociology*, 6, pp. 479–508.

Callan, E. (1985) 'Moral Education in a Liberal Society', *Journal of Moral Education*, 14, 1, pp. 9–22.

Charvet, J. (1981) *A Critique of Freedom and Equality*, Cambridge, Cambridge University Press.

Coates, B. (1972) 'White Adult Behaviour towards Black and White Children', *Child Development*, 43, pp. 143–154.

Cohen, E.G. (1968) 'Interracial Interaction Disability', *Stanford University School of Education. Technical Report 1*.

Cohen, E.G. (1972) 'Interracial Interaction Disability', *Human Relations*, 25, 1, pp. 9–24.

Cohen, E.G. (1973) 'Modifying the Effects of Social Structure', *American Behavioural Scientist*, 6, pp. 861–879.

Cohen, E.G. (1975) 'The Effects of Segregation on Race Relations', *Law and Contemporary Problems*, 39, pp. 271–299.

Cohen, E.G. (1980) 'Design and Redesign of the Desegregated School: Problems of Status, Power and Conflict', in W.G. Stephenson and J.R. Faegin (Eds), *School De-segregation: Past, Present and Future*, New York, Plenum Press.

Cohen, E.G. (1982) 'Expectation States and Interracial Interaction in School Settings', *Annual Review of Sociology*, 8, pp. 209–235.

Cohen, E.G. (1984) 'The Desegregated School: Problems in Status, Power and Interethnic Climate', in N. Miller and M.B. Brewer (Eds), *Groups in Conflict: The Psychology of Desegregation*, New York, Academic Press.

Cohen, E.G. and Roper, S.S. (1972) 'Modification of Interracial Interaction Disability: An Application of Status Characteristics Theory', *American Sociological Review*, 37, 6, pp. 643–657.

Cohen, E.G., Lockheed, M.E. and Lohman, M.R. (1976) 'The Centre for Interracial Co-operation: A Field Experiment', *Sociology of Education*, 49, pp. 47–58.

Cook, S.W. (1978) 'Interpersonal and Attitudinal Outcomes in Co-operating Interracial Groups', *Journal of Research and Development in Education*, 12, 1, pp. 97–113.

Crain, R.L., Mahard, R.E. and Narot, R. (1982) *Making Desegregation Work*, Cambridge, Mass., M.A. Ballinger.

Deutsch, M. (1949) 'An Experimental Study of the Effects of Co-operation and Competition upon Group Process', *Human Relations*, 2, pp. 199–231.

Dovidio, J.F. and Gaertner, S.L. (1981) 'The Effects of Race, Status and Ability on Helping Behaviour', *Social Psychology Quarterly*, 14, pp. 192–203.

Dovidio, J.F. and Gaertner, S.L. (1983) 'Race, Normative Structure and Helpseeking', in B.M. DePaulo, A. Nadler and J.P. Fisher (Eds), *New Direction in Helping*, 2, New York, Academic Press, pp. 285–303.

Entwisle, D.R. and Webster, M., Jr (1974) 'Expectations in Mixed Racial Groups', *Sociology of Education*, 47, pp. 302–318.

Entwisle, D.R. and Webster, M., Jr (1978) 'Raising Expectations Indirectly', *Social Forces*, 57, pp. 257–264.

Gaertner, S.L. and Dovidio, J.F. (1977) 'The Subtlety of White Racism, Arousal and Helping Behaviour', *Journal of Personality and Social Psychology*, 35, pp. 691–707.

Johnson, D.W. (1975) 'Co-operativeness and Social Perspective Taking', *Journal of Personality and Social Psychology*, 31, pp. 241–244.

Johnson, D.W. and Johnson, R. (1975) *Learning Together and Alone: Co-operation, Competition and Individualization*, Englewood Cliffs, N.J., Prentice-Hall.

Johnson, D.W., Johnson, R. and Maruyama, G. (1983) 'Interdependence and Inter-Personal Attraction among Heterogeneous and Homogeneous Individuals: A Theoretical Formulation and a Meta-analysis of the Research', *Review of Educational Research*, 52, pp. 5–54.

Johnson, D.W., Johnson, R. and Maruyama, G. (1984) 'Goal Interdependence and Interpersonal Attraction in Heterogeneous Classrooms: A Metanalysis', in N. Miller and M.B. Brewer (Eds), *Groups in Conflict: The Psychology of Desegregation*, New York, Academic Press.

Johnson, J.H. (1987) 'Values, Culture and the Effective School', *NASSP Bulletin*, 71, pp. 79–88.

Joseph, P.S. (1986) 'Like It or Not, Your Schools Are Teaching Values, So Emphasise These', *American School Board Journal*, 173, May, pp. 35–46.

Katz, D. and Braly, L. (1933) 'Racial Stereotypes of One Hundred College Students', *Journal of Abnormal Social Psychology*, 28, pp. 280–290.

Katz, I. and Benjamin, L. (1960) 'Effects of White Authoritarianism in Biracial Work Groups', *Journal of Abnormal Social Psychology*, 61, pp. 448–456.

Katz, I. and Cohen, M. (1962) 'The Effects of Training Negroes upon Co-operative Problem Solving in Biracial Teams', *Journal of Abnormal Social Psychology*, 64, pp. 319–325.

Katz, I., Goldstone, J. and Benjamin, L. (1958) 'Behaviour and Productivity in Biracial Work Groups', *Human Relations*, 11, pp. 123–141.

Katz, I., Henchy, T. and Allwitt (1968) 'Effects of Race of Tester Approval-Disapproval and Need of Negro Children's Learning', *Journal of Personality and Social Psychology*, 8, pp. 38–42.

Lohman, M.R. (1972) 'Changing a Racial Status Ordering: Implications for Desegregation', *Journal of Education and Urban Sociology*, 4, pp. 382–402.

McCarthy, C. (1988) 'Re-thinking Liberal and Radical Perspectives on Racial Inequality in Schooling: Making the Case for Non-Synchrony', *Harvard Educational Review*, 58, 3, pp. 265–279.

McDougall, D. (1983) 'Co-operation and the Reduction of Prejudice', *Multiculturalism*, 6, 3, pp. 3–7.

MacIntyre, A. (1982) *After Virtue: A Study in Moral Theory*, London, Duckworth.

Milner, D. (1983) *Children and Race Ten Years On*, London, A Linq Kee.

Pyszkowski, I.S. (1986) 'Moral Values and the Schools: Is There a Way Out of the Maze?', *Education*, 107, 1, pp. 41–48.

Rosenthal, R. and Jacobson, L. (1968) *Pygmalion in the Classroom*, New York, Holt, Rinehart and Winston.

Rubovits, P.C. and Maehr, M.L. (1973) 'Pygmalion Black and White', *Journal of Personality and Social Psychology*, 25, pp. 210–218.

Secord, P.F. and Backman, C.W. (1974) *Social Psychology*, 2nd ed., New York, McGraw-Hill.

Slavin, R.E. (1983) *Co-operative Learning*, New York, Longman.

Slavin, R.E. (1985) 'Co-operative Learning: Applying Contact Theory in Desegregated Schools', *Journal of Social Issues*, 41, 3, pp. 45–62.

Walkling, P.H. and Brannigan, C. (1986) 'Anti-sexist/Anti-racist Education: A Possible Dilemma', *Journal of Moral Education*, pp. 16–25.

Williams, B. (1962) 'The Idea of Equality', in P. Laslett and W.G. Runciman (Eds), *Philosophy, Politics and Society*, 2nd Series, Oxford, Basil Blackwell, pp. 110–131.

Wills, T.A. (1983) 'Social Comparison in Coping and Help-seeking', in B.M. De Paulo, A. Nadler and J.D. Fisher (Eds), *New Directions in Helping: Help-Seeking 2*, New York, Academic Press.

Wright, D. (1986) 'An Outline of an Approach to Moral Education in Schools', *Westminster Studies in Education*, 9, pp. 45–55.

Zimet, C.N. and Zimet, S.G. (1978) 'Educators View People: Ethnic Group Stereotyping', *Journal of Community Psychology*, 6, pp. 189–193.

# 12. The Jigsaw Classroom: A Cooperative Strategy for Reducing Prejudice

ELLIOT ARONSON AND RUTH THIBODEAU

This chapter focuses on the Jigsaw method, a cooperative teaching technique for reducing intergroup prejudice in the classroom. The first part looks at the historical conditions leading up to the Jigsaw method's development, as well as the theory and research behind it. This discussion also touches briefly on a selection of similar cooperative teaching strategies that have proved successful in fostering more harmonious relationships between minority and majority school children. Part 2 offers practical guidance for teachers wishing to implement the Jigsaw technique.

## BACKGROUND: SCHOOL DESEGREGATION

In 1954, when the US Supreme Court outlawed school desegregation, hopes ran high that we might be on our way to a better society. At that time many of us believed that if only youngsters from various ethnic and racial backgrounds could share the same classroom, negative stereotypes would fade and crossethnic friendships would take root and flourish under the warm glow of face-to-face contact. Ultimately, we believed, these young people would grow into adults who would be largely free of the racial and ethnic prejudice that has plagued American society since its inception.

The case that brought about the court's landmark decision was that of *Oliver Brown vs The Board of Education of Topeka, Kansas*. The decision reversed an 1896 ruling (in *Plessy vs Ferguson*), which held that racially segregated schools were permissible as long as equal facilities were provided for all races. In the *Brown* case the court held that, psychologically, there could be no such thing as 'separate but equal' because the forced separation — in and of itself — implied to the minority group in question that its members were inferior to those of the majority. To quote from the *Brown* decision:

Does segregation of children in public schools solely on the basis of race, even though the physical facilities and other 'tangible' factors may be equal, deprive the children of the minority group of equal educational opportunities? We believe that it does ... to separate Negro school children from others of similar age and qualifications solely because of their race generates a feeling of inferiority as to their status in the community that may affect their hearts and minds in a way unlikely ever to be undone.... We conclude that in the field of public education the doctrine 'separate but equal' has no place. Separate educational facilities are inherently unequal.

As Stephan (1978) spelled out, the language of the court in the *Brown* decision reflects the influence of a group of distinguished American social psychologists, led by Kenneth Clark, Stuart Cook and Isidor Chein, who testified as 'friends of the court' in this case, as well as in previous cases in state supreme courts. These social psychologists testified to the effect that in segregated schools Black children 'learn the inferior status to which they are assigned', leaving the Black child to wonder 'whether his group and he himself are worthy of no more respect than they receive. This conflict and confusion leads to self-hate' (Stephan, 1978).

Thus the logic implicit in the *Brown* decision went as follows: because segregation lowers self-esteem, desegregation would eventually produce an increase in the self-esteem of minority students. Furthermore, because segregation deprived minority group members of equal educational opportunities, desegregation should result in improved education for these students. Thus the *Brown* decision was not only a humane interpretation of the US Constitution; it also marked the beginning of a profound and exciting social experiment with three clear hypotheses: that desegregation would (1) reduce prejudice; (2) raise the self-esteem of minority students; and (3) improve the classroom performance of minority students.

## THE EFFECTS OF DESEGREGATION

More than thirty-five years have passed since the *Brown* decision, and it appears that some of us may have been overly optimistic about the benefits of desegregation. Things did not work out exactly as we had hoped. For example, in a longitudinal study in Riverside, California, Gerard and Miller (1975) found that long after the schools had been racially integrated, Black, White and Mexican-American children remained segregated in settings outside the classroom. They socialized in their own ethnic clusters on the playgrounds, in the lunch room and in other informal settings. Moreover, anxiety among minority students had increased and remained high long after desegregation. These trends were echoed in several other studies. Indeed, the most careful scholarly reviews of the research show few, if any, benefits (see St John, 1975; Stephan, 1978). For example, according to Stephan's review, there was not a single non-experimental study that found a significant increase in the self-esteem of minority children after desegregation. In fact, in fully 25 per cent of the studies desegregation was followed by a significant decrease in the self-esteem of young minority children. Stephan also reported that desegregation reduced the prejudice of Whites toward Blacks in only 13 per cent of the school systems studied. Moreover, the prejudice of Blacks toward Whites increased in about as many cases as it decreased. Similarly, studies of the effects of desegregation on the academic performance of minority children present a mixed and highly variable picture.

What went wrong? First of all, it is important to note that the social psychologists who testified in these cases were sophisticated and properly cautious. They neither stated nor implied that the predicted benefits of school desegregation would occur automatically. Certain preconditions would have to be met. These preconditions were most articulately stated by Gordon Allport in *The Nature of Prejudice* (1954), published the same year as the Supreme Court decision:

> Prejudice ... may be reduced by equal-status contact between majority and minority groups in the pursuit of common goals. The effect is greatly enhanced if this contact is sanctioned by institutional supports (i.e., by law, custom, or local atmosphere), and provided it is of a sort that leads to the perception of common interests and common humanity between members of the two groups. (p. 281)

Thus, according to Allport, positive results could be expected when desegregation occurs in the context of equal status contact in pursuit of common goals, sanctioned by authority. It is our contention that very few of the studies reviewed by Stephan and by St John involved an educational environment in which all three of these prerequisites had been met. Let us look at each of these three factors separately.

## Sanctioned by Authority

In some school districts there was clear acceptance and enforcement of the desegregation ruling by responsible authority; in others acceptance was not as clear. In still others (especially in the early years) local authorities were in open defiance of the law. As early as 1961, Pettigrew demonstrated that desegregation proceeded more smoothly and with less violence in those districts in which local authorities sanctioned integration. However, such variables as self-esteem and the reduction of prejudice do no necessarily change for the better, even when authority clearly supports desegregation. Although sanction by authority may be necessary, it is clearly not a sufficient condition for desegregation to yield positive effects.

## Equal Status Contact

The definition of 'equal status' has been difficult to establish in the context of desegregation. For example, one might claim that equal status exists on the grounds that all children, in, say, the fifth grade have the same 'occupational' status; that is, they are all fifth-grade students. On the other hand, if the teacher is prejudiced against minority children, he or she may treat them unfairly, thereby lowering their perceived status in the classroom (see Gerard and Miller, 1975). Moreover, if minority students are initially handicapped by an inferior education (before desegregation) or language difficulties (as in the case of Mexican-

Americans), their classroom performance will in all likelihood suffer — a fact which may also result in lower status among their peers.

An important insight by Cohen (1972) points to a more subtle complication regarding equal status contact. Although Allport (1954) predicted that positive interactions would result if cooperative, equal status conditions were achieved, Cohen's formulation of expectation theory predicts that even in such an environment, biased expectations by both majority and minority group members may lead to sustained White dominance and subordinate status for minority children. Cohen reasoned that both of these groups have accepted the premise that the majority group's competence results in social dominance and superior academic achievement. She suggested that alternatives be created to dismantle these entrenched expectations. According to Cohen, at least a temporary exchange of majority and minority roles is required as a prelude to equal status. A study by Cohen and Roper (1972) provides evidence to support this claim. In their experiment Black children were taught how to build radios and how to teach this skill to others. Then a group of White children and newly trained Black children viewed a film of themselves building the radios. After the film, one group of Black children taught the White children how to build the radios, while a comparison group of Black children taught a Black administrator how to construct the radios. Finally, all the children were assigned to small, racially integrated groups. Equal status interactions were observed in the groups in which Black children had trained White children. In the comparison group, however, the usual White dominance prevailed.

## In Pursuit of Common Goals

If there is one statement we can make unequivocally about the typical American classroom, it is that children are almost never engaged in the pursuit of common goals. In recent years we and our colleagues have systematically observed scores of American classrooms at all grade levels. We have found that in the vast majority of cases the process of education is highly competitive. Children vie with one another for good grades and for the respect of the teacher. This occurs not only during quizzes and exams, but also in the informal give-and-take of the classroom. In the typical classroom the scenario is as follows: children raise their hands (often frantically) in response to questions from the teacher; they groan when someone else is called on and answers the question correctly; and they revel in the event that their classmate's answer is incorrect. The competitive atmosphere that pervades the classroom encourages children to view each other as foes to be heckled and vanquished. In a newly desegregated school this atmosphere could easily exacerbate whatever prejudice existed before desegregation.

A dramatic example of dysfunctional competition was demonstrated by Sherif *et al.* (1961) in their classic 'Robber's Cave' experiment. In this field study the investigators used a variety of strategies to encourage intergroup competition between two teams of boys at a summer camp. This created fertile ground for anger and hostility between the groups, even in previously benign, non-competitive situations — such as when watching a movie together. Positive relations between the groups were ultimately achieved only after both groups had been required to work cooperatively to solve a common problem.

It is our contention that the competitive environment of the classroom undermines the potential for 'equal status contact', to the detriment of minority student achievement and positive intergroup relations. That is, any differences in skills and ability that existed between minority and White children before desegregation are aggravated by the competitive structure of the learning environment. Because segregated school facilities are rarely equal, minority children often enter the newly desegregated school at a distinct academic disadvantage, which is made more salient by the competitive atmosphere. In sum, the interacting dynamics of classroom competition and unequal preparation for school serve to sabotage the potential benefits of desegregation.

## THE JIGSAW METHOD

It was this reasoning that first led us to develop the hypothesis that interdependent learning environments would establish the conditions necessary for desegregation to succeed (Aronson *et al.*, 1975, 1978). To this end we developed a highly structured method of interdependent learning, designed to enhance self-esteem and academic performance, while also reducing prejudice. We then systematically tested the effects of our method in a number of elementary and secondary school classrooms. The aim of this research programme was not merely to compare the effects of cooperation and competition in a classroom setting. Such a comparison had been made competently by other investigators dating as far back as Deutsch's (1949) classic experiment. Rather, our intent was to devise a cooperative classroom structure that could be used easily by teachers on a long-term basis, and to evaluate the effects of this intervention via a series of controlled field experiments. In short, this was an action research programme aimed at developing and evaluating a technique for creating a cooperative classroom atmosphere that could be sustained by teachers long after the researchers had packed up their questionnaires and returned to the more sterile and precise world of social-psychological laboratory. We dubbed our invention the 'Jigsaw method' for reasons that will soon become clear.

The Jigsaw method is described in detail elsewhere (Aronson, 1984; Aronson and Goode, 1980; Aronson and Yates, 1983; Aronson *et al.*, 1978). To summarize, students in the Jigsaw classroom are placed in six-person learning groups. The day's lesson is divided into six paragraphs, so that each student has one segment of the written material. Thus each student owns a unique and vital part of the class lesson, which — like the pieces of a jigsaw puzzle — must be joined with the others before any of the students can learn the whole picture. The individual must master her or his own section and teach it to other members of the group. Consequently, every student spends some of the time in the role of *expert*, a condition that incorporates Cohen's (1972) suggestion that a temporary exchange of status between minority and majority group members is a necessary prelude to equal status contact. The most important aspect of the Jigsaw method (and the one that makes it unique among cooperative techniques) is that each student has a special, vital gift for the other group members — a gift that is unattainable elsewhere. It is this factor that contributes to the gains in self-esteem and feelings of efficacy experienced by children exposed to Jigsaw. In sum, the method works by changing the *way* material is learned, rather than by changing the material itself. Unlike the traditional classroom which has only one expert, the teacher, the Jigsaw classroom has as many knowledgeable resources as it has students.

An example will clarify. In our initial experiment we entered a fifth-grade classroom in a newly desegregated school. The children were studying the biographies of famous Americans, and the next lesson happened to be a biography of Joseph Pulitzer, the famous publisher. First, we constructed a biography of Pulitzer consisting of six paragraphs: Paragraph 1 was about his ancestors and how they came to this country; Paragraph 2 was about Pulitzer as a little boy and how he grew up; Paragraph 3 described him as a young man, his education and his early employment; Paragraph 4 was about his middle age and how he founded his newspaper; and so on. Each major aspect of Joseph Pulitzer's life was contained in a separate paragraph.

We made copies of our biography of Pulitzer, cut each copy into six one-paragraph sections, and gave every child in each of the six-person groups one paragraph about Pulitzer's life. Thus each learning group had within it the entire biography of Joseph Pulitzer; but each individual child had no more than one-sixth of the story. To learn the complete biography, each child had to master a paragraph, teach it to the others and listen carefully while each of the other children presented their portions.

### The Expert Group

Each student took his or her paragraph and went off to master it. The child then consulted with fellow 'experts' from the other learning groups. That is, if Bill had been dealt Joseph Pulitzer as a young man, he would then consult with Nancy, Carlos and Samantha, who were in different Jigsaw groups and had also been assigned the paragraph about Joseph Pulitzer as a young man. In the expert groups the children used one another as consultants, to rehearse and clarify for themselves the important aspects of that phase of Pulitzer's life.

The expert group is of great importance in providing time, space and practice for the less articulate and less skilful students to learn the material. It also affords them an opportunity to make use of the more adept students as models for organizing and presenting the report. Without the expert group, the Jigsaw experience might easily backfire. That is, as Brown (1986) pointed out, the Jigsaw classroom can be a little like baseball: if the boy playing right field keeps dropping fly balls, it hurts your team and you might begin to resent him. Similarly, if you must depend on the performance of a Mexican-American child whose command of English is less than perfect, you might resent him — unless he had a clear idea of how to present the material. Thus practice in the 'expert' groups is crucial to the success of the Jigsaw technique. Even so, things rarely go as smoothly in practice as on the drawing board — as we shall see.

### The Jigsaw Group

After spending from ten to fifteen minutes with their fellow experts, the students returned to their original six-person groups, and the teacher informed them that they had a certain amount of time (usually from twenty to thirty minutes) to communicate their knowledge to one another. They were also informed that at the end of the time, or soon after, they would be tested on the material.

When thrown on their own resources, the children eventually learned to teach and to listen to one another. They gradually realized that none of them could do well without the help of each child in the group — and that each member had a unique and essential contribution to make. Nevertheless, old habits die hard. The students in our experimental group had grown accustomed to competing during all of their years in school. As a result, for the first few days most of the youngsters tried to compete, even though competitive behavior was dysfunctional.

Let us illustrate with an example, typical of the way the children stumbled toward mastery of the cooperative process. In one of our groups there was a Mexican-American boy, whom we will call Carlos. Carlos was not very articulate in English, which was his second language. He had learned over the years how to keep quiet in class because, when he had spoken up in the past, he had often been ridiculed. In the Jigsaw group he initially had a little trouble communicating his paragraph to the other children, and was very uncomfortable about it. This was not surprising because, under the system we introduced, Carlos was forced to speak, whereas before he had always been able to keep a low profile in the classroom. However, the situation was even more complex than that: long before Jigsaw had been introduced, the teacher and Carlos had unwittingly entered into a conspiracy of sorts. Carlos was perfectly willing to be quiet. In the past, when the teacher had occasionally called on him, he would stumble, stammer and fall into an embarrassed silence. Several of his peers would make fun of him. Consequently, the teacher had learned not to call on him anymore. The decision probably came from the purest intentions: in all likelihood, the teacher simply did not want to expose the child to further humiliation. However, by sparing his feelings and ignoring him, she had also written him off. Her actions implied that he was not worth bothering with; at least, the other students in the classroom got that message. In their eyes there was one good reason that the teacher was not calling on Carlos: he was stupid. Indeed, even Carlos began to draw this conclusion. This incident illustrates the dynamic of how desegregation, when coupled with a competitive process, can generate unequal status contact, resulting in even greater enmity between groups and a loss of self-esteem for the members of disadvantaged ethnic minorities.

Returning to our six-person group, Carlos was having a hard time presenting his report on Joseph Pulitzer's young manhood. Although he had learned the material quite well in his expert group, when it was his turn to recite in his Jigsaw group, he grew very nervous. He stammered, hesitated and fidgeted. The other youngsters in the circle were not very helpful. They had grown accustomed to a competitive process, and they responded out of this old, overlearned habit. They knew what to do when a fellow student stumbles, especially a student whom they believed to be stupid. They ridiculed and teased him. During our experiment it was Mary who was observed to say, 'Aw, you don't know it, you're dumb, you're stupid. You don't know what you're doing.' When this incident occurred, our research assistant, who was monitoring the groups, made one brief intervention: 'OK, you can do that if you want to. It might be fun for you, but it's not going to help you learn about Joseph Pulitzer's young manhood — and the exam will take place in an hour.' Notice how the reinforcement contingencies have shifted. No longer does Mary gain much from putting Carlos down. In fact, she now stands to lose a great deal. After a few days and several similar experiences, it became increasingly clear to the students in Carlos's group that the only way they could learn about his part of the lesson was by paying attention to what Carlos had to say.

Moreover, they gradually developed into rather competent interviewers. Instead of ignoring or ridiculing Carlos when he was having a little trouble communicating what he knew, they began asking friendly, probing questions — the kind of questions that made it easier for Carlos to communicate what was in his head. Carlos responded to this treatment by becoming more relaxed; with increased relaxation came an improvement in his ability to communicate. After a couple of weeks the other students concluded that Carlos was a lot smarter than they had thought he was. They discovered qualities in him that they had never seen before. They began to like him. Carlos began to enjoy school more and started seeing the students in his group not as tormenters, but as helpful and responsible people. Moreover, as he became increasingly comfortable in class and started to gain more confidence in himself, his academic performance improved. The vicious cycle had been reversed; the elements that had been causing a downward spiral had been changed, and the spiral now began to move upward.[1]

Working with the Jigsaw technique, children soon realize that their old competitive behaviour is no longer appropriate. Rather, in order to learn all the material, each student must listen to the others, ask appropriate questions and in other ways contribute to the group. As children begin to pay more attention to each other, they come to value one another as potentially valuable resources. It is important to emphasize that students' greater appreciation of one another is *not* motivated by altruistic concerns. Rather, the Jigsaw process is fuelled primarily by self-interest, which in this case also happens to produce outcomes that are beneficial to others.

### Generalization of Positive Attitudes

In our initial study each group remained intact for approximately six weeks. The groups were then dissolved and reformed. The purpose of this procedure was to increase the diversity of contacts each student experienced, so that each child would have an opportunity to interact with several students of various ethnic groups. Such diversity plays a key role in breaking down prejudiced attitudes toward outgroup members in general. As Brewer and Miller (1988) have argued, cooperative interactions can be successful in reducing negative stereotypes attributed to *particular* members of another group, but they are less likely to lead to generalization outside the specific encounter. That is, individuals who have had positive interactions with an outgroup member are likely to modify their prejudiced attitudes toward that specific individual, but not necessarily toward the outgroup as a whole. Nevertheless, Brewer and Miller also argue that cooperative interactions, such as those provided by Jigsaw, stand a good chance of reducing intergroup conflict in the long run because 'frequent individualization of outgroup members results in a loss of the meaning and utility of broader category distinctions' (1988, p. 320) that reflect negative stereotypes regarding the out-group in general.

We agree with Brewer and Miller. It is important that cooperative experiences with outgroup members include a continually changing cast of characters. Indeed, this is why the Jigsaw method calls for dissolving and reforming Jigsaw groups at regular intervals, thereby ensuring that positive experiences with an outgroup member would not be narrowly attributed to specific non-stereotypical aspects of that particular person. In our experience, students initially resist the dissolution of their group ('just when we're beginning to feel comfortable') but quickly learn that their new partners can be just as interesting and helpful.

## EXPERIMENTS IN THE CLASSROOM

Since the mid-1970s, methodologically rigorous experiments on the Jigsaw method have produced consistently positive results. Typical of this research is an early field experiment that we conducted in Austin, Texas (Blaney *et al.*, 1977). The recent desegregation of the Austin schools had generated a great deal of tension as well as some interracial skirmishes throughout the school system. In the midst of this crisis we introduced the Jigsaw technique in ten fifth-grade classrooms in seven elementary schools. Three classes from among the same schools were used as controls. The control classes were taught by teachers who, although using traditional techniques, were rated very highly by their peers. The experimental classes met in Jigsaw groups for about forty-five minutes a day, three days a week, for six weeks. The curriculum was basically the same for the experimental and control classes.

### Self-Esteem, Liking School and Liking One Another

Students in the Jigsaw groups expressed significantly greater liking for their groupmates both within and across ethnic boundaries. Moreover, the children in Jigsaw groups experienced a significantly greater increase in self-esteem than the children in the control classrooms. This was true for both White majority and ethnic minority students. Most children in the Jigsaw classrooms also reported greater liking for school than those in traditional classrooms.

The major results were replicated and refined in several experiments in school districts throughout the United States. For example, Geffner (1978) introduced Jigsaw in Watsonville, California. As a further control (for the possibility of a Hawthorne effect), Geffner compared the behaviour and attitudes of children in classrooms using Jigsaw with those of children in highly innovative (but not interdependent) classroom environments, as well as with traditional classrooms. Geffner found consistent and significant gains only in the cooperative classrooms. Specifically, the children in these classes showed increases in self-esteem as well as increases in liking for school. Negative ethnic stereotypes were also diminished: compared to children in traditional and innovative classrooms, Jigsaw students experienced a far greater increase in positive attitudes toward their own ethnic group as well as toward members of other ethnic groups.

### Academic Performance

Conventional wisdom has long held that if one designed a classroom structure that increased the joy of education or enhanced students' respect for themselves and each other, these benefits would occur at the expense of fundamental learning. Thus, when the American public is periodically made aware of the fact that our children are not learning as much in school as they might, there is usually an outcry to eliminate the 'frills' (such as cooperative learning) and 'get back to basics'. Research on Jigsaw and other cooperative techniques has proved this popular notion to be bankrupt.

We made our first systematic attempt to assess the effects of Jigsaw learning on academic performance in Austin, Texas (Lucker *et al.*, 1977). The subjects were 303 fifth- and sixth-grade students from five elementary schools. Six class-rooms used the Jigsaw method, and five classrooms were taught traditionally by highly competent teachers. For two weeks the children were taught a unit on colonial America taken from a fifth-grade textbook. All the children were then given the same standardized test. The Anglo students performed just as well in Jigsaw as they did in traditional classes (means = 66.6 and 67.3, respectively). The minority children, however, performed much better in Jigsaw classes than in traditional classes (means = 56.6 and 49.7, respectively), demonstrating a highly significant improvement in academic achievement. Indeed, only two weeks of Jigsaw activity had narrowed the performance gap between majority and minority students from more than 17 percentage points to about 10 percentage points. Moreover, it is worth noting that the Jigsaw method apparently does not work a special hardship on high ability students: the students in the highest quartile in reading ability benefitted just as much as the students in the lowest quartile.

Since that experiment, a number of additional experiments have evaluated academic performance, comparing the effects of Jigsaw (as well as other coopera-tive methods) with learning in the traditional, competitive classroom. Overall, these studies have provided striking support for the academic benefits of coopera-tive classroom structures (see Slavin, 1983). Later in this chapter we will briefly examine other cooperative learning methods and the research that supports them. First, however, we will discuss some of the social-psychological processes that lie at the heart of the Jigsaw method, in particular, the impact of Jigsaw on children's role-taking ability.

## PROCESSES UNDERLYING JIGSAW

### Empathic Role-Taking

We believe that people who work in interdependent groups, such as those found in the Jigsaw classroom, gradually become more adept at taking one another's perspective. For example, suppose that Jane and Carlos are in a Jigsaw group.

Carlos is reporting and Jane is having difficulty following him. She does not quite understand because his style of presentation is different from that to which she is accustomed. Not only must she pay close attention but, in addition, she must find a way to ask questions that Carlos will understand and that will elicit the additional information she needs. To accomplish this, she must get to know Carlos, put herself in his shoes — in short, she must begin to empathize with him.

This notion was systematically tested by Diane Bridgeman (1981). She reasoned that if taking the perspective of other students is required and practised in Jigsaw learning, students with exposure to the Jigsaw process should display greater role-taking abilities than students who have not participated in Jigsaw. In her experiment Bridgeman administered a revised version of Chandler's (1973) role-taking cartoon series to 120 fifth-grade students. Roughly half of the students spent eight weeks in a Jigsaw learning environment, and the others were taught in either traditional or innovative small-group classrooms.

Each of the cartoons in the Chandler test depicts a central character caught up in a chain of psychological cause and effect, so that the character's subsequent behaviour is shaped by and fully comprehensible only in terms of the preceding events. In one of the sequences, for example, a boy who has been saddened by seeing his father off at the airport begins to cry when he later receives a gift of a toy airplane similar to the one that had carried his father away. Midway into each sequence a second character is introduced in the role of a late-arriving bystander who witnesses the resultant behaviours of the principal character but is not privy to the preceding causal events. As a result, the subject is in a privileged position relative to the late-coming story character, whose role the subject is later asked to assume. The cartoon series measures the degree to which one is able to set aside facts known only to oneself and to adopt the perspective different from one's own. Thus in our example the subject knows why the child cries when he receives the toy airplane, but the postal worker who delivered the toy lacks this knowledge. What happens when the subject is asked to take the postal worker's perspective?

After eight weeks students in the Jigsaw classrooms were better able to see things from the bystander's point of view than students in the control classrooms (Bridgeman, 1981). For example, when the postal worker delivered the toy airplane to the little boy, the students in the control classrooms were more likely to assume that the postal worker knew that the boy's father had recently left town on an airplane — simply because they (the subjects) had this information. On the other hand, the students who had participated in the Jigsaw group were much more successful in taking the postal worker's role, realizing that he could not possibly understand why the boy would cry upon receiving a toy airplane.

Bridgeman's data confirm the notion that the interdependent structure of the Jigsaw classroom promotes each child's ability to take the perspective of other group members. Moreover, the successful achievement of the group's goals rests, at least in part, on the extent to which group members acquire and exercise these role-taking skills. Working together toward common goals enhances role-taking ability which, in turn, feeds back into and facilitates the group's (and hence the individual's) performance. We believe that the dynamic interplay between cooperative effort and role-taking serves as an important mediator of Jigsaw's positive effects on intergroup relations, self-esteem and academic performance. Again, it is important to note that these dynamics are initially set into motion by each child's desire to do well in school. Thus perspective-taking that begins in pure self-interest ultimately generates the conditions under which genuine empathy and warm feelings can flourish.

## Attribution of Success and Failure

Highly related to its impact on role-taking abilities, interdependent work in the pursuit of common goals also influences the kinds of attributions people make about their own and others' performances. Experimental evidence indicates that in general people tend to make dispositional attributions when they succeed at a task (e.g., they attribute their success to skill or talent) and situational attributions when they fail (e.g., they attribute their failure to bad luck). In other words, people often explain their successes and failures in a self-enhancing or self-protective manner (e.g., Zuckerman, 1979). In one of our experiments (Stephan *et al.*, 1978) we found that individuals engaged in an interdependent task made similar attributions regarding their partner's performance as they did for their own. That is, they treated their partners with the same generosity typically reserved for themselves alone. This was not the case in competitive interactions.

## Self-Esteem and Academic Performance

Our general assumption is that various consequences of Jigsaw learning can become antecedents for one another. This orientation is evident in our earlier discussion of the dynamic interplay of cooperative activity and role-taking skills. A similar argument can also be made for the reciprocal effects of self-esteem and academic performance. Just as low self-esteem can inhibit a child from performing well, anything that increases self-esteem is likely to improve academic performance among underachievers. Conversely, as Franks and Marolla (1976) have observed, increases in performance should bring about increases in self-esteem. Being treated with greater respect by one's peers (as almost inevitably happens in Jigsaw groups) is another important antecedent of self-esteem, according to Franks and Marolla. Indeed, the two-way causal connection between performance and self-esteem is supported by research (see Covington and Beery, 1976; Purkey, 1970).

## OTHER COOPERATIVE STRATEGIES

Our results offer substantial evidence for the value of the Jigsaw methods in raising self-esteem and academic performance, in reducing intergroup enmity and in increasing the attractiveness of school. However, we hasten to add that Jigsaw is merely one of several cooperative strategies developed more-or-less independently by Robert Slavin and his colleagues at Johns Hopkins University, Stuart Cook and his colleagues at the University of Colorado, David Johnson and his colleagues at the University of Minnesota, Shlomo Sharan and his colleagues in Israel, and others.

Based on social-psychological theory and research, these techniques have been evaluated in field experiments conducted in a variety of school settings and a wide range of grade levels. Although each technique has its own unique flavour and its own special advantages and disadvantages, they all essentially involve a far greater degree of interdependence than is found in traditional classrooms. A full discussion of these methods is beyond the scope of this chapter. However, we will briefly focus on one set of cooperative learning strategies called 'Student Team Learning'. Developed by Slavin (1980) and his colleagues, these techniques include Student Teams-Achievement Divisions (STAD), Teams-Games-Tournament (TGT) and Jigsaw II (a spinoff of our original method).

*Student Teams Achievement Divisions.*  In the STAD method students meet in teams of four or five members to learn a set of worksheets that are based on the teacher's lesson for that day. Students then take individual quizzes on the material. Individual scores are used to compute a team score, with each student's contribution based on the degree to which he or she has improved over his or her past average. High scoring teams receive recognition in a weekly class newsletter.

*Teams-Games-Tournament.*  Similar to STAD, TGT substitutes academic games for individual quizzes. As representatives of their teams, students compete in tests of academic skills with members of other teams who are roughly equal in ability and achievement. Thus both STAD and TGT learning strategies provide a combination of cooperative and competitive activities, with the latter designed to allow students to perform well — either by competing with an equal, or by making a contribution to the team score that reflects the student's individual improvement over time.

*Jigsaw II.*  Based on our original technique, Jigsaw II (Slavin, 1980) is a modification designed to allow Jigsaw to work better with the other Student Team Learning methods discussed above. As in regular Jigsaw, students in each group become experts on special topics and then teach this information to other members of the group. After individual quizzes are taken, the scores of each student are used to compute a team score, as in the STAD technique.

*Commentary.*  The most notable difference between regular Jigsaw and the various methods that make up the Student Team Learning approach is that the latter strategies explicitly combine elements of both cooperation and competition. Competition at the individual level, which so often marks the traditional classroom, is replaced in these methods by intragroup cooperation and intergroup competition. This competitive component, however, is structured in a fashion that allows students who devote effort to their studies to perform well — either by competing with an equal, or by contributing a 'personal best' to their team's score. In original Jigsaw, competition is largely eliminated from the *process* of learning. Still, rivalry may persist in comparisons of academic achievement, which remain based on tests of individual performance. In the Student Team Learning approach, achievement is assessed at both individual and group levels.

Regardless of their differences, nearly all methods of interdependent learning face similar problems — problems associated with the dynamics of cooperation itself. As Slavin (1985) has observed, the differences among various techniques reflect each method's attempt to address the same set of concerns. For example, a central problem associated with cooperative techniques is the need to maintain individual accountability so that all members of the group share roughly the same amount of work. Thus Jigsaw and Jigsaw II circumvent the problem of 'social loafing' primarily by requiring each student to make a unique contribution to offer the group as a whole, and also by having students take quizzes alone.

Another problem Slavin notes is the need to compensate for the fact that low achieving students may start with less to contribute to the group than their high achieving counterparts. In such cases students may devalue or ridicule the efforts of low achieving groupmates. Techniques associated with the Student Team Learning approach avoid this difficulty by basing students' contributions to team scores on their performance as measured against their own past achievements or as measured against the performance of students of roughly equal ability. Both these strategies involve giving low achieving students a 'handicap', which allows them to be regarded as important resources to their groupmates.

Getting students to care about the success of their group is an essential element in promoting cooperative learning. According to Slavin (1985), many students will resist cooperative activities unless some kind of incentive — such as group recognition and praise — is provided. In regular Jigsaw, of course, the incentive to cooperate is based on self-interest; that is, each student's academic performance will suffer if the group fails to function in a cooperative manner. The Student Learning Teams approach, on the other hand, introduces explicit rewards on the group level, which complement individual motivations to succeed.

*Research Support.*   Studies evaluating the effects of Student Team Learning techniques and other cooperative methods have yielded results consistent with those reported in our earlier discussion of research on Jigsaw. Overall, most studies find that cooperative learning in ethnically diverse groups has a positive impact on self-esteem, intergroup relations and academic achievement, compared to learning in a traditional classroom.

In a review of forty-six methodologically sound field experiments, Slavin (1983) reported that cooperative classrooms produced higher academic performance in twenty-nine studies, whereas only two studies favoured traditional, competitive classrooms. In fifteen studies no differences were found. Moreover, there was some evidence that the achievement of Blacks and other minority students was especially likely to benefit from a cooperative classroom structure. These studies lasted at least two weeks and were conducted in elementary and secondary schools.

Similarly, cooperative learning was associated with improved relationships among members of diverse ethnic groups, including Blacks, Whites, Hispanics and Middle Eastern and European Jews in Israel (Slavin, 1983). Out of fourteen studies on the impact of cooperation on crossethnic relationships, twelve revealed positive outcomes. In two of these studies beneficial effects persisted up to nine months after the cooperative programme ended (Slavin, 1979; Ziegler, 1981, cited in Slavin, 1985).

## SUMMARY

The merits of cooperative learning environments in reducing prejudice and improving academic performance are supported by a substantial body of evidence gleaned from carefully conducted social-psychological experiments. It should be clear, however, that we are not suggesting that Jigsaw learning or any other cooperative method constitutes *the* solution to our problems with intergroup relations. What we have shown is that highly desirable results occur when children spend at least a portion of their time in the pursuit of common goals. These effects are in accordance with predictions made by social scientists in their testimony favouring school desegregation in the United States over thirty-five years ago.

It is also worth emphasizing that the Jigsaw method has proved effective even when used for as little as 20 per cent of a child's time in the classroom. Moreover, it has been shown that cooperative techniques have produced beneficial results even when accompanied by competitive activities (Slavin, 1980). Thus the data neither support the elimination of classroom competition nor interference with individually guided education. Cooperative learning can and does coexist easily with almost any other method used by teachers in the classroom. Practical guidance on how teachers can implement the Jigsaw method in their classrooms is the subject of the next section of this chapter.

## A PRACTICAL GUIDE TO THE JIGSAW CLASSROOM

Students rarely become magically cooperative and helpful the first time they work in a Jigsaw group. Because they have spent many of their school years in a competitive environment, competition is a familiar and natural mode for them, and not one that is instantly abandoned. Gradually, however, they learn that in a situation of structured interdependence — such as the Jigsaw group — competition does not pay off. Thus an essential part of the Jigsaw process is the time spent learning cooperative skills *before* actually learning academic material using the Jigsaw method. We have termed this process 'team-building'.

### Team-Building: Planting the Seeds of Cooperation

Children who have no previous training in cooperative skills should not be expected to cooperate successfully in learning a difficult lesson. This would be asking them to master content and process at the same time, a request that will lead to frustration, boredom and failure to learn either content or process very well. Whatever amount of time the teacher plans to spend using Jigsaw, he or she should provide a chance for students to work together through team-building exercises before approaching the curriculum material in the Jigsaw format. Ordinarily, a short period each day for one or two weeks is sufficient for this purpose. We have found it useful to conduct these team-building activities with the children already assigned to their Jigsaw groups. This allows the groups to develop a cohesiveness that will help when they begin to use Jigsaw to learn academic material.

Most students have only a vague notion of cooperative and constructive behaviour. They understand, for example, that shouting or punching each other probably has no place in a cooperative activity, but they are not certain which positive actions help to create a good group atmosphere. The purpose of team-building exercises is to develop communication skills and to promote understanding of group process, both of which allow students to assume responsibility for their own behaviour and to help their group to function more productively. We have found several exercises useful in teaching children cooperative skills, and these are described in *The Jigsaw Classroom* (Aronson *et al.*, 1978). Here we will present a few examples to illustrate the goals of the team-building period.

The Broken Squares game (Bavelas, 1973) is a cooperative task analogous to the Jigsaw procedure. In the Broken Squares game each group member receives six pieces of a puzzle. The participants are told that the object of the game is for each person to end up with a completed square. The pieces that each person needs are scattered among the group members, so the individual is unable to complete his or her own square without their help. Simply taking a piece from another person in the group is not allowed. All group members can do is give away their own pieces, one by one, to help others in the group complete their squares. Moreover, to encourage each person to be actively helpful to other members instead of waiting to see who can help him or her, no communication is allowed. A participant may not signal or ask for a needed piece of the puzzle. Thus all members of the group must take the initiative for each member to end up with a completed square. If even one person decides to work only with his or her own pieces, and ignores the needs of the others in the group, the task may never be completed.

The Broken Squares game emphasizes giving and cooperating. No reinforcement is given for being the fastest, smartest or best in the group. On the contrary, success becomes possible only when participants realize that the task's completion depends on the group's ability to work together. Following this exercise, time is provided for a discussion of the procedure. Participants are encouraged to talk about how they completed the squares, what feelings they experienced, and what frustrations they encountered (if any). Discussing the process often is as important as the exercise itself. It makes students aware of how the group functioned as a whole, and gives them a chance to talk about effective strategies within the cooperative structure.

One of the most important skills team-building can help to develop is effective or *active listening*. Many students (and adults as well) have developed the habit of not listening to one another. This is often overlooked in the competitive classroom because success depends on listening to the teacher rather than to other members of the class. In the Jigsaw classroom the opposite is true. Listening attentively to fellow group members is the only way to learn the material that each student has to teach, and each student's material is an essential part of the whole lesson. For the speaker, making a presentation to students who are throwing spitballs and doodling in their notebooks is bound to be a frustrating and discouraging experience. When making subsequent presentations, that speaker is likely to be less than enthusiastic. Concentrating on listening skills during the team-building period helps to prevent this kind of discouragement from developing.

Perhaps the most important aspect of Jigsaw is the *distribution of responsibility* among group members. Instead of having a director who can be praised when things go well or blamed when they go poorly, every group member is partly responsible for how the group functions. Developing this sense of responsibility in students is the primary goal of the team-building exercises. The more engaged and responsible students feel, the more exciting education becomes; students feel they have some control over the learning process. Indeed, a successful Jigsaw group is not one without problems, but one in which all members take some responsibility for improving the dynamics of the group and for solving problems when they arise.

A technique called 'brainstorming' encourages students to develop their own criteria for a good group process. In brainstorming, participants think of as many suggestions and ideas about a particular topic as they can within a short time. These ideas are written down without discussion or evaluation. After this brainstorming period the ideas and suggestions are ranked according to priority. For example, if the topic under discussion is 'How to show your groupmates you're listening to them', a group lists as many positive behaviours as they can think of in five or ten minutes. Since people learn more from thinking about what they can or should do than from dwelling on the things they should not do, listing behaviours in a positive way is important. The behaviours listed should also be as specific as possible. To illustrate with the topic we have mentioned, a list might include the following:

nod at the speaker to show you understand him;

look directly at the speaker when she is speaking;

summarize what the speaker says;

rephrase what the speaker has just said;

try to reflect the feeling the speaker is expressing (for example, if Peter says, 'My part was much harder to learn than the part you guys got,' the listener might respond, 'It sounds like you're feeling you got an unfair share of the work.');

build on the speaker's ideas by taking them a step further;

smile at the speaker in a reassuring way;

lean toward the speaker while you are listening.

We have presented only a few examples of team-building exercises; others can be found in *The Jigsaw Classroom* (1978). In addition, teachers are encouraged to develop and implement exercises that draw from their own experience and imagination.

## Putting Together the Jigsaw Group

A Jigsaw group can be made up of five or six members, depending on the size of the class. In our experience having six children in each group works well. The teacher is responsible for assigning children to groups and for choosing one student to serve as the leader of each group. We have found three factors to be important in constructing the membership of a group: (1) general scholastic ability; (2) leadership ability; and (3) affective bonds between and among students. In general, the Jigsaw groups should have roughly equal distribution of resources (readers and non-readers, articulate speakers and those who have difficulty speaking, and so forth). Clearly, a group composed of six poor readers would be a disaster. A mixture of skill levels provides bright students with the challenge of developing effective teaching skills and slower students with readily available assistance from their peers.

If possible, the teacher should avoid having best friends or worst enemies in the same group. Although Jigsaw is often successful in helping to restore amicable relations, a neutral group will facilitate learning the method in the beginning stages. In addition, the most popular students in the class should be distributed evenly among the groups, and each group should reflect a diversity of racial or ethnic backgrounds and include members of both sexes.

Particularly in the initial stages of implementing Jigsaw, leadership ability is an important factor in making up the group. Each group should have at least one member the teacher feels will be an effective group leader. Ideally, this should be someone who is on good (or at least neutral) terms with other group members, is a good reader, and is responsible and easy for the teacher to work with. This last characteristic is especially important since the teacher will make suggestions about the group's process through the group leader.

## Jigsaw Curriculum: Constructing the Puzzle

A carefully planned curriculum can go a long way toward making students' introduction to Jigsaw proceed smoothly. Ideally, the teacher will have prepared the curriculum during a school vacation or other non-teaching time, giving the task uninterrupted attention and making the process a pleasant one. If this is not feasible, we strongly recommend that the preparation of the curriculum be completed — at the latest — before Jigsaw begins. On the whole, narrative material that emphasizes reading and comprehension skills is the easiest to work with in groups. Because of this, the area of social studies, including history, civics and geography, is perhaps the most naturally suited to the technique. Jigsaw has been successfully used, however, in teaching mathematics, language arts and biology, although these subjects are more difficult to adapt.

Whatever material is used must be divided into coherent segments that can be distributed to members of the Jigsaw group. That is, an individual piece of the lesson must be understandable to a student without knowledge of the portions given to his groupmates. We have found that Jigsaw works best with material that is *not* conceptually novel (i.e., requiring students to use skills they have yet to learn). Introducing addition or subtraction for the first time in the context of a Jigsaw group is probably not a good idea, although Jigsaw could be used for practising those skills once they are established.

To provide for maximum interdependence among group members, each student should have access to other parts of the lesson *only* through other group members. If students have already had experience with the lesson material, they will be less dependent on listening to their groupmates. If standard texts are used, the material must be cut out or reproduced, divided, and the texts collected and stored away.

It is advisable for teachers to do weekly lesson planning to determine the material to be covered daily in the Jigsaw group and to provide additional time for curriculum preparation. Homework assignments and material to supplement the basic lesson should also be organized well in advance. The amount of material used and how it is broken up are both important aspects of curriculum preparation for Jigsaw. In the first few weeks students are still adjusting to the process, as well as learning content material. We suggest that, at least initially, the amount of information be kept quite light. After two weeks the workload can be gradually increased until a full load is reached. We have found that time lost early in the process is made up later — with interest.

How much material constitutes a full load? In our experience students can be given as much or more material using Jigsaw than using traditional teaching methods. Even when a large amount of material is to be mastered, the students seem to rise to the occasion. The decision about how much material should be contained on each Jigsaw 'card' is an important one. If there is consistently too little material, there will be little challenge for the students, and they will quickly become bored with the process. On the other hand, if there is too much material, it will be difficult to cover all parts within the allotted time. This is bound to be a frustrating experience for the group. One way to avoid these extremes is to equate the Jigsaw cards for the number of important facts that each card contains. Thus one student may read three paragraphs and another five, but both will be responsible for the same number of important facts. Using this method results in a student's workload varying from day to day, but we have not found this to impede the successful working of the group.

Another helpful practice is to break up material such that a separate subject is covered each day. For example, on Monday students might learn about the geography of China, on Tuesday they might study Chinese family structure, and so forth. The best general advice we can give concerning the division of material is to strive for a balanced distribution among individual students and over the course of the unit.

Our research team has prepared a sample curriculum in multicultural social studies that can be found in *The Jigsaw Classroom* (Aronson *et al.*, 1978). For detailed information about making up Jigsaw cards, see Aronson and Goode (1980).

### The Jigsaw Hour: Teaching Jigsaw to Students

If a class is to use Jigsaw an hour a day, twenty minutes of the hour should be spent in 'expert' groups and the remaining forty minutes in the Jigsaw group. At the beginning of the hour students gather in their Jigsaw groups to receive their cards and any special instructions from their group leader. They then break into 'expert' groups, consisting of students who have identical material to learn, and plan their presentations. They then return to Jigsaw groups to present their material and to listen to the presentations of others in their group. A short time (roughly five to ten minutes) should be reserved at the end of the hour for the group to discuss any problems that might have arisen during the hour.

**Teacher as Facilitator: Teaching through Intervention**

The role of the teacher and that of the group leader parallel each other: both serve as facilitators. If the class is of average size, it probably will be divided into four to six Jigsaw groups. Even with a teacher's aide, the teacher cannot be everywhere at once. The group leaders function as additional assistants to the teacher, channelling group process skills to group members and helping to organize the activities of the day.

The Jigsaw teacher's goal is to have students regard each other as learning resources rather than depend solely on the teacher as an instructor and leader. Teachers do not abandon all authority in the classroom, however. Instead, they act as backstage directors, creating a structure in which the students may learn how best to make use of each other's knowledge and skills. In addition, the teacher plays an important role as an information resource, one we will discuss in more detail later. The teacher moves around the room, from one Jigsaw group to another, listening, observing, keeping alert for any problem that may develop. Whenever possible, the teacher should make interventions through the group's leader, thereby validating the leader's authority in the eyes of the other students. Since developing the group's capacity for self-regulation is the goal, interventions should help the group discover its own solutions. The teacher may phrase interventions as requests or suggestions to the group leader (for example: 'Jane, perhaps you should check to see if everyone feels they understand all the parts well enough to take the test tomorrow' or, 'Peter, maybe you should ask the group if telling John that he's stupid is helping them learn the material').

If a group member complains directly to the teacher about someone in the group ('Mr Pike, Jane is drawing funny pictures instead of listening!'), it is *not* the responsibility of the teacher to solve the problem directly. The Jigsaw teacher refers the problem back to the group to have them solve it themselves. In the above example Mr Pike might ask the group leader whether group members have any ideas about why Jane is drawing pictures instead of listening. Perhaps the presentations are going too fast for her to understand, or perhaps she is bored because the speaker is reading his card in a dull tone of voice. Once the source of the problem is identified, the teacher may take the group leader aside and suggest ways of solving it, or the students may be ready to take responsibility for providing their own solutions.

Ultimately, the teacher's interventions are designed to help students learn the content of their lessons more effectively, and to assist them in developing an efficient, comfortable and cooperative group process. Perhaps more importantly, the teacher serves as model for the students, demonstrating effective communication and problem-solving skills. Through such interventions — even the phrasing, tone of voice and the kinds of suggestions offered — the teacher provides an example students can eventually imitate in their roles as group members.

The first time 'expert' groups meet, students may have difficulty finding proficient and interesting ways of presenting their material. The teacher can help them learn how to identify and extract important points from the printed information, and to think of creative ways to present what they have learned. The first time students present, they often simply read their paragraphs aloud, an experience that quickly bores the listeners. Below are some examples of teacher interventions that we have found useful in the initial expert sessions:

Can you think of a way to put the information you just learned into your own words?

Can you think of how the material you just read is related to your own life? Are there any examples in your own life that you could use in explaining this information to your groupmates?

Do you know what you are going to say when you go back to your Jigsaw group?

Once students return to their Jigsaw groups, the teacher may need to offer assistance during their presentations. At the beginning some children may have difficulty summarizing material in their own words. Even after practising in the expert groups they may simply read the paragraph aloud in the Jigsaw group. In such cases the teacher will need to remind them gently that putting the information in their own words makes their presentations more interesting and easier to follow. The teacher should also encourage students to include the examples and interesting points discussed in the expert group, and to comment on the presentations of other members.

Initially, in both expert and Jigsaw groups, students may stop working together and become merely six individuals working alone who happen to be sharing a space. This may happen because they are practising their own parts while others are talking. The teacher must emphasize that the purpose of the expert groups is for students with the same material to help each other learn it, and that Jigsaw groups are also meant to be situations where the students learn from each other. The following interventions are useful in reminding students of this:

Are you helping one another learn the material?

Is everybody in this group understanding the material you covered today?

Sometimes very bright students finish learning the material early and withdraw from the rest of the discussion, leaving other group members to struggle by themselves. At this point the teacher needs to emphasize the student's role as a teacher as well as a student. The bright student need not disappear when she or he has learned the material. Rather, such students should be encouraged to spend the extra time helping other students learn. We have found that adopting this role in the group can be very rewarding for bright students and prevents them from becoming bored. Having students fulfil this function also helps narrow the communication gap — as well as the social distance — between high achievers and low achievers that is often found in traditional classrooms. The following intervention is designed to encourage more competent students to help their groupmates:

Now that you've finished the material, can you help John learn it so he can teach it to his groupmates?

Perhaps the most important intervention the teacher will make is convincing students that fighting, teasing and insulting each other are dysfunctional behaviours. Working in groups invariably involves some conflict. The teacher will find that some of the quicker students become impatient with those who learn more slowly; that fourth-, fifth- and sixth-grade students have definite misgivings about cooperating with (or even sitting next to) classmates of the opposite sex; and that existing rivalries tend to become exaggerated in the group setting. Jigsaw, however, can be an excellent place to work out some of these conflicts and build understanding and harmonious relations. Getting students to express their emotions, including negative ones, can help this process. The teacher will need to point out, however, that insulting the other person is not a useful way to express negative emotions. In communicating this, the teacher may want to appeal to the students' sense of kindness ('I think Linda must feel pretty rotten when you say that to her'); to their need to be constructive and helpful ('Is there a way you could help Jody understand the part she is having trouble with?'); to their sense of practicality ('Insulting each other may be fun, but it doesn't seem to be helping you to learn the material'); or to their need for personal achievement ('There's a test tomorrow, and if you keep insulting Kim you're never going to be able to learn her part'). These interventions teach students to avoid destructive, cruel behaviours and work toward a process emphasizing cooperation, consideration and learning the content of the lesson.

**Teacher Training Workshops**

When we began conducting research on the Jigsaw technique, we considered it essential to provide teachers with special training. For our research it was important not only that Jigsaw be implemented as effectively as possible, but also that there be some consistency of implementation across classrooms. With this in mind we developed a one-day, in-service training workshop introducing Jigsaw through demonstrations and lectures describing the technique. Over the years we have trained several groups of teachers using the workshop format. We have found that workshops can play an important role both in familiarizing teachers with the Jigsaw process and in giving them an experiential understanding of the approach that they did not get reading about it or studying the research and theory behind the technique. This experiential understanding facilitated their own and their students' adaptation to the Jigsaw technique. Back in their classrooms, teachers were better able to anticipate difficulties and help students acquire team-building skills. Moreover, they were able to empathize with the students' introduction to the approach rather than merely direct it.

We highly recommend that teachers wishing to use the Jigsaw method in their classrooms undergo the training these workshops provide. A step-by-step description of a typical one-day workshop can be found in Aronson and Goode (1980).

**Postscript: The Future of Cooperative Learning**

Our work on Jigsaw began almost twenty years ago, when we intervened in the Austin, Texas, school system at the urgent request of local administrators. We came at a time of turmoil, at a time of crisis in American race relations, at a time when the ideals of the civil rights movement were on the line. For us, as social scientists, it was also a time of great challenge, a rare opportunity to take our theories out of the lab and test them in the real world, in the very institution that symbolizes the American ideal of equality: the public schools.

When we first entered the schools, the upheaval over desegregation in Austin was so great that we were given extraordinary freedom to propose and implement changes in the way classrooms had traditionally been run. Indeed, in their urgent quest for solutions, local officials granted us free rein in restructuring the dynamics of the classroom in the interests of improving race relations while upholding academic standards. Casting modesty aside, we felt our mission had succeeded: not, certainly, in solving the problem of interracial strife, but in making an important difference in the lives of hundreds of youngsters who otherwise might have been deprived of healthy self-respect and a decent education.

In the immediate aftermath of the Austin crisis we continued our research on cooperative education, set up workshops for teachers in school systems around the nation and in general endeavoured to give away what seemed to us a very valuable addition to learning methods already in practice. But a strange thing happened. Once the storm of desegregation had passed, we found doors closing instead of opening. As things settled down, most school administrators turned a deaf ear, content to return to business as usual — to the zero-sum game of the competitive classroom. In the absence of a crisis, few schools were receptive to any change in the status quo.

At first we were puzzled by the cool response to Jigsaw. Although we developed the technique in the context of improving intergroup relations, it was abundantly clear that its potential applications were much more general. We had demonstrated that competitiveness was not a deeply ingrained trait, but rather an overlearned orientation that could be modified by altering the structure of the classroom. Surely, we thought, no one could fail to see the value in teaching children to work together productively, and to respect themselves and each other more, especially since academic standards were not compromised and in some cases were even improved.

What we failed to realize, however, was that change — even when it looks like change for the better — is scarcely a high priority for the majority of school administrators, beholden to parents who want the 'best' for their children. Seeing themselves as realists, many parents may consider the ability to cooperate as having only secondary importance, as an optional set of skills with little to contribute to their child's future. Indeed, most parents want their children's elementary and high school years to leave them well prepared. But, we might ask, well prepared for *what*? For competing for admission to the best colleges and universities? For competing for the best jobs? For competing for the best promotions? For competing for the best homes and schools for *their* children, who in turn can go out into the world well prepared?

In a very profound sense the idea of cooperative education is at odds with the intensely competitive ethos as well as the values associated with individualism (first observed by de Tocqueville in 1831) that have prevailed in America from its very inception. Indeed, the idea of cooperative education might even be subversive. However, one might also ask: just how realistic is the notion that a highly competitive learning environment is vital to our children's future? How adaptive is this one-sided emphasis on competitive skills? Recent research suggests that even in the business world, where the competitive spirit has historically reigned supreme, competition does not always pay off. Rather, there is evidence for just the opposite: individuals who are the most competitive are not, in fact, those who are most likely to succeed.

To illustrate, research by Helmreich and his colleagues (e.g., Helmreich *et al.*, 1978, 1986; Spence and Helmreich, 1983) indicates that highly competitive people do not perform as well academically and in the workplace when compared to less competitive individuals. In one study, business school graduates were given ranks in three categories: (1) mastery (taking on new challenges), (2) work (the amount of time and effort expended), and (3) competitiveness (the desire to outperform others). Individuals ranked high in mastery and work, but low in competitiveness, earned roughly $6000 a year more than their highly competitive counterparts (Helmreich and Spence, 1978, cited in Sit, 1989).

These findings are consistent with recent observations of seasoned business experts, who point out that a cooperative atmosphere boosts workers' self-esteem, improves relationships among workers and promotes higher productivity (Kohn, 1986). These observations parallel our research findings on the benefits of Jigsaw learning. Moreover, the need to foster cooperation in the workplace has received serious attention from corporations, with some employers spending large sums of money on workshops and other forms of cooperative training for managers and other works. Somewhat ironically, however, the call for a more cooperative workplace has been sounded in response to the growing recognition that only by getting employees to pull together in the workplace can American companies compete successfully in the global marketplace. Here, once again, we find self-interest as the motivating force behind the need for greater cooperation — albeit self-interest on an entirely different level from that in the Jigsaw classroom.

In any event it appears that the highly competitive environment of our schools has reached a point of diminishing returns, has become dysfunctional in preparing youngsters for adulthood. Fortunately there are signs that educators and parents are beginning to reconsider the merits of cooperative learning — that is, if the recently rekindled interest in Jigsaw is any indication of a larger trend.

Finally, it bears repeating that the goal of Jigsaw and other cooperative learning techniques is not to eliminate the ability or the desire to engage in competitive pursuits — far from it. Rather, we see Jigsaw as a supplementary teaching method that allows children to develop important social skills as well as a greater appreciation of individuals from racial and ethnic groups different from their own. It is our belief that such skills will leave children well equipped to function happily and productively in the increasingly diverse world that awaits them — a world that will surely demand a more evenly balanced combination of competitive and cooperative skills.

## ACKNOWLEDGMENTS

Portions of this article were adapted from previous articles written by the senior author in collaboration with several of his former graduate students. We especially wish to thank Diane Bridgeman, Robert Geffner, Erica Goode, Alex Gonzalez and Neal Osherow for their earlier contributions.

## NOTE

1 Our choice of a Mexican-American child named 'Carlos' to illustrate the positive effects of the Jigsaw method was not an arbitrary one. Indeed, Jigsaw appears to offer special benefits to Mexican-American children, largely because of the cooperative, group oriented nature of Mexican-American socialization practices. For a discussion of this issue, see Aronson and Gonzalez (1988).

## REFERENCES

Allport, G.W. (1954) *The Nature of Prejudice*, Reading Mass., Addison-Wesley.

Aronson, E. (1984) 'Modifying the Environment of the Desegregated Classroom', in A.J. Stewart (Ed.), *Motivation and Society*, San Francisco, Calif., Jossey-Bass.

Aronson, E. and Gonzalez, A. (1988) 'Desegregation, Jigsaw, and the Mexican-American Experience', in P. Katz and D. Taylor (Eds), *Eliminating Racism*, New York, Plenum Press.

Aronson, E. and Goode, E. (1980) 'Training Teachers to Implement Jigsaw Learning: A Manual for Teachers', in S. Sharan, P. Hare, C. Webb and R. Hertz-Lazarowitz (Eds), *Cooperation in Education*, Provo, Utah, Brigham Young University Press.

Aronson, E. and Yates, S. (1983) 'Cooperation in the Classroom: The Impact of the Jigsaw Method on Inter-Ethnic Relations, Classroom Performance, and Self-Esteem', in H. Blumberg and P. Hare (Eds), *Small Groups*, London, Wiley.

Aronson, E., Blaney, N., Sikes, J., Stephan, C. and Snapp, M. (1975) 'Busing and Racial Tension: The Jigsaw Route to Learning and Liking', *Psychology Today*, 8, pp. 43–50.

Aronson, E., Stephan, C., Sikes, J., Blaney, N. and Snapp, M. (1978) *The Jigsaw Classroom*, Beverly Hills, Calif., Sage.

Bevelas, A. (1973) 'The Five-Squares Problem: An Instructional Aid in Group Cooperation', *Studies in Personnel Psychology*, 5, pp. 29–38.

Blaney, N.T., Stephan, C., Rosenfield, D., Aronson, E. and Sikes, J. (1977) 'Interdependence in the Classroom: A Field Study', *Journal of Educational Psychology*, 69, pp. 139–146.

Brewer, M.B. and Miller, N. (1988) 'Contact and Cooperation: When Do They Work', in P. Katz and D. Taylor (Eds) *Eliminating Racism*, New York, Plenum.

Bridgeman, D.L. (1981) 'Enhanced Role-taking through Cooperative Interdependence: A Field Study', *Child Development*, 52, pp. 1231–1238.

Brown, R. (1986) *Social Psychology*, 2nd ed., New York, Free Press.

Chandler, M.J. (1973) 'Egocentrism and Antisocial Behavior: The Assessment and Training of Social Perspective-taking Skills', *Developmental Psychology*, 9, pp. 326–332.

Cohen, E. (1972) 'Interracial Interaction Disability', *Human Relations*, 25, 1, pp. 9–24.

Cohen, E. and Roper, S. (1972) 'Modification of Interracial Interaction Disability: An Application of Status Characteristics Theory', *American Sociological Review*, 6, pp. 643–657.

Covington, M.V. and Beery, R.G. (1976) *Self-Worth and School Learning*, New York, Rinehart and Winston.

Deutsch, M. (1949) 'An Experimental Study of the Effects of Cooperation and Competition upon Group Process', *Human Relations*, 2, pp. 199–231.

Franks, D.D. and Marolla, J. (1976) 'Efficacious Action and Social Approval as Interacting Dimensions of Self-Esteem: A Tentative Formulation through Construct Validation', *Sociometry*, 39, pp. 324–341.

Geffner, R.A. (1978) 'The Effects of Interdependent Learning on Self-Esteem, Inter-Ethnic Relations, and Intraethnic Attitudes of Elementary School Children: A Field Experiment', Unpublished doctoral thesis, University of California, Santa Cruz.

Gerard, H. and Miller, N. (1975) *School Desegregation*, New York, Plenum Press.

Helmreich, R.L. and Spence, J.T. (1978) 'The Work and Family Orientation Questionnaire: An Objective Instrument to Assess Components of Achievement Motivation and Attitudes toward Family and Career', *JSAS Catalog of Selected Documents in Psychology*, 8, p. 35.

Helmreich, R.L., Beane, W.E., Lucker, G.W. and Spence, J.T. (1978) 'Achievement Motivation and Scientific Attainment', *Personality and Social Psychology Bulletin*, 4, pp. 222–226.

Helmreich, R.L., Spence, J.T., Beane, W.E., Lucker, G.W. and Matthews, K.A. (1980) 'Making It in Academic Psychology: Demographic and Personality Correlates of Attainment', *Journal of Personality and Social Psychology*, 39, pp. 896–908.

Kohn, A. (1986) *No Contest: The Case against Competition*, Boston, Mass., Houghton Mifflin.

Lucker, G.W., Rosenfield, D., Sikes, J. and Aronson, E. (1977) 'Performance in the Interdependent Classroom: A Field Study', *American Educational Research Journal*, 13, pp. 115–123.

Pettigrew, T. (1961) 'Social Psychology and Desegregation Research', *American Psychologist*, 15, pp. 61–71.

Purkey, W.W. (1970) *Self-Concept and School Achievement*, Englewood Cliffs, N.J., Prentice-Hall.

St John, N. (1975) *School Desegregation: Outcomes for Children*, New York, Wiley.

Sherif, M., Harvey, O.J., White, J., Hood, W. and Sherif, C. (1961) *Intergroup Conflict and Cooperation: The Robber's Cave Experiment*, Norman, Okla, University of Oklahoma, Institute of Intergroup Relations.

Sit, M. (1989) 'Cultivating a Corporation Culture of Cooperation', *San Jose Mercury News*, 13 August, pp. 1–2.

Slavin, R.E. (1979) 'Effects of Biracial Learning Teams on Cross-Racial Friendships', *Journal of Educational Psychology*, 71, pp. 381–387.

Slavin, R. (1980) 'Student Team Learning', in S. Sharan, P. Hare, C. Webb and R. Hertz-Lazarowitz (Eds), *Cooperation in Education*, Provo, Utah, Brigham Young University Press.

Slavin, R. (1983) 'When Does Cooperative Learning Increase Student Achievement?' *Psychological Bulletin*, 94, pp. 429–445.

Slavin, R. (1985) 'Introduction to Cooperative Learning Research', in R. Slavin, S. Sharan, S. Kagan, R. Hertz Lazarowitz, C. Webb and R. Schmuck (Eds), *Learning to Cooperate, Cooperating to Learn*, New York, Plenum Press.

Spence, J.T. and Helmreich, R.L. 'Achievement-Related Motives and Behavior', in J.T. Spence (Ed.), *Achievement and Achievement Motives: Psychological and Sociological Approaches*, San Francisco, Calif., Freeman.

Stephan, W. (1978) 'School Desegregation: An Evaluation of Predictions Made in Brown versus the Board of Education', *Psychological Bulletin*, 85, pp. 217–238.

Stephan, C., Presser, N.R., Kennedy, J.C. and Aronson, E. (1978) 'Attributions to Success and Failure in Cooperative, Competitive, and Interdependent Interactions', *European Journal of Social Psychology*, 8, pp. 269–274.

Tocqueville, A. de. (1981) *Democracy in America*, Westminster, Md., Random House.

Ziegler, S. (1981) 'The Effectiveness of Cooperative Learning Teams for Increasing Cross-Ethnic Friendship: Additional Evidence', *Human Organization*, 40, pp. 264–268.

Zuckerman, M. (1979) 'Attribution of Success and Failure Revisited, or: The Motivational Bias is Alive and Well in Attribution Theory', *Journal of Personality*, 47, pp. 245–287.

# 13. Educational Interventions for Prejudice Reduction and Integration in Elementary Schools

YAACOV J. KATZ

Six issues, broadly related to educational interventions designed to achieve prejudice reduction and integration in elementary school, are dealt with in this chapter. The first part deals with the evolution of prejudice reduction and integration policies in Western countries which absorbed mass immigration, such as the United States, the United Kingdom and Israel; the second describes the initial results of integration in the 1960s and 1970s; the third refers to the psychoeducational principles involved in integration and prejudice reduction; the fourth defines classroom interventions that are thought to facilitate prejudice reduction and integration; the fifth centres on teacher training for the purpose of achieving prejudice reduction and integration within the classroom; and the last part is concerned with empirical evidence from a prejudice reduction and integration project in an Israeli elementary schools.

Many scholars use the term 'desegregation' interchangeably with the terms 'integration' and 'prejudice reduction'. There are others who use the term 'desegregation' to designate physical changes that transform homogeneous into heterogeneous groups and the terms 'integration' and 'prejudice reduction' to denote positive cognitive, affective and conative changes that transpire in newly formed heterogeneous social groups. In this chapter all three terms are used interchangeably, based on the premise that in the ideal situation desegregation should lead to integration and prejudice reduction which conceivably occur simultaneously.

## DEVELOPMENT OF INTEGRATION AND PREJUDICE REDUCTION POLICIES

In countries such as the United States, Great Britain and Israel, where masses of immigrants from different cultures and socio-economic backgrounds were and are

257

still being absorbed into society, dissatisfaction with inequality — which developed in society to the detriment of the relative newcomers — served as a catalyst for the implementation of integration programmes. The school system soon became the principal agency for inducting the immigrant children or children of immigrant families, who usually belonged to lower socio-economic levels, into the social and cultural norms of their newfound countries of residence. Schools were called upon to facilitate scholastic achievement of lower socio-economic status pupils, as well as to engineer social procedures that would lead to a feeling of greater equality and well-being within society.

Hendrick (1975) noted that schools, historically, have been expected to serve as agencies for social preservation as well as for inducting youth into the ways of society. At present, especially in those countries which have absorbed mass immigration, schools are also being called upon to help produce a basic reform in the way people behave toward one another. Hendrick declared that in the United States, following the historic *Brown vs Board of Education* decision of the US Supreme Court in 1954, school authorities were slowly forced into an awareness that racially and ethnically separate schooling cannot result in education of equal quality.

In most countries with heterogeneous population groups, such as the US, Great Britain and Israel, there are elements of inequality in society. Gerard (1984) pointed out the existence of a significant correlation between the person's socio-economic status and the adequacy of his or her educational background. Gerard said that in the 1960s the first intervention projects were undertaken in the United States in an attempt to reduce group-related educational deficits. According to Stephan (1980), a gradual process of desegregation, mediated by the courts, was set in motion in the US following the *Brown* decision. Desegregation in the US progressed primarily when lawsuits were brought or threatened against local school boards.

Jeffcoate (1979) reviewed the need for combatting segregation and inequality in the school system in Great Britain. He reviewed a number of reports dealing with scholastic achievement of Black pupils, and found that Blacks were generally classified as underachievers who did less well on standardized tests and examinations than their White counterparts. Blacks were also overrepresented in schools for special education and in remedial units.

Gurnah (1987) addressed issues that led to resentment with the traditional school system and acted as catalysts for school desegregation and multicultural education in Great Britain. Gurnah stated that Black parents felt — and still feel — that schools directly cause underachievement in their children's scholastic performance. In addition, Black parents feel that many teachers hold stereotypes of their children, schools remain aloof and, as a result, few Black parents are prepared to become involved in school affairs either as governors or as members of parent committees. Black parents feel that the school curriculum is Eurocentred and does not cater for the history and culture of Black children. There is also a dearth of good quality action research on Black educational needs in teacher training.

Troyna (1987) described the 1944 Education Act as the cornerstone of the organization and thrust of the current educational system in Great Britain. The Act gave expression and legitimacy to two closely linked principles: first, that social advancement should be available to all; and second, that the meritocratic structure of the education system would guarantee that personal achievement and talent would be rewarded within a competitive setting, irrespective of the age, sex and ethnic or class origin of individual pupils. Halsey, Heath and Ridge (1980) conclude that despite the aims of the 1944 Act and a range of subsequent reformist measures and interventions, there remained a tenacious pattern of class inequality in educational achievement and attainment.

Schwarzwald (1989) dealt with the issue of integration in Israel. He said that the political decision of 1968 to reform the educational structure in Israel and impose ethnic integration in junior high schools sought to improve relations between Oriental and Western pupils and to reduce the achievement gap between them. The thesis was that direct contact between individuals from different groups would lead to better relations and understanding. Amir, Sharan and Ben-Ari (1984) pointed out that the fostering of interethnic integration in the Israeli educational system is desired to facilitate the entry of the lower status ethnic subgroups (Orientals) into the mainstream of Israel's social life. The aim of ethnic integration in the national school system, therefore, is to create a society that grants all subgroups equal access to public resources.

In addition to the issue of integration in the school system, the related topic of multicultural education surfaced as a means to achieve the goals of social integration. Banks (1981) envisaged multicultural or multiethnic education as a process of accommodation or acculturation, whereby both teachers and pupils maintain separate cultural identities, interacting with each other in creative harmony. School and society are interdependent, and both must legitimate and respect the cultures of all concerned and share power before accommodation can take place. Lynch (1986) asserted that the task of multicultural education is to assist the individual to reach out and achieve a higher stage of ethnic and cultural existence so that there exists a sufficient cultural and social overlap for society to function.

Lynch (1987) added that multicultural education aims at three main goals: education for a shared political and economic value system; education for cultural diversity; and education for greater equality of educational opportunity. According to Lynch, these goals are to be realized while ethnic groups have the right to maintain attachments and identifications with their native cultures, and it is the duty of the school of reflect this right in the school curriculum. Grant and Sleeter (1986) indicated that the multicultural curriculum must encompass content addressing knowledge of society to ensure that prejudice reduction can take place. The curriculum must, among other things, provide accurate information and correct misinformation about the different ethnic groups, as well as promote a feeling of human empathy and increasing comfort with different cultures.

From the above it appears that in Western heterogeneous societies, such as those in the United States, Great Britain and Israel, the major reasons for embarking on programmes of integration as well as of multicultural and multiethnic education in the respective school systems stem from common principles. These principles deal with ethnic and racial equality, the equality of educational opportunity and the social necessity to deal fairly with all population subgroups in heterogeneous societies. The legislators in those countries interested in undertaking integration programmes, for example, the US, Great Britain and Israel, felt that the educational system was most suited for the implementation of integration policies, and thus affirmative action was undertaken in the respective school systems, each system undertaking interventions best suited to its particular needs.

## DISAPPOINTMENT WITH INITIAL RESULTS OF INTEGRATION

Crain and Mahard (1978) stated that desegregated schools should provide a higher level of educational services for lower-class pupils than segregated schools. Consequently, one may expect some positive effect of these improved resources, both material and human, on the achievement level of minority group pupils in contrast with those in segregated schools. However, in heterogeneous Western societies, such as the United States, Great Britain and Israel, there is evidence that the initial results of desegregation, integration and prejudice reduction were disappointing. Significant change was not engineered, and researchers levelled many criticisms at the methods employed to achieve the set goals of integration. Graglia (1980) noted that the court decisions in the United States prohibited segregation of schools but did not actually address the issue of integration. The school boards were instructed to desegregate their schools by populating them with pupils from different ethnic groups, with each ethnic group constituting a certain proportion of the school's overall population. However, none or very few educational interventions designed to promote integration were instituted.

According to St John (1975), who reviewed over 120 integration studies conducted between 1965 and 1975, while desegregation did not lead to lowered academic achievement for either Black or White pupils in the US, no other positive results emerged. The self-concept and aspiration of Black pupils tended to be stronger in segregated rather than desegregated schools. St John concluded that interethnic contact alone in the desegregated schools, usually achieved by bussing, did not promote a better sense of psychological feeling on the part of Black pupils, indicating that the desegregation process was dysfunctional for minority pupils. Feagin (1980) noted that in the 1970s desegregation in the US slowed down mainly as a result of White opposition and a conservative trend in decisions by the US Supreme Court. In addition, Feagin pointed out that the achievement and social results of desegregation in the 1970s were disappointing and equality of educational opportunity was not attained by the lower-class communities — usually Blacks and Hispanics — even if they attended desegregated schools. Stephan (1980) said that from 1954 to 1969 certain negative outcomes resulted from the desegregation process. Often Black schools were closed down, Black children were bussed to White schools and Black teachers were dismissed from their jobs as a result of desegregation. Bitterness was felt by the Black community because of the methods used to achieve desegregation.

McConahay (1978) and Miller (1980) attempted to explain the insignificant results of desegregation during the 1970s. McConahay stated that one of the prominent goals of ethnic integration in the schools is to foster positive social-emotional attitudes among pupils from different social groups and a willingness to maintain relationships with children from different social settings. However, interethnic contact alone, which represented the major and usually only intervention designed to achieve integration, usually has no effect on ethnic attitudes and may produce attitudes more negative than those held before the contact began. In a similar vein Miller said that distributing pupils in each school in proportion to their frequency in the district as a whole without simultaneous initiation of other interventions is unlikely to provide a desirable kind of integrated learning experience or to improve academic achievement of minority pupils, their self-concepts or intergroup relations.

Collett (1985) reviewed the situation in Great Britain, and like his American counterparts, came to disappointing conclusions regarding integration and the promotion of prejudice reduction in the British school system. He pointed out that Black and Asian parents despaired of their ability to persuade the educational system to effect changes for the good of their children. Very little consultation took place between school authorities and minority parents with the result that schools continued to function in the traditional fashion which did not take the needs of the minorities into account. Jeffcoate (1979) corroborated the conclusions reached by Collett, and suggested that racism was the main reason that progress toward integration and prejudice reduction was not being made in British schools. Although the central authorities provided for equality of educational opportunity, local educational authorities were usually slow in implementing the interventions designed for prejudice reduction and integration.

In Israel Amir (1976) as well as Sharan and Rich (1984) concluded that although in many junior high schools interethnic contact took place, this was not enough to promote integration or positive interethnic attitudes. According to Amir, the Israeli experience in the early 1970s raised doubts as to whether interethnic contact in school can be described as the ultimate tool in improving attitudes and ethnic relations between children. Katz, Schmida and Dor-Shav (1986) confirmed that in junior high schools where interethnic contact in heterogeneous classrooms took place, no changes were effected in the ethnic prejudices of the participants in the contact situation.

The overall picture that emerged in the US, Great Britain and Israel after the attempts to effect integration and prejudice reduction in schools during the 1970s was one that provided little comfort for those who advocated the principles of integration. Whatever interventions were undertaken, and these usually involved various types of interethnic or intergroup contact, little was achieved regarding positive ethnic attitude change. It became increasingly evident that more needed to be done to achieve the goals of integration and prejudice reduction.

## KEY PSYCHO-EDUCATIONAL INTERVENTIONS DESIGNED TO PROMOTE INTEGRATION AND PREJUDICE REDUCTION

The major issue that must be clarified relates to the psycho-educational principles that underlie the integration and prejudice reduction process. Amir (1969), Ben-Ari and Amir (1988) and Sharan (1980) delineated a list of psycho-educational conditions designed to facilitate the integration process. Among these conditions are equal status contact between the members of the interacting groups; intergroup cooperation in the pursuit of common goals; intergroup contact actively supported by school authorities; and intergroup contact of an intimate rather than a casual nature. Under such circumstances minority group pupils could satisfactorily experience some enhancement of their ethnic and personal self-esteem as well as their attitudes toward themselves and toward pupils from other ethnic groups in the class.

McConahay (1981) described additional conditions which should facilitate integration. Integrated schools should be relatively small and approximately equally proportioned between the different ethnic groups; children should be brought into contact with other ethnic groups at as young an age as possible; multiethnic textbooks and curricula should be used to give a more accurate picture of the multiethnic society; and non-racist attitudes on the part of administrators and teachers should promote non-racist attitudes on the part of the pupils. Cohen and Sharan (1980) and Epps (1981) indicated that middle-class pupils from the majority group occupy a higher level of social and academic status in the integrated class. However, the self-esteem of lower-class pupils can be raised only if they compare themselves to middle-class pupils under favourable conditions in the heterogeneous classroom. The majority group then serves as a positive reference group or model for the minority group, thereby motivating and attracting the minority group pupils to learning and academic pursuits. Lower-class pupils may strive to raise their status in the classroom through improved academic achievement, in order to be more like their higher status counterparts.

Lynch (1987) suggested a number of working principles of multicultural education and prejudice reduction. Among the principles are the following: prejudice reduction should be viewed as a normal part of the education of all children; as prejudice comprises both informational and emotional factors, strategies to correct for prejudice need to include both cognitive and affective attitudinal components; the self-concept of the individual pupil needs to be raised; and the school must aim for mutual and multiple acculturation by pupils and teachers. Cook (1984) summarized a great deal of empirical evidence to demonstrate that, given favourable conditions (such as those mentioned in this section of the chapter), significantly positive integrational results are yielded. Members of the minority group acquire characteristics which disconfirm previously held negative stereotypes; the contact situation holds high acquaintance potential with participants receiving a positive opportunity to get to know one another as individuals; and the contact takes place in a situation in which social norms encourage friendly associations.

The psycho-educational interventions appearing in this section emanated from the initial disappointment with integration in the Western countries with heterogeneous societies, such as the US, Great Britain and Israel, in the 1960s and 1970s. The scholars involved in research on integration and prejudice reduction suggested the implementation of psycho-educational interventions in the hope that they would contribute significantly to an improved integrational process. They realized, albeit belatedly, that legislation and interethnic contact alone could not successfully promote significant increments in integration and positive interethnic attitude change. Therefore, the psycho-educational interventions suggested here were perceived as vital additional steps to be taken to facilitate integration and prejudice reduction.

## CLASSROOM INTERVENTIONS DESIGNED FOR INTEGRATION
## AND PREJUDICE REDUCTION

Educational psychologists and educators came to the conclusion that classroom interventions should be instituted in accordance with the psycho-educational principles suggested in the previous section to facilitate the prejudice reduction and integration process. The measures described in this section are those to be implemented in the interethnic heterogeneous classroom.

Crowfoot and Chesler (1981), Crain, Mahard and Narot (1982) and Lynch (1987) said that on the classroom level the multicultural character of the population must be considered to promote good interethnic relations. It is imperative to prepare culture-fair tests for the ethnically heterogeneous classroom population, and curricula that focus on the history and traditions of the different ethnic groups are to be adopted. Regarding classroom organization, pupils from different ethnic groups and levels should cooperate on a broad range of tasks so that each and every pupil can add from his or her own personal experience and knowledge to the task solution. In addition, participation of pupils in ethnically heterogeneous extracurricular activities will help produce improved interethnic contact.

Sharan, Amir and Ben-Ari (1984) stated that collective group efforts by pupils in the multiethnic class, cooperative interaction and a division of learning tasks appear to create a learning environment conducive to social integration and supportive of pupils' learning efforts on a range of academic levels. Ramsey (1987) said that in the heterogeneous classroom it is essential that students participating in cooperative learning are shuffled frequently from group to group to provide for maximum intergroup and interpersonal contact. Competition must be eliminated to reduce anxiety and to facilitate a feeling of self-esteem among pupils from the different ethnic groups.

Johnson and Johnson (1979) stated that there is a greater likelihood of success in cooperative than in competitive and individualistic learning situations. Cooperative learning experiences, compared with individualistic ones, result in more intrinsic motivation. The cooperative experiences encourage the relationship between peers of different intellectual levels and promote more positive attitudes toward members of different ethnic groups and contribute to higher self-esteem. Slavin (1981) concluded that only by instituting instructional methods that foster and improve integration will any headway be made. According to Slavin, all cooperative methods are designed to provide long-term daily opportunities for intense interpersonal contact between students of different ethnic groups and social levels. The cooperative methods which promote interethnic contact are Student Teams-Achievement Divisions (STAD) (Slavin, 1978), Teams-Games-Tournament (TGT) (De Vries and Slavin, 1978) and Jigsaw (Aronson *et al.*, 1978). Slavin contended that a review of research results indicates that the above-mentioned cooperative learning methods, on the whole, contribute to a higher achievement level and to positive interethnic contact.

Sharan (1984) studied peer cooperation in mixed ethnic groups assigned to cooperative and whole-class learning situations. Results of the study indicate that the pupils in the cooperative learning classes achieved higher scores in language than those in the whole-class situations. Sharan concluded that the cooperative classrooms fostered improved interethnic attitudes compared with whole-class classrooms in which pupils perceived the other ethnic group more negatively as time went by. Sharan and Shachar (1988) reported the results of a similar study in which cooperative learning groups were compared to whole-class groups. Academically speaking, both lower-class (Oriental) and middle-class (Western) pupils gained considerably in the cooperative groups when compared with the whole-class groups. Social relations in the cooperative groups were far more equitable and symmetrical, and lower-class pupils in the cooperative groups offered significantly more support to their own ethnic peers than their ethnic counterparts in the whole-class groups.

Harrison and Glaubman (1981) studied the effects of the open classroom method designed to facilitate integration in the lower classes of Israeli elementary schools. They found that open heterogeneous classrooms facilitated academic achievement, especially for lower-class pupils. The achievement gap between lower-class and middle-class pupils was stabilized in the open classroom, whereas in the traditional classroom it continued to grow. Klein and Eshel (1981), in another study conducted in Israeli elementary schools, reported that the combined effect of interethnic classroom integration and activity oriented classrooms produced significant gains in academic achievement for the lower-class pupils. In addition, significantly more interethnic friendships were forged in the activity oriented heterogeneous classroom than in the traditional heterogeneous classroom.

From the evidence presented above it is apparent that, in addition to the psycho-educational principles involved in facilitating prejudice reduction and integration, certain classroom methods contribute to positive integrational changes. The major principle underlying these methods is that of interethnic cooperation. Cooperative learning methods, open classrooms and activity oriented classrooms must be based on ethnically integrated pupil populations. When the learning groups are heterogeneous and cooperative methods are used, then both academic achievement and social relations improve. In addition, multicultural curricula dealing with the culture and history of the different ethnic groups promote a feeling of self-esteem among members of the different ethnic groups and are vital for the integrated classroom. A feeling of self-esteem, especially among lower-class pupils, is an imperative condition for successful cooperative learning.

## TEACHER TRAINING FOR PREJUDICE REDUCTION AND INTEGRATION

After dealing with classroom interventions designed to promote integration, it is of importance to review teacher training that can contibute to successful prejudice reduction and social integration. Insel and Jacobson (1975), after reviewing a number of studies, said that teachers are more likely to express expectations for higher level academic achievement from lower-class pupils in integrated middle-class schools than in segregated lower-class schools. This is because they adjust their teaching levels to some mean level of ability and not to the lowest common denominator of ability in the class. Epps (1981) said that to maintain teacher belief in the ability of lower-class pupils in the integrated classroom, in-service training centring on the academic and social potential of lower-class pupils should be organized. McConahay (1981) suggested teacher workshops designed to reduce bias in teacher behaviour and prejudice.

Sharan, Amir and Ben-Ari (1984) declared that school principals and teachers must make major accommodations in role definition and performance that differ radically from the role models they learned during their professional training. They must acquire a variety of new competences needed to meet the needs of an ethnically mixed student body. Alternative and innovative teaching methods, such as cooperative learning strategies, small-group learning, open classrooms and activity oriented classrooms, are to be adopted if the principals and teachers wish to cope adequately with ethnically and socially heterogeneous classroom populations. Teachers must also master subject matter dealing with the cultural and social needs of the different ethnic groups in the integrated classroom situation. Gay (1983) summarized a number of essential components to be included in courses for teachers involved in integration and prejudice reduction programmes. The components include basic information about ethnic and cultural pluralism; knowledge acquisition and values clarification about ethnic groups and their cultures; psychology and sociology of ethnicity; and competence in teaching and learning activities that promote integration and prejudice reduction.

There is no doubt that teacher training is an important aspect of prejudice reduction and school integration. In addition to the various topics suggested above, principals should consult with teachers on policy issues concerning integration, to make the teachers part of the decision-making process. This in itself can help bring about positive changes in teachers' ethnic and social attitudes and motivate them to cooperate on the integration issue. The school as a whole must be positively involved in the promotion of integration, and only by teacher training and staff consensus can this be achieved.

## EMPIRICAL EVIDENCE FROM AN ISRAELI ELEMENTARY SCHOOL INTEGRATION PROGRAMME

An elementary school integration programme was undertaken at the Gush Etzion Regional Elementary School in Israel. Pupils of Oriental ethnic origin from the Adullam region, which is a lower achievement oriented environment and of a lower socio-economic level, were placed in the first grade of the school, together with higher achievement oriented and higher SES level pupils of Western ethnic background, resident in the seven rural settlements in Gush Etzion. All those involved in decision-making, namely the municipal authorities, the school administration and faculty and the school parent body, with the approval of the Ministry of Education and Culture, undertook the project voluntarily, bearing in mind the conditions necessary for the success of the project as presented in the previous sections of this chapter. A parallel four-phase study was conducted to evaluate the success of the integration programme in the areas of academic achievement, social integration, parental satisfaction and teacher attitudes.

The integration programme was conducted under conditions that took much of the research evidence and conclusions into consideration. A mandatory intensive year-long in-service training course in cooperative learning methods and prejudice reduction was attended by the teachers involved in the integration programme. The major aims of the course were to prepare the teachers psycho-educationally for the integration programme, and to provide them with interventions designed to promote positive interethnic contact in the heterogeneous classroom. Emphasis was placed on cooperative instructional methods which were implemented in the classes participating in the project. The small groups were formed, each comprising six pupils of whom a majority were resident in the Gush Etzion area and a minority in the Adullam region. Study in most subject matter was undertaken in the small groups, with the brighter pupils helping those who were weaker in any particular subject. Thus cooperation was fostered within the small groups in the routine learning process. STAD, Jigsaw and Small-Group Learning were among the cooperative methods used in the interethnic classrooms.

In those classes where the integration programme was conducted, a multicultural curriculum was introduced. This curriculum included intensive study of the history, folklore, religious traditions and culture of the two ethnic groups assigned to the ethnically heterogeneous classrooms. To facilitate teacher orientation to the multicultural curriculum, teachers were coached about the cultural, traditional and religious customs of the ethnic groups.

On the organizational level, fortnightly staff meetings were held, when members of the school counselling department advised the class teachers on problems arising from the interethnic oriented activities. Teachers were encouraged to raise any difficulties encountered in their work in the integrated classrooms, and visiting experts made suggestions to help teachers overcome these difficulties. To make things easier for the teachers and to provide reasonable chances for success, each class was limited to a maximum of thirty pupils, with only 30 per cent of the pupils in each class coming from the lower SES Adullam region. In addition to the organizational efforts made by the school, the Ministry of Education and Culture as well as the municipal authorities provided full backing for the programme. A committee of experts was appointed to supervise the integration project and to assist the school authorities and staff in their execution of the project.

Additional measures were undertaken to rectify language deficits which characterized the pupils of Oriental ethnic origin. Two hours a week were devoted to vocabulary enrichment and auditory word comprehension for the lower SES pupils. A qualified teacher encouraged the pupils to read recommended books, after which the contents were discussed in group meetings. In addition, two weekly sessions were held, each of one hour's duration, with a 'big brother' tutor who assisted each pupil from the Adullam region with homework and preparation for class tests. These sessions were designed to promote a higher level of academic achievement as well as to instil a feeling of self-confidence and self-esteem in the lower-class population.

Parents were also involved in the programme by school initiative. Four parent evenings were organized during the school year. At these meetings the parents of all pupils were briefed on the integration project and were given the opportunity to voice their opinions about the project. Two additional workshops for parents of all children participating in the integration programme were held. In these workshops topics such as developmental problems, learning difficulties and disabilities, and social issues were discussed.

One hundred and ninety-two Israeli first-grade pupils, who had successfully completed compulsory kindergarten education, served as the sample in the first phase of the study, conducted by Katz and Ben-Yochanan (1988a). This phase of the study dealt with the academic achievement of participants in the programme. All were declared eligible for first grade after successfully completing a battery of school readiness tests. The sample was subdivided in the following manner: thirty-nine first-grade pupils, resident in the rural Adullam region and placed in the first grade at the Gush Etzion Regional Elementary School, served as the experimental group in this research. These pupils would under normal circumstances have studied at the Elah Valley Elementary School, but due to the initiation of the integration project were accepted for studies at the school where the project was conducted. Their selection for participation in the integration project at Gush Etzion Regional Elementary School, from the total first-grade population resident in the Adullam region, was totally random. The remaining seventy-five pupils resident in the Adullam region and from a similar demographic background attended first grade at the Elah Valley Elementary School and served as the control group for the research. The assignment of these pupils to the control group was based on random selection. Seventy-eight pupils, resident in the Gush Etzion region and assigned to the first grade in the Gush Etzion Regional Elementary School, served as a comparison group in this study. Thus, in addition to the experimental group being compared with a control group, it was also compared with a comparison group.

The Israel Reading Comprehension Test, compiled by Ortar and Ben-Shacher (1972), served as the research measure. As Israeli first-grade pupils are usually administered this test to ascertain their reading level towards the end of the first grade, the researchers decided to use this measure in the present study. To gauge the achievement of Adullam resident pupils in the experimental group as compared with their first-grade counterparts in the control group and their Gush Etzion resident classmates in the comparison group, the scores obtained by the three groups on the Israel Reading Comprehension Test at the end of first grade were compared.

The second phase of the study was conducted by Katz and Ben-Yochanan (1988b). In this phase, which evaluated social integration, 108 subjects served as the research sample. They came from lower SES Oriental ethnic backgrounds characterized by what the Israeli Ministry of Education and Culture designated as culturally disadvantaged environments. All were screened for school readiness by standardized readiness tests and were found to be eligible for acceptance in the first grade of an Israeli elementary school.

The experimental group was made up of forty pupils from the lower SES, ethnically Oriental background who were assigned to the ethnically integrated Gush Etzion Regional Elementary School (School *A*). There were two control groups, the first of which was made up of thirty-five lower SES and Oriental pupils who were placed in an ethnically integrated elementary school (School *B*) in the Jerusalem district which did not initiate any active integration interventions. The second control group was comprised of thirty-three lower SES and Oriental pupils who were assigned to the first grade of a non-integrated Jerusalem district school (School *C*), which catered mainly to culturally disadvantaged students and where integration was in no way part of the school's goals.

A questionnaire, examining teacher evaluation of perceived social change occurring during the course of the year the pupils spent in the first grade, was compiled for the express purpose of evaluating social attributes of the research samples. The questionnaire contained items built around four major factors, namely social image, social confidence, social acceptance and social leadership. The concepts were operationalized for the teachers as follows: social image was defined as the way the subjects' peers from all types of social and ethnic groups related to them in social interaction situations; social confidence was described as the ability of the subjects to behave confidently within the school setting; social acceptance was explained as the ability of the subjects to forge friendships with students from different ethnic groups; and social leadership was defined as the ability of the subjects to make a decision which was then adopted by the group. The class teachers were first asked to evaluate all subjects by means of the research questionnaire at the end of the first month of the school year, and for the second time during the last week of the same school year.

The third phase of the study, as yet unpublished, consisted of an evaluation of parental satisfaction with the integration programme. One hundred and eighty-two parents of lower SES and ethnically Oriental pupils served as the research sample. The schools in this phase of the study were those in which the subjects who participated in the second phase of the study were placed. The experimental group was made up of sixty-seven parents whose children studied in the integration programme at the Gush Etzion Regional Elementary School (School *A*). As in the second phase of the study, there were two control groups. The first consisted of fifty-two parents of Oriental ethnic origin and lower SES whose children studied in the first grade of the ethnically integrated elementary school (School *B*) in the Jerusalem district, which had no active integration interventions. The second control group consisted of sixty-three Oriental, lower SES parents whose children studied in the first grade of the non-integrated Jerusalem district school (School *C*), which did not promote integration at all.

A ten-item questionnaire comprising three factors, namely academic satisfaction, social satisfaction and satisfaction with the staff-pupil relationship, was compiled for use in this phase. The questionnaire was administered to the subjects after their children had spent one year in first grade at the respective schools.

The fourth phase of the study, also as yet unpublished, consisted of an examination of teacher attitudes toward integration. Forty-two teachers at the Gush Etzion Regional Elementary School served as the research sample. Each of the teachers taught in the integrated classes and participated in a year-long in-service training programme which consisted of instruction in psycho-educational interventions and cooperative learning strategies designed to promote prejudice reduction and social integration among the pupils. A twenty-item questionnaire, which consisted of two factors, namely attitude toward academic achievement and attitude toward social integration of the pupils participating in the integration programme, was administered to the teachers at the beginning of the integration programme (which coincided with the beginning of the in-service training course) and at the end of the first year of the programme.

Results of the four parallel phases of the study indicate that thus far the integration programme has met with a measure of success. Significant differences were found among the three groups for the academic achievement variable. Although the middle-class ethnically Western comparison group was found, as expected, to have achieved significantly higher scores than both the experimental and control groups on the Israel Reading Comprehension Test, the experimental group was found to have scored significantly higher than the control group on the same measure, indicating that the integration programme interventions promoted improved academic achievement in the lower-class pupil population.

For the second phase of the study designed to examine the social increments of the integration programme, statistical analyses demonstrated that, for all four factors, the experimental group placed in School *A* achieved significantly higher increments than those achieved by both control groups. Mention should be made of the fact that control group subjects in School *B* had a significantly greater increment on all four research factors than control group subjects placed in School *C*. Once again it appears that the interventions undertaken in the programme facilitated improved social performance of the lower SES participants.

In the third phase of the study parental satisfaction with the integration programme was examined. Significant intergroup differences were yielded for academic satisfaction, social satisfaction and satisfaction with staff-pupil relationship. Parents of pupils at the Gush Etzion Regional Elementary School were significantly more satisfied with the school than parents of School *B*, who in turn were significantly more satisfied than parents of School *C*. These results indicate that the interventions on the parent level had the same positive effect as those implemented on the pupil level.

Statistical analyses were computed to ascertain possible differences between beginning-of-year and end-of-year teacher attitudes examined in the fourth phase of the study. Results of the analyses indicated that end-of-year teacher attitudes toward academic achievement and attitudes toward social integration of the Oriental pupils were significantly more positive than teacher attitudes on the same two factors at the beginning of the year, indicating that the in-service training programme achieved a measure of success.

## CONCLUSION

The results of the statistical analyses of the data yielded in all four phases of the empirical examination of the integration programme at the Gush Etzion Regional Elementary School overwhelmingly indicate that the programme has been successful thus far. The interventions undertaken in the integration programme were all based on suggestions made by numerous researchers whose studies were reviewed in this chapter. Educational interventions, which included cooperative learning methods (Aronson *et al.*, 1978; De Vries and Slavin, 1978; Sharan and Shachar, 1988; Slavin, 1978), a multicultural curriculum (Banks, 1981; Lynch, 1987; McConahay, 1981), a balanced proportion of pupils from the different ethnic and SES groups in the heterogeneous classroom (McConahay, 1981), staff consultation on issues directly affecting the integration programme (Ben-Ari and Amir, 1988; Sharan, 1980), intensive teacher training for prejudice reduction and the promotion of integration (Epps, 1981; Gay, 1983; McConahay, 1981), active involvement of parents in the integration programme (Collett, 1985; Gurnah, 1987), full backing by the municipal and education authorities (Amir, 1969; Ben-Ari and Amir, 1988; Sharan, 1980), as well as special language help and 'big-brother' tutoring for pupils of Oriental ethnic origin (Katz and Ben-Yochanan, 1988a), paved the way for the programme's success.

From the result of the integration programme at the Gush Etzion Regional

Elementary School, it is apparent that if the suggestions recommended by scholars involved in research on integration and prejudice reduction are applied, then success in the promotion of integration and prejudice reduction will become a real educational possibility.

# REFERENCES

Amir, Y. (1969) 'Contact Hypothesis in Ethnic Relations', *Psychological Bulletin*, 71, pp. 319–342.

Amir, Y. (1976) 'The Value of Intergroup Contact in Change of Prejudice and Ethnic Relations', in P.A. Katz (Ed.), *Towards the Elimination of Racism*, New York, Pergamon Press, pp. 245–308.

Amir, Y., Sharan, S. and Ben-Ari, R. (1984) 'Why Integration?', in Y. Amir and S. Sharan (Eds), *School Desegregation: Cross-Cultural Perspectives*, Hillsdale, N.J., Lawrence Erlbaum Associates, pp. 1–19.

Aronson, E., Blaney, N. Stephan, C. Sikes, J. and Snapp, M. (1978) *The Jigsaw Classroom*, Beverly Hills, Calif., Sage Publications.

Banks, J.A. (1981) *Multiethnic Education: Theory and Practice*, Boston, Mass., Allyn and Bacon.

Ben-Ari, R. and Amir, Y. (1988) 'Intergroup Contact, Cultural Information and Change in Ethnic Attitudes', in W. Stroebe, A.W. Kruglanski, D. Bar-Tal and M. Hewstone (Eds), *The Social Psychology of Intergroup Conflict*, Berlin, Springer-Verlag, pp. 151–165.

Cohen, E. and Sharan, S. (1980) 'Modifying Status Relations in Israeli Youth', *Journal of Cross-Cultural Psychology*, 11, pp. 364–384.

Collett, R. (1985) 'Consultation: Participation and Control', *Multicultural Teaching*, 3, pp. 19–20.

Cook, S.W. (1984) 'Cooperative Interaction in Multiethnic Contexts', in N. Miller and M. Brewer (Eds), *Groups in Contact: The Psychology of Desegregation*, New York, Academic Press, pp. 155–185.

Crain, R.L. and Mahard, R.E. (1978) 'Desegregation and Black Achievement: A Review of the Research', *Law and Contemporary Problems*, 42, 3, pp. 17–56.

Crain, R.L., Mahard, R.E. and Narot, R. (1982) *Making Desegregation Work*, Cambridge, Mass., Ballinger Publishing.

Crowfoot, J.E. and Chesler, M.A. (1981) 'Implementing Attractive Ideas: Problems and Prospects', in W.D. Hawley (Ed.), *Effective School Desegregation*, Beverly Hills, Calif., Sage Publications, pp. 265–295.

De Vries, D.L. and Slavin, R.E. (1978) 'Teams-Games-Tournament (T.G.T.): Review of Ten Classroom Experiments', *Journal of Research and Development in Education*, 12, pp. 28–38.

Epps, E.G. (1981) 'Minority Children: Desegregation, Self-Evaluation and Achievement Orientation', in W.D. Hawley (Ed.), *Effective School Desegregation*, Beverly Hills, Calif., Sage Publications, pp. 85–106.

Feagin, J.R. (1980) 'School Desegregation: A Political-Economic Perspective', in W.G. Stephan and J.R. Feagin (Eds), *School Desegregation*, New York, Plenum Press, pp. 25–50.

Gay, G. (1983) 'Why Multicultural Education in Teacher Preparation Programs?' *Contemporary Education*, 54, pp. 79–85.

Gerard, H.B. (1984) 'Introduction', in Y. Amir and S. Sharan (Eds), *School Desegregation: Cross-Cultural Perspectives*, Hillsdale, N.J., Lawrence Erlbaum Associates, pp. xi–xiii.

Graglia, L.A. (1980) 'From Prohibiting Segregation to Requiring Integration', in W.G. Stephan and J.R. Feagin (Eds), *School Desegregation*, New York, Plenum Press, pp. 69–96.

Grant, C.A. and Sleeter, C.E. (1986) *After the School Bell Rings*, Philadelphia, Pa., Falmer Press.

Gurnah, A. (1987) 'Gatekeepers and Caretakers: Swann, Scarman and the Social Policy of Containment', in B. Troyna (Ed.), *Racial Equality in Education*, London, Tavistock Publications, pp. 11–28.

Halsey, A.H., Heath, A.F. and Ridge, J.M. (1980) *Origins and Destinations*, Oxford, Clarendon Press.

Harrison, J. and Glaubman, R. (1981) 'Who Benefits from the Open Classroom?' *Journal of Educational Research*, 75, pp. 87–94.

Hendrick, I.G. (1975) 'The Historical Setting', in H.B. Gerard and N. Miller (Eds), *School Desegregation*, New York, Plenum Press, pp. 22–51.

Insel, P. and Jacobson, L. (1975) *What Do You Expect?* Menlo Park, Calif., Cummings Publications.

Jeffcoate, R. (1979) *Positive Image*, Richmond, Surrey, Chameleon Books.

Johnson, D. and Johnson, R. (1979) 'Cooperation, Competition and Individualization', in H. Wahlberg (Ed.), *Educational Environments and Effects*, Berkeley, Calif., McCutchan, pp. 105–108.

Katz, Y.J. and Ben-Yochanan, A. (1988a) 'Academic Achievement as a Function of Integration in an Israeli Elementary School', *British Educational Research Journal*, 14, 3, pp. 311–318.

Katz, Y.J. and Ben-Yochanan, A. (1988b) 'Social Interaction as a Function of Active Intervention in an Israeli Elementary School', *Journal of Social Psychology*, 128, 1, pp. 89–96.

Katz, Y.J., Schmida, M. and Dor-Shav, Z. (1986) 'Two Different Education Structures in Israel and Social Integration', *Educational Research*, 28, 2, pp. 141–146.

Klein, Z. and Eshel, Y. (1981) *Integrating Jerusalem Schools*, New York, Academic Press.

Lynch, J. (1986) *Multicultural Education*, London, Routledge and Kegan Paul.

Lynch, J. (1987) *Prejudice Reduction and the Schools*, London, Cassell.

McConahay, J.B. (1978) 'The Effects of School Desegregation upon Students' Racial Attitudes and Behaviour: A Critical Review of the Literature and a Prolegomenon to Future Research', *Law and Contemporary Problems*, 42, 3, pp. 77–107.

McConahay, J.B. (1981) 'Reducing Racial Prejudice in Desegregated Schools', in W.D. Hawley (Ed.), *Effective School Desegregation*, Beverly Hills, Calif., Sage Publications, pp. 35–53.

Miller, N. (1980) 'Making School Desegregation Work', in W.G. Stephan and J.R. Feagin (Eds), *School Desegregation*, New York, Plenum Press, pp. 309–348.

Ortar, G. and Ben-Shachar, N. (1972) *Israel Reading Comprehension Test*, Jerusalem, Ministry of Education and Culture.

Ramsey, P.G. (1987) *Teaching and Learning in a Diverse World*, New York, Teachers College Press.

St John, N. (1975) *School Desegregation Outcomes for Children*, New York, John Wiley and Sons.

Schwarzwald, J. (1989) 'Interethnic Contact under Differing Circumstances', Paper presented at the Second Regional Conference of the International Association for Cross-Cultural Psychology, Amsterdam.

Sharan, S. (1980) 'Cooperative Learning in Small Groups: Recent Methods and Effects on Achievement, Attitudes and Ethnic Relations', *Review of Educational Research*, 50, 2, pp. 241–271.

Sharan, S. (1984) *Cooperative Learning in the Classroom: Research in Desegregated Schools*, Hillsdale, N.J., Lawrence Erlbaum Associates.

Sharan, S. and Rich, Y. (1984) 'Field Experiments in Ethnic Integration in Israeli Schools', in Y. Amir and S. Sharan (Eds), *School Desegregation: Cross-Cultural Perspectives*, Hillsdale, N.J., Lawrence Erlbaum Associates, pp. 189–217.

Sharan, S. and Shachar, H. (1988) *Language and Learning in the Cooperative Classroom*, New York, Springer-Verlag.

Sharan, S., Amir, Y. and Ben-Ari, R. (1984) 'School Desegregation: Some Challenges Ahead', in Y. Amir and S. Sharan (Eds), *School Desegregation: Cross-Cultural Perspectives*, Hillsdale, N.J., Lawrence Erlbaum Associates, pp. 219–235.

Slavin, R.E. (1978) 'Student Teams and Achievement Divisions', *Journal of Research and Development in Education*, 12, pp. 39–49.

Slavin, R.E. (1981) 'Cooperative Learning and Desegregation', in W.D. Hawley (Ed.), *Effective School Desegregation*, Beverly Hills, Calif., Sage Publications, pp. 225–244.

Stephan, W.G. (1980) 'A Brief Overview of School Desegregation', in W.G. Stephan and J.R. Feagin (Eds), *School Desegregation*, New York, Plenum Press, pp. 3–23.

Troyna, B. (1987) 'A Conceptual Overview of Strategies to Combat Racial Inequality in Education: Introductory Essay', in B. Troyna (Ed.), *Racial Inequality in Education*, London, Tavistock Publications, pp. 1–10.

# Part Four: Values and Prejudice Reduction

# 14. Values Education and Attitude Change: The Need for an Interdependent Approach

MIKE BOTTERY

## THE POWER OF STRUCTURE AND THE INEQUALITY OF POSITION

The publication of *The Satanic Verses* has aroused the passions of the public, politician and academic alike, and then has, for the general public, but not for the Muslim minority in the UK, been superseded by more immediately pressing concerns.[1] Yet it is more than merely a newsworthy incident which can be forgotten, for it goes to the heart of racial and cultural tolerance, in that it pinpoints specific problems which prevent the resolution of two intractable issues. These are, first, that wrongs and rights are embedded in a sociological context, in which minorities may have right on their side, but not be granted that precisely because they are minorities. The second concerns the nature of the values upon which a society, composed of different groups with different values, must found a consensus.

In the Rushdie affair the issues at stake seem to be these: has an individual the right to express what he feels about a particular religious/cultural/racial group, and for this expression to take precedence over the outraged feelings and sensibilities of that group, in this case members of the Muslim community? Should Salman Rushdie, or anyone else for that matter, be allowed to publish materials which are perceived as blasphemous to a religion, deeply hurtful to believers, and liable to distort outsiders' views of the meaning and purpose of that set of beliefs, that way of life? What appears to be at stake is the freedom of individuals to express opinions which might not agree with those of another body of opinion, when that other body may be hurt or aggrieved by them. If one accepts Voltaire's dictum that one need not agree with other people's opinions to fight to the death for them to hold them, then Salman Rushdie's right to publish seems to be cast iron.

Indeed, the case for Salman Rushdie was painted in rather benign terms by the British media and political establishment, being portrayed as a clear example of the right of the individual to free speech against a hostile larger body. Further, there is considerable doubt as to whether Rushdie meant anything malicious in

**275**

what he was doing. The author's motives may be as complex as the writer and the book itself. Bhiku Parekh has argued persuasively that the book is a revealing portrait of an immigrant torn between identifying with his adopted culture, and the rootlessness that this entails, and identifying with the culture left behind, with all its archaic certainties.[2] It is not a book of understanding and compassion, but a book of self-doubt, of personal torment, and of a search for understanding and roots. People in this situation have a tendency not only to hurt themselves but to hurt those around them as well, if for most of the time unintentionally.

However, even granted this, the situation is still not simple. There are structural, institutional and sociological issues here which need to be addressed as much as the rational, logical and ethical ones. Thus the victim in the Salman Rushdie case, until fundamentalist calls for banning and burning of the book and fanatical calls for the author's assassination, was not Salman Rushdie, but the Muslim community. Yet in Great Britain neither the popular press, nor the politicians, nor the majority of the academic community picked up this grievance. The matter simply was a non-event until the aggrieved became the aggressors. Why, one must ask, was so little notice paid to the issue at first?

*The* major factor appears to be the situation of the Muslims in this country. Despite being the largest Muslim community in Western Europe, their beliefs, thoughts, values, practices and way of life are generally seen as of marginal concern or interest by 'mainstream' Britons. Most could not tell the difference between the Koran and the Kaaba. Most have no understanding or interest in Muslim customs and practices, ignore or repudiate the unfamiliar, and totally fail to see that customs and practices are more tightly clung to, the more that minority groups see their disregard by the majority culture. This is not an unusual phenomenon in Western societies, but the Rushdie affair brings out the implications of this indifference with some poignancy. For what is disregarded is disvalued. The lesson the Muslims learnt — if they did not already know it — was that right may initially have been on their side, but that this counts for little when they count for little.

The reaction of the Muslim community — and of any community in this situation — is predictable and understandable. Disregard fuels resentment, and resentment fuels polarization. Polarization, inevitably, eliminates the voice of the moderate. When only the extreme are heard, the British media pick up the story. Now, rather than being the sinned against, the Muslim community become the sinners. Even those who distance themselves from the Iranian calls for Rushdie's death — and the vast majority did — still find themselves branded as the trouble-makers in the story. The recipe for racial disharmony is easily mixed.

It is this kind of large-scale reaction which, more than the individual act, foments distrust and obliterates attempts at understanding and mutual benefit. It is for this reason that an initial spirit of open enquiry into the unfamiliar, as well as the elimination of institutionalized perceptions and inequalities must be seen as essential parts of an attempt to change attitudes — of both minority and majority cultures in any country. It will be argued, however, that as majority cultures hold the reins of power, in this respect they must change the most.

# A HISTORY OF REPUDIATION AND STRUCTURAL NEGLECT

Both repudiation of the unfamiliar and structural and institutional neglect by the majority culture can be seen in the matter of educational policies towards ethnic minorities. The survey by Banks and Lynch of the appreciation and application of policies towards minority groups in Western societies is saddening in the repetition of fine words and lack of delivery.[3] Each of the major countries covered — the UK, US, Canada and Australia — has moved at different times through much the same educational phases in dealing with ethnic minorities. It is clear that the evolution of these policies has been more a reactive matter than a proactive response, and so has consistently failed to deal with the issue in any planned or coordinated manner. It is instructive to look at these responses in a little detail.

Each country covered by Banks and Lynch has started with an assimilationist approach, where factors such as home background, restricted linguistic codes and poor parental attitudes have been used to ascribe failure to the cultures themselves. Ideas of genuine empathic concern for minority needs, or of structural or institutional change do not enter the debate. Early in this kind of attitude is the American approach. In the words of one state board of education in 1884:

> The danger to civilisation is not from without, but from within, the heterogeneous masses must be made homogeneous. Those who inherit the traditions of other and hostile nations; those who bred under diverse influences and hold foreign ideas; those who are supported by national inspirations not American must be assimilated and Americanized. The chief agency to this end has been the public school and popular education. No better agency has every been devised by man.[4]

Much later, but still very typical, is that in the UK of the Commonwealth Immigrants Advisory Council report:

> ... a national system of education must aim at producing citizens who can take their place in a society property equipped to exercise rights and perform duties which are the same as another citizen's. If their parents were brought up in another culture or another tradition, children should be encouraged to respect it, but a national system cannot be expected to perpetuate the different values of immigrant groups.

However, the effective teaching of English necessitates its bedding in some kind of material, and what better materials could be used than those of the immigrants' own country or culture? This was the integrationist approach, which, because its aim was merely to make the immigrant's transition easier for both immigrant and host, was still very much assimilationist, and so essentially lacked a structural element. However, the integrationist approach at least drew attention to home backgrounds and culture, placing them on the educational map.

From both theoretical and practical perspectives, policy and practice are unlikely to remain at this stage. Such an approach in no way understands and accepts a community's need for continuity and security of social custom and practice. It tends to be — and is perceived by minority cultures — as superficial, stereotypical, patronizing and dismissive. In the UK there was also the fact that within a generation a different problem was presenting itself. No longer was the majority of minority culture children in school born outside the host country. Such children presented different needs and different demands. Something much more wide-ranging and comprehensive was needed. This was the beginnings of the multicultural response.

The aims and objectives of multicultural education programmes are based very much upon the three key assumptions which Bullivant specified after his empirical studies in six countries in the 1970s:[6]

1   that an ethnic minority pupil will improve his educational achievement by learning about his country and culture of origin;
2   that learning about one's country and culture of origin will improve equality of opportunity;
    and differently
3   that learning about other countries and cultures will reduce the prejudice and discrimination by children, and ultimately adults, of the majority culture.

There is, then, still a primary orientation towards the definition of the problem in minority culture terms, though this is now expanding towards a recognition of the equality of cultures, a recognition that lifestyles and values are different, but that each has a right and a need to existence and equal participation in society. In educational terms this means not only the broadening and rethinking of the curriculum, but also practical and philosophical changes on the part of the majority culture. Theirs is no longer seen as the culture to which one assimilates, but one of many which exist on equal terms in the same geographical space. As the Swann Report said in its opening chapter:

> We consider that a multiracial society such as ours would in fact function most effectively and harmoniously on the basis of pluralism, which enables, expects and encourages members of all ethnic groups, both minority and majority, to participate fully in shaping the society as a whole within a framework of commonly-accepted values, practices and procedures, whilst allowing, and where necessary, assisting the ethnic minority communities in maintaining their distinct ethnic identities within this common framework.[7]

Reactions to multiculturalism have come from many quarters, but this article will focus upon three, before pointing up a fourth, and perhaps the most important issue which tends to have been neglected.

First, there has been the right-wing backlash. The move to the political right world-wide during the 1980s has seen an increased self-confidence in assimilationist and integrationist approaches as well. This would seem to be due to a number of factors which might include:

1   a perception that, contrary to Swann's belief, we are *not* a multiracial society, but a predominantly White, Western, English society, which has (relatively) small minorities of immigrants; a fundamental belief that 'when in Rome, do as the Romans do', is thus supplemented by the belief that nearly everyone in the UK is a 'Roman';[8]
2   the fact that the prevailing socio-political philosophy — free market economics – has little or nothing to say on the subject, precisely because it is not concerned with it; a policy of no-policy can be clearly perceived in the fact that the Swann Report was greeted so critically by the government, and that there have been no initiatives or major formal statements on the issue since;
3   an awareness that multiculturalism precisely places demands upon the

dominant culture to make moves of accommodation itself, and to place itself on an equal footing with other cultures: it implicitly suggests structural and institutional changes;

4    following from this is an awareness that the road does not necessarily stop at multiculturalism: it follows logically to an antiracist stance, which demands not only changes in curricular policies, but also explicit and fundamental structural and institutional changes, not only in schools, but economic and political ones in society as a whole; this can be perceived as a clear threat to those holding the reins of such power;

5    the perception that antiracist strategies have been adopted by Marxist thinkers precisely as a means to the end of undermining the present structure of society, with its perceived inequalities;

6    the tendency for a snowball effect: that if respect and rights through explicit structural changes are granted to one minority, others will follow. This was clearly the case in the US, where the upsurge in granting Negro rights led to demands from other minority groups like the American Indian, women's movements, and homosexual and lesbian groups. Allowing one group fairer access may be tolerable, for this only takes so much adjustment; allowing a whole variety of groups is much more stressful and threatens instability.[9]

Many of the right-wing criticisms are aimed at the antiracist approach. This approach, as we have seen, is in some ways a fairly natural outgrowth of multiculturalism. To the extent that multiculturalism posits equality of respect, existence and opportunity for ethnic minorities, and argues the need for change in the White majority culture, it implicitly suggests that goal of equality through structural changes in White society. Antiracism takes this aspect, but argues that it is not taken far enough. Two aspects are paramount. The first is the fact of racism within White society. If this does not change, it is argued, nothing will change, and curricular emphasis on cultural differences really fails to address this problem directly. What is needed is a considerably more systematic and thorough attack on the problem, which involves not only curricular reform and a change in White people's attitudes, but also an examination and reform of the institutions of White society itself, for it is these which mediate much of the racism. A distinction is drawn in many studies between *conscious* and *unconscious* racism. The former is seen most often at the personal level, and is perhaps that more easily confronted. More difficult is the latter, which may be seen at the personal level, but is as likely, if not more so, to be seen at institutional levels, in the very way institutions function, provide and select. Unintentional racism, then, is not normally seen as an object of censure in quite the same way as intentional racism, but is as profoundly unjust and hurtful, and all the more dangerous because it is unrecognized. It is for this kind of reason that Lynch suggests that an agenda for change needs to address three different levels: *societal* (that of the nation state), *systemic* (that of the education system) and *institutional* (that of the educational institution).[10]

The second major aspect, as described by Cohen and Cohen, is that: 'Preoccupation with culture ... tends to obscure or to avoid the more fundamental issues to do with *race, power* and *prejudice*' (italics in original).[11] They go on to describe the four key questions it fails to address:

1  the economic position of Black people in relation to White people;
2  differences in access to resources and in power to affect events;
3  discrimination in employment, housing and education;
4  relations with the police.

All four are seen as structural and institutional in origin, and it is clear that their eradication will involve considerably more than curricular innovation in schools.

This is an area of considerable polemic, not only in the attacks that right-wing critics have made upon the entire concept,[12] but also in that there is a variety of opinions within the antiracist movement as to the fundamental causes of these inequalities. Some, like Milner, Craft, or Yinger, argue that the economic factors can be seen as but one (though very important) element in an overall strategy which has to be as catholic and eclectic in its analysis of the problem as in its prescriptions for remediation.[13]

Others, like Mullard, Hatcher or Troyna and Williams, argue that these economic factors are the central and fundamental cause.[14] This latter approach is very much class-based and Marxist, in that the inferior position of minority groups is seen as but a reflection of the power structures within society. Minority groups, on this analysis, are kept in a subordinate and inferior position precisely to supply a source of cheap labour to the capitalist system, and therefore differ little in their injustice and exploitation from, say, the White working class and women. With this scenario, the answer is clear: the only way to change the situation is to change society. This does not mean changing people's attitudes towards one another, but changing the power relationships within society. It means nothing less than revolution, bloody or bloodless; anything less is cosmetic and pointless. One of the major reasons for a right-wing backlash will now be apparent.

A third reaction to multiculturalism has come, again at the structural level, from the ethnic minorities themselves. Part of the impetus comes from a perspective not radically different from the antiracist one: that the problem is not primarily theirs, but is one of the White majority, in terms of intended and unintended racism, and in terms of wider societal and institutional inequalities. This no doubt reinforces the kind of perception which was forced upon Muslims by the Rushdie affair: that rhetoric and reality do not often match one another. After decades of indifference and attempted assimilation, talk at policy level may now be one of multiculturalism, of cultural pluralism, even of selected and acceptable doses of antiracism, but the sheer overwhelming experience is still one of indifference and intended assimilation by the dominant culture, with little or no attempt to change by *them*. Lynch's summary of the state of play in Western Europe is not untypical:

> With the notable exception of Sweden ... the other nations of Western Europe [are] pursuing simultaneously policies of social exclusion and cultural assimilation, cloaked by an expressed commitment to an innocuous intercultural education to salve their continued commitment to democratic values. Once again, issues of the underachieve-ment of migrant workers' children and the inadequacy of teacher preparation are highlighted at the side of wider social phenomena such as economic and legal marginalisation and discrimination.[15]

While criticism by ethnic minorities has developed towards a structural perspec-tive, it is important to note that it was precisely and paradoxically a structural effect which slowed down their response to it. Thus a vitally important aspect of the negative assessment of multiculturalism as an education policy by many members of ethnic minority groups was the development of their self-esteem and positive image in virtually all Western democracies. Milner describes clearly how the picture has changed over the last twenty years or so.[16] Before the struggle for civil rights, the Black Power movement, the 'Black is beautiful' view, and an emergent African continent, the Negro had no positive image by which to identify himself. As Clark put it:

> Human beings who are forced to live under ghetto conditions and whose daily experience tells them that almost nowhere in society are they respected and granted the ordinary dignity and courtesy afforded to others, will, as a matter of course, begin to doubt their own worth.... These doubts become the seeds of a pernicious self- and group-hatred, the Negro's complex and debilitating prejudice against himself.[17]

Thus the Negro in the US and Blacks in the UK were pictured, because of their structural situation, as facing the unenviable choice of identifying with the outgroup, the dominant White culture, or the ingroup, the subordinate Negro culture. If they identified with the former, they denied their true identity; if they identified with the latter, they accepted themselves as of little worth. If neither was accepted, then a state of unresolved and continued internal tension existed. While the picture portrayed was perhaps a little too dramatic and stereotypical, there seems little doubt that this situation was the case for many Negroes. The implications for all other ethnic minorities are clear.

However, there has been a marked change since the late 1960s, precisely because of the changes in society and the world noted above. The standard assessment of self-worth — responses on the Black and White doll tests, wherein Black children were more likely either to identify themselves with White dolls, or to prefer them to Black dolls — began to subside and to change in favour of the Black doll, which tended to indicate a much higher self-regard.[18] The situation had changed: there was now an ingroup with which to identify, an ingroup of which one could be proud. The consequences seem to have been twofold. The first has been precisely this reaction to multicultural policies. As with assimilation and integration, so now multiculturalism may be rejected. Separate identity, in terms of values, attitudes, customs and social practices, can now be confidently asserted, for there is confidence in that identity.

The second reaction, and one simultaneous with the first, is anger. Silent, bitter but passive acceptance of majority policy is replaced by vocal, bitter and active rejection, and an identification with those elements of ethnic culture most different from the majority culture. This is hardly surprising. When the very roots of one's being have been dismissed, then there can be little wonder that groups withdraw into their own enclaves and cease to engage in dialogue. Indeed, not only does dialogue tend to be dropped, but examination of one's culture and beliefs tends to be dropped as well. Ideas, notions, customs and values become entrenched and fossilized for fear that examination of them will be seen as an admission of weakness. Those aspects of a cultural tradition which might be the first to be discussed, reflected upon and modified are aggressively paraded as badges of identity. If stability, continuity and security cannot be found by dialogue with the dominant culture, then such things will be found precisely through the assertion of the permanence of both trivial and crucial features of cultural life.

The result is that the dominant culture forces entrenched attitudes by its own lack of movement, and then expresses surprise and indignation with the fundamentalism and hostility it finds. This only sets in train a further round of labelling by the mass circulation media, and a self-fulfilling prophecy is created, with a vicious circularity worked in. This is healthy for neither dominant nor minority cultures. It fuels prejudice, intolerance and racism on both sides. It destroys understanding, cooperation and social development on both. The necessary spirit of open enquiry into the unfamiliar is extinguished.

## FOUR DIFFERENT VALUE ORIENTATIONS

How does one break the circle? How does one come to terms with other beliefs? Part of the necessary remediation lies in a philosophy of openness and empathic concern, and in institutional and structural reforms so conspicuously avoided in Western societies, reforms essential to any change in attitudes by members of majority and minority cultures alike. But more than this will be required. There are logical as well as empathic and sociological questions here. To explain this further, let us return to the opening paragraphs of the Swann Report, when it talks about:

> ... members of all ethnic groups, both minority and majority, to participate fully in shaping the society as a whole within a framework of *commonly-accepted values*, practices and procedures, whilst also allowing, and where necessary, assisting the ethnic minority communities in maintaining their distinct identities within this common framework. (italics added)[29]

This sounds very nice, but there is a real problem here. It is quite possible for there to be a disturbing tension between those 'commonly-accepted values' which are intended to underpin this multicultural society and those 'distinct ethnic identities' which are to be maintained within it. For what if some or part of these distinct ethnic identities are grounded in values which cannot be commonly accepted? What if values which define a particular ethnic identity clash with values from other ethnic identities? What happens then? What yardstick does one use to evaluate which should be kept and which should be jettisoned in the name of commonly accepted values? Take four, very possible (and existing) value orientations in Western countries at the present time. I shall call these the Fundamentalist, the Objectivist, the Subjectivist and the Relativist. While they are no more than caricatures, they represent nodal points of argument, and if a multicultural education is to be a possibility, then communication among them must be seen as possible, and ways of productive dialogue described.

Fundamentalists knows that their values, customs and social practices are not only correct for them in this time and place, but are correct for everyone in all times and all places. They know this because these values have been passed down by God, or some other unarguable authority, through a text which is not open to criticism or correction. Its pronouncements are revealed truth. All of life is permeated by these values, even much of the mundane, and much of the mundane, therefore, cannot be challenged or changed, because it is a part a larger picture, whose colours have already been decided. There can be little or no distinction between sacred and profane, for all is sacred. Toleration of others, for such people, must be extremely circumscribed. One cannot tolerate the unbeliever, and so much must be believed. Those who are unbelievers but are willing to learn may be tolerated so long as they show a desire to learn the truth, but toleration of the person who does not is not possible. Fundamentalists see assimilation or integration as a good thing if it is other cultures, faiths, beliefs assimilating to theirs, but a bad thing if this means dropping the truth and adopting false beliefs and practices. Multicultural education, for the Fundamentalist, makes little or no sense, for why would one want one's children exposed to belief systems which clearly are false? When one has the truth, what is the point of exposing children to anything else? Indeed, to do so amounts to gross moral dereliction. Racism is generally seen as a bad thing. If they are the minority culture, it is obviously grossly unjust. If such fundamentalists are the dominant culture, and other minority cultures are classed as false believers, they may be viewed as not worthy of equal respect as persons, and therefore be treated in a racist manner. On the other hand, they may still be granted equal respect as persons, and therefore be worthy of equal political, economic and social treatment.

Objectivists, like fundamentalists, believe in certain values being applicable to all people at all times and in all places. They may come to this belief through a belief in the revealed truth of a similar text, through simple intuition that some things are positively good or positively bad, or through a rational comparison of cultures, in which it becomes clear that certain practices are needed by all societies. But, unlike the Fundamentalist, the Objectivist believes that besides these core values, there are many things which are purely customary, and which can and should be varied from society to society. There is a fairly clear gap between the sacred and the profane, and it is important to know of that gap, of which things belong to God and which things belong to Caesar. Toleration, then, depends upon the beliefs one is talking about. There can be no toleration of those who break fundamental universal rules, but there can be toleration of those who are seeking them. There can also be toleration of people who adopt different social customs and practices, as long as these do not incorporate any of the fundamental ethical practices. Objectivists would see assimilation and integration as being acceptable to the extent that those who were assimilating were eschewing abhorrent practices and adopting objectively good ones. They would also want to examine the assimilating culture and see whether there was anything within *that* culture to which one should not assimilate. They would, however, believe that the assimilation of custom or social practice is neither necessary nor desirable, as they do not express any profound universal values. The Objectivist would view multicultural education in much the same way. It would only be seen as a 'good thing' to the extent that these universal values were adhered to by all cultures within this multicultural framework. The Objectivist would see as undesirable anything which smacked of cultures sharing the same geographical territory but failing to adopt an overarching set of values for all of them, precisely because it would show that there had been no serious attempt to address the question of what values a society should espouse. *Laissez-faire* is no more an option for the Objectivist than the Fundamentalist. For much the same reasons as the Fundamentalist, antiracism would be seen as being self-evidently a good thing, whatever the society.

Subjectivists, if pressed, would probably say that they agree with a great deal of what the Objectivist says, but they have not the Objectivist's confidence in their assertions. Like the Objectivist, they believe that there are certain fundamental moral truths for all people in all societies, but they are much more reticent to name them. Constantly in front of them and everyone else, they believe, are the layers upon layers of distorting factors which prevent a person from ever being certain of the truth.[20] It is like a person walking down a tunnel towards the light. The light is certainly there, and so one knows which way to walk, but the exact description of the end of the tunnel is not open to the observer. It is a matter of tentative, sensitive guesswork and testing. There is truth, but no one person or culture will ever have total knowledge of it. Tolerance, for the Subjectivist, is therefore one of the cornerstones of living, for there is always the chance — a very good chance — that one's beliefs may be wrong, may need correction, and the person you thought was wrong may indeed be nearer to the truth. Tolerance of others, and of one's own fallibility, is therefore essential. It is clear, then, that notions of assimilation and integration cannot be right, for no one person or group has the monopoly on insight. Only a genuine multiculturalism, where all parties learn from one another in the perennial pursuit of the truth, is possible. Antiracism is a stand which can be taken by the Subjectivist with confidence, for even if the absolute truth is not open to the Subjectivist, there are *degrees* of subjectivity and objectivity, and this is clearly a more objective case of injustice and immorality.

Relativists see no revealed truths in holy books, only the expressed beliefs of a particular person in a particular culture at a particular time, whose words may or may not have relevance for other people living in other cultures. That, however, is their choice. Similarly, the Relativist has no profound intuitions that certain actions are fundamentally good or bad, nor even that some are more likely to be better or worse than others. Relativists are aware of the power of conditioning and socialization pressures, and are convinced that these intuitions are no more than this. Finally, they have looked at the anthropological and sociological evidence, and agree that there are some comparabilities, but this is empirical evidence, not logical evidence; it suits societies to adopt or prohibit certain practices and adopt certain values, but this does not make them *right*: it just makes them right for society if you want a particular kind of society. This being the case, the Relativist feels no one has the right to tell anyone else how to live. All values are of equal value, all practices, norms and customs are equally valid. The message is clear: take what you will. Toleration is a word and a deed that comes easy, for as none can be judged better than another, so all must be tolerated. For the Relativist, then, assimilation and integration are anathema. By what right, they demand, does one culture impose its practices and values on another? If it comes down to sheer power, might or numbers, this is no ethical argument, but it is the only one, they argue, that could be given. On the same principle, multiculturalism can only be acceptable if it is precisely a form of cultural pluralism, where each culture does as it pleases with no interference from any other. If, of course, the members of a culture wish to adopt certain values or practices from another, they may do so, but that is their choice. There can be no fundamental justification for their doing so, or not doing so, save merely their preference. Antiracism as a policy is rather tricky for the relativist. If it is the practice of one culture, then it must be only as acceptable as the practice of any other, so it cannot be inveighed for or against. Antiracist policies could not be supported, any more than racist policies could: they are of equal value.

Now the crucial question becomes: how do Fundamentalists, Objectivists, Subjectivists and Relativists communicate with each another? A brief examination of their likely views of one another will indicate that this is a desperately difficult thing to achieve.

Fundamentalists will probably view Relativists as the most reprehensible of opponents, for here are people who not only do not acknowledge the truth of Fundamentalists, but go so far as to say that their truth is no better than the most ethically retarded society. Fundamentalists will view Relativists as people who fail to provide moral guidance to the young of society, and in so doing, abnegate their responsibilities. With them Fundamentalists would see little point of dialogue. Their views are anathema.

They will view Subjectivists as slightly better, for these people believe that there is light at the end of the tunnel, whereas Relativists do not believe in any light. But not much else can be said. Subjectivists are far too tolerant of wrong opinions. They may be searching, and this is laudable, but when one has the truth, why place any trust or credence in people who have not?

Fundamentalists may view Objectivists in a slightly kindlier light, being glad to see that they at least acknowledge the existence of fundamental values, and will specify them. There can be dialogue over which values are fundamental. But they are wary of them, for Objectivists have started on the slippery slope to amorality by declaring that most cultural practices and customs are not subject to the same timeless rules. Fundamentalists see Objectivists as weak, providing a tempting but false model to the young in the assertion that some things do not matter. All things matter, for all practices are part of the seamless robe of the sacred. At least with Relativists you know where you stand; with the Objectivist there is a slipperiness you find disturbing and dangerous for the unwary. The Fundamentalist might well judge that the best policy is not to get entangled in Objectivist seductions, but to cut off all communication completely.

If Fundamentalists view Objectivists with suspicion, the feeling is more than reciprocated. How do you communicate with people who are not prepared to give an inch? How do you communicate with people who are so sure of everything? How do you communicate with people so dogmatic, so clearly authoritarian in outlook? For the Objectivist there is something deeply alarming and unforgiving about the Fundamentalist. There is also something deeply irritating. Debate hardly gets off the ground. You might agree on certain core values, perhaps even on how you arrived at the list, but when you move onto the customs of Fundamentalist society, you get an answer which prohibits debate — the book tells me it must be so. To a person who has been brought up in a society which values the place and need for rational debate — which argues for the ethical basis of rationality — to be told simply that certain things are beyond the bounds of discussion is anathema.

Objectivists have a certain sympathy for Subjectivists, for they are on the road to enlightenment, even if they have not reached it. What perhaps irritates Objectivists is the Subjectivists' simple insistence that they will never reach the end of that road, and, by implication, this the Objectivist should admit as well. The Objectivist has certainties, and therein lies security. The Subjectivist makes a virtue out of insecurity, and expects others to do so as well. For one who knows the way this blind refusal to see can be rather galling.

But Objectivists finds Relativists even more irritating. Can they not see that the adoption of such a stance is self-refuting? Why accept a Relativist position when, by their own theory, this can be no better than any other? And does the relativist *really* want to say that all practices are equal in commendation or criticism? Is treason really on a par with truth-telling, murder with marital fidelity? Do Relativists really believe in what they say? Objectivists have the suspicion that Relativists are really very tolerant people, who, because of a desire to be fair to all sides, and to show that their understanding of other cultures is limited by their own cultural upbringing, are leaning too far towards them in tolerance. There must come a limit to what one tolerates, and the Relativist has passed that limit a long time ago.

The Subjectivist agrees with the Objectivist about the Relativist. The position is self-defeating. The Relativist's position is initially attractive, but is fatally flawed with any serious examination. But the Subjectivist is as worried by the Objectivist and the Fundamentalist. While acknowledging the existence of the 'good', the Subjectivist is deeply distrustful of those who claim to have found it. People who know they are right are just as dangerous as those who know there is not a right. On the foundations of certainty are religious wars, intolerance and cruelty built.

The Relativist agrees with the Subjectivist about the other two. They are both immensely dangerous in their passionate espousal of one way. The Relativist feels a little sorry for the Subjectivist, for there is an admission of uncertainty, but still a constant striving. The lack of attainability is accepted, but the struggle goes on. The Relativist just does not see the point. The Subjectivist would be far better off admitting the futility of the search and getting on with the things of this world.

The tensions are clear. All four positions may exist within the one society, and, at first blush, there is no necessary communication or understanding among them. It might well be replied that *in real life* this situation is not likely to occur, for what will happen is the step-by-step approach of reconciliation, of each position fudging the issue slightly, of compromise. The crucial point surely, however, is that there is no logical reason why compromise should occur. Given a particular personality, a certain institutional make-up, such positions, such attitudes become rigidified, and intolerance and cruelty rather than compromise are the result. There are too many examples from history, both ancient and modern, for anyone to be comfortable with a 'step-by-step fudge' reaction to be acceptable. Where are the grounds for genuine communication — and then compromise — to take place?

To put this dilemma into practice, take, for example, the place of women in different societies. One Fundamentalist perspective might see men and women as equal but different, and therefore needing different treatment, which locates people within particular social roles and educates to the fulfilment of that role. Human happiness, then, is perceived not as an individual pursuit, but as attainment through a prescribed social role.

A Western Objectivist or Subjectivist might take a very different perspective. While it is still the case that in Western societies women are not given equal treatment in terms of job opportunities, recognition or ability to realize their potential to the extent that men are, yet their treatment is determined by the ethics of equality and individualism. It is held, in theory if not in fact, that not only should men and women be treated equally in terms of life opportunities, but that they should be able to come to a decision themselves about what they wish to do within their society. If they decide to stay at home and raise children, this should not be because they have been socialized into accepting this position, or simply forced into it by expectation and custom, but because they have freely chosen to do so. If they decide to marry early or late, or not at all, this again should be because they have so decided, not because this is decided for them. One, therefore, has a morality of equality, individual choice and decision-making.

Relativists have little to contribute to this debate, because their prescriptions would be that there can be no prescriptions. They would not support the Fundamentalist, the Objectivist, or the Subjectivist, nor would they criticize any of them. This is a fundamentally unhelpful stance, and consequently the following discussion will deal only with the other three stances.

The tension between them is precisely the problem which Walkling and Brannigan highlight when they suggest that antiracist and antisexist policies do not always sit easily together.[21] As they say:

> What makes a particular culture identifiably that culture might include essentially sexist or racist practices and principles ... sexism can be rooted in beliefs which are among the most strongly held and which are crucial to cultural identity.[22]

Ignoring for the moment the fact that by describing practices as 'sexist' or 'racist' they have already determined the rightness and wrongness of these actions, the point is still well made. If Fundamentalists argue that certain customs are fundamental to their culture, and they happen to be (in the Objectivist's or the Subjectivist's eyes) sexist in that they do not grant the same opportunities to women as to men in that society, what are the others to say, and not be accused of being ethnocentric and racist? It is this kind of dilemma to which a resolution is urgently needed, and until one can be proposed, an uneasy compromise is all that is possible, for, crucially, no meeting ground can be identified.

Not all, however, have agreed with the foregoing analysis. Troyna and Carrington, for instance, in a detailed critique of Walkling and Brannigan suggest that there are three weaknesses to this position:

1 that their arguments may be used by right-wingers for less than ethical reasons;
2 that one should concentrate on the structural and institutional features of racism;
3 that it misrepresents minority group practices, and in particular Muslim attitudes in this country to single-sex schools.[23]

As Walkling and Brannigan point out, none of these objections materially affects the points they raise.[24] The first argument is not really an argument as such. A concern for the truth cannot be watered down because of how someone may use this truth. The second argument focuses upon precisely those aspects which the first half of this chapter has been at pains to point out: the structural and institutional features of racism in UK society. It does not, however, follow that a belief in such features should deter one from isolating and ameliorating other factors. There is nothing incompatible in holding both points of view. Indeed, this chapter argues that the two are interdependent. The final argument may be true for some sections of the Muslim community, is clearly not for others, but in any case does not touch the *logical* point that antiracist and antisexist stances may find themselves in opposition in practice.

If an opposition between antiracism and antisexism is perceived, this may well indicate a problem with both concepts. Antiracism is a concept which, in Western society at least, has been adopted by White middle-class intellectuals more than any others, in an attempt to acknowledge the discriminatory practices against ethnic groups within Western societies as part of an attempt to remediate these practices. As we have seen, it can and does have a variety of hues in its interpretation, but one of the less sensible (if understandable) features has been an unwillingness to criticize other cultures, precisely because of the recognition of their own culture's poor record. Some writers have even gone so far as to say that racism can only be performed by White people. This is logically ludicrous, and cannot be pardoned, even if it does express the simple observation that in a White-dominated society White people are more likely to be able to exercise racist practices. This sensitivity to criticizing other ethnic groups is the major reason for the difficulty in admitting the simple logical point that *any* culture is capable of racist practices.

The second conceptual problem comes in terms, however, of antisexism. If, as defined above, this means that women should be given equal opportunities and equal life chances to men, it cannot be doubted that some cultures do not do this (White majority cultures included). If, however, it is argued (as it is) that men and women are physiologically, biologically and psychologically different, and so should be treated differently, then to treat them differently is not unethical but simply sensible. This could be a matter of discussion, dispute and testing; there is room for discussion and communication. If, more problematically, a holy text declares men and women to be different, and therefore to be treated differently, the room for debate is eliminated. What is to be done here?

The tension between antiracism and antisexism seems to boil down to three possible problems:

1   a misguided, overrelaxed view of tolerance, where it is felt that criticism of another culture is by definition racist;
2   an (arguable) belief in the essential similarities or dissimilarities between men and women;
3   a (non-arguable) belief in the truths of a sacred book which states these differences and places such belief beyond argument.

The first *is* both misguided and overrelaxed. As long as one is suitably aware of the biases and distortions of one's own culture — and hence the need for the policies in the first half of this chapter — then informed constructive criticism of all ways of life is both possible and necessary. The second is a clear area for disagreement, but also for communication; and while communication is possible, so cultural tolerance is as well. The third is the core of the problem, but there is some room for manoeuvre in terms of: discussion of the grounds for unarguability; discussion of humanity's fallibility in perceiving the message objectively; discussion of different interpretations of the message.

However, these are discussions which accept the essential truth of the revelation, and of the correctness in holding such an intellectual position. It comes down to a question of toleration. I suggest that in a society founded upon tolerance, discussion of differences, and the use of reason and communication, any stance which denies them should not be allowed within an educational institution. As Walkling and Brannigan said: 'The beginnings of a solution to the liberal's conflict turn upon the question of what is meant by toleration.'[25] And as G.K. Chesterton put it: 'There is a thought that stops thought. That is the only thought that ought to be stopped.'[26] It is to be hoped that the situation never gets as far as this. It is suggested that where structural and institutional inequalities are remediated, it is much more unlikely to happen.

What is needed is not surety by any party, but a spirit of enquiry into an examination of both sides for the greater benefit of both. What a multicultural society — or any society for that matter — needs to do is to give its children the tools to reflect upon their own and other societies, and proceed to build ones which incorporate the best of all, ones which are caring, understanding, tolerant and capable of discerning and repudiating practices which are not.

## CONCLUSION: FEATURES FOR ATTITUDINAL CHANGE

The Salman Rushdie affair was created by tensions within a society which contains a variety of cultures and conflicting values, where majority and minority cultures have failed to communicate and understand one another. Examples of such conflicts have been considered in this chapter; while resolution of them is seen as neither quick nor simple, neither is remediation seen as impossible. If examples of such mutual hostility are to be prevented, and if a multicultural policy is to be possible — and by this I mean where people celebrate differences precisely because of the acceptance of core values — then five fundamental changes are necessary.

The first part of such a philosophy demands institutional and structural changes in existing societies to remediate social, political and educational injustices. Without such changes minority cultures will not trust majority cultures and will not enter into dialogue. Nor will the populations of majority cultures realize that their society has these faults, and that there is a need for reflection. In this respect political change may well have to precede popular opinion.

The second part must involve an increased recognition that despite the fact that some practices within cultures are variable, these practices serve the function of giving continuity and security to members of those cultures. An attitude of assimilation by majority cultures simply shows a lack of understanding for the needs of others. When people cling grimly to apparently inappropriate practices, it may well be a need for secure psychological ground which motivates this, much more than any belief in the sacred permanence of such rites. An empathic understanding of this by the majority culture, and concomitant structural changes, may in many cases be all that is needed to begin an intelligent and mutually beneficial dialogue.

A third part is a further empathic development in values education. It involves a commitment by both majority and minority cultures to listening and trying to understand others' beliefs and values. Providing a framework for this to happen is a crucial part of teaching, but it necessarily involves the other changes detailed in this conclusion at the same time.

A fourth part is to provide children with the critical tools to understand and change society. This is only possible if the three above are in place. Only where it is clear that majority structures are open to change will minority cultures enter dialogue, and only when dialogue is in progress will minority cultures feel sufficiently secure to look at the adjustments *they* need to make. Education and culture can then be seen as part of a dialectic of life, a dialogue of acculturation, of what to retain and what to change. It does not demand change for change's sake, but it does prevent the fossilization of attitudes and the rigidification of positions.

A final part of an educational programme must be an appreciation of others' points of view, Fundamentalist, Objectivist, Subjectivist, or Relativist, of why they think the way they do. This should lead to the perception that any individual's understanding of the 'truth' is necessarily veiled, that there is room for dialogue. The individual must struggle through the veils of personal and social limitations, and have to think within the biological constraints of the human organism. The individual is permanently faced with looking through layer upon layer of distorting prisms. The recognition of this should move people to understand their and anyone else's fallibility. It should indicate the need for an openness to criticism and change, for no one person is going to be wholly right. It should also indicate a need for tolerance, for criticism itself is probably flawed and capable of being criticized. In a multicultural context it suggests these for all parties, majority and minority cultures alike.

This account has implications for a multicultural curriculum. First, it suggests an appreciation of human knowledge and culture as a progressive, expanding, but always limited endeavour. It asks for a critical, open attitude to both. This is only possible in an educational context where majority and minority cultures feel comfortable with themselves and each other. It cannot be conducted properly with an attitude of superiority and neglect on one side, and alienation and distrust on the other.

Second, it suggests that part of the educative process, part of the teacher's, part of the parent's duty, is to help the child to develop his own style and understanding, with a corresponding tolerance of others. An appreciation of each individual's limited attainment becomes a vital lesson to be taught. It is because of this that '... teaching is seen as a mode of being with, a positive mode of solicitude in which one leaps ahead of the other so as to open his possibilities for him, but never leaps in for the other, for this would be to deprive him of his possibilities.'[27] This has profound implications for the beliefs of all cultures, for it suggests change rather than stasis, but in a considered and considerate manner.

Finally, this concept of education suggests that any area of the curriculum, including the study of other cultures' values, beliefs and ways of life, should be viewed through an understanding of the subjectivity of human understanding. This means that both the perceiver and the object of perception could be in error. It assumes, demands, tolerance and humility in its undertaking; it insists on empathy, for if you:

> See yourself in others.
> Then whom can you hurt?
> What harm can you do?[28]

Any substantial development in relations between cultures is going to need these changes in attitude: changes in attitude to the fairness of institutions, to the impermanence of knowledge, to the needs of each other, to the value of criticism. A change in one is not sufficient, for all are interdependent.

## NOTES

1  S. Rushdie (1988) *The Satanic Verses*, Harmondsworth, Penguin Books.
2  B. Parekh (1989) 'Between Holy Text and Moral Void', *New Statesman and Society*, 23 March.
3  J.A. Banks and J. Lynch (Eds) (1986) *Multicultural Education in Western Societies*, Eastbourne, Holt.
4  Annual Report of the Rhode Island School Board 1884, quoted in R.H. Hersh, J.P. Miller and G.D. Fielding (1980) *Models of Moral Education*, New York, Longman, p. 18.
5  Commonwealth Immigrants Advisory Council (1964), p. 7, quoted in B. Troyna and J. Williams (1986) *Racism, Education, and the State*, London, Croom Helm, p. 12.
6  B.M. Bullivant (1981) *The Pluralist Dilemma in Education: Six Case Studies*, London, George Allen and Unwin.
7  *Education for All: The Swann Report* (1985) London, HMSO, p. 5.
8  As an example of this approach, see R. Scruton (1986) 'The Myth of Cultural Relativism', in F. Palmer (Ed.), *Anti-Racism: An Assault on Education and Value*, London, Sherwood Press.
9  See J.A. Banks (1986) 'Race, Ethnicity and Schooling in the United States: Past, Present and Future', in J.A. Banks and J. Lynch (Eds), *Multicultural Education in Western Societies*, Eastbourne, Holt.
10  J. Lynch (1986) 'Multicultural Education: Agenda for Change', in Banks and Lynch, *op. cit.*
11  L. Cohen and A. Cohen (Eds) (1986) *Multicultural Education: A Sourcebook for Teachers*, London, Harper, p. 4.
12  See the readings in Palmer, *op. cit.*
13  D. Milner (1983) *Children and Race Ten Years On*, London, Ward Lock; M. Craft (1984) 'Education and Diversity', in M. Craft (Ed.), *Education and Cultural Pluralism*, Lewes, Falmer Press; J. Milton Yinger (1986) 'Intersecting Strands in the Theorisation of Race and Ethnic Relations', in J.A. Rex and D.J. Mason (Eds), *Theories of Race and Ethnic Relations*, Cambridge, Cambridge University Press.
14  C. Mullard (1980) *Racism in Society and Schools: History, Policy and Practice*, London, University of London Institute of Education; R. Hatcher (1985) 'On Education for Racial Equality', *Multiracial Education*, 13, 1; Troyna and Williams, *op. cit.*
15  Lynch (1986) *op. cit.*, p. 178.
16  Milner, *op. cit.*
17  K. Clark (1965) *Dark Ghetto*, Gollancz, pp. 63–64.
18  Ably described in Milner, *op. cit.*, Ch. 6.
19  *Education for All: The Swann Report*, *op. cit.*
20  See M.P. Bottery (1988) 'Education, Objectivity and Tolerance', *Westminster Studies in Education*, 11.
21  P.H. Walkling and C. Brannigan (1986) 'Anti-Sexist/Anti-Racist Education: A Possible Dilemma', *Journal of Moral Education*, 15, 1.
22  *Ibid.*, p. 21.
23  B. Troyna and B. Carrington (1987) 'Anti-Sexist/Antiracist Education: A False Dilemma; A Reply to Walkling and Brannigan', *Journal of Moral Education*, 16, 1, pp. 5.
24  P. Walkling and C. Brannigan (1987) 'Muslim Schools: Troyna and Carrington's Dilemma', *Journal of Moral Education*, 16, 1.
25  Walkling and Brannigan (1986) *op. cit.*, p. 23.
26  G.K. Chesterton (1909) *Orthodoxy*, John Lane Company, p. 58.
27  J. Macquarrie (1972) *Existentialism*, London, Hutchinson, p. 205.
28  *The Dhammapadama* (The Sayings of the Buddha), quoted in *Profile on Prejudice*, Minority Rights Group, p. 10.

# 15. Moral Education, Values Education and Prejudice Reduction*

JOHN WILSON

Philosophers should be able to help educators in two ways. First, there are some very general points to be made about education and human differences, particularly about the application of various criteria and the status of different kinds of arguments. Second, there are more specific problems clustering round the notions of attachment, identity and rationality in relation to race and culture. I deal with these below; but I must forewarn the reader that I can only draw a very rough map of a terrain which is still largely uncharted, and shall be content if I can at least make more explicit some problems and difficulties that are usually glossed over.

## CRITERIA OF DIFFERENTIATION

I have eschewed terms like 'multiethnic' and 'multicultural' in my title, because one of the most important (and most neglected) problems for educators consists in determining what criteria of differentiation to use for (1) their pupils and (2) their own enterprises. In practice, (1) pupils are classified according to such criteria as age, ability, sex, colour, creed, race, etc. Sometimes these criteria are institutionalized in particular groupings of pupils (single-sex schools, remedial classes, 'special' schools): sometimes they may be used just to take note, as it were, of the existence of certain classes ('disruptive pupils', 'racial minorities'). But there is, of course, an infinite number of ways in which people can be classified, because there is an infinite number of human differences. We could, for instance, classify (and even group) pupils according to social class, motivation, psychological type, physical strength, moral beliefs, etc. Similarly (2) we have titles which, however roughly, we use to describe and classify different parts of the general enterprise of education: 'the curriculum', 'pastoral care', 'sex education' and so forth. These classifications are not god-given, and their descriptions are often vague. (Does 'pastoral care' include 'discipline'? Does 'sex education' include 'the education of the emotions' or is it just a part of 'biology'?)

* A version of this chapter was printed in the *Oxford Review of Education*, 12, 1, 1986, to which acknowledgment is made here.

There are certain principles which apply to any classification or taxonomy: the items must be *clearly described* (otherwise we do not know what we are talking about under particular headings), and must be *discrete* from each other (otherwise there are confusing overlaps). Educational taxonomies fail badly on both grounds, but the problems here could, in principle at least, be solved simply by the application of logic and common sense. More controversial is the question of what basic values or purposes underlie the taxonomy: what the taxonomy is *for*. This causes some trouble even in elementary cases: we need to classify whales as fish for some purposes, as mammals for other purposes. But in education we have to ask the question, 'What differences, both in our pupils and in our various tasks, are *educationally important?*' Any set of educational practices gives at least a tacit answer to that question. Simply by using certain descriptions, and still more by engaging in certain practices under those descriptions, we commit ourselves to singling out certain things as worthy of particular attention.

We have thus to answer nasty questions like (1) 'Are we right to underline (emphasize, highlight) features in our pupils like being Black, or female, or Jewish, or working-class?', and (2) 'Are we right to delimit (as it were, draw a circle around, even perhaps put on the curricular map) areas of learning under the headings of "humanities", "religion", "sex", "morality", "racialism", "feminist studies"?' The answers to these questions are not obvious. But what we actually do under these headings may be less important than the fact of adopting the headings themselves; moreover, the mere fact of adopting them brings certain values and practices with it. This occurs partly because the delimitations themselves are educationally potent (just by having *something called* 'sex education' — rather than, say, dealing with sexuality *en passant* during some more general course about the education of the emotions or about the human body — we convey a message to our pupils: the message that sexuality is something special, in need of peculiar treatment, which is of course controversial); and partly because the descriptions are value-laden ('pastoral care' implies a certain tendermindedness, a 'caring' rather than a stern attitude, etc.: also controversial).

Most practical educators will probably not begin by considering this problem in the a priori way which I have (deliberately) used above; but they will be obliged to face it, sooner or later in their thinking, even if they start with particular cases. A teacher concerned, for instance, with certain children in a particular school will soon find himself asking: 'Is it really their *colour* that causes the trouble? Or their *racial origins*? Or is it rather their way of life, their *culture* (and just what does "culture" mean, anyway)? Or maybe it's just their social class, or their social position?' He will also think: 'Should I have special classroom periods about this, try to tackle it head-on? Or should I try to play it down, help them to forget it (whatever it is)? Is it really important, or does it only seem important to them?' These thoughts, however particularized or random, lead us (and him, if he has the time and energy to pursue them) straight back to the basic questions.

## EDUCATIONAL AND SOCIAL VALUES

In determining whether something is 'important', a reasonable candidate for singling out in accordance with a particular criterion, educators are commonly (and rightly) influenced by social or political facts. These facts vary, sometimes dramatically. Any serious educator would want his pupils, if they were living in a racist society, to appreciate certain facts which pupils in other circumstances would not need to appreciate. Pupils come from certain backgrounds into school, and will have to live in certain backgrounds when they leave school. We need not teach them to endorse or agree with all or even much of what happens in society; but if they are to survive, we have to teach them what the prevailing features and norms of society are. None of that (I imagine) is seriously in dispute.

Nor is it in dispute that governments, representing particular societies, have an obligation (putting it at its lowest) to avoid certain kinds of trouble. We do not want civil war, race riots, the oppression of particular groups, various kinds of crime. More positively, there are certain basic goods (of a fairly down-to-earth utilitarian kind) which we want established: health, a decent standard of living and so on. To avoid the troubles and achieve the goods, pupils will have to learn certain things, and the educators will have to teach them those things.

However, few educators believe (at least on reflection) that their task is wholly exhausted by the demands of government or society. They believe — and this belief is encapsulated by the term 'educate', when contrasted with such terms as 'socialize' or 'indoctrinate' — that their pupils should learn certain things which are good or important or worthwhile in themselves, or for their pupils as people in their own right, not just for their pupils as members of a particular society at a particular time. We do not (I hope) teach our pupils about music or literature or religion or morality just because this will be useful to them as social functionaries. These and other types of learning, or other aspects of the learning, are not justified by social values; they are justified by other kinds of values.

Like any other educational question, a question like 'How important is it that these pupils are Black (Jewish, Asian, female, etc.)?' has to be answered in (at least) two different ways. First, we have to consider what we may call the *contingent* importance of these criteria, which would vary considerably depending on whether the pupils were in Alabama, South Africa, Iran or North Oxford. Second, we would also have to consider how important the criteria were *sub specie aeternitatis*, so to speak, or in the eyes of God: whether (to use less grand language) we want the pupils to think that, irrespective of what their particular neighbours or societies may think, it is a matter of great importance *to themselves* that they are Black (Jewish, etc.). There is a *general* question about how much weight or value a person should (for instance) attach to his ancestry, or racial origins, or culture, or class, or creed, which is not exhausted by — not really even touched by — the question of how much importance these features may have in the eyes of others. Whether to 'be Jewish' (whatever that means), or how Jewish to be, and what to do about it if one is brought up as a Jew, are all matters which are relevant to a person's life in a general way: not only relevant if one is being persecuted.

## PSYCHOLOGICAL VALUES

'Social values' is a vague phrase; and we ought at least to recognize that 'importance', even contingent importance, is not exhausted by purely social considerations. A person's identity (sense of security, self-esteem, self-confidence, or whatever phrase we may want to use here) is not purely social; indeed, a great many of the factors that go to make or mar that sense operate on the person at a very young age, before he is significantly affected by anything we could reasonably call 'society' — how he is handled as an infant, his relationships with parents and so on. It is difficult, even in theory, to distinguish 'psychological' from 'social' features; but at least matters of individual psychology must be taken into account.

The distinction above applies equally here. It may be, contingently and as the result of particular facts, 'important' for an individual to see himself as coming from a distinguished ancestry, or as White (Black, etc.), or as anything else. But it is another question, distinct from the first even if connected with it in educational practice, whether it is right or reasonable or desirable for that individual to do so. (A somewhat insecure aristocratic acquaintance of mine would only pay attention to history lessons in which his aristocratic ancestors figured. The history teacher said words to the effect of 'Do forget about your blasted ancestors and try and be a historian.' He thought that attachment to doing history was more worthwhile than attachment to one's family tree.)

It might be possible here — with 'social values' it seems harder — to run some kind of developmental stage theory; and that would be very useful, if it gave us reason to believe that the criteria of 'importance' were to some degree fixed or given for all individuals, from a psychological viewpoint. For instance, it might be held that young children inevitably used visible or physical criteria (strength, colour) at a certain stage, before they could graduate to what some might regard as more sophisticated criteria (intelligence, kindness, being a historian). Such a theory might have a sociological counterpart, as it were: one might think that insecure or oppressed people in society would be bound, at an early stage of their 'liberation', to identify themselves in simple, perhaps purely physical, terms — as Black, or female, or advanced in years ('ageism'), or Aryan, or something of that kind: rather than as members of a group defined by more sophisticated criteria (historians, lovers of classical music).

The significance of any such theory is clear: it would commit us, as educators, to accepting as inevitable certain developmental stages which (however undesirable) were not contingent, but had to be gone through step by step. If we had — as I am trying to suggest we must have — certain well-based views on how people *ought* to define themselves, it would still be no good trying to sell these views to individuals irrespective of their developmental stage. We should say to ourselves something like 'Whatever we do, we have to accept that people will first define themselves in reference to criteria *ABC*: then later thay may be moved to, or grow towards, criteria *DEF*: and much later, if we're lucky and educate them properly, they may end up with the criteria we think best for them (*XYZ*).'

I do not believe in any such theory; and it is at least plain that no simple version of it, of the kind mentioned above, seems immediately plausible. Prima facie, in the light of history, people can and do identify themselves very potently in non-physical terms — as Christians or followers of Islam, for instance, or as Marxists or members of some gang whose identity is obscure but may be to do with common tastes or values as much as with physical identity. Such a theory would have to show not only (what may well be true) that children or simple-minded adults *notice* physical differences more readily than non-physical ones, but that they *put more weight* on such differences, which is a very different matter. It may be that particular societies (or particular parents) operate régimes that virtually force individuals to put weight on certain differences: you cannot help but put weight on the criterion of being Black in South Africa, for example. But that seems to be a contingent, and therefore a mutable, matter: something to be questioned, perhaps changed, not just taken as given or inevitable.

## AIMS OF MULTIETHNIC (MULTICULTURAL) EDUCATION

We should now be in a better position to tackle the question of what the aims of multiethnic (multicultural) education should be. For we can at least see two reasonably clear types of justification: first, justification in terms of contingent facts — the particular features of particular societies, or of particular individuals; and second, justification in terms of what is universally desirable for non-contingent reasons. This distinction may still seem too vague or (as people say) 'abstract' or 'theoretical' to be of much use: but it is easy to think of examples. If, for instance, we are thinking of appointing someone as a member of some committee, we commonly have two criteria in mind. We may think of a candidate *X* as likely to advance some *political* (in a broad sense) good: thus the committee may carry more weight in the public mind, or satisfy various pressure groups better, if *X* is a well-known public figure, or is Black, or female, or whatever. This is a perfectly respectable criterion: committees have to cut ice in the real world, and the contingent facts of that world have to be taken into account. But we may also think of *X* as more or less likely to perform well in the non-political aspects of the work, aspects which have nothing to do with public relations or other such contingent facts: and here whether *X* is Black, or a peer of the realm, or representative of certain group interests, is irrelevant. Similarly, it may be desirable to appoint someone as a policeman because he is Black, and hence can do his job better in certain areas; but no one can think that the notion of 'a good policeman' is exhausted by such considerations. There are aspects of being a policeman which are not affected by contingent circumstances: aspects which are, as it were, inherent in the enterprise itself.

So, a fortiori, with any concept of the educated person: the educated person is not only (though he may be this) someone who can function well in a particular society, or with reference to his own particular psychological and idiosyncratic feelings. Such a person has to measure himself, and his society, against certain transcultural and transpersonal norms and standards. He must have, and live up to, some idea of what is right, or appropriate for any human being, or good, or sane, or true; and (*pace* relativists) terms like 'right', 'sane' and so on do not translate into 'what such-and-such a person (society) takes to be right (sane, etc.)'. They are, to use a grand word, transcendental: time-free and non-contingent. That is not to say that educators have the job of browbeating pupils into accepting what the educators think is right: it is to say that they have the (much more difficult) job of helping them to decide *reasonably* for themselves what is right.

Hence multiethnic education, indeed any education which highlights certain criteria, has to justify itself not only (1) at the bar of contingent facts, political or otherwise, but also (2) at the bar of culture-free rationality. I stress (2) here, partly because I think it likely that (in a relativistic climate) (2) is likely to receive insufficient attention, partly because there is not much that can be said in a *general* way about (1). Precisely because justifications of type (1) rest on contingent facts, it is hard to generalize. Some societies, in which people have strong and potentially dangerous self-identifications in terms of race and colour, may need multiracial education; others, in which their affiliations are (say) religious, would profit more from a certain kind of religious education. We would need a lot of information from sociologists and others about the nature, and in particular the durability, of the empirical facts which are relevant to specific social needs at any one time. There is also the point, commonly neglected, that it might be better to use non-educational methods to satisfy these needs, or at least not to confine ourselves to educational ones. It might well be that a well-organized advertizing campaign, plus a judicious distribution of rewards and punishments, plus certain other 'brute' moves of that kind, would do more to avoid racial trouble than any amount of *education*.

If we tackle the aims of multiethnic education head on — and it is best, as I have (too briefly) tried to show, not to do this too quickly — we shall find it difficult to rise above the level of the obvious or merely banal. Thus it is obvious (i) that we shall encourage pupils to reflect upon, and (we hope) accept the reasonableness of, certain propositions about the equal value (worth, rights, importance) of human beings as such, irrespective of race (creed, sex, colour, etc.). Moral philosophers have expended a lot of ink on this topic (see particularly Hare, 1981) and I need not enlarge on it here. We may also reasonably want (ii) members of one race (culture, etc.) to learn something about members of other races: perhaps as an objective in its own right (a kind of anthropological education) or perhaps as a reinforcement to (i). These aims are fairly non-controversial. Much more difficult are the questions (iii) how far ought an individual to find his identity (sense of security, etc.) as a member of a particular race? and (iv) what is to be said about the merits and demerits of particular ethnic cultures?

I stress that these questions arise in the minds of pupils, however much educators may try to sidestep them. A girl brought up in a strict Islamic family, a boy brought up in a Jewish family, is bound to ask how far she/he wants or ought to follow the particular precepts and behaviour patterns laid down by these environments. Such conflicts occur more obviously in a multiracial or pluralist society, but (particularly with increased communication in a shrinking world) the possibility of conflict is always there. Unless educators do something to steer pupils through such conflicts, they are not likely to do more than utter platitudes about human equality (i), or offer a shop-window tour of various races and cultures, without giving the pupils any reasons for preferring one to another (ii).

Questions (iii) and (iv) are clearly linked, at least in that the merits and demerits of particular cultures must have *some* bearing on whether or not to identify oneself as a member of this or that culture. People who like to think of themselves as English (Aryan, African, etc.) do not attach themselves to the *word* 'English'; they characteristically think there is something about English culture, traditions, history, etc. which is meritorious, or anyway which they have some *reason* for adhering to and identifying with. The pretence, often indulged in by multiethnic educators, that 'one culture (race, etc.) is as good as another' is no more than relativist rhetoric: no one seriously believes that (for instance) a belief in Aryan supermen, or female circumcision, or other such cultural items is just a matter of taste or morally neutral. We think they are *wrong*; or at the very least we think that the question of their rightness or wrongness is a real question.

So far I have done no more than point to some issues which (in my limited experience) are commonly evaded. Even this may be of some practical value: if they were put on the multicultural agenda, so to speak, and actually *discussed with the pupils* (rather than played down for fear of giving offence), much would be gained. However, there is a good deal more to be said about these questions; and it may help to say some of it here, however tentatively.

## RACE, CULTURE AND 'BECAUSE IT'S MINE'

I have used terms like 'race', 'ethnic', 'culture', etc. somewhat indiscriminately; but anyone seriously facing the question of what to put his psychological money on (so to speak) would demand much more precision. Even 'race' alone is obscure: are we to say that the English are a single race, or a blend of different races (Celts, Angles, Saxons, Normans, etc.)? Different from this is the notion of colour or physical appearance: different again, though commonly confused, is some supposed similarity in terms of geographical area ('Caribbean' or 'Indian' may be used like this). 'Culture' is worse still: I have seen no definition of this term with any serious pretension to clarity.

This matters because we should be inclined to make very different judgements about 'importance' depending on what we were supposed to be judging. Thus prima facie, and in the light of pure reason rather than prevailing social facts (which we have, at this stage of the argument, put on one side), there seems nothing particularly important about just being Black: one has to find very specific contexts, such as casting *Othello* or distributing suntan lotion, even to see any relevance in having a black skin. 'Because $X$ is Black', in other words, is a reason with very limited application. At the other end of the scale, 'being a Christian' or 'being a good all-American democratic guy' ('English gentleman', etc.) seems much more important, since the values and behaviour enshrined in these phrases can at least be plausibly represented as good reasons for a great many contexts in life.

Two temptations meet us at this point, both of which have to be resisted. One, well expressed by Mishler (1978), is to take the view that education should give no weight at all to individual attachments and put all the weight on impersonal criteria of relevance and merit. If, for instance, we are concerned with selecting and training a football team, then our practice should be guided solely by the criteria relevant to football: whether particular individuals are psychologically attached to other criteria — whether they are or see themselves as Black, Christian, all-American, etc. — is simply not to the point. Relevant considerations in educational grouping and other practice would, on this view, be derived only from what was to be learned: the standards inherent in the particular subject. If we teach mathematics or musical appreciation, then it is simply irrelevant that some mathematicians are Jewish, or that particular kinds of music have particular psychological or social connotations for various people. ('They're playing our tune, darling' is of interest to someone involved in a personal relationship, irrelevant to someone judging the aesthetic merit of the tune.)

The attraction of this view is that it leaves the educator free to disregard (again, except insofar as he has to serve contingent social or other interests) *all* the criteria we have been talking about. He can say something like, 'Look, we live in a prejudicial society, about which you need to know some facts (some people are barmy and hate Blacks/Christians get better treatment, etc.): we will spend a bit of time preparing you for the society you'll have to face later. But apart from this, *just forget* whether you're Black/Jewish/Asian/Christian, and concentrate on learning various things in their own right — mathematics, not "Black mathematics"; literature, not "feminist literature"; religion, not specifically the Christian religion. We shall try to get you to see and love what is *good*, not what happens to be the possession of any particular social or other group — not even if it is *your* group. Of course, as sensible educators, we shall take full account of (as the Americans say) "where you're coming from": we are not so stupid as to think that your cultural (national, racial, etc.) background makes no difference to *how* we teach you. But it makes no difference to our educational *aims*.'

Unfortunately, there is a snag with this. Briefly, 'Because it's mine' does seem to be a satisfactory reason for certain kinds of attachment, even if I recognize that what I am attached to lacks public merit. In *As You Like It* Touchstone describes his wife Audrey as 'a poor thing, but mine own'; even granted the correctness of his judgment, we still think it right that he should love her as his wife. I am attached to my home, country, children, even my cat, not because I think them better than others but because they are mine. 'Breathes there a man with soul so dead/That never to himself hath said "This is my own, my native land"?' Well, many may so breathe; but we pity them. Love, as Iris Murdoch says in one of her not infrequent novels, has nothing to do with merit. Children, as Aristotle says, are seen as extensions of their parents: a friend, as he also says, is *allos autos*, another self. It is difficult to see how such local attachments could be wholly absent from any form of human life; and even if they could, human life would be much the poorer.

This throws us into the arms of the second temptation, which is (briefly) to adopt a wholly relativist position. We are to take 'important' simply as 'important to $X$' (where $X$ is some individual or social group). That would demolish both the problem of what categories or criteria of demarcation to use (because each person could choose his own criterion and be beyond the reach of criticism), and the problem of what to judge good or bad within each category. Thus we should, on this view, have no objection either to a person finding his identity primarily in terms of his ancestry or colour, nor to him thinking that (for instance) white was good and black bad.

There are more objections to this than can be mentioned here — not least the point that no one really adopts the position: it would remove the whole idea of acting for a reason, something which is just as firmly written into any form of human life as the idea of local attachment. Here it needs only to be pointed out that the concept of education itself involves the notion of truth or reason, via the concept of learning. To learn something is not merely to change one's mind or behaviour: it is to change them in the direction of truth. If we abandon this idea, we have as educators no reason for doing anything: for choosing one book to put in the school library rather than another, for saying certain things about the physical world rather than certain other things, still less for expending large sums of money on schools. If no change has the backing of reason, there is no need to learn anything. Certainly there is no point in taking the education of racial or cultural groups seriously: for to take anything seriously implies that there are things that stand in need of improvement, and if the criteria for improvement are purely relative, we have no ultimate reason for backing one set of practices against another.

We are thus obliged in education, as we are in life as a whole, somehow to put together or do justice to both local attachments — 'Because it's mine' — and public criteria of merit — 'Because it's good'. Some palliation of our difficulties may be found in the fact that some attachments are non-negotiable. We cannot, for instance, escape from our own bodies, or our own parents: and one educational aim must be to help pupils to achieve at least good working relationships (to put it rather absurdly), if not a loving attitude, towards these. But the palliation is a small one. It is an open question, much canvassed in the history of philosophical and religious thought, just how attached one should be to one's body, or indeed to one's parents. A fortiori attachments to a particular nation, race or culture are profoundly in question. Hence it seems better to accept two different, though ultimately connected, types of educational aim. Roughly, we want the pupils (1) to be able to love and feel loved — to have the capacity to form local attachments rather than (as it were) being nomadic, unable to see anything or anyone as 'theirs', with that peculiar sense of 'belonging' which is at the heart of love; but also (2) to be able to make proper judgments about the merits not only of colour or culture or race but of other things that may be more or less worthwhile or trivial.

I must belabour the point (even if its screams may weary some readers) that we must not, as educators, foreclose these matters by making overt or concealed assumptions about the general *form* of a person's identity. In much education today, indeed in much of life generally, it is taken for granted that 'social' identity and position are all-important, and that 'society' (whatever that term may mean: I have seen no satisfactory account) must somehow come into all education. (At a university where I once taught this became a joke in the course titles: 'Mathematics and Society', 'Beethoven and Society', Greek Grammar and Society'. . . .) 'Society' has, it might be said, come to occupy a place previously occupied by other candidates — God, nature, the soul, truth, reason, beauty. How far pupils ought to define themselves socially, how much money they should put on social as against other features of their lives, must be put to them as open questions. Matters of race and culture are just one instance of a general problem here. Of course we are not educating potential hermits; but neither, I hope, are we educating people who see themselves only, or even primarily, as members of this or that society or group, particularly since not a few such groups seem, to put it mildly, somewhat less than satisfactory.

It follows from this that education aiming at (1) and (2) above — the ability to form attachments, and the ability to make judgments of merit — cannot be *based on* any particular social, racial, cultural or other kind of grouping: for to do that would be, precisely, to foreclose these issues by predetermining the criteria for the pupils. Certainly we may use such groupings as subject matter for discussion, just as we may consider other possible groupings (a club of stamp collectors, a football team, membership of a school); but that is a very different matter. A first step here would be to make an adequate set of categories of attachment, which could be used as something to put before pupils for discussion and experience. We could then have some hope of answering the question: 'What kinds of attachments are there, and what value can we reasonably place on each?'


## THE POTENCY OF THE SCHOOL

It will be said, of course, that schools *as they are* (an important qualification) are comparatively impotent, and are forced to accept prevailing social criteria, so that the question is not in fact open — the pupils arrive with particular identities ready-made. That is not entirely true; but even if it were, it would be a powerful argument for greatly increasing the potency of schools as institutions. For unless an educational institution is capable of providing a background strong enough to override the pupils' external emotional investments, it can hardly hope to educate in this area at all. Relativistic temptations make us hesitate here, because we find it hard to conceive of a potent school apart from a particular and questionable ideology. But a moment's thought is enough to show us that the values inherent in education itself demand *both* extremely potent institutions *and* institutions devoted to developing reason rather than ideological commitment. A good family is an obvious example (not all good families share a common ideology, in any serious sense of 'ideology': they are potent because they are fraternally binding and their members love each other).

Schools as they could be (and could be without the need for greater financial support or total reorganization) would have something of the potency — not necessarily the partisan values — of the family, of certain schools in the independent sector, or of other institutions that have refused to sell out to 'society' and are unwilling to lie down under social pressure. Such institutions exist, and I have described elsewhere (1972) what I take to be their crucial features — a strong house system or 'pastoral' base which overrides the classroom, a full-time investment on the part of the pupils, a deliberate shielding or separation of the institution from external practices and values. These notions, once traditional, are not currently fashionable: the obsession with 'society', together with relativistic temptations, have produced a strong if miasmic desire to 'integrate', 'break down barriers', and 'be open'. That, I am arguing, is logically inconsistent with any serious educational aims: education which simply reflects or plays along with 'society' is not education. The educator *withdraws* (to a greater or lesser extent) his pupils from the world, and asks his pupils to reflect upon it and upon themselves, to pursue knowledge and to develop powers of ratiocination which will enable him to see the world differently and more clearly. That task has to be done *in the teeth of* external pressures whether of ideological intervention or the values of the marketplace.

Such an institution is, in any case, required for the aims in (1) and (2). For only there can pupils (1) form the personal attachments and loyalties which will enable them to develop their ability to love (to form other attachments), just as only a genuinely potent and fraternal family can do this; and (2) gain the knowledge and powers of judgment which will enable them to free themselves from those social or other criteria which they may not wish to accept. This is true of any serious form of moral, personal, social, political or emotional education: unless the institution gives pupils a firm and secure base of personal relationships and institutional loyalty, they will not have the moral strength to make any real changes in their hearts and minds. Something can, of course, be done in class-room discussion and by other forms of overt education; but these will merely scratch the surface unless they appear as a natural extension of a proper educational background — that is, of an institution whose values and practices are potently and obviously devoted to *learning* rather than social reinforcement.


## DESIRABLE AND UNDESIRABLE ATTACHMENTS

Granted that some attachments are non-negotiable, and granted also that we can love where there is no merit, there is still considerable latitude for choosing what we shall be attached to. What criteria are we to use? What makes an attachment desirable or undesirable? It is difficult to divorce such questions from even vaster questions about the meaning of life, or what we should count as of ultimate importance. Nevertheless, some separation (if not total divorce) is possible. Thus Richard Peters in a well-known book (1966) argues for attachment to 'curricular activities' (science, history, mathematics, etc.) on the grounds that the goods they offer are (1) varied and less boring than those on offer elsewhere, (2) non-perishable, and (3) non-competitive; and those are, at least, significant arguments whether or not we agree with the conclusion.

There are three criteria which seem to have some merit in the light of what we should actually say about particular cases.

1 The object of attachment should be something of central importance to human life, or at least not too peripheral. We incline to look with favour on attachments to one's wife, children, parents, friends, home and native land because it is hard to see how these could be anything other than central to any normal person. Human beings have to some extent a given nature, and what is central is also given: we cannot just *choose* that something be central. Hence if someone has immensely strong attach-ments to (say) stamp collecting, or having red hair, or eating off solid silver plates, we feel suspicious and may use terms like 'fanatical' or 'obsessive'. We suspect, perhaps, that the man's natural affections have been blocked or (in a literal sense) perverted. Of course, we should make such judgments with caution; but we recognize, for instance, the differ-ence between a miser's attachment to money and the attachment of a normally prudent man.

2 The attachment should be to something which is, as it were, rich and not empty or boring. There is, as we say, 'more in' some things than others; and this again is not a matter of choice. There is more in the relationship of a successful marriage than there is in a one-night stand, or even in a relationship which (so to speak) amputates a large part of a woman's personality. There is more in people than there is in dogs, more in Shakespeare than in most other writers, more in advanced mathematics than in the mere recitation of one's multiplication tables.

3 The attachment should be to something *outside the self*. We need to love ourselves, but a person capable of love will direct it outwards as well. He

will find, respect and value things *in the world* — not just in his own body or mind — that exist in their own right. That might help us to distinguish the ability to love and relate from some kind of autism. Here the reason 'Because it's mine' is harmless, since it enshrines the feeling of belonging to, or with, something that exists in its own right, independently of my will or desire. We find happiness by contemplating and caring for things that are real, not by dreaming or concocting fantasies.

A good deal more needs to be said about such criteria; but if we accept anything at all on these lines, it is hard to see how either race or culture could be very plausible candidates for educators to emphasize. To make race plausible, one would have (like the Nazis) to build up the idea of race to include all sorts of other goods (the 'Aryan ideal'); this is false to fact, and anyway cheats because it is really the other goods that are worthy of admiration. Race is (1) peripheral, (2) empty, and (as normally used) (3) autistic. Culture is prima facie more plausible, because some cultures at least — not all — may contain much that fits the three criteria: 'the culture of the Italian Renaissance', for instance. But that is, again, a long way from valuing one's own culture just because it is one's own; and we have, and should give our pupils, the chance to opt for cultures other than their own which may contain more that is of merit. In any case, the culture of the *school* (as I hinted above) must presumably be based not upon reflections or microcosms of particular social groups, but upon whatever norms, values and practices are best for education; *that* is what we must, as educators, insist on initiating our pupils into, so that we cannot accept their own particular cultures as having any priority (though we shall not want to trample on them).

## CONCLUSIONS

The general trend of my argument has proved hostile to anything seriously to be called 'multicultural *education*' or 'the *education* of ethnic minorities', because it turns out that there is a mismatch between the concept of education and the use of criteria which have nothing necessarily to do either with learning or with personal security (the criteria of race and culture). Educating people has no logical connections with the use of educational institutions for other purposes — to guard, integrate, socialize, indoctrinate or achieve some other political or social end — any more than it has logical connections with the use of these institutions to store arms, for instance, in time of war or food in time of famine. Not everything that goes on in schools is education.

That is not to say that different sorts of people (including different cultures) may not need different kinds of education: of course they do. Very stupid children, deaf children, children with outstanding musical talent, children who will have to spend a lot of time catching seals in Greenland, indeed every and any real or notional group of children brings its own peculiar endowment to school, and leaves school to go into its own particular milieu. That is a conceptual truth; and it follows that they must be handled differently. Nevertheless, the aims of education remain constant, and must include the idea of helping pupils stand back, in the light of reason, from all particular backgrounds or commitments, so that they may make up their own minds autonomously and on the basis of certain general truths about what is important.

If some government or other agency wishes to use educational institutions for some other purpose, the onus of proof is on it. We should need to be persuaded that, for instance, only bussing Black children to White schools would avoid race riots, or that only certain programmes in the schools would keep blood off the streets of Brixton. Politics is politics: if it wants to invade education (or the practice of science, religion, the arts or any other enterprise), it must declare its hand and prove its case. I do not, myself, regard the political case for multiracial or multicultural education (if that education underlines, as surely it must, criteria of race and culture) as anywhere near proven; and the educational case seems to me logically incoherent.

We may still ask ourselves, at a very practical level, how we are to handle prejudice and other undesirable things that go on in schools as well as outside them; but the answer to this is not far to seek. We might ask ourselves how these things are avoided, or dealt with, in a loving and well organized family. The answer is that the structural and other features of the family *override* the possibilities of prejudice or culture-clash. The children are profoundly engaged in other activities, they invest in the institution, and (if they were to show absurd prejudice) would be reprimanded or punished, and run the risk of forfeiting the love of the parental figures. In any efficiently run family a great many of the problems which beset schools are solved, as it were, *en passant*. Of course, the family is not immune from jealousy, hatred, fear and so forth; but it offers an arena in which these are (1) contained within reasonable bounds, and (2) made subject to education. If we fail to improve the potency of schools, as described above, we shall not be saved by any amount of special educational initiatives under such headings as 'multicultural'.

To put this less sentimentally, in producing categories like 'multicultural education', 'special needs', 'remedial education', 'life skills' and so forth, we become victims to a kind of terror. Like one who patches a leaky boat, we look round in alarm in case certain groups are not being done social justice to, or certain needs not socially catered for. (This is a never-ending task, since there is an infinite number of groups and an infinite number of needs.) Then we invent special educational programmes to cater for them and salve our consciences. Our feelings here are really (and honourably) political, or social, not educational. In doing all this, we lose sight of more important educational categories. 'Multicultural education', for instance, insofar as it means anything clear at all, must presumably be a kind of moral education, and ought to be classified as such: it has something to do with gaining a proper concept of a person, being aware of certain kinds of facts, having the ability to relate to other people (of different backgrounds) in certain ways, etc. (for all this, see Wilson, 1973); just as 'sex education', insofar as it is not just elementary biology, must presumably be a kind of moral or psychological education, or education of the emotions.

The intrusion of political worries into education thus causes us to lose grip both of certain structural or general features necessary to educational institutions (on the analogy of the family), and of certain basic categories of what it is important to learn (on the analogy of Hirst's forms of thought: see Hirst, 1970). These two losses are in process of making education even more of a rarity, and educational institutions even more feeble than they already are. The circle is at present vicious, such feebleness encourages governments and other agencies to increase the pressure and hence disable the institutions still further, particularly by displaying a lack of trust. We may be able to reverse this, by thinking hard about the concept of education and what it implies; but I am not sanguine about this, since thinking hard about concepts is not a popular activity.

**REFERENCES**

Hare, R.M. (1981) *Moral Thinking*, Oxford, Oxford University Press.
Hirst, P.H. (1970), with R.S. Peters, *The Logic of Education*, London, Routledge and Kegan Paul.
Mishler, M.M. (1978) 'Education and Identity', *Oxford Review of Education*, 4, pp. 197–203.
Peters, R.S. (1966) *Ethics and Education*, London, Allen and Unwin.
Wilson, J. (1972) *Practical Methods of Moral Education*, London, Heinemann.
Wilson, J. (1973) *The Assessment of Morality*, Windsor, NFER.

# 16. Prejudice and Moral Education

FRITZ K. OSER

How many times can a man turn his head pretending that he just doesn't see ...?
(Bob Dylan)

## DEVELOPMENT AND PREJUDICE: A PROMISE WAITING FOR REDEMPTION

In a recent experiment we confronted children, adolescents and adults with nine photographs of different male persons on a tableau. The appearance of these men differs greatly. They wear dissimilar clothes, have different hair styles, their faces vary in shape and expression. One of them looks very sinister, has long hair and a cigarette in the corner of the mouth; another has a moustache and is very skinny; one is a laughing Black person, one a policeman, one a priest; one of the men carries glasses while talking, another resembles Fidel Castro. We told our subjects that one of these persons is a criminal, and we asked them to guess who it could be.

With respect to the smaller children, aged 6 and 7, the results are very clearcut: these children made their decision without further questions and without hesitation. They were sure what a criminal looks like. Here is an extract from one of the interviews:

Q.: Which one do you think is the criminal?
A.: This one [points to photograph No. 9].
Q.: Why do you think it is this man?
A.: Because this one looks like many of them ... or this one, too [points to another photograph].
Q.: Why do you believe it could be No. 4?
A.: From my books. In children's books or elsewhere they are mostly like this.
Q.: Yes?
A.: But this one here could also be one [points to No. 6].
Q.: And why do you think this one could be a criminal?
A.: Because, because he, eh, he has such long hair.
Q.: Try to tell me exactly what you mean.
A.: Because he looks so special, like a thief.
Q.: You mentioned his long hair; could you say that again, please?

*A.*:   Eh, with the face ... it looks like this, he looks so dangerous.
*Q.*:   ... And what do you think these three men have done, what kind of deed?
*A.*:   Maybe they stole money, or, eh ... [laughs].

This experiment was conducted following partly the experimental design of a study by Hofstätter (1962) that will be reported later in this chapter. It shows that children of this age may sound very prejudiced. Normally, this is not because of negative socialization effects, however, but because they lack reversibility of categories. Their 'prejudice' is caused by the fact that they believe in the outside, physical or expressive aspects of the phenomenon only. They are unable to combine intention with expression and to separate internal features, such as character traits, from the external appearance of a person.


## EDUCATIONAL MEANS TO REDUCE PREJUDICE: PRELIMINARY THESES

The conclusions from the above research example lead to a number of theses that could provide a basis for an educational programme aiming at a reduction of prejudice in social reasoning.

1   It seems that any education to reduce prejudice should be related to a developmental theory. Lower social cognitive stages are more susceptible to prejudice than higher stages. The structural theories of cognitive, social-cognitive and moral development can serve as a link for such a connection.

2   The fostering of unprejudiced action (e.g., sharing without consideration of racial, ethnic or social factors, etc.) in educational settings can be based on direct stimulation of action tendencies as well as on developmental growth. From a developmental standpoint, good action must not necessarily wait for the emergence of cognitive preconditions. Thus a child can learn to act free from prejudice without understanding in a deep sense why prejudice is unethical, i.e., without having attained a level of full ethical reversibility.

3   Education for tolerance and understanding can only succeed in educational settings that are informed by high moral standards warranting an unprejudiced social climate. Such high moral standards can only be vitalized where a rational, discourse oriented attitude among the members of the community is cultivated, a major example for such an endeavour being the 'just community' concept of democratic schooling. Morality and unprejudiced ways of social interaction can never be secured once and for all time by law and authoritarian decision-making; they cannot be enforced primarily by means of social control. Rather, a vivid situational context must be created in which processes of moral searching can be stimulated and discursive strategies of interaction and problem-solving can be made possible.

4   Social psychological research gives strong suggestions as to what factors can help to reduce prejudice in society (for an overview, see Gergen and Gergen, 1986, pp. 149–156): intense social contact between alien groups,

consciousness-raising experiences and nomological knowledge transformation, development of social identity without a need to define oneself or the ingroup in terms of scapegoating and outgroup hostility (as attempts to counterbalance lowered self-esteem or sense of inferiority). As will be shown, these factors are most clearly provided in two specific models of moral and social education, the just community approach and the complex approach to moral education suggested by Solomon and collaborators.

In the final section these four theses are further differentiated. In advance, however, an overview of the major approaches to moral education in general is provided to indicate which is most likely to enhance tolerance and to diminish prejudice.

## APPROACHES TO MORAL EDUCATION AND CRITERIA FOR THEIR EVALUATION

A look at various literature reviews and descriptions of the field (e.g., Hersh *et al.*, 1980; Morrill, 1980; Arbuthnot and Faust, 1981; Beck, 1983; Chazan, 1985; Oser, 1986; Oser and Althof, 1989; Leming, 1989) reveals at least five global approaches and two special models of moral education. The general approaches considered here are (1) the progressive approach in the Deweyan tradition ('development as the aim of education'; Kohlberg and Mayer, 1972); (2) the romantic approach, particularly the values clarification movement (Simon *et al.*, 1972); (3) the norm transmission approach or the traditional concept of character education (e.g., Educational Policies Commission, 1951; Faust and Feingold, 1969; Holmes, 1980); (4) McPhail's 'Startline' and 'Lifeline' projects in Britain (McPhail *et al.*, 1972, 1978); and (5) the discourse approach. The most interesting additional, unique models are: (6) Kohlberg's just community concept (Power *et al.*, 1989; Oser, 1988, 1989); and (7) the Child Development Project in San Ramon, California (Solomon *et al.*, 1989). In terms of goals and methods, additional concepts in this area can normally be subsumed under one of these approaches or models or be considered as a combination of several of them.

To evaluate these seven forms of moral education, I shall outline some criteria for a powerful global concept. First, we need a developmental frame; autonomous morality can only be achieved through a number of transformations of moral cognitive structures that are related to concepts of the good and the evil, the right and the wrong. Second, an action-related frame must be provided; actual conditions for real moral action must exist — in the simple sense that 'good' acting has its proper chance and is not automatically disillusioned. Third, opportunities of norm generation and norm integration must be provided; moral norms can become more understandable through role-taking and empathy training. Fourth, procedural ways of moral decision-making must be emphasized; the evaluation of individual claims and the search for the best solution to a moral problem can function as a facilitator for moral development when it is combined with a willingness to understand the needs of those who are involved in the conflict and with a willingness to enter a respectful and open discourse among all interested parties.

These are the minimal conditions for effective moral education in families and classrooms. The developmental frame helps us in considering typical features of evolving world-views, and thus keeps us from judging children's opinions in a prejudiced way ourselves. Knowledge with respect to developmental facts is a precondition for developmental support in educational settings, aiming at a form of social and moral reasoning that is more and more reversible and differentiated. Considering the action dimension increases the probability that students care for each other in practical real-life situations. The norm integration rule is necessary for reflecting the content of social standards (and for evaluating them according to their degree of prejudice) and to regulate social and interpersonal action. The quest for a discursive mode of decision-making aims at warranting a humane, impartial and just (that is, unprejudiced) criterion for interpersonal problem-solving.

In the following, the seven approaches and models of moral education will be evaluated against the background of these minimal conditions. On this basis I will then relate this discussion to the task of reducing the emergence of prejudiced thought.

## Development as the Aim of Education

The first approach was 'development as the aim of education'. The main goal here is to stimulate higher, more complex and differentiated forms of reasoning, the stimulation being oriented to the next higher stage on a developmental scale, like the Kohlberg scheme of moral judgment development. To reach this goal, children, adolescents and adults must be confronted with manifold conflictual situations (dilemmas), be they artificial or of a real-life type (Walker *et al.*, 1987); students must be confronted with others' views and with reasoning of different stages (Turiel, 1966); they can be trained to use transactional argumentation strategies (Berkowitz *et al.*, 1987). Meta-analyses of intervention studies (e.g., Schläfli, 1985) show that these educational strategies allow for significant progress in moral stage development in a major portion of subjects, provided that the intervention is not only of a short-term type (the effects of programmes that have been conducted over about three months do not differ from those of long-term interventions). With adults, it is easier to reach significant effects; in work with younger children educators must be prepared for a cognitive ceiling inhibiting further moral reasoning development.

Let us make use of the criteria outlined above. In this approach there is a good possibility of a transformation toward a higher (more autonomous) stage of moral reasoning; but at least in the 'traditional' cognitive developmental moral education programmes there is no focus on moral action, no attempt to integrate normative orientations; procedural problem-solving strategies may play a role, but they must not have any real meaning to the subject him- and herself. In fact, even if Kohlberg shows that there is what he calls a 'monotonic' relationship between moral judgment development and the increase of morally responsible action (Kohlberg and Candee, 1984), from an educational standpoint it is important to see that it cannot be warranted that certain action decisions necessarily result from certain levels of moral reasoning competence.

Kohlberg himself has self-critically renounced his early focus on the cognitive and formal aspects in moral education. From the mid-1970s on he emphasized the integration of education for moral reasoning development in a wider frame of real-life morality, of moral action and of norm integration. Autonomous moral judgment competence without integration in life produces the danger of cynical segmentation of life spheres and of moral hypocrisy; the educational significance of simple classroom moral discussion programmes can easily be overestimated.

## Values Clarification

The second approach listed above was 'values clarification'. Its main goal is to support people in processes of evolving and evaluating their own values, to stimulate higher consciousness in dealing with value questions. Raths *et al.* (1966, p. 30) state that something can only be considered a value if it is chosen (1) freely, (2) from alternatives and (3) after thoughtful consideration of each alternative's consequences, if the subject (4) cherishes the choice and is (5) willing to affirm it publicly, if s/he is (6) acting in accordance with the choice, and (7) not only once but repeatedly. Values clarification programmes train students and adults by use of a series of group dynamic exercises designed to reveal the participants' value systems and to give subjects a chance to rethink personal priorities.

When evaluated on the basis of the three criteria from the first section, the concept of values clarification lacks a developmental frame to aid understanding of the emergence of particular forms of value reasoning, and it lacks a distinction between moral values on the one hand and personal, aesthetic or conventional values on the other. While the value definition quoted above emphasizes the action side, the educational strategies typically do not. Evaluation of norms from any objective standard is not among the goals of this approach, as is norm integration. Discussions in groups and classrooms focus on exchange, but not on the procedural search for a consensus with respect to the most moral or just solution. As to this approach, the only criterion for the adequacy of a value is personal conviction. Thus the fundamental standpoint of the values clarification movement is relativistic. In its overall feature it is an incomplete approach to moral education; the social reality of life worlds (in family, school, workplace and surrounding society) is not opened to moral scrutiny, the constitution of a moral self is not a main target of educational enterprises.

## Character Education

A third approach was called 'character education'. Traditionally, the most prominent means of this approach were preaching of values, modelling (influencing children by good examples), training and practising of given standards; indoctrination was not considered a threat to the educational goals. Even though the non-efficiency of those strategies was proved by numerous studies, beginning with Hartshorne and May's (1928) large-scale investigation, the idea of normative transmission has had its protagonists time and again (e.g., Burton, 1984). The major weaknesses of this method are a lack of justification of the learning process, of the central norms and virtues themselves, and of the interpersonal constellation between norm-giver and norm-taker. Punishment, threat, appeals to conscience and self-punishment tendencies, non-rational persuasion and indoctrination are bad means, even if the goals can be justified as good.

Furthermore, the value transmission concept normally is not embedded in a developmental frame; action is only conceived as practical conformity to norms or rules but is not subject to cooperative reflection. Evidently, there is no focus on procedural problem-solving, but, instead, the belief that norm integration or 'internalization' is a matter of mere instruction.

### The Consideration Model

The fourth approach is characterized by its focus on interpersonal sensitivity and respect. Peter McPhail was the director of two large-scale moral education projects funded by the British School Council. On the basis of research regarding children's and adolescents' needs and expectations in their social life two detailed sets of curriculum materials were constructed and published under the title 'Lifeline' and 'Startline' (McPhail *et al.*, 1972, 1978). The theoretical underpinnings of this approach are rather weak, though the material itself is creative and abundant. The authors try to show how students can develop a 'considerate lifestyle' (a term that mingles moral issues with other dimensions of social behaviour). A variety of methods is proposed, including role-playing, creative attempts at social understanding and problem-solving, analysis of novels, short stories and documentary reports. The emotional component is emphasized more strongly than the rational or cognitive component of morality; the approach is oriented to a concept of being a good person while more or less denying the moral reasoning dimension.

Nonetheless, the four criteria are partially applied in this model. There is an implicit (though not elaborated) developmental frame insofar as the authors have investigated a lot of real-life problem situations children and adolescents have to face and have used those experiences as a database for their educational material. Classroom strategies are directed toward exchange and a cooperative search for right action; the legitimacy of particular problem solutions is also an issue in role-plays and position games. Norm integration by active participation in decision-making regarding school affairs is a very strong point in McPhail's general concept. However, development towards a procedural stance in moral reasoning and action is less visible in this conception.

### The Discourse Approach

The fifth approach, called the discourse model, is procedural by its very nature. From the standpoint of this approach, whatever is taught, discussed, proposed, whatever conflicts are reflected and opened for some kind of resolution, everyone involved should be viewed as having the potential for autonomy, commitment, reliability and true moral competence (cf. Oser, 1986; Oser *et al.*, 1989). The coordination of validity claims in a decision-making situation becomes a just procedure in itself when each participant is encouraged to consider empathically the best for all others.

As introduced by Habermas (e.g., 1981) and Apel (e.g., 1988), 'discourse' is a central concept in deontological post-Kantian ethics. Related to educational processes, one can understand it as an ideal form of open, impartial moral argumentation against which all actual and restricted forms of moral argumentation should be assessed. In dialogical problem-solving all participants should contribute equally, and their truthfulness and commitment should be presupposed. The discourse perspective to moral education then focuses on the stimulation of those elements that describe moral discourse in general. It emphasizes that moral and values education should remain a cognitive, reflective enterprise and that justice, human freedom and dignity should be the indispensable categories of each moral evaluation.

While the concept of 'moral discourse' has been introduced as an ideal, there are practical implications for everyday teaching. Whatever we do in moral education (transferring moral knowledge, stimulating moral reasoning and action competence, etc.), the student should be supported in developing his or her personal point of view and at the same time considering the other's point of view, in order to establish the basis for engaging in a dialogical exchange. He or she should learn to prepare for moral decision-making by learning that the experience of concrete disagreement cannot abrogate a rational practice of communication. On the other hand, teachers must learn what it means to presuppose students' reliability, truthfulness, commitment and interest in just solutions in everyday interaction — even if their logical or social-cognitive competences still lack maturity, and even if uncontrolled, irrational or strategic behaviour still is predominant in certain situations.

Discourse oriented pedagogy is directed towards ethical sensitivity, awareness of possible consequences of acting, the justification of moral claims, the implementation of collectively elaborated solutions. Justice and interpersonal respect are central when moral rules and principles are reflected upon. Growing competence in the use of moral discourse components enables a person to apply those moral principles and rules to decision-making processes. Therefore, whatever teaching methods are intended, they have to be selected prior to the application, and with the discourse in mind, in order to be compatible. There must be a congruence between means and ends, there can be no inculcation or indoctrination of moral values or of the discourse idea itself. But teachers have to be aware that there is a difference between concrete decision-making situations and moral discourse. The discourse is always a step back from the reality of the situation, which is necessarily bounded by time and other pressures — a decision must be made, an action taken, here and now. The discourse stays an ideal form of solving a moral problem; on a concrete level it serves as a criterion for the justifiability of educational strategies.

Evaluated with respect to the above general criteria, the discourse approach (1) does have a developmental frame because it builds upon 'progressive', developmental notions of moral education; furthermore, the capacity even of children to take responsibility and to participate actively is stressed. This approach (2) shows a relative lack of the action dimension, although fundamentally it emphasizes that effective moral learning takes place in relevant situations where true moral decisions with real consequences are made. The discourse approach (3) also cares about norm integration only implicitly, whereas (4) procedural morality is its core notion.

These five approaches have now to be questioned with respect to their power to reduce prejudice. In doing this, I only implicitly refer back to the social-psychological and sociological literature on the nature of prejudice and the factors affecting its occurrence and stabilization (see, for instance, Allport's, 1954, classic; see also Adorno *et al.*, 1950; Bandura *et al.*, 1961; Panahi, 1980; and many textbook introductions, notably Gergen and Gergen, 1986). While I would reject some positions of other authors (e.g., the non-developmentalism of most social psychology), I would stress that this contribution is not to be a critical review of this literature but a first attempt to integrate its essential features with viewpoints on moral education.

## MORAL EDUCATION APPROACHES AND THEIR POWER TO REDUCE PREJUDICE

Which moral educational approach is most effective in reducing prejudice?

### 'Development as the Aim of Education' and Reduction of Prejudice

Very little research has been done concerning the developmental aspects of prejudice. This is a failure, in my view, because even if most children and adolescents do behave in a non-racist, non-aggressive, helping and caring way most of the time, these behaviour tendencies are rooted in sand as long as the current developmental level does not allow for a deep and reversible substantiation of the moral necessity of such behaviour on behalf of the student him- or herself. A direct dealing with issues of prejudice should be a crucial aspect of educational work. We cannot wait for the emergence of mature moral reasoning to begin with attempts to reduce prejudiced thinking. We cannot resign ourselves to stimulate moral reasoning development. Instead, we have to face the delicate task of framing children's practical readiness to replace prejudice by tolerance.

On the other hand, it is a fact that higher stage moral reasoning is more and more incompatible with prejudice. One reason is that higher stages include more reversible, more differentiated thinking, more awareness that only universal principles can give guidance in the diversity of practical values and contexts. The higher the moral judgment stage, the less differences in status, sex or race count in issues of justice — for instance, in decisions regarding the distribution of resources. Full impartiality of judgment can only be expected, if at all, at Stage 5 (Kohlberg scheme), where systematic reversibility of perspectives is achieved and 'ideal role-taking' is understood as a major means of arriving at the moral point of view. However, each structural change in moral reasoning is an important step towards these features of Stage 5. Thus it makes sense to stimulate structurally higher forms of reflection in the educational process.

There is another reason why the growth of moral reasoning competence is educationally desirable: the relationship of moral judgment level and moral action tendencies mentioned above. There is much support for what Kohlberg called the 'monotonic relationship' between increases in moral reasoning and the practical readiness to consider or abandon certain courses of action (Kohlberg and Candee,

1984; Blasi, 1980, 1983; Kutnik, 1985; Oser, 1987, 1989). If the monotonic relation hypothesis is right, there is reason to believe that as moral reasoning becomes more and more reversible, concrete judgment and action will become less affected by egocentric or ethnocentric or group-centred views. Whenever an action is preceded by reflection, the higher judgment stage is in itself a help in structuring the situation in a less racist, intolerant, unpeaceful way.

A developmental conception of the evolution of prejudice in social thinking can also help educators to understand the way children construct reality, and thus can prevent them from oversimplification in separating the 'nice guys' and the 'bad guys'. We should be careful not to judge children's thinking merely in categories of personality differences. A developmental view would interpret prejudiced thinking in terms of the natural properties of reasoning stages, and would look for the implications of Stage 2 tit-for-tat reasoning or of Stage 3's intertwining of the morally good with group interests. Children will not learn to orient themselves in the complicated world of values if they are not allowed to make their own experiences, to evaluate the implications of their spontaneous judgments, and eventually to overcome their egocentric thinking in a structural transformation.

Rokeach's (1956) assumption that it is not the 'preaching' of equality and liberty that is significant, but the mobility of thinking in practising these virtues (which also refers to the fact that the 'preachers' themselves may be extremely intolerant), can also be informed by a developmental viewpoint. How does such mobility (flexibility, situational awareness) emerge? The developmental position is most important when we attempt to arrive at a comprehensive understanding of the child's thinking. Domain-specific analyses did not generate a clear picture of prejudiced thinking. We can only say that at lower stages children refer to the physical (superficial) features and observable consequences of action in evaluating persons and deeds, whereas later they make more and more use of psychological knowledge and intentional criteria. While this holds strongly for face-to-face interactions, on a more abstract level of social judgment stereotyping may last for a long while. Generalized concepts of social groups arise, the use of 'us' and 'them' categories allows for conceiving foreigners, outsiders and every sort of alien people as potential enemies. Later, social thinking (with respect to moral and conventional standards) is regulated by a societal perspective. While a certain degree of diversity may be tolerable or even desirable under the perspective of the stability and integrating force of the societal system, certain specifics of personal or cultural lifestyle are viewed as potentially endangering to the system, and thus to one's self-understanding as a member of the system. Only on the highest stages does human dignity become incontestable. From a principled but not absolutist standpoint, human beings are viewed as equal in their right to pursue happiness and self-actualization; they are viewed as equally valuable and just, notwithstanding differences in personal and group values.

From a developmental standpoint there is reason to be cautious with respect to the results of much social-psychological research. If, for instance, members of the ingroup develop self-glorifying attitudes (cf. Brewer, 1974; Triandis *et al.*, 1982), this is associated not only with context factors and social pressure but also with the developmental state of persons within this group.

These glimpses help us to understand why a certain developmental precondition is necessary for education aiming at the reduction of prejudice. A later section refers more directly to the question of how effective the classical Kohlbergian dilemma discussion strategy is in cutting the roots of prejudice.

### Values Clarification and the Reduction of Prejudice

My hypothesis is that values clarification — as presented in the current instructional programmes of the values clarification group — does not help much to reduce prejudice. To clarify personal values does not mean to change values in the direction of tolerance and interpersonal understanding. Having a clear concept of what is important to the self does not mean that one gives up stereotyped ideas about alleged differences between self and others, between 'my people' and 'strangers'. Hofstätter (1962) conducted a classical experiment that may be relevant here. He confronted subjects with portraits of several persons and asked them to judge which of them had a 'face like a government official'. In a second step, subjects were assembled in a group and had to decide who among themselves had faces like government officials and who probably had such a person among his or her relatives. Typically, subjects did cooperate in the first step of the experiment, but not in the second. The disclosure of personal values and concepts can be really perplexing for people, but it does not necessarily affect their stereotypes. Consciousness is one precondition of a transformation of the value concept, but it is not sufficient in setting this transformation in motion.

### Character Education and the Reduction of Prejudice

Character education can have a positive influence on a child if — and only if — the value of tolerance is applied in real-life situations, that is, when it can be experienced and reflected upon. But in general, these conditions do not hold. Typically, tolerance is preached as one of many virtues, and prejudice is condemned as one of many vices. Attitudes are categorized as 'good' and 'no good' from the beginning. The probability of a transfer to the level of personal experience, doubt and action is very small. Practical efforts at non-rational inculcation tend to create a hiatus between the 'thou shalt' messages and the practice of social life as perceived by students. Moreover, virtues like 'tolerance' are only consensual as long as they are vague. When it comes to concrete rules of acting, the meaning of 'tolerance' tends to be understood in very different ways. When preachers preach values that are too general to become immediately relevant and then interpret them contradictorily, education gives way to hedonistic and relativistic countermovements. The most important failure of this approach, however, is its ignorance of children's active structuring and restructuring tendencies. If children are not given the opportunity to construct, deplore and evaluate norms themselves, they are cheated of an opportunity for real growth. When they are put off instead with advice and commands, traditions and conventions, their moral reasoning potential is repressed, be the norms in question more or less authoritarian, or more or less democratic. A main characteristic of indoctrination is its bypassing of rationality and the need for justification. When subjects' active rationality does not get its way, words and deeds can easily become very distant things, and prejudice is not far off.

## The Consideration Model and the Reduction of Prejudice

The 'Startline' and 'Lifeline' curricula and instructional materials put much emphasis on interpersonal sensitivity, consideration of viewpoints and care for other persons' needs and circumstances. Morality is defined as an encompassing 'considerate lifestyle' (McPhail *et al.*, 1972, p. 3) based on flexibility of attitudes, imagination and interpersonal commitment. Obviously, these ideas are in strong opposition to every form of prejudice, stereotyping and discrimination. However, the consideration model does not go far enough. Moral reflection and problem-solving in situations with conflicting values are not stressed. As in the values clarification approach, a clear distinction between moral and non-moral aspects of social situations cannot be found; thus it is not very likely that students will conclude that prejudice is not just 'not nice' but immoral. McPhail's psychology is more or less based on a conventional conception of virtues and vices that tends to equate certain social attitudes with moral maturity while ignoring issues of justice. After passing through the Schools Council curriculum, students can be expected to be relatively immune against forms of active discrimination against other people in face-to-face interactions. I am not very sure, however, that they will have the reasoning competence and the active decision-making experiences needed to deal with complex and more abstract societal issues calling for principles of justice as a guide for procedures of conflict solution

## The Discourse Approach

The notion of discourse is an absolute precondition for the understanding of other persons in conflict situations calling for some kind of negotiation. If subjects are able to participate actively in decision-making processes as well as to presuppose a decent amount of responsibility, commitment and truthfulness, this is in itself a force leading to mutual understanding and a sense of obligation to put into practice what was found to be the right thing to do. Discourse is communicative morality, and communicative morality stands in strong opposition to outgroup labellings, discrimination, social deprivation and any kind of action guided by jealousy or hatred. As soon as a person is oriented towards a fundamental discourse attitude, he or she can no longer subscribe to material or cultural separation, to racial, ethnic, social or political repression, to violent forms of conflict solution. In this sense, the degree of discourse — as procedural morality — is *the* measure of success in superseding prejudice as a starting point of social action. To move towards a discourse orientation means to open oneself to the needs and sorrows of other people concerned in attempting to find a moral point of view in the vast realm of contradictory claims. Viewed this way, the discourse model is not an approach comparable to the others discussed here; rather, it is a state of readiness and of offering humanity to human beings and courage to the burdened.

## THE JUST COMMUNITY APPROACH AND THE REDUCTION OF PREJUDICE

Prejudice is not only an attitude but also forms a part of the cognitive map that guides situational judgment and action in the diversities of social life. If we do not want prejudiced judging to play this role, we have to help children in developing more sound strategies of orientation in the social world. To build up a map that serves as a useful guide and at the same time avoids stereotypical shortcuts is a challenging educational task. This task means that we have to help children from an early age not to distinguish in terms of race, sex, social status and brightness when judging the worth, attitude or performance of a person. We want children not to make this kind of distinction even before they can fully understand what could be wrong in making that distinction.

There is a lot of support for the assumption that social experience is the major condition for the growth of interpersonal understanding and tolerance — given that this experience is of a certain kind, namely, cooperative and not competitive, empathy enhancing and not empathy undermining. Interpersonal care, truthfulness and justice do not develop in classroom situations characterized by mere talk about values or by self-centred reflection on personal values. They do not develop without active interpersonal exchange, dialogue and negotiation. They do not develop when students are deprived of real influence in the formation of their social worlds. Children and adolescents need the possibility to participate in real decision-making processes; hence the democratization of school settings is a major factor in students' social and moral development.

A most interesting attempt to combine aspects of interpersonal understanding and participatory experiences under a moral education perspective is the 'just community' approach put forward by Lawrence Kohlberg and collaborators. What are the special elements in a just community school? I shall give an example to illustrate the educational focus and procedural structures from a school in West Germany where I serve as a scientific project counsellor.

As in comparable programmes, the so-called community meeting is the core institution of this just community school. It takes place every two or three weeks and is attended by the whole faculty and about 120 students. Discussion is directed by members of an agenda committee, typically by two students and two teachers.

> Participants meet in the assembly hall; teachers and students from different grades mix, there is no block seating. The agenda is proposed by the committee. Today, incidents of theft in school will be the main issue. Those students who introduce the topic express their sorrow; they are concerned about minor and major thefts happening time and again. Some of the participating students describe their own experience of being robbed; they talk about how it felt to find out that a nice pen, a precious jacket or a purse were missing. After a period of discussion someone suggests establishing a common fund to pay damages to a certain degree, to decrease the harm to victims of theft. This suggestion stirs up heated and emotional responses. If it is accepted, everyone would be obliged to make a contribution to the fund, be it only some pennies. The pro and con debate is transferred to smaller discussion groups for a while, and then continued in the general session. The con-

troversy is hot-tempered. There are students who emphasize that we belong together, that we should help one another. Others argue that this decision would eventually increase the problem: everyone, including the thieves themselves, could show up and report something missing so that amends will be made.

The participants become more and more engaged in the debate. The teachers are split in their opinion, too. It is a general experience from just community schools that in most cases there is no block voting — teachers on one side, students on the other — but a diversity of opinions among both groups. Today, some of the teachers plead for the support fund. Others make the same reservation as some of the students: the danger of misuse. Others argue that the law does not give this assembly the competence to force anyone to contribute to the fund. Notably, some of the students respond that this argument shows how much the school still lacks a sense of community, how little one cares for the other. On the other hand, many participants are not content with this line of argument. For them, cases of theft are no one's business except from the two people directly concerned.

It comes to a vote. A relatively small majority succeeds over a relatively large minority: the establishment of the fund is accepted. The close result of the vote makes it immediately evident that further clarifying decisions are needed. Many of those decisions are made: a lost property office is installed; rules of control are decided upon to make sure that something really was robbed and not simply forgotten somewhere. Nonetheless, there is still much agitation among the students. What about minority rights? Is it just when those who voted against this decision are forced to share in following it through? I try to explain that democracy cannot function without consensus on this point. But I also draw their attention to the right of democratic recourse against decisions. One possibility could be a campaign to collect signatures for a renewed discussion of the issue at the next community meeting. This line of reasoning sounds intelligible to my discussion partners. In each classroom the event is debated again. Many students grimly fight for a motion of recourse. They collect signatures, try to convince comrades and teachers.

At the beginning of the next community meeting a student reads the motion of recourse. The agenda committee was prepared to accept it without a formal vote in order to avoid a display of opposition. However, the student who introduced the recourse insists on a vote. The motion of recourse is passed. Now some of those students who were in favor of the fund show that they are prepared, too. They present their reasons once again. The same with the opponents. Again, the meeting breaks up into small discussion groups. I join a group of seven students, all of them against the fund. When I make my appeal for a sense of community, they call me a utopian, a dreamer. Their experiences, they explain, have not been like this. They have been deceived more than once. How can I expect that there will be no misuse of the money they are to collect among themselves? I try to explain that there must be someone who starts doing good, that there are situations when you just have to act in order to help someone: a physician helping the victim of an accident does not have to check if this person might be a murderer or a terrorist.

In the full assembly the discussion seesaws fiercely, though in a disciplined manner; 120 students and thirty teachers are in suspense, following the discussion in a most motivated atmosphere. At the peak of the debate a student makes a mediating proposal that turns the crisis towards the direction of community progress and consensual resolution. It is proposed that money should be collected for the victims of theft, but that there should be no easy access to the fund. Instead, it should be decided from case to case if the respective person really needs help. This would, the student explains, give individual members of the school community more freedom to participate in the evaluation and in the decision whether the current case is 'true' or 'false'. This suggestion has a very relieving effect on the atmosphere in the assembly hall. Spontaneously, it is proposed to decide upon this proposal immediately. But the crisis has not yet been overcome fully. A lengthy discussion on the mode of decision-making evolves. Finally, it is decided with a vast majority that a voluntary collection of money should take place to help victims of theft under specific circumstances. Evidently, this is less than the revised prior resolution wanted; but evidently, too, this is the optimal result given the state of the community.

Relieved and exhausted at the same time, teachers and students stand in groups in the corridors and in the school yard for a long while after the meeting, discussing what has happened. The students felt that they had made *their* decision; there was a strong feeling that today this school has also been *their* school — a place where they have a say, where significant issues can be decided upon in a just manner. The teachers discuss what they could have done better, where pedagogical failures might have happened. All of them are excited: they have had the experience that these meetings make school life a lively matter, give opportunities to understanding the thinking of individuals more fully, elaborate and elucidate features and groups of opinion, construct common plans of action and allow the possibility of developing shared norms.

This example shows the principle behind the just community model, which is directed to moral education as well as to school reform. When students get a real chance to participate, to contribute to decision-making and to take responsibility, they perceive the school as a space of social living with which they can identify. This social space can become a source for the growth of democratic behaviour, pro-social attitudes, moral reasoning and shared norms, i.e., a self-constructed, lived system of values and rules that are conceived of as binding, because they are understood. Just communities do not claim to be 'just' by mere definition, and they are certainly not more just than many other communities. The notion is programmatic: justice is created by the community members themselves, on the basis of a participatory model of democracy.

It is neither necessary nor possible to elaborate on the rationale and the principles of this approach here (for further descriptions, see Oser, 1988, 1989; Power *et al.*, 1989). Its most important psychological elements are: the genesis of accepted norms through democratic participation; the identification with a school community through responsibility sharing; the connection between judgment and action through community commitment and control; the development towards higher moral judgment stages through controversial negotiations and thought processes; and the enhancement of role-taking capacities through real interactional problem-solving. Various studies show significant positive effects with respect to all of these variables.

The prejudice issue is very closely related to these variables, as can be shown by the following example. In the school introduced above, a very important discussion about culture specifics and the meaning of the word 'integration' took place when the students of the Turkish minority (children of so-called 'guestworkers', actually immigrants, most of them born in Germany) for the first time raised their hands and began to fight for their cultural rights. These students had not participated in a school-wide festivity, and they were being criticized and even insulted for their collective absence. The reason for this absence was that the party took place on a Friday, the Muslim feast-day. The Turkish children stood up and explained their behaviour, arguing convincingly and suggesting politely that the whole problem could be settled and the school community could have common experiences if events like this took place on some other day. The effect of this intervention was enormous: 120 German children not only learnt much about the significance of religious traditions within another ethnic and cultural background, but also understood the message of having been thoughtless, unwilling to discuss and prejudiced, and of having lacked a sense of community in their planning and in their reactions to their Turkish comrades.

The process of the just community life confronted the students with manifold issues they had to resolve in a conscious, differentiated, impartial, nonstereotypical way in order to let the community grow. Members gained understanding of global differences between 'the' girls and 'the' boys, 'the' teachers and 'the' students, 'the' older kids and 'the' small ones, between parents, teachers, administration, principal and themselves as to their realities, complexity and respective history. Students — like teachers — had to learn to consider more viewpoints, not to let themselves be led by pre-fixed assumptions and priorities. The organigram of the just community participation and decision-making structure (Figure 1) shows that one and the same problem (if it is important enough) can be at stake in a number of different social constellations and on different levels of analysis, ensuring that there will be no easy and premature 'settling' of the problem that is often more likely to stabilize than to break up prejudiced reasoning.

Problems can be made the issue of a classroom dilemma discussion (which is designed to promote the development of social understanding and moral reasoning), the matter for the Agenda Committee (concerned with the preparation of the community meeting and authorized to choose topics according to their significance), for the Just Community Meeting, where everyone is involved and definite steps towards responsible action must be taken; the Fairness Committee is charged with following through decisions and has to deal with cases of transgression; the Faculty Meeting not only allows for discussion of pedagogical issues (goals and methods) but also provides teachers with an opportunity to reflect on their stereotypes or openness themselves.

In the just community process many of the dangerous effects described in the social-psychological literature can be diminished or avoided: e.g., the effect of 'illusory correlation' (Hamilton *et al.*, 1985), where information that opposes a certain stereotyping is avoided and the stereotype itself is protected against any counter-idea, or the effect of group protection and outgroup exclusion (Reid,

*Figure 1.   Core Components of the Just Community Model*

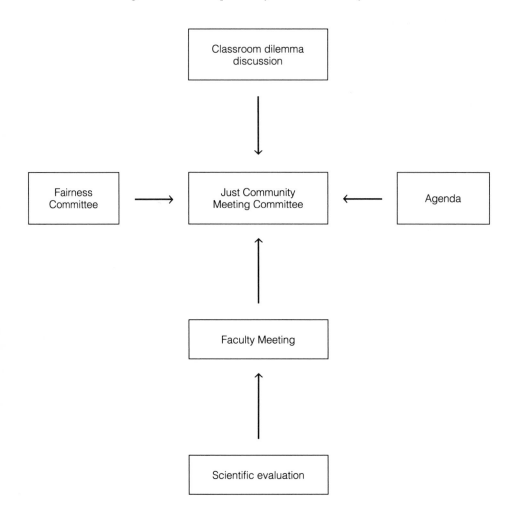

1983; Mackie and Cooper, 1984; Wilder, 1984), where people adopt the opinion of a party or group they belong to or would like to belong to, or the self-diminishing effect, where a person likes the preferred toys, clothing, food, etc. of the other person because of identity doubts (Clark and Clark, 1947, found that Black children chose White baby dolls for play because they found them to symbolize something nicer, healthier, richer than Black dolls), the well-known effects of labelling, or, finally, negative expectation effects (familiar as 'Pygmalion' effects, cf. Rosenthal and Jacobson, 1968; Brophy and Good, 1974), where uncommunicated expectations in the behaviour or academic performance of someone lead to self-fulfilling prophecies. The just community is a place where self-esteem can be enhanced, where social contact among all group members is increased, where authoritarian leaders have no chance to push others in the direction of their own prejudices, where an individual conscience and a public consciousness is built up to oppose discrimination against minorities in thinking and behaviour. Thus the just community can provide an ideal surrounding for the reduction of prejudice. The interactive setting urges everyone to interrelate in a true way, to respect human dignity, to try to understand every (and even an apparently absurd) position and hence to abandon racial, ethnocentric, sexist or other clichés.

The major difference between the just community approach and many other approaches is that active participation in the formation and development of school life is made possible by institutions like the community meeting. In his book, *Better Schools: A Value Perspective*, Beck (1990) provides some relevant suggestions. In the chapter entitled 'Dealing with Racism in Schools' it is recommended that the school structure be changed by increasing the racial mix among teaching and administrative staff and in the student body, and caring about the language people use in communicating with one another. A further means, says Beck, is to focus more heavily on the particular features of other cultures. Additionally, it is recommended that textbooks be carefully chosen and lacking racial bias, and that curricula be checked for racial bias. Beck summarizes the aim of those revisions: 'The central teaching task of the school in this area, I believe, is to challenge systematically the notion that racial distinctions are important and that some races are superior to others' (1990, p. 103).

These recommendations are acceptable, but they lack the active component emphasized with respect to the just community programme. In a just community school there is much more active role-taking, active striving for consensus (including consensual rules for interracial relationships), and stimulation of active consideration of each other's feelings and needs. If we want an unprejudiced attitude to become a basis of everyday social acting, we must provide students with the possibility (and the challenge) of putting themselves in other people's shoes in many real and relevant situations. Most schools are in need of a stronger sense of community, they have to open themselves for justice oriented evaluations. This holds in general, and it especially holds if the aim is a reduction of prejudice. A rational community fosters interpersonal understanding and leaves no room for discrimination and prejudice; a focus on just forms of conflict resolution makes the injustice of prejudiced decision-making immediately evident. The notion of a 'just community' combines the most important conditions for an education that can succeed in diminishing prejudice.

## THE BERKELEY MODEL AND THE REDUCTION OF PREJUDICE

Having put the emphasis on the degree of student activity in school settings, let us look at an additional school project from the activity point of view. The Berkeley Prosocial Behavior Model is a long-term programme designed to enhance children's pro-social development. This programme was implemented in three suburban elementary schools and evaluated for five consecutive years, focusing primarily on a single cohort of children as it moved from kindergarten through fourth grade (Solomon *et al.*, 1989; Battistich *et al.*, 1990; Watson *et al.*, 1988).

This programme's basic premise is that pro-social reasoning and behaviour can best be promoted in an educational setting that emphasizes and exemplifies commitment to shared values, mutual responsibility and concern, and a sense of

*Figure 2.  Teacher's Implementation of Cooperative Learning in Programme and Comparison (Class-rooms — Grades K-4 Combined)*

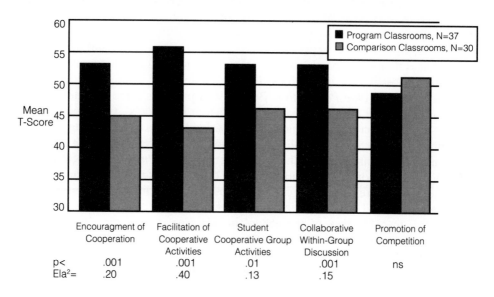

| | Encouragment of Cooperation | Facilitation of Cooperative Activities | Student Cooperative Group Activities | Collaborative Within-Group Discussion | Promotion of Competition |
|---|---|---|---|---|---|
| p< | .001 | .001 | .01 | .001 | ns |
| Ela²= | .20 | .40 | .13 | .15 | |

*Source*: Solomon *et al.* (1989), p. 3.

community. Manifold activities aim at supporting cooperation, social understanding and pro-social values like an active willingness to help people in need. Figure 2 shows some of the central activity dimensions.

Repeated measurement compared programme feasibility and interpersonal behaviour of the experimental and three control schools. Results are in strong support of the means-end relation assumed in this programme; e.g., analyses indicate significantly higher scores for students participating in the programme on two indices of interpersonal behaviour: supportive and friendly behaviour and spontaneous pro-social behaviour.

Even though this programme uses a mixture of various methods and does not rely on a single educational rationale, it can be expected to provide an enormous help in reducing prejudice. Unlike the just community approach (and similar to the McPhail programmes), subjects' reasoning competences and issues of justification are not stressed heavily. When a Black child guides a White newcomer to the eating room, this behaviour will be reinforced by the teacher. The act is viewed as positive in itself, regardless of further motives, factors in decision-making and degree of justification. This approach focuses more on action without referring to the rationality of the single act. We could say that in the just community setting the practical rationality precedes the act, while in the Berkeley project the act precedes the practical rationality. The approaches can be viewed as complementary, and may inform each other. The just community approach refers to development as the aim of education and constructs a viable model of moral discourse and decision-making. The Berkeley project refers to the act and to positive interpersonal experiences as necessary preconditions for a comprehensive moral consciousness. Both methods are highly effective, both are models of special value in reducing prejudice, both include the same core elements (act, development, discourse). The differences in the relevance subscribed to these elements and in the practical order of their stimulation and application may define the starting point of a fertile educational competition within the same general paradigm.

## CONCLUSION

I would like to refer back to the four hypotheses presented in the opening section of this chapter. First, the necessity of a developmental frame for educational work was mentioned. While the character education approach, the concept of values clarification and the McPhail model do not consider this aspect explicitly and thoroughly enough, the original Kohlbergian concept neglected the significance of the act, the content and the rule system in a given context. Only the just community model and the Berkeley project explicitly combine the activity dimension with a sound developmental frame as essentials of comprehensive educational enterprises. In these projects developmental knowledge is used (1) to understand the deep structure of the child's socio-moral reasoning (and hence the roots of his or her eventual social stereotyping and prejudice); (2) to help children develop this structure in a purposeful way, through active experience and discourse; (3) to go consciously beyond this reasoning structure by mediating action and judgment. We can only regret that developmental psychology has not yet applied the social cognitive and moral judgment stage models seriously to the ontogenesis of prejudice, stereotyping and discrimination.

Second, it was hypothesized that there cannot be effective moral education for reducing prejudice without action and interpersonal encounter, without real moral problem-solving. In the just communities acts are enforced by responsibility of the group and towards the group; in the Berkeley schools the act is implemented by playing, modelling, reinforcement and subsequent justification. In acting situations the child experiences the joy of being together with others, including those of other race, sex and social background, without losing one's own identity. Acting means concrete changing, concrete pro-social and moral decision-making and concrete emotional experience of the reversibility of rights, duties and affiliations. In the alternative moral/values education concepts (character education, values clarification, consideration), acting tends to remain unconsidered or unreal, without practical consequences, thus eventually undermining success in terms of reducing prejudice. The judgment-action gap is untouched, and subjects may feel protected from the call of duty, from the need to put into practice what has been discussed or even planned and justified.

Third, it was hypothesized that morally high standards of a whole system are an important condition for the viability of impartial, moral procedures of decision-making and problem-solving, and, for that reason, a precondition for the development of a procedural understanding of morality in the subjects involved. When the system allows for the employment of practical reason, it challenges its members to come up with well thought out, unprejudiced suggestions. Such a system is incompatible with hierarchies of command and obedience and with bureaucratic delegation of responsibility. In this sense reduction of prejudice as an aim of education calls for a dissolution and reconstruction of traditional school structures. Put into practice, discourse as a major principle of democratic schooling can help to overcome prejudice in serving several individual functions, such as: (1) the function of orientation in social life, (2) the function of adaptation, (3) the function of utility, (4) the function of self-representation, and (5) the function of self-assertion (cf. Bergler and Six, 1972; Barres, 1978). The realignment of the function of orientation consists in overcoming subjective uncertainty not by stereotyped judgment but by rational analysis of facts, relations and interactional or structural constraints. If subjects can listen to the arguments and viewpoints of others in conflict situations, they can learn to find procedural ways of problem-solving and resist the tendency to categorize and label persons, groups, cultures or societies. Again, among the models analyzed, only the just community approach and the Berkeley programme clearly provide the necessary setting.

The function of adjustment also becomes more transparent — and thus accessible to rationality — in a discourse oriented environment. As in every relevant life sphere, subjects adopt group norms; but additionally, in the openness and trustfulness of the interactional climate of such a setting they can reflect on the genesis and appropriateness of such norms. McGuire (1969, p. 158) stated that anti-Semitism often is not a result of real hate against Jews but rather of seeing them better integrated in a social/societal context and reacting to this threat to the self's hidden values in a defensive way. Such a mechanism can only work in an unquestioned manner when the environment does not make dialogical exchange and evaluation of claims obligatory or a matter of course. Procedural morality makes those hidden adaptation norms reflective and establishes the possibility of consciously denying their power.

Probably the most important subjective function of prejudice is utility in the sense of taking direct or — more often — indirect advantage of discrimination against minorities, such as persons with low income or power. Once again, the most explicit struggle against this aspect of discrimination can be observed in the just communities and the Berkeley project. Here a central notion is to give minorities a voice, to integrate them in participatory processes and to proceed on the assumption that they are fully committed and responsible in their reasoning and doing. This is precisely the main idea of procedural morality: to presuppose participants' readiness and competence to have a voice in any decision-making concerning issues of relevance for them. Evidently, children must learn to work out a standpoint and to articulate it in front of other people in a discourse situation. Educators must help them in developing these competences, hoping that later they will be able to create and arrange such discourse situations themselves. The just community is essentially a place for transcending and removing strategic and utilitarian concepts. Think about how many times in a child's school career grading and selection are misused as means of punishment. In a discourse oriented school environment this would never be the case.

I mentioned fourth and fifth functions of prejudiced thinking, self-representation and self-assertion. The latter is a form of protecting oneself by defending one's own position by way of devaluing the other. It seems to be a most difficult enterprise to destroy the old and familiar prejudices built up in childhood. Self-defence is a bastion against changes in world-views. This is why any educational attempt to change a prejudice directly is without chance. No one can transform a fixed attitude and a hidden normative concept directly, in the sense of traditional character education programmes. We can only provide some conditions for the subject's own reworking of attitudes and concepts, and these conditions are more likely to be effective in a discursive context, in open and interactive situations with everyone having his or her voice, in a setting where moral standards are not alien but rather perceived as essential and applied in a procedural way. Education against prejudice can be effective when turned into a positive direction. Merely preaching against apartheid and against everyday discrimination, merely talking about artificial dilemmas, does not relate to children's and adolescents' need for self-assertion.

My fourth and last hypothesis should have become quite obvious by now, and I would only like to underscore its significance. I do not believe in any method resorting to consciousness-raising techniques or to knowledge or values transmission if it is not embedded in concrete interactional situations, in procedural and moral solution-finding, in a participatory and dialogical frame. Morality has to be created by the students themselves, and it can only be created in processes of high activity and operational integration of self-chosen norms and rules. Educational work aiming at reducing prejudice needs concreteness: families must invite other families; groups must share their traditions and cultural peculiarities with other groups; school classes must interact with other classes and with wider parts of the community; decisions must be made by way of democratic — and often exhausting — participation; and schools must open their own problems and conflicts as issues for moral experiences and as a material for the development of discursive rationality: 'Why do you see the speck that is in your brother's eye, but do not notice the log that is in your own eye. Or: How can you say to your brother, "Let me take the speck out of your eye", when there is the log in your own eye?' (Matt. 7:3).

# REFERENCES

Adorno, T.W., Frenkel-Brunswick, E., Levinson, D.J. and Sanford, R.N. (1950) *The Authoritarian Personality*, New York, Harper and Row.

Allport, G.W. (1954) *The Nature of Prejudice*, Reading/Mass., Addison-Wesley Publishing Company.

Apel, K.O. (1988) *Diskurs und Verantwortung: Das Problem des Übergangs zur postkonventionellen Moral*, Frankfurt am Main, Suhrkamp.

Arbuthnot, J. and Faust, D. (1981) *Teaching Moral Reasoning: Theory and Practice*, New York, Harper and Row.

Bandura, A., Ross, O. and Ross, S.A. (1961) 'Transmission of Aggressive Models', *Journal of Abnormal and Social Psychology*, 63, pp. 575–582.

Barres, E. (1978) *Vorurteile. Theorie — Forschungsergebnisse — Praxisrelevanz*, Opladen, Leske and Budrich Verlag.

Battistich, V., Watson, M. and Solomon, D. (1989) 'The Child Development Project: Comprehensive Program for the Development of Prosocial Character', in W.M. Kurtines and J.L. Gewirtz (Eds), *Moral Behavior and Development: Advances in Theory, Research, and Application*, New York, Erlbaum.

Battistich, V., Solomon, D., Watson, M., Solomon, J. and Schaps, E. (1990) 'Effects of an Elementary School Program to Enhance Prosocial Behavior on Children's Cognitive Social Problem-Solving Skills and Strategies', *Journal of Applied Developmental Psychology*, 10.

Beck, C. (1983) *Values and Living: Learning Materials for Grades 7 and 8*, Toronto, OISE Press.

Beck, C. (1990) *Better Schools: A Values Perspective*, Lewes, Falmer Press.

Bergler, R. and Six, B. (1972) 'Stereotype und Vorurteile', *Hdb. der Psychologie*, Bd. 7, 2, Hdb. Sozialpsychologie.

Berkowitz, M., Oser, F. and Althof, W. (1987) 'The Development in Sociomoral Discourse', in W.M. Kurtiner and J.L. Gewirtz (Eds), *Moral Development through Social Interaction*, New York, Wiley, pp. 322–352.

Blasi, A. (1980) 'Bridging Moral Cognition and Moral Action: A Critical Review of the Literature', *Psychological Bulletin*, 88, pp. 1–45.

Blasi, A. (1983) 'Moral Cognition and Moral Action: A Theoretical Perspective', *Developmental Review*, 3, pp. 178–210.

Brewer, M.B. (1974) 'Cognitive Differentiation and Intergroup Bias: Cross-Cultural Studies', Paper presented at the Symposium on the Development and Maintenance of Intergroup Bias, Annual Meeting of the American Psychological Association, New Orleans.

Brophy, J.E. and Good, T.L. (1974) *Teacher-Student Relationships*, New York, Holt, Rinehart and Winston.

Burton, R.V. (1984) 'A Paradox in Theories and Research in Moral Development', in W.M. Kurtiner and J.L. Gewirtz (Eds), *Morality, Moral Behavior, and Moral Development*, New York, Wiley, pp. 193–207.

Chazan, B. (1985) *Contemporary Approaches to Moral Education: Analyzing Alternative Theories*, New York, Teachers College Press.

Clark, K.B. and Clark, M.P. (1947) 'Racial Identification and Preference in Negro Children', in T.M. Newcomb and E.L. Hartley (Eds), *Readings in Social Psychology*, New York, Holt, Rinehart and Winston.

Educational Policies Commission (National Education Association of the United States) (1951) *Moral and Spiritual Values in the Public Schools*, Washington, D.C., NEA-Self-Print.

Faust, C.H. and Feingold, J. (1969) *Approaches to Education for Character: Strategies for Change in Higher Education*, New York, Columbia University Press.

Gartner, J. (1985) 'Religious Prejudice in Psychology: Theories of Its Cause and Cure', *Journal of Pastoral Care*, 4, pp. 16–23.

Gergen, J.G. and Gergen, M.M. (1985) *Social Psychology*, 2nd ed., New York, Springer Verlag.

Habermas, J. (1981) *Theorie des kommunikativen Handelns*, 2nd ed., Frankfurt am Main, Suhrkamp.

Hamilton, D., Dugan, P. and Trolier, T. (1985) 'The Formation of Stereotypic Beliefs: Further Evidence for Distinctiveness-Based Illusory Correlations', *Journal of Personality and Social Psychology*, 48, pp. 5–18.

Hartshorne, H. and May, M.A. (1928) *Studies in the Nature of Character*, Vol. 1, New York, Macmillan.

Hersh, R.H., Miller, J.P. and Fielding, G.D. (1980) *Models of Moral Education: An Appraisal*, New York, Longman.

Hofstätter, P.R. (1962) 'Eliten und Minoritäten', *Kölner Z. f. Soziologie und Sozialpsychologie*, Vol. 14, pp. 59–86.

Holmes, M. (1980) 'Forward to the Basics: A Radical Conservative Reconstruction', *Curriculum Inquiry*, 10, pp. 383–418.

Kohlberg, L. and Mayer, R. (1972) 'Development as the Aim of Education', *Harvard Educational Review*, 42, pp. 449–496.

Kohlberg, L. with Candee, D. (1984) 'The Relationship of Moral Judgment to Moral Action', in L. Kohlberg, *The Psychology of Moral Development*, San Francisco, Calif., pp. 498–581.

Kutnik, P. (1985) 'The Relationship of Moral Judgment and Moral Action: Kohlberg's Theory, Criticism and Revision', in S. Modgil and C. Modgil (Eds), *Lawrence Kohlberg: Consensus and Controversy*, Lewes, Falmer Press.

Leming, J.S. (1989) 'Curricular Effectiveness in Moral/Values Education: A Review of Moral Education', 10, pp. 147–164.

Mackie, D. and Cooper, J. (1984) 'Attitude Polarization: Effects of Group Membership', *Journal of Personality and Social Psychology*, 46, pp. 575–585.

McPhail, P., Middleton, D. and Ingram, D. (1972) *Moral Education in the Middle Years*, London, Longman.

McPhail, P., Ungoed-Thomas, J.R. and Chapman, H. (1978) *Moral Education in the Secondary School*, London, Longman.

Morrill, R.L. (1980) *Teaching Values in College*, San Francisco, Calif., Jossey-Bass.

Oser, F. (1986) 'Moral Education and Values Education: The Discourse Perspective', in M.C. Wittrock (Ed.), *Handbook of Research on Teaching*, 3rd ed., New York/London: Macmillan.

Oser, F. (1987) 'Das Wollen, das gegen den eigenen Willen gerichtet ist: Über das Verhältnis von Urteil und Handeln im Bereich der Moral', in H. Heckhausen, P.M. Gollwitzer and F.E. Weinert (Eds), *Jenseits des Rubikon: Der Wille in den Humanwissenschaften*, Berlin, Springer, pp. 255–285.

Oser, F. (1988) 'Die Gerechte Gemeinschaft und die Demokratisierung der Schulwelt: Der Kohlberg-ansatz, eine Herausforderung für die Erziehung', in *Vierteljahresschrift für wissenschaftliche Pädagogik*, 64, Bochum, Ferdinand Kamp, pp. 59–79.

Oser, F. (1989) 'Lernen durch die Gestaltung des Schullebens: Der Ansatz der "Gerechten Gemein-schaft"', *Berichte zur Erziehungswissenschaft des Pädagogischen Instituts der Universität Freiburg/ Schweiz*, Nr. 82.

Oser, F. and Althof, W. (1989a) 'Moralerziehung durch Gerechte Gemeinschaft und Demokrati-sierung. Schule nach innen: Eine praktische Theorie der Bildung', Fernbriefe der Universität Hagen.

Oser, F. and Althof, W. (1989) *Moralische Entwicklung und Erziehung*, 4 Bd, Fernbriefe der Universität Hagen.

Oser, F., Ammann, B., Aufenanger, S., Klaghofer, R., Patry, J.-L. and Zutavern, M. (1989) 'Zwischenbericht zum Nationalfondsprojekt: Fürsorge, Gerechtigkeit und Wahrhaftigkeit. Zur Stimulierung des Berufsethos von Lehrern', Pädagogisches Institut der Univeristät Freiburg.

Oser, F., Dick, A. and Patry, J.L. (1992) *Effective and Responsible Teaching: The New Synthesis*, San Francisco, Calif, Jossey Bass.

Panahi, B. (1980) *Vorurteile. Rassismus, Antisemitismus, Nationalismus ... in der Bundesrepublik heute: Eine empirische Untersuchung*, Frankfurt am Main, S. Fischer Verlag.

Power, C., Higgins, A. and Kohlberg, L. (1989) *Lawrence Kohlberg's Approach to Moral Education*, New York, Columbia University Press.

Raths, L.E., Harmin, M. and Simon, S.B. (1966) *Values and Teaching*, Columbus, Ohio, Merrill.

Rokeach, M. (1956) 'Political and Religious Dogmatism: An Alternative to the Authoritarian Perso-nality', *Psychological Monographs*, 70.

Rosenthal, R. and Jacobson, L.F. (1968) 'Teacher Expectations for the Disadvantaged', *Scientific American*, 4, pp. 19–23.

Schläfli, A.R. and Thoma, S. (1985) 'Does Moral Education Improve Moral Judgment? Meta-analysis of Intervention Studies', *Review of Educational Research*, 55, pp. 319–352.

Simon, S.B., Howe, L.W. and Kirschenbaum, H. (1972) *Values Clarification: A Handbook of Practical Strategies for Teachers and Students*, New York, Hart.

Solomon, D., Watson, M., Schaps, E., Battistich, V. and Solomon, J. (1989) 'Cooperative Learning as Part of a Comprehensive Classroom Program Designed to Promote Prosocial Development', in S. Sharan (Ed.), *Current Research on Cooperative Learning*, New York, Praeger.

Solomon, D., Watson, M.S., Delucchi, K.L., Schaps, E. and Battistich, V. (1988) 'Enhancing Children's Prosocial Behavior in the Classroom', *American Educational Research Journal*, 25, pp. 527–554.

Triandis, H., Lisansky, J., Setiadi, B., Chang, B.-H., Marin, G. and Betancourt, H. (1982) 'Stereo-typing among Hispanics and Anglos: The Uniformity, Intensity, Direction and Quality of Auto- and Heterostereotypes', *Journal of Cross-Cultural and Social Psychology*, 47, pp. 1363–1375.

Turiel, E. (1966) 'An Experimental Test of the Sequentiality of Developmental Stages in the Child's Moral Judgments', *Journal of Personality and Social Psychology*, 3, pp. 611–618.

Walker, J., DeVries, B. and Trevethan, S.D. (1987) 'Moral Stages and Moral Orientations in Real-Life and Hypothetical Dilemmas', *Child Development*, 58, pp. 842–858.

Watson, M.S., Hildebrandt, C. and Solomon, D. (1988) 'Cooperative Learning as a Means of Promoting Prosocial Development among Kindergarten and Early Primary-Grade Children', *International Journal of Social Education*, 3, pp. 34–47.

Widaman, K.F. and Little, T.D. (1985) 'Contextual Influences on Sociomoral Judgment and Action', in J.B. Pryor and J.D. Day (Eds), *The Development of Social Cognition*, New York, Springer-Verlag.

Wilder, D.A. (1984) 'Predictions of Belief Homogeneity and Similarity Following Social Categoriza-tion', *British Journal of Social Psychology*, 23, pp. 323–333.

# Part Five: Cooperative Learning, Prejudice Reduction and Effective Education

# 17. Cooperative Learning: Applying Contact Theory in Desegregated Schools[*]

ROBERT E. SLAVIN

The year 1984 marked the thirtieth anniversary of *Brown vs Board of Education* (1954) and the twentieth anniversary of the 1964 Civil Rights Act, the two most important events in the dismantling of legal barriers to racial integration. This year also saw the thirtieth anniversary of one of the most important events in the study of dismantling interpersonal barriers to racial integration: the publication of Gordon Allport's *The Nature of Prejudice* (1954). As the *Brown* decision set the tone for later judicial action against school segregation, and as the Civil Rights Act set the tone for later legislative action against segregation and discrimination in society as a whole, *The Nature of Prejudice* has served for thirty years as the basis for the study of intergroup relations.

At the time that Allport was writing, social scientists were debating the potential impact of desegregation in general, particularly of *school* desegregation, on intergroup relations. Allport's work was central to the social science statement (*Minnesota Law Review*, 1953), which played an important role in the deliberations of the court in the *Brown* case (see Cook, 1984).

In *The Nature of Prejudice*, Allport evaluated the experience of desegregation in industrial, military and other non-school settings to anticipate the effects of school desegregation on intergroup relations and other outcomes. In the early 1950s integrated schools were illegal in the seventeen states (plus the District of Columbia) in which most Blacks lived, and they were rare elsewhere, so that direct study of integrated schools was difficult. However, Allport did have available enough experience and research on various integrated settings to derive a set of principles to explain when interracial contact would lead to improved relationships and when it would not. He cited research that indicated that superficial contact could be detrimental to race relations, as could competitive contact and

* This slightly edited version is reprinted with permission from the *Journal of Social Issues*, 41, 1985, pp. 45–62. The original paper was prepared under funding from the National Institute of Education, No. NIE-G-83-0002. However, the opinions expressed are those of the author and do not represent NIE policy.

contact between individuals of markedly different status. However, he also cited evidence to the effect that when individuals of different racial or ethnic groups worked to achieve common goals, when they had opportunities to get to know one another as individuals, and when they worked with one another on an equal footing they became friends and did not continue to hold prejudices against one another. Allport's contact theory of intergroup relations, based on these findings, has dominated social science enquiry on race relations for three decades. His own summary of the essentials of contact theory is as follows: 'Prejudice ... may be reduced by equal status contact between majority and minority groups in the pursuit of common goals. The effect is greatly enhanced if this contact is sanctioned by institutional supports ... and if it is of a sort that leads to the perception of common interests and common humanity between members of the two groups' (Allport, 1954, p. 281).

## SCHOOL DESEGREGATION AND INTERGROUP RELATIONS

Thirty years after the *Brown* decision, social scientists have had ample opportunity to study the effects of school desegregation on intergroup relations. In one sense this is a difficult topic to study, because before desegregation there are few if any intergroup relations among students, and attitudes toward students of other races may be quite unrealistic (whether positive or negative). However, researchers and reviewers are generally pessimistic about the effects of desegregation per se on intergroup relations, at least in the short run (e.g., Cohen, 1975; St John, 1975; Stephan, 1978). Even though students in desegregated schools do have friends of different ethnicities, these do not approach the number of friends they have within their own ethnic group, and this situation does not generally change of its own accord (e.g., Gerard and Miller, 1975).

Do these disappointing findings confirm or discredit contact theory? In general they confirm it. The traditional school setting hardly fulfils the conditions outlined by Allport. Interaction between students of different ethnicities is typically superficial and often competitive.

Black, Anglo, Hispanic and other groups compete for grades, for teacher approval, for places on the student council or on the cheerleading squad. Interaction between students of different ethnic groups is usually of a superficial nature. In the classroom, the one setting in which students of different races or ethnicities are likely to be at least sitting side by side, traditional instructional methods permit little contact between students that is not superficial. Otherwise, Black, Anglo and Hispanic students usually ride different buses to different neighbourhoods, participate in different kinds of activities and go to different social functions. Thus opportunities for positive intergroup interaction are limited. One major exception is sports; sports teams create conditions of cooperation and non-superficial contact among team members.

Correlational research by Slavin and Madden (1979) has shown that students who participate in sports in desegregated high schools are much more likely to have friends outside their own race group and to have positive racial attitudes than students who do not participate in integrated sports teams. Sports teams fulfil the requirements of contact theory in that interaction among teammates tends to be non-superficial, cooperative and of equal status. However, there are only so many positions on teams, and schools below the high school level may not have sports teams at all.

Is there a way to change classroom organization to allow meaningful, co-operative contact to take place between students of different ethnicities? This chapter describes the results of several research programmes designed to answer this question by systematically applying interventions based on Allport's contact theory to academic classrooms. The methods evaluated in this research are referred to collectively as 'cooperative learning' (Slavin, 1980a, 1983a). This chapter reviews the research on cooperative learning methods, with an emphasis on understanding the complex changes in both classroom organization and student friendship patterns when cooperative, integrated learning teams are used in the desegregated classroom.

## Cooperative Learning

Cooperative learning methods explicitly use the strength of the desegregated school — the presence of students of different races or ethnicities — to enhance intergroup relations and other outcomes. The groups in which students work are made up of four to five students of different races, sexes and levels of achievement, with each group reflecting the composition of the class as a whole on these attributes. In most cooperative learning methods the groups receive rewards, recognition and/or evaluation based on the degree to which they can increase the academic performance of each member of the group. This is in sharp contrast to the student competition for grades and teacher approval characteristic of the traditional classroom. Cooperation between students is emphasized both by the classroom rewards and tasks, and by the teacher, who tries to communicate an 'all for one, one for all' attitude. The various methods are structured to give each student a chance to make a substantial contribution to the team, so that team-mates will be equal — at least in the sense of role equality specified by Allport (1954). The cooperative learning methods are designed to be true changes in classroom organization, not time-limited 'treatments'. They provide daily opportunities for intense interpersonal contact among students of different races. When the teacher assigns students of different races or ethnicities to work together, this communicates unequivocal support on the teacher's part for the idea that inter-racial or interethnic interaction is officially sanctioned. Even though race or race relations per se need not be mentioned (and rarely are) in the course of coopera-tive learning experiences, it is difficult for a student to believe the teacher supports racial separation when the teacher has assigned the class to multiethnic teams.

Thus, at least in theory, cooperative learning methods satisfy the conditions outlined by Allport (1954) for positive effects of desegregation on race relations: cooperation across racial lines, equal status roles for students of different races, contact across racial lines that permits students to learn about one another as individuals, and the communication of unequivocal teacher support for interracial contact.

The conditions of contact theory are not difficult to achieve in the laboratory. However, as Harrison (1976) points out: '200 million Americans cannot be run through the laboratory one by one [to reduce prejudice]' (p. 563). If a programme designed to implement contact theory in classrooms is to be anything but an academic exercise, it must not only improve intergroup relations, but must also accomplish other educational goals. For example, research on cooperative learning would be of little relevance to schools if the methods did not also improve (or at least not hinder) student achievement, or if they were too expensive, too difficult, too narrowly focused or too disruptive of school routines to be practical as primary alternatives to traditional instruction. As a consequence, features of cooperative learning methods other than the degree to which they are designed to improve race relations are of great importance.

Seven principal cooperative learning methods embody the principles of contact theory, have been researched in desegregated schools, and have the practical characteristics outlined above: they are cheap, relatively easy to implement, widely applicable in terms of subject matter and grade levels, easily integrated into an existing school without additional resources, and (for four of the seven methods) have been shown to improve achievement more than traditional instruction (see Slavin, 1980a, 1983a). Three of these methods were developed and evaluated at the Center for Social Organization of Schools at Johns Hopkins University. These are Student Teams-Achievement Divisions (Slavin, 1978), Teams-Games-Tournament (DeVries and Slavin, 1978) and Team-Assisted Individualization (Slavin, Leavey and Madden, 1984). These methods are both the most extensively studied of the cooperative learning techniques and the most widely used in American schools. A fourth technique, 'Jigsaw teaching' (Aronson *et al.*, 1978), has been evaluated in several desegregated schools and is widely used both in its original form and as modified by Slavin (1980b). Methods developed and assessed at the University of Minnesota (Johnson and Johnson, 1975) have been studied in desegregated schools, and Group Investigation (Sharan and Sharan, 1976) has been studied in Israeli schools that include European and Middle Eastern Jews. In addition, Weigel, Wiser and Cook (1975) evaluated a cooperative learning method in tri-ethnic (Black, Hispanic, Anglo) classes. These techniques are described below (see Slavin, 1983a, for more detailed descriptions).

1  *Student Teams-Achievement Divisions (STAD).* In STAD the teacher presents a lesson, and then students study worksheets in four-member teams heterogeneous on student ability, sex and ethnicity. Following this, students take individual quizzes, and team scores are computed based on the degree to which each student improved over his or her own past record. The team scores are recognized in class newsletters.

2  *Teams-Games-Tournament (TGT).* TGT is essentially the same as STAD in rationale and method. However, it replaces the quizzes and improvement score system used in STAD with a system of academic game tournaments, in which students from each team compete with students from other teams of the same level of past performance to try to contribute to their team scores.

3  *Team-Assisted Individualization (TAI).* TAI combines the use of cooperative teams (like those used in STAD and TGT) with individualized instruction in elementary mathematics. Students work in four- to five-

member heterogeneous teams on self-instructional materials at their own levels and rates. The students themselves take responsibility for all checking, management and routing, and help one another with problems, freeing the teacher to spend most of his or her time instructing small groups of students (drawn from the various teams) working on similar concepts. Teams are rewarded with certificates if they attain preset standards in terms of the number of units mastered by all team members each week.

4 *Jigsaw and Jigsaw II.* In the original Jigsaw method (Aronson *et al.*, 1978) students were assigned to heterogeneous six-member teams, and each team member was given a unique set of information on an overall unit. For example, in a unit on Spain one student might be appointed as an 'expert' on Spain's history, another on its culture, another on its economy and so on. The students read their information and then discuss it in 'expert groups' made up of students from different teams who have the same information. The 'experts' then return to their teams to teach the information to their teammates. Finally, all students are quizzed, and students receive individual grades.

Jigsaw II modifies Jigsaw to correspond more closely to the Student Team Learning format (Slavin, 1980b). Students work in four- to five-member teams (as in STAD, TGT and TAI). All students read a chapter or story, but each team member is given an individual topic on which to become an expert. Students discuss their topics in expert groups and teach them to their teammates as in original Jigsaw. However, quiz scores in Jigsaw II are summed to form team scores, and teams are recognized in a class newsletter as in STAD.

5 *Johnson Methods.* In cooperative learning methods developed by David Johnson and Roger Johnson (1975) students work in small, heterogeneous groups to complete a common worksheet, and are praised and rewarded as a group. These methods are the least complex of the cooperative learning methods, and the closest to a pure cooperative model, as the other methods contain individualistic and/or competitive elements.

6 *Group Investigation.* Group Investigation (Sharan and Sharan, 1976), developed by Shlomo Sharan and his colleagues in Israel, is a general classroom organization plan in which students work in small groups using cooperative enquiry, group discussion and cooperative planning and projects. In this method students form their own two- to six-member groups. The groups choose subtopics from a unit being studied by the entire class, further break their subtopics into individual tasks, and carry out the activities necessary to prepare a group report. The group then makes a representation or display to communicate its findings to the entire class, and is evaluated based on the quality of this report.

7 *Weigel et al. Methods.* In one study in junior and senior high schools containing Black, Hispanic and Anglo students, Weigel *et al.* (1975) used a combination of cooperative learning methods, including information gathering, discussion and interpretation of materials in heterogeneous groups. Prizes were given to groups on the basis of the quality of the group product.

## RESEARCH ON COOPERATIVE LEARNING AND INTERGROUP RELATIONS

The remainder of this chapter reviews the field experiments evaluating the effects of cooperative learning methods on intergroup relations. This review emphasizes studies in which the methods were used in elementary or secondary schools for at least three weeks (median duration = 10 weeks), and in which appropriate research methods and analyses were used to rule out obvious bias. Study *Ns* ranged from 51 to 424 (median = 164), grade levels from 4 to 12, and per cent minority from 10 to 61 per cent. Most of the studies used sociometric indices (e.g., 'Who are your friends in this class?'), peer ratings, or behavioural observation to measure intergroup relations as pairwise positive relations between individuals of different ethnic backgrounds. A few studies defined intergroup relations in terms of attitudes toward various ethnic groups. Several studies used such sociometric questions as 'Who have you helped in this class?' Because only students in the cooperative learning classes are likely to have helped their classmates, such measures are biased toward the cooperative learning treatments; thus the results of these measures will not be discussed. Also, observations of crossracial interaction during the treatment classes, another measure of implementation rather than outcome, are not considered as intergroup relations measures.

### Main Effects on Intergroup Relations

The experimental evidence on cooperative learning has generally supported the main tenets of contact theory (Allport, 1954). With only a few exceptions, this research has demonstrated that when the conditions outlined by Allport are met in the classroom, students are more likely to have friends outside their own racial groups than they would in traditional classrooms, as measured by responses to such sociometric items as 'Who are your best friends in this class?'

*STAD.* The evidence linking STAD to gains in crossracial friendships is strong. In two studies Slavin (1977, 1979) found that students who had experienced STAD over periods of ten to twelve weeks gained more in crossracial friendships than did control students. Slavin and Oickle (1981) found significant gains in White friendships toward Blacks as a consequence of STAD, but found no differences in Black friendships toward Whites. Kagan *et al.* (1985) found that STAD (and TGT) reversed a trend toward ethnic polarization of friendship choices among Anglo, Hispanic and Black students. Sharan *et al.* (1984) found positive effects of STAD on ethnic attitudes of both Middle Eastern and European Jews in Israeli schools.

Slavin's (1979) study included a follow-up into the next academic year, in which students who had been in the experimental and control classes were asked to list their friends. Students in the control group listed an average of less than one friend of another race, or 9.8 per cent of all of their friendship choices; those in the experimental group named an average of 2.4 friends outside their own race, 37.9 per cent of their friendship choices. The STAD research covered grades 2–8, and took place in schools ranging from 13 per cent to 61 per cent minority.

*TGT.*  DeVries, Edwards and Slavin (1978) summarized data analyses from four studies of TGT in desegregated schools. In three of these, students in classes that used TGT gained significantly more friends outside their own racial groups than did control students. In one, no differences were found. The samples involved in these studies varied in grade level from 7–12 and in percentage of minority students from 10 to 51 per cent.

*TAI.*  Two studies have assessed the effects of TAI on intergroup relations. Oishi, Slavin and Madden (1983) found positive effects of TAI on crossracial nominations on two sociometric scales, 'Who are your friends in this class?' and 'Whom would you rather *not* sit at a table with?' No effects were found on crossracial ratings of classmates as 'nice' or 'smart', but TAI students made significantly fewer crossracial ratings as 'not nice' and 'not smart' than did control students. In a similar study Oishi (1983) found significantly positive effects of TAI on crossracial ratings as smart and on reductions in ratings as not nice. The effect on smart ratings was due primarily to increases in Whites' ratings of Black classmates.

*Jigsaw.*  The effects of the original Jigsaw method on intergroup relations are less clear than those for STAD, TGT or TAI. Blaney *et al.* (1977) did find that students in desegregated classes using Jigsaw preferred their Jigsaw groupmates to their classmates in general. However, since students' groupmates and their other classmates were about the same in ethnic composition, this cannot be seen as a measure of intergroup relations. No differences between the experimental and control groups in interethnic friendship choices were reported.

Gonzales (1979), using a method similar to Jigsaw, found that Anglo and Asian-American students had better attitudes toward Mexican-American class-mates in the Jigsaw groups than in control groups, but he found no differences in attitudes toward Anglo or Asian-American students. In a subsequent study Gonzales (1981) found no differences in attitudes toward Mexican-Americans, Blacks or Anglos between Jigsaw and control bilingual classes.

The most positive effects of a Jigsaw-related intervention were found in a study of Jigsaw II by Ziegler (1981) in classes composed of recent European and West Indian immigrants and Anglo-Canadians in Toronto. She found substantial-ly more crossethnic friendships in the Jigsaw II classes than in control classes both on an immediate post-test and on a ten-week follow-up. These effects were for both 'casual friendships' ('Who in this class have you called on the telephone in the last two weeks?') and 'close friendships' ('Who in this class have you spent time with after school in the last two weeks?').

*Johnson Methods.*  Two of the Johnsons' studies have examined intergroup rela-tions outcomes. Cooper *et al.* (1980) found greater friendship across race lines in a cooperative treatment than in an individualized method in which students were not permitted to interact. However, there were no differences in crossracial friendships between the cooperative condition and a competitive condition in which students competed with equals (similar to the TGT tournaments). Johnson and Johnson (1981) found more crossracial interaction in cooperative than in individualized classes during free time.

*Group Investigation.* In a study in Israeli junior high schools Sharan *et al.* (1984) compared Group Investigation, STAD and traditional instruction in terms of effects on relationships between Jews of Middle Eastern and European backgrounds. They found that students who experienced Group Investigation and STAD had much more positive ethnic attitudes than students in traditional classes. There were no differences between Group Investigation and STAD on this variable.

*Weigel et al. Method.* One of the largest and longest studies of cooperative learning was conducted by Weigel *et al.* (1975) in tri-ethnic (Mexican-American, Anglo, Black) classrooms. They evaluated a method in which students in multiethnic teams engaged in a variety of cooperative activities in several subjects, winning prizes based on their team performance. They reported that their cooperative methods had positive effects on White students' attitudes toward Mexican-Americans, but not on White-Black, Black-White, Black-Hispanic, Hispanic-Black or Hispanic-White attitudes. They also found that cooperative learning reduced teachers' reports of interethnic conflict.

The effects of cooperative learning methods are not entirely consistent, but sixteen of the nineteen studies reviewed here demonstrated that when the conditions of contact theory are fulfilled, some aspect of friendship between students of different ethnicities improves.

It is important to note that in addition to positive effects on intergroup relations, cooperative learning methods have positive effects on student achievement. This is particularly true of STAD, TGT and TAI — highly structured methods that combine cooperative goals and tasks with a high degree of individual accountability (see Slavin, 1983b). Thus it is apparent that cooperative learning methods have positive effects on relationships among students of different races or ethnicities, while also increasing their achievement. These main effects are the most important findings in terms of implications for the practice of education. However, additional research has further explored the effects of cooperative learning on variables related to contact theory. The following section discusses this research.

## CONTACT THEORY IN THE CLASSROOM

As noted above, the theory linking cooperative learning methods to improvements in intergroup relations is derived from Allport's (1954) contact theory. Contact theory has been studied in the social-psychological laboratory for many years (e.g., Cook, 1978). The field experimental research on cooperative learning methods in the classroom offers a new opportunity to explore many of the components and assumptions behind contact theory. Clearly, the cooperative learning research confirms the expectation that a treatment based on contact theory would improve intergroup relations. The following sections consider how cooperative learning affects the conditions for contact, cooperation, equal status, and normative climate in the classroom, which are the major dimensions of contact theory.

### How Close Are the New Crossethnic Friendships?

It is not surprising that friendships across racial or ethnic boundaries are rare, compared to friendships within these groups. Black, Hispanic and Anglo students typically live in different neighbourhoods, ride different buses and prefer different activities. Secondary school students of different ethnicities often come from different elementary schools. Socio-economic and achievement differences further separate students. These factors work against friendship formation even when race is not a factor (see Lott and Lott, 1965). Racial differences accentuate students' tendencies to form homogeneous peer groups, and sometimes result in overt prejudice and interracial hostility.

Given the many forces operating against the formation of crossracial friendships, it would seem that if cooperative learning influences these friendships, it would create relatively weak relationships rather than strong ones. On first thought, it seems unlikely that a few weeks of cooperative learning would build strong interracial relationships between students in the classroom at the possible expense of prior same-race relationships.

A secondary analysis of the Slavin (1979) STAD study by Hansell and Slavin (1981) investigated this hypothesis. Their sample included 424 seventh- and eighth-grade students in twelve inner-city language arts classrooms. Classes were randomly assigned to cooperative learning (STAD) or control treatments for a ten-week programme. Students were asked on both pre- and post-tests, 'Who are your best friends in this class? Name as many as you wish', in a free-choice format. Choices were defined as 'close' if they were among the first six made by students, and 'distant' if they ranked seventh or later. The reciprocity and order of choices made and received were analyzed by multiple regression.

The results showed that the positive effects of STAD on crossracial choices were primarily due to increases in *strong* friendship choices. Reciprocated and close choices, both made and received, increased more in STAD than in control classes. Contrary to what might have been expected, this study showed positive effects of cooperative learning on close, reciprocated friendship choices, the kind of friendships that should be most difficult to change.

*Equal Status.* One of Allport's (1954) theoretical criteria for contact to improve intergroup relations is that it occur between individuals of equal status. Equal status has been emphasized by many in recent years as a critical aspect of contact theory as it relates to school desegregation (e.g., Amir, 1969; Cohen, 1975). In Allport's use of the term students in the same grade level have equal status, regardless of race, sex or achievement level. Allport was concerned more with occupational status (e.g., the status differences between supervisors and workers, or between sergeants and privates) than with status associated with ascribed characteristics or abilities. This kind of equal status is referred to by Cook (1969) as 'situational equal status'.

However, Cohen's (1975) research introduces a new meaning to the term 'equal status'. She is interested in the perceptions of competence that students of different ethnicities have about each other, and whether students of different races and ethnicities have equal performance expectations for each other. In Cohen's sense equal status may be impossible to achieve in an American school, because Blacks are often seen as lower in competence, and low expectations for Blacks by Whites generalize beyond situations in which they may in fact be lower in achievement. Cohen states:

> The inference may be drawn that even though blacks and whites might be brought together in a desegregated school in an 'equal status' manner, it is still quite possible for the racial difference to act as a strong status differential triggering expectations for whites to do better in a new situation and for blacks to do less well. If this occurs in the school situation, then the racial stereotypes which contribute to these expectations are only reinforced and confirmed by the interracial interaction in the desegregated school. It should be a matter of great concern if the process of desegregation actually does result in reinforcing such stereotypes of racial incompetence. (p. 294)

The implication of Cohen's argument is that equal status interaction between Black and White students is unlikely, particularly when actual Black-White differences in reading and mathematics performance confirm racial stereotypes. Cohen has voiced a concern that placing students in joint work groups would make racial achievement differences even more salient, thereby diminishing any chance that Black and White students might treat one another as equals.

If, as Cohen suggests, minority students are perceived as less competent, then they should be less well liked by their groupmates as a consequence of a cooperative learning intervention. However, data from the field experiments on cooperative learning directly contradict this expectation. Improvements in majority-minority friendships are even more consistently seen than are increases in minority-majority friendships (e.g., Slavin and Oickle, 1981).

There are several possible reasons why Cohen's predictions are not borne out by the data. First, her demonstrations that Whites have low performance expectations for Blacks (e.g., Cohen and Roper, 1972) involve one-time observations in laboratory settings. Having had the experience of working together in small groups over a longer period of time, White students might learn that their Black groupmates do in fact have much to contribute to the group, and are no less able than themselves. In fact, Oishi (1983) found that White students in TAI significantly increased their ratings of their Black classmates as smart. Even when there are differences in the average achievement levels of Blacks and Whites in the same class, there will be Blacks among the highest-performing students and Whites among the lowest-performing students, making a racial generalization difficult. Further, two studies of STAD (Slavin, 1977; Slavin and Oickle, 1981) found that initial significant achievement differences between Black and White students were eliminated in the STAD groups while they remained in the control groups; this suggested that even if there are perceptible racial differences in achievement, the experience of working in cooperative groups may diminish them.

Another reason that Cohen's fears about cooperative learning have not been realized may be that the most frequently evaluated cooperative learning methods — STAD, TGT, TAI and Jigsaw II — use equal opportunity scoring systems intended to diminish the salience and the effect of ability differences within the cooperative activities. For example, the scores students contribute to their teams in STAD are based on the students' improvement over their level of past performance. This ensures that no student is automatically a drag on the team score. At present the evidence about the role of equal status and of equal opportunity scoring in cooperative learning interventions is unclear. Unfortunately, cooperative learning researchers have not measured status perceptions directly, and Cohen and her colleagues have not measured race relations (at least in the sense of interracial liking or friendship). It seems unlikely that positive race relations require equal performance status (as opposed to situational status) between Blacks and Whites, but future research could establish this link.

*Institutional Norms.*   Allport (1954) hypothesized that crossrace contact would be more likely to improve race relations if the institutions in which the contact took place clearly supported racial interaction and equality. Allport felt most Whites have conflicting feelings about desegregation. On one hand they may be uncomfortable about interacting with others different from themselves; on the other hand they feel shame about this discomfort, because they share the American belief in fair play and equality. Allport reasoned that Whites will accept desegregation best when they themselves do not have to initiate interracial contact, and when such contact is strongly supported by institutional norms and policies.

In schools one might assume that institutional support for interracial contact would be present. Certainly, few school officials openly advocate segregation. However, teachers and administrators are often quite uncomfortable about the issue of race, being unsure whether race should simply be ignored ('We're all the same here') or whether race relations should be openly discussed and dealt with. Students may get the idea that while racial conflicts are not permitted in school, positive crossracial contacts are not really encouraged.

One simple change that cooperative learning methods may make in the desegregated classroom is to legitimize positive interracial contact. Students of different races may hold few overt prejudices, but still may be reluctant to take the first step toward making friends of another race. Such students might welcome having a teacher who establishes a climate that supports and encourages interracial interaction, and who labels it as normal and desirable. This climate may be created without speaking a word about race; the fact that the teacher assigns students to racially mixed learning groups clearly indicates teacher approval of interracial interaction. If the teacher allows students to choose their own teams (which would often result in racially and sexually homogeneous teams), the opposite message might be communicated.

No research at present bears directly on the issue of institutional support as a contributor to the effects of cooperative learning on intergroup relations, and such effects are difficult to separate from the effects of contact per se. However, this is an important issue for a theory of cooperative learning and intergroup relations.

*Perceived Similarity.* One of the strongest determinants of friendship in general (after contact) is a perception on the part of two individuals that they share important characteristics, world-views, favourite activities and so on (Lott and Lott, 1965). One problem of race relations is that students of different races or ethnicities are likely to be dissimilar in many important attributes, such as socio-economic status, values and preferred activities. Even if students could be made colour-blind, these differences would continue the tendency for students to make friends primarily within their own racial groups.

Allport (1954) referred to perceived similarity as a criterion for contact to lead to improved race relations in his emphasis on equal status and on crossracial contact that leads to a perception of common interests and common humanity. However, few of the basic racial dissimilarities likely to exist in desegregated classrooms can be easily overcome.

In one sense cooperative learning methods create a new basis for perceived similarity among dissimilar students. The assignment of students to teams automatically gives them a common identity. Social-psychological laboratory research has shown that simply announcing group assignments induces individuals to evaluate groupmates more positively than non-groupmates, even before they meet them (Brewer, 1979; Gerard and Hoyt, 1974). Particularly as they enter adolescence, students seek an identity and a peer group with which to affiliate. In some cases crossracial friendships that existed in elementary school are broken in junior high as students come to identify more with their own ethnic group. Cooperative learning provides each student with a group based less on ethnicity or sex than on shared goals: the mere announcement of group assignments begins to break down racial barriers to friendship as students perceive their shared identity.

*Effects on Social Networks.* One limitation of existing research on cooperative learning and on contact theory in general is the concentration on dyadic relationships across racial lines or (to a lesser extent) attitudes toward entire racial groups. However, the impact of cooperative learning almost certainly involves networks of friendships rather than simple dyadic friendships. Secondary analyses of the data from Slavin's (1979) STAD study have revealed that many of the new crossracial friendships made over the course of the STAD intervention were formed between students who had never been in the same cooperative group. A moment's reflection would support the inevitability of this result; in a four-member team that has two Blacks and two Whites, each student could only make two new friends from a different race if he or she made new friends only within the team. At least one of those teammates from a different race would also be likely to be of a different sex; norms against Black-White dating aside, cross-sex friendships are even less frequent than are crossrace friendships (Cooper *et al.*, 1980; DeVries and Edwards, 1974). It is also possible that two or more teammates of different races were already friends, further restricting the possible number of new crossrace, within-team choices, and any deviation from a 50–50 racial split reduces the possibilities still further.

Apparently, crossrace friendships formed outside cooperative groups account for some of the effects of cooperative learning on dyadic interracial friendships. In theory this should not happen. After all, the teams are usually in competition with each other. Laboratory research (e.g., Miller, Brewer and Edwards, 1985) often finds that intergroup competition is detrimental to attitudes between members of different groups.

However, there are at least two ways in which cooperative learning might increase crossrace friendships outside particular cooperative groups. First, a cooperative learning experience often offers students their first (or best) crossrace friendships. Racial groups in classrooms are characterized by many friendship ties within each race group but few outside it. However, once a crossrace friendship is formed, the new friend's friends (of his or her own race) also become likely friendship candidates. For example, if a White student makes his or her first Black friend, this relationship bridges between formerly isolated Black and White peer groups. It opens a new pool of potential Black friends, possibly reaching even beyond the confines of the classroom.

Second, even a small number of crossrace friendships may create less well defined peer group boundaries, formerly based on racial (and sexual) criteria, thereby allowing new, smaller cliques to form based more on mutual liking than on race and sex. This pattern was found in an analysis of sociometric data conducted by Hansell, Tackaberry and Slavin (1981); clique size tended to diminish as a result of a cooperative intervention similar to STAD.

There is an interesting discrepancy between the results of laboratory studies (see Cook, 1978; Miller *et al.*, 1985) and the results of the cooperative learning studies involving intergroup competition. Some of the laboratory evidence would suggest that any gains in crossracial friendships within competing groups would be achieved at a cost in friendships toward students in other groups. Yet the strongest evidence for the positive effects of cooperative learning on intergroup relations comes from studies of methods using intergroup competition, such as STAD, TGT and Jigsaw II. For example, the two studies that found maintenance of increased intergroup friendships many months after the end of the interventions were studies of Jigsaw II (Ziegler, 1981) and of STAD (Slavin, 1979) — both of which involved intergroup competition.

This discrepancy is probably due to differences between laboratory studies and field experiments. In laboratory studies interactions are very brief. Subjects have little information about one another, except that introduced by experimental manipulations. If the only knowledge a subject has about another is that he or she is on an opposing team, then the subject has little basis for a positive attitude toward that person. However, the classroom experiments are done in real settings over many months, during which time students have many opportunities to get to know one another. The mechanisms suggested above that explain positive effects of cooperative learning on crossracial choices outside cooperative groups take time to operate. They depend on changes in behaviour, not short-lived changes in perceptions or attitudes.

## CONCLUSIONS

The results of the studies relating cooperative learning to intergroup relations clearly indicate that when students work in ethnically mixed cooperative learning groups, they gain in crossethnic friendships. This research indicates that the effects of cooperative learning on intergroup relations are strong and long-lasting, and are more likely on close, reciprocated friendship choices than on distant or unreciprocated choices. There are no clear patterns indicating more consistent results for some methods than for others. All methods have had some positive effects on intergroup relations.

The evidence discussed in this article generally supports contact theory. However, it raises some important questions about contact theory and related issues. For example, Allport (1954) emphasizes equality of status between individuals of different races as a precondition of positive relations between them. His reference was to situational status (Cook, 1969), by which definition all students in the same grade have the same status. However, Cohen (1975) has suggested that perceived (or actual) performance differences between students of different ethnicities interfere with the development of positive relationships between them. On this basis she has expressed concern that cooperative learning, by making performance differences more salient, may be detrimental to interethnic relations. Positive effects of cooperative learning methods on intergroup relations provide little support for Cohen's concerns, supporting instead Allport's focus on situational rather than performance or ability status. However, this issue needs further study.

Additional research is also needed to discover the effects of cooperative learning on actual intergroup behaviour, particularly behaviour outside school. A few studies (e.g., Oishi, 1983; Ziegler, 1981) have found positive effects of cooperative learning on self-reported crossracial friendships outside class, but behavioural observation in non-classroom settings is still needed. Also, additional long-term follow-up data are needed to establish the duration of the effects of cooperative learning.

The practical implications of the research reported in this chapter are unambiguous. There is a strong positive effect of cooperative learning on intergroup relations. Thirty years after Allport laid out the basic principles, we finally have practical, proven methods for implementing contact theory in the desegregated classroom. These methods are effective for increasing student achievement as well as improving intergroup relations. However, much more work is needed to discover the critical components of cooperative learning and to inform a model of how these methods affect intergroup relations.

## REFERENCES

Allport, F.H. and thirty-four cosigners (1953) 'The Effects of Segregation and the Consequences of Desegregation: A Social Science Statement', *Minnesota Law Review*, 37, pp. 429–440.

Allport, G. (1954) *The Nature of Prejudice*, Cambridge, Mass., Addison-Wesley.

Amir, Y. (1969) 'Contact Hypothesis of Ethnic Relations', *Psychological Bulletin*, 71, pp. 319–343.

Aronson, E., Blaney, N., Stephan, C., Sikes, J. and Snapp, M. (1978) *The Jigsaw Classroom*, Beverly Hills, Calif., Sage.

Blaney, N.T., Stephan, S., Rosenfield, D., Aronson, E. and Sikes, J. (1977) 'Interdependence in the Classroom: A Field Study', *Journal of Educational Psychology*, 69, 2, pp. 121–128.

Brewer, M. (1979) 'In-group Bias in the Minimal Intergroup Situation: A Cognitive-Motivational Analysis', *Psychological Bulletin*, 86, pp. 307–324.

*Brown vs Board of Education*, 347 US 483 (1954).

Cohen, E.G. (1975) 'The Effects of Desegregation on Race Relations', *Law and Contemporary Problems*, 39, pp. 271–299.

Cohen, E.G. and Roper, S. (1972) 'Modification of Interracial Interaction Disability: An Application of Status Characteristics Theory', *American Sociological Review*, 37, pp. 643–657.

Cook, S.W. (1969) 'Motives in a Conceptual Analysis of Attitude-related Behavior', in W. Arnold and D. Levine (Eds), *Nebraska Symposium on Motivation*, Vol. 17, Lincoln, Neb., University of Nebraska Press, pp. 179–236.

Cook, S.W. (1978) 'Interpersonal and Attitudinal Outcomes of Cooperating Interracial Groups', *Journal of Research and Development in Education*, 12, pp. 97–113.

Cook, S.W. (1984) 'The 1954 Social Science Statement and School Desegregation: A Reply to Gerard', *American Psychologist*, 39, pp. 819–832.

Cooper, L., Johnson, D.W., Johnson, R. and Wilderson, F. (1980) 'Effects of Cooperative, Competitive, and Individualistic Experiences on Interpersonal Attraction among Heterogeneous Peers', *Journal of Social Psychology*, 111, pp. 243–252.

DeVries, D.L. and Edwards, K.J. (1974) 'Student Teams and Learning Games: Their Effects on Cross-Race and Cross-Sex Interaction', *Journal of Educational Psychology*, 66, pp. 741–749.

DeVries, D.L. and Slavin, R.E. (1978) 'Teams-Games-Tournament (TGT): Review of Ten Classroom Experiments', *Journal of Research and Development in Education*, 12, pp. 28–38.

DeVries, D.L., Edwards, K.J. and Slavin, R.E. (1978) 'Biracial Learning Teams and Race Relations in the Classroom: Four Field Experiments on Teams-Games-Tournament', *Journal of Educational Psychology*, 70, pp. 356–362.

Gerard, H.B. and Hoyt, M.F. (1974) 'Distinctiveness of Social Categorization and Attitude toward Ingroup Members', *Journal of Personality and Social Psychology*, 29, pp. 836–842.

Gerard, H.B. and Miller, N. (1975) *School Desegregation: A Long-range Study*, New York, Plenum Press.

Gonzales, A. (1979) 'Classroom Cooperation and Ethnic Balance', Paper presented at the annual convention of the American Psychological Association, New York.

Gonzales, A. (1981) 'An Approach to Interdependent–Cooperative Bilingual Education and Measures Related to Social Motives', Unpublished manuscript, California State University at Fresno.

Hansell, S. and Slavin, R.E. (1981) 'Cooperative Learning and the Structure of Interracial Friendships', *Sociology of Education*, 54, pp. 98–106.

Hansell, S., Tackaberry, S.N. and Slavin, R.E. (1981) 'Cooperation, Competition and the Structure of Student Peer Groups', *Representative Research in Social Psychology*, 12, pp. 46–61.

Harrison, A.A. (1976) *Individuals and Groups: Understanding Social Behavior*, Monterey, Calif., Brooks Cole.

Johnson, D.W. and Johnson, R.T. (1975) *Learning Together and Alone*, Englewood Cliffs, N.J., Prentice-Hall.

Johnson, D.W. and Johnson, R.T. (1981) 'Effects of Cooperative and Individualistic Learning Experiences on Interethnic Interaction', *Journal of Educational Psychology*, 73, pp. 444–449.

Kagan, S., Zahn, G.L., Widaman, K.F., Schwarzwald, J. and Tyrell, G. (1985) 'Classroom Structural Bias: Impact of Cooperative and Competitive Classroom Structures on Cooperative and Competitive Individuals and Groups', in R.E. Slavin, S. Sharan, S. Kagan, R. Hertz-Lazarowitz, C. Webb and R. Schmuck (Eds), *Learning to Cooperate: Cooperating to Learn*, New York, Plenum, pp. 277–312.

Lott, A.J. and Lott, B.E. (1965) 'Group Cohesiveness as Interpersonal Attraction: A Review of Relationships with Antecedent and Consequent Variables', *Psychological Bulletin*, 64, pp. 259–309.

Miller, N., Brewer, M.B. and Edwards, K. (1985). 'Cooperative Interaction in Desegregated Settings: A Laboratory Analogue', *Journal of Social Issues*, 41, 3, pp. 63–79.

Oishi, S. (1983) 'Effects of Team Assisted Individualization in Mathematics on Cross-Race Interactions of Elementary School Children', Unpublished doctoral dissertation University of Maryland.

Oishi, S., Slavin, R. and Madden, N. (1983) 'Effects of Student Teams and Individualized Instruction on Cross-Race and Cross-Sex Friendships', Paper presented at the annual meeting of the American Educational Research Association, Montreal, Canada.

St John, N.H. (1975) *School Desegregation: Outcomes for Children*, New York, John Wiley and Sons.

Sharan, S. and Sharan, Y. (1976) *Small-Group Teaching*, Englewood Cliffs, N.J., Educational Technology Publications.

Sharan, S., Kussell, P., Hertz-Lazarowitz, R., Bejarano, Y., Raviv, S. and Sharan, Y. (1984) *Cooperative Learning in the Classroom: Research in Desegregated Schools*, Hillsdale, N.J., Lawrence Erlbaum Associates.

Slavin, R.E. (1977) 'How Student Learning Teams Can Integrate the Desegregated Classroom', *Integrated Education*, 15, 6, pp. 56–58.

Slavin, R.E. (1978) 'Student Teams and Achievement Divisions', *Journal of Research and Development in Education*, 12, pp. 39–49.

Slavin, R.E. (1979) 'Effects of Biracial Learning Teams on Cross-Racial Friendships', *Journal of Educational Psychology*, 71, pp. 381–387.

Slavin, R.E. (1980a) *Using Student Team Learning*, Rev. ed., Baltimore, Md, The Johns Hopkins University, Center for Social Organization of Schools.

Slavin, R.E. (1980b) 'Cooperative Learning', *Review of Educational Research*, 50, pp. 315–342.

Slavin, R.E. (1983a) *Cooperative Learning*, New York, Longman.

Slavin, R.E. (1983b) 'When Does Cooperative Learning Increase Student Achievement?' *Psychological Bulletin*, 94, pp. 429–445.

Slavin, R.E. and Madden, N.A. (1979) 'School Practices that Improve Race Relations', *American Educational Research Journal*. 16, 2, pp. 169–180.

Slavin, R.E. and Oickle, E. (1981). 'Effects of Cooperative Learning Teams on Student Achievement and Race Relations: Treatment by Race Interactions', *Sociology of Education*, 54, pp. 174–180.

Slavin, R.E., Leavey, M. and Madden, N.A. (1984) 'Combining Cooperative Learning and Individualized Instruction: Effects on Student Mathematics Achievement, Attitudes, and Behaviors', *Elementary School Journal*, 84, pp. 409–422.

Stephan, W.G. (1978) 'School Desegregation: An Evaluation of Predictions Made in *Brown vs Board of Education*', *Psychological Bulletin*, 85, pp. 217–238.

Weigel, R.H., Wiser, P.L. and Cook, S.W. (1975) 'Impact of Cooperative Learning Experiences on Cross-Ethnic Relations and Attitudes', *Journal of Social Issues*, 31, 1, pp. 219–245.

Ziegler, S. (1981) 'The Effectiveness of Cooperative Learning Teams for Increasing Cross-Ethnic Friendship: Additional Evidence', *Human Organization*, 40, pp. 264–268.

# 18. Involuntary School Desegregation versus Effective Education

HERBERT J. WALBERG

This chapter begins with a brief account of the early research on segregation cited in the landmark US Supreme Court decision *Brown vs Board of Education of Topeka* of 1954, and summarizes thirty-five years of results of major empirical studies and scholarly commissions on the controversial question of the possible dependence of Black students' learning on the student racial composition of schools. The inconsistency and inconclusiveness of research are traced from the early research to recent work that appears to present a reasonable resolution of the question.

In the US student desegregation generally means moving Black students to majority-White schools and White students to majority-Black schools to attain school quotas close to the overall percentage of students within a school district (or local educational authority). The scholarly literature on school desegregation is vast; and the present review is restricted mainly to effects on Black students' learning. Relatively little research is available concerning desegregation effects on Asian, native American, Hispanic and White students; and this review has little to say about them. Educators, psychologists, social scientists and legal scholars have offered voluminous (though conflicting) opinions about desegregation; this review, apart from the introductory historical section, is an attempt to summarize the factual findings rather than the wide web of value judgments and commentary. Several historical and recent court orders, however, are mentioned in conclusion that may have set important judicial precedents.

**Preliminary Definitions**

Several definitions may be helpful at the outset. In the context of race relations in US schools, de jure ('of law') segregation is the unlawful separation of Black from White students by federal, state or local governmental agencies. It originally involved the denial of Black students' right to go to White public schools nearest their homes, as in *Brown vs Board*; early in the century, for example, several state legislatures in the US enacted laws forbidding local boards of education to allow Black and White students to attend school together.

De jure segregation, however, also included instances of restrictive housing covenants as in northern cities, city annexation or non-annexation of suburban areas, the siting of public housing for poor Blacks in Black rather than White neighbourhoods, and other possibly segregative public laws and acts. De facto segregation, by contrast, is the 'naturally occurring' separation of races attributable to such things as private discrimination; immigration patterns to northern cities from the south; housing choices due to racial differences in income; and personal preferences of Blacks and Whites to live near relatives, friends, churches and other institutions of their own race.

When the courts have found school districts and states liable for segregation, they have often ordered mandatory or voluntary desegregation plans as remedies. Some school districts have also instituted desegregation plans under the threat of lawsuit, or without coercion. Desegregation plans range widely in scope: some allow students to attend voluntarily the schools nearest their homes; others allow voluntary transfers, perhaps induced by distant magnet schools, designed to attract students by distinctive educational programmes.

Mandatory plans, however, may require all schools to be within several percentage points from the total racial percentage in a district by pairing schools or redrawing attendance boundaries. Mandatory plans in larger cities that have neighbourhood racial concentrations are often controversial since they usually require long distance and cross-town transportation that neither Black nor White parents may desire. Nonetheless, since many cities in the US are increasingly racially concentrated, two remedies have recently been urged: the consolidation of city and suburban districts, and magnet schools to attract students across district attendance boundaries.

Those who hold that racial mixing improves Black achievement or confers other special benefits on Black students often use the term 'racial balance'. Sceptics often use the term 'bussing', since it is the usual and often disliked consequence of court orders. The term 'changing racial composition', perhaps less ideologically loaded, is preferred in this review.

### Historical Meanings of *Brown*

Now, more than thirty years after *Brown*, it seems useful to put desegregation research in brief historical context. For additional book-length perspective, see Wolters' (1984) legal history and five case studies of desegregation, including Topeka. See also Anderson's (1984) historical summary of social science research on Black children's educational opportunities from 1900 to 1954, and Bartz and Maehr's (1984) historical account of the development of court remedies for adjudicated Constitution-violating school districts.

In *Brown*, the Supreme Court struck down the 'separate but equal' doctrine of *Plessy vs Ferguson* (1896); and it has been called 'the case of the century' because its principle helped to terminate Jim Crow practices. *Brown* began major changes in American race relations, but it also foreshadowed thirty years of continuing litigation and scholarly controversy about the definition, effects and remedies of educational segregation, and the role of courts and schools in society (Bartz and Maehr, 1984).

As a Black 8-year-old, Linda Carol Brown crossed a railroad yard to catch a bus that brought her twenty-one blocks to a school where she often had to wait half an hour until it opened. Her father, Oliver Brown, felt, as she herself did, that she should have been able to attend a neighbourhood school five blocks from their home. As a mother, she later said:

> I don't want my kids bused. I know what that's like. One of the reasons I went to court back in the 1950s was to escape busing and all the hassle it causes. Kids like me were taken out of our neighborhoods and bused across town. I still feel kids should be able to attend schools in their own neighborhoods. (quoted in Wolters, 1984, p. 270)

Plaintiffs' chief argument in *Brown* was that racial classifications for school assignments implied government approval of the doctrine of Black inferiority and that such classifications are unconstitutional. Said the plaintiffs to the Supreme Court: 'That the Constitution is *color-blind* is our dedicated belief' (Kurland, 1975, p. 49; emphasis added). Further:

> 'What we want from this Court is the striking down of race.... Do no deny any child the right to go to the school of his choice on the grounds of race or color within the normal limits of your districting system.... Do not assign them on the basis of race.... If you have some other basis ... any other basis, we have no objections. But just do not put in race or color as a factor.' (quoted in Wolters, 1984, p. 4)

In his opinion for the Court, moreover, Chief Justice Earl Warren wrote that *Brown* concerned the 'segregation of children in public schools solely on the basis of race' (*Brown vs Board*, 1955, p. 301), which seemed to imply that de facto school segregation resulting from colour-blind district policy was lawful when the reasons were non-racial, such as de facto segregated housing patterns (Wolters, 1984, p. 6).

Yet elsewhere in the opinion Justice Warren wrote that 'separate educational facilities are inherently unequal' and cause 'a feeling of inferiority as to [the Blacks'] status in the community that may affect their hearts and minds in a way unlikely ever to be undone' (p. 298). Indeed, the facilities were clearly unequal; Anderson's (1984) historical studies show that Blacks, particularly in the south, had extremely poor facilities and few years of schooling during the first half of the century. Just as clearly, they were denied the opportunity to go to superior White schools in their neighbourhoods. Equalization of facilities and services, together with racially non-discriminatory, 'colour-blind' assignments would solve these problems (even though large variations in spending and other resources would remain among districts within and among states).

But were White schools superior for another or additional reason — because they were attended by White students? If so, as Wolters points out, the Court's statements imply that only the 'colour-conscious' remedy of changing the racial composition of schools would be acceptable as a remedy. Colour-blind or colour-conscious? Perhaps it was Justice Warren's ambivalence or equivocation that led three decades of scholarly controversy, policy disputes and continuing litigation and court supervision of hundreds of districts affecting millions of children.

After *Brown*, a colour-blind policy was adopted with great success in hotels, restaurants, parks and other public facilities. But with respect to schools, many courts went beyond non-discriminatory, colour-blind policy and called for mandatory changes in the racial composition of schools, seemingly on the theory that racial isolation damages self-concept and therefore educational opportunities and achievement of Black students. This theory, of course, was far from the pleading of *Brown*; it was analogous to assigning Blacks and Whites to eat at restaurants in fixed quotas no matter where they live or work.

At first it appeared to courts that the Constitution required that each person be treated as an individual without regard to race, and that colour-blind remedies would suffice. In *Briggs vs Elliott* (1955), for example, Circuit Court Judge John J. Parker wrote what is sometimes called the *Briggs* doctrine: 'Nothing in the Constitution or in the decision of the Supreme Court takes away from the people the freedom to choose the schools they attend. The Constitution, in other words, does not require integration. It merely forbids discrimination' (p. 777). Congress, moreover, authorized the US Attorney General to initiate desegregation litigation, and defined desegregation as follows: ' "Desegregation" means the assignment of students to public schools without regard to their race, color, religion, or national origin, but "desegregation" shall not mean the assignment of students to public schools in order to overcome racial imbalance' (Public Law 88-352, 1964, p. 246).

This Civil Rights Act, however, was in place for only a few years when the Supreme Court struck down the *Briggs* doctrine and returned to the second apparent meaning of *Brown* (*Green*, 1968). It accepted the views that the Constitution is colour-conscious and that desegregation means colour-conscious involuntary changes in racial composition of schools.

### Contact Theory

Apparently decisive in this second meaning of *Brown* was testimony by Professor Kenneth B. Clark of City College of New York (see Bartz and Maehr, 1984, pp. 144–146). In testimony cited in a famous footnote in *Brown*, he described an experiment in which he had asked Black children questions about the relative attractiveness of a black and a white doll. Between 59 and 67 per cent preferred to play with the white doll, indicated it was a 'nice colour', and said the black doll looked 'bad'. Children from non-segregated schools more frequently chose the white doll and less frequently indicated the black doll looked bad. About one-third of the children said the white doll looked doll looked bad. About one third of the children said the white doll looked like them, and the non-segregated children said so somewhat more often. From these results Clark concluded that de jure segregated schools had a detrimental effect on the self-esteem of Black children:

> I think it is the desire of the Negro to be a human being and to be treated as a human being without regard to skin color. He can only have pride in race — and a healthy and mature pride in race — when his own government does not constantly and continuously tell him, 'Have no pride in race,' by constantly segregating him. (quoted in Kluger, 1976, p. 498)

In his review of this study Stephan (1980) suggested that Clark's data show that segregated children were less rejecting of the black doll, which might lead to higher self-esteem. Lightfoot (1980), moreover, pointed out several vitiating flaws in the methodology, analyses and causal inferences in Clark's study, although she viewed the impact of his testimony as enormous.

If de jure segregation were the sole source of district liability, then non-discriminatory, colour-blind assignments would be a proper remedy. But if Black students were injured by isolation from Whites, then Gordon Allport's (1954) 'contact theory of intergroup relations' might be a proper remedy. This theory had some support in research on adult intergroup relations in housing projects and other settings. According to analogous application of Allport's theory to schools, contact with Whites raises Black self-esteem and reduces hostility toward the self and others under the conditions that: the two groups are of equal status; and have common goals, institutional support and a non-competitive atmosphere. A later version of the theory (Cook, 1969) suggested that the necessary conditions for contact benefits are: equal status and mutual dependence of majority and minority groups; favourable attitudes toward interracial association; behavioural contradiction of prevailing stereotypes of minority group members; and contacts conductive to treating group members as individuals.

These ideal conditions, however, were not and are not easy to establish. If Blacks and Whites differ in socio-economic status and achievement, for example, they could hardly be said to be equal in two critical respects relevant to educational performance. Nor can it be assumed that schools are or should be non-competitive; that parents put desegregation above other considerations such as their children's academic learning and the convenience of neighbourhood schools; that the groups see themselves as mutually dependent; and that colour-conscious racial identification for transportation fosters views of individuality. Indeed, as indicated in subsequent sections of this review, research on educational circumstances at the time of *Brown* as well as later research contradicted these assumptions.

This brief account hardly does justice to the early meanings of segregation and the early ideas and research. Nonetheless, it sets the stage for questions that have since preoccupied the courts and scholars. Does de jure or de facto segregation affect Black achievement, self-esteem and other educational outcomes? Does mandatory or voluntary desegregation improve the achievement outcomes? In addition to these questions that can now be reasonably answered, research of the last two decades yields answers to related questions that deserve consideration: do Blacks and Whites, in fact, want their children to be desegregated? at what cost? and what best raises achievement of children in schools?

## RACIAL COMPOSITION AND BLACK LEARNING

Post-*Brown* research concerned the effects of both naturally occurring and contrived school racial mixing on Black learning — both measured achievements on tests and other school outcomes. Since this research evolved through the decades, it seems most comprehensible to present the major scholarly works in chronological order. It can be seen that several distinguished scholars disagreed with one another, and changed their views. Early points were forgotten; and participants and issues dropped in and out of the continuing debate. Various unconnected arguments rather than cohesive debate took place. Yet, as studies accumulated, more massive evidence could be compiled.


### The Coleman Report and Reanalyses

About a decade after *Brown*, the Congress, under the US Civil Rights Act, commissioned the Equality of Educational Opportunity survey, often called the 'Coleman Report' after its principal author, James S. Coleman (1966), then at Johns Hopkins University. The survey of more than 645,000 students in about 4000 schools was possibly the largest national survey ever conducted (aside from the census). It showed that, within regions of the country, roughly equal facilities, staff and programmes were available to Black and White students. With respect to some educational resources Whites were slightly advantaged on average over Blacks; but with respect to other resources Blacks were advantaged; no discernable pattern of resource discrimination seemed apparent. This was not to say that resources within the country were equal; in the deep south and border states that had the highest concentration of Black students, tangible resources were clearly inferior to those in other parts of the country. Surprisingly, however, the survey also suggested that costly school resources made little difference in learning.

The original report showed that average Black students in all-Black schools did better than those in which they were in the minority, even though Blacks in White schools were superior to other Blacks in socio-economic status. Although Coleman first concluded that desegregation improves Black achievement, later analyses suggested to him that racial desegregation does not help Black learning (see, for example, Bailey's (n.d.) report for the National Academy of Education and the US Department of Health, Education, and Welfare on the twenty-fifth anniversary of *Brown*).

The Coleman Report revealed that roughly equal resources were being expended within regions only a decade after the *Brown* decision; but it generated considerable controversy with respect to (1) the possible influence of racial composition on Black achievement, and (2) the apparent lack of association of tangible educational resources and learning. For the next two decades scholars debated these two points.

The corpus of Coleman data was so massive and complex that other investigators took about eight years to reanalyze it and publish their work. Two groups acquired the data and published extensive reports on them in 1972. Mosteller and Moynihan's report confirmed Coleman's conclusions of equal resources for Blacks and Whites, and of an apparent small positive effect of racial mixing on learning. They also found that Black students scored substantially below Whites in first grade and fall further behind in the later grades — a phenomenon sometimes called 'the cumulative deficit' or 'the Matthew effect', named after the passage in the Bible about the rich getting richer. The other group, led by Christopher Jencks, however, found the racial mixture effects to be small and inconsistent. They concluded that neither Coleman nor any other investigator had ever shown definite positive effects of racial mixture on Black achievement. They attributed school success and social mobility to family socio-economic influence and personal luck rather than to educational quality or equality.


## Early Reviews of Desegregation Studies

Coleman and subsequent reanalysts were trying to determine, among other things, the possible influence of 'naturally occurring' racial mixtures on Black learning; these were naturally occurring in the sense of reflecting racial composition of schools determined by such causes as personal choice, private discrimination and historical immigration. But by 1972 several 'contrived' desegregation plans had been implemented by districts and metropolitan clusters of districts voluntarily or under court order; and these had been evaluated. In some respects evidence from the longitudinal evaluations could in principle be more telling than the Coleman survey because several studies assessed the learning gains of desegregated and control group children over periods of time.

Two groups attacked the question by compiling and assessing the evidence concerning contrived desegregation on Black learning. David Armor (1972) reviewed the evaluations and found no evidence for its positive desegregation effects on Black learning, self-concept and racial attitudes. Thomas Pettigrew and others (1972) re-examined the research compiled by Armor and several other studies. They concluded that Armor was wrong and that school desegregation had a positive effect on average.

At about this time Black educationist Ronald Edmunds (1973) returned to an earlier question raised by Coleman about the lack of systematic school effects on learning. He and several other Black scholars wrote an article criticizing the Jencks group for overemphasizing luck in the determination of Black achievement. They concluded that the Jencks group had given insufficient attention to school quality and educational effectiveness as determinants of Black achievement and life success. (Edmunds later led the 'effective schools' movement in New York City and later the nation before his untimely death.)

Three reviews of the possible influences of desegregation (including natural and contrived) on Black learning appeared in the period 1975 through 1977. In a 1975 book Nancy St John gathered sixty-four available studies of the possible influence of racial mixture and desegregation on Black learning. She found the evidence inconclusive, and noted that White learning may be hurt in desegregated settings. In 1977 Meyer Weinberg reviewed forty-eight studies of desegregation and found that twenty-nine, or 60 per cent, showed positive effects on Black achievement. Since, however, 40 per cent of the studies showed no significant effect or a harmful effect of desegregation on learning, the evidence appeared mixed at best. In 1977 Lawrence and Gifford Bradley reviewed the literature on the subject and concluded that there are sometimes positive and sometimes negative effects, and that the evidence is inconsistent and inconclusive.


## Black Perspectives

Thomas Sowell (1974, 1976), a Black economist writing for the *Public Interest*, reported his studies of eight schools that were outstandingly productive of members of the Black élite. Of the schools he studied, four (located in Atlanta, Baltimore, New Orleans and Washington) educated a long list of graduates that made outstanding Black breakthroughs, including the first Black state superintendent of schools, Supreme Court Justice, and military general, as well as the discoverer of blood plasma, a Nobel Prize winner, and the only Black US Senator in this century.

Sowell (1976) attributed the outstanding success of these schools neither to random events nor to natural abilities of their students but to the social order of these institutions and concerted, persevering educational efforts: 'Each of these schools currently maintaining high standards was a very quiet and orderly school, whether located in a middle-class suburb of Atlanta or in the heart of a deteriorating ghetto in Brooklyn' (p. 54). Strong principals concentrated on achievement and discipline:

> 'Respect' was the word most used by those interviewed to describe the attitudes of students and parents toward these schools. 'The teacher was *always* right' was a phrase that was used again and again to describe the attitude of the black parents of a generation or more ago.... Even today, in those few instances where schools have the confidence of black parents, a wise student maintains a discrete silence at home about his difficulties with teachers, and hopes that the teachers do the same. (p. 54)

In 1978 two Black sociologists at the University of Chicago wrote important works on the subject of racial mixing and Black learning. The first confirmed an earlier suspicion that non-cognitive outcomes such as motivation and self-concept may be unrelated to racial composition. In 'The Impact of School Desegregation on the Self-Evaluation and Achievement Orientation of Minority Children' Edgar Epps concluded: 'It seems clear that generalizing about the impact of desegregation on self-concept is unwarranted. As Christmas and Weinberg concluded after reviewing the literature, the findings are generally inconclusive' (p. 71).

The second Chicago sociologist, William Julius Wilson (1978), raised the question of whether an individual's race is the critical determinant of opportunity and achievement. In *The Declining Significance of Race* he retraced the history of the slave economy of the south and the immigration of Blacks to industrialized northern cities during the two world war periods. He pointed out today's vast differences between Blacks of higher and lower socio-economic status. Wilson argued that it is misleading to categorize people racially because socio-economic status is the far more important determinant of behaviour:

> To say that race is declining in significance, therefore, is not only to argue that the life chances of blacks have less to do with race than with economic class affiliation but also to maintain that racial conflict and competition in the economic sector — the most important historical factors in the subjugation of blacks — have been substantially reduced. (p. 152)

These insights suggested that socio-economic status and other variables had to be taken into consideration more explicitly. Perhaps the possible effects of racial composition on Black achievement were different depending on the socio-economic status of schools. Perhaps, also, the possible effects differed in the north and south, since the south was generally more poor and had historically more extensive de jure segregation. In addition, many Black families in the north had migrated from the south; they may have been different in initiative and self-concept, and were demonstrably different in socio-economic status from those in the south.

Several sociological surveys described in the next section were to study these possibilities. These surveys are admitedly complex, tedious and inconclusive. Less patient readers may wish to skip to the subheading on policy implications.


## SOCIOLOGICAL SURVEYS

Crain and Mahard (1978) reported an extensive racial composition survey that examined not only achievement but also later outcomes such as college attendance. They started with the following observation about racial composition:

> The general conclusion seems to be that the differences in achievement between black students in predominantly white schools and those in black schools was on the order of one-fifth of a standard deviation net of individual social class differences. However, there was little agreement among the analysts about how to interpret this, with many arguing that problems in the low reliability of social class measurement, coupled with the self-selection of high ability black students into white schools, might explain the difference.

Thus highly motivated Blacks may have anticipated better college preparation in White schools; their slight average superiority to other Blacks on achievement and other outcomes, occasionally observed, may have been attributable to pre-existing differences in motivation and social class, not to attending predominantly White schools. Crain and Mahard noted that scholars had raised but not tested these possibilities.

They also pointed to a National Opinion Research Center analysis of 200 southern schools that 'found relatively weak effects of school racial composition' and that 'black males performed poorly in schools which were overwhelmingly white' (p. 82). Aside from race, they pointed out that the effects of social class composition of the school upon college attendance were controversial, and that in some cases attending a middle-class high school had a negative effect on working-class students' college attendance: 'One of the reasons for this', in their reasoning, 'is that a middle-class school serves both to encourage and to discourage a working-class student from higher education. This discouragement occurs because the middle-class students are likely to be of higher academic ability than their working-class peers, and the working-class students, doing badly in competition for grades, may decide that they do not have college potential' (p. 83).

Crain and Mahard abstracted their survey findings as follows:

> [S]outhern black students graduating from predominantly white high schools are less likely to attend and survive in college. Southern black achievement is not related to school racial composition. In the North, black achievement, college attendance and college survival are all higher in predominantly white schools.

Further, with respect to the self-selection hypothesis: 'An attempt is made to test the hypothesis that the higher outcomes for black students in predominantly white schools are due to the "self selection" of the more motivated black students into the white schools. The test reveals some evidence of self-selection in the South' (p. 81).

Their analysis that controls for such self-selection (Table 5) showed that the higher the segregation, the higher the mean college attendance and persistence rates of Black students in the south. Black achievement in the south was highest in the most highly segregated schools. Referring to a National Opinion Research Center study (1973) showing that southern Blacks graduating from predominantly White high schools were less likely to attend college than those who attended segregated schools, Crain and Mahard noted the 'unfortunate irony that the region of the country which has experienced the greatest amount of desegregation is also the one where the effects of desegregation are negative' (p. 98).

In summarizing their conclusions, Crain and Mahard wrote: '[B]lacks attending predominantly white schools in the South are 5 per cent less likely to attend college. We find that only 10 per cent of the blacks graduating from predominantly white schools are college juniors three years later, compared to 16 per cent of the graduates from all-black schools.... We cannot decide from these data whether attending a predominantly white school does not help blacks, or whether it harms them' (p. 98).

### Complications and Challenges

It seemed odd that segregation would hurt learning in the south but help in the north. Indeed, Crain and Mahard's findings were soon challenged in the same journal, *Sociology of Education*, in which they originally published their findings. Eckland (1979) summarized his contradictory results as follows:

> Crain and Mahard recently reported that the effects of high school desegregation for blacks on school achievement and college attendance were negative in the South and positive in the North. Using the same data but re-specifying the model, i.e., introducing curriculum and grades and relocating the test scores, leads to markedly different results. The negative consequences for blacks of attending a predominantly white high school are not on college attendance but on high school grades and curriculum placement. Contrary to Crain and Mahard's conclusions, moreover, the deleterious effects of school desegregation not only appear in the North but are more severe there than in the South. (p. 122)

The data then from this large survey seemed to shift the research question. Earlier it had been asked if increasing White racial composition would help Black learning, and under what circumstances? Crain and Mahard, and Eckland seemed to raise the question of when it did harm, and under what circumstances?

Similarly, in 1980 Patchen, Hofmann and Brown reported a particularly comprehensive analysis of racial composition and Black learning. They collected data from eleven Indianapolis, Indiana public high schools ranging in racial composition from over 99 per cent Black to 99 per cent White, and they considered the joint effects of racial and socio-economic composition, as well as educational programmes and interracial friendships, on student effort, grades, academic values and achievement scores. What their survey lacked in size, it made up for in having more measures and in testing the possible differential effects of White schools of higher and lower socio-economic status on Black learning.

With ability and socio-economic status controlled, neither school racial composition nor friendship with Whites had statistically significant effects on effort, grades and academic values of Black students. Curriculum programme, however, had large, consistent and highly significant effects on these outcomes: students in the academic programmes did consistently better than those in the general, practical and fine arts programmes. Thus, when compared in the same study, the quality of the education (even crudely indicated by programme type) had a large effect; and racial composition had an insignificant effect.

Moreover, contrary to what earlier had been thought, 'attending mostly white classes was associated with higher effort among blacks whose [white] peers were from lower-education families and were not academically oriented. However, the impact of interracial contact on academic outcomes was small' (p. 33). Thus the small benefits to Blacks arose from contacts with White students of lower socio-economic status; educational harms to Blacks arose from school contacts with White students of higher socio-economic status (interracial contacts had a small negative effect on academic outcomes for White students, as St John had tentatively concluded from her earlier review).

### Policy Implications

In sum, these analyses seemed to have the following implications. From Crain and Mahard: segregate Blacks in the south; desegregate them in the north; from Eckland: segregate Blacks in the north and south; from Patchen and others: mix Blacks with poor and academically unmotivated Whites (although it would harm White students, and although educational factors were far more beneficial for all, whatever the racial composition of their schools).

Given the conflicting findings and implications of the surveys, as well as from the earlier Coleman Report and from the compilations of evaluations of desegregation programmes, it may have been too much to hope that the results might somehow be sorted out and put in plain language with clear and constructive policy implications. At the time large cities such as Boston and Los Angeles, as well as many small cities, were undergoing court-ordered desegregation with mandatory cross-town transportation, despite the mixed results and the controversial and inconclusive history of research.

A series of national Gallup polls, moreover, showed that although the public favoured integration (mutual, positive racial attitudes), 75 per cent of public school parents favoured a Constitutional amendment prohibiting involuntary bussing to achieve desegregation; and the bulk of Whites and the majority of Blacks were against such transportation. Second only to discipline, moreover, the public most frequently mentioned desegregation as the major problem facing the schools (see, for example, Gallup, 1974). Policy-makers craved answers, but even the most distinguished scholarly group at the time could not agree on the major questions of fact and implication.

## THE NATIONAL ACADEMY REPORT

On the twenty-fifth anniversary of *Brown*, the National Academy of Education, commissioned by the US Department of Health, Education, and Welfare, appointed a panel to examine the meaning of the case and its subsequent history

(Bailey, n.d.). Under the chairmanship of the distinguished urban educator Robert J. Havighurst, the eighteen-member panel attempted to settle the difficult questions raised by subsequent controversy. In the panel's words, however, they found 'themselves deeply divided over the historical reality, the contemporary meaning, and the future portent of that luminous Constitutional lodestar' (p. 1). Not even the original meaning of *Brown* seemed clear. Panelist Diane Ravitch wrote:

> The social science testimony introduced in the *Brown* case in Topeka consisted of statements by educators and psychologists, who expressed their views rather than introducing specific research findings. Their views were of two kinds: one, that there was no significant difference between children of different races, so that there was no rational basis for assigning children to school on the basis of their color; and two, that black children were deprived by lack of contact with white children, since interracial experience was valuable in itself. Thus the social science testimony was essentially ambivalent.... What was left unresolved by the social scientists' testimony was a dilemma: should school-assignment be color-blind or color-conscious? Were black parents suing for the right to send their children to the nearest school or for the right to an integrated education? Was the constitutional wrong to blacks the denial of liberty or the denial of integration? (p. 7)

On the other hand, rapporteur Stephen Bailey noted:

> This strict construction of *Brown* — that *Brown* was concerned essentially with the 'color-blindness' of the law and with *de jure* segregation only — is countered by those Panel Contributors who, as we have seen, stress the *Brown* dictum that 'separate schools are inherently unequal.' It is, they argue, the 'separatism' that is the underlying evil — even when that separatism emerges from constraints that are not specifically segregationist in a legal sense. Furthermore, they argue, there is no way of making color irrelevant until there is enough racial integration to prove in fact that 'unequal history' has been overcome. (p. 7)

The group could reach little consensus on other questions related to desegregation and Black achievement. Was desegregation diverting attention from the quality of Black schools? Was it causing self-defeating White light from mandatory bussing in the cities? Finally and most relevant to this review, 'The Panel Contributors are also divided as to whether desegregation policies have in fact had a beneficial effect on the scholastic achievement of black children.' Thomas Pettigrew claimed positive effects, and James Coleman argued that about as many studies showed negative as those that showed positive effects. Benjamin Bloom, however, put forward evidence that superior instruction clearly helps all students (Bailey, n.d., pp. 17–18).

## RESEARCH SYNTHESIS

Beginning about 1975, educational psychologists began employing standard statistical techniques to synthesize quantitatively the findings in collections of many studies of instruction and other learning influences. Bloom (1976), for example, compiled the results of dozens of studies of personal and educational effects on learning. Such things as motivation, time on task, corrective feedback, reinforcement, tutoring and gearing the difficulty of lessons to individual learners' needs, and particularly parental involvement, turned out to have very large beneficial effects, and they almost always worked effectively (Walberg, 1984). That is, average educational effects from six to more than twelve months[1] of extra educational achievement growth (beyond conventionally instructed control groups) were found with some educational treatments; experimental groups exceeded control groups in as many as 95 per cent of the comparisons.

Many of the studies of these factors, moreover, employed random assignment of students to experimental and control conditions, and pre-tests and post-tests to measure actual gains, instead of using controversial assumptions and statistical adjustments to eliminate biases of correlational surveys. The same could be done for studies of racial composition and Black achievement, and it soon was.

Krol (1984), for example, compiled seventy-one comparisons from fifty-five studies of desegregation effects on Black learning; 61 per cent of the studies favoured desegregated groups, and the average gain was 1.6 months (averages close to zero, of course, mean that some comparisons revealed harms, in fact, 39 per cent in this case). Crain and Mahard (1982) assembled ninety-three studies of the effects of school desegregation on Black achievement. The overall average effect suggested that desegregated students differed by less than a month (.07 standard deviations) from segregated students. The total percentage of studies with positive effects (under their definition) among 321 comparisons was 54 per cent — close to the 50 per cent expectation of a coin toss.

## A Resolution

In 1982 the National Institute of Education (NIE), then the research arm of the US Department of Education, commissioned a panel of six scholars to try to settle the question by the technique of quantitative synthesis. These included two who had previously claimed or believed that the effects were positive (Robert Crain and Paul Wortman), two who espoused no effects (David Armor and Norman Miller) and two who were sceptical or open-minded (Walter Stephan and Herbert Walberg). Thomas Cook served as a methodological consultant.

A total of 157 studies were identified; but the panel agreed to include only the nineteen most rigorous and methodologically acceptable studies and to allow each scholar to add or subtract from that core based upon departures from their standards, such as the use of achievement pre-tests and post-tests before and after segregation to measure gains over control groups. Since it is filled with many numbers, the resulting 224-page volume cannot easily be summarized. Nonetheless, summaries by two non-participating reviewers are worth quoting.

Dennis Cuddy (1983) of the US Department of Education reviewed the work of the group and wrote: 'The conclusion to be drawn from these 19 best studies is that desegregation has not significantly improved black achievement levels. What slight positive nonsignificant gains there were in the 19 studies came from the 14 voluntary programmes, as the five mandatory programmes showed collectively either no gain or an actual decline in academic achievement' (p. 26).

Writing for the US Commission on Civil Rights, Max Green (1984) summarized the answers of the NIE panel to 'one of the great social science questions of our time' (p. 35).

> There was a variety of views:
> Armor: 'The conclusion is inescapable: the very best studies available demonstrate no significant and consistent effects of desegregation on black achievement.'

Walberg: 'School desegregation does not appear promising in the size or consistency of its effect on learning of black students.'

Stephan: 'These results appear to indicate that verbal achievement improves somewhat but math achievement shows little effect as a result of desegregation.'

Miller: 'The desegregation studies that met the NIE minimal criteria show some moderate academic benefit to black children when they attend desegregated schools. . . . the magnitude of these effects translates into the rather trivial increase of about twenty points on the typical SAT.'

Wortman: 'The effect size found in both (math and reading) analyses . . . indicates about a two-month gain or benefit for desegregated students.'

Cook [the methodological watchdog]: 'Desegregation probably does not increase math achievement, . . . it probably raises reading scores between two and six weeks.'

Of the seven panelists only Crain came to different conclusions, and he was specifically criticized by four of his colleagues for using the data of studies that the others threw out for methodological deficiencies. Both Armor and Cook pointed out that if these weak studies were eliminated from Crain's analysis, his conclusions would 'have been roughly equivalent to those of the other panel members' (p. 36). Assuming Cook's estimate of two to six weeks in reading for purposes of discussion, Green noted that desegregation

will just begin to close the more than one year gap now separating white and black children.

In fact this minimal gain may be an illusion. Most studies that were reviewed showed no effects whatsoever. This may mean, as David Armor suggests, that the few studies that reported large effects were picking up the impact of special educational programs that were implemented simultaneously with integration plans. (p. 36)

Cook himself noted that studies that showed reading gains tended to involve desegregated children who outperformed their segregated counterparts even before desegregation began, who were voluntarily desegregated, and who, unlike their control groups, had educational enrichment programmes simultaneously with their desegregation experience. Thus the apparent effect in reading observed in a few cases that showed slight differences was probably caused by pre-existing group differences in ability or motivation, or improved quality of instruction. Indeed, as indicated previously, strong evidence for these alternative explanations had appeared in previous large-scale surveys and well-designed instructional experiments.

## DESEGREGATION, EDUCATIONAL EFFECTIVENESS AND THE COURTS

In his NIE paper Walberg summarized the overall estimates of Krol, Crain and Mahard, and the set of nineteen studies acceptable to the panel; he carried out standard tests of their statistical significance, and compared the estimates to effects of well-known educational factors. By the standards of percentage of positive results and magnitude of effects, none of the desegregation syntheses yielded statistical significance at the standard (two-tailed .05) level. Nor were desegregation effects comparable to the consistency and magnitude of even mediocre educational effects. On the contrary, some educational techniques such

as reinforcement, acceleration, mastery techniques, cooperative learning, tutoring, parent involvement programmes and graded homework had effects up to
eight or more times larger than the estimates of desegregation effects.

The estimates of the educational effects were derived from more than 2500
small-scale experiments carried on in schools during the previous thirty years, as
well as recent statistically controlled survey estimates from large surveys including
the National Assessment of Educational Progress, High School and Beyond, and
the International Association for the Evaluation of Educational Achievement
(Walberg, 1984). These experiments and surveys showed consistent, strong effects
of quite plausible educational and social factors, namely, the amount and quality
of instruction, and parental encouragement of the child's intellectual growth at
home and intensive involvement in their children's educational activities at
school.

In 1984 John Hattie, an Australian, also reviewed available syntheses of
desegregation and educational factors. He attributed the very small average effect
of desegregation to only a few studies that were inconsistent with the others. He
concluded: 'It appears that desegregation, at least as far as it has been operationalized, is not related to increasing academic or self-concept outcomes'
(p. 13).


**Recent Court Rulings**

Despite much hope and considerable research, despite authoritative commissions
and lengthy deliberation, no consistent evidence of the positive effects of school
racial composition or desegregation on Black learning has been forthcoming.
Where small effects had been shown, some were positive and some were negative.
The positive effects were convincingly accounted for by other explanations with
clearcut empirical support; notably, desegregated children were superior to their
counterpart control groups at the outset, or were given superior instruction.
Quality educational programmes, without desegregation, moreover, showed far
larger effects on both Black and White learning than quality education programmes with desegregation.

Reflecting this new knowledge, the tide in courts seems to be turning toward
education and away from racial composition as an answer to the learning problems of Black children, perhaps because of the great concern in the public and
among policy-makers about improving educational achievement among all US
children, but especially poor children in cities. The US Supreme Court, for
example, refused to order an injunction against the plan of Norfolk, Virginia
public schools, led by a Black superintendent, to terminate mandatory cross-town
bussing, leave ten schools racially concentrated and launch educational and parent
involvement programmes in neighbourhood schools (*New York Times*, 23 June
1986). The appeals court had also refused to overturn the federal court's order:

> We agree with the district court that the evidence reveals that Norfolk's neighbor-
> hood school assignment plan is a reasonable attempt by the school board to keep as
> many white students in public education as possible and so achieve a stably inte-
> grated school system. It also represents an attempt to improve the quality of the
> school system by seeking a programme to gain greater parental involvement. While
> the effect of the plan in creating several black schools is disquieting, that fact alone is
> not sufficient to prove discriminatory intent. (*Riddick*, p. 59)

Similarly, the appeals court supported the federal district court order against special pleadings by the Richmond, Virginia Public Schools for extra desegregation funds. The lower court had reached the following conclusion:

> Plaintiffs contend that the State should be required to provide additional funding to the Richmond Public Schools because improved programs would attract more white students to RPS. Plaintiffs allege that the achievement levels of black students in RPS have been adversely affected by the low percentage of white students currently in the school system. The Court finds, however, that this assertion is unsupported by, and actually contrary to, the evidence introduced at trial, for there is no correlation between the ratio of blacks to whites in RPS and the performance levels of RPS students. Moreover, in examining the performance levels of students in school districts Statewide, it is clear that performance is unrelated to racial composition. (*Bradley*, 1986, p. 33)

Similarly, in *Dowell* (1987) the federal district court found Oklahoma City unitary or non-discriminatory. Praising the district's 'effective schools' and related programmes, the judge ruled as follows:

> 'Plantiffs further contend that young black students cannot achieve academically in schools which are not racially balanced. A substantial amount of evidence and expert testimony was offered on this subject at the hearing, and the court concludes that this suggestion is without merit. Any suggestion that young blacks are intellectually inferior to young whites is contrary to empirical evidence. Socioeconomic status and the level of parental involvement, rather than the degree of racial balance, are the primary factors which impact student achievement'. (p. 1523)

## NOTE

1  Since they may be intuitively simpler to understand, gains are sometimes expressed in months rather than the roughly equivalent tenths of standard deviation units. Other time units such as weeks and years may be similarly employed for purposes of illustration, under the crude equivalence of a twelve-month gain and one unit of standard deviation.

## REFERENCES

Allport, G.W. (1954) *The Nature of Prejudice*, Reading, Mass., Addison-Wesley.

Anderson, J.D. (1984) 'The Schooling and Achievement of Black Children: Before and after *Brown v. Topeka*, 1900–1980', in D.E. Bartz and M.L. Maehr (Eds), *The Effects of School Desegregation on Motivation and Achievement*, Greenwich, Conn., JAI Press.

Armor, D.J. (1972) 'The Evidence on Busing', *The Public Interest*, 28, Summer, pp. 90–126.

Bailey, S.K. (Rapporteur) (n.d.) *Prejudice and Pride: The Brown Decision after Twenty-Five Years May 17, 1954–May 17, 1954, Report from the National Academy of Education*, Washington, D.C., US Department of Health, Education, and Welfare.

Bartz, D.E. and Maehr, M.L. (Eds) (1984) *The Effects of School Desegregation on Motivation and Achievement*, Greenwich, Conn., JAI Press.

Bloom, B.S. (1976) *Human Characteristics and School Learning*, New York, McGraw-Hill.

*Bradley vs Baliles, Final Order*, US District Court for the Eastern Division of Virginia, 10 July 1986.

Bradley, L.A. and Bradley, G.W. (1977) 'The Academic Achievement of Black Students in Desegregated Schools: A Critical Review', *Review of Educational Research*, 47, pp. 399–451.

*Briggs vs Elliott*, 926 F. Supp. 36 1955.

*Brown vs Board of Education of Topeka* (1954) 347 US 483; (1955) 349 US 295.

Clark, R.M. (1983) *Family Life and School Achievement: Why Poor Black Children Succeed or Fail*, Chicago, Ill., University of Chicago Press.

Coleman, J.S., *et al.* (1966) *Equality of Educational Opportunity*, Washington, D.C., US Department of Health, Education, and Welfare and US Government Printing Officer.

Cook, S.W. (1969) 'Motives in a Conceptual Analysis of Attitude-related Behavior', in W.J. Arnold and D. Levine (Eds), *Nebraska Symposium on Motivation*, Lincoln, Neb., University of Nebraska Press.

Crain, R.L. and Mahard, R.E. (1978) 'School Racial Composition and Black College Attendance and Achievement Test Performance', *Sociology of Education*, 51, pp. 81–101.

Crain, R.L. and Mahard, R.E. (1982) *Desegregation Plans that Raise Black Achievement: A Review of the Research*, Santa Monica, Calif., Rand Corporation.

Cuddy, D.L. (1983) 'A Proposal to Achieve Desegregation through Free Choice', *American Education*, 19, 4, pp. 25–31.

*Dowell vs Board of Education of Oklahoma City*, 677 F. Supp. 1503 (Western District of Oklahoma) 1987.

Eckland, B.K. (1979) 'School Racial Composition and College Attendance Revised', *Sociology of Education*, 52, pp. 122–125.

Edmunds, R., *et al.* (1973) 'A Black Response to Christopher Jencks's *Inequality* and Certain Other Issues', *Harvard Educational Review*, 43, 1, pp. 76–91.

Epps, E.G. (1978) 'The Impact of School Desegregation on the Self-Evaluation and Achievement Orientation of Minority Children', *Law and Contemporary Problems*, 42, 3, pp. 57–77.

Gallup, G. (1974) 'Major Problems Confronting the Public Schools, and Busing to Achieve Racial Integration', *Phi Delta Kappan*, 56, 1, pp. 21–26.

*Green vs County School Board of New Kent County* (1968) 391 US 430.

Green, M. (1984) 'Thinking Realistically about Integration', *New Perspectives*, Fall, pp. 35–36.

Hattie, J.A. (1984) *Identifying the Salient Facets of a Model of Student Learning: A Synthesis of Meta-Analyses*, Armidale, Aust., University of New England, Centre for Behavioural Studies.

Jencks, C., *et al.* (1972) *Inequality: A Reassessment of the Effect of Family and Schooling in America*, New York, Harper and Row.

Kluger, R. (1976 ) *Simple Justice*, New York, Knopf.

Krol, R.A. (1984) 'Desegregation and Academic Achievement', in Bartz, D.E. and Maehr, M.L. (Eds), *The Effects of School Desegregation on Motivation and Achievement*, Greenwich, Conn., JAI Press.

Kurland, P.B. (1975) *Landmark Briefs and Arguments of the Supreme Court*, Arlington, Va., University Publications of America.

Lightfoot, S.L. (1980) 'Families as Educators: The Forgotten People of Brown', in D. Bell (Ed.), *Shades of Brown*, New York, Teachers College Press.

Miller, V.R. (1979) 'The Emergent Patterns of Integration', *Educational Leadership*, February, pp. 308–312.

Mosteller, F. and Moynihan, D.P. (Eds), (1972) *On Equality of Educational Opportunity*, New York, Vintage Books, Random House.

National Institute of Education (1984) *School Desegregation and Black Achievement*, Washington, D.C., US Department of Education.

National Opinion Research Center (1973) *Southern Schools: An Evaluation of Emergency School Assistance Program and of School Desegregation*, Chicago, Ill., University of Chicago.

Patchen, M., Hofmann, G. and Brown, W.R. (1980) 'Academic Performance of Black High School Students under Different Conditions of Contact with White Peers', *Sociology of Education*, 53, pp. 33–51.

Pettigrew, T.F., Smith, M., Useem, E.L. and Normand, C. (1973) 'Busing: A Review of "the Evidence",' *The Public Interest*, 30, Winter, pp. 88–118.

*Plessy vs Ferguson* (1896) 163 US 537.

*Riddick vs School Board of the City of Norfolk* (6 February 1986) US Court of Appeals for the Fourth Circuit, No. 84-1815.

St John, N.H. (1975) *School Desegregation: Outcomes for Children*, New York, John Wiley and Sons.

Sowell, T. (1974) 'Black Excellence: The Case of Dunbar High School', *Public Interest*, 35, Spring, pp. 1–21.

Sowell, T. (1976) 'Patterns of Black Excellence', *Public Interest*, 43, Spring, pp. 26–58.

Stephan, W.W. (1980) 'A Brief Historical Overview of School Desegregation', in W.G. Stephan and

J.R. Fegin (Eds), *School Desegregation: Past, Present, and Future*, New York, Plenum Press.

*US Civil Rights Act* (1964) Public Law 88-352.

Walberg, H.J. (1984) 'Improving the Productivity of America's Schools', *Educational Leadership*, 41, 8, pp. 19–27.

Weinberg, M. (1977) *Minority Students: A Research Appraisal*, Washington, D.C., US Department of Health, Education, and Welfare and US Government Printing Office.

Wilson, W.J. (1978) *The Declining Significance of Race*, Chicago, Ill., University of Chicago Press.

Wolters, R. (1984) *The Burden of Brown: Thirty Years of School Desegregation*, Nashville, Tenn., University of Tennessee Press.

# 19. Pride, Prejudice and Power: The Mass Media as Societal Educator on Diversity

CARLOS E. CORTÉS

18 September 1986. Relaxing in my Riverside, California, home, enjoying my customary third cup of morning coffee and scanning the daily newspapers, I chanced to turn on the popular American daytime television game show, *The $25,000 Pyramid*.

*Pyramid* provides the ideal combination of background distraction and distracting challenge for a committed media double-dipper who enjoys basking in a TV ambience while reading. Competition in *Pyramid* involves two pairs of contestants. For each team, a series of words appears on a screen in front of one player, who then gives clues to guide the partner into correctly identifying the maximum number of words within the time limit. The team that gets the most correct words wins.

Then it happened. As I watched, the word 'gangs' popped onto one cluer's screen. Without hesitation, he shouted, 'They have lots of these in East LA' (a heavily Mexican-American section of Los Angeles). Responding immediately, the guest celebrity partner answered, 'Gangs'. Under competitive pressure, two strangers had instantly achieved mental communion through their coinciding visions of a Chicano community as being synonymous with gangs. Moreover, they had transmitted this ethnic stereotype to a national television audience.

Unfortunately, East Lost Angeles does have Chicano gangs. But it also has a multitude of far more prevalent elements, like families, schools, business, churches and socially contributing organizations. Yet gangs, not such other aspects of East LA life, had rapidly and reflexively linked these total strangers. Why?

The answer lies with the media, whose continuous fascination with Latino gangs — from new reports and documentaries to TV series and feature films — has elevated and reinforced them as *the* quintessential popular vision of East LA (and many other Latino communities). *Pyramid* both dramatized this media impact and added to the media bombardment. The media, in short, have created a gang-featuring public curriculum on Latinos.

Moreover, the *Pyramid* episode illustrates an even broader phenomenon: the power of the media to influence public perceptions, not just of Latinos, but of any ethnic or racial group — and not just racial and ethnic groups, but also foreign nations and world cultures. Conceived as an educational metaphor, the media provide a public curriculum on myriad topics, including race, ethnicity, culture and nationality.

The degree to which the media actually *create* intercultural visions and stereotypes, pride and prejudice, can be debated. Beyond debate, however, is the fact that they *contribute* to intercultural, interracial and interethnic beliefs, perceptions and attitudes, including prejudice, as well as to group self-image, including pride (or lack of it). This power to influence rests not only with those involved in the so-called news or factual media, but also with those who create so-called entertainment.

No matter how vociferously mediamakers may disclaim their educational power and no matter how obstinately entertainment mediamakers, in particular, may claim that they merely provide diversion, evidence clearly demonstrates that the media, including the entertainment media, teach. Identifying what different individuals learn from the media, however, poses a considerable challenge.

Numerous complexities arise concerning the media's role in contributing to ethnic pride and intergroup prejudice. This essay deals briefly with five of these questions. How do the media fit within the larger process of educating the public about race, ethnicity, culture and foreignness? What dilemmas must be faced in attempting to assess media impact in these areas? What is the nature of that media influence? What forms of evidence provide insight into that influence? What effective actions can be adopted to address that influence?

## THE MEDIA CURRICULUM

The mass media as a social force should be examined within the broader context of societal education. Discussions of education often, and erroneously, use schools and education as synonymous concepts. Certainly schools comprise a powerful component of the educational process. However, they do not monopolize education, nor could they even if they wished.

People learn through schools. But they also learn outside schools through what I have termed the 'societal curriculum' — that massive, ongoing, informal curriculum of families, peer groups, neighbourhoods, churches, organizations, institutions, mass media and other socializing forces that educate all of us throughout our lives.[1] Through the societal curriculum, as well as through the school curriculum, people learn language and culture, acquire beliefs and attitudes, and develop patterns of behaviour. They learn about themselves and others. They learn about the groups to which they and others belong. They learn about their nation and other nations and cultures of the world. In short, they learn about diversity, including racial, ethnic, cultural, gender, religious, regional and national diversity.

As a major element of societal education, the media curriculum — through such avenues as newspapers, magazines, motion pictures, television and radio —

disseminates information, images and ideas concerning race, ethnicity, culture and foreignness. Educating both for better *and* for worse, this media curriculum about diversity functions whether or not individual mediamakers actually view themselves as educators, whether or not they are aware that they are spreading ideas about diversity, and whether or not they operate in the realms of fact or fiction.

This media curriculum can contribute to ethnic pride, but it can also erode self-esteem through the repetition of negative themes or demeaning images. It can contribute to intergroup understanding through sensitive examinations of ethnic experiences and problems, but it can also contribute to intergroup misunderstanding through the repeated presentation of derogatory stereotypes and an over-emphasis on negative themes about selected groups or nations. It spreads fact and fiction, at times striving for truth, accuracy, sensitivity and balance, while at other times consciously distorting for purposes of sensationalism and commercialism. By operating in this dual manner, the media curriculum both challenges and hypertrophies intergroup prejudice.

Moreover, an analysis of the media curriculum must involve both the news and entertainment media. Audiences learn not only from programmes and publications intended to provide information, but also from media presumably made only to entertain (as well as to make money). Moreover, it has become increasingly evident that audiences have great difficulty distinguishing media fact from fiction. For example, a 1989 survey revealed that 50 per cent of US television viewers considered *America's Most Wanted* to be a news programme, while 28 per cent thought it entertainment.[2] My own research on feature films reveals that crosscultural learning from fictional media has become an international phenomenon.

While some members of the so-called entertainment media proclaim that they merely offer diversion, in fact they simultaneously teach, whether intentionally or incidentally. Let us reverse the equation. Whatever the stated or unstated goals of the media, audiences learn from both fictional and non-fictional media, although in the case of fictional media they usually do not realize that such media-based learning is occurring.[3]

As entertainment packaged, often unintended multicultural textbooks, feature films and television have been a major part of the century-long teaching-learning environment in which people develop intercultural beliefs and attitudes. Plato recognized the power of fictional narrative when he asserted, 'Those who tell the stories also rule the society.' In more recent times George Gerbner of the University of Pennsylvania's Annenberg School of Communications proclaimed hyperbolically, but with a core of truth, 'If you can control the storytelling of a nation, you don't have to worry about who makes the laws.'

Television, including cable, has dominated recent media analysis. Experts concur that television viewing has been growing around the world. In the United States, for example, average household TV viewing time has been climbing steadily — from five hours per day in 1956 to six hours per day in 1971 and to seven hours per day in 1983. As early as 1961 scholars concluded that young Americans between the ages of 3 and 16 were devoting one-sixth of their waking hours to television.[4] According to another estimate, by the time of high school graduation the average US student will have spent 11,000 hours in the classroom and 22,000 hours in front of the television set.[5] Sometimes movie viewing and television watching become synonymous, particularly with TV, cable and videocassettes now serving as prime recyclers of feature films.

Likening television to schools and television programmes to school courses, sociologist Herbert J. Gans argued:

> almost all TV programs and magazine fiction teach something about American society. For example, *Batman* is, from this vantage point, a course in criminology that describes how a superhuman aristocrat does a better job eradicating crime than do public officials. Similarly, *The Beverly Hillbillies* offers a course in social stratification and applied economics, teaching that with money, uneducated and uncultured people can do pretty well in American society, and can easily outwit more sophisticated and more powerful middle-class types.... And even the innocuous family situation comedies such as *Ozzie and Harriet* deal occasionally with ethical problems encountered on a neighborhood level.... Although the schools argue that they are the major transmitter of society's moral values, the mass media offer a great deal more content on this topic.[6]

I have come to similar conclusions through my own decade-long research on the history of the US motion picture treatment of race, ethnicity and foreignness. At present I am completing a book on the history of the US feature film treatment of race and ethnicity, which will be followed by two more book-length studies: the American movie depiction of foreign nations (Hollywood's textbook on the world); and the evolution of interracial love as an American movie theme that serves as a revealing barometer of the tenacity of racial prejudice, provides insight into media efforts to inculcate social behaviour, and offers unique perspectives on the ramifications of changing racial attitudes. Because of my special interest in the attitude-shaping role of the entertainment media — the power of entertainment media to influence ethnic pride and prejudice — I will emphasize that theme in this chapter.[7]

## THE DILEMMA OF ASSESSING MEDIA IMPACT

Despite the extensiveness of the media curriculum on race, ethnicity, culture and nationality, caution must temper assertions concerning the *precise* content of audience learning. In particular, we must avoid falling into the common trap of media determinism, assuming the 'hypodermic needle' effect so popular (and so fallacious) in many early media studies and still rampant in protest group proclamations.

As all educators know, teaching and learning are not synonymous. We teach and then through examinations, often to our chagrin, we discover great variations in the extent, content and quality of student learning. With that in mind, while recognizing the teaching power of the media, we must also respect the conscious and unconscious filtering power of the learner. To assume and make definitive assertions concerning media impact based only on an examination of content, as some scholars and many public pundits have done, is a fallacy equivalent to assessing student learning on the basis of analyzing reading assignments and professorial lectures (in the words of Samuel Butler, 'drawing sufficient conclu-

sions from insufficient premises'). Identifying the exact content of learning —
from whatever source — can be frustratingly elusive.[8]

Scholarly and popular analyses of the societal impact of the media, particularly the entertainment media, have tended to become polarized on the issue of
the media influence on public perceptions and attitudes. Many analysts, including
some scholars, have taken a nearly deterministic position, drawing direct causal
(sometimes unicausal) links between media and the development of individual,
group and national attitudes and behaviour. At the opposite extreme stand most
feature filmmakers and creators of entertainment television, who generally claim
that they make fictional media merely to entertain, reject responsibility for what
their films might incidentally or unintentionally teach, and at times even deny
their teaching potential. In the middle stand those scholars who agree that media,
including movies and fictional television, do teach, but argue that research to date
has generally failed to reveal the precise nature of audience learning. For example, in *The Media Monopoly* Ben Bagdikian argues, 'It is a truism among political
scientists that while it is not possible for the media to tell the population what to
think, they do tell the public what to think about.'[9]

Assessing media impact, therefore, poses a major challenge, but research to
date does provide some insights. Scholarship on the impact of movies and television on intergroup perceptions has been sporadic and temporally limited, focusing
almost entirely on short-range effects of specific films or television shows, often
in empirically controlled settings. While research results vary, they do coalesce
around two basic conclusions. First, these studies make it clear that feature films
and fictional television do influence interethnic perceptions; viewers do learn
about race and ethnicity from the entertainment media. Second, the nature of
that influence varies with the individual viewer, who provides a key variable
concerning the extent, content and tenacity of that conscious or unconscious
learning. In short, scholarship confirms that old social science axiom, '*Some*
people are influenced by *some* media, at *some* time.'

Research has identified the influence of selected films and television shows on
intergroup attitudes and perceptions, sometimes reinforcing prejudices, other
times modifying them.[10] One pioneering study of the 1930s involved the classic
1915 silent film, *The Birth of a Nation*, which included a degrading portrayal of
Black Americans during the post-Civil War reconstruction period of US history.
That research revealed that when students viewed *Birth* as part of their study
of US history, an increase in student prejudice toward African-Americans
resulted.[11]

But entertainment media can also reduce prejudice. Another study found
that the 1947 anti-anti-Semitism film, *Gentleman's Agreement*, had such an effect.
Students who saw it reported improved attitudes toward Jews, even though most
of the surveyed students stated that the film *had not* influenced their attitudes![12]

Other analysts have taken a broader view of the media's impact on intercultural perceptions. Sam Keen's *Faces of the Enemy: Reflections of the Hostile
Imagination* and Vamik Volkan's *The Need to Have Enemies and Allies: From
Clinical Practice to International Relationships* argue that people *need* to hate and
that 'the other' — the racial other, the ethnic other, the cultural other, the
national other — serves as a convenient outlet for that hate.[13] In his article, 'The
Convenient Villain: The Early Cinema Views the Mexican-American', Blaine

Lamb asserts that Mexican characters served that 'other' role for early US movie audiences, who needed an easily identified, easily despised foil.[14]

Other scholars have examined media impact on pride and prejudice within the context of larger intergroup and international themes. For example, in his *War without Mercy: Race and Power in the Pacific War* historian John Dower identifies the nature of racial pride and crosscultural stereotypes of the enemy that developed in both Japan and the Allied nations prior to and during World War II. He does so by exploring multiple Japanese and Allied sources — from scholarly studies to propaganda tracts, from government reports to military training materials, from popular periodicals to motion pictures. But Dower takes an additional step, pointing to political and military decisions made by both sides that reveal how these stereotypes became operationalized, even when operating on those stereotypes led to military and diplomatic excesses and blunders.

While research has demonstrated conclusively that people learn about race, ethnicity, culture and foreignness from the media, including the entertainment media, it has also demonstrated that learner responses vary, even to the same media stimulus. Analyses of two highly acclaimed US television comedy series — Norman Lear's *All in the Family* and *The Cosby Show* — have teased out this content-impact gap.

In 1971 *All in the Family* burst onto the American television scene. This popular weekly series portrayed anti-hero Archie Bunker as a classic bigot — racist, sexist and just about every other kind of anti-'ist' imaginable. The show sought to critique racial and ethnic prejudice by making Bunker's expressions of bigotry appear to be comically absurd. Viewers would laugh at Archie, bigotry would appear to be imbecilic, and prejudice would be reduced. The ploy succeeded ... but only for *some* viewers. Unfortunately, other viewers identified with the cuddly, ingratiating laugh-provoking Archie, the lovable racist, and found his expression of bigoted beliefs to be a confirmation of the validity of their own prejudices.[15] One study of *All in the Family* confirmed the operation of the 'selective perception hypothesis' — that is, already 'high prejudiced viewers' tended to admire Bunker and condone his racial and ethnic slurs.[16]

The far less controversial *The Cosby Show* has even drawn mixed responses. At first glance *Cosby* would appear to be the ideal pride producing, positive role model minority show, featuring a well-educated, sophisticated, financially successful African-American family. Yet it has drawn its share of concerned reactions. In particular, some analysts have expressed reservations on the grounds that the show's concentration on well-heeled African-Americans might unintentionally encourage viewers to ignore the fact that the majority of American Blacks still face tremendous social and economic problems. As media scholar Paula Matabane wrote:

> 'The Cosby Show,' for example, epitomizes the Afro-American dream of full acceptance and assimilation into US society. Both the series and Bill Cosby as an individual represent successful competitors in network television and in attaining a high status. Although this achievement is certainly not inherently negative, we should consider the role television plays in the cultivation of an overall picture of growing racial equality that conceals unequal social relationships and overestimates of how well blacks are integrating into white society (if at all). The illusion of well-being among the oppressed may lead to reduced political activity and less demand for social justice and equality.[17]

While come scholars have addressed media impact by examining individual shows, other have examined the process of media learning by posing and applying different theories of audience reception. Some use schema theory, according to which each learner (viewer) develops an internal mental and emotional schema based on his or her own personal experiences, including school and societal learning. This personal schema then becomes the reception framework by which learners process, interpret and organize new information, idea and images, including those disseminated by the media. Psychologist Leon Festinger proposed his 'theory of cognitive dissonance', according to which once an individual's cognitive structure takes firm shape, it tends to repel those ideas that seem too dissonant.[18] The application of this theory suggests that media or school frontal assaults on firmly rooted prejudices, when those attacks lack subtlety, may well be rejected by some because they create too much dissonance.

Moreover, learners are not usually aware of either their reception schema or many of their prejudices, including those learned, reinforced or shaped by the media. Psychologist Albert Bandura, for example, has described the 'sleeper effect', which may provide a key to understanding how media teaching/learning works.[19] In relation to the media, the 'sleeper effect' suggests that ideas, clothed as entertainment, can subconsciously enter and become part of a viewer's cognitive or affective storehouse, then lie dormant until provoked by some external stimulus, like an event, a personal contact or even another media presentation. For example, people may not realize that they have prejudices, including media-fostered prejudices, about a certain group until they encounter individuals from that group, at which point these 'sleeping' beliefs and attitudes awaken and move into action.

## THE NATURE OF MEDIA INFLUENCE

Given these dilemmas of assessing media impact, what can be said with some degree of certainty (or at least reasonably hypothesized) about media impact, including the impact of feature films and fictional television? How do media contribute to pride, prejudice and other aspects of self-concept or intergroup perceptions, particularly to the reinforcement or modification of racial or ethnic bigotry? My own research suggests at least five basic types of media influences on the creation, strengthening, and reduction of ethnic pride and intercultural prejudice.

1 *Media Provide Information about Race, Ethnicity, Culture and Foreignness.* People cannot be at all places at all times, so they must rely on the media to bring the world to them. Because they cannot develop in-depth knowledge about each and every racial or ethnic group or nation on the basis of personal experience, they necessarily acquire much of what they know about race, ethnicity, culture and foreignness through what historian Daniel Boorstin has termed the 'pseudoenvironment', principally the mass media.[20]

Certainly newspapers, magazines, television news and documentary films provide information (selected, organized, edited, filtered and often decontextualized information of varying accuracy and quality), but so do the entertainment media. Some years ago an elementary school teacher, with whom I had been working, came to me with consternation. Preparing to teach about Gypsies to her fourth-grade class, she began by asking students if they knew anything about them, only to be overwhelmed by the flood of Gypsy 'information' that students 'knew'. When she asked where they had obtained that information, they cited old Wolfman and Frankenstein movies among their main sources.

Moreover, the issue of media as an information source about race, ethnicity, culture and foreignness goes well beyond the question of accuracy. In news, the constant reiteration of certain themes, even when each story is accurate in and of itself, may pound home an image of an ethnic group, with the relentless drumming of negative themes likely to contribute both to prejudice against the group and to the decline of group pride. Similarly, the repetition of ethnic images by the entertainment media adds to viewers' pools of 'knowledge', particularly if news and entertainment treatment coincide in theme, approach and frequency.

2 *Media Help Organize Information and Ideas about Racial, Ethnic, Cultural and National Groups.* More than providing information, media help shape viewer and reader structures for perceiving, receiving and thinking — the way people organize information. Movies and television, for example, perform the same roles that folk stories and fairy tales have done for years.[21] They provide a type of 'ritualized glue' that helps audiences make sense of the pseudoenvironment's increasing information overload, which assaults and often overwhelms readers, viewers and listeners. In his recent book, *Information Anxiety*, Richard Saul Wurman opines that the amount of information now doubles every half decade, while a single weekday issue of *The New York Times* contains more information than the average resident of seventeenth century England was likely to encounter in a lifetime.[22]

Reporting that there had been more than 2300 research papers on television and human behaviour, social psychologist George Comstock addressed the relationship of media to the reification of social structures:

> Several writers have argued that television is a powerful reinforcer of the status quo. The ostensible mechanisms are the effects of its portrayals on public expectations and perceptions. Television portrayals and particularly violent drama are said to assign roles of authority, power, success, failure, dependence, and vulnerability in a manner that matches the real-life social hierarchy, thereby strengthening that hierarchy by increasing its acknowledgement among the public and by failing to provide positive images for members of social categories occupying a subservient position. Content analyses of television drama support the contention that portrayals reflect normative status.[23]

To the degree that media express and reiterate the normality of racial, ethnic and social hierarchies, the more they legitimize taboos and reinforce the validity and even the naturalness of these relationships. When news media present a pattern of thinking about race and ethnicity, they contribute to reader and viewer frameworks for organizing future information and ideas about these groups. When the entertainment media repeatedly depict ethnic or racial dominance or subservience, present ethnic slurs as an acceptable form of expression (for example, when uttered by movie heroes), or portray members of specific ethnic groups in limited spheres of action, they contribute to the formation of viewer schema for absorbing future images into a meaningful, consistent, if distorted, mental framework.

3 *Media Help Create Values and Attitudes.* Critics of the media have been asserting this for decades. The Payne Fund studies of the 1930s, for example, included Henry James Forman's provocatively titled *Our Movie Made Children*.[24] As recently as 1975 media historian Robert Sklar chose *Movie-Made America* as the title for his widely read cultural history of US motion pictures, although in his book he avoids the 'hypodermic' leanings that pervade the Payne Fund studies.[25]

Hollywood's 1930 Motion Picture Production Code (the Hays Code) provides a primer on Hollywood's recognition both that movies teach and that filmmakers should take cognizance of the values they are disseminating. One of the Code's value positions, its opposition to interracial love, appeared in its Section II, Rule 6, which read, 'Miscegenation (sex relationship between the white and black races) is forbidden.' Until the 1950s Hollywood drummed home the repeated message that miscegenation should be avoided. In those rare screen instances where it occurred or seemed about to occur, punishment and retribution predictably arrived. To an extent this element of Hollywood movie textbook values reflected widespread American social mores. After all, when surveys conducted for Gunnar Myrdal's 1944 classic, *An American Dilemma: The Negro Problem and Modern Democracy*, asked southern Whites what discriminatory lines must be maintained, their most common answer was 'the bar against intermarriage and sexual intercourse involving white women.'[26]

On the other hand, interracial marriage had long occurred in the United States. However, Hollywood chose value lessons over the presentation of reality. In adopting this pattern of portrayals, moviemakers functioned simultaneously as learners (reacting to the presence of such social mores among many Americans and fearing that movies with interracial love might not 'sell' in the south) and as teachers of values (creating and operating within these miscegenation 'curriculum guidelines').

4 *Media Help Shape Expectations.* Ruling Hollywood since 1934, before beginning its slow decline in the mid-1950s and being extinguished in 1968, the Hays Code ordained that crime could not pay in American films. All screen criminals must ultimately receive their just desserts. So it came as a shock to audiences who 'expected' screen crime to lead to inevitable punishment when Steve McQueen flew away to Europe to enjoy the fruits of his masterfully engineered bank robbery as the 1968 film, *The Thomas Crown Affair*, came to an end.

With the burying of the Hays Code, Hollywood moved from a crime-cannot-pay to a crime-may-or-may-not-pay position of expectation shaping. Ironically and unfortunately, this more permissive instructional position concerning the expected results of criminality occurred simultaneously with the rise in ethnic theme films spurred by the civil rights movements of the 1960s. The result has been a flood of movies with ethnics as the principal perpetrators of crime. In

recent years, for example, Italian-Americans and Hispanic-Americans have become nearly synonymous with screen crime — ergo, *The $25,000 Pyramid* caper
that began this essay.

*5 Media Provide Models for Action.*   Anecdotal evidence provides myriad examples of movies and television popularizing clothing styles, verbal expressions
('Make my day') and other forms of behaviour. Aware of this penchant for
imitation, protesters have railed against the release of such youth gang films as *A
Clockwork Orange* (1971), *The Warriors* (1979) and *Colors* (1988) for fear that
young people would imitate the screen gang violence. Although a few fights did
break out near theatres, massive waves of imitative gang violence did not occur,
which came as a shock to those who proclaimed such media deterministic
positions.

But more critical and also more difficult to handle is the issue of 'disinhibit-
ing' effects. The question is not do the entertainment media provoke people into
action? More important and more subtly, do they remove inhibitions to previously repressed actions? Some African-American comedians, for example, who had
repeatedly used the word 'nigger' in their routines, have dropped it because of
their concern that they may have unwittingly and unintentionally helped lower
public inhibitions against employing this brutalizing word.

## RESPONDERS AS EVIDENCE OF MEDIA IMPACT

While precise empirical data on media impact — as contributors to pride and to
prejudice — have inevitably been elusive, responses to the media by scholars,
governments, groups and even the media themselves reveal both a recognition
and an expression of that teaching power. Three examples — one racial, one
ethnic and one international — provide glimpses into the stereotype and
prejudice-producing potential of the media. Moreover, they illustrate the five
types of media influence that I have proposed: providing information; helping to
organize information and ideas; contributing to values and attitude formation;
helping to shape expectations; and providing models for action.

*1 Racial.*   Media-honed audience preconceptions about 'other' groups can lead to
viewer expectations about their screen behaviour. When moviemakers do not
fulfil these audience predispositions and expectations, viewers may respond with
disappointment, cynicism or even outrage. Such occurred in 1989 with *Do the
Right Thing*, the perceptive examination of interracial conflict, intraracial diversity and urban pressures in the primarily Black Bedford-Stuyvesant section of
Brooklyn.

Written and directed by the brilliant young African-American filmmaker,
Spike Lee, *Do the Right Thing* received lavish praise from some White critics.
However, others challenged its authenticity, on the grounds that Lee did not
address the issue of drugs — and what's a movie about an African-American
community without drugs in the forefront? These White critics brought their

media-massaged ghetto preconceptions to the theatre, and when Lee failed to deliver, *he* was at fault. (That same criticism descended on the 1990 African-American teen comedy film, *House Party*, which also did not deal with drugs.) Certainly, Black communities have a drug problem, but so do middle- and upper-class White communities, not only in the United States but in many other nations. Yet when was the last time that a White filmmaker received a critical roasting for making a drug-free movie about a White community?

2 *Ethnic.*    Sometimes media themselves provide begrudging recognition of their power to contribute to intergroup stereotyping. For example, prior to the 1977 US national network television showing of Francis Ford Coppola's *The Godfather Saga* (a revised and expanded version of the two theatrical motion pictures, *The Godfather* and *The Godfather: Part II*), the following words appeared on screen, simultaneously intoned by a solemn voice: '*The Godfather* is a fictional account of the activities of a small group of ruthless criminals. It would be erroneous and unfair to suggest that they are representative of any ethnic group.'

Forewarned that the characters were not 'representative of any ethnic group', a nation-wide audience watched the violent, multigenerational saga of the Corleone family. The film began in Sicily, large segments were spoken in Italian with English subtitles, and most of the characters bore such names as Clemenza, Barzini, Tattaglia and Fanucci. Of course, the film and the television showing could not possibly contribute to Italian-American stereotyping, because the disclaimer had inoculated viewers against thinking of the characters as members of any specific ethnic group![27]

Moreover, those worthless words became the model for future media disclaimers. Subsequent controversial films that exploited criminal violence in presenting other ethnic groups, such as the 1983 *Scarface* (Cuban-Americans) and the 1985 *Year of the Dragon* (Chinese-Americans), copied and only slightly modified the 'Godfather disclaimer'. While these words could not mitigate the image-influencing impact of these films (in fact, howls of laughter from audiences when I watched the disclaimer suggest that the warnings may have done more harm than good), the disclaimer did serve as a media admission that feature films do, in fact, teach. They can create, reinforce and modify public images about ethnic groups. In other words, the 'Godfather disclaimer' and its clones provide additional evidence that media have the power to demean group images.

3 *International.*    In the popular 1980 movie satire, *Airplane!*, an airline pilot continually tries to seduce a little boy passenger, using subtle and not-so-subtle laugh-provoking advances. At one point he asks the boy, 'Have you ever stayed in a Turkish prison?', inciting uproarious audience laughter. Would that line have been as funny if it went, 'Have you ever stayed in a prison?' No. How about a 'Swedish prison?' Nothing funny there. An 'Argentine prison?' No again. But Turkish prison worked as humour. Why? It drew laughter not only because of the movie's content, but also because of the information, ideas, mental schema and expectations that movie audiences brought into the theatre. It worked because the filmmakers had identified audience 'sleeping' predispositions and cleverly played upon them. The filmmakers presumed — and they were proven correct — that

audiences would respond to 'Turkish prison' as a humorous metaphor for homosexuality.

But how could the filmmakers have predicted that response? Did they assume that most viewers had learned in school about Turkish prisons as centres of homosexuality? Of course not. Few schools (at least American schools) teach *anything* about Turkey. Or that most viewers had read scholarly books about Turkey containing discussions of Turkish prisons? Dubious. Or that they had read articles about Turkish prisons? A few viewers, maybe.

But the makers of *Airplane!* did know that millions of moviegoers had recently been exposed to the powerful imagery of Turkish prisons in the 1978 film hit, *Midnight Express*, adapted from American Billy Hayes' best-selling account of his imprisonment in and escape from Turkey. Simultaneously skilful in execution and sensationalistic in conception, the movie took Hayes' gruelling narrative and reshaped it further to dehumanize Turks (in contrast, while the book excoriated Turkish prison conditions, it also presented Turks in a far more human and diverse manner). Moreover, the movie accentuated the themes of prison homosexuality and Turkish brutality.

With *Midnight Express* priming audiences on Turkish prisons, *Airplane!* merely had to present the 'Turkish prison' line. Media-prepared audiences did the rest. In other words, rapidly and reactively drawing upon their own pre-existent internal images, audiences functioned as co-creators in the production of the film's meaning. (According to one Chinese proverb, 'We see what is behind our eyes.')[28]

Lest this essay be misinterpreted as media bashing, let me assure you that it is not. As I said earlier, media have sometimes been in the forefront of the struggle against prejudice while at other times functioning as purveyors of bigotry. Media have simultaneously contributed to improved interethnic understanding and to hypertrophied intercultural misunderstanding. They have both built and battered group pride, and have even played a role in fostering positive intercultural action.

Media coverage of Ethiopia provides a cogent example of the positive intercultural role of the media. Famine had ravaged Ethiopia for years. Yet despite many stories written by print journalists, most people paid little attention to the Ethiopian tragedy until the moving-image media succeeded in capturing the horror and pathos of the famine. The resulting television dissemination of the famine story awakened the world to this catastrophe. Suddenly everyone wanted to help Ethiopia: 'We are the world, we are the children'; 'Hands across America.' The visual media had begun the process; music further spread the message. The war against the Ethiopian famine was 'in'. But what the media place on the agenda, the media can remove by disuse. Famine in Ethiopia continues, but it has receded in media attention and, as a result, the public agenda has moved on, with other media-designated human dramas taking Ethiopia's place.

Or take Richard Attenborough's 1987 film, *Cry Freedom*, an anti-apartheid celebration of the friendship between South African Black Consciousness Movement leader Steve Biko and liberal White South African newspaper editor Donald Woods. Opening on 29 July 1988 in thirty packed South African theatres, *Cry Freedom* was confiscated later that day by the police, fearful of its teaching power — what both Black and White South Africans might learn from it about national racial conditions. In February 1990, in the wake of the release of Nelson

Mandela, the government permitted the film's renewed showing, deeming it now appropriate for South African audiences to be exposed to the film's potential impact as a media textbook on the nation's history.


## THE MEDIA CHALLENGE


In short, the mass media teach, although we can never be certain what any one individual may learn from the media. In dealing with race, ethnicity, culture and foreignness, the media have the power to contribute to pride and to prejudice, to intergroup understanding and to intergroup stereotyping. Both fact and fictional media provide information, help viewers, readers and listeners to organize that information, contribute to values and attitudes, help shape expectations and provide models for behaviour. But action can be taken to deal with the intercultural teaching power of the media. Action can and should occur in various sectors of society, but three areas stand out as particularly important.

First, the media need to become more responsible in dealing with race, ethnicity, culture and foreignness. News media should become more self-critical concerning their news selection, balance and manner of presentation of different groups. Entertainment media should continuously examine their own tendencies in order to identify patterns of ethnic and foreign images that they disseminate, patterns of intergroup relationships that they portray, and patterns of group behaviour that they repeatedly present. Simultaneously, they should strive to create character diversity and human complexity in their portrayal of members of all ethnic groups and nations.

The public at large should become more activist. Public awareness of the teaching power of the media appears to be growing, as reflected in a variety of forms. Protest groups have monitored the media and have challenged what they perceive to be 'negative images' or distortions of various ethnic themes. Conversely, ethnic groups have presented awards to mediamakers who have contributed 'positive images' to the media curriculum on ethnicity. Other groups have worked closely with the media in an attempt to improve images or mitigate negative treatment, while magazines such as the American quarterly, *Media and Values*, for which I wrote a column on minorities and the media, provide discussions of media issues as well as suggestions for teachers, counsellors, religious leaders and others active in working with youth in particular.

Finally, school educators need to dedicate themselves to integrating media analysis into their teaching. Long after school education has ended, each individual will experience life-long learning through the media. To prepare students for this eventuality, schools need to help develop their media analytical literacy, including multicultural media literacy. 'To read without reflecting is like eating without digesting', Edmund Burke once opined ... but so are mindless viewing and listening.

The struggle against prejudice, bigotry and discrimination may be eternal. Those engaged in this crusade need to dedicate themselves not to spurious quick-fix efforts to eradicate prejudice, but rather to the unending battle for understanding and equity. As English historian, E.P. Woodward, once wrote, 'Everything good has to be done over again, forever.'

## NOTES

1 Carlos E. Cortés (1981) 'The Societal Curriculum: Implications for Multiethnic Education', in James A. Banks (Ed.), *Education in the 80s: Multiethnic Education*, Washington, D.C., National Education Association, pp. 24–32.
2 Thomas B. Rosenstiel (1989) 'Viewers Found to Confuse TV Entertainment with News', *Los Angeles Times*, 17 August, I, p. 1.
3 Garth Jowett (1976) *Film: The Democratic Art*, Boston, Mass., Little, Brown and Company; Robert Sklar (1975) *Movie-made America: A Cultural History of American Movies*, New York, Random House; and Robert Singer and Robert Kazdon (Eds) 'Television and Social Behavior', *Journal of Social Issues*, Fall. (1976).
4 Wilbur Schramm, Jack Lyle and Edwin B. Parker (1961) *Television in the Lives of Our Children*, Stanford, Calif., Stanford University Press.
5 Jack G. Shaheen (1984) *The TV Arab*, Bowling Green, Ohio, Bowling Green State University Popular Press.
6 Herbert J. Gans (1967) 'The Mass Media as an Educational Institution', *Television Quarterly*, 6, pp. 21–22.
7 I would like to thank Charles Wetherell, Director of the University of California, Riverside's Laboratory for Historical Research, for his comments on this paper and his valuable recommendations on my long-term film research.
8 I address the issue of assessing what I term 'potential impact' in my (1984) article, 'The History of Ethnic Images in Film: The Search for a Methodology,' *MELUS: The Journal of the Society for the Study of the Multi-Ethnic Literature of the United States*, 11, 3, pp. 63–77.
9 Ben Bagdikian (1983) *The Media Monopoly*, Boston, Mass., Beacon Press, p. xvi.
10 Louis E. Raths and Frank N. Trager (1948) 'Public Opinion and "Crossfire"', *Journal of Educational Sociology*, 21, 6, pp. 345–368.
11 Ruth C. Peterson and L.L. Thurstone (1933) *Motion Pictures and the Social Attitudes of Children*, New York, Macmillan.
12 Irwin C. Rosen (1948) 'The Effect of the Motion Picture "Gentleman's Agreement" on Attitudes toward Jews', *Journal of Psychology*, 26, pp. 525–536.
13 Sam Keen (1986) *Faces of the Enemy: Reflections of the Hostile Imagination*, New York, Harper and Row; and Vamik Volkan (1988) *The Need to Have Enemies and Allies: From Clinical Practice to International Relationships*, Northvale, N.J., J. Aronson.
14 Blaine S. Lamb (1975) 'The Convenient Villain: The Early Cinema Views the Mexican-American', *Journal of the West*, 14, 4, pp. 75–81.
15 John D. Leckenby and Stuart H. Surlin (1976) 'Incidental Social Learning and Viewer Race: "All in the Family" and "Sanford and Son"', *Journal of Broadcasting*, 20, 4, pp. 481–494.
16 Neil Vidmar and Milton Rokeach (1974) 'Archie Bunker's Bigotry: A Study in Selective Perception and Exposure', *Journal of Communication*, 24, 1, pp. 36–47.
17 Paula W. Matabane (1988) 'Television and the Black Audience: Cultivating Moderate Perspectives on Racial Integration', *Journal of Communication*, 38, 4, pp. 21–31.
18 Leon Festinger (1957) *A Theory of Cognitive Dissonance*, Evanston, Ill., Row, Peterson.
19 Albert Bandura (1977) *Social Learning Theory*, Englewood Cliffs, N.J., Prentice-Hall.
20 Daniel J. Boorstin (1961) *The Image or Whatever Happened to the American Dream?*, New York, Atheneum.
21 Bruno Bettelheim (1976) *The Uses of Enchantment: The Meaning and Importance of Fairy Tales*, New York, Knopf.
22 Richard Saul Wurman (1989) *Information Anxiety*, New York, Doubleday.
23 George Comstock (1977) *The Impact of Television on American Institutions and the American Public*, Honolulu, East-West Communications Institute, East-West Center, pp. 20–21.
24 Henry James Forman (1933) *Our Movie Made Children*, New York, Macmillan.
25 Sklar (1975) *op. cit.*
26 Gunnar Myrdal (1944) *An American Dilemma: The Negro Problem and Modern Democracy*, New York, Harper and Brothers, p. 60.
27 For a more detailed discussion of the evolution of the Italian-American movie image, see Carlos E. Cortés (1987) 'Italian-Americans in Film: From Immigrants to Icons', *MELUS: The Journal of the Society for the Study of the Multi-Ethnic Literature of the United States*, 14, 3–4, pp. 107–126.

28  For an analysis of the history of movie shaping of one nation's image, see Carlos E. Cortés (1989) 'To View a Neighbor: The Hollywood Textbook on Mexico', in John H. Coatsworth and Carlos Rico (Eds), *Images of Mexico in the United States*, La Jolla, Calif., University of California, San Diego, Center for US-Mexican Studies, pp. 91–118.

# Epilogue

# Prejudice Reduction:
# Retrospect and Prospect

JAMES LYNCH, CELIA MODGIL AND SOHAN MODGIL

It cannot be said that the theme of this volume is a source of popular and passionate debate on the world scene. It cannot even be said that there is any individual country which has taken seriously the need to address issues of prejudice reduction through the medium of its educational system. In that context the various contributors to this volume have taken on the thankless role of the intellectual pioneer, in seeking to follow routes explored many years ago and left untrodden, and to map often uncharted arguments, in penetrating to frontiers of theory and action which are not yet in vogue. Thus, while they have built on the work of others, stretching back almost fifty years, they are in a sense before their time. As with all voyages of discovery, there are many bystanders to prejudice, who will argue that there can be no positive outcome to our endeavours to identify the seeds of human bigotry and to seek by deliberate strategies to overcome the insidious growth of prejudice in individual nations and across the globe.

The purpose of education for such critics may be the advancement of science and technology, economic progress leading to higher standards of living for some, or socialization into élite positions, which brook no prejudice against themselves. Such critics will accept no relationship between the profligate consumerism of the rich nations and the continued destitution of the majority poor. They will be unable to perceive the role of prejudice in legitimating the status of the poor in the eyes of the rich, nationally or internationally. Others may argue that while we do have evidence of the efficacy of certain strategies in overcoming prejudice and amending antisocial attitudes on a localized and short-term basis, there is no certainty as to their long-term or broader effects. We should, therefore, continue to declaim polemic against prejudice, rather than commence the more difficult and expensive road of progress in combatting it.

The message of this book is a very different one, at the same time optimistic but urgent. The volume is the second in a series devoted to greater engagement with the complexity of cultural diversity world-wide. In Volume One contributors engaged with issues of alternative perceptions, definitions and responses to cultural diversity. They addressed problems caused by alternative social constructions of the reality of cultural diversity, and weighed the ways in which warring antagonists in the struggle to secure both the meaning and social reality of cultural diversity proposed sometimes mutually exclusive theoretical approaches and political strategies to respond to the phenomenon. Labels such as 'integration', 'assimilation' and 'separation', 'unity' and 'diversity', 'cohesion' and 'pluralism' were the stock-in-trade of their deliberations and advocacy. Key words, such as 'multiculturalism', 'interculturalism' and 'antiracism', were their intellectual banners. Their common denominator, however, was a conviction that measures to combat prejudice and discrimination were desirable. For that reason it is important to review briefly the content of that volume as a context to the current volume.

In that volume authors provided analyses of the core issues and dilemmas in a culturally diverse society, its values and moral bases, their function, utility and potential elasticity in embracing the many ideologies resident within those societies, while guaranteeing the same access to human rights, dignity and justice for all members. They highlighted the many dilemmas which those twin goals carry with them, and they focused in particular on the problematic nature of all judgments, not least in education, in the legitimation as much as in the making. In particular, they considered the role and weaknesses of formal examinations, tests, assessments and judgmental decisions and evaluations in the allocation of life chances, and the way in which they may be culturally skewed and thereby fundamentally flawed. Most strategies and approaches contain such dilemmas and the need was to make them as culture-fair and free of prejudice as possible.

In detail, Part One of that volume sought to provide varied perceptions of the three basic policy options open to democratic societies in response to cultural diversity: integration, separation, or the fostering of some form of structural and cultural pluralism. By and large, contributors envisaged their options as located between the two poles of the continuum of policy options available to pluralist societies: social assimilation or cultural mosaic. These are not presented as absolutes, but rather as tensions of prevailing and countervailing social tendencies and attendant ideologies. At any one time an individual society may be at several different points along that continuum in different social sectors, and it is not unusual for societies to be simultaneously pursuing contrasting, incompatible or divergent policies in different sectors.

Nomenclature is always a problem, not least where the underlying assumptions and values are as hotly contested as they are in the field of cultural diversity. For this reason, contributors attempted to move from epistemological absolutism in the use of the terms 'integration' and 'assimilation', dominant in the contemporary debate, to greater sensitivity to the many dimensions and nuances of these words. They envisaged gradations and calibrations to the social construction of these terms for different people in different sectors at different times. Some degree of integration within the labour force is essential for individual and societal wealth production, just as for personal identity, some degree of apartness is necessary with family and community, whether the locus for separation is basically religious, linguistic, ethnic or more broadly culturally conceived, or all of these dimensions. In this respect the case was advanced that schools have the role of advancing a society's policy in this area, and exemplifications of this role were given, as well as details of the techniques and intervention approaches, through which schools may advance and promote those broader social endeavours.

One major issue was the extent to which schools and other educational institutions might be regarded as the handmaidens of broader social policy or, looked at from the other end, the margin which schools may have to influence broader policies or diverge from them in accordance with their own cultural biographies and exigencies. They were not seen solely as 'state ideological institutions', but as having a less absolutist and more interactive relationship with their communities and societies. The second contribution to Part One made clear that policies and practice in this respect were neither constant nor uncontested, but were subject to the changing weather patterns of ideological legitimation within the broader society, seen both historically and contemporaneously across different societies and regions. One of the major opinion-builders in this respect is the mass media. Their role in the formulation, location and maintenance of policy in this area was discussed, and a shift was noted in their ideological support for policies of cultural diversity, from an ideology of access, equity and participation to an ideological nexus focusing on the economic benefits of immigration. It was also felt to be not unconnected with the ideological sea-change in Eastern Europe, which has brought a movement from planned to market economies and from democratic centralism to pluralist democracy.

This resort to greater economic functionality as a legitimation of provision was also considered to be part of a world-wide phenomenon and to be at the base of an economic efficiency approach to responses to cultural diversity, as manifest in the growth of separate schools for and among ethnic minorities. Greater economic and political functionality, one might almost say the greater acceptance of the need for consumer and citizen choice, which may bridge the dilemma of apart or together, has stimulated the growth in a number of societies of such separate schools. They do not, however, necessarily replace the available state schools, but enhance, extend of otherwise cover needs not adequately responded to by those state schools. Three major functions of these schools do appear to be (1) to provide religious socialization, (2) to afford opportunities not available in the state system for mother-tongue teaching and learning, and (3) to compensate for the shortcomings of the state schools in other directions, such as out-of-school support for academic work. Examples were given of the types of provision, from evening and weekend classes to the provision of full-time independent schools in parallel and in competition with the state schools, with a view to achieving state support or subsidies after subsequent recognition.

The possibility of greater responsiveness in the state system as an inducement to minorities to send their children to state schools was proposed through the reorganization of the school day to accommodate greater flexibility across the domains offered by supplementary provision. But the assumption underlying such efforts is that a state system is or should be able to offer the diversity of provision required by an educational market economy. The counterargument might be that there should be a greater specialization of function, so that market forces can influence what is offered, rather than either sector seeking to pre-empt that market. The ideology of the marketplace may well be the most flexible way of bridging the gap between the liberal desire to cover all educational demands for all children within the state system and the apparent incapacity of state systems to fulfil that promise, a concern with which the final contribution in Part One sought to come to grips, pointing out the way in which liberal ideology has led to a focus on inputs and their equality rather than on processes and the equality of outcomes, which might lead to a challenging (might one say overthrow?) of existing hegemonies.

Part Two of the first volume focused even more closely on the ideologies supportive of, resistant or even antipathetic to existing constructions of cultural diversity. Here the ideological Tower of Babel *vis-à-vis* cultural diversity came to expression quite clearly. There are many competing interpretations and aspirations, and there is only the first faint light of the will or ability to bridge these interpretations. But the paradigm war which is ensuing should not be considered in any sense undesirable, unusual or dysfunctional. Rather, it is both functional and desirable if policies and solutions are not to become flaccid and simplistic, and if monism is not to take over from pluralism. It is the paradox of the debate on pluralism that so many have sought to achieve unanimity. In other words, the diversity of social constructions of pluralism is to be welcomed and encouraged, because it sharpens the debate and provides an unending quarry of intellectual stimulation, as well as a power generator of new policy ideas and practices: necessary critical arenas and testing grounds for their institutionalization.

The first contribution in Part Two sought to document this interminable debate through the consideration of three major approaches to multiculturalism found in the United States: curriculum content, achievement and intergroup education, and the extent to which each has become institutionalized. The driving forces behind that process of institutionalization as well as the factors inhibiting its achievement were considered. Possible approaches were suggested which may make the paradigm more accessible for all teachers and, therefore, more susceptible to institutionalization. None of the three dominant approaches carried the label of antiracist education, although all contained the commitment to eradicate racial and other prejudices.

Other societies have focused their attention more sharply on this aspect of discrimination, suggesting the need for radical political as well as economic change. On the other hand, and levying a marketplace reason, one contributor argued that antiracist education was not even in the interests of the poor and unempowered that its declared aim is to serve. The implicit assumption of antiracist education, it was argued, is the indoctrination of children into a futile commitment to the destruction of inequalities in modern Western capitalist societies through the destruction of the current economic order. On the other hand, another contributor argued that there is a paramount need to choose between antiracist and other pluralist paradigms, which are not capable of adequately serving the objective of combatting racism, and particularly structural racism, held in place by the values and class interests of capitalist society. Claiming the high moral ground, such a case implies that we must choose for antiracist education, or at least a loose confederation of like focused forces to achieve greater social justice and the human rights of disadvantaged minorities. Here, as on many future occasions in this series, commitments to greater equity, social justice and human dignity vie uncomfortably with the overall ideological commitment to a capitalist economy and the associated need to pursue excellence. On the other hand, the evidence from Eastern Europe is not encouraging on the ability of socialist societies to overcome prejudice and discrimination of long-standing historical aetiology by an alternative route.

Finally, in Part Two of the first volume two francophone contributions raised the flag of an alternative paradigm to both antiracist and multicultural education: interculturalism. This term expresses the dominant approach in the francophone world, including francophone North America, and it focuses on the micro level of interaction between individuals, groups and cultures. Here the values and socially constructed norms and mores of the three cultural partners in migration, represented by the terms 'emigration', 'immigration' and 'migration', are considered through a sensitive lens which can evoke the mutual construction of reality and the problems faced by individuals and groups in achieving sufficient cultural commonality to communicate and interact. What macro strategy can achieve that kind of fine-grained cultural and social rapport is the pertinent question to those who wish for grand designs to respond to cultural diversity and to eradicate prejudice and injustice: grand designs which are matched only by the failure to find grand theories. Within the context of contributions focusing more closely on prejudice and its eradication, this theme was taken up again in the second volume, through a consideration of the contribution of intercultural education to the training of educators.

Part Three of the first volume addressed the issue of the values and morality which may be necessary to bind together a culturally diverse society sufficiently to provide for social and economic cohesion and adequate social harmony. The first contribution in this part highlighted the problematic nature of values education within multicultural societies, because of the diverging subcultural perceptions of the goals of such an enterprise. One might add that it is not just the divergence of perceptions of the goals of values education, but also the overall goals of society which are thus rendered problematic. A moral curriculum, expressive of Western democratic ideology, which seeks to foster the autonomous selection of primary social identities and values, may be seen as challenging the apparent theological certainty of some religions, or even perhaps as a corrupting blasphemy. The very liberalism of such a curriculum may be radically at variance with the conservatism and illiberalism of some branches of some religions. For example, orthodox Muslims increasingly reject the dominant Western cultures' liberal values, as well as the penetration of that ideology into the curriculum and teaching methods. They demand instead traditional Islamic instruction in values, and in some cases the inception of separate schools which can achieve that goal — an approach which may exclude some children from the core democratic values of their own society and exclude the sharing of a basic normative framework which could reduce destructive interethnic conflicts.

Within pluralist democracies, on the other hand, even those interests which are perceived to be irreconcilable are considered to have the right to a legitimate and peaceful voice and to be taken account of. For that, in turn, every citizen needs an awareness and understanding of the complexity of the issues and the means to prevent such differences being creative of violence. Thus, unless the state regulates education (not necessarily providing it in its entirety), it is difficult to envisage any mechanism which will guarantee the attenuation of intercommunal strife and the human rights of all. Democratic societies have been dangerously reluctant to grasp the nettle of this dilemma and fulfil their obligation to secure the continuation of democracy for their citizens, either through the provision of an appropriate moral education directly or through the indirect regulation of what is taught and how. Such societies have to come to creative and democratic terms with the fact that some of their citizens will not wish to perpetuate the very values which sustain democratic pluralist society, but that fact does not release them from the responsibility which they hold to the majority of their citizens.

This objective may imply the introduction of a new model of religious education, as one contributor to this volume has suggested, or it may imply a modification of that model with a greater orientation to the concept of moral education in democratic societies, emphasizing a common destiny centred on human rights, reciprocity of human behaviour and mutuality of human endeavour. To achieve such an objective, consideration would be necessary of the moral development of children and a synthesis of current knowledge of development education and much of what has come to be included in multicultural education.

Part Four of Volume One offered a sharper focus on some of the major issues which have occupied the pluralist debate over the last half-century. Given the destructive world and regional conflicts which have occupied most of this century, should peace education be a more prominent part of the educational fare of democratic societies? Certainly, human harmony is necessary for development, and the burden of development still hangs heavily on two-thirds of the world's population. Even within the individual society, education for conflict resolution, harmony and peace is necessary if useless strife is to be avoided. Thus, although everyone does not need to be alike, it is essential that all are committed against the arousal of hatred and contempt against other people and for the peaceful resolution of conflict.[1] To achieve that, in some cases it will be necessary to develop bilingual and/or bicultural models of schooling, grounded in their own cultural context. For, while many societies may be multicultural, the composition of that multiculturalism, the seedbed from which development grows, differs widely. Such an identification with the specific cultural context is necessary not only in bilingual contexts but in all school contexts, given that each represents a different identikit of the factors which go to make up cultural diversity. A whole curriculum may have the same outer parameters in two schools, but its meaning will be reinterpreted by the students and educators who daily act out the social construction of the reality that we call a curriculum. Should the whole curriculum include what has come to be called affirmative action or positive discrimination?

The final section of Part Four contained two contrary views on the issue. On the one hand, equity, human justice and individual creativity, as well as the correction of past injustices, may seem to demand affirmative action. On the other hand, it can be argued that they emphasize apartheid, destroy excellence and carry the seeds of injustice to those who are excluded from affirmative action. It is an interesting dilemma, faced in micro form by all teachers in their daily work. Should they give more time to the less able, or those who may have missed some work through illness, at the cost of giving less time to other children? Perhaps, as mostly happens in daily classroom life, professional pragmatism and choice will provide a series of constantly differing resolutions of this dilemma for pluralist societies. The important thing is that educators are maximally accountable for those choices and are able and willing to correct for incorrect judgments and fallacious choice. Perhaps systems, schools and educators will seek to maximize choice by parents and pupils, through a more market oriented approach to what is offered in education, either within the state system or between it and a private sector, which includes separate ethnic or religious schools, as well as within the individual school and classroom. Differentiated electives within schools and grouping within classrooms, however, raise the dilemma of how students are allocated to groups and tracks and on the basis of what evidence and how informed a personal choice.

The final part of the first volume was concerned with the abiding dilemmas surrounding the making of judgments by educators and others in contexts of cultural diversity: IQ and cultural distance, ethnicity and intelligence, assessment and examinations, achievement tests and impressionistic judgments of behaviour in multicultural contexts. The unreliable nature of IQ scores and tests and the values and assumptions underlying them led to a conclusion of the inadequacy of such tests for crucial life chance decisions. This is particularly so in view of the contradictory evidence about between-group and intergenerational achievement — evidence which may provide more of a confirmation of ethnic stereotypes than a validated assessment of human potential.

The contrary case was also advanced, namely that environmental factors alone cannot explain the whole of the differences in mean IQ scores between different ethnic groups. Thus it is likely that a genetic-environmental factor is at work. All contributors acknowledged the clouded nature of the evidence about achievement comparisons even within one society. At the same time it is possible even statistically to detect certain patterns of deficits in achieving certain educational goals, and more importantly educational and economically consequential outcomes. This system malfunction implies the need for much more attention to the way in which pupils from particularly at-risk groups are channeled and allocated through the school system and grouped within it. This view was endorsed by the penultimate contribution to the volume, which argued that tests are telling us nothing useful about pedagogy and how to improve it and therefore the learning of children and schools.

The final contribution then argued that assessment and judgments about achievement are inherently interpretive processes, and that they are particularly open to bias in crosscultural contexts. Assessment processes and procedures may, of course, be subject to unconscious distortion by the cultural biography and presuppositions of the assessor, of which that person may be totally unaware. Equally, they may be the subject of deliberate bias because of the racist, credist or ethnicist values nd prejudice which a teacher, administrator, social worker, educational welfare officer or educational psychologist may explicitly or implicitly espouse. Consequently, the judgments of underachievement of minority pupils are misleading, not necessarily because of the culture bias of the test, but because of the inbuilt and taken-for-granted frames of reference of those involved. To counter this, that culture needs to be explicitly addressed through the training of those involved, in a conjoint way, involving the teaching and testing processes seen as a unity, and a wide range of contexts, contents, approaches, formats and modes of communication needs to be adopted. Significantly, this theme of prejudice, conscious and subconscious, implicit and explicit, individual, group and systemic, national and international, is the major theme of this, the second volume in this series.

From the very diversity of the contributions to the first volume a number of commonalities arose. First, there was a recognition of the continuing need to learn from each other, and thus to deepen and extend the dialogue. This does not necessarily involve giving up one's own ship, although it may, of course, result in a change in the colours under which it sails. Second, there was an acknowledgment of the need for more sensitive and more intensive dialogue, to tease out what are the real differences and what is their essence as well aś their appearance. Third, there was an acceptance of the value of discourse among and within groups and for minorities to be potently involved, but not to be led to believe that they have the power or right to establish a dictatorship of the minority, to veto on all occasions that with which they do not agree. Fourth, there was a realization that it may not be functional to seek to eradicate the differing perceptions of cultural diversity and the varying responses which those perceptions evoke. Fifth, there was a sensitivity to the bluntness of our present means to make judgments about other human beings, not least those from cultural groups substantially different from our own. While the contributors acknowledged that teachers will continue to need to make judgments for a host of reasons, they also need to be more circumspect, and their judgments need to be more easily reversible.

Finally, among the contributors to that first volume there was unanimity on the value of democratic means and more accountable professionalism to consider differences and conflicts. In this respect the greatest guarantor of the rights of minorities to the same justice and equity that majorities enjoy was considered to be the anchoring of the values of that majority within democratic traditions of human rights, which are secured at least in part by covenants beyond and above the boundaries of the nation state. While democracy may not always function perfectly, and while a reappraisal of the meaning of democracy in the social and economic structures of Western societies must also be part of the ongoing debate about responses to cultural diversity, care is needed to avoid the facile assumption that a less pluralist form of government can better solve the problems which diversity so creatively generates. Experience, not least in Eastern Europe, persuades us to an alternative conclusion. Pluralism cannot be successfully coerced, nor can it be ignored. The first volume in the series thus sought to lay the groundwork for succeeding volumes. Its basic message was that homogeneity of views on cultural diversity is not even a utopian dream, but rather the pursuit of a dangerous totalitarian illusion and illogical contradiction, resembling chasing after a millennial chimera and trampling everyone else in pursuit of it.

This volume, the second in the series, picks up the relay by arguing that there can be no real human rights, justice and progress where human bigotry and its corollaries, discrimination, exploitation and enslavement, hold sway. Neglect of the currently burgeoning diversity of human culture and its scope for prejudice 'production' is a highway to disaster and human misery. Down that road lies the legitimation of existing inequity, injustice and denial of human dignity and rights, above all to those who 'are different' in skin colour, ethnicity, religion, language, and not least in economic possessions and might. Down that road lies continued human, economic and environmental degradation, ultimately for all humankind, because education is silent on the pollution, deprivation and human misery visited on the poor by the rich. Down that road is continued underinvestment in human potential for reasons of gender, race, class, caste or other cultural factors.

In response to that challenge, Part One of this volume has advanced the argument that to tackle prejudice, you need to know about its evolution and cause. Some contributors have argued that prejudice derives from environmental factors, others that its cause is in part genetic. Others still advance the case that it is through a complex process of interaction between the cultural biography of an individual and the socialization process which the individual experiences that human prejudice grows. That cultural biography is not static, but through interaction with the environment accretes to itself new dimensions and perspectives. The very diversity of socialization processes in culturally pluralist societies leads to the development of attitudinal and behavioural preferences, which make it more difficult for an individual to accept the values and behaviour, sometimes even the existence, of others who have been significantly differently socialized.

An understanding of how these 'preferences' develop and lead to prejudice and discrimination against others, different in gender, language, creed, ethnicity, race or physical or mental capacity, is thus essential to the development of strategies aimed at modifying attitudes, values and behaviour. The development of prejudiced beliefs, such as racism, not only facilitates perceptions of inferiority, but also legitimates for the oppressor the exploitation or subhuman treatment of those who are considered to be significantly inferior by dint of their racial or other appurtenance. Men continue to legitimate their gender hegemony, in spite of legal constraints in many democratic societies, by subtle strategies of bracketing out, avoidance and jealously coveting crucial empowering information or positions.

In many developing countries gender inequity is supported or connived at by the external agencies of nations, which are themselves apparently committed to equity for their own citizens, regardless of gender. Women may not travel without their husband's or father's permission; they may not possess independent wealth. In some cases they may not even open an independent bank account without the endorsement of their father or husband. International commerce or politics may frequently blind trading partners, economic fellow-travellers, but also aid agencies to issues of human rights. International organizations may have two levels of commitment: ideological and practical; the one to be declared and the other to be practised, for others as for themselves. Even through non-verbal communication, prejudice may be mediated and absorbed as justification for considering other humans as less human than oneself. Silence may indeed be eloquent consent.

The phenomenon of prejudice should not be seen as a uniquely individual one, and several contributors to this series have posited the existence of two or three levels of prejudice and discrimination: *individual*, *systemic*, variously described as societal or structural as well, and *group*. This tripartite theme also arises in slightly different form in succeeding volumes, where contributors consider the need for different levels of citizenship, including international or world citizenship. They thus challenge the conventional wisdom that prejudice is individual *or* group *or* national. Each of the different levels may well be interrelated and act to reinforce the other.

Prejudice may thus be reinforced through group pressures and anxieties, which in turn distort further the perceptions of intergroup relations, augmenting prejudiced perceptions and further polarizing evaluations of those belonging to different groups. Thus, in adopting ethnic contact as a strategy to overcome prejudiced and polarized perceptions, it is important to understand and implement the contingencies surrounding successful utilization of heightened contact to overcome prejudice, or further regression in attitudes will take place. Forming and maintaining positive crossethnic relationships (including crossnational ones) demand skill and expertise, if they are to be successful. Those who adopt such approaches need to know of the stage of our knowledge in the field and to be aware of the validated experience of others, to be aware of the pitfalls and dangers, as well as of the promise and potential. As always, a balance is needed between inertia induced through the modesty of our knowledge and overprecipitate action through ignorance.

Educators in particular need to accept that schools instil moral values and perceptions, not only of right and wrong, but also of other human beings and groups. Connivance or passive acceptance of prejudiced behaviour by teachers and schools is reinforcement of it. Cooperative methods of working in schools have been shown to assist in establishing more harmonious intergroup relationships, and experimental field research has found relatively consistent positive effects on intergroup relations. But there are other educational interventions which can be efficacious in combatting prejudice, changing values and altering socially dysfunctional attitudes, and one contributor points to the utility of intercultural approaches in this respect. But for how long do such approaches remain potent? Not only is the process complex, requiring synergy, if progress is to be made, but long-term effects are unknown, and independently implemented policies are unlikely to succeed. What is needed is a coordinated approach which addresses not only structures and values, but also the often taken-for-granted social controls which hold prejudice and discrimination in place, even when structures have been changed, approaches and content amended, and policy statements produced.

One of these major controlling agencies is represented by the conglomeration that we call the mass media. However much they disclaim responsibility for society's values, including its prejudiced ones, the mass media are potent purveyors of values — and of prejudices. In this sense they are the world's corporate educators. They endorse or demolish the characteristics which make up the identities of individuals, groups and nations, as they are permitted to be perceived by society. Just as educators in schools must be called to the bar of unprejudiced policy and action, so also must the ever more powerful educators of the mass media. This process involves, for both, questioning the very idea that the identity of individuals should be conceived racially or culturally, thus institutionalizing and making more salient the very categories, paradigms and epistemologies which generate prejudice and discrimination. This, in turn, implies the generation of alternative criteria for the differentiation of pupils in schools and individuals in society, a terra incognita which has long been implicitly mapped but never explored.

The contributions to this volume chart and illuminate what we know of prejudice. They identify theories of causation and policies for action. Cautiously, they gently highlight what appear to be tried and tested principles for practice. In a circumspect way they propose promising initiatives for further research, policy and action. For all their differences of national biography, cultural perception and disciplinary approach, there is a striking unanimity about their objectives and message. They admonish that educators do not need to continue to sit on the sidelines while the game of prejudice is played to the same rules from one generation to the next. They argue that educators can potently influence intergroup relations and the development of a more harmonious society and international community. Indeed, educators have a responsibility to do so. Certainly, they accept, educators are not omnipotent, but they can make a difference, and have done so in the past. First, however, they must learn. They must learn to build their teaching on the kinds of principles and objectives identified in this volume, and to consider their own professional practice against those principles.

We do not know everything about combatting prejudice, nor do we know nothing. Already codifications of what effectiveness may mean in strategies for achieving greater gender equity as part of development work are appearing and pointing the way in which other areas of prejudice and inequity may be addressed.[2] Perhaps industrialized nations must look again at what they can learn from development education to achieve their own goals and rejuvenate their own democratic values.

For their part, educators must not be overwhelmed that they know nothing about prejudice reduction, but equally they must not be encouraged into the dangerous belief that they know all. They have to learn to learn from the experiences, research and pioneer development work of others, as well as relying on the accumulated wisdom of their own and their colleagues' folk intuition. For that process, educators need to be accurately informed about the dimensions, growth and combatting of prejudice. They must be empowered by their training, their administrators and their political masters to interlearn with their learners and to conduct a dialogue with the ends of education as much as with the means. One of those major ends or goals must surely be to combat the lamentable growth and effects of human prejudice and discrimination. Educators have to be recognized as more than the mere passive operants for the implementation of the political will of society, let alone any group within it, however vociferous. Rather, they need once again to become partners in the ongoing dialogue about the purposes of human education, where the dignity, responsibilities and rights of those humans are the central yardstick for professional action, decision and for the evaluation of both policy and practice.

Translating that vision into reality, however, cannot be achieved by educators alone. Therefore, equally eloquently, the contributions to this volume address policy-makers and administrators in education. They speak emphatically of neglect of the evidence, based on silent prejudice against the discussion of prejudice, not least where it is compounded as in race, class and gender. There is an economic cost to prejudice and discrimination, in denied investment opportunities, wasted talent and lower tolerated levels of growth and standards of living than could be achieved without prejudice, as well as economic loss due to such phenomena as underutilization of women in the workforce at a time when there is an imminent shortage within the labour force.[3]

Thus, for reasons ideological and ethical, social and economic, contributors advocate multiple strategies for combatting prejudice at individual and structural levels and the inception of system-wide legal, social and educational measures to confront it. Their contributions are an invitation to those with power over education to survey the evidence and to provide democratic and accountable policies, based on that research and development work, which recognize the intricate but not insuperable nature of prejudice. The contributors chart over fifty years of endeavour against prejudice. They map an agenda for individuals, groups, nations and the international community, which educators neglect at their peril and that of humankind. In that sense their response to the question of this volume title is that the time is now for progress in attacking prejudice by rational, systematic means. Where the rhetoric has failed, scientific research and pioneer development work, carefully targeted innovation and development could succeed. Their contributions have shown the way, politicians need to provide the means and educators the will.

## NOTES

1   It is now over fifty years since the establishment of the Council for Education in World Citizenship by the League of Nations Union; see D. Heater (1984) *Peace through Education*, Lewes, Falmer Press.
2   See, for example, E.M. King and M.A. Hill (Eds) (1990) *Women's Education in Developing Countries: A Review of Barriers, Benefits and Policy*, Washington, D.C., World Bank, Education and Employment Division, Population and Human Resources Department.
3   H. Metcalf and P. Leighton (1989) *The Under-Utilization of Women in the Labour Market*, IMS Report No. 172, Brighton, Institute of Manpower Studies/Equal Opportunities Commission.

# Author Index

Abdallah-Pretceille, M., 191, 198
Abercrombie, D., 121, 124
Aboud, F., 43, 44, 57, 58, 78, 134
Abramenkova, V.V., 50, 51
Acton, H.M. and Zarbatany, L., 67, 68
Adorno, T.W., *et al.*, 26, 76, 314
Agras, S., 153
Aiken, L., 110
Albert, A.A. and Porter, J.R., 55
Albert, M. and Derby, B., 12, 93–106
Albert, M.A., 101
Allen, V.L.
    *see* Asher and Allen
Allen, V.L. and Wilder, D.A., 166, 168
Allport, G.W., 13, 15, 21, 22, 43, 44, 95,
    100, 101, 119, 134, 153, 159, 168, 170,
    213–14, 233, 234, 314, 333–4, 335, 338,
    340, 341, 343, 344, 346, 353
Althof, W.
    *see* Oser and Althof
American Council of Education, 103
Amir, Y., 6, 167, 214, 261, 269, 341
    *see also* Ben-Ari and Amir
Amir, Y., *et al.*, 221–2, 259
Ammons, R.B., 76
Anderson, C.A.
    *see* Bowman and Anderson
Anderson, J.D., 350, 351
Anderson, J.P. and Perlman, D., 168
Andrews, P., 45
Annis, R.C.
    *see* Berry and Annis
Antia, S.D., 62, 63–4
Apel, K.O., 312–13
Arbuthnot, J. and Faust, D., 309
Argyle, M., 120, 121, 122, 123, 124, 126,
    131
Argyle, M. and Tower, P., 124, 133
Argyle, M., *et al.*, 122, 123, 124
Armor, D.J., 355, 361, 362
Aronson, E., 187
Aronson, E. and Goode, E., 235, 249, 252
Aronson, E. and Thibodeau, R., 14,
    231–56
Aronson, E. and Yates, S., 235

Aronson, E., *et al.*, 162, 235, 246, 249, 263,
    269, 336, 337
Asante, M.K., 136
Asante, M.K., *et al.*, 133
Ashear, V.H.
    *see* Snortum and Ashear
Asher, S.R.
    *see* Singleton and Asher
Asher, S.R. and Allen, V.L., 98
Ashmore, R.D., 21

Backman, C.W.
    *see* Secord and Backman
Bagdikian, B., 371
Bagley, C. and Young, L., 59
Bagley, L., *et al.*, 28
Bailey, S.K., 354, 360
Bak, J.J. and Siperstein, G.N., 65, 66, 68
Bandura, A., 373
Bandura, A., *et al.*, 314
Banks, J.A., 259
Banks, J.A. and Lynch, J., 277
Banks, W.C., 102, 103
Banks, W.C., *et al.*, 103
Bar-Tal, D., *et al.*, 21
Barakat, R.A., 132
Barna, L., 146
Barres, E., 326
Bartz, D.E. and Maehr, M.L., 350–1, 352
Battistich, V., *et al.*, 323
Bavelas, A., 246
Bayton, J.A., 215
Bayton, J.A., *et al.*, 215
Beck, C., 309, 323
Beckman, P.J. and Kohl, F.L., 67
Beery, R.G.
    *see* Covington and Beery
Bem, D., 85
Ben-Ari, R. and Amir, Y., 261, 269
Ben-Ezer, G., 121, 127, 130
Ben-Shacher, N.
    *see* Ortar and Ben-Shacher
Ben-Yochanan, A.
    *see* Katz and Ben-Yochanan

# Subject Index